Lecture Notes in Computer Science 11576

Commenced Publication in 1973
Founding and Former Series Editors:
Gerhard Goos, Juris Hartmanis, and Jan van Leeuwen

More information about this series at http://www.springer.com/series/7409

Pei-Luen Patrick Rau (Ed.)

Cross-Cultural Design

Methods, Tools and User Experience

11th International Conference, CCD 2019
Held as Part of the 21st HCI International Conference, HCII 2019
Orlando, FL, USA, July 26–31, 2019
Proceedings, Part I

 Springer

Editor
Pei-Luen Patrick Rau
Tsinghua University
Beijing, China

ISSN 0302-9743   ISSN 1611-3349   (electronic)
Lecture Notes in Computer Science
ISBN 978-3-030-22576-6   ISBN 978-3-030-22577-3   (eBook)
https://doi.org/10.1007/978-3-030-22577-3

LNCS Sublibrary: SL3 – Information Systems and Applications, incl. Internet/Web, and HCI

This Springer imprint is published by the registered company Springer Nature Switzerland AG
The registered company address is: Gewerbestrasse 11, 6330 Cham, Switzerland

Foreword

The 21st International Conference on Human-Computer Interaction, HCI International 2019, was held in Orlando, FL, USA, during July 26–31, 2019. The event incorporated the 18 thematic areas and affiliated conferences listed on the following page.

A total of 5,029 individuals from academia, research institutes, industry, and governmental agencies from 73 countries submitted contributions, and 1,274 papers and 209 posters were included in the pre-conference proceedings. These contributions address the latest research and development efforts and highlight the human aspects of design and use of computing systems. The contributions thoroughly cover the entire field of human-computer interaction, addressing major advances in knowledge and effective use of computers in a variety of application areas. The volumes constituting the full set of the pre-conference proceedings are listed in the following pages.

This year the HCI International (HCII) conference introduced the new option of "late-breaking work." This applies both for papers and posters and the corresponding volume(s) of the proceedings will be published just after the conference. Full papers will be included in the *HCII 2019 Late-Breaking Work Papers Proceedings* volume of the proceedings to be published in the Springer LNCS series, while poster extended abstracts will be included as short papers in the HCII 2019 *Late-Breaking Work Poster Extended Abstracts* volume to be published in the Springer CCIS series.

I would like to thank the program board chairs and the members of the program boards of all thematic areas and affiliated conferences for their contribution to the highest scientific quality and the overall success of the HCI International 2019 conference.

This conference would not have been possible without the continuous and unwavering support and advice of the founder, Conference General Chair Emeritus and Conference Scientific Advisor Prof. Gavriel Salvendy. For his outstanding efforts, I would like to express my appreciation to the communications chair and editor of *HCI International News,* Dr. Abbas Moallem.

July 2019   Constantine Stephanidis

HCI International 2019 Thematic Areas
and Affiliated Conferences

Thematic areas:

- HCI 2019: Human-Computer Interaction
- HIMI 2019: Human Interface and the Management of Information

Affiliated conferences:

- EPCE 2019: 16th International Conference on Engineering Psychology and Cognitive Ergonomics
- UAHCI 2019: 13th International Conference on Universal Access in Human-Computer Interaction
- VAMR 2019: 11th International Conference on Virtual, Augmented and Mixed Reality
- CCD 2019: 11th International Conference on Cross-Cultural Design
- SCSM 2019: 11th International Conference on Social Computing and Social Media
- AC 2019: 13th International Conference on Augmented Cognition
- DHM 2019: 10th International Conference on Digital Human Modeling and Applications in Health, Safety, Ergonomics and Risk Management
- DUXU 2019: 8th International Conference on Design, User Experience, and Usability
- DAPI 2019: 7th International Conference on Distributed, Ambient and Pervasive Interactions
- HCIBGO 2019: 6th International Conference on HCI in Business, Government and Organizations
- LCT 2019: 6th International Conference on Learning and Collaboration Technologies
- ITAP 2019: 5th International Conference on Human Aspects of IT for the Aged Population
- HCI-CPT 2019: First International Conference on HCI for Cybersecurity, Privacy and Trust
- HCI-Games 2019: First International Conference on HCI in Games
- MobiTAS 2019: First International Conference on HCI in Mobility, Transport, and Automotive Systems
- AIS 2019: First International Conference on Adaptive Instructional Systems

Pre-conference Proceedings Volumes Full List

1. LNCS 11566, Human-Computer Interaction: Perspectives on Design (Part I), edited by Masaaki Kurosu
2. LNCS 11567, Human-Computer Interaction: Recognition and Interaction Technologies (Part II), edited by Masaaki Kurosu
3. LNCS 11568, Human-Computer Interaction: Design Practice in Contemporary Societies (Part III), edited by Masaaki Kurosu
4. LNCS 11569, Human Interface and the Management of Information: Visual Information and Knowledge Management (Part I), edited by Sakae Yamamoto and Hirohiko Mori
5. LNCS 11570, Human Interface and the Management of Information: Information in Intelligent Systems (Part II), edited by Sakae Yamamoto and Hirohiko Mori
6. LNAI 11571, Engineering Psychology and Cognitive Ergonomics, edited by Don Harris
7. LNCS 11572, Universal Access in Human-Computer Interaction: Theory, Methods and Tools (Part I), edited by Margherita Antona and Constantine Stephanidis
8. LNCS 11573, Universal Access in Human-Computer Interaction: Multimodality and Assistive Environments (Part II), edited by Margherita Antona and Constantine Stephanidis
9. LNCS 11574, Virtual, Augmented and Mixed Reality: Multimodal Interaction (Part I), edited by Jessie Y. C. Chen and Gino Fragomeni
10. LNCS 11575, Virtual, Augmented and Mixed Reality: Applications and Case Studies (Part II), edited by Jessie Y. C. Chen and Gino Fragomeni
11. LNCS 11576, Cross-Cultural Design: Methods, Tools and User Experience (Part I), edited by P. L. Patrick Rau
12. LNCS 11577, Cross-Cultural Design: Culture and Society (Part II), edited by P. L. Patrick Rau
13. LNCS 11578, Social Computing and Social Media: Design, Human Behavior and Analytics (Part I), edited by Gabriele Meiselwitz
14. LNCS 11579, Social Computing and Social Media: Communication and Social Communities (Part II), edited by Gabriele Meiselwitz
15. LNAI 11580, Augmented Cognition, edited by Dylan D. Schmorrow and Cali M. Fidopiastis
16. LNCS 11581, Digital Human Modeling and Applications in Health, Safety, Ergonomics and Risk Management: Human Body and Motion (Part I), edited by Vincent G. Duffy

http://2019.hci.international/proceedings

11th International Conference on Cross-Cultural Design (CCD 2019)

Program Board Chair(s): **Pei-Luen Patrick Rau, *P.R. China***

- Sangwoo Bahn, South Korea
- Chien-Chi Chang, Taiwan
- Na Chen, P.R. China
- Zhe Chen, P.R. China
- Zhiyong Fu, P.R. China
- Paul Fu, USA
- Toshikazu Kato, Japan
- Rungtai Lin, Taiwan
- Dyi-Yih Michael Lin, Taiwan
- Na Liu, P.R. China
- Cheng-Hung Lo, P.R. China
- Yongqi Lou, P.R. China
- Liang Ma, P.R. China
- Alexander Mädche, Germany
- Katsuhiko Ogawa, Japan
- Taezoon Park, South Korea
- Chunyi Shen, Taiwan
- Huatong Sun, USA
- Hao Tan, P.R. China
- Pei-Lee Teh, Malaysia
- Lin Wang, South Korea
- Hsiu-Ping Yueh, Taiwan

The full list with the Program Board Chairs and the members of the Program Boards of all thematic areas and affiliated conferences is available online at:

http://www.hci.international/board-members-2019.php

HCI International 2020

The 22nd International Conference on Human-Computer Interaction, HCI International 2020, will be held jointly with the affiliated conferences in Copenhagen, Denmark, at the Bella Center Copenhagen, July 19–24, 2020. It will cover a broad spectrum of themes related to HCI, including theoretical issues, methods, tools, processes, and case studies in HCI design, as well as novel interaction techniques, interfaces, and applications. The proceedings will be published by Springer. More information will be available on the conference website: http://2020.hci.international/.

General Chair
Prof. Constantine Stephanidis
University of Crete and ICS-FORTH
Heraklion, Crete, Greece
E-mail: general_chair@hcii2020.org

http://2020.hci.international/

Contents – Part I

Cultural Differences, Usability and Design

Aesthetics and Mindfulness

Contents – Part II

Cross-Cultural Product and Service Design

Intercultural Learning

Cross-Cultural Design Methods and Tools

The Study of Developing Innovation on Technology-Enabled Design Process

Chiui Hsu[1]([✉]), Claudia Wang[2]([✉]), and Rungtai Lin[3]([✉])

[1] Department of Material and Fiber,
Oriental Institute of Technology, Taipei, Taiwan
hsu.chiui@msa.hinet.net
[2] Interactive Design, National Taipei University of Technology, Taipei, Taiwan
w93524@yahoo.com.tw
[3] National Taiwan University of Arts, Taipei, Taiwan
rtlin@mail.ntua.edu.tw

Abstract. The worldwide industries are pondering how to redefine the domain they belong to. The industry, by taking views from functional approach, has shifted from "What equipment is doing" to "What equipment is representing?" Therefore, from the status of the equipment itself, the instant visibility of the design, to the data of the first-draft, etc., all these elements are required to be united, communicated and innovated. The philosophy behind this study is "technology alignment, product innovation, and service integration." It will introduce research and development applications such as interconnection with 3D software, etc., which means to apply the "Virtual-design System" as its conceptual foundation and to reach cross-domain applications in conventional industries with animation tools, such as iClone and Clo 3D. Hence, it allows free communication between science and technology, humans and machines, people and people. With the help of the cutting-edge equipment of digital process in production line, it innovates design process. To save time and cost of design and creation, by applying technology alignment and verification, the innovation process will become a complete medium for just-in-time customization. The design will no longer be fettered by complicated and tedious techniques. Designers can realise his original contents by utilize various materials and technology to express their ideas more effectively and efficiently. Further, the conclusion by the applications with Clo3D and iClone technology, accelerates design innovation mechanisms, speeds up production and delivery while instantly meets customer satisfaction with "Virtual communication production;" therefore, enhances the design services.

Keywords: Virtual-design · Digital process ·
The instant visibility of the 3D design · High customization

1 Introduction

1.1 Fashion Industry Status

Innovative design and management are common in international fashion brands. Development models constructed in response to the trends and difficulties in the

P.-L. P. Rau (Ed.): HCII 2019, LNCS 11576, pp. 3–17, 2019.
https://doi.org/10.1007/978-3-030-22577-3_1

fashion industry are not limited to application solely in fashion design fields. Focusing on creating original interdisciplinary products on the basis of the brand's image and value, international fashion brands are integrating art, technology, and culture to customize services and reach out to consumers through diverse methods. This approach not only impresses consumers but also enhances brand value.

Although fashion products are rich in cultural and artistic elements, fashion design is time-consuming and complex. However, designers have to produce collections twice a year to keep up with trends. From the setting of a theme to fabric planning, product planning, pattern development, style development, and series sampling, innumerous iterations of the process of trying on, adjusting, resampling, and readjusting are required. When the designs of the garments have been finalized, processes including promotion, photographing, dynamic and static exhibition, order receiving, stock preparation, production confirmation, and shipment are required for the final product to reach consumers. Despite stagnant global economies, fashion designers must still launch a new collection every season, which is highly costly. Designing apparel can itself deplete a designer's resources. Moreover, designers have to market their products and increase their popularity by holding fashion shows or attending international fashion shows [1] in addition to selling their products through consignment, online shops, and brick-and-mortar shops. Because of the environment and their limited resources, designers worldwide are confronted with the challenge of survival and development. Therefore, solving the problem of lengthy and costly development processes is a critical issue for the global fashion industry.

1.2 Emerging Virtual Design Technology

Fashion design and the practice of making garment samples is a highly professional field that requires interdisciplinary techniques. Computer-aided design (CAD) systems and computation technologies for fashion design have long been developed. In 1990, the first accurate garment simulation application was developed, with many complementary technologies being considered in addition to fabric simulation [2]. Among the technologies used are body modeling and animation [3] and fabric layers [4]. One study used geometrics to process grid positions and speed [5]. In recent years, each specific system has been successfully integrated into separate stages of product design processes. Three-dimensional (3D) virtual simulation software has advanced to the point that it can simulate realistic effects of products to reduce or eliminate lengthy time spent sampling and without needing to create actual garments. The simulation software provides an opportunity to view a design or produced pattern in a 3D environment immediately during virtual garment sampling and fitting [6].

Because CAD has been an advanced technology in the field of garment design, research institutes and manufacturers worldwide have endeavored to integrate 3D garment virtual simulation software with fashion design, patterning, sewing, printing and laminating, and other production tasks. Computers have been used to simulate the entire garment production process. Well-developed 3D scanning and human body data analysis and processing have been combined with management applications and 3D design of garments. Through the combination of multidisciplinary theoretical knowledge and multiple technical fields and methods, a digitized model has been established for constructing and simulating fitting and garment demonstration [4, 7]. Virtual garment fit technologies were first developed in western research. Example systems include <u>MIRACloth</u> developed by <u>MIRALab in Switzerland</u>, the virtual garment fitting software developed by the Fraunhofer Society in Germany, the cross-platform system developed by those companies of PAD producer in Canada, the E-Design system developed by lectra in France, and the virtual fitting room jointly developed by Gerber and Browzwear in the United States [8]. Companies in various countries continue to develop advanced 3D software for the virtual garment fitting; for example, PGM 3D Runway in the United States and CLO3D by CLO Virtual Fashion in South Korea. Although the 3D Runway has stronger application functions and more refined settings than other software, CLO3D has easy and intuitive operation to facilitate learning and comprehension; moreover, the garment sizes and virtual contour effects in CLO3D are close to those of real garments [9]. Among the numerous software programs, CLO3D is an outstanding technical software package that provides complete garment simulation, high-quality fabric simulation editing, and technical effects, imitating garment manufacturing [10, 11].

Fashion designing is a charming, diverse, and large industry. During the process of fashion design, each step from patterning to material selection, size measuring, sewing, and sampling requires repeated revisions and approvals, which is extremely time-consuming. In the increasingly challenging global economy, strategies tailored to current market or industrial needs and involving 3D virtual simulation functions are crucial to achieving rapid improvement in the fashion industry. CLO3D virtual design technologies enable simultaneous 2D and 3D simulation. Users can immediately see the effects of pattern, color, texture, and detail revisions [12]. During the design process, software users can examine and revise the style and fit of a garment quickly. This reduces the preparation time required for designs. Existing modules can be used for combinational design. Users may also swiftly design garments on a virtual model to produce garment patterns automatically. This is a near zero cost method and creates numerous possibilities such as the generation of patterns, color set samples, pattern and print alignments, and layouts. Immediate examination of the revisions to 3D garments can reduce the number of unnecessary processes and transportation costs that are required in actual sample creation. A reduction of the production time leads to lower costs. The process from sketching to 3D virtual simulation and the sampling and production of finalized products is illustrated in Fig. 1. The proposed design method not only overhauls the materials (e.g., paper, brushes, and pigment) required from those in traditional design drawing but also considerably reduces the patterning, sampling, and material costs. Using the CLO virtual design technology to develop designs can save time and money and enable fashion designers to create products of higher quality [13]. In addition, options including concept communication, explanation, color, fabric, print pattern, and design styling provide opportunities for fashion designers to innovate and be more creative.

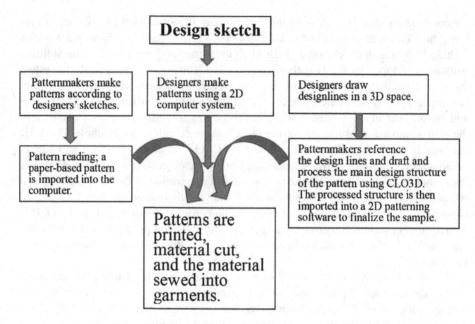

Fig. 1. Process of 3D sampling

1.3   E-Marketing in the Fashion Industry

In October 2018, the 30th anniversary of its founding, the luxury fashion retailer I.T (ithk.com), headquartered in Hong Kong [14, 15], declared for the first time that future digitization of the fashion industry is a keynote idea. I.T requested digital fashion companies to create a new promotional collection symbolic of its 30 years of devotion to the Chinese fashion industry. The promotional collection was designed by brands such as Marques Almeida, Helmut Lang, and Alexander McQueen. Customers can only view digital forms of the products before purchasing them in I.T concept stores. The collection was presented in a 60-s film made by The Fabricant and through static images obtained using CLO3D. This method of presentation indicates that virtual and digital technologies will lead e-commerce in the 21st century. A trend has formed for the use of applications that enable fast communication and visual garment revision by incorporating relevant virtual software. Such applications solve cost and time problems for the fashion industry. Under the momentum of Industry 4.0, design, production, and marketing are commonly being performed using virtual approaches to communicate advanced concepts. The integrated application of CLO3D and other animation software packages has resulted in the novel concept of garment customization within micro factories. The demand for such applications and concepts is increasing [16].

2 Research Process

The research framework had three steps. Step 1 involved a review of the literature to analyze the fashion trends and status quo of digital software in practical operations. Step 2 involved design development based on original themes. Step 3 involved verification of the process from designing to sampling. The benefits obtained using the process and the comprehensive procedural analysis were used to make suggestions for optimizing innovative design and production processes.

2.1 CLO3D and Key Integration Software

The CLO3D, Alembic Importer, and iClone 7 Pro 3D software tools were considered in this study.

CLO3D. This tool has various functions useful for fashion design, including drawing high-quality curves, partial sewing, free sewing, folding, and inserting flexibility effects. The drawing tool can be used along with 3D patterning and cutting. The physical properties of fabric are digitized and parameterized to facilitate the editing of fabric flexibility, cutting, curvature, friction, density, and thickness to simulate the textures of different materials. Various functions, such as examining points of contact and fabric pressure, can be used to measure the fit of a designed garment to a model [9] to achieve accurate fitting.

Alembic Importer. The objective of using this software is to completely display the detailed fabric simulation effects of CLO3D in iClone and further optimize the instantaneous display performance. In addition to fabric simulation, the Alembic format is suitable for processing various types of dynamic and static topological grid information such as fluid and particle effects. Use of this function enhances integration with other mainstream tools of the fashion industry.

iClone 7 Pro. This is a 3D animation software package that can be used to create 3D animations by integrating various fine art materials, movement performance, and lighting effects. It also exports various technological materials for the development of other digital content (e.g., virtual reality and augmented reality).

To clarify the process through which these integrated software tools can be applied, this study analyzed the contexts of the 3D digital software tools. We estimate that during the design and technology application communication process of CLO3D, few scholars have proposed the concept of integrated design, customization, and microfactory production from the perspective of the designer as the innovative organizer. This study employed innovative and practical methods in the design process by importing virtual and digital technologies as a solution to problems in fashion production processes. Table 1 shows the research steps of the design process and software integration application.

Table 1. Steps in the research methods

Research	Steps
1	Literature review of key concepts related to the application of CLO3D and iClone in production processes and product demonstration
2	Learning of software tool application (added-value application) technologies and suitable software integration applications
3	Create the design structure of "real-time virtuality" and actual sampling procedures
4	Verification that original content is convertible into visualized fashion design proposals and innovative sampling processes
5	Concept connection, design simulation, product sampling, demonstration, and experience of interactive virtual reality
6	Construction of innovative work models of the "cyber-design process" serving as the reference for the industry, government, and academia

Source: this study

3   Framework for Studying the Virtual Design System

3.1   A Design Services of a Real-Time Virtual Design Model

Using the communication of CLO3D, the author proposed a real-time virtual design system structure that integrates multiple software tools (Fig. 3). The system combines CLO3D, Alembic Importer, Character Creator, and iClone to facilitate product design and sampling and is an example of an innovative fashion production process. The potential users of the system include designers and design customers. Through the real-time virtual effect, users can complete communication and revision without wasting time and money. The proposed system structure focuses on the operation sequence and technologies between the users and software as well as the sequence between software applications and the production processes. The new process improves the development and communication methods in traditional design, providing designers with the ability to customize garments in detail. Designers can thus design freely, unlimited by materials and technologies. Multiple concept generation and real-time communication can enhance the essence of design services, freeing fashion designers from their previous constraints. In future, real-time and effective communication methods can help create new work modes of design in the fashion industry. Advancement of multimedia technologies and interpersonal and human–machine communication and cooperation can promote increasing the application of interactive designs in innovative demonstration.

3.2   Unified Procedure of Design Production and Showcasing

The method used by designers to express an original concept involves their overall conception of the garment. Garment showcasing is a method of presenting a designer's ideas and is thus necessary for converting designs into fashion products. In addition to having aesthetic value, effect drawings demonstrate a designer's intentions regarding their design. Accurate comprehension of the structure of a fashion design can help turn the drawing into a physical garment. Therefore, creating high-quality effect drawings is a requirement before interaction between designers and customers. Additionally, it is a critical problem in fashion design.

Traditional 2D drawings often neglect the rear and lateral views of garments, as well as the aesthetics when the garment view is turned from the front to the back. The powerful 3D virtual simulation performance of CLO3D enables designers to create complete, 3D fashion designs. The software is also convenient for designers, pattern-makers, and consumers because it can display eye-catching designs created by changes to pattern structures. This study examined how garments are created. The first stage focused on the development planning of original content and established figure model dimensions. The key software technologies and the application of future product showcasing were then evaluated. This study secondly analyzed the functions and technical aspects of CLO3D, CC, iClone animation, and plug-in software tools that facilitate practical learning and operation. The tools were then integrated to form a digital tool for idea conception, design planning, construction and showcasing of 3D patterns, real-time virtuality, and cyber-design processes. As well as, convert into a plug-in for iClone to construct dynamic and static figure models according to the garments' characteristics and styles. (e.g., personality and posture) The unified tool can be further integrated with interactive virtual reality to construct an integral part of the fashion industry ecosystem. The predetermined procedure is illustrated in Fig. 2.

4 Real-Time Design and Work Procedure

The process from virtual fitting and revision to practical sampling emphasizes consensus on humanistic theme exploration, followed by software technology examination. Because CLO3D can simulate garments realistically, designers can revise and design patterns in a 2D right-side view. After pattern revision is complete, the result can be previewed in 3D left-side view instantly. Garment fit is crucial to fashion design; therefore, placing garments on virtual models and viewing from multiple angles can serve as an effective reference for reviewing the designed garments. With 360° observation of a garment, designers, customers, vendors, and technicians can identify more defects in the design. Revisions can then be immediately made to improve the garment design. The steps with which innovative design can be implemented using a unified design and showcasing process are detailed in the following sections.

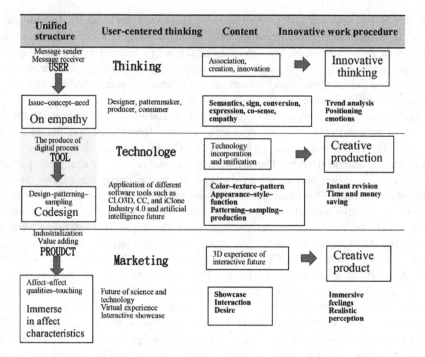

Fig. 2. Unified work modes of cyber-design processes to marketing

4.1 Creative Thinking—Original Content Converted into Design Elements

See Table 2.

Table 2. Thematic elements and patterns

Item	Content
Creative thinking Theme (concept) Color (image) Appearance (pattern form)	1. Taiwanese mountain landscape patterns: Inspired by an old song, *Qing Chun Ling*, which describes birds, red springtime flowers, bees, herbs, and wings. Like the song, the patterns describe the flow of youth and freedom. 2. The graffiti spirit of the youth never dies. From one end of the street to the other, spirits and fashion monsters look for sprouting contexts, becoming the new-generation contexts and textures of Taiwan.

4.2 Practical Operation of CLO3D Pattern Production Process

See Table 3.

Table 3. Pattern and garment design and print simulation

Item	Content
	1. Sample drawing: 2D garment patterns are drawn in the right-hand window to fit the human model. Digital information is displayed in the steps presented on the left sample.
	a. In CLO3D, design drawings and 2D patterns are created.

	b. Placement of sample: After completion of sample drawing, "synchronization" is activated. The pattern is displayed in the left-hand window. Users can then select the "point alignment" mode to align surrounding sample pieces. The sample on the left is a better fit to the model.
	c. Sewing: Smart sewing tools are selected to perform virtual sewing along the shoulder line, lateral line, and segmentation line of the front and rear patterns.
	d. Revised pattern
	2. Pattern sample design:
2.Creative production	a. Pattern design
	Photoshop/Ai is used to process and edit patterns [2]. Fashion design requires personalized effects, and fabric pattern design is the key element. When designing fabric patterns, fashion designers tend to borrow from art graphics or modern images, signs, or markings. They then simplify and summarize the patterns. The use of computers can greatly increase their work efficiency.
	b. Digital print pattern output
	The designed CLO3D fabric pattern is edited into fabric samples. The density and pattern size of the cloth are edited to sufficiently express the art effect of the garment.

	3. Print simulation:
	The left-hand picture is a manual illustration. The picture in the center is the 2D sample, and the right-hand picture is a 3D preview of the garment on the model. In addition, in the virtual garment showcase, the virtual model displays the design effect simultaneously. Discarding unfavorable designs during the design process limits development costs and shortens the development period. Plug-ins and iClone animation software can be used to distribute a virtual showcase through the Internet, facilitating dynamic display of virtual fashion designs and combining design and marketing.
	This CLO3D intuitive garment showcase method is different from the traditional plan symmetry fabric design in terms of pattern application. Thus, the proposed method is suitable for highly customized designs. The pattern arrangement can be adjusted according to customer preference and at any time.

The author also discovered that when the proportion of the sample in the right-hand window is correct, marking can be used to edit the pattern and position it optimally. Set patterns can be adjusted by changing the pattern size. Thus, pattern designs and print patterns can be printed once to create innovative digital print patterns, thereby saving money, time, and materials. Reflective items, Perler beads, and embroidered accessories can also be appropriately positioned.

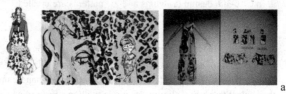

a

4. Pattern design and virtual fitting

a.3D pattern design and pattern mapping

Digital print patterns can be arranged in the preferred manner and marked before being printed out.

Source: this study

4.3   Creative Product—Simulation Design and High-Order Practice

See Table 4.

4.4   Innovative Showcase: CLO3D-Based Fashion Design and Added-Value Application of Digital Animation

Based on the cyber-design system, new digital technologies were explored along with CLO3D, iClone, and other augmented reality and virtual reality software applications. The Alembic plug-in tools are suitable for processing dynamic and static topological grid information [8], such as fluid and particle effects. Import of this function can improve the iClone function as a comprehensive instant animation tool, as shown in figures below. iClone was used to create animal-faced characters, postures, and runway paths for innovative product marketing and showcasing.

Table 4. Virtuality simulation and sampling procedure

Item	Content
3. Creative products High-order 3D practice based on simulation try-on designs	CLO3D offers fast and stable virtual simulation, instantaneous revision and preview, and simulation of the textures of different materials. Different functions can be used to measure garment fit to the model. Designers can draft the design and set model sizes and postures and render the draft in the preview mode. Detailed effect simulation is also available, such as wrinkles, tension, folding, ironing lines, multilayer garments, jackets, and coats. Multilayer garments including hoods, jackets, and stuffed jackets can also be simulated. Because the simulated garments have realistic details, a design can be changed at the last minute if the market or customer demands change. After approval of the design, the sample and printed patterns are exported.  a Simulation  b Sampling

Source: this study

Fig. 3. The design of the runway paths and innovative characters

5   Conclusion and Suggestion

5.1   From User-Centered Thinking to Simulation and the Actual Production Process

In the design and development procedure of the fashion industry chain, design planning and pattern design are the core elements of product development. Although various digital application devices are available, the processes of drawing communication, patterning, printing, and sampling have not been integrated. Interdisciplinary cooperation is common in the fashion industry; however, integration of technology into the industry's production processes is currently primitive. Multiple software technologies and design practices were integrated with instantaneous virtual design to present products immediately to the customer. This method enables rapid communication, immediate adjustment, and precise revision, thereby reducing the time and cost of repeated communication on colors, shapes, patterns, and sampling and optimizing service applications for high-order customization. Users can be designers, pattern-makers, customers, or customers with customization needs. User operation interfaces are simulations on software applications. With the combination of virtuality and reality, simulated human figure or model forms and the physical properties, style, and print of the garment can be adjusted in accordance with user and designer needs and communication. The size, proportion, and position of the elements can also be adjusted anytime to reduce the time required for sampling, increase the communication efficiency, and improve the existing work sequence. The proposed system can be used by the designer, producer, and user because it combines virtuality and practice. The system conforms with user-centered design thinking. It facilitates barrier-free communication, revisions, and cocreation designing through digital simulation tools. By decreasing the gap between imagination and reality, designers can strengthen their connections with customers and those with customization needs, creating a new market trend.

5.2   Optimization of Highly Customized Service

1. The system reduces the time designers spend on planning drafts and that pattern-makers spend on communicating with customers, effectively shortening the process time.
2. Instantaneous arrangement function combined with print patterns: The 3D garment fitting simulation function facilitates timely revision according to customer needs, optimizing communication over digital prints and the materials used.
3. Instantaneous design assists communication, solves the complex work procedure problem in traditional designing, and improves design processes. Simulated fabric patterns can be placed on animated runways with realistic features (such as garment movement) to help marketing and product showcasing. The innovative process becomes a real-time customization process that enables consumers and developers to satisfy their desire for smart communication in production and customization. The mode can be used in future client-to-client interactions to expedite the development of design innovation and innovative marketing.

5.3   Environmentally Friendly Process Integration

Using the proposed process to create a garment saves one-third of the amount of fabric used in marking. The time saved in the production process was four times that in the traditional process. To ensure the innovative process runs smoothly, the operations of pattern designers, sample makers, and the digital software are required. The traditional process of making a dress from patterning to sampling and production takes approximately one month or longer (depending on the complexity from size measurement to design drafting, patterning, sampling, fitting, revision, and sample delivery). Using

CLO3D, the process took only 27 h from size measurement to 3D design, 3D simulated patterning, 3D simulated sampling, pattern/print approval, pattern export, and sample creation. The sample acceptance rate was 55%, with a sample creation time of approximately 7 days. The proposed method substantially reduced the time designers spent on planning drafts and that patternmakers spent on communicating with customers, effectively shortening the process time.

6 Recommendation for Innovative Fashion Production Processes

6.1 A Garment Design Database Can Be Established

The interdisciplinary empirical results of this study verify that the proposed innovative design and showcasing process can serve as a reference for the fashion industry and relevant academic collaborators. Designers can use Gerber or Lactra patterning software to input their original concepts into CLO3D and arrange patterns in the correct positions in the 2D window. The design pattern size can be adjusted in the 2D window to determine the visual effect of the garment. In the 3D window, sewing and pattern adjustment can be performed and a preview of the design is displayed. Once the design pattern is approved (a garment design database can be established simultaneously), the pattern to be created is exported. Photoshop/AI image layout software is used to adjust the print pattern and marking. The process not only saves materials used in printing but also enables unified export of products with customized prints, customized patterns, or both. Eventually, the proposed system can provide services for fabric developers, fabric vendors, illustrators, artists, galleries, and customers with customization needs while creating a relevant image database (Fig. 4).

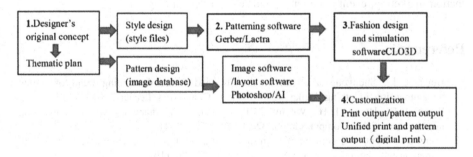

Fig. 4. Fashion design sampling process

6.2 A Digital Marketing Is a Precursor Viewpoints

The second suggestion of this study regards digital marketing and the showcase of fashion concepts. Designers first input their original ideas into Character Creator in iClone 3D to create 3D virtual human characters with varying appearance. The

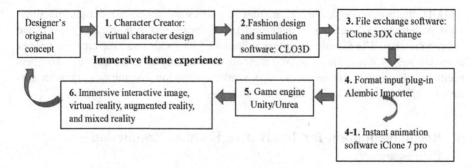

Fig. 5. Process of fashion concept digital marketing

characters are then sent to iClone (with one click) for movement addition. The characters and character movements are sent in .fbx format to CLO3D for garments to be added. The characters with garments then perform movements. The dynamic simulation results (with garments of the designed patterns on the virtual characters) are then calculated. CLO3D is used to export the characters and character movements in .fbx format to 3DXchange*, which then exports the outcome in .iProp item format. CLO3D is then used to export the dynamic simulation results in .abc (ogawa) format. The .iProp item containing the characters, character movements, and garment data is input into iClone. The Alembic plug-in of iClone is used to simulate the dynamic fabric simulation results in the .abc file. The movement and material dynamics of the virtual characters are consistent. The animation resulting from the Alembic plug-in can be used by Unity/Unrea to create immersive interactive virtual reality, augmented reality, and mixed reality images. The service targets can be virtual runway shows, interactive experiences, precursor viewpoints, concept marketing, and other media output related to project proposals, design concepts, expected development, popular projects, animation marketing, event experience, and fashion design (Fig. 5).

References

1. Huizhen, L., Shouyong, Z.: Current situation and future developing trend of virtual threedimensional clothing displaying technology. China Text. Leader **3**, 019 (2015)
2. Breen, D.E., House, D.H., Wozny, M.J.: Predicting the drape of woven cloth using interacting particles. Comput. Graph. **32**(4), 365–372 (1994)
3. Yang, Y., Magnenat-Thalmann, Y.: An improved algorithm for collision detection in cloth animation with human body. Comput. Graph. **1**, 237–251 (1993)
4. Volino, P., Magnenat-Thalmann, N.: Developing simulation techniques for an interactive clothing system. In: Proceedings of Virtual Systems and Multimedia (VSMM 1997), pp. 109–118. IEEE Press, Geneva (1997)
5. Volino, P., Magnenat-Thalmann, N.: Implementing fast cloth simulation with collision response. In: Proceedings of Computer Graphics International, pp. 257–266. IEEE Press, New York (2000)

6. Power, J., Apeagyei, P., Jefferson, A.: Integrating 3D scanning data & textile parameters into virtual clothing. In: Proceedings of the 2nd International Conference on 3D Body Scanning Technologies, Lugano, Switzerland (2011)
7. Mu, S., Cao, W.: Virtual fashion design with CLO3D. J. Electron. Sci. Technol. **2**, 366–371 (2015)
8. Yishan, W., Zengbo, X.: Shanghai 2016 key technology of virtual garment fitting system. Shanghai University of Engineering Science, Fashion College, China (2016)
9. Hailian, Y., Yilei, C.: Application of three-dimensional virtual fitting designs. Des. J. (11) (2018)
10. Yufei, Z., Shijian, L.: Micro plant of virtual apparel customization based on industrial design. Ind. Des. Res. Zhejiang Univ. (2017)
11. Magnenat-Thalmann, N., Volino, P.: From early draping to haute couture models: 20 years of research. Vis. Comput. **21**, 506–519 (2005). Springer. https://doi.org/10.1007/s00371-005-0347-6. Accessed 1 Sept 2005
12. Yibo, C.: Photoshop image processing techniques. Sci. China Technol. Sci. 76–78 (2009)
13. CLOEnterprise V2.3.135 (X64). http://room715.hatenablog.com/entry/2015/12/31/040602
14. The Fabricant x I.T Hong Kong Digital Collection Made w/CLO. https://www.facebook.com/clo3d/videos/322895858294989/
15. I.T Shop Lifestyle Collection. https://www.thefabricant.com/it-hong-kong
16. Liqiang, D.: J. Zhejiang Fashion Inst. Technol. (2014). cqvip.com
17. GPU Emulation, Fastest Simulation Speed, Ver 5.0. https://www.clo3d.com/promotion/5_0

Advanced Designing Assistant System for Smart Design Based on Product Image Dataset

Yi Li[1], Yong Dai[2,3(✉)], Li-Jun Liu[1], and Hao Tan[1]

[1] School of Design, Hunan University,
Changsha, Hunan, China
{2012171,sallyliu,htan}@hnu.edu.cn
[2] School of Electrical and Information Engineering, Hunan University,
Changsha, Hunan, China
chd-dy@foxmail.com
[3] Key Laboratory of Visual Perception and Artificial Intelligence of Hunan Province,
Changsha, Hunan, China

Abstract. Existing product images are very important references for designing a new scheme. However, the designers have to collect and organize the product image data manually without proper tools, which may be time-consuming, inefficient and expensive. The rapid growth of product design has called for a smart system to assist designers with a quick start in designing a new product. Therefore, we propose an advanced designing assistant system (ADAS) to help the designers handle the large-volume product images more efficiently and create better design. The ADAS utilizes big data and artificial intelligence technology to achieve mass product data acquisition, analysis, retrieval, and design scheme generation. The ADAS utilizes builds a product image dataset firstly to decrease high cost of time and money in images collection task. Furthermore, based on this dataset, the ADAS develops three applications: (1) image retrieval and infringement analysis, (2) multi-label semantic annotation, (3) automatic design scheme generation. Experiments are conducted to validate the merits of the proposed system. And the results show that the ADAS could support designers with high quality from initial data collection to image retrieval, infringement analysis, semantic learning, and design scheme generation throughout the entire flow of the design task, greatly shortening the design period and improving efficiency.

Keywords: Product image dataset ·
Advanced designing assistant system · Retrieval ·
Multi-label semantic annotation · Automatic design scheme generation

Supported by the National Natural Science Foundation of China (No. 61772186).

P.-L. P. Rau (Ed.): HCII 2019, LNCS 11576, pp. 18–33, 2019.
https://doi.org/10.1007/978-3-030-22577-3_2

1   Introduction

Existing products are very useful resources for designers in product design, which could inspire designers to come out the new concepts and achieve a preliminary design scheme more quickly. The product images are the most intuitive expression of products which contain the basic design rules, the historical and current popular design of a certain product. In the era of rapid update of product design, such information is very useful for a quick start in developing a new product and grasping the design trend of a certain product.

Traditionally, the designers have to collect and organize the product image data manually, which may be time-consuming, inefficient and expensive. And most importantly, the manually collected data cannot cover most of the product images [12]. Hence, it is difficult to grasp the current product design trend and design concept with only a small number of product data, resulting in the appearance of the same design and bad law consequences [15]. What's more, it not only limits the speed and quality of product development but also increases the cost and risk of design innovation. At present, enterprise official websites and shopping platforms offer a huge amount of product data which are enormous, extensive and fast updating. But the data volume may be too large for the designers to process without proper tools. With the development of information technology, advanced intelligent acquisition of big data and deep learning technology can be utilized to handle these problems [3,4,6,25].

Motivated by this, an advanced designing assistant system (ADAS) is proposed which utilizes big data and artificial intelligence technology to help the designers with mass product data acquisition, analysis, retrieval, and design scheme generation. The rapid development of information technology represented by the Internet has promoted the formation of big data of products and provided an information basis for the research and development of new products. Image retrieval could find similar images with designers' target product image, which could help them to seek inspiration or prevent the infringing act before or after design work, respectively. Multi-label annotation could be applied to describe design schemes with several features such as time, style, function, etc., which could better describe the schemes. After reviewing and analysing the previous product, automatic generation algorithms can be applied to assist designers to find the features and styles from skilled designers to seek for the inspiration and then propose the initial design scheme.

To the best of our knowledge, this is the first work to present such kind of advanced designing assistant system based on product image dataset for product design. The key contributions of our work are as follows:

1. The construction of the dataset to speed up the data collection task, and an efficient procedure for image preprocess which can be easily generalized to augment and update the dataset.
2. A different method for infringement analysis based on product features present in images, and the architecture of automatic design scheme generation part which can support designers to create new design schemes quickly.

3. The formulation of the ADAS which could support designers with high quality from initial data collection to image retrieval, infringement analysis, semantic learning and design proposal generation throughout the entire flow of the design task, greatly shortening the design period and improving efficiency.

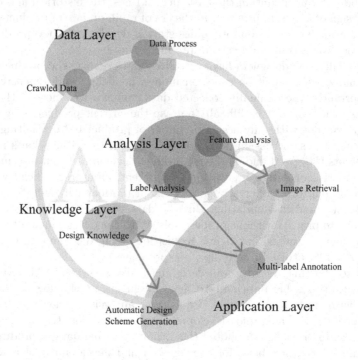

Fig. 1. The framework of the advanced designing assistant system (ADAS).

The rest of the paper is organized as follows. Section 2 gives an overview of the ADAS. Section 3 presents how we obtain the images and preprocess them. Section 4 is devoted to the introduction of three applications in the application layer and their corresponding preparation work in the analysis layer and the knowledge layer of ADAS system. Conclusions and future work are finally reported in Sect. 5.

2   Advanced Designing Assistant System

Figure 1 illustrates the framework of the proposed ADAS system which consists of four layers: the data layer, the analysis layer, the knowledge layer, and the application layer. The data layer can support designers in handling the data collection task with a data acquisition and preprocessing step. The major sources of data acquisition step are official websites of the related enterprises and the online stores. The sources can cover most of the product data, which are enough to grasp the current product design trend. And the "cluttered" and duplicate images are removed in preprocessing step to get the product images with high quality. The analysis layer is an intermediate layer to make preparations for the application layer. This layer can assist designers to analyze the key features of the products which users want and the attribute that can display design elements and describe products better. The knowledge layer mainly helps designers to check the design trend including time, style, function, etc. based on product images, since they contain the most critical features of the product intuitively.

The application layer is an integration layer with multiple functions. Firstly, the annotation part can help designers to annotate the product images with multiple labels based on the attribute of the product analyzed in the analysis layer. Secondly, image retrieval and infringement analysis are carried out by using the annotated labels and features analyzed before. This function can help designers to find the most suitable images for their demands, and also help them seek inspiration or compare the similarity with their design schemes before or after design work, respectively. The most important part is the design scheme generation part which is developed to assist designers to improve the efficiency of product design. This part is achieved by integrating an automatic scheme generation step and optimization step. The generation step utilizes the Generative Adversarial Networks to capture the statistical distribution and features from the existing product images and generate new design schemes based on the learned distribution and features. The generated schemes have a similar distribution but are different from the existing product. Finally, the optimization step develops a sketch inversion model to transfer the hand-drawn sketches, inspired by generated schemes before, to photorealistic design schemes.

This ADAS system can easily and quickly augment and update the product data using data acquisition and preprocessing procedure, avoiding high labor, time and money cost in images collection task. Meanwhile, the system can also support designers from semantic learning, to image retrieval, design scheme generation and infringement analysis throughout the entire flow of the design task, freeing the designers from the specific algorithms which are complicated and elusive and providing them with visual design scheme and greatly shortening the design period and improving efficiency.

3   Data Acquisition and Preprocessing

In this section, the proposed methods for image acquisition and preprocessing will be presented in detail. More than 160 thousand images are crawled from several big online shopping websites. It is observed that: (a) some images have inappropriate size, (b) some images have cluttered background which is useless to be the reference for design work, (c) some images are same. So firstly, the images whose sizes are inappropriate or have bad length-width ratios are resized to the size of 200×200 pixels. Next, images are put into a "cluttered" removal procedure. This step uses frequency-tuned salient region detection [9] to get salient

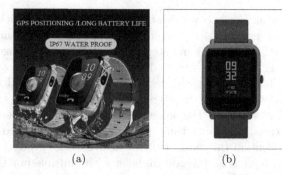

(a)   (b)

Fig. 2. An example of "cluttered" and "pure" images. (a) The "cluttered" image with poor background or unclear edge of the product; (b) "pure" image with pure white background and clear edge of the product.

Table 1. Several examples of categories and their corresponding amounts and brands number.

Category	Sample number	Brand number
Interphone	5156	151
VR glasses	2560	181
Earphone	7699	971
Bluetooth audio	6995	621
Mobile phone	2491	184
Smart watch	5459	412
Band	3672	365
Headset	5284	556
Radio	5346	260
MP4	2015	81

objects since it could achieve the best results among several saliency detection algorithms [1,2,5,30]. Feature extraction of the inter and outer area of the salient objects are judged to classify whether the backgrounds of images are pure and white or not. The images with pure and white backgrounds remained, others are removed. Taking smart watch as an example, Fig. 2 shows the examples of "cluttered" (a) and "pure" (b) images.

The comparison of similarity based on dhash is put forward to remove the duplicated images to get rid of data redundancy. Firstly, perceptual Hash Algorithm [26,27] is used to computer dhash value for the remained images after "cluttered" removal. Then we successively select pairwise images to calculated Hamming distance (L) among them to obtain their similarity. Finally, one of them is removed when their similarity is above 0.95, note that the more similar images are, the bigger similarity between two images is. And when the images are the same, the similarity is 1. The formal steps are achieved automatically using data analysis algorithms coded by Python, decreasing several hundred worker hours. This procedure for image preprocess can be easily employed to add more categories to augment the dataset.

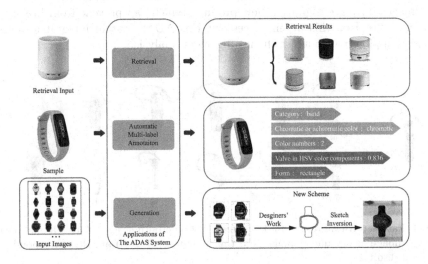

Fig. 3. The overview of the applications in the proposed ADAS system.

The remaining set contains 64893 images including a total of sixteen categories of daily electronic products with more than four thousand brands, 76.3% of the products have more than 5 images including front view, top view, left view and some local view in detail. And the images with the same view of products are put into the same folders. This step is carried out to prepare for the automatic generation of design schemes. Table 1 gives several examples of categories and their corresponding amounts and brand numbers.

4   Applications of the ADAS System

Figure 3 shows the overview of the applications in the ADAS system. Retrieval part can be used to retrieve similar images with the query image, results are given after the query image inputted to the retrieval part of the ADAS system. And multi-label part is actually a pre-trained model that could annotate new images with their own corresponding labels. Finally, new design schemes could be generated after inputting images of a certain category to the generation part of the ADAS system.

4.1   Image Retrieval and Infringement Analysis

In the industrial design field, designers usually need to collect and analyse the images of the existing product since they are very important references for designing a new scheme. However, without proper tools, designers have to search for target images manually with much time and money consuming. Based on this, image retrieval technology is urgently needed to support designers to handle this problem. Besides, it is also important to analyse the degree of similarity between two images during designing a new product, which can prevent from breaking tort law. Based on this urgent necessary, this ADAS system integrates image retrieval application to assist the infringement analysis.

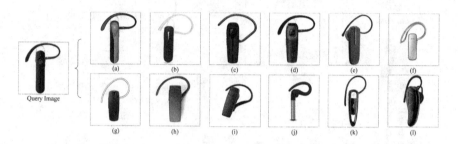

Fig. 4. Partial retrieval results for the category of bluetooth headset. Given a bluetooth headset image as the query image, and the subfigure (a) to (l) are the corresponding retrieval results.

Retrieving the New Image. Due to the high computational cost, traditional similarity search methods such as the nearest neighbor search and tree-based techniques are not suitable for large-scale image retrieval [14,22]. In order to achieve efficient image retrieval, hashing methods that construct similarity-preserving binary codes for efficient image search have drawn significant attention in this field [8,14]. And roughly speaking, learning-based hashing methods can generate more comparable and efficient binary codes for the retrieval task among the hashing methods.

For learning-based hashing methods, extracting discriminative feature representation of images is important for subsequent hashing transforming. For most conventional hashing methods, the image is first encoded into a vector with hand-crafted visual descriptors. However, the representative ability of such hand-crafted features is limited, which may result in poor retrieval performance [16,23,24]. Recently, deep learning, as a robust feature extraction tool, has achieved many significant breakthroughs in computer vision field. Compared with conventional machine-learning methods, deep learning can automatically extract high-level feature via a series of hierarchical layers. Hence, in the analysis layer, features are extracted by deep learning methods.

In this paper, a deep hashing network is proposed to achieve efficient image retrieval on this new dataset. This proposed method makes full use of the advantages of deep learning and hash technique. In this framework, the image features and hash codes can be simultaneously learned via a designed deep convolutional neural networks. In addition, the pairwise sample similarity is considered to obtain similarity preserving binary codes. The whole image retrieval framework is divided into three components. The first one is supervised pre-training on the larger-scale ImageNet dataset [21]. The second component is to fine tune the pre-trained model on the target dataset. In the last stage, given a query image, the similar images are ranked based on the minimal Hamming distance via the well-trained network. The retrieval performance can be significantly improved via combining deep learning with hashing learning. Partial retrieval results for the category of bluetooth headset is given in Fig. 4.

Table 2. The similarities between the object and other images corresponding to the retrieval results for the category of bluetooth headset.

Retrieval results	a	b	c	d	e	f
Similarity	0.85	0.82	0.80	0.80	0.78	0.77
Retrieval results	g	h	i	j	k	l
Similarity	0.76	0.73	0.71	0.65	0.64	0.61

Infringement Analysis. With the formation of the global economic integration, the domestic and overseas markets are changing rapidly and the product update speed is accelerating. Hence, new design schemes are apt to be the same with the existing design without efficient infringement analysis approaches, resulting in tort or bad law consequences after the new design scheme marketed. Traditionally, infringement analysis mainly depends on the similarity analysis by sophisticated designers through the view of design style, form, color assortment *etc*. However, the methods cannot be carried out accurately and effectively, which is one of the weakest links in product design.

Most of the time, the tort is analysed based on the reference of the degree of similarity. The proposed retrieval method extracts high-level features for the product images via a series of hierarchical layers. After binarizing the features using hash code technology, the similarity between images can be preserved in binary codes. Hamming distance, which is usually employed in hash technology, calculated between the binary codes is further figured as the similarity. Note that the proposed method use extracted features instead of original images. Extracted features can better represent the product images, since the same original product may have high Hamming distance when their images are in different size while extracted features still remain similar. Specifically, the more similar images are, the smaller Hamming distance between binary codes is.

The similarities between the query image and the corresponding retrieval results in Fig. 4 are given in Table 2. It is observed that the top four similarities are all above 0.80, which means these products are more similar to the object than others. The similarities can be referred for designers or analysis organization to provide assistant infringement analysis to some extent.

4.2   Multi-label Semantic Learning

After obtaining a large amount of image data, designers need to retrieve the images according to product attributes for reference. However, designers usually find pictures with little relevance or low quality when searching without proper tools, which reduces the design efficiency. Based on this, multi-label learning technology is needed to better structure the image data with multiple labels such as time, style and function [11]. So that images can be described more intuitively and retrieved accurately according to labels.

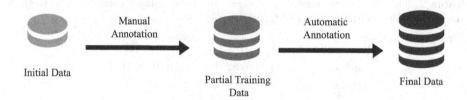

Fig. 5. The flow of the multi-label semi-manual annotation procedure.

Labels Analysis. Multi-label learning algorithms should be trained with a part of images with ground-truth to automatically generate labels for a product image [7,28]. Traditionally, images with ground-truth were always annotated by the annotator, but it is a time-consuming work when the amount of the data is very extensive.

Motivated by this, this paper develops a model based on machine learning algorithms to assist the annotation task. Below, to overcome the subjective feelings of annotators so as to increase the annotation precision of algorithms. A set of basic objective labels are firstly select which are picked from attributes of the product and the elements of industrial design. With the addition of the categories of products, the number of labels is extended to 20.

- Category
  As mentioned before, the dataset contains a total of 16 categories of daily electronic products with more than three thousand brands. Categories are selected instead of brands into the annotation task since there are too many brands to annotate.
- Chromatic or achromatic color
  Achromatic color is a combination of white, black, and a variety of degree of gray that are formed from white and black. On the contrary, chromatic includes spectral color, natural object color, and artificial color etc.
- Color numbers
  When designing products, designers usually need to consider the color assortment. So the number of colors is also a design element that should be taken into consideration.

- Value of HSV color components

  The value indicates the bright degree of color. For the light source color, the value is tied to the luminosity of the light body. For object color, this value is tied to the transmittance or reflectance of an object.

- Form

  The form is another kind of design element that is usually considered when designing a product. Common form usually contains two kinds such as circular type and rectangle type.

Image Annotation. Due to the characteristic of objective labels, these labels should be able to be annotated automatically by code. But sometimes, some categories' images may affect the results, taking mobile as an example, the picture shown in mobile's screen may decrease the precision of annotation for the label of color numbers and chromatic or achromatic color. Hence, the annotation task is divided into two parts, one part is annotated by code, and the other one part is annotated by annotator with the help of a trained model.

Fig. 6. Several samples with their corresponding labels which are generated from multi-label annotation part of the ADAS system.

(a) Automatical annotation

  For the labels of category and value of HSV color components, programs are written to annotate the labels automatically. It's easy to annotate the labels of the category since the data are managed into its corresponding folders of category when crawled from webs. For the labels of the value of HSV color components, we refer to the preprocessing step which is discussed in Sect. 3. Saliency detection is applied first to get the region of objects, and then the value of the certain region of the image could be obtained.

(b) Semi-manual annotation

  Next, Fig. 5 introduces the semi-manual annotation procedures for annotating the multiple labels. The annotators manually view and annotate about a half of all images for each category. If the annotator sees a certain concept exist in the image, label it as positive. Otherwise, label it as negative. These portion of annotated images are used as the training data to perform multi-label induction on the remaining unlabeled images. After applying automatic annotation, final data with labels can be obtained. Final data are much bigger than initial manually annotated data.

Semantic Labels Generation. After revising the final data, the big amount data with labels can be applied to optimize the automatic annotation model. This model is embedded in the multi-label annotation part of the ADAS system. Just as Fig. 3 shows, given a new image, the multi-label annotation part can automatically output its corresponding labels. Figure 6 shows several samples with their corresponding labels which are generated from multi-label annotation part of the ADAS system. By the way, designers can also retrieve images from the final data based on annotated labels. Images with the same label can help designers better analysis the features and learn to how to use the features in their own design works.

Fig. 7. Examples for the category of the watch in the front view.

4.3 Automatic Design Scheme Generation

The rapid update of products in the current era requires designers to accurately grasp the design trend and design products in line with market demands faster and better. However, due to the incomplete data acquisition in the research process and the limitation of the designer's personal level, the designers are often unable to design products quickly which keep up with the trend of products and the needs of users. Based on this urgent need, automatic design scheme generation could support designers to predict trend and propose new product schemes with a quick start.

Image Preprocessing. In Sect. 3, after the images are completely preprocessed, the dataset is classified properly according to their own categories. And for each category, the images with the same view of products have put into the same folders. These images in the same view can be fed into the training set for generative adversarial networks which can learn specific object representations for products. Figure 7 gives the partial samples which are in the front view for the category of the watch.

The quality of the generations depends on two aspects, first is the amount and quality of images, second is the performance of the algorithms. For the first aspect, there still remains one step to be processed. The images with the same view of products could be regarded with good quality, but the amount of these images is still small. For the second aspect, advanced algorithms which have satisfied performance could be utilized to overcome the negative effects of algorithms.

Augmenting images is a good way and often used by researchers for machine learning when training data are in shortage. Most used augmentation techniques include image rotated, image resized, image blurred and adding different kinds of noise to images. However, images with good quality and the same view are needed in this paper. Hence, image blurred and adding noise techniques which can decrease the quality of images are not appropriate. Besides, generation algorithms have to model the distribution without rotation invariance. In this way, image rotated technique is also inappropriate. Considering the situation of our research, We finally decide to use the image resized technique. To ensure the integrality of the product, two provisos are defined, including: (1) the size of salient object is not allowed to be bigger than the size of 200×200 pixels, (2) the size of salient object is limited to be bigger than the size of 160×160 pixels to prevent the product becoming too small. All resized images will be cropped or filled to the size of 200×200 pixels.

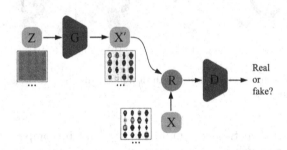

Fig. 8. The framework of generative adversary network (GAN), including the discriminator (D) and the generator (G). X means the real data sample, Z represents noise source and X′ is the synthetic data sample generated by the Generator (G). X′ and X are combined after X′ is generated in R, then the combination is discriminate by D.

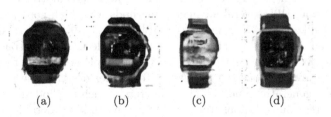

Fig. 9. Generated new schemes by DCGAN (a), LSGAN (b), WGAN (c, d).

Scheme Generation. Figure 8 shows the whole framework of generative adversary network. Setting capital X as the real data sample and capital Z as the noise source, X′ is the synthetic data sample generated by the Generator (G). By the way, images can be regarded as a kind of noise distribution, and the generator is trained to map a noise sample to a synthetic data sample that can deceive the discriminator (D). The generator has no direct access to real images, the only way it learns is through its interaction with the discriminator. The discriminator has access to both the synthetic samples and samples drawn from the stack of real images. Both real data sample X and synthetic data sample X′ are transferred to the discriminator. The discriminator is trained to distinguish real data sample from synthesized samples. The real or fake result is provided through the real data with ground truth of knowing whether the image came from the real stack or from the generator. If the synthetic data sample X′ is discriminated as the real data sample, then it can be used to train the generator, leading it towards being able to produce forgeries of better quality.

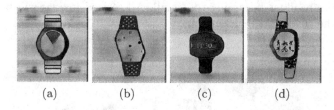

(a)   (b)   (c)   (d)

Fig. 10. Partial results of generated watch design scheme by the design scheme generation part of ADAS.

Both G and D are trained simultaneously, and in competition with each other. Generative models learn to capture the statistical distribution of training data, allowing us to synthesize samples from the learned distribution. With the training times increasing, the distribution of the synthetic data sample X′ will have more and more similar distribution of the real data sample X. Using this method, the synthetic data sample X′ is our new generated design scheme which has combined the distributed features but is different with the real product data.

From 2014 when the generative adversary network was firstly put forward by Goodfellow et al. [10], several advancing methods with high generation quality were present, like DCGAN [20], LSGAN [18], WGAN [19] *etc.* In this paper, we try to use these advanced methods to generate a design scheme based on our product dataset. Taking smart watch as the example, we select front view of images which are preprocessed in Sect. 3. To further describe the possibility of automatically generating, individual parameters of each method are instantiated according to recommendations from the literature. And in general for these algorithms, the batch size is fixed at 64, the learning rate is set at 0.0002. To decrease the cost, images are all resized to 64×64 pixels from the size of 200×200 pixels.

Figure 9 shows the partially selected results of generation by DCGAN (a), LSGAN (b) and WGAN (c, d), respectively. The results are of low resolution than the results when the algorithms are adapted to the LSUN [29] dataset or the CelebA dataset [17] present in the corresponding literature. The numbers of the LSUN dataset and the CelebA dataset reach to more than one hundred thousand, however, from Table 1, we can see that the number of smart watch is of shortage to some extent, so this may be the reason for lower resolution than the expectation.

Optimization. Karras *et al.* [13] proposed a method which can improve quality, stability, and variation by a progressive growing of GANs, unfortunately, this method still improve little for the resolution due to the inadequate data of some certain categories. Therefore, an optimization step is carried out to further obtain design schemes with high quality. In this step, sophisticated designers draw the sketches based on the form of generated results before. However, sketches are achromatic and do not contain color information. On the contrary, the visual effect of the product rendering is closer to the final product which is more attractive. We consider the method that design renderings are generated from their corresponding sketches. Hence, a sketch inversion model is developed to transfer the hand-drawn sketches to photorealistic design schemes. Taking the watch as an example to validate the merits of the proposed system, partial results of generated watch design scheme are given in Fig. 10.

5   Conclusions and Future Work

In this paper, an advanced designing assistant system (ADAS) is proposed to help the designers handle the large-volume product images more efficiently and create better design. A product image dataset is firstly built by the ADAS to decrease high cost of time and money in images collection task. After removing the "cluttered" and duplicate images, the ADAS develops three applications based on this dataset including image retrieval and infringement analysis, multi-label semantic annotation, and automatic design scheme generation. System test results reported in this paper shows the merits of the proposed system. Image retrieval could accurately find similar images with designers' target product image, which could help them to seek inspiration or compare the similarity with their design schemes before or after design work, respectively. The multi-label semantic learning could correctly generate labels for new product images which can better semantically describe the products. And most importantly, the application of automatic design scheme generation could assist the designers to easily propose new design schemes.

Future work will mainly focus on the following aspects. Firstly, more product images for more categories will be obtained to augment the dataset. Secondly, more subjective elements of industrial design will be done in the future annotation to better semantically describe the design scheme. Finally, more algorithms will be further discussed from the aspects of getting better design scheme with the designers' intervention.

Acknowledgements. This work is supported by the National Natural Science Foundation of China (No. 61772186). The authors would like to thank following persons who put a lot of valuable effort throughout the processes of collecting the dataset and annotation: Liu Yang (Hunan Univ., China), Xiangmei Xiao (Hunan Univ., China), Yeye Li (Hunan Univ., China).

References

1. Achanta, R., Estrada, F., Wils, P., Susstrunk, S.: Salient region detection and segmentation. In: International Conference on Computer Vision Systems, vol. 5008, pp. 66–75 (2008)
2. Achanta, R., Hemami, S., Estrada, F., Susstrunk, S.: Frequency-tuned salient region detection. IEEE Conference on Computer Vision and Pattern Recognition, pp. 1597–1604, June 2009
3. Calderaro, A.: Book review: big data: a revolution that will transform how we live, work, and think. Media Cult. Soc. **37**(7), 1113–1115 (2015)
4. Chen, C., Jiang, S.: Research of the big data platform and the traditional data acquisition and transmission based on sqoop technology. Open Autom. Control Syst. J. **7**(1), 1174–1180 (2015)
5. Cheng, M., Mitra, N.J., Huang, X., Torr, P.H.S., Hu, S.: Global contrast based salient region detection. In: IEEE Conference on Computer Vision and Pattern Recognition, pp. 409–416, June 2011
6. Fan, J., Han, F., Liu, H.: Challenges of big data analysis. Natl. Sci. Rev. **1**(2), 293–314 (2014)
7. Fan, J., Yang, C., Shen, Y., Babaguchi, N., Luo, H.: Leveraging large-scale weakly-tagged images to train inter-related classifiers for multi-label annotation. In: ACM Workshop on Large-Scale Multimedia Retrieval and Mining, pp. 27–34, January 2009
8. Gong, Y., Lazebnik, S.: Iterative quantization: a procrustean approach to learning binary codes. In: IEEE Conference on Computer Vision and Pattern Recognition, pp. 817–824 (2011)
9. Hou, Q., Cheng, M., Hu, X., Borji, A., Tu, Z., Torr, P.H.S.: Deeply supervised salient object detection with short connections. IEEE Trans. Pattern Anal. Mach. Intell. **41**(4), 815–828 (2019)
10. Goodfellow, I.J., Jean Pouget-Abadie, M.M.: Generative adversarial networks. Adv. Neural Inf. Process. Syst. **3**, 2672–2680 (2014)
11. Jia, D., Russakovsky, O., Krause, J., Bernstein, M.S., Berg, A., Li, F.F.: Scalable multi-label annotation. In: SIGCHI Conference on Human Factors in Computing Systems, pp. 3099–3102, April 2014
12. Jihyun, L., Chang, M.L.: Stimulating designers' creativity based on a creative evolutionary system and collective intelligence in product design. Int. J. Ind. Ergon. **40**(3), 295–305 (2010)
13. Karras, T., Aila, T., Laine, S., Lehtinen, J.: Progressive growing of GANs for improved quality, stability, and variation. arXiv abs/1710.10196, October 2017
14. Kulis, B., Grauman, K.: Kernelized locality-sensitive hashing for scalable image search. In: IEEE International Conference on Computer Vision, pp. 2130–2137 (2010)
15. Kusiak, A., Salustri, F.: Computational intelligence in product design engineering: review and trends. IEEE Trans. Syst. Man Cybern. Part C **37**(5), 766–778 (2007)

16. Liu, W., Wang, J., Ji, R., Jiang, Y., Chang, S.: Supervised hashing with kernels. In: IEEE Conference on Computer Vision and Pattern Recognition, pp. 2074–2081 (2012)
17. Liu, Z., Luo, P., Wang, X., Tang, X.: Deep learning face attributes in the wild. In: International Conference on Computer Vision, pp. 3730–3738 (2015)
18. Mao, X., Li, Q., Xie, H., Lau, R.Y.K., Wang, Z.: Multi-class generative adversarial networks with the L2 loss function. arXiv abs/1611.04076, November 2016
19. Arjovsky, M., Chintala, S., Bottou, L.: Wasserstein GAN. In: International Conference on Machine Learning, pp. 214–223 (2017)
20. Radford, A., Metz, L., Chintala, S.: Unsupervised representation learning with deep convolutional generative adversarial networks. arXiv abs/1511.06434, November 2015
21. Russakovsky, O., et al.: ImageNet large scale visual recognition challenge. Int. J. Comput. Vis. 115(3), 211–252 (2015)
22. Shanmugapriya, N., Nallusamy, R.: A new content based image retrieval system using GMM and relevance feedback. J. Comput. Sci. 10(2), 330–340 (2014)
23. Shen, F., Shen, C., Liu, W., Shen, H.T.: Supervised discrete hashing. In: IEEE Conference on Computer Vision and Pattern Recognition, pp. 37–45 (2015)
24. Shi, X., Xing, F., Cai, J., Zhang, Z., Xie, Y., Yang, L.: Kernel-based supervised discrete hashing for image retrieval. In: Leibe, B., Matas, J., Sebe, N., Welling, M. (eds.) ECCV 2016. LNCS, vol. 9911, pp. 419–433. Springer, Cham (2016). https://doi.org/10.1007/978-3-319-46478-7_26
25. Sivarajah, U., Kamal, M.M., Irani, Z., Weerakkody, V.: Critical analysis of big data challenges and analytical methods. J. Bus. Res. 70, 263–286 (2017)
26. Wen, Z., et al.: A robust and discriminative image perceptual hash algorithm. In: International Conference on Genetic and Evolutionary Computing, pp. 709–712, December 2011
27. Weng, L., Preneel, B.: A secure perceptual hash algorithm for image content authentication. In: De Decker, B., Lapon, J., Naessens, V., Uhl, A. (eds.) CMS 2011. LNCS, vol. 7025, pp. 108–121. Springer, Heidelberg (2011). https://doi.org/10.1007/978-3-642-24712-5_9
28. Wu, F., et al.: Weakly semi-supervised deep learning for multi-label image annotation. IEEE Trans. Big Data 1(3), 109–122 (2015)
29. Yu, F., Zhang, Y., Song, S., Seff, A., Xiao, J.: LSUN: construction of a large-scale image dataset using deep learning with humans in the loop. arXiv abs/1506.03365, June 2015
30. Yun, Z., Mubarak, S.: Visual attention detection in video sequences using spatiotemporal cues. In: ACM International Conference on Multimedia, pp. 815–824, October 2006

A Study on Application of Enclothed Cognition in Apparel Design

Szuyao Lin[✉]

Graduate School of Creative Industry Design,
National Taiwan University of Arts, New Taipei City, Taiwan
cynszlin@gmail.com

Abstract. This study is designed to investigate the application of enclothed cognition in apparel design based on the study that extended from clothing psychology. Using the potential of the systematic influence that clothes have on wearers' psychological process, the purpose is to seek the relationship between clothing, psychology, and cognitive and behavioral response. The study explores the current influence and interpretation of clothing on psychology, and by taking the perspective of enclothed cognition to make further relevant acknowledged and developmental research. In addition, with the goal of implementing affecting factors for apparel design, and to refer to product design concept. This study verifies not just the visual impacts that clothing bring to the wearers, but also the spiritual satisfaction. Then, by the process of re-designing the clothing, this study attempts to arouse the public awareness and reinterpret the meaning for apparel design in a social and cultural aspect. The study integrates the literatures reviews on the application for clothing psychology, cultural product design model and emotional design for developing the research framework. Through case study of two apparel brands, the study analyses and explores the use of their current designing process in a literary framework. This study is attempted to provide a farsighted thinking method for the apparel design industry. The contribution of this study lies in: (1) Expanding the multi-directional plasticity development of apparel design and psychology at the academic and practical levels. (2) Through the research and exploration of this study, constructing the framework for apparel design that go beyond the function and usability benefit and also bring emotional benefit for the product as a reference in relevant creative fields.

Keywords: Clothing psychology · Enclothed cognition ·
Cultural product design · Emotional design

1 Introduction

1.1 Background

Nowadays, the modern society is changing faster and in the age of advance in information technology, everyone has the opportunity to appear oneself. Usually when observing a person, at the first glance, our subconscious mind will depend on the first impression: appearance. Regardless of whether the person is aware or not, the

P.-L. P. Rau (Ed.): HCII 2019, LNCS 11576, pp. 34–45, 2019.
https://doi.org/10.1007/978-3-030-22577-3_3

appearance also affects our perception and judgment of others. Many people know how we wear that affecting how others perceive themselves. There have been many researches on clothing psychology which is mainly to explore how to use clothing to shape the way that others see themselves. The most common example is the clothing for business wears. Theoretical studies have shown that proper dressing in particular occasion is important for the social relationship, and that the choice of clothing is actually more than expected [5].

As they say, "Clothes are the second layer of skin" can be explained as clothing is an extension of oneself, which is also the medium used to show oneself to the outside world. However, a new study by the APS-The Association for Psychological Science found that clothes may not only affect the way others see us but the clothes people wear will also affect how the wearer perceives oneself. Through out the cognitive process, we influence the way we think [14]. Therefore, in the relationship between clothing, psychology, and cognition and behavior, there are many potential possibilities and it is an area worthy for further discussion.

What if we can change our mood simply depending on what clothes we wear? A recent research called enclothed cognition by Northwestern University, which is the systematic influence that clothes have on wearers' psychological process: what you wear influence how you think and feel [1]. Clothing can both reflect and generate an emotional state [11]. Whether the clothes can be used to influence the thinking and feelings of the wearers, such as the function that many emotion design products in the market or not. The study is characterized to research the emotional concern in the process of conception and production for apparel design.

1.2   Motivation and Objective

Clothing is ubiquitous. It is in touch with our body almost every moment. The majority of people face the situation everyday: what to wear. Enormous researches have shown that clothing is more than simply a trend comes and goes as a material benefits [2]. The intimate connection between clothing and wearers could be considered deeply more as a spiritual satisfaction. With the development of society, clothing has long been more than just a tool to protect the body, protect the cold from the heat, and defend against external aggression. In the fast fashion era, clothing has gradually become a symbol of people's self-expression. In daily life, through various styles of dressing, different clothing can be chosen according to different occupations, personality, age and other factors [6].

Clothing can be said to be omnipresent, and it is in contact with our bodies almost every moment. It can be seen that its influence and importance cannot be neglected, and there is an absolute mutual influence between clothing and human emotions. Mostly everyday, the first choice that most people face to start the day is: "What do you want to wear today?" Therefore, what if we can affect our feeling simply depends on the "clothes" we wear on our bodies? Using clothing as a medium to influence one's own cognition and even behavior, the standard of wearing clothes is not only one's "current feelings" but the concept of "hoping how to feel" toward you is the main motivation to this study.

Buying clothing is a very common consumer behavior nowadays. People might purchase them on impulse or perhaps in order to meet the needs of special occasions, but people buy a piece of clothing for certain reason at that moment. Every piece of clothing carries a story or gives a specific emotion. However, with the fast fashion culture that under the condition of lowering the quality to maintain the speed of changing seasons, the emotional added value that clothing should have has gradually lose its meaning just like any other disposable products. This study aims for the motives to change the public's awareness and reinterpret the meaning of clothing that it can bring people not only the visual influence but also show the spirit of satisfaction and execution in the real industry.

This study explores the possibility for application of enclothed cognition in apparel design. In the conception and production process of cultural product design that adding the emotional connection between the clothing itself and the wearers. The objectives of this study is to (1) Adding value to the emotional cognition in design process through the relationship between clothing and psychology. (2) Introducing emotional design attributes into apparel design. (3) Providing new innovative thinking and design framework for the apparel industry. (4) Based on experimental results and conclusions that might develop industrial business model that meets the needs of market demands.

2 Literature Review

2.1 Clothing Psychology/Enclothed Cognition

Karen Pine, the famous British psychologist has discovered through more than five years of researches that people's dressing is closely related to their mental state. What one's wearing can not only reflect wearer's psychological changes but also regulate one's emotions to achieve special effects of improvement [4]. As early as 2012, the study by Northwestern University proposed the theory that clothing affects people's psychological state is called Enclothed Cognition. It is found the subjects who are dressed in laboratory white coat that they think its the doctors' coat performance is better than the one who think its the painters' coat, as shown in Fig. 1.

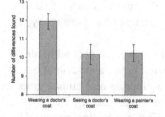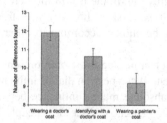

Fig. 1. Sustained attention: number of differences found in the comparative visual search tasks, as a function of experimental condition [1]

The results show that people's acknowledge toward the dressing's characteristics which in turn that affects their cognition and behaviors afterward. The study presents a potentially unifying framework to integrate the past findings and captures the diverse influences that clothing have on the wearers by proposing that enclothed cognition involves the co-occurrence of two independent factors: (1) the symbolic meaning of the clothes and (2) the physical experience of wearing them [1]. This theory is widely used in many clothing-related researches in the apparel industry for dressing effects, casual dresses, sportswear, and professional uniforms. By mean of giving the clothing a specific identity which could guide the behavior and the differences in dressing is equivalent to a sign of different identity of conversions [13].

2.2　Cultural Product Design

Cultural product design, which is a process of rethinking the cultural features and then redefining them for the purpose of designing the product that can in accordance with the society and at the meanwhile can satisfy consumers culturally and aesthetically [3]. By using the cultural features to add non-rational value to the products could increase the economic of the society over the market, and also connect the specific characteristics of a particular culture. As cultural creativity has became a critical issue among the design industry, a cultural product design framework is shown as Fig. 2, which is proposed for combining cultural levels, layers and design features in order to facilitate the understanding of cultural product design [9].

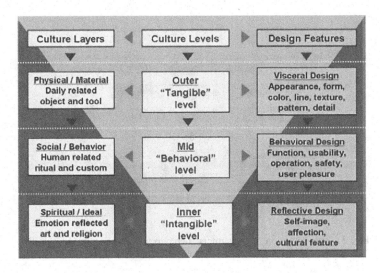

Fig. 2. Three layers and levels of cultural objects and design features [9]

As shown in Fig. 2 offers the framework for cultural objects, in this study would be the clothing and in which is classified into three layers: (1) physical or material culture, (2) social or behavioral culture, and (3) spiritual or ideal culture. Furthermore, these three layers of culture can be matched into three cultural levels as shown. While three design features can be identified according to the corresponding cultural objects as:

(1) the intangible level, containing reflective emotions and feelings, (2) the behavioral level, dealing with function and usability, and (3) the tangible level, handling with color, texture, shape, decoration, pattern, quality, and surface detail [9]. While cultural factors have became important issues for various design fields, this study attempts to take the cultural product design model as a valuable reference and use in apparel design, as clothing is a major cultural objects widely as it is an universal design.

2.3   Emotional Design

Understanding the emotions consumers feel about the products can help the designers make the most of its designs in the market. Emotional Design by Donald Norman states why attractive things work better in which he explains the important of aesthetics in inducing an emotional judgment that would enhances the products' usability. The emotions which affect the consumers' behaviors are based on three aspects of design: (1) visceral, the pre-conscious reaction, mostly are the product appearance, (2) behavioral, the conscious use and experience with the product like functionality and usability, and (3) reflective, the interpretation and understanding of the product, including both the emotional and cognitive reaction like personal memories and experiences [12]. His theory interprets how design affects emotions and how emotions affect consumers' decisions which has changed the designing process in the industry.

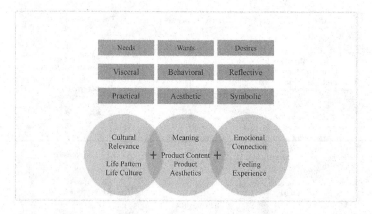

Fig. 3. The evolution of consumers' behaviors from needs to desires [8]

The purpose of products design is to meet the physiological and psychological needs of human beings through conception and production of designing. Therefore, in addition to the functions that the products are designed and manufactured according to engineering, whether the products can meet the expectations of users psychologically should be importantly considered as well during the designing process [8]. By taking Norman's idea and to refer to product design, the mutual relations is shown as Fig. 3, where the product functions are divided into three categories: (1) practical function that meet the visceral needs, (2) aesthetic function that accomplish the behavioral wants, and (3) symbolic function that fulfill the reflective desires. The emotional design has established a crucial relation between affective and cognitive reaction, thus cognition drives our affective states, our emotions, and hence influencing our behavior [12].

3   Methodology

The study integrates the literatures reviews on the application for clothing culture and psychology, cultural product design model and emotional design for the conceptual model of the research process, as shown in Fig. 4. Various informations are collected academically and industrially in order to form useful knowledge toward the study. By applying the acknowledge of enclothed cognition and adding the creative value which referring to emotional design to developing the research framework. Furthermore, through case study of two apparel brands that originated from the concept, the study analyses and explores the use of their current design process to evaluate within a literary framework as the research assessment. The study attempts to use the four steps scenario method for the design process and validate the prototype using evaluation grid method.

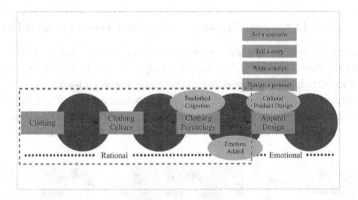

Fig. 4. A broad overview of the research process

3.1   Research Framework

The framework of the study is revised and combined from Lin's cultural product design and Norman's emotional design as shown in Fig. 5. Considering apparel for not just rational consume which only fulfill consumers' expectation and cognition in visceral and behavioral design aspect, it is more importantly for the emotional experience that focus in reflective design aspect for the wearers. Through the research, the idea of designers' creativity toward the sensibility of inner emotion for the users are become a crucial added value for apparel design. As the concept of enclothed cognition is to describe the systematic influence that clothing have on the wearers' psychological processes [1]. The study offers a potentially integrated framework to combine the past acknowledge and examine three different design impacts though the design process.

And thus the research particularly will focus on the reflective design which includes both the emotional and cognitive reaction between the designers and the product which emphasizes the wearers' self-images, memories, experiences, and culture [9].

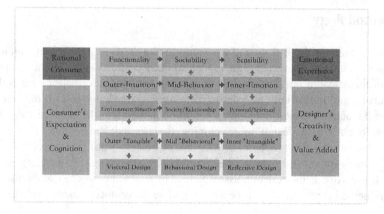

Fig. 5. Research framework for application of enclothed cognition in apparel design

3.2   Case Study-1 "Abstract_": Clothes Made from Your Emotional Data

Danish designers, Bjørn Karmann in interaction design, Kristine Boesen in textiles design and Julie Helles Eriksen in fashion design together created with a concept that they thread your feelings into customized and unique piece of ready-to-wear garments. Instead of only designers participating in the design process before the manufacturing, the idea is to let the end-users involved in the design process simply by collecting data into generating patterns from their own personal stories and face expression, as shown in Fig. 6.

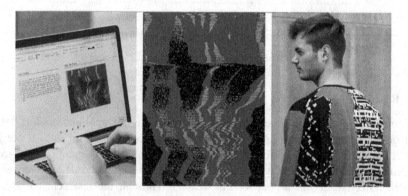

Fig. 6. The design process of "Abstract_"

The concept offers the customers a different connection to the clothing they are purchasing in which that gives reflective aspect of their inner emotion for the sensibility. This design process that involved typing a story about your own, and then following up the data gained from the pace of keystrokes (what and how is written) combined with facial expression. The picked up data will then translate into an unique patterned material, as shown in Fig. 7 only from this specific information [7].

Fig. 7. Color samples and textiles made from user-generated stories

The data affects all the elements, such as color, thread thickness and knitted rhythm in order to make a piece of garment. The material is then transformed from the customers' personal pattern into a textiles piece of garment, as shown in Fig. 8. With "Abstract_", the clothes are produced on the demand of personal desires in which it at the basis of the concept is a deeper concern for human nature as they said. For the garment silhouette, it even reflects human error and features the uneven shapes in asymmetrical cuts, as shown in Fig. 8.

Fig. 8. Final outfit; materials created from user-generated stories

3.3   Case Study-2 "Enclothed Cognition": Clothes Inspired from Behavioral Psychology

Enclothed Cognition is an experimental project from fashion designer Bregje Cox and visual artist Mark King. They created the collection which is inspired by the theory of Enclothed Cognition. The concept of the design process is particularly about the garment's symbolic meaning combined with the physical experience of wearing it and how it affect the wearer's performance both in cognition and behavior. They also attempt to increase the public awareness within the clothes we wear, the environment we at, and the human mind we are [10].   Human behavioral psychology and biology are crucial elements in their design process which that offers behavioral and reflective aspects of physical and emotional response for the sociability and sensibility: how clothes impact our everyday performance and how we feel. During the design process, the garment's meaning is formed with the physical experiences of wearing it and the space relationship with the environment. Furthermore, for the symbolic meaning of the garment, they enrich the pattern inspired from the human nature and scientific principles, such as cell migration and landscape surface, as shown in Fig. 9.

Fig. 9. Final outfits, materials created from cellular pattern and spatial concern

Behavioral psychology are a great source for pattern. As shown in Fig. 10, the collection takes the imitation that the pattern occurring at the cellular level to create the feeling of wearing a second skin to bring the awareness that are happening subconsciously guide our behavior.

Fig. 10. Menswear collection for Summer/Spring 2019

Although the collection is more like an experimental concept, it surely arouse the public acknowledge in the apparel industry. As they mentioned, it not just the patterns: but also the silhouettes of the clothes, the design structures, how the fabric feels on the skin and what experience that provides the wearers a different but significant way of thinking in the design process in apparel design. By adding the behavioral and reflective aspect in the design, the clothes are evolved from purely functional aesthetics.

4   Discussion

The result and analysis from both case studies show that the apparel industry is taking a different pathway for the design process. The concept that takes the meaning of design into a different level of what the end-users can have influence on from the product consumed. The value in apparel design for the primitive purpose, which is mainly physical and functional are taking over by the innovation in design that are more social and spiritual satisfaction. As clothing is the most approachable products and applied to mostly each one of us, the emotional design aspect should be considered more in a sustainable and conscious way. As shown in Fig. 11, the research purpose and future conception for this study is listed as the conceptual framework. What we are wearing is a more powerful way not just to express one's personality and style, but on a higher level there might be something to convey and to put to use as a spiritual product. At the meantime, if people could build a stronger emotional connection to the product personally, the usage term of it might last longer in a better environmentally friendly way.

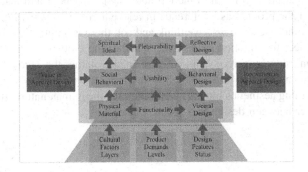

Fig. 11. Research future conception

5   Conclusion and Suggestion

As we continue to develop the potential framework around clothing psychology and apply into for academic and industrial design purpose. This study aims to arouse public consumers with awareness that how we could affect oneself purely by what we are using and surrounded by. Norman has addressed that the role of appealing aesthetic in eliciting a positive emotional state resulting in enhanced usability and user performance

[12]. Nowadays with the rapid developed technologies, design has become omnipresent in mostly every objects. That is in the case we should emphasize the element of human nature in design, which is design for feeling. The study attempt to execute the product design for future implementation that generated by the study result and combined with scenario method for design process. The evaluation grid method revised for the apparel design, as shown in Fig. 12 will be taken as the validation for the prototype.

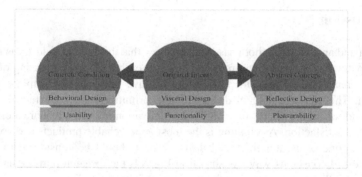

Fig. 12. Validation concept for apparel design product

The contribution of this study lies in: (1) Expanding the multi-directional plasticity development of apparel design and psychology at the academic and practical levels. (2) Through the research and exploration of this study, constructing the framework for apparel design that go beyond the function and usability benefit and also bring emotional benefit for the product as a reference in relevant creative fields. Furthermore, as what we wear could affect the way we think and act, there is a potential to use clothing as a healing object for emotion controlled. Whether the clothes to uplift depression, inspire attention, slow anger or achieve calm in the status, the study has aimed to discourse to the apparel industry that this research framework as a reference for designing something aesthetics but also well-being for the human nature. It is the future vision cross over between design and social science.

References

1. Adam, H., Galinsky, A.: Enclothed cognition. J. Exp. Soc. Psychol. **48**(4), 918–925 (2012). https://doi.org/10.1016/j.jesp.2012.02.008
2. Baumgartner, J.: You are What You Wear: What Your Clothes Reveal About You, 1st edn. Da Capo Lifelong Books, New York (2012)
3. Ho, M.C., Lin, C.H., Liu, Y.C.: Some speculations on developing cultural commodities. J. Des. **1**(1), 1–15 (1996)
4. Howlett, N., Pine, K., Cahill, N., Orakçıoğlu, I., Fletcher, B.: Unbuttoned: the interaction between provocativeness of female work attire and occupational status. Sex Roles **72**(3–4), 105–116 (2015). https://doi.org/10.1007/s11199-015-0450-8

5. Hutson, M., Rodriguez, T.: Dress for success: how clothes influence our performance. SA Mind **27** (2016). https://doi.org/10.1038/scientificamericanmind0116-13a (2016)
6. Karl, K., Hall, L., Peluchette, J.: City employee perceptions of the impact of dress and appearance. Publ. Pers. Manag. **42**(3), 452–470 (2013). https://doi.org/10.1177/0091026013495772
7. Kesa, I.: Wear clothes made from your emotional data (2015). https://www.vice.com/en_us/article/qkwwbq/wear-clothes-made-from-your-emotional-data. Accessed 30 Jan 2018
8. Lin, R., Hsieh, H.-Y., Sun, M.-X., Gao, Y.-J.: From ideality to reality - a case study of Mondrian style. In: Rau, P.-L.P. (ed.) CCD 2016. LNCS, vol. 9741, pp. 365–376. Springer, Cham (2016). https://doi.org/10.1007/978-3-319-40093-8_37
9. Lin, R.: Transforming Taiwan aboriginal cultural features into modern product design: a case study of a cross-cultural product design model. Int. J. Des. **1**(2), 45–53 (2007)
10. Martin, N. (ed.): Science in Style (2018). http://designerisland.com/stories/science-in-style. Accessed 30 Jan 2018
11. Moody, W., Kinderman, P., Sinha, P.: An exploratory study. J. Fashion Mark. Manag.: Int. J. **14**(1), 161–179 (2010). https://doi.org/10.1108/13612021011025483
12. Norman, D.A.: Emotional Design: Why We Love (or Hate) Everyday Things, 3rd edn. Basic Books, New York (2003)
13. Sarada-Joshi, G.: 7 ways your clothes change the way you think (2016). https://brainfodder.org/psychology-clothes-enclothed-cognition/. Accessed 30 Jan 2018
14. Slepian, M., Ferber, S., Gold, J., Rutchick, A.: The cognitive consequences of formal clothing. Soc. Psychol. Pers. Sci. **6**(6), 661–668 (2015). https://doi.org/10.1177/1948550615579462

Persuasive Design and Application of Intelligent Healthcare Product

Hongyu Liu and Zhirong Li[(✉)]

School of Architecture and Art, Central South University,
932 Lushan Street, Changsha 410083, Hunan, China
905410578@qq.com, 172677569@qq.com

Abstract. Intelligent healthcare is an emerging interdisciplinary field combining medical field, network technology and interaction and service design (Joseph, Ahn, Kim et al. 2005; Ma, Wang, Zhou et al. 2018). It is also an innovation to the clinical treatment with which patients actively cooperate at a specific time and place. At present, in view of the physical health problems, researchers have put forward design methods of behavior intervention, behavior modification and behavior prevention, such as self-shaping design, temptation-resistant design, behavior-changing design and emotion design (DeVries and Chevaux 2014; Mo, Xu, Duan et al. 2016). However, the formation and transformation of healthy behaviors are a gradual process of mental cooperation. Persuasion theory suggests that the user can be induced and persuaded to develop or change behavior through design intervention, so as to achieve the goal of fitness and develop healthy behaviors (Rebecca and Tobias 2001; Stephen 2004; Chris 2006). To summarize, the structure of this paper is as follows. First, based on persuasion theory, the behavior model is investigated and the design factors of persuasion are put forward. Second, persuasive behavior components are studied to build a persuasion design model for intelligent health-care products, and persuasive design strategies are proposed in this part. Third, the above design factors and strategies are analyzed in combination with design cases. Finally, this paper will summarize and put forward the future research direction.

Keywords: Persuasion theory · Intelligent health-care product ·
Behavior model · Design strategies

1 Introduction

Persuasion theory has attracted widespread attention in various fields such as e-commerce, app development, product design, and architectural design [1]. One of the important application areas is intelligent health-care product design. Intelligent health care is an emerging interdisciplinary field combining medical field, network technology, interaction and service design [2–4]. It is also an innovation to the clinical treatment with which patients actively cooperate at a specific time and place. Persuasion theory suggests that the user can be induced and persuaded to develop or change behaviors through design intervention, so as to achieve the goal of fitness and develop healthy behaviors [5–7].

Persuasive technology is usually defined as a technology to change the attitude or behavior of users through persuasion and social influence rather than coercion [8].

© Springer Nature Switzerland AG 2019
P.-L. P. Rau (Ed.): HCII 2019, LNCS 11576, pp. 46–56, 2019.
https://doi.org/10.1007/978-3-030-22577-3_4

Persuasive theory was first proposed by Fogg, an experimental psychologist at Stanford university. He defined it as any interactive computing system used to form, change or enhance people's attitudes and behaviors. On the basis of this research, he further integrated computer technology in practical application and put forward Captology theory – "computers as persuasive technology". As the name implies, Captology focuses on how to make a computer persuasive, thus changing the behavior or attitude of users [9]. It emphasizes the initial purpose of the design and persuades the sub-jectivity and directness of the result. Compared with human persuasion, the theory features the following advantages: (1) computer persuasion is of longer duration; (2) the computer can carry out anonymous persuasion; (3) the computer can store, acquire and process a large amount of persuasion data; (4) the computer can persuade in various forms; (5) large-scale persuasion can be carried out through computer software; (6) ubiquitous computer technology can be used to persuade people every-where [10]. From the intention of persuasion, it can be divided into explicit persuasion and implicit persuasion. The former one means that the purpose of designing inter-active products is to persuade users to change their attitude and behavior, while the latter means that the design of products is mainly for commercial purposes and per-suasion is complementary. In the process of persuading users, computers have three forms of tools, simulations and members of society, that is, the so-called "functional iron triangle", which can be understood as a conceptual framework describing the three roles that computer technology can play.

Persuasive design is the practice and application of persuasion theory, which is a form of changing the will of the persuaded person through non-mandatory guidance. Persuasive design can also be called "influence design" or "persuasion design", a method using persuasive techniques to change a user's attitude or behavior, that is, design with intention of persuasion [11]. Interactive design puts emphasis on the relationship between people and machines. Designers are more concerned with the users' task execution process and user behaviors. Persuasion design focuses on whether or not the user does something, and what impact the design will have on the user. Therefore, persuasive design pays attention not only to the behavior process of human-computer interaction, but also to the situation in which the interaction occurs, espe-cially the motivation and users' behavior ability required to facilitate the behavior.

After more than 20 years of development and improvement, the current typical persuasive design model mainly involves four types [12]. The first model refers to the intersection of different disciplines to help designers produce a highly usable method called design with intent (DWI) [13, 14]; the second model is called persuasive sys-tematic design(PSD) that provides systematic analysis and design methods for the persuasive design requirements of software [15]; the third model is FBM based on the understanding of human behaviors [16]; the fourth model is the behavior Wizard model [17]. The PSD model is an interpretation of specific persuasive principles based on Fogg's theory. FBM theory is the basic support of persuasive principle of PSD model. FBM model believes that a behavior contains three dimensions, namely motivation, ability, and triggers. In order to implement a certain behavior, the individual must have sufficient motivation, ability and triggers to implement this behavior at the same time.

The purpose of this paper is to make an investigation of user's demand and pro-poses persuasive design strategies for intelligent health-care product on a basis of persuasion theory. It puts forward the strategies of persuasive design from such major perspectives as target behavior, motivation, ability and triggers: 1. product strategy based on user's goals. 2. product strategy for improving user's motivation. 3. product strategy for developing user's ability. 4. product strategy for enhancing triggers. In this paper, case study method is used to analyze the above design strategies, and the effectiveness of the strategies is verified via real application. To conclude, the research ideas of this paper are laid out as follows. Firstly, based on persuasion theory, the behavior model is studied and the factors of persuasive design are put forward. Secondly, persuasive behavior components and model of persuasive design for health-care product are studied, and persuasive design strategies are proposed in this part. Third, the above design factors and strategies are analyzed in combination with design cases. Finally, this paper will make a summary and point out the future research direction.

2 FBM and Factors of Persuasive Design

2.1 Behavior Model for Persuasive Design

As a tool for analyzing behavioral changes, FBM is designed to help designers understand both the opportunities and obstacles in design. In this way, they can establish a link between target behavior and the design of intelligent health-care product, analyze relevant cases of smart product design, and make persuasive design be used in the construction of a conceptual model of intelligent health-care products. The model should be able to answer what design will improve users' execution, what type of design or technology can give users encouragement and guidance, as well as what design and technology will motivate users for continued use [18] (Fig. 1).

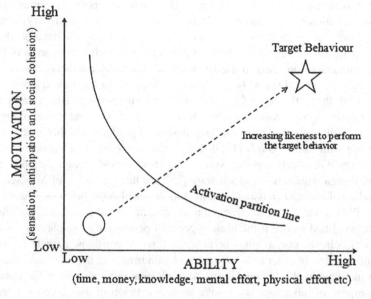

Fig. 1. Behavior model for persuasive design [Adapted from Fogg [11, 16]]

2.2   Design Factors

This model concludes four design factors which will search for strategies of intelligent health-care products from four perspectives.

The first factor is target behavior, which is the specific design purpose for the users. The purposes generally include correcting existing unhealthy behaviors, preventing unhealthy behaviors that may occur, motivating users to maintain existing healthy behaviors, raising health awareness, and increasing social connections. Products need to be clear about their emphasis so as to avoid confusion when users choose them. Meanwhile, users may have second thoughts about whether the product can produce target behavior or the completion effect after that. These are all the factors that designers need to take into consideration.

The second factor is motivation. That is, the internal reason why the user is operating or generating usage behavior. Fogg divides motivation into three groups: sensation, anticipation, and social cohesion. Sensation refers to happiness, disappointment, pain, etc. Anticipation stands for the observation of good or bad results for the future: hopeful or fearful; social cohesion refers to social recognition, rejection or social influence.

The third factor is ability. Ability, regarded as the most scarce resource for users, includes various contents such as time, money, physical expenditure, energy consumption, related skills, resilience, etc. All of these, to a certain extent, constitute a hindrance to the user's inability to accomplish the intended objectives.

The fourth factor is the trigger, which means when both motivation and competence are available, an effective stimulus is needed to trigger the behavior. The triggers are classified by situations: (1) Unable to trigger: either motivation or competence is too low to trigger a behavior. (2) Incentive triggers: for object with lower motivation yet higher ability. For instance, the motivation of the target users is enhanced by positive reactions from other users. (3) Counseling triggers: triggers that help users with lower ability and higher motivation, such as providing health counseling and other scientific methods to improve competence. (4) Indication triggers: triggers working as a reminder or instruction that help users with both stronger motivation and higher ability.

Some people with relatively low motivation and ability may need to combine incentive triggers with counseling triggers. Therefore, in order to trigger effective target behavior, some relevant incentive methods or strategies are needed to enhance the user's motivation and improve the user's competence to complete the target behavior, and give appropriate stimulation at right times. Such mathematical models enable behavioral changing theory with computer technology to be better applied into practice. In practical applications, the degree of motivation and ability indicates the probability of behavioral occurrence, while the stimulus, with the help of persuasive strategies, can generate and promote the behaviors.

3 Persuasive Design Strategy for Intelligent Health-Care Products

Persuasive strategy is a specific strategy and method to make persuasive technology into practice and real application. In order to achieve the ultimate goal that persuasive design can change the behaviors or habits of target users, a series of persuasive strategies are needed to embody the model and improve its usability. This paper will propose corresponding design strategies based on factors in FBM model. 1. considered from the perspective of user's goal (Table 1), the product should have market positioning and provide expected results, etc. 2. considered from the perspective of improving user's motivation (Table 2), it covers the four phases between the user and the product, which are the processes from impression of the product, product usage, performing the behavior to maintaining the behavior. The contact phase includes visual attraction, function attraction, etc. The using phase includes user experience, social connection, value improvement, etc. The behavior completion phase contains target reward and establishment of new target and so on; The behavior maintenance phase includes emotional maintenance, social maintenance, long-term goal attraction, etc. 3. designed from the perspective of developing user's ability (Table 3), it concludes content design, behavioral design, and feedback design. 4. from the perspective of improving the effectiveness of triggers (Table 4), it involves visual performance, cultural associations, and feedback timing, etc. is shown in Fig. 2.

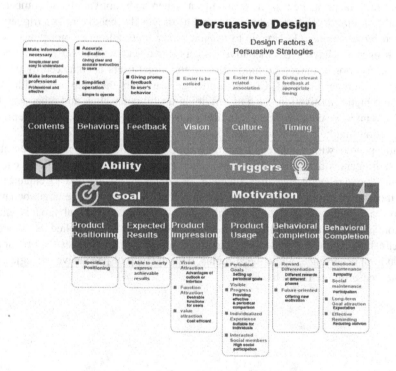

Fig. 2. Persuasive design factors & strategies

Table 1. Persuasive strategies for defining user's goal

Design factor	Design aspects	Persuasive strategies	Explanation
User's goal	Product positioning	Specified positioning	Having emphasis and clear function
	Expected results	Predictable results	Able to clearly express achievable results

Table 2. Persuasive strategies for improving user's motivation

Design factor	Design aspects	Persuasive strategies	Explanation
User's motivation	Product impression	Visual attraction	Advantages of outlook or interface
		Function attraction	Desirable functions for users
		Value attraction	Cost efficient
	Product usage	Periodical goals	Setting up periodical goals
		Visible progress	Providing prompt, effective and periodical comparison
		Individualized Experience	Suitable for individuals
		Interacted social members	High social participation
	Behavioral completion	Reward differentiation	Different rewards at different phases
		Future-oriented	Offering new motivation
	Behavior maintenance	Emotional maintenance	Sympathy
		Social maintenance	Participation
		Long-term goal attraction	Expectation
		Effective reminding	Reducing oblivion

Table 3. Persuasive strategies for improving user's ability

Design factor	Design aspects	Persuasive strategies	Explanation
User's ability	Contents	Make information necessary	Simple, clear and easy to understand
		Make information professional	Professional and effective
	Behaviors	Simplified operation	Simple to operate
		Accurate indication	Giving clear and accurate instruction to users
	Feedback	Prompt feedback	Giving prompt feedback to user's behavior

Table 4. Persuasive strategies for activating users

Design factors	Persuasive strategies	Explanation
Triggers	Vision	Easier to be noticed
	Culture	Easier to have related association
	Timing	Giving relevant feedback at appropriate timing

4   Case Study on Persuasive Design of Intelligent Health-Care Products

Recently, as intelligent health-care products have enjoyed wide varieties, and the most popular type is the product that records human bodies, several smart scales have been selected for case analysis.

4.1   Smile Scale

QardioBase scale is elegant in shape and simple in performance. It can measure the proportion of body components, be connected to mobile phones via Bluetooth and WiFi. The necessary data of the body can be displayed on the mobile phone in a graphical form, enabling people to have a quick understanding of their current health condition. Meanwhile, QardioBase scales give users encouragement through the interaction between people and scales, prompting users to enhance their self-confidence and perseverance. When the user stands on a QardioBase scale, the touching feedback system of the scale will gently remind the user that his or her weight has been recorded is shown in Fig. 3.

Fig. 3. QardioBase scale smile-face feedback

The intelligent feedback mechanism of the scale is divided into three types. When the user gradually moves toward the set health goal, the QardioBase scale will give the user a visual smile feedback (Fig. 2). If the weight keep unchanged during a set of time, the expression image on the scale will remain the same. However, when the user's weight exceeds the set or standard number, the image on scale will become a crying face. Users can grasp their current weight quickly through the changes of these three expressions, and also protect their own weight privacy. What's more, QardioBase scales also have functions such as target setting and reminding, which can be used by the whole family, thus avoiding the limitation of single user brought by the products. In addition, the reminding function is convenient for users to carry out phased data recording, which improves the user's motivation and helps them form a long-term using habits.

User's goals, user's motivation, user's ability, and triggers are well designed respectively. Elegant outlook and superior functions can enhance purchase desire; smile-face feedback, family participation and privacy protection during usage are able to improve user's motivation; simple and indispensable forms and images can save users from too much analysis and improve ability. At last, necessary reminding function can work as a trigger of usage.

4.2   Fitbit Aria Smart Scale Weight

Apart from the interaction between products and users, the scale can also implement the reward function in the weight-loss and fitness process through an additional program in the app. For example, as Fitbit Aria scales in Fig. 3, equipped with a small challenge program, users can compete with friends and families and play various fun games like "Match of the Day" in the process, from which users can win badges, red envelopes or in-kind incentives. At the same time, social participation and user's stickiness can be strengthened by daily sharing on social media. Users' determination, enthusiasm and mobility on losing weight can all be enhanced is shown in Fig. 4.

Fig. 4. Fitbit Aria scale and challenge program

For such product, weight control is undoubtedly a factor of target behavior. To improve user's motivation, the product has been upgraded in terms of its outlook, reward mechanism and deepening social connections. It has gained quite popularity among users especially due to its different reward rules compared with her similar products. The user loyalty maintained by this special reward mechanism will also improve their ability to use the product in long-term run. Due to the observable nature of the real prizes, it constitutes the triggers for continuous use in users' lives.

4.3 Huawei Smart Scale Weight

Users are expected to get an accurate value when measuring physical data, however, the tilt or unevenness of the site will bring errors in the reading of the scale. Currently, few products on the market solving the problem from this aspect, mostly start from the product itself, which means focusing on addressing functional or outlook problems. But the places for use should not be neglected. is shown in Fig. 5.

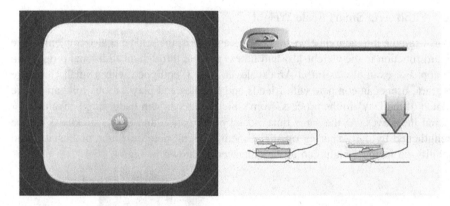

Fig. 5. Huawei smart scale 360° adjustable scale feet

Huawei smart scales can also measure the ratio of body composition, have a body composition ratio measurement function, and can display physical changes of the user through various charts in the app of the phone. In addition, it supports the identification of 10 users, and can share measurement data through multiple mainstream social media. This is similar to the previous two scales, but this scale weight has a new highlight in user's experience. Thanks to the adjustable 360° support frame, it guarantees the usability of the scale in most places, reduces errors during measurement.

This product basically share exact functions and features of the target behavior with the first ones, but in light of improving user's motivation, apart from providing social connections, simplifying the display mode, etc., it offers more precise measurement and intensifies user's motivation accordingly. Concerning use's ability, this design also enhances the adaptability of scales to the environment, eliminating the trouble from seeking for suitable placement, thus user's ability are improved. Regular timed reminders can be used as a trigger for this type of product.

From the above case analysis, we can see that the application of persuasive-designed products with different factors will affect and guide users' behavior to different extents. Similar products can also find targets using persuasive design strategies with different factors to overshadow its counterparts. Similarly, due to the difference between target users and positioning of the products, there will be some emphasis on the specific application of the strategy. In the process of subsequent evolution, based on the previous strategies, the product can strengthen and supplement corresponding visual presentation, content structure, behavior flow so as to enhance the user's behavior motivation and ability to a greater extent, thereby achieving the purpose of persuasion.

5 Conclusion

Even there are plenty of factors impairing health, most of the diseases are caused by users' own reasons. Therefore, the health self-management of intelligent health-care products is particularly important. To achieve health self-management, a quite effective way is to help users establish healthy behaviors using persuasive technology. As intelligent health-care products become a hot spot of current product design and development, persuasive technology will also be an essential part in the product development process. Hence, it is practical and worthwhile to probe design strategies that can assist designers find enlightenment and come up with solutions in a short time. Certainly, a series of design strategies proposed for intelligent health-care products in this paper are not a complete fixed mechanism. Different products need to be designed with different emphasis depending on the user positioning.

Acknowledgement. This research is supported by National Social Science Fund of China program (12BJL047). We also gratefully acknowledge the financial support.

References

1. Fogg, B.J.: Persuasive Technologies, 1st edn. Communications of the ACM, New York (1999)
2. Jiao, M.: Application research of persuasive design theory through products relating to forming healthy lifestyles. Design **4**, 95–96 (2015)
3. Joseph, V.C., Ahn, S.H., Kim, J.Y.: Intelligent healthcare systems: re-defining personal healthcare solutions. In: International Conference on Advanced Communication Technology no. 1, pp. 424–427. IEEE, Phoenix Park (2005)
4. Ma, X., Wang, Z., Zhou, S.: Intelligent healthcare systems assisted by data analytics and mobile computing. Wirel. Commun. Mob. Comput. **2018** (2018)
5. Hansson, R., Skog, T.: The LoveBomb: encouraging the communication of emotions in public spaces. In: CHI 2001 Extended Abstracts on Human Factors in Computing Systems, pp. 433–434. ACM, Seattle (2001)
6. Stephen, S.: A new research challenge: persuasive technology to motivate healthy aging. IEEE Trans. Inf. Technol. Biomed. **8**(3), 235–237 (2004)

7. Creed, C.: Using computational agents to motivate diet change. In: IJsselsteijn, W.A., de Kort, Y.A.W., Midden, C., Eggen, B., van den Hoven, E. (eds.) PERSUASIVE 2006. LNCS, vol. 3962, pp. 100–103. Springer, Heidelberg (2006). https://doi.org/10.1007/11755494_14

8. Fogg, B.J.: Persuasive technology: using computers to change what we think and do. Ubiquity, **5** (2002)

9. Fogg, B.J.: Persuasive computers: perspectives and research directions. In: Proceedings of the SIGCHI Conference on Human Factors in Computing Systems, pp. 225–232. ACM Press/Addison-Wesley Publishing Co., Los Angeles (1998)

10. Yuxia, J.: The persuasive research and design of e-commerce web sites. In: CHCI. PCC

11. Fogg, B.J.: A behavior model for persuasive design. In: Fourth International Conference on Persuasive Technology, Xi'an (2009)

12. Torning, K.: A review of four persuasive design models. Int. J. Conceptual Struct. Smart Appl. **1**(2), 17–27 (2013)

13. Lockton, D., Harrison, D., Stanton, N.: Design with intent: persuasive technology in a wider context. In: Oinas-Kukkonen, H., Hasle, P., Harjumaa, M., Segerståhl, K., Øhrstrøm, P. (eds.) PERSUASIVE 2008. LNCS, vol. 5033, pp. 274–278. Springer, Heidelberg (2008). https://doi.org/10.1007/978-3-540-68504-3_30

14. Lockton, D., Harrison, D., Stanton, N.: The design with intent method: a design tool for influencing user behaviour. Appl. Ergon. **41**(3), 382–392 (2010)

15. Oinas-Kukkonen, H., Harjumaa, M.: Persuasive systems design: key issues, process model and system features. In: Routledge Handbook of Policy Design, 1st edn. Routledge, London (2018)

16. Fogg, B.J.: A behavior model for persuasive design. In: Proceedings of the 4th International Conference on Persuasive Technology, vol. 40. ACM, New York (2009)

17. Fogg, B.J., Hreha, J.: Behavior wizard: a method for matching target behaviors with solutions. In: Ploug, T., Hasle, P., Oinas-Kukkonen, H. (eds.) PERSUASIVE 2010. LNCS, vol. 6137, pp. 117–131. Springer, Heidelberg (2010). https://doi.org/10.1007/978-3-642-13226-1_13

18. Shih, L.: Persuasive design for products leading to health and sustainability using case-based reasoning. Sustainability **8**(4), 318 (2016)

A Review of the DesignX Discourse: Knowledge Diffusion and Integration Across Disciplines

Jin Ma[✉]

College of Design and Innovation, Tongji University,
281 Fuxin Road, Shanghai, China
majin.sheji@icloud.com

Abstract. Design research and practice is increasingly expanding into new areas and merging with other disciplines, yet empirical research that investigates the interdisciplinary knowledge structure of these emerging areas remains scarce. This paper explores a novel front in design research inspired by Norman and Stappers's 2015 article "DesignX: Complex Sociotechnical Systems." The aim here is to depict the transient knowledge structure of an interdisciplinary domain started from inside design. The present empirical study uses mixed methods combining the VOSviewer knowledge mapping technique with text-based qualitative analysis. Results from these quantitative and qualitative methods frame rich insights into patterns of knowledge diffusion and integration in DesignX-related research. I argue that knowledge mapping techniques and qualitative analysis complement each other and can yield not only macro knowledge patterns about the examined area but more fine-grained meso- and micro-level knowledge of that area. The paper further reflects on the development of the DesignX approach.

Keywords: DesignX · Sociotechnical systems · Mixed methods ·
Knowledge mapping · Design discipline · Interdisciplinarity

1 Introduction

Collaboration and the integration of learnings across the boundaries of individual disciplines gives rise to interdisciplinary domains and expertise uniquely suited to addressing multilayered and multifaceted challenges. The design discipline can be applied across countless domains, and its scope continues to expand, reaching beyond its conventional, artifact-centric focus to address complex systems for living, working, playing, and learning. The pragmatic nature of design supports the quest for connection and the integration of useful knowledge from other disciplines "for new productive purposes" [1]. This understanding has gradually grown into a common view in the design field, though not without a certain degree of friction. And yet, the ambiguity clouding the ontology of design means design faces constant challenge. Two questions have plagued the design community for decades: If design is inherently interdisciplinary, what constitutes the unique body of knowledge that makes design different

© Springer Nature Switzerland AG 2019
P.-L. P. Rau (Ed.): HCII 2019, LNCS 11576, pp. 57–78, 2019.
https://doi.org/10.1007/978-3-030-22577-3_5

from other disciplines? And, how interdisciplinary *is* design, in fact? Both questions beg for inquiries into design knowledge, its structure and foundation, and its evolution.

As a small, experimental response to this broad topic, here I attempt to depict the transient knowledge structure of an interdisciplinary area initiated from inside design—specifically an emerging research domain related to a position article in design published in 2015. I adopt a quantitative knowledge mapping technique called VOSviewer in addition to a textual analysis-based qualitative review approach to explore the feasibility of studying the interdisciplinarity of the design discipline using mixed methods.

2   What is DesignX?

2.1   A Brief Account

In October 2014, a small group of design scholars and educators[1] announced their determination to explore how design can address the complex issues the world faces today. They called their initiative "DesignX," with "X" referring to the turbulent, unknown future of design. The fruit of their first discussion was a document called "DesignX: A Future Path for Design" [2].

A two-day follow-up working conference on DesignX was hosted by Tongji University in 2015, aiming to advance understandings about how design and designers can contribute to tackling complex sociotechnical systems problems. Norman and Stappers invited around 30 scholars and practitioners from the design, systems theory, cybernetics, computer sciences, and cognitive sciences domains to participate. They were experienced in working with complex issues ranging from health care, education, urban systems, financial service, etc. The multi-disciplinary perspectives on DesignX triggered debates, and the participants found it extremely challenging to arrive at a clearly articulated, unified understanding. Norman acknowledged that the complex problems design aims to deal with today were not new, but that implementing solutions in the real world was and is the biggest challenge to designers in that it requires interdisciplinary collaboration. Based on these developments, Norman and Stappers penned an article titled "DesignX: Complex Sociotechnical Systems" [3] and published it in *She Ji: The Journal of Design, Economics, and Innovation* in December 2015.

2.2   Norman and Stappers on DesignX

In 2014, the DesignX Collaborative defines DesignX as "a new, evidence-based approach for addressing many of the complex and serious problems facing the world today" [2]. In the follow-up article, Norman and Stappers [3] map out the context from which DesignX emerged, elaborate on its subject matter, outline the characteristics of the problems DesignX aims to address, and argue for a possible approach to designing for complex sociotechnical systems.

---

[1] The initial DesignX Collaborative includes (in alphabetical order) Ken Friedman, Yongqi Lou, Don Norman, Pieter Jan Stappers, Ena Voûte, and Patrick Whitney.

Norman and Stappers situate DesignX where complex challenges arise: at the crossroads of all kinds of sociotechnical systems used to support our caring, feeding, dwelling, moving, and policymaking. According to Norman and Stappers [3], DesignX problems have nine principal properties that they organize into three categories: human, social/political/economic, and technical. To appropriately address DesignX problems we need knowledge and expertise from a variety of disciplines and multi-stakeholder collaboration. This implies a shift in focus from inside the design discipline as well.

For Norman and Stappers, DesignX practice is a muddling-through. It involves a modular approach with incremental steps which break up the whole into an assembly of more manageable and relatively independent parts. The authors emphasize that real world solutions implementation is of central concern in DesignX, and that designers must play a more active role in implanting and developing their solutions—"the design process never ends" [3]. The implications of the DesignX arguments require the design discipline to develop new expertise and call for design education to prepare future designers with adequate knowledge and skills.

As the managing editor of *She Ji*, I witnessed the birth and the ensuing discourse surrounding DesignX.[2] I became curious about the influence the DesignX article had on the research fields where it had been cited. Has the idea of DesignX spread into any other disciplines during the past three years? Is the research area inspired by DesignX an interdisciplinary one? What kind of knowledge supports such a discourse? And, has the idea of DesignX evolved? I wanted to explore the possibility that there might be a new frontier in design research related to DesignX.

3   Methodology

There is a robust body of research on the development of science, knowledge, and interdisciplinary trends. One of the best known fields supporting such studies is scientometrics [4]. However, there are very few studies dealing directly with the design discipline in this field. The ambiguous boundary surrounding design and the absence of a subject category compatible with design in dominant science databases are probably significant barriers. For example, there are no ready-made subject categories available in the current 254 subject categories listed in the core collection of Web of Science (2018) covering the three major indexes (SCI-E, SSCI, and A&HCI). Scientometric studies on interdisciplinary trends rely on using subject categories assigned to each publication indexed by the dominant citation indexing services (Web of Science and Scopus) [5]. Hence, this well-established approach to interdisciplinary studies cannot be directly applied to design.

Within design, there is a plethora of literature emphasizing the viewpoint that design is interdisciplinary, but there are few empirical studies examining its interdisciplinary characteristics. Some scholars have undertaken the task of constructing a framework of design knowledge, however. Most of these are expressed via viewpoint articles [6, 7], while existing empirical studies on design and the emerging knowledge

---

[2] This article has been downloaded 23,138 times globally via ScienceDirect by October 2018.

areas within it rely largely on qualitative approaches based on guidelines derived from expert interviews [8, 9] and textual analysis [10].

Scientometric studies can measure the development of disciplines based on quantitative features at a macro level. They focus on information about a discipline, not the contents of the discipline per se. Qualitative literature review based on textual analysis captures fine-grained knowledge and deep insights of a specific research field at the micro level, but its capability to grasp disciplinary patterns tends to be weak due to limitations in data size and time-consuming methods.

The powerful scientometric tools used for knowledge mapping seem to have started to attract design researchers' attention recently. The results of these pioneering studies [11, 12] do not seem to differ greatly from a scientometric researcher's inquiry. Finding ways to link macro level findings with the discourse taking place within the discipline on a micro level is a valuable direction that I attempt to explore through combining the two approaches in this study.

3.1   Collecting Data

I searched publications that cited Norman and Stappers's DesignX article. The first difficulty I encountered was that there were too few design journals indexed by major indexing sources Web of Science (WoS) and Scopus [13]. My search in WoS only resulted in 17 articles. So I widened my search to include results from Scopus, Google Scholar, and CNKI and expanded the types of publication I included from journal articles and conference papers to books (book chapters) and theses. The initial, expanded search resulted in a list of 82 documents (February 24, 2019). I then downloaded all available full texts, read the title and abstract of each, and verified whether the DesignX article was properly cited in the text and listed in the references. After removing 5 items that were repeatedly indexed by Google Scholar, I further eliminated the following

- 6 documents whose complete texts were not available;
- 1 thesis in Swedish and 2 journal articles in Spanish and Japanese, which remain beyond my language capability;
- 1 Google Scholar indexed journal article showing problematic referencing;
- 2 conference papers (Google Scholar) that were published as indexed journal articles with minimum revision.

I then added 10 *She Ji* articles (6 full-length articles and 4 short communications) that cited the DesignX article. Although *She Ji* is indexed by Scopus, the bibliometric information offered by Scopus excludes cited references. This is possibly due to the fact that *She Ji* uses a footnotes system and does not include a reference list at the end of each article. That lack of bibliometric data also exists on Google Scholar.

The final dataset contains 75 full-text DesignX-related documents (17 indexed by WoS, 23 indexed by Scopus, 35 indexed by Google Scholar).

Among the set, there were 10 documents that had no keywords, as they were either viewpoint journal articles (non-peer reviewed) or book chapters. Since keywords analysis is critical to reveal the knowledge clusters in the examined field, I decided to construct keywords for these items by carefully reading them entirely. I identified the most relevant subject terms for each document as "added keywords." My status as a journal editor comes with the capacity to accomplish this step.

The scientometric tool requires all bibliographic information formatting to be consistent. Converting incompatible data formats and completing missing information is crucial if the results are to express the examined area as accurately as possible. WoS is the best source for scientometric data, because it carries the most accurate and complete documentation information as compared to Scopus and others. So I converted bibliographic information obtained via Scopus into the WoS format manually, and coded by hand information from documents that were indexed by Google Scholar. To do this I searched the website of each document's source publication, collecting as much publishing information as possible. Although it was time-consuming, it was doable due to the modest size of the DesignX-related document set.

3.2   Analysis Using Mixed Methods

Data analysis was divided into two parts: (1) experimental analysis using the VOS-viewer knowledge mapping tool to visualize the resulting knowledge networks and decipher their meanings, and (2) coding of the 75 documents based on a set of DesignX themes through textual analysis. VOSviewer is a software offering a relatively easy way for visualizing bibliometric networks [14].

The first stage of the research (Part 1) sought to reveal

- which disciplines had incorporated the DesignX concept
- the kind of knowledge being used to support DesignX as a research field, and
- the research communities who were using the DesignX concept.

The second stage of the research (Part 2) looked at

- how the Norman and Stappers DesignX article was used in the literature.

Part 1 and Part 2 together provide a holistic view of

- the interdisciplinary structure of emerging DesignX-related research
- whether the DesignX concept had evolved or not.

These two parts of analysis unfolded in parallel. Insights obtained from reading and qualitatively analyzing the documents informed the interpretation of the results presented by VOSviewer. And the VOSviewer results provided insights into the structure of the examined area and clarified the patterns embedded in the qualitative analysis. They became mutually supporting phases of study.

4 Results and Analysis

4.1 Part 1: Mapping the Knowledge of DesignX-Related Research

Norman and Stappers's article envisions a potentially new research frontier related to design. The 75 papers citing the work published in the three years after its date of publication implies considerable interest in the topic—although this number may seem small for the sciences, it is nonetheless notable for a developing discipline such as design. This small but important body of literature signals an emerging research area, which I have tentatively labelled DesignX-related research.

In information science, a specialty is conceptualized as a time-variant duality between research fronts—frontiers in research—and intellectual bases [15]. Price [16] first introduced the concept of a research front to characterize the transient nature of a research field. Persson [17] coined the concept of an intellectual base to clarify the nature of a research front. A research front therefore represents the state of the art of a line of research; what this research front cites forms its intellectual base [15].

On the other hand, rather than delimiting the boundary of a research front in terms of collection of state-of-the-art articles, Chen [15] defines a research front as "an emergent and transient grouping of concepts and underlying research issues" and its intellectual base as "an evolving network of scientific publications cited by research-front concepts." This understanding supports the design of the knowledge mapping part of the current study.

The keywords extracted from the 75 documents examined represent a research front. The publications co-cited by these documents can be regarded as the intellectual base, i.e., the knowledge underpinning ongoing DesignX-related research. Both can be visualized by VOSviewer.

4.1.1 The Research Front of DesignX-Related Studies

The 75 DesignX-related documents (spanning from 2015 to 2019) contain 386 keywords employed by 139 authors from 73 organizations and 20 countries. There are 2,992 references cited by these 75 documents, and 2,088 authors cited in total.

Keyword co-occurrence mapping resulted in clusters of themes and topics. Given the small size of the data, I set the keyword occurrence threshold at 2. Figure 1 lists a total of 9 clusters of 58 keywords co-occurring with other keywords in the same network in at least 2 DesignX-related documents. The links (L), link strength (LS) value, and number of occurrences (O) of a keyword indicate how many other keywords it is related to, its total strength of co-occurrence relations with other keywords, and how many documents it appears in, respectively. These keywords form concepts and represent the underlying research concerns of DesignX-related research, denoting its research front.

VOSviewer provides distance-based visualizations of bibliometric networks, i.e., the distance between two nodes approximately indicates the relatedness of the nodes [14]. Figure 2 shows the network of keywords. The size of the keyword indicates the frequency of its occurrence, its amount of links, or total link strength; the thickness of the line connecting two keywords indicates the number of co-occurrences one word has with another, i.e., it illustrates the strength of relational co-occurrence between the pair.

The resulting network, when visualized, looks relatively sparse. Among the nine clusters, seven contain only a couple of keywords that are strongly co-occurring with another keyword. This lack of occurrences implies that DesignX-related research is still in its infancy. On a separate note, the transient structure indicates an interdisciplinary character, rather than one that is discipline focused.

Cluster 1	L*	LS	O	Cluster 2	L	LS	O	Cluster 3	L	LS	O
co-design	5	3	3	**complexity**	8	6	7	Constructivism	6	2	2
community	4	2	2	context variation	3	2	2	embodied sensemaking	3	2	2
emergency department	7	2	2	engineering design	5	2	2	multi-stakeholder	4	3	3
experience	5	2	2	design methodology	4	2	2	product-service system	6	3	3
health care	7	3	3	emotion	1	1	2	sensemaking	6	2	2
hospital	7	2	2	innovation	5	3	3	social systems	10	3	3
human engineering	9	3	3	interaction design	5	2	2	**systemic design**	9	3	4
human-centered design	11	5	5	performance	5	2	2	systems thinking	6	2	2
human-computer interaction	6	4	4	systems	4	2	2	visualization	6	2	2
human-systems integration	7	2	2								
service design	6	4	4								

Cluster 4	L	LS	O	Cluster 5	L	LS	O	Cluster 6	L	LS	O
complex adaptive systems	2	1	2	community of practice	5	2	2	**design thinking**	7	4	4
design activism	4	2	2	**design education**	9	5	6	socio-technical transitions	3	2	2
design-led innovation	3	1	2	design method	4	2	2				
designX	16	10	10	design practice	4	2	2	**sustainability**	8	6	6
resilience	1	2	2	design research	5	2	2	transition design	4	3	3
social innovation	4	2	2	public sector innovation	4	2	2	**wicked problem**	7	5	6
sociotechnical systems	16	10	12								

Cluster 7	L	LS	O	Cluster 8	L	LS	O	Cluster 9	L	LS	O
applied computing	4	2	2	**design**	15	7	7	community energy storage	3	2	2
decision-making	4	2	2	failure	3	3	3				
e-government	4	2	2	ubiquitous computing	6	3	3	energy transition	3	2	2
multi-criterion optimization	4	2	2	user study	3	3	3	responsible innovation	3	2	2

* L = number of links; LS = link strength; O = number of occurrence.

Fig. 1. The 9 clusters of keywords that occur in at least 2 out of the 75 DesignX-related documents based on the co-occurrence algorithm of VOS.

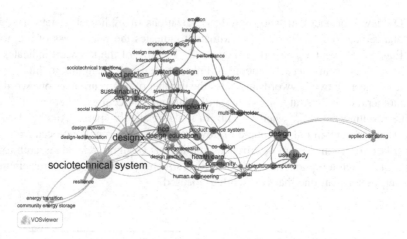

Fig. 2. The network mapping of keywords from DesignX-related documents (occurrence threshold 2) using VOS approach. (Color for each cluster: C1—red; C2—green; C3—blue; C4—yellow; C5—purple; C6—sky-blue; C7—orange; C8—brown; C9—pink.) (Color figure online)

Unsurprisingly, two core terms—"DesignX" and "sociotechnical systems"—are the most popular ones and appear in the same cluster (4). Their family members include "design activism" (the argument that designers must play a more active role tackling complex problems [18]); "social innovation" [19] and "design-led innovation" [20] (approaches to address the complex problems society and organizations face); "resilience" (a key characteristic for society and communities to respond to complex challenges [21]); and "complex adaptive systems" (used to design for governance structures [22]). Clearly, this cluster emphasizes the social dimension of the DesignX approach. Cluster 6's terms, "sustainability," [23] "transition design," [24] and "wicked problems," [25] can be seen as an extension of Cluster 4, with a specific focus on the social sphere.

The strong link between "DesignX" and "complexity" bridges the social concerns with the technological world of DesignX. With "complexity" as the keystone of Cluster 2, this group of keywords penetrates an engineering-based area that focuses on, for example, "engineering design," "systems' performance," and the "context variation" for such performance. The inclusion of "design methodology" and "design method" echoes the long tradition in engineering seeking robust methods and methodologies [26].

Between the "DesignX" and "complexity" groups sits Cluster 3, which explores various topics within systems theory ranging from "systems thinking," to "social systems," "product-service systems," and "multi-stakeholders." The biggest node in this cluster is called "systemic design" [27]—a research area aiming to relate systems thinking with design to address social issues.

Interestingly, although Cluster 4—the DesignX cluster—contains the biggest nodes with the strongest relationships, the cluster does not sit at the heart of the map (Fig. 2). It is on the fringe of other clusters that represent the dominant focuses of the design discipline, for example, the "human-centered design" group (Cluster 1) and the "design education" group (Cluster 5). This location implies the body of research that focuses on DesignX (and hence adopting DesignX and sociotechnical systems as its keywords) emerges at the intersection between design and other possible disciplines.

The keywords "design" and "user study"—two most familiar keywords to the design discipline—locate in Cluster 8, which unexpectedly sits between the main network and the island-like Cluster 7 (bottom right, Fig. 2). By tracing their source documents, I found this cluster of publications to be mainly papers from ACM conferences such as CHI and UBICOMP on applied computing. This might explain the strategy of choosing "design" as a keyword when introducing design concepts or research into a field outside of design. I suspect the big node of "design" is a footprint of design's landing in computer science. Currently, this cluster is small and mainly focused on lessons learned through designing intelligent systems within healthcare environments [28].

Unlike the above seven clusters, Clusters 7 and 9 carry a small number of keywords that are evenly connected to the others. Figure 2 clearly shows that the two clusters (orange and pink) are located in the remotest places on the map, almost cast away from the main network. I went back to the source documents where these keywords emerged and found that Cluster 7 derived from 2 articles [29, 30] on sensemaking of complex systems in the context of public sector innovation; Cluster 9 from two articles [31, 32] on community energy storage. Although the source article numbers are small, these two clusters reflect that the notion of DesignX is drawn on by social science studies examining governance innovation and science, technology, and policy studies on energy systems—two disciplines that are not part of design's foundation, and are probably the remotest disciplines to design so far. The authors' affiliations also suggest the same insight: leading authors respectively come from Data Science Institute, NUI Galway, Ireland; and University of Twente Department of Science, Technology and Policy Studies, the Netherlands. However, the small number of documents supporting these two clusters and the limited author groups also suggests a possibility that these are just incidental, ephemeral cases.

VOSviewer can also visualize the same network based on a given timeline. "Human-centered design" is the oldest keyword in the cluster network (average publishing year 2016.33). This approach is the bedrock of the design discipline. While the notion of wicked problems [33] has a history longer than human-centered design, the keyword "wicked problems" entered into the DesignX-related research lexicon more recently (average publishing year 2017.50). Here I offer a hypothetical explanation for the lag: while DesignX was first manifested as a "new, evidence-based approach" [2], people soon realized that the issues DesignX purported to address are not new—many of them "fall under the rubric of 'wicked problems,' long a staple of economists, management science, operations researchers, and design theorists" [3]. It takes time for researchers to come aware of wicked problems' relevance to designing for complex sociotechnical systems in today's context, and to seek new methods and processes to resolve such problems. Therefore, "wicked problems" appears relatively late. The keywords "design methodology" that it relates to appeared around the same time, and later on "design methods" appeared.

VOSviewer's clustering provides a snapshot of the current structure of the emerging DesignX-related research front. The clusters form an interdisciplinary discourse at the intersections of design, the social sciences, engineering, and computer science. When looked at more closely, the configuration of the clusters points to some noteworthy possibilities.

(1) Within the "human-centered design" cluster (1) health care ("health care," "hospital," and "emergency department") takes a significant place. Healthcare systems are one of the most complex sociotechnical systems that exist, and one wherein designers are called to intervene on a more regular basis. It is probably one of the few areas that provides evidence demonstrating the effects of design interventions, be they positive or negative [34]. It remains to be seen whether more areas will adopt DesignX approaches to problems as part of a human-centered design approach, and the emergence of any convergences merits ongoing surveillance.

(2) Some keywords that are usually closely related (and therefore part of the same cluster) from a design perspective were divided into different clusters. For example, "emotion," which is often examined together with "experience," "human-computer interaction," and "service design," now sits at the edge of a cluster that is tilted to engineering and systems studies. This implies two possibilities: either it signals a novel emphasis on emotional aspects of engineering research as an approach to "innovation" (also categorized in the same cluster); or its occurrence in engineering and systems research is just incidental due to the small size of data and low threshold, and all these terms will be eventually integrated into the foundational definition of design.

4.1.2 The Knowledge Underpinning DesignX-Related Studies

As introduced above, a research front is the state of the art of a line of research—what researchers at this frontier cite forms its intellectual base [15]. Following Chen [15], the intellectual base of the keyword network identified above are the references cited by papers carrying these keywords. This requires a further shrinking of the dataset. I took an approximate approach here, i.e., I used the co-citation network established by all 75 documents to imply a possible body of knowledge underpinning DesignX-related research. Table 1 shows the 10 references most frequently cited (more than 4 times) by the 75 documents.

Table 1. The body of knowledge supporting DesignX-related research.

	Most frequently co-cited references	Links	Total link strength	Citations
1	Norman and Stappers [3], "DesignX: Complex Sociotechnical Systems"	9	35	75
2	Rittel and Webber [33], "Dilemmas in a General Theory of Planning"	8	15	15
3	Dorst [35], *Frame Innovation*	7	9	9
4	Buchanan [1], "Wicked Problems in Design Thinking"	8	7	7
5	DesignX Collaborative [2], "DesignX: A Future Path for Design"	6	6	6
6	Manzini [36], *Design, When Everybody Designs*	5	6	6
7	Brown [37], *Change by Design*	7	4	4
8	Buchanan [38], "Worlds in the Making"	5	4	4
9	Lindblom [39], "The Science of 'Muddling Through'"	3	4	4
10	Snowden and Boone [40], "A Leader's Framework for Decision-Making"	4	4	4

The full DesignX article by Norman and Stappers is of course the most cited article, given that I used it to demarcate the set of DesignX-related documents. The DesignX Collaborative 2014 manifesto "DesignX: A Future Path for Design," which gave rise to Norman and Stappers' article, is closely related. However, this document was not officially published (distributed via Norman's online blog instead) and it carries initial ideas about DesignX that are less well articulated than those in the full length article by Norman and Stappers. These factors might restrict the manifesto paper's visibility and influences in the literature. Lindblom's article (1959) on what they called "muddling-through" supports one of the core arguments in Norman and Stappers' DesignX approach— adopting small, incremental steps to muddle through the complex situation. These three seem to be the base for understanding Norman and Stappers' DesignX concept.

Rittel and Webber's seminal article on wicked problems is a classic, recently reviving in DesignX-related studies. The close relationship between DesignX problems and wicked problems calls for new approaches to old issues. When allied with the rest of the publications on the list, this article serves to support DesignX-related studies in at least two pivotal ways: it enriches design thinking, as in Buchanan [1] and Brown [37]; and addresses organizational or social innovation, as in Buchanan [38], Snowden and Boone [40], Dorst [35], and Manzini [36].

4.1.3   Research Communities

To understand the research communities who are using the notion of DesignX, I chose bibliographic coupling, which is a method that clusters a set of documents based on the number of references co-cited by each two articles in the set [41]. It can reveal the relations between the examined documents in terms of their authors, sources, organizations, and countries. Figure 3 shows the network of authors and that of organizations in the 75 DesignX-related documents based on bibliographic coupling.

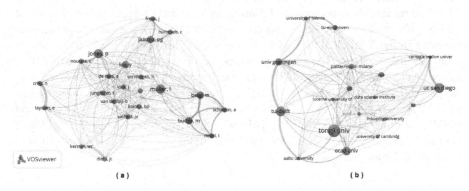

(a)   (b)

Fig. 3. (a) Authors' network and (b) organizations network based on bibliographic coupling (minimum documents of each node above 2).

In Fig. 3a, the four clusters of authors lying at the edges of the network have the strongest internal links, because they co-authored multiple publications. Aside from these authors, the connections between the other authors remain weak. However, some of these authors are more connected than the map shows, because of the research activities they were engaged in. Peter Jones, based at OCAD University, Canada, for example, is the co-founder of the systemic design symposium RSD. He was invited to attend the DesignX working conference at Tongji in 2015, and later he edited a themed issue of *She Ji* on the topic of systemic design. This also explains a portion of the 75 documents are from the systemic design community (including ones authored by Eloise Taysom, Nathan Crilly, Mieke van der Bijl-Brouwer, Susu Nousala, etc.).

The organizational network in Fig. 3b describes the connections among authors' affiliations. Tongji University contributed 8 documents, UC San Diego 6, and Delft University of Technology 6. Five out of the six DesignX initiators (DesignX Collaborative) come from these three universities. They play an important role in promoting DesignX in their home organizations and research networks. Since the DesignX position article was published these communities have expanded, engaging more universities in Europe and North America in the past three years. The Dutch university cluster stands out significantly, as does the United States cluster linking UC San Diego and Carnegie Mellon University. Tongji University College of Design and Innovation seems to be most productive probably because it is the location where DesignX first started and the faculty is inspired by the DesignX community, especially one of DesignX's leading proponents Yongqi Lou, who is dean of the school.

4.2   Part 2: A Closer Look at the DesignX-Related Studies

Although the knowledge mapping tool is able to visualize who is citing the DesignX article, the maps tell little about how people actually employ this article in their own research. Therefore, I carried out a text-based analysis of the 75 DesignX-related documents. Here I report a few important results.

While reading these documents, I found people tended to refer to distinct facets of the DesignX article for different purposes, and that the depth of use varied significantly. From the DesignX article, I derived 3 categories that I felt constitute a holistic view of what DesignX is about. The three categories are (1) its intervention context; (2) its subject matter and problems; and (3) its practical approach and arguments. Under these categories, there are 13 codes including "challenges"; "the shift of the design discipline"; "sociotechnical systems"; "human aspect"; "social sphere"; "technological world"; "9 properties of DesignX problems"; "human-centered design"; "muddling through"; "evidence-based"; "implementation'; "designers' active role"; "new design expertise and education."

Level of Use	Author(s), Year	Context: Complex challenges	Context: Shift of design discipline	Subject and Problems: Sociotechnical systems	Subject and Problems: Human	Subject and Problems: Social	Subject and Problems: Technological	Subject and Problems: 9 Properties of DX problems	Approach and Arguments: HCD perspective	Approach and Arguments: Muddling-through	Approach and Arguments: Evidence-based	Approach and Arguments: Implementation	Approach and Arguments: Designer's active role	Approach and Arguments: New expertise & education
Level 3. Integrating	51. Allen,2017	•		•	•	•	•			•				
	52. Budde, Schankin, & Hoffmann et al., 2017				•	•			•	•				
	53. Cipriani & Rossi, 2018			•						•		•	•	
	54. Davis, 2016	•	•	•				•		•	•			•
	55. Fehr, Müller, & Aronoff-Spencer, 2017	•		•	•	•	•	•		•				
	56. Huang, Poderi, & Šćepanović et al., 2019			•	•	•	•		•	•		•		
	57. Jaasma, Wolters, Frens, Hummels, & Trotto, 2017	•		•		•						•		
	58. Lupetti, Yao, Gao, Mi, Germak, 2017			•	•	•	•	•	•					
	59. Malan, 2018			•		•				•				
	60. Nousala, Ing, & Jones, 2018	•	•	•		•		•		•				•
	61. Aronoff-Spencer, 2018			•	•	•	•		•			•		
	62. van der Bijl-Brouwer, 2017b			•						•				
Level 4. Reflecting & Developing	63. Flach, 2015	•	•	•	•	•	•			•				•
	64. John & Pam, 2018			•				•		•				
	65. Jones, 2015			•	•	•	•	•		•				
	66. Junginger, 2017b			•	•	•	•							
	67. Kersten, Long, Diehl et al., 2017									•				
	68. Kersten, Diehl, & Engelen, 2018									•				
	69. Lou, 2018a	•		•	•	•	•							
	70. Lou, 2018b	•				•					•	•	•	•
	71. Lou, 2017	•	•	•	•	•	•	•			•	•	•	•
	72. Ma, 2017	•		•						•		•		•
	73. Mulder & Loorbach, 2018	•	•	•		•						•	•	•
	74. Myerson, 2015		•	•					•	•				
	75. Nousala, 2016			•	•	•	•							

Fig. 4. Coding results about how the notion of DesignX is used in the literature (in part).

I coded the 75 documents based on this set of codes. Then I identified 4 ways that DesignX was used in the documents, ranging from (1) labeling and annotating; (2) introducing; (3) integrating; and (4) reflecting and developing. Figure 4 demonstrates part of these coding results.

To sum up, the whole set of 75 DesignX-related documents indicates a pattern in which DesignX aspects have attracted attention from various domains. The most salient aspect of DesignX is the domain of its identity as primarily the area of complex sociotechnical systems (referred to 53 times). The social dimension (involving multidisciplinary and multi-stakeholder perspectives) of such systems (31 times) and complex challenges our society faces (30 times) follow immediately. The muddling-through approach involving incremental and modular strategy (28 times) indicates intensive attention also paid to methodological considerations. The human psychological and cognitive dimension (21 times) and human-centered design (7) show this traditional design focus is also influential to shape DesignX concerns. It is noteworthy that evidence-based (4 times) is mentioned the least. This probably because "evidence-based" was advocated in the first DesignX manifesto but was not emphasized in Norman and Stappers' article.

I fully recognize that this coding scheme is highly analytic, and does not fully represent the real use of the DesignX article in these 75 documents. Many authors synthesized several aspects as an argument in their inquiries. Therefore the following elaboration helps to build a holistic idea how DesignX is used.

4.2.1   Level 1. Labeling and Annotating

Among the 75 documents, 37 documents referred to the DesignX article briefly by using it as either a quick label or an annotation without further introduction.

The article is used to label a distinct aspect of an approach to complex sociotechnical systems, for example, people and technology [42]; or to label a certain kind of complex problem [43]; or to indicate an increasing research interest from a specific domain [44]; or, as a means of echoing a shift within the design discipline [45].

It is also used as an annotation supporting characteristics of complex sociotechnical systems. For example, "there are complex and non-linear interactions and dynamics among different layers, actors, and technological components of CES (Norman and Stappers 2015)" [31].

In this Level 1 group, most documents cited the DesignX article in their introduction or literature review sections, locating the study in the context of sociotechnical systems or defining what such a system is. Some use the article when discussing their research's implications and future direction, drawing on DesignX's call to change design practice and education. Some refer to its muddling-through, incremental approach. The Level 1 group does not look into the notion of DesignX deeply, and only touches upon very limited aspects among the 13 codes.

4.2.2   Level 2. Introducing

The Level 2 group embraces a deeper or more holistic understanding of DesignX, by considering detailed dimensions spanning across the 13 codes. Barbara McCombs [46], for example, introduces DesignX as it is originally defined: as a sociotechnical systems approach characterized by the human-centered design perspective that includes a muddling-through process of taking small, incremental steps within a modular approach so as to divide the whole into more manageable components. Peppou [47] delves more into the intertwining human, social and technical spheres of DesignX problems. Vornhagen [30] further illustrates the difficulties in making sense of complex sociotechnical systems by referring to the 9 properties of DesignX problems. The call for new skills for designers to tackle complexity is also presented more clearly in this group of documents [48].

4.2.3   Level 3. Integrating

In the Level 3 group, the DesignX article is more comprehensively and deeply used, and referred to in various places in the document including the introduction, methods, discussion, and conclusion. These authors show an observable inclination to integrate some of the essential DesignX arguments into their studies. For example, Fehr and colleagues [49] adopt DesignX as the methodology guiding their study on design for computing in health care. Allen [50] uses DesignX's modularity and incremental process as the guiding principle to align the implementation of an open professional development strategy. Jaasma and colleagues [51] emphasize the necessity of incorporating multi-stakeholder interaction—a very important feature of DesignX in the social sphere—in the framing of their study on a product-service system design for participatory sensemaking for public issues. Mieke van der Bijl-Brouwer [52] draws on DesignX's call for "the continuous development of multiple interventions" to explain the findings of her empirical study in service systems design.

Compared to the Level 1 group, the 25 documents on both Levels 2 and 3 exhibit a wider and deeper interest in DesignX. They are more inclined to use this notion to explain or support their arguments. However, a critical reflection and development of the DesignX notion is not really present. The articles in the Level 4 group fill this vacancy.

4.2.4   Level 4. Reflecting and Developing

There are 13 documents that directly reflect on the idea of DesignX, and some of them shed light on dimensions that DesignX could possibly flesh out.

While they accept the nine properties of DesignX problems, John and Pam [22] challenge the notion that the muddling-through approach is "unnecessarily defeatist" and would be "cause for alarm" if institutionalized in medical care. They assert that DesignX fails to consider some advanced tools available now including Axiomatic Design, Cynefin, Agent Base Modeling, and data sciences, which can offer workable holistic heuristics while also being able to resolve local and emergent difficulties.

Kersten and colleagues [53] question the operational characteristic of muddling through also, this time from an engineering design perspective. They argue that strategic intent can steer one through uncertainty when such intent is more explicitly present from the outset, as it empowers designers to develop scenarios to guide them through.

These two criticisms seem controversial to me, because DesignX does not ignore the capability of technology or deny the advantage of design being explicitly strategic. The question is whether advanced techniques and strategic intent are sufficient to address DesignX challenges, especially given that complexity and uncertainty are central characteristics of the design context. Such debates need evidence to support any position.

Mulder and Loorbach [24] offer a comprehensive account of DesignX and observed valuable discussions, for example, on the PhD-Design mailing list inspired by the DesignX article. However, the authors criticize the more or less design expert-dominant context of the discussions, as the DesignX article seems to cast the designer as the central figure "in the proposed path-dependent optimization of a design regime" [24]. They argue that for design to deliver more value to society, engaging more with society is inevitable. This possibly implies that although DesignX emphasizes multi-stakeholder involvement in the social sphere of complex systems, the political issues and how to handle such challenges deserve further examination.

Ma [54] notes that DesignX (2015) is too focused on issues of "how" without sufficiently exploring the fundamental question of "what is a system?" Drawing on Buchanan's [55] schema of systems being based on distinct design strategies, the author attempts to understand DesignX problems (which are not new) from a fresh perspective to enrich the ongoing conversation.

She Ji published invited commentary articles on Norman and Stappers' DesignX article. The purpose was to reflect on and expand the DesignX conversation. All 3 commentary authors participated in the DesignX working conference. Their distinct perspectives helped the future journey of DesignX unfold by looking deeper into cognitive systems engineering, the design tradition, and socioecological systems.

Flach [56] argued that we must recognize that all agents—including the smartest human beings and the most advanced technological systems—are confined by "bounded rationality." He warns of the danger of reinforcing "a tendency ... to identify the human as the 'weakest link' that is often the source of 'errors' in complex systems" [56]. His cognitive systems engineering perspective adds an alternative view to more classical approaches in the DesignX agenda such as human factors or human-computer-interaction.

Myerson [57] discusses the difficulties design has embarking on the X journey due to a double mismatch. On the one hand, complex sociotechnical issues require a big picture thinking broader than specialized silos where designers were educated and where they traditionally intervene; on the other hand, the muddling-through approach of taking small, modular steps seems to go against designers' tendency to "think big and bold outside the constraints of any systems," a habit reinforced by project-based design education.

Jones [58] emphasized that understanding the social sphere of DesignX (social, cultural, and political issues) requires a socioecological systems perspective. It deserves its own methodological exploration that Norman and Stappers did not sufficiently cover.

In addition, Lou's effort to develop DesignX is noteworthy. Firstly, he points out that efforts to achieve sustainability involve the most complex sociotechnical systems issues that also need design intervention [59]. Second, he advocated a type of design activism [18] that opens up the DesignX call for designers' to be more active in the implementation phase. Rather than being problem-solving service providers, designers should create visions, initiate projects, integrate resources, drive innovation aimed at social wellbeing, and implement the solutions [60]. Thirdly, evidence-based [18] research is a feature that Lou believes distinguishes DesignX from conventional practices that are largely based on trial-and-error and rule of thumb. All these aspects call for a cultural shift of the design discipline [61].

5   Findings

5.1   Patterns of Knowledge Diffusion and Integration

When combining the results of study Part 1 and Part 2, a more meaningful pattern emerges. Almost half of the DesignX-related studies (37 docs) refer to this notion in a light manner. In Fig. 2, the two keyword clusters that are relatively distanced from the main network—"applied computing" and "energy transition"—come from studies that used "DesignX" as a label. This implies that the DesignX notion has scratched but the surface of such disciplines as computer science and energy engineering, but the seed has not been deeply sown. However, this label use possibly also implies that, although the DesignX notion is alien to many disciplines, it is so well synthesized—articulating the challenges and problems—that it acts as a kind of ready-made shorthand to indicate a complex (design) situation. Such clarity helps design to communicate with other disciplines.

Not all interdisciplinary encounters remain on the surface level. Some authors from cognitive engineering systems and engineering design did start to weave the DesignX notion into their studies and offered insightful reflections on DesignX. These authors were either invited to participate in the DesignX working conference or had an experience of working with *She Ji*, the journal that published the DesignX article. Collaborative activities and publication platforms (including journals and conference proceedings) help a new design idea to spread beyond disciplinary boundaries and evoke deeper responses. In particular, the close communication between *She Ji* and the systemic design community led by Jones and colleagues resulted in a significant portion of DesignX-related studies across Levels 2 to 4, which better integrate DesignX into other fields and critically reflect on it.

I held a hypothesis before the analysis that documents from disciplines outside design would tend to use the DesignX article in a relatively light manner (on Level 1); those from inside design would be more likely to look deeper into DesignX. However, the qualitative analysis results do not necessarily support this hypothesis. All the four distinct levels of use include many design studies. A more fine-grained pattern of DesignX use—one that is able to clearly illustrate the relationships brought together by DesignX within design disciplines and between design and other disciplines—will require a subject categorization that works for design. This categorization is beyond the scope of the current study but will be further explored in my future work.

The academic impact of DesignX Collaborative scholars has been indispensable to the course of knowledge diffusion and integration of DesignX. Don Norman in particular is one of the best known design theorists and human-centered design promoters. His work, whose topics range from psychology and engineering to design and design education, was cited 94 times in the 75 documents included in this study. His multidisciplinary experience and expertise translates extremely fluidly across various disciplines. In addition, the organizations where he and the other Collaborative scholars are based have become the most influential places supporting DesignX-related studies. These loci of DesignX research include the Design Lab, UC San Diego led by Don Norman; Delft University of Technology where Stappers and Voûte are based; and Tongji University College of Design and Innovation led by Lou. These organizations have served as DesignX ground zeroes: places where these pivotal scholars can develop the emerging DesignX "research community of practice" [62] engage in the early stages of knowledge diffusion, and open the DesignX discussion to their research networks.

5.2   A Future Path for DesignX

Insights obtained through this study on developing DesignX are multi-faceted, and can be summarized as follows.

(1) A better understanding of the technological aspect of the DesignX domain is needed. As evidenced by the results from Part 2, most of the documents in this study emphasize the social and human-centeredness of DesignX issues. The technical aspect is sorely lacking. In fact, all three dimensions of DesignX problems require advanced exploration supported by cutting-edge knowledge from the social sciences, computer sciences, systems studies, engineering, and many more domains in addition to design. Norman and Stappers acknowledged designers' ignorance of knowledge about complex systems that other disciplines have been accumulating for decades [3]. To add to this observation, Lou [59] advocates involving the most advanced technology at our disposal including data science techniques and Artificial Intelligence to address complexity, ambiguity, and uncertainty.

(2) The methodology is ready for further advancement. Re-examining what constitutes "wickedness" in DesignX problems comes with significant implications. Without a methodology that actually works to design for complex sociotechnical systems, the DesignX discourse probably will not be able to move forward. It is an optimistic sign to see that keywords such as "design methodology" and "design methods" recently joined in the conversation. The dialectic on the muddling-through approach and its reductionist feature deserves exploration of a more empirical nature.

(3) A cultural shift in design must be fostered. To tackle complex sociotechnical issues, DesignX must emphasize an evidence-based approach, interdisciplinary collaboration, the goal of sustainability, the spirit of design activism, and more rapid uptake of cutting-edge technologies [61]. All these require a new culture, different from the one reinforced by conventional design practice and research.

The above points offer a rough outline of a possible future path for DesignX. Their implications for design education are massive.

6 Concluding Remarks

This paper has explored an emerging front in design research inspired by Norman and Stappers's seminal 2015 article entitled "DesignX: Complex Sociotechnical Systems." This empirical study adopts a mixed methods approach combining the knowledge mapping technique VOSviewer with textual-based qualitative analysis. Results from both quantitative and qualitative methods disclose the transient structure of DesignX-related research in its knowledge and research communities. Although relatively few documents have become available during a short (±3-year) period, a preliminary interdisciplinary pattern is discernible. Rich insights arising from these results support interpretation and understandings about patterns of knowledge diffusion and integration in DesignX-related research. This paper advances understandings about how a new, interdisciplinary concept, first initiated in one discipline, slowly migrates to other disciplines and evokes studies at their intersections.

However, the domain of DesignX-related research has not reached a saturated and stable state. Based on a very small data set, mapping the DesignX-related research front is explorative at best. The risk lies in how much the structure is disturbed by the noises that were not filtered out by low threshold settings when applying knowledge mapping technique. The patterns reported in this study are experimental snapshots of a changing area, and are subject to further examination. If the dataset expands, the clustering of emerging thematic topics in this area might change and be able to represent the interdisciplinary structure more accurately. Also more knowledge mapping techniques should be experimented to identify tools that work best for small and medium sized datasets coming from mixed indexing sources. Techniques for correcting and formatting documents' bibliographic information also require further study.

Bibliometric and scientometric knowledge mapping methods and tools work well for revealing structures at the macro-level, and are particularly useful for detecting research fronts for knowledge management and policymaking purposes. To achieve insights that make sense to design researchers on a micro and meso level, I argue that when applying knowledge mapping techniques to the design discipline, researchers should consider complementing perspectives or approaches to help interpretation of the macro views by eliciting more fine-grained findings from within the disciplines concerned.

The systematic review of DesignX-related studies is an experimental attempt to describe the interdisciplinary structure of an emerging research area. The insights and lessons learned contribute to further studies on the interdisciplinarity of design discipline.

Acknowledgments. I would like to thank Gang Sun for giving me tutorials on VOSviewer, Ying Liu and Fei Lin for searching a preliminary set of documents via Google Scholar, and Huilin Zhou for her assistance to quicken my formatting bibliographic information for non-WoS indexed documents.

References

1. Buchanan, R.: Wicked problems in design thinking. Des. Issues **8**(2), 5–21 (1992). https://doi.org/10.2307/1511637
2. DesignX Collaborative: DesignX: A Future Path for Design. jnd.org. http://www.jnd.org/dn.mss/designx_a_future_pa.html. Accessed 1 Mar 2019
3. Norman, D.A., Stappers, P.J.: DesignX: the design of complex sociotechnical systems. She Ji: J. Des. Econ. Innov. **1**(2), 83–94 (2015). https://doi.org/10.1016/j.sheji.2016.01.002
4. Porter, A.L., Rafols, I.: Is science becoming more interdisciplinary? Measuring and mapping six research fields over time. Scientometrics **81**(3), 719–745 (2009). https://doi.org/10.1007/s11192-008-2197-2
5. Leydesdorff, L., Rafols, I.: A global map of science based on the ISI subject categories. J. Am. Soc. Inform. Sci. Technol. **60**(2), 348–362 (2009)
6. Friedman, K.: Models of design: envisioning a future for design education. Visible Lang. **46**(1/2), 128–151 (2012)
7. Murphy, P.: Design research: aesthetic epistemology and explanatory knowledge. She Ji: J. Des. Econ. Innov. **3**(2), 117–132 (2017). https://doi.org/10.1016/j.sheji.2017.09.002
8. Ahmed, S.: Encouraging reuse of design knowledge: a method to index knowledge. Des. Stud. **26**(6), 565–592 (2005). https://doi.org/10.1016/j.destud.2005.02.005

9. Carvalho, L., Dong, A., Maton, K.: Legitimating design: a sociology of knowledge account of the field. Des. Stud. **30**(5), 483–502 (2009). https://doi.org/10.1016/j.destud.2008.11.005
10. Hernández, R.J., Cooper, R., Tether, B., Murphy, E.: Design, the language of innovation: a review of the design studies. She Ji: J. Des. Econ. Innov. **4**(3), 249–274 (2018). https://doi.org/10.1016/j.sheji.2018.06.001
11. Li, N., Kramer, J., Gordon, P., Agogino, A.: Co-author network analysis of human-centered design for development. Des. Sci. **4**(e10), 1–24 (2018). https://doi.org/10.1017/dsj.2018.1
12. Xu, J.: Knowledge Mapping of Design Science. Science and Technology Press, Beijing (2018). (in Chinese)
13. Gemser, G., de Bont, C., Hekkert, P., Friedman, K.: Quality perceptions of design journals: the scholars' perspective. Des. Stud. **33**(1), 4–23 (2012). https://doi.org/10.1016/j.destud.2011.09.001
14. Van Eck, N.J., Waltman, L.: Visualizing bibliometric networks. In: Ding, Y., Rousseau, R., Wolfram, D. (eds.) Measuring Scholarly Impact, pp. 285–320. Springer, Cham (2014). 10.1007/978-3-319-10377-8_13
15. Chen, C.: CiteSpace II: detecting and visualizing emerging trends and transient patterns in scientific literature. J. Am. Soc. Inform. Sci. Technol. **57**(3), 359–377 (2006). https://doi.org/10.1002/asi.20317
16. Price, D.J.D.S.: Networks of scientific papers. Science **149**, 510–515 (1965)
17. Persson, O.: The intellectual base and research fronts of JASIS 1986–1990. J. Am. Soc. Inf. Sci. **45**(1), 31–38 (1994)
18. Lou, Y.: DesignX, an era of new design activism. Creation Des. **11**(1), 25–29 (2018). (in Chinese)
19. Ni, M.: Open your space: a design activism initiative in Chinese urban community. In: Rau, P.-L.P. (ed.) CCD 2017. LNCS, vol. 10281, pp. 412–431. Springer, Cham (2017). https://doi.org/10.1007/978-3-319-57931-3_33
20. Price, R., Straker, K.: The design movement: two case studies from the edge of the discipline. Des. J. **20**(Suppl. 1), S4565–S4574 (2017)
21. Eloise, T., Crilly, N.: Resilience in sociotechnical systems: the perspectives of multiple stakeholders. She Ji: J. Des. Econ. Innov. **3**(3), 165–182 (2017). https://doi.org/10.1016/j.sheji.2017.10.011
22. John, T., Pam, M.: Complex adaptive blockchain governance. In: MATEC Web of Conferences, vol. 223, p. 01010. EDP Sciences, London (2018). https://doi.org/10.1051/matecconf/201822301010
23. Blevis, E., Preist, C., Shien, D., Ho, P.: Further connecting sustainable interaction design with sustainable digital infrastructure design. In: Proceedings of the 2017 Workshop on Computing Within Limits, pp. 71–83. ACM, New York (2017). https://doi.org/10.1145/3080556.3080568
24. Mulder, I., Loorbach D.: Rethinking design: a critical perspective to embrace societal challenges. In: Kossff, G., Potts, R. (eds.) Proceedings of Transition Design Symposium 2016, Dartington, UK, pp. 16–24 (2016)
25. Irwin, T.: The emerging transition design approach. In: Proceedings of the Design Research Society 2018, vol. 3, pp. 968–990. (2018). https://doi.org/10.21606/drs.2018.210
26. Bayazit, N.: Investigating design: a review of forty years of design research. Des. Issues **20** (1), 16–29 (2004). https://doi.org/10.1162/074793604772933739
27. Jones, P.: Preface to systemic design: theory, methods, and practice. In: Jones, P., Kijima, K. (eds.) Systemic Design: Theory, Methods, and Practice, pp. vii–xvi. Springer, Tokyo (2018)

28. Müller, L., Budde, M., Weibel, N., Aronoff-Spencer, E., Beigl, M., Norman, D.: Learning from failure: designing for complex sociotechnical systems. In: Proceedings of the 2017 ACM International Joint Conference on Pervasive and Ubiquitous Computing and Proceedings of the 2017 ACM International Symposium on Wearable Computers, pp. 988–991. ACM, New York (2017). https://doi.org/10.1145/3123024.3124460

29. Vornhagen, H.: Effective visualisation to enable sensemaking of complex systems. The case of governance dashboard. In: Proceedings of the International Conference EGOV-CeDEM-ePart 2018, pp. 313–324 (2018)

30. Vornhagen, H., Davis, B., Zarrouk, M.: Sensemaking of complex sociotechnical systems: the case of governance dashboards. In: Proceedings of the 19th Annual International Conference on Digital Government Research: Governance in the Data Age, Article no. 101. ACM, New York (2018). https://doi.org/10.1145/3209281.3209392

31. Koirala, B.P., van Oost, E., van der Windt, H.: Community energy storage: a responsible innovation towards a sustainable energy system? Appl. Energy 231, 570–585 (2018)

32. Koirala, B.P., van Oost, E., van der Windt, H.: Socio-technical innovation dynamics in community energy storage. In: CESUN Global Conference 2018, pp. 1–8 (2018)

33. Rittel, H.W.J., Webber, M.M.: Dilemmas in a general theory of planning. Policy Sci. 4(2), 155–169 (1973)

34. Müller, L.: A cognitive assistant for the emergency department. In: Proceedings of the 2016 ACM International Joint Conference on Pervasive and Ubiquitous Computing: Adjunct, pp. 1062–1067. ACM, New York (2016). https://doi.org/10.1145/2968219.2968569

35. Dorst, K.: Frame Innovation—Create New Thinking by Design. MIT Press, Cambridge, MA (2015)

36. Manzini, E.: Design, When Everybody Designs: An Introduction to Design for Social Innovation. MIT Press, Cambridge, MA (2015)

37. Brown, T.: Change by Design: How Design Thinking Transforms Organizations and Inspires Innovation. Harper Business, New York (2009)

38. Buchanan, R.: Worlds in the making: design, management, and the reform of organizational culture. She Ji: J. Des. Econ. Innov. 1(1), 5–21 (2015). https://doi.org/10.1016/j.sheji.2015.09.003

39. Lindblom, C.E.: The science of "muddling through". Public Adm. Rev. 19(2), 79–88 (1959)

40. Snowden, D.J., Boone, M.E.: A leader's framework for decision making. Harvard Bus. Rev. 85(11), 68–77 (2007). https://hbr.org/2007/11/a-leaders-framework-for-decision-making

41. Kessler, M.M.: Bibliographic coupling between scientific papers. Am. Doc. 14, 10–25 (1963). https://doi.org/10.1002/asi.5090140103

42. Boy, G.A.: Human-centered design of complex systems: an experience-based approach. Des. Sci. 3, e8 (2017). https://doi.org/10.1017/dsj.2017.8

43. Müller, L.: Solving the wrong problem: when technology is making us blind. In: Proceedings of the 2017 ACM International Joint Conference on Pervasive and Ubiquitous Computing and Proceedings of the 2017 ACM International Symposium on Wearable Computers, pp. 1012–1015. ACM, New York (2017). https://doi.org/10.1145/3123024.3124396

44. Jaasma, P., van Dijk, J., Frens, J., Hummels, C.: On the role of external representations in designing for participatory sensemaking. In: Proceedings of the Conference on Design and Semantics of Form and Movement-Sense and Sensitivity, DeSForM 2017, pp. 281–295. IntechOpen, London (2017)

45. Cheatham, D.M.: A multiple intelligences model for design: developing the ways designers think as design disciplines expand. Dialectic 1(2), 75–100 (2017)

46. McCombs, B.L.: Historical review of learning strategies research: strategies for the whole learner—a tribute to Claire Ellen Weinstein and early researchers of this topic. Front. Educ. **2** (2017). https://doi.org/10.3389/feduc.2017.00006

47. Peppou, G., Thurgood, C., Bucolo, S.: Designing competitive industry sectors. Des. Manag. J. **11**(1), 3–14 (2016)

48. Brambila-Macias, S.: Early Stages of Designing Resource-Efficient Offerings: An Initial View of Their Analysis and Evaluation. Linköping University Electronic Press, Linköping (2018)

49. Fehr, Í., Mueller, L., Aronoff-Spencer, E.: DesignX in the emergency department: requirements of a digital antibiogram. In: Duffy, V., Lightner, N. (eds.) AHFE 2017. AISC, vol. 590, pp. 406–414. Springer, Cham (2018). https://doi.org/10.1007/978-3-319-60483-1_42

50. Allen, W.S.: Open professional development as a sociotechnical design challenge. In: Proceedings of the 2017 CHI Conference Extended Abstracts on Human Factors in Computing Systems, pp. 1478–1485. ACM, New York (2017)

51. Jaasma, P., Wolters, E., Frens, J., Hummels, C., Trotto, A.: [X] Changing perspectives: an interactive system for participatory sensemaking. In: Proceedings of the 2017 Conference on Designing Interactive Systems, pp. 259–269. ACM, New York (2017)

52. van der Bijl-Brouwer, M.: Designing for social infrastructures in complex service systems: a human-centered and social systems perspective on service design. She Ji: J. Des. Econ. Innov. **3**(3), 183–197 (2017). https://doi.org/10.1016/j.sheji.2017.11.002

53. Kersten, W., Diehl, J.C., van Engelen, J.: Facing complexity through varying the clarification of the design task: how a multi-contextual approach can empower design engineers to address complex challenges. FORMakademisk **11**(4), 1–28 (2018)

54. Ma, J.: What is a system?: a lesson learned from the emerging practice of DesignX. In: Rau, P.-L.P. (ed.) CCD 2017. LNCS, vol. 10281, pp. 59–75. Springer, Cham (2017). https://doi.org/10.1007/978-3-319-57931-3_6

55. Buchanan, R.: Systems and the environments of experience: design thinking and systems analysis. She Ji: J. Des. Econ. Innov. **5**(2) (2019, forthcoming)

56. Flach, J.M.: Supporting self-designing organizations. She Ji: J. Des. Econ. Innov. **1**(2), 95–99 (2015)

57. Myerson, J.: Small modular steps versus giant creative leaps. She Ji: J. Des. Econ. Innov. **1**(2), 99–101 (2015)

58. Jones, P.: Designing for X: the challenge of complex socio-X systems. She Ji: J. Des. Econ. Innov. **1**(2), 101–104 (2015)

59. Lou, Y.: Designing interactions to counter threats to human survival. She Ji: J. Des. Econ. Innov. **4**(4), 342–354 (2018). https://doi.org/10.1016/j.sheji.2018.10.001

60. Lou, Y., Ma, J.: Growing a community-supported ecosystem of future living: the case of NICE2035 living line. In: Rau, P.-L.P. (ed.) CCD 2018. LNCS, vol. 10912, pp. 320–333. Springer, Cham (2018). https://doi.org/10.1007/978-3-319-92252-2_26

61. Lou, Y.: The expanding scope and paradigm shift of design. Time Arch. **35**(1), 11–15 (2017). (in Chinese)

62. Poggenpohl, S.H.: Communities of practice in design research. She Ji: J. Des. Econ. Innov. **1**(1), 43–56 (2015). https://doi.org/10.1016/j.sheji.2015.07.002

Designing Co-design: Addressing Five Critical Areas to Increase the Experience of Participants and Facilitator in a Co-design Session

Paola Trapani[✉]

College of Design and Innovation, Tongji University,
281 Fuxin Road, Shanghai, China
paola@tongji.edu.cn

Abstract. *Background:* In recent years, the practice of co-design has gained proper attention for it can provide innovative approaches to complex societal problems through the participation of all stakeholders. Usually, designers focus on arranging methods and tools to support participants' ideation and expression trying to overcome the barriers resulting from differences in background, skills, attitudes, and expertise (Sanders and Stappers 2012). However, acting as facilitators or team leaders without specific training on individual and group dynamics can lead to overlooking tacit or latent aspects that can eventually drag the team into tiresome quicksand during the sessions. *Methods:* interpretive concepts and theories describing individual transformation processes in the context of small groups are taken from relevant literature in the field of management development and applied psychology. *Results:* a light conceptual framework spots five critical areas that professional designers need to pay attention to when planning and conducting a co-design activity, if they want to keep the participation and involvement alive: (1) Motivation; (2) Focus; (3) Boundaries; (4) Rumination; (5) Transformation. *Conclusion:* An area for further research and theory ground for group-based co-design practice is outlined.

Keywords: Co-design · Co-creation · Participatory design ·
Collective creativity · Group dynamics · Group processes ·
Small groups · Personal transformation · Transdisciplinarity

1 Introduction

1.1 Co-creation and Co-design Today

Areas of application. Today, co-creation is emerging in increasingly broader contexts because it seems an appropriate approach to address open, complex, dynamic, and networked problems thanks to the involvement of all stakeholders in an extended problem context (Dorst 2015). According to Sanders and Stappers (2012), from in-house co-creation within a company or organization, we have moved on to the involvement of external stakeholders, whether they are customers or other companies in the supply chain. Public administration and civil servants, especially in Western

© Springer Nature Switzerland AG 2019
P.-L. P. Rau (Ed.): HCII 2019, LNCS 11576, pp. 79–93, 2019.
https://doi.org/10.1007/978-3-030-22577-3_6

countries affected by spending review, are increasingly inclined to involve citizens and communities in the creation of targeted policies, in an attempt to oppose the progressive reduction of financial resources available for public services (Meroni et al. 2018).

Through co-creation it is possible to produce added value at different levels: financial, experiential, and social (Sanders and Stappers 2012). This practice can, in fact, help companies to increase sales thanks to user feedback on a product, service, or brand; it can involve people in the expression of practices that are still latent and unexpressed, it seems a suitable methodology in all cases where the product/service innovation happens at the level of meanings (Norman and Verganti 2012) so that it is wise to envisage new wanted meanings that do correspond to an emerging user practices, although yet in the bud; can finally give people the tools and methods to express new lifestyles more sustainable and in line with a new environmental and social sensitivity.

Stages of the Design Development Suitable for Collaborative Development. According to Sanders and Stappers (2012), co-design can be applied to any phase of a product or service development: from the initial stages of context analysis to the definition of an opportunity, from concept development to prototyping, to conclude with marketing, sales, distribution, and after-sales. If more revenue is the objective, then co-design should be introduced in the final stages of the development process; if the design team is looking for more experiential value, it is appropriate from the intermediate steps; it must be used from the beginning if a social value is pursued. Other authors, including Dorst (2015) and Meroni et al. (2018), consider the collaborative approach as the only possible way to attack contemporary problematic contexts, which have an original status and are resistant to any traditional problem-solving approach. Discussing of a collaborative approach extended to each phase of the design process, Lou and Ma (2018), presenting NICE2035, propose the Living Lab model as an example of complex socio-technical systems in which the creation and experimentation of innovation goes beyond the traditional epicenter of its production, the university college, to involve the community of the surrounding neighborhood.

How Co-design Affects the Role of the Professional Designer. As expected, the participatory approach to design has generated a heated debate in the scientific community about the radical reconfiguration of the role of the professional designer. Experts from different sides questioned his part and legitimacy in a context where everyone has some expertise to bring to the table.

According to Dorst (2015), among the pioneers of a collaborative approach to complex urban issues would be the Young Design Foundation in Europe and the Designing Out Crime Center in Australia. In both institutions, the methodology differs from the traditional problem-solving approach in proposing a much more ambitious and complex model of "frame creation" in which designers and all stakeholders are more in search of questions, continually refined and redefined, than pretentiously resolutive answers. Looking for a solution to the issues as the problem-owner formulates them usually leads to a dead end road already traveled many times without success. The question is vicious at the beginning and carries within itself only the symptom of the problem, never the root, which must come to light through a sophisticated and complex method of re-framing the question. This alternative way is usually all uphill because it means that each actor sitting at the table renounces their established position.

Manzini (2015) considers the designer as a "mediator" and "facilitator" who uses his creativity and culture to guide the social conversation between very heterogeneous actors. Even for Sanders and Stappers (2012), the role of professional designers has extended considerably beyond the limits of current specializations. Today it is no longer enough to be an expert in interior design, communication, product, service, or system of products/services, fashion, jewelry, etc. Designers need to know how to develop methods and tools that allow people to express their creativity at all levels, as well as being able to organize and conduct fruitful and transformative conversations between experts and non-experts.

However, the emphasis on change should not be alarming because some fixed points remain: society will always need an excellent product or interior designers. Too much stress on the shift from expert designer to facilitator only polarizes the discussion: the enthusiasts of the new course end up arousing the defense mechanisms of the knowledge gatekeepers, acquired at the cost of years of study and professional practice. As always, the formation of opposing barriers does not benefit the necessary co-evolution of the figure of the designer and society.

The paper contributes to the area that Meroni et al. (2018) identify as "designing co-design": in particular, we want to deepen the role of the professional designers in the co-design setting by focusing on some basic skills for which there is no training in the curriculum. Hopefully, a discussion can be opened between those in charge so that these gaps are revealed and filled.

If proficiency with relevant design methods and tools generally do suffice in the traditional professional/client setting, to co-design a product/service in real time, along with the users or the client, not to mention a scattered cloud of multiple stakeholders, can be a dreadful experience for designers. In fact, in these cases, a new layer of sensitivity is required to detect and interpret subtle individual behaviors and group's dynamics. Co-designing in real time is a journey for which no map can be provided because it must be constructed on the go as the result of a purposeful interaction and conversation among the parties. Participants find themselves in a typical situation that, in each moment, can present the project team with unexpected circumstances - both positive and negative- affecting the emotional state at any level: visceral, behavioral and reflective (Norman 2007). Past frustrating experiences and bitter memories can block the endeavor at any time Sanders and Stappers (2012).

On the other hand, the occurring challenges are unpredictable and can cement or disintegrate not only the bonds within the group but also self-esteem, identity, awareness, etc. According to Tonkinwise (2013), in this case, designers must have a very refined and sensitive knowledge of human beings, they must understand psychology, even psychoanalysis, if they need to take into account also the signs that are still latent as unconscious, including body language, and attitudes. Unfortunately, designers do not receive any specific training to manage these aspects with the result that carefully planned and professionally conducted activities often fail because of the "human factor." Let's, therefore, proceed to a literature review on individual and collective creativity, to understand to what extent the skills and tools typical of designers can be useful, and to highlight any shortcomings that should be addressed through targeted curricular pathways.

1.2   Individual Creativity

Diffused Creativity in Daily Life. Human creativity is a trans-disciplinary subject on which there is no agreement between psychologists, designers, neuroscientists, psychoanalysts, anthropologists, sociologists, etc. In common sense, a solution to a problem is creative when it is both new and appropriate. Sanders and Stappers (2012) distinguish different levels of individual creativity. At the simplest level, creativity means *doing*: any practical activity is at this level, e.g., buying a ready-to-wear garment. Above this, is the level of *adapting*: one buys the clothing and makes changes to better tailor it to individual sizes or tastes. Then comes the level of *making*: purchasing the fabric and a pattern and engaging in the execution of the garment. Finally, at the top level of *creating*: one buys the material, draws and makes the garment from scratch. From here the authors derive that everyone is creative, at least at the first levels of the scale. Everyone has dreams and aspirations that can trigger acts of creativity in everyday life in the form of doing, adapting, making, or creating. It is not at all easy for designers to make such needs and desires explicit because often people would not be able to express them verbally during interviews or focus groups.

The wealth of knowledge that each of us has is similar to an iceberg stratified on four levels, of which the two lower ones plunge in the unconscious. The emerged tip represents the *explicit* knowledge of which we are aware and which we can communicate to others. Below it, we find the layer of *observable* knowledge that can be grasped by others but not form us. From this level onward, we are below the level of consciousness. The third layer is that of *tacit* knowledge, the set of all the concepts that make sense to us but which we are not able to communicate in words to others. Finally, at the base of the pyramid, there is the most substantial layer of *latent* knowledge consisting of all those concepts that we have not yet experienced, but that we can imagine, even if confusedly, based on past experiences. Latent knowledge could become explicit or observable in the future. The more designers are interested in discovering future scenarios, the more they have to do "data mining" from the pre-verbal submerged layers, where desires, needs, and values float and are difficult to make explicit and shared. Presenting incomplete and ambiguous tools during a co-design workshop is the most effective way for designers to bring such content to consciousness. Faced with such stimuli, in fact, everyone will tend to project their needs into it because of the human being's irrepressible tendency to make sense meaning. In other words, everyone will manage to fill in the gaps (i.e., what is unexpressed) with their content.

Emotions then influence creativity. Positive emotions favor the ramification of creative associations and cognitive flexibility. However, it is unpleasant that during co-creation and co-design sessions, especially if extended in time, negative emotions are not generated in the group originating from frustration, disillusionment, conflict, disengagement, etc. For this reason, the ability of designers to recognize, intercept, and channel them most properly can be a decisive factor in the success of the activity.

Discovering how past emotions influence a future expectation is another puzzle for designers. Sanders and Stappers (2012) recommend that participants prepare themselves on the subject for at least a couple of weeks before the workshop using the "path of expression" framework. Through sensitizing activities, participants may be asked to write down observations and reflections on a specific experience on personal journals to facilitate the triggering of creative associations during the workshop. They are also invited to reflect and record relevant past experiences for sharing during the workshop. Sharing helps to access fundamental values (silent or latent) and unexpressed needs and to project these into future aspirations.

Creativity can also be stimulated by the place where the co-design activities take place. For example, the presence of modular furniture that can be assembled at will, walls on which it is possible to post materials for collective discussion, corners suitable for moods and different attitudes (reflection, discussion, relaxation, mess-making, etc.), spaces for individual and/or group work, reconfigurable external permeability, etc. are all elements that designers should carefully prepare.

1.3 Collective Creativity

Fostering Groups' Creativity. When involving multiple people in co-creative working groups, the considerations about individual creativity are always valid. However, the variety of profiles and mutual interaction make the context much more complicated. For example, it may be appropriate to balance people who have mainly the typical left brain hemisphere skills such as logic, numeracy, literacy with others who perform best in the capabilities of the right one: rhythm, Gestalt, visual and three-dimensional composition, etc. Some think, others see, others act first of all (Mintzberg and Westley 2019).

Dorst (2015) sees design as a form of reasoning. Therefore, referring to the three models of thinking introduced by Charles Pierce, deduction, induction and abduction, the author states that designers use all three. However, designers are the only ones to present a peculiar variant of adduction. The traditional problem-solving activity in design is based on the classic model of adduction: to achieve a wanted result, we don't question the procedures or the patterns of behavior; we change the elements that can be combined to get the results. Often we create a solution within a fixed mode of practices (the "how"). When we don't question the "how," we exclude the creation of new scenarios. Sooner or later, routine reasoning will not lead to the desired value anymore and we must think about the problem again. At this point, designers can turn to a more powerful adduction version: we only know something about the outcome that we want to achieve. So the challenge is to figure out "what" new elements to create, while there is no known "how," no pattern of behavior that can lead to the desired outcome. As "what" and "how" are wholly interdependent, they should be developed in parallel. This double creative step requires the designers to devise proposals for both the unknowns, and test them in conjunction.

In conclusion, the co-design group should be formed by people with different skills and attitudes in terms of reasoning, making decisions, thinking styles, etc. Diversity must be managed, because it can lead to contrast and unproductive blockage. Here lies the ability of designers to act as mediators and facilitators of a social conversation with very different profiles, which Manzini (2015) addresses.

2 Diagnosing the Problem

2.1 Designer's Traditional Skills

After briefly mentioning some salient aspects of human creativity, both individual and collective, we review the skills that designers traditionally acquire to assess whether they are necessary and sufficient to address co-design activities with reasonable expectations of success. According to Mulgan (2011), designers are typically proficient in the use of three kinds of methods and tools.

Ethnographic Tools to Explore a New Context. To design in a collaborative setting, it is mandatory to start inquiring the field to get an understanding of the big picture, including the gaps: there are unknown unknowns that will not be grasped in any way. Therefore, it is not only acceptable but also mandatory to adopt an iterative approach that can refine at each loop ambitions and realistic opportunism.

Mapping and System Thinking Tools are useful to bring to light the right connections and relationships between elements of complex systems. The strategic mind required to envision an innovative frame (Dorst 2015) must be able to generate and visualize its element (e.g., primary and secondary stakeholders, flows of goods and materials, facilities, flows of information and financial resources) based on the data collected in the previous stage. Here the attention focuses on connections (e.g., cause-effect relationships, or connections based on meaning) between elements. The three forms of logical thinking and intuition should alternate through deliberate phases of intuitive expansion and analytical contraction.

Prototyping Tools can make ideas tangible and measurable. In this regard, there is a considerable difference between services, which are complex systems made of composite components scattered through space and time, and products. One thing is prototyping a tangible object like a chair, less obvious is how to make concrete the experience of a new service. Rough prototypes should be iterated to evaluate in real-time the progress made through the map and to uncover issues related to its usability and responsiveness to the scope.

Co-design Requires the Acquisition of New Skills. To a professional designer specialized in co-design, further competencies to size, evaluate, and manage personality traits, attitudes, interaction styles, motivations, group dynamics, etc. are as critical as the aforementioned hard skills. Although these competencies are in high demand, given the escalating market expansion of co-design, still are difficult to find also due to the deficient academic training in this regard. Often the team leader is called to lead the group in the exploration of an unknown territory without having the support of a map already drawn, because this must be built during the trip, procedurally. Any radical innovation of complex systems, in fact, is a long and uncertain journey due to the lack of structural conditions (including legislation, policies, and access to capital) that usually are still locked into old systems.

Consequently, failure is the rule and may arrive after years of roadblocks. Most likely, the whole quest could end up being perceived by the participants as a frustrating activity. As soon as the original optimistic plan fails and the expected "new Eldorado" will appear not so straightforward, members could suddenly plunge into chaos or the underworld with the consequent release of negative emotions that can jeopardize the goal (Peterson 1999). Designers usually find themselves ill-equipped in dealing with unpredictable psychological, perceptive, and behavioral response to a moving target.

3   Methods

3.1   Literature Review

By searching online for some of the keywords relevant to the paper, such as "group dynamics theory," Google scholar generates 4,370,000 entries, while the British Library returns a list of 4,645 entries. Looking for "group behavior" we get 4,000,000 results in Google Scholar. Repeating the procedure for all the indicated keywords, the quantity of bibliographic references becomes unmanageable. Texts have been published in sectors as diverse as social psychology, education, management development, health and wellness, occupational psychology, etc. over a while from the early '900 to today.

Faced with the impossibility of managing such a multitude of references, we have resorted to designerly adduction (Dorst 2015). We know that we want to create a working framework that allows designers engaged in co-design to manage external change and at the same time to keep an eye on the internal transformation of participants so that the former does not block the latter but instead favors it (desired outcome). To better explain this working framework, we have tried to represent it in Fig. 1. In the continuation of the research, we will remain open to the hypothesis of disposing of the model for a better one. However, in this initial phase, it guides us in the identification of the type of references to be reviewed in search of the conceptual underpinnings useful for the subsequent refining of the framework.

Given this desired result, we proceed to search for concepts in disciplinary areas other than design in which the authors already provide a comprehensive survey of the literature in the field of interest before providing their contribution. In particular, we investigate literature that discusses the connection between the external changes of a context and the possible internal adaptive transformations of individuals in response to those. For example, the essay by Breu and Benwell (1999) reports a good literature review on the experience of managers engaged in cases of change management in particularly critical situations. We then explore a second aspect, namely the influence of group dynamics on the internal transformation of individual group members. To this end, the Borek and Abraham paper (2018) provides a detailed review of group-based behavior-change interventions (GB-BCIs) experiments before proposing their original framework.

After that, we try to synchronize the various aspects in a framework for the use of designers, such as the one in Fig. 1, supported by the underpinnings assumed by the literature review. Finally, we identify some critical areas to which designers should pay attention during the entire performance of the activities, depending on the current design development phase.

Conceptual Underpinnings from Management Development. In the area of management development, Bridges (1980, 1986) studied the adaptive strategies of managers in the face of radical change management in a company operating in turbulent market conditions. In making a distinction between *change* that is always relative to the *external* context, and *transition* that is *intern* to the individual, the author links the two dimensions, for the individual failing to move successfully through the transition, context's change efforts will fail.

Nortier (1995), based on studies carried out on a sample of about 1500 managers engaged in change management processes in different western countries, expands Bridges' theory of individual transition and consolidates it into an articulated model in 5 phases: *balance, separation, crisis, rebirth, new balance.* In short, every time managers are faced with a management change, it is possible to reconstruct a typical cyclical pattern: the initial and final phases see managers operating in a situation of external balance, which allows them to continue to adopt the usual patterns of behavior, ways of thinking, and make decisions. At some point, the change begins to emerge but is underestimated or judged irrelevant, so that managers continue to proceed as usual but with decreasing effectiveness and success. This is the separation phase. Things fall into the crisis phase where it is clear that the previous balance has vanished. All attempts to apply consolidated strategies go awry, and managers begin to experience the loss of meaning in a situation of chaos and disintegration. The old ways of filtering, acquiring, and interpreting reality are no longer, and no new ones have been found. In the best cases, after a period of discouragement, it follows that the change in external circumstances can be an opportunity to rethink and question the operating methods. In this phase, called rebirth, the behavior returns to be exploratory and, even if aware of the possibility of failure, at least the motivation to experiment and test new frameworks of thought and action returns. With the first successes, it begins to appear clear that the worst is behind the back and one is again in control of the situation. Usually, the transition is remembered as a positive period and an opportunity for growth and learning.

Breu and Benwell (1999), studying the adaptive behavior of CEOs and senior managers of East Germany at the time of opening to Western market logic, focus on a variable so far little studied: the impact of the order of magnitude of change during epochal shifts in the State and global economy. In that case, the change has been multi-dimensional, multi-component, and multi-aspectual because it forced managers to move from a socialist management model to a capitalist one within a few months. From the field research conducted on a sample of 73 managers from 61 companies, it emerges that the most significant impact occurred in three areas: the perception of the external environment, the self-perception at the individual level, and the change in their behavior. After analyzing the data collected through interviews and structured questionnaires, the authors develop a model of transformative transition that is divided into five phases: *disintegration, euphoria, crisis, development, redefinition.* They then analyze the transformation of the external environment, self-perception, and behavior during the stages.

Conceptual Underpinnings from Group-Based Behaviour Change Intervention.
In the field of psychology applied to health, trying to induce changes in individual

habits and lifestyles within small therapeutic groups has been the subject of many experiments since the beginning of the 20th century. There are many empirical and experimental studies on the management of the most different chronic pathologies caused by harmful lifestyles or addictions, in which researchers have shown the greater effectiveness of interventions on groups of patients compared to one-to-one ones not only for economic reasons but also because they are often more effective. Positive changes can be triggered by the support received from the group and the facilitator, by the assumption of a new social identity within the group, by the adoption of group rules, by the virtuous circle triggered by the mechanism of feedback and further challenge, etc.

Borek and Abraham (2018) investigated the optimal characteristics of the group and the facilitation styles that seem to be most effective in inducing individual change within a therapeutic group. The authors propose a model of the mechanisms of change in groups, articulated in 5 all-comprehensive categories: (1) group development; (2) dynamic group processes and properties; (3) social change processes (or inter-personal processes between group members); (4) personal change processes as individual (or intra-personal) change processes; (5) group design and operating parameters. The 5-step model may seem simplistic, but it shows that personal change must be facilitated differently throughout the life of the group.

The first encounter is crucial because it can trigger a sense of belonging and reduce ambiguity, detachment, and artificiality. The transformation from a simple aggregate of individuals to a cohesive group capable of pursuing a common goal occurs through the development of some group dynamics explicitly desired and sought, including the development of social identification, group cohesion, the establishment of rules, roles and statutes and a peculiar climate of the group. The group, once established, can trigger changes identified through peer-to-peer interaction of members. They can trigger mechanisms of social comparison, both incremental and diminutive, of social learning, social power and influence, and mutual support. The expected results at the individual level are of various types: personal cognitive change (e.g., change of attitude, development of motivation, awareness of making&breaking deals, etc.), skill development, self-disclosure, feedback, and challenge.

Finally, the authors propose five guidelines for those who have to design self-help groups: (1) purpose of the group; (2) group composition and size; (3) leadership processes; (4) facilitator characteristics; and (5) group and interaction management. Establishing group objectives rather than individual ones, as long as they are realistic, facilitates group cohesion and identity. The composition, the size, the even or odd number of members, the prevalence of the male or female gender, as well as the personal characteristics, the cultural background, the gender of the facilitator are discussed with evidence in the literature. The style of communication used in the group is decisive. Sometimes, a pyramid model in which the facilitator always mediates interaction can be more effective; other times a circular model in which the members communicate directly with each other is more suitable. The facilitator must, in any case, be able to intercept and channel potentially dangerous single behaviors: according to Benne and Sheats (1948), patterns can include blocking, aggression, recognition-seeking, special pleading, withdrawing, and dominating.

4   Research Questions

From Naive to Realistic Co-design. Co-design, not differently from overly positive group management practices, is still mainly relying on the belief that the careful, preventive planning of a chain of activities subsequently implemented, given a wanted goal, is all that is required from designers. This empirical vision shows how persistent is the faith in the stability of a thoroughly prepared co-design setting and the predictability of planned activities on future success. The truth is that, when it comes to complex processes, in which heterogeneous actors interact for a long time, the stability and certainty of the result are not granted, and this can trigger internal resistance reactions that will make the situation worse.

For this reason, designers must be careful to catch the first signs of discontent, disappointment, bitterness, before they propagate to the rest of the group by sabotaging the efforts made. If the traditional skills of ethnographic exploration, mapping and prototyping are sufficient to manage the phases of external change, they do not seem useful to intercept and manage the internal transition of the participants. On this front, designers need skills for which they do not receive specific training.

We are interested in the link between external change and personal transformation within a group, and the effects of the group's dynamics and behavior on personal transformation. We want to find out what can favor or block own transition so to figure

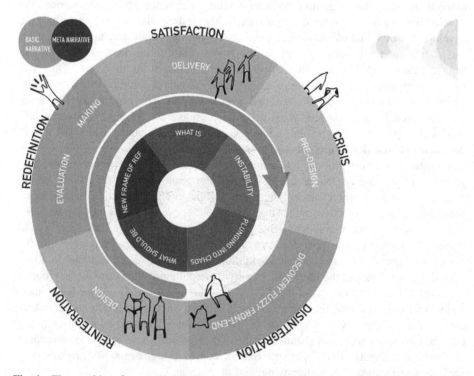

Fig. 1. The working framework of the co-design path development that synchronizes the narrative and meta-narrative levels. (Color figure online)

out how to fix or improve the management of group dynamics and intercept harmful behaviors early on. Updating academic programs to teach new skills is another hoped-for outcome.

Proposing a New Framework as a Working Hypothesis. The model in Fig. 1 introduces a frame, even though speculative, of development of the co-design path that synchronizes the external changes of the context in the various design phases with the probable internal transitions of the participants in response to those. At the level of the external environment, the process is articulated in a succession of phases that we can define as basic narrative represented (in the yellow ring): *pre-design* and *discovery fuzzy front-end, design, evaluation, making, delivery.* To operate at this level, the design group uses ethnographic, mapping, and prototyping tools and methods. In the case of radical innovation, establishing the sequence of the core narratives equals to exploring unknown territory. On this front, there is vast and ever-expanding literature, to which we do not claim to contribute.

Instead, we are interested in focusing on the internal transition of the participants. In response to the changing external conditions that the co-design group will encounter during the course, there will be internal reactions to which designers must be able to pay attention and intervene to avoid the failure of the experiment. By integrating the underpinnings derived from the literature review and Peterson's model "The Metamythological Cycle of the Way" (Peterson 1999), we indicate (blue ring) the dimension related to the internal transition of the participants as meta-narrative or the level of self-perception concerning individual and group behavior. We distinguish 5 phases: [*what is*] participants feel satisfied with the current state of planned activities, they act with confidence because they have negotiated attainable goals, a roadmap to reach them that seem to protect the group from chaos; [*instability*] timid signs that the plans will not lead to the expected result within the established time frame generate at first "surprise" that Peterson (1999) defines as "instinctive emotional response to the occurrence of something we did not desire" and that can turn out scary. Sooner or later, someone in the group, under the effect of negative emotions (e.g. scare, disengagement, boredom, disempowerment, etc.), can start acting passively or undermining the group's cohesion and confidence; [*plunging into chaos*] if negativity is not detected and con-tained early on, can fall the entire group into chaos where only panic reigns and all plans seem disrupted for good; [*what should be*] if the team leaders are capable of detecting the crisis, they can steer the efforts toward a more realistic goal: a new desirable state can be imagined by integrating the lesson learned; [*new frame of reference*] eventually, a new prototype of a more desirable state of the art rises out of a trade-off between realism and opportunism. However, it is only a matter of time for the cycle to start again, because every situation, however good it may be, can always be improved.

5   Defining the Specific Opportunity

5.1   Five Critical Areas to Improve the Designer's Capabilities

The model in Fig. 1 could easily lead us to think that the two processes, the narrative, and the meta-narrative, are not only distinct and synchronized with each other, but also take place according to a linear scan of phases linked in a precise order. For instance, the fuzzy front-end discovery phase may seem a chaotic time - during which the group wanders in total darkness and is at the verge of collapse and disintegration- but if the group endures the struggle, the design phase always follows. Now the group, happily reintegrated, has found the energy to explore what does not yet exist but should exist, to improve the real world. Unfortunately, we know that not all trips end in the Eldorado, the happy conclusion is not guaranteed at all, the mortality of the co-design groups is very high and comes before any result is reached. Moreover, no stage can ever be said concluded and passed for good, and it could reoccur and explode in the middle of a subsequent step. Finally, it is never possible to separate the level of activities under development, which cause changes in the external context, from internal changes as an adaptive response to those.

For this reason, instead of insisting too much on the DOs and DONTs of each phase of the meta-narrative level, we think it's more useful that designers always have five critical areas in mind that intertwine, present themselves, and fade intermittently throughout the process.

Motivation. One area concerns motivation, passion, liveliness, attraction, urgency, and appetite for the exploration at hand. How can we sustain the participants' motivation along the journey? It seems unlikely that motivation will be at the highest level at all stages of the quest for each member of the group. However, this is not necessarily a bad thing: a motivation that is always at its peak is not only not credible but is also counterproductive in the long run. Instead, it would be appropriate for designers to be able to detect the "temperature" of the group and manage it with wisdom: as long as there is a flame, there is always combustion in place. To keep the fire of motivation in place, designers will have to find strategies and tactics to lower it when it is too high, foment it when it is pale, make it twinkle at times, etc.

Focus. However, to keep motivation alive it is not enough because it must be addressed. People's desire to participate can be sustained only to a limited extent; therefore, it needs careful direction, or the team will run out of steam. "Focus" means direction, aim, purpose, or concentration (Hillman 2009). The motivation must be targeted and concentrated, or it risks being dispersed. How can we hone methods and tools to retain the group's focus?

Boundaries. A way to retain the focus is to establish proper "boundaries" for the experience. Meroni et al. (2018) suggest performing ceremonies for activity beginning and end, to suggest the "different" nature of the experience compared to the normal flow of daily life. We have seen that designing an appropriate location for the co-design session means establishing a delimited and separate spatial niche. Should other types of boundaries be created, different than space-time ones? An important kind of edge is the one that delimits the content to be dealt with at each stage of design development. Without this outline, there can be no focus. Dorst (2015) brings the intractability of contemporary problems back to the fact that they are often "open" so the boundary of the issue is either unclear or permeable. When you try to encircle the problem to define the included and excluded elements, you are immediately in trouble. However, the effort is necessary because human perception has such limits that it cannot grasp reality in all its complexity. If this is true about what already exists and observable through the senses, it will be even more true for what does not yet exist but is under development in the collective imagination of the group. Designers must facilitate the adoption by the group of a frame of reference through which to look at the new reality in the process of formation, that is, a sort of "visual cone" through which to observe the problem.

Dorst (2015), as we have seen, considers the designer's visual cone as a kaleidoscope: not only does it include some elements to look at but also the rules of assembling them in narrative chains of relationships and actions because of the desired end.

Peterson (2015) suggests starting by considering the reality included in the cone as predictable, while always keeping in mind that it is not predictable at all. In general, the group should deal with the minimum number of elements and relationships that will reasonably lead to the desired result. In other words, the group will only deal with an unexpected and adverse event if it constitutes a severe threat to the achievement of the outcome. In that case and just in that case, the reality in the visual cone will no longer be a predictable world. An event is positive and will generate positive emotions if it helps to advance the group towards the goal. Otherwise, it will be negative and will create negative emotions in the group. If the size of the adverse event is such that it does not allow the advancement, it may be wise to change the visual cone. In any case, the fact remains that the existence of a visual cone maintains the focus.

Rumination. Common sense and a touch of everyday life make events sensed and felt. A fully lived experience touches us personally, changing the innermost core of our essence. Ways to knit and knot the actual events that occurred during the session, no matter how disappointing or frustrating, into the fabric of a meaningful experience should be envisaged. "Preserving under salt," what happened during the day allows going back, ruminating and digesting the experience. The process of digestion of events in co-design is as if it happened in the stomach of a cow, so some "indigestible" elements return to be processed for further refinement of matter (Hillman 2009). How can designers develop tools and techniques to "preserve" experiences for subsequent ruminations?

Designers' Transformation. The designer is also transformed internally by the co-design process and should receive specific training to deal with this aspect. According to Broadbent (2018), the designers trained in the tradition of the American school of Human Centered Design are experts who externally observe the participants in their context. Designers trained in the North European "participatory" tradition are, on the contrary, participating observers. In the latter case, the clear distinction between context, participants, observation methods and researcher is impossible. Therefore, designers themselves, who are immersed in a prolonged co-evolution with the group, will undergo a specific internal transition to adapt to the evolution of the group. For example, when the activity does not give tangible results, the group proceeds in a slow, repetitive, gripped, dark, thick, and obstinate way. The designer may feel exhausted, stuck, entangled, frustrated. When the group shows signs of recovery, no longer turns in circles and seems to have guessed a way out of the stalemate, the designer can mediate the discussions thanks to his detachment. He can mirror any given situation. His reasoning can have a cold and dry quality because every trace of phlegmatic stickiness typical of the previous phase has been purged. As the group proceeds, some hypotheses begin to turn yellow and to decay; others instead begin to mature slowly. The designer favors this necessary transition, etc.

Facilitators are responsible for ensuring that the group develops optimally over time. To this end, they should consider ways of resolving conflicts constructively, establishing rules that encourage personal change. It would be beneficial for their training to observe the most experienced facilitators, to undergo observation and receive critical and supportive feedback, to exchange ideas with other group facilitators and to have access to qualified people. Senior supervisors can help develop facilitation skills. The limits imposed by this paper do not allow us to go into detail on this point, which deserves an article on its own.

6   Conclusive Discussion and Future Work

We have highlighted five critical areas that designers must always consider to improve the internal response of participants to co-design activities, to make the subjective experience more adaptive and fluid and facilitate changes in attitudes and behavior. The tools and techniques that are used in co-design today are not suitable to address this dimension. The designer's toolkit is usually useful on the narrative level (Fig. 1) to explore unknown territory, map the relationships between the elements contained in it and prototype proposals for interventions. The toolbox usually has no useful tools to manage the meta-narrative level. Consequently, the five areas are a new field of exploration for the future creation of new operational tools.

Finally, our ambition would be to open the discussion among those in charge of updating design programs to evaluate the prospect of including the skills needed to manage the meta-narrative level according to the modalities and prerogatives of designers.

References

Benne, K., Sheats, P.: Functional roles of group members. J. Soc. Issues **4**, 41–49 (1948)

Borek, A.J., Abraham, C.: How do small groups promote behaviour change? An integrative conceptual review of explanatory mechanisms. Appl. Psychol.: Health Well-Being **10**(1), 30–61 (2018)

Breu, K., Benwell, M.: Modeling individual transition in the context of organisational transformation. J. Manag. Dev. **18**(6), 496–520 (1999)

Bridges, W.: Transition - Making Sense of Life's Changes. Addison-Wesley, Reading (1980)

Bridges, W.: Managing organisational transitions. Org. Dyn. **15**, 24–33 (1986). Summer

Broadbent, S.: Anthropology, ethnography and massive codesign for complex services. In: Meroni, A., Selloni, D., Rossi, M. (eds.) Massive Codesign: A Proposal for a Collaborative Framework. Franco Angeli, Milan (2018)

Dorst, K.: Frame Innovation: Create New Thinking by Design, Kindle edn. The MIT Press, Cambridge (2015)

Hillman, J.: Alchemical Psychology (Uniform Edition of the Writings of James Hillman Book 5), Kindle edn. Spring, Thompson (2009)

Lou, Y., Ma, J.: Growing a community-supported ecosystem of future living: the case of NICE2035 living line. In: Rau, P.-L.P. (ed.) CCD 2018. LNCS, vol. 10912, pp. 320–333. Springer, Cham (2018). https://doi.org/10.1007/978-3-319-92252-2_26

Manzini, E.: Design, When Everybody Designs. The MIT Press, Cambridge (2015)

Meroni, A., Selloni, D., Rossi, M.: Massive Codesign. A Proposal for a Collaborative Framework. Franco Angeli, Milan (2018)

Mintzberg, H., Westley, F.: Decision making: it's not what you think. MIT Sloan Manag. Rev. (2001). https://sloanreview.mit.edu/article/decision-making-its-not-what-you-think/. Accessed 15 Feb 2019

Mulgan, G.: Foreword to Boyer, B., Cook, J.W., Steinberg, M.: In Studio: Recipes for Systemic Change. Sitra, Helsinki (2011)

Norman, D.A.: Emotional Design. Why We Love (or Hate) Everyday Things. Basic Books, New York (2007)

Norman, D.A., Verganti, R.: Incremental and radical innovation: design research versus technology and meaning change. Manuscript submitted to Design Issues. Based on a talk by Norman and Verganti (2011) at the Designing Pleasurable Products and Interfaces Conference in Milan, Italy (2012)

Nortier, F.: A new angle on coping with change: managing transition! J. Manag. Dev. **14**(4), 32–46 (1995)

Peterson, J.B.: Maps of Meaning: The Architecture of Belief. Routledge, London (1999)

Peterson, J.B.: 2015 maps of meaning lecture 03: narrative. Neuropsychol. Mythol. I (Part 1) (2015). https://www.youtube.com/watch?v=6NVY5KdSfQI&index=2&list=PLYRAIpZh7SWhf-pgT8 1hOqaFaiPygfbL1&t=2941s. Accessed 15 Feb 2019

Sanders, E., Stappers, P.J.: Convivial Toolbox: Generative Research for the Front End of Design. BIS, Amsterdam, (2012)

Tonkinwise, C.: Design thinking as a radical form of disruptive innovation. In: Yee, J., Jefferies, E., Tan, L. (eds.) Design Transitions: Inspiring Stories, Global Viewpoints. How Design is Changing. BIS, Amsterdam (2013)

The Design Thinking Between Man-Made and Natural – Taking Jewelry as an Example

I-Ting Wang[✉], Hsienfu Lo, and Gao Yang

Graduate School of Creative Industry Design, College of Design,
National Taiwan University of Arts, New Taipei City, Taiwan
etinw@ms43.hinet.net, hsienfulo@gmail.com,
Lukegao1991@gmail.com

Abstract. This study is concerned with the thinking process and the role of symbiosis in jewelry design. By investigating the connections between the natural and the artificial, this study builds a theoretical foundation for creating jewelry works based on imitation of the nature and for finding a balance between natural and artificial creations with the messages manifested in the nature. A qualitative approach combined with document analysis and case research method is adopted to develop the principles for creative design.

In the development of the principles, this study proposes a Function Follows Form (FFF) model to overcome some of the drawbacks of design-led innovation. Under the natural guidance of objects and based on the concepts of FFF, this study develops the model and process of applying FFF and discusses the feasibility of applying it in jewelry design. The result can also be a reference for development of creative ideas. In addition, a declining industrial technique, electroforming, is utilized in the design of jewelry works to find the value co-creation possibilities with craft and an industrial process. This study attempts to develop an innovative design thinking process and evaluate the feasibility of this process by applying it in the design of jewelry works. Through mapping of the views of the creator and observers, this study further provides a new perspective on the relationship between the natural and the artificial in art creation, which can be an issue worth further investigation by future researchers.

Keywords: Design thinking · Function Follows Form (FFF) ·
Innovative design process

1 Introduction

1.1 Background and Motivation

As a metalworking teacher, I understand that instruction, demonstration, and practice of techniques are not simply for one-way training of students. After students have achieved a certain stage in their learning, I need to focus my instruction on shift of thinking and implementation of methods. Through thinking and repetitive training of hands, the easily perceived sensations and guidance can enable a switch of roles, like a swap of roles between a teacher and students. This allows one to virtually play both the role of an observer and the role of the observee.

© Springer Nature Switzerland AG 2019
P.-L. P. Rau (Ed.): HCII 2019, LNCS 11576, pp. 94–104, 2019.
https://doi.org/10.1007/978-3-030-22577-3_7

In art creation, one may easily follow a pre-established design thinking process or even be trapped in a state of self-drowning confusion. This study is intended to analyze the process, status, form, and logic of my creations and summarize the context and features of related arguments proposed by numerous scholars. Starting with imitation of the nature, I attempt to re-create the beauty of nature using metalworking techniques. After an analysis of archetypes, Function Follows Form theory, and the symbiosis principle, I explore the possibilities of or foundation for applying a novel design thinking process between natural and artificial creations. The goal is to highlight the interdependencies in nature and evaluate the feasibility of an innovative design process.

1.2 Objectives

Through application of the Function Follows Form theory, this study attempts to explore a thinking process that can be applied in jewelry design. The objectives of this study are as follows:

1. To develop and analyze a design thinking process between natural and artificial creations.
2. To explore the possibilities of applying the Function Follows Form theory.

2 Literature Review

2.1 When Metalworking is Viewed as a Language

Jewelry tells one's thinking and is viewed as a new form of communication in the society. However, metalworking creates a space of expression for objects (the media). In such space, a replicated image and the content of a container, for example, need different instruments (i.e. craft and techniques) to describe how they should be observed. Art creators relying on use of "hand" choose not to express "verbally" but to view "the works they create" as a language. They use a more intuitive way of communication than verbal expression to respond, describe, and interpret the world they perceive. As mentioned in the beginning of *Ways of Seeing* by Berger, "Seeing comes before words. The child looks and recognizes before it can speak" [1]. Idealist aesthetics suggests that art creation is a subjective, conscious activity in which artists express their minds. Leo Tolstoy conceptualizes art as any activity that communicates emotion. Artists use sounds, colors or forms expressed in words as a means to express a feeling they have once experienced. The work they have created then becomes an instrument for communicating emotion that allows others to experience the same feeling by observing (or experiencing) the work. According to Renesette Croce and R. G. Collingwood, the work of art is located in the artist's spirit or mind. Through expression of intuitions or imaginations, and even without use of external media, the art process can be completed in the artist's mind [2].

In the making of art, artists use their hands to touch the object and feel the texture. Subsequently, through a comparison with their memories, they identify the common experiences between the object before them and the objects in their memories to support creation of a new image of the object. Berger mentions in Ways of Seeing that "We only see what we look at. To look is an act of choice. As a result of this act, what we see is brought within our reach. To touch something is to situate oneself in relation to it. (Close your eyes, move round the room, and notice how the faculty of touch is like a static, limited form of sight)"

2.2   The Relationship Between Nature and Artificial Creations

In the nature, the growth, integration, symbolization, corruption, and fading of biological entities always follow a certain law of life. The features of natural creations, such as browning, rough and layered texture, and fading of leaves, are always so astonishing. Through our sight, these features can be collected for use as design elements. People have imaginations about the world of minerals and look for the signs of natural creation. By describing the intuitive image of objects with our senses, transcribing their textures, and expressing emotions, we can create the imaginary images of nature.

In the *Record on the Subject of Music* (Yue-ji) chapter of *Book of Rites* (Li-ji), it is mentioned that the poem expresses man's ambitions; the song sings man's heartfelt wishes; the dance expresses man's sentiments. All of them come from man's inner world, and then musical instruments follow [3]. "The poem expresses man's ambitions" refers to the sensual experiences of seeing. Through making, conversion of thoughts or intuitive delivery of thoughts, one can create a work and then exhibit the work to have dialogues with observers, in hope of arousing different perceptions. Herbert Read states in his book *Art and Society* that "the image seems to accurately match with his impression of the object, rather than with the thing he sees with the eyes" [4]. This explains that primitive artists and child artists use their observations and sensations to represent their lives. The realist images they create are inevitably abstract, but because of the gap, the artistic image of the work no longer equates to an archetype of life. Musical scholar Yan-jiang Che mentions in "*On the history and development of variations*" [5] that "Variation is a type of music characterized by using limited materials to present unlimited imaginations. Whether the result of the presentation can open everyone's eyes and attract endless appraise is the greatest challenge for the creator of the variation. Arnold Schoenberg (1874–1951) describes the technique that Brahms used in developing variations (*entwickelnde Variation*) as a process of unfolding basic materials, motifs, and intervals into large pieces. Brahms' use of this technique is largely related to the secular music he was exposed to and the environment where he grew up. It was such environment that allowed him to absorb the "variations" in music in bars and coffee shops. Repetitions are common in original folk music. In the continuous diffusion of the repetitive parts of music, there might be some changes or variations to the original version. Brahms developed his improvising style and creativity in this background. With a special ability of developing variations, he created music with unique ethnic features and achieved a height in musical achievement that is hard to reach by later musicians.

3 Method

3.1 Model Development

Using the author's works as examples, this study discusses the relationship between natural and artificial creations along three dimensions, including archetypal analysis, Function Follows Form (FFF), and the symbiosis principle. By extending the FFF theory, this study attempts to develop from the relationships between function and form and between techniques and concepts an experimental model that can be applied in research and development of a design thinking process. In the following figures, Fig. 1 shows the framework of this study, and Fig. 2 presents how this model can assist design thinking using jewelry design as an example.

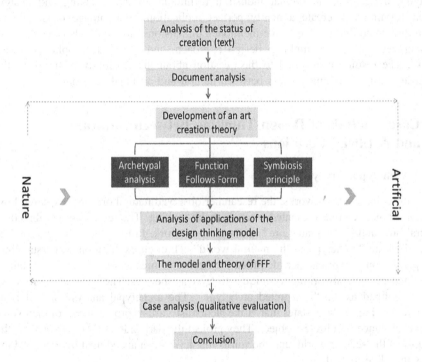

Fig. 1. The research framework (illustrated by the author)

3.2 Method, Case Analysis, and Subjects

The subjects are three jewelry works created with the same theme by the researcher, including "Memory replication I", "Memory replication II", and "Symbiosis". These works are first analyzed along three dimensions, including "archetypal analysis", "FFF", and "symbiosis principle". In addition, according to the rough model of contemporary jewelry design (Wang, Ni, and Lo 2018), revisiting industrial techniques and making breakthroughs in traditional techniques are among the approaches of contemporary jewelry design. Therefore, the researcher explored the possibilities of

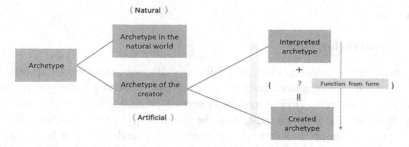

Fig. 2. The archetypal analysis model

applying a declining traditional industrial technique, in craft making and design. Electroforming can create a nearly perfect replication of an image or an object. Therefore, in addition to the above-mentioned dimensions, this study also analyzes and summarizes the design thinking, design approach, and techniques applied in these works. The result can respond to the question about the feasibility of applying the proposed design thinking process between natural and artificial creations.

4 Case Analysis of Design Thinking Between Natural and Artificial Creations

4.1 Archetypal Analysis

In creating this series of works, the researcher observed natural ores and explored how a natural object can be presented in an artificial making. The researcher combined "a natural ore" and "a simulated ore" into a piece of work. In this study, "natural ore" is defined as the "archetype in the natural world". Through exploration, understanding, and perception, the researcher identified the beauty of ores and used haptic sensations combined with metalworking techniques to recreate the ores. The recreated "simulated ore" is defined as the "interpreted archetype". The archetypal analysis model is as illustrated in Fig. 3. Jaffe states that "Like alchemists, artists project a part of their souls onto a substance or a lifeless object. They project the dark side of their personality, the shadow of the secular world, and the spirits that have been abandoned by them and the times they live in" [6].

The natural world has abundance of materials, waiting to be explored and recognized by observers. As shown in Table 1, the "Memory replication I" series of works is characterized by use a withered branch and application of electroforming. Through an electrodeposition process, the metallic deposits will be attached to the negative cavity side. After the deposits accumulate to a certain thickness, the cavity side can be separated to form the electroform, which is the recreated archetype. Roger Resenblatt mentions in *All the Days of the Earth* that "However we frenetically we get and spend, an attachment to the natural life of the plant remains fixed in our system… One cannot think of a single composer, painter or writer who has not tracked at least one major inspiration to a bird, a tree or a rose. People automatically lose themselves in wordless

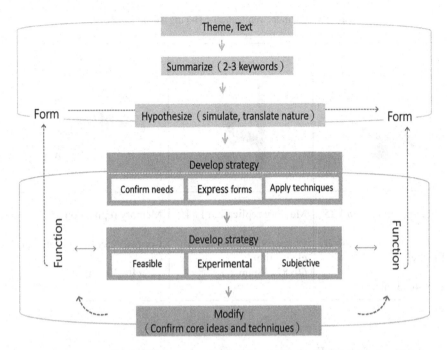

Fig. 3. Discussion of the design thinking process

reverence at the sight of a curlew or a silver cloud of anchovies or at the mournful wail of howler monkeys. Or they stare dumbly out at oceans, as if longing for their microbial past" [7]. Creation is oftentimes done through intuitive matching of self-perceptions. In Carl Jung's map of the soul, this process seems to fall in the border areas of conscious and unconscious, between personal unconscious and non-personal unconscious, and in the intersection of complex, archetypal image, and instinct. It is a turning point between soul and non-soul, bridging the inner and the outer worlds. According to the theory of synchronicity proposed by Carl Jung, there are meaningful connections between the subjective and the objective worlds. As a theory extended from the theories of id and the universe, synchronicity suggests that there is a hidden order and unity among all the existences. More specifically, there is a meaningful order between two coincidences which appear to have randomly occurred; spiritual images (subjective) and objective events may sometimes appear in an exact order.

Jung proposes that archetypes are transcendental and not limited to the psychological field. In terms of their transcendability, they can enter our consciousness from the soul, from the outside world or from both channels. Synchronicity refers to the situation when it enters our consciousness from both channels. The spiritual image (including abstract scientific thoughts) may reveal the actual reasons in the reflections of human consciousness. The soul and the world are inter mapping as in a certain dimension. Art makers can follow this process to interpret their "creative archetypes".

Table 1. Memory replication I (I-Ting Wang 2018)

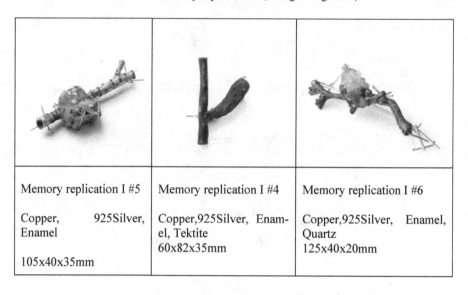

Memory replication I #5	Memory replication I #4	Memory replication I #6
Copper, 925Silver, Enamel 105x40x35mm	Copper,925Silver, Enamel, Tektite 60x82x35mm	Copper,925Silver, Enamel, Quartz 125x40x20mm

4.2   Function Follows Form

Form Follows Function or Functions Follows Form. Where does "form" come from or why? In the 19th century, Louis Sullivan, a master of the Chicago School of architecture, proposed the Form Follows Function theory, stressing that form can be designed and altered depending on functions and is not just tended for ornament. The concept of Form Follows Function does not oppose ornament but proposes that the establishment of an ornament system must conform to and present the meanings of the archetypes. Sullivan mentions that "All things in nature have a shape, that is to say, a form, an outward semblance, that tells us what they are, that distinguishes them from ourselves and from each other." The goal of creating is to make each artificial creation (not incompatible with nature) harmonious and appropriate.

However, in the early 1990s, a group of psychologists led by Ronald Finke had an interesting discovery. They found creating a virtual form and then exploring its potential functions can lead to more possibilities of innovation. Therefore, they proposed the Function Follows Form theory, suggesting that functions are variable, and by shifting the focus onto innovation and by exploring or challenging cognitions, one can discover hidden possibilities or new models of creation.

In the creating process, artists are not only an observer who watches how the work is made (objective) but also an observer involved in the making (subjective). Based on an experimental creation method, the researcher learned about the "archetype in the nature world" through observation, exploration, and dialogues in creating the "Memory replication II" series of works, as shown in Table 2. By interpreting and translating the "archetypes of the creator" the researcher derived the "interpreted archetypes" and provided support to restore the archetypes to the pattern as remembered in the brain. It was hoped that this humble attitude, as that of the nature, can be directly reflected on the works. Using the minimum amount of substrate (support), the researcher reduced the add-ons to the "interpreted archetypes" to demonstrate the maximum sensations that initially motivated the making of this work. Besides, for each archetype, the researcher also created an exclusive structure with a once-in-a-lifetime spirit.

Table 2. Memory replication II (I-Ting Wang 2018)

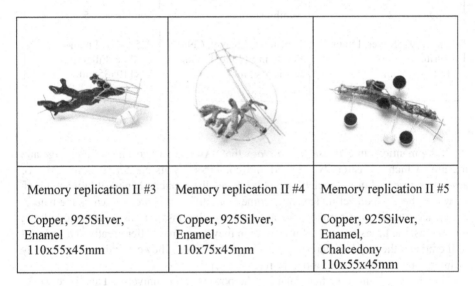

Memory replication II #3	Memory replication II #4	Memory replication II #5
Copper, 925Silver, Enamel 110x55x45mm	Copper, 925Silver, Enamel 110x75x45mm	Copper, 925Silver, Enamel, Chalcedony 110x55x45mm

4.3 Symbiosis Principle

Among these series of works, the archetypes in the natural world, the interpreted archetypes, and structure (form) are equally important, interdependent, and supportive of each other. On condition that the viewing angle for the archetype is unaffected and maximized, this study applies the structural trap to linearly connect the three elements and use the rules of counterbalancing—maintain flexible, calculate the tension, and set the pull distance, to define an appropriate role for each element such that all of them can harmoniously exist and support each other. According to National Academy for Education Research, symbiosis is a relationship between two different species. It includes three relationships, namely mutualism, commensalism, and parasitism. In this study, the relationship between design elements is defined as a "symbiosis" (Table 3).

Table 3. Symbiosis series (I-Ting Wang 2018)

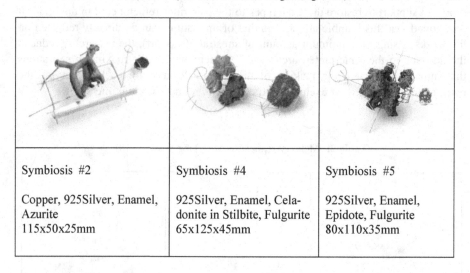

Symbiosis #2	Symbiosis #4	Symbiosis #5
Copper, 925Silver, Enamel, Azurite 115x50x25mm	925Silver, Enamel, Cela-donite in Stilbite, Fulgurite 65x125x45mm	925Silver, Enamel, Epidote, Fulgurite 80x110x35mm

Yang mentions in *Chinese Narratology* that "An imagery consists of an image and meaning which are carefully selected and combined by its creator. It is a carrier of aesthetics accepted in the society and culture and also a phenomenon of human spirits. However, because object images may come from different sources, such as the nature, the society, traditions or myths, the author's intuitive inspirations or historic culture, the sounds, the tastes or types of imagination they carry may differ greatly. The interest of literati and the secular interest in them may also differ. They can induce a wide array of interpretations and associations in readers" [8].

There is a certain force that balances the powers in the universe. This force works like dancing with a partner. Where one steps forward, the other steps back, and vice versa. In creating a work, visualizing symbiosis can bring observers or readers back to the state where they and other beings were mutually dependent and benefiting. German artist Wolfgang Laib mentions that "If you feel part of a whole that what you are doing is not just you. The individual, but something bigger then all these problems are not there anymore. Everything is totally different." When we are able to feel and achieve this state of mind, it is the moment our soul can humbly rest. "Pride brings a person low, but the lowly in spirit gain honor" (Proverbs 29:23). Taichi has a similar conception, that is, all the things in the world follow a certain principle and are related in certain ways. They all prosper and decline. Sometimes, retreating is moving forward, and advancing is deteriorating. If we can return to the original state—restoring our attitude toward the archetype (as a humble observer) and using the approach for dealing with the archetype (symbiosis), maybe we can find an alternative option for the future (Fig. 4).

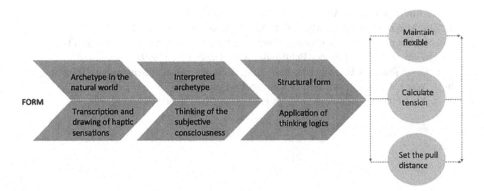

Fig. 4. The model of the symbiosis principle

5 Results and Findings

Artificial making relies on inspirations from the nature. In this study, the researcher attempted to recreate the beauty of nature using an imitation approach. The researcher converted the visual and haptic senses into ideas and integrated them into the development of Function Follows Form model. Based on the inspirations from the nature, the researcher sought the balance between natural and artificial when making the jewelry works. By means of the counterbalancing approach, the researcher demonstrated a context where the archetype in the natural world, the interpreted archetype, and the structural form are equally important, mutually dependent, and benefiting from each other.

In contemporary jewelry design, more and more artists have attempted to employ various techniques to express their ideas. Based on the principles of FFF, the researcher took on a perspective of observers and employed an experimental method of art creation to learn the archetype being created through observation, exploration, and dialogues, and then create the interpreted archetype through interpretation and translation. The researcher seemed to have captured the messages from the nature. Through touch and the feel of electricity on the skin, lines were sketched on a paper. Then, the researcher closed her eyes and let the hands freely guide the development of ideas. That was a type of unlimited output of ideas, solidified in a state called "sketch". The researcher realized that when learning from the nature, humble confrontation, counterbalancing, restoring the original motivation and the pursuit for aesthetics can lead to more creations and implementation.

References

1. Berger, J.: Ways of Seeing (Trans. by. L. Wu). Rye Field Publishing Co., Taipei (2010)
2. Liu, C.: An Introduction to Western Aesthetics, pp. 149–170. Linking Publishing, Taipei (1994)
3. Cho, H.: Poetry: The Nobles of Literature. The Commercial Press, Shanghai (2003)

4. Yi, Z.: Anthropology of Art. Fullon Culture, p. 196 (2006)
5. MUZIK Magazine Issue 97. MUZIK & ART Publishing, Taipei (2015)
6. Jaffe, A., Jung, C. (eds.): Symbolism in the visual arts. In: Man and His Symbols. (Trans. by, Z. Long), p. 322. New Century Publishing, New Taipei City (1999)
7. Love, G.A.: Practical Ecocriticism: Literature, Biology, and the Environment (Trans. by, Z. Hu, J. Wang, C. Xu), p. 65. Beijing University, Beijing (2010)
8. Yang, Y.: Chinese Narratology, p. 313. College of Management, Chiayi (1998)

A Study on Integrated Design Process of Software and Hardware Interfaces for Automotive Human-Machine Interaction

Qingshu Zeng[✉] and Qijun Duan

School of Design Arts and Media, Nanjing University of Science and
Technology, 200, Xiaolingwei Street, Nanjing 210094, Jiangsu, China
qingshuzeng@qq.com

Abstract. The design of automotive human-machine interface has become an important topic in the field of automotive design. It is closely related to the styling design of automotive interiors, construction of information models, and process for user operation and interaction. It is also an important source of the user's sense of driving, safety, and experience. The purpose of this paper is to establish an integrated design process for automotive human-machine interface that integrates hardware interface (styling design) with software interface (interaction design) in order to improve design efficiency and optimize design effects. The structure of the research is as follows: Firstly, logical cues for the integrated design process for automotive human-machine interface that integrate software and hardware were proposed through the analysis of research on and the development process of "software and hardware" products; secondly, the temporal structure of the integrated design process for automotive human-machine interface that integrates software with hardware was presented through the analysis of the design process of automotive styling and interaction; thirdly, the objects and tasks of the integrated design for automotive human-machine interface were provided through the analysis of the objects of automotive styling design and interaction design; fourthly, the integrated design process for automotive human-machine interface was constructed based on the logical cues, temporal structure, and objects of the design process, and the application practice of the design process was implemented with reference to design project cases from the self-developed "Human-Machine Interface for Electrical Vehicles" for mass production. The final sections discuss the contributions of this research and present the conclusions and future research directions.

Keywords: Integrated design process · Software and hardware interfaces · Automotive human-machine interaction

1 Introduction

With the widespread application of information technology and intelligent system and network technology in the field of transportation, as well as the development of in-vehicle information technology, the interior space, human-machine interface, and the processes of operation and interaction of automobiles are undergoing revolutionary

© Springer Nature Switzerland AG 2019
P.-L. P. Rau (Ed.): HCII 2019, LNCS 11576, pp. 105–123, 2019.
https://doi.org/10.1007/978-3-030-22577-3_8

changes; the display and control interfaces are also going through a fundamental transformation [1, 2]. Therefore, the design of automotive human-machine interface has become an important topic in the field of automotive design. It is closely related to the styling design of automotive interiors, construction of information models, and process for user operation and interaction. It is also an important source of the user's sense of driving, safety, and experience. In particular, after a large amount of In-Vehicle Information Systems (IVISs) were introduced to the driving space, the automobile is gradually transforming from a simple transportation tool with the function of transfer to an interactive space that integrates information retrieval, transmission, communication, and entertainment. The automotive human-machine interface also presents the characteristic of integrating styling (hardware) design with interaction (software) design. The traditional interface that separates software from hardware has gradually been replaced by integrated interfaces with enriched interactive experiences and technological complexity. In fact, there are differences in the interactive media of "software" and "hardware," and their design methods and interactive styles are also different.

2   Related Work

Research on the design of automotive human-machine interface can be seen as a study of automotive styling design, human-machine interaction design, automotive human-machine engineering science, and traditional automotive human-machine interface; it is closely related to the field of automotive human-machine engineering science. It mainly conducts qualitative and quantitative research on the automotive interior space, display and control devices, vision, and lighting of the vehicle from the perspective of the driver in order to ensure the functionality, comfort, convenience, safety, and manufacturability of the product. It involves conducting research on the driver's visual model, performance evaluation, and workload measurement. Hammouded proposed a model for the visibility of a visual display that is predictable and identifiable [3]. Hankey et al. provided a calculation model for evaluating the design of IVISs as well as for demand modeling in order to predict thedriver's distraction level associated with in-vehicle devices [4]. In addition, Tijerina et al. evaluated four commercial navigation systems based on test vehicles [5]; Owens et al. conducted task evaluation based on the usage of mobile phones and MP3 players in the vehicle [6]. Drews assessed the impact of texting while driving based on arriving simulator [7]. All of the studies mentioned above have compared the user's driving behavior under standard conditions to that under dual-task conditions and have conducted research on the design of in-vehicle systems from the perspective of the driver's workload.

Relevant studies and the establishment of standards for human-machine engineering science provide the design of human-machine interface with principles and specifications [8]. The Society of Automotive Engineers (SAE) handbook (SAE 2009) lists explicit regulations for the design of vehicles' passenger placement, primary vehicle control devices, bodywork, and decorative accessories. For example, the SAE Standard J1138 provides recommendations on the placement of various primary and secondary manual control devices, as well as requirements for identification signs and labels; the SAE Standard J11050 provides procedures for the determination of unobstructed areas in order to ensure the visibility of the display devices [9]. Van Cott conducted research on display devices in the vehicle and presented design principles for the design of the scale marks as well as the number system on simulating indicators [10]. Bhise examined the panels on the dashboard, display interface of the central control radio, and control buttons, and pointed out design issues related to visibility and identifiability [11].

With the infiltration of information products, the automotive human-machine interface presents the characteristics of Internet interactive products and attracts a large amount of attention in the field of human-machine interaction. Aaron Marcus proposed design principles for the automotive human-machine interface by comparing it with the human-machine interface; these include the safety of design, reducing complexity, using GUI only when necessary, proper use of physical control, avoiding cognitive load, and allowing user-customized information visualization interfaces [12]. He believed that the traditional process of research and development driven by technology and the market should be transformed into one that is user-centered and presented new testing technology and a rapid prototyping tool. Dagmar Kern proposed the design space of the automotive user interface through the analysis of the input and output modes of driving tasks, and prospective studies on display and control devices in the vehicle as well as their relationship [13]. Schmidt et al. suggested that the critical issues and challenges in research on automotive user interface include the design space, techniques and tools, new methods for user research, interaction and distraction, and multimodal feedback [14]. Tan studied the influence of the factors related to automotive human-machine interaction on cognitive indicators such as driving distractions, driver workload, and situational awareness, and presented the key design elements of human-machine interface inside the vehicle [15]. They also explored and conducted the design practice of a multi-channel human-machine interactive mode. Sun studied the key design elements of touch-free hand gestures, and proposed application principles for gesture interaction in the automotive human-machine interface [16]. Thomas analyzed and designed a logical framework for the automotive human-machine interface based on analytic hierarchy process theory [17].

The 2009 AUI Conference (International Conference on Automotive User Interfaces and Interactive Vehicular Applications) can be seen as a milestone that established an international platform for research and sharing in this field. The annual academic conference gathers the leading research results from academia and industry. The scope of research on automotive human-machine interface was classified by the conference into four categories, namely devices and interfaces, automation and instrumentation, evaluation and benchmarking, driver performance and behavior. In addition, the domestic research direction of transportation user interface (TUI) at Hunan University started to conduct exploratory research in the field in 2009 and began to design and develop automotive human-machine interface products based on brand new interactive modes. In March 2012, the Hunan University School of Design successfully hosted the first National Seminar on Automotive User Interfaces and Interaction Designs. In 2018, the Hunan University School of Design and Baidu jointly released the "Smart Automotive human-machine Interaction Design Trend White Book." Furthermore, Tsinghua University, Tongji University, Guangzhou Academy of Fine Arts, and other Chinese universities have also conducted prospective design exploration on the automotive human-machine interface.

The research field of automotive human-machine interface has been constantly expanding and presents cross-disciplinary and interdisciplinary characteristics. Therefore, the critical issue in current innovative design of automobiles is to conduct research on design process, design tools, and design methods based on the transformation of the objects of automotive human-machine interface design [18].

The purpose of this paper is to establish an integrated design process for automotive human-machine interface that integrates hardware interface (styling design) with software interface (interaction design) in order to improve design efficiency and optimize design effects. The structure of the research is as follows: Firstly, logical cues for the integrated design process for automotive human-machine interface that integrate software and hardware were proposed through the analysis of research on and the development process of "software and hardware" products; secondly, the temporal structure of the integrated design process for automotive human-machine interface that integrates software with hardware was presented through the analysis of the design process of automotive styling and interaction; thirdly, the objects and tasks of the integrated design for automotive human-machine interface were provided through the analysis of the objects of automotive styling design and interaction design; fourthly, the integrated design process for automotive human-machine interface was constructed based on the logical cues, temporal structure, and objects of the design process, and the application practice of the design process was implemented with reference to design project cases from the self-developed "Human-Machine Interface for Electrical Vehicles" for mass production. The final sections discuss the contributions of this research and present the conclusions and future research directions.

3   Integrated Design Processes of Automotive Human-Machine Interaction Interfaces

The typical processes of product development and software engineering were investigated, and the relationship and constraints among the elements of the two processes were analyzed to explore the integrated design framework for the design process of automotive human-machine interaction software and hardware interfaces.

3.1   Clues: Logical Clues to the Integrated Design Process of Automotive Human-Machine Interaction Software and Hardware Interfaces

The internal relationship between the design tasks and their mutual constraints are called "clues." They specifically refer to the logical clues to problem solving in design and are the logical clues to design tasks based on the design processes of software and hardware interfaces. Chandrasekaran et al. proposed a general task structure for design tasks, namely recommendation, evaluation, and modification [12]. Jones tried to establish a so-called design technical theory system, and proposed a design logical mechanism of "divergence, transformation and convergence." He posited that design consists of three links—idea-divergence, association-transformation, and evaluation-convergence—and he realized design logic mechanism through strategy control [19]. Lawson believed that the essence of design process is "analysis, synthesis and evaluation [20]." This paper compared and analyzed the design process of software and hardware products and proposed the following based on the design tasks and design solution paths: design problem analysis, design scheme synthesis, logic structures for design result evaluation and iteration, and combing the logical clues of conception, evolution, construction, and refinement for integrated design of software and hardware interfaces is shown in Fig. 1.

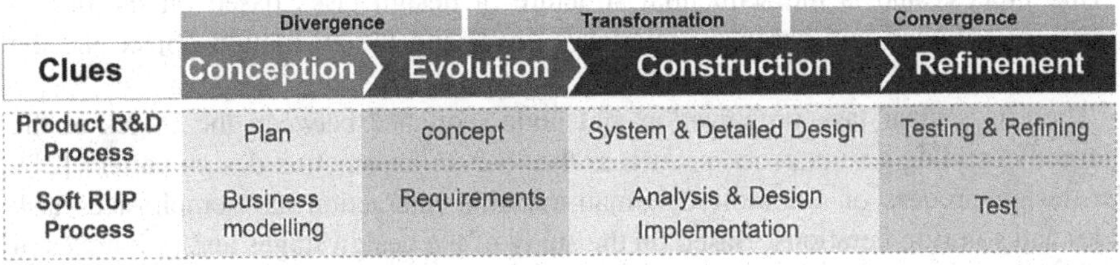

Clues	Divergence		Transformation	Convergence
	Conception	Evolution	Construction	Refinement
Product R&D Process	Plan	concept	System & Detailed Design	Testing & Refining
Soft RUP Process	Business modelling	Requirements	Analysis & Design Implementation	Test

Fig. 1. Logical clues to the integrated design process of automotive human-machine interaction

- **Conception:** Mainly refers to clarifying design tasks, design problems, design boundaries and design goals through design analysis and divergent thinking, among which design boundaries and design goals are the key.
- **Evolution:** Refers to the conception, deduction and transformation of the design scheme within the scopes of goals and boundaries. The essence is to produce creative solutions that emphasize the deduction and iteration of design ideas and design concepts.
- **Construction:** Refers to the materialization of design and corresponds to the "system design, detailed design" and "analysis and design, implementation" of the hardware and software design process. In the clues of integrated design, construction means a divergence-convergence process accompanied by decision-making activities.

- **Refinement:** Refers to the test and modification of the design and is the process of designing iteration and freezing, corresponding to "testing" in the hardware and software design process. In the clues of integrated design, refinement means convergence, dominated by assessment and decision-making activities.

Conception, evolution, construction, and refinement can be further summarized into three processes: divergence, transformation and convergence. After one convergence, the design scheme is evaluated and can be returned for divergence again or frozen as the final design scheme. The integrated design process clues consisting of conception, evolution, construction, and refinement reflect the internal relationship among design tasks and their mutual constraints in the hardware and software design process, and constitute the common, abstract logical clues of the integrated design process of "software and hardware" products.

3.2 Framework: Sequential Structure of Integrated Design Process of Automotive Human-Machine Interaction Software and Hardware Interfaces

The organization and management framework for design activities and design tasks is called "framework." It specifically refers to the sequential structure of the problem-solving process and is the sequential structure of design tasks based on the design process of software and hardware interfaces, involving the evaluation object and the decision mode.

There is a clear task organization and node sequence between the stages of the automotive styling design process, such as the "9-3-1" automotive design pattern [21]. The design process of automotive human-machine interaction also emphasizes task nodes and solution iterations. Based on the study of the design stages and task nodes of automotive styling and interaction design process, this paper proposes the following: the sequential structure of the design definition, concept and system construction, detailed design, prototype and evaluation test of software, and hardware interface integrated design, as a system framework is shown in Fig. 2.

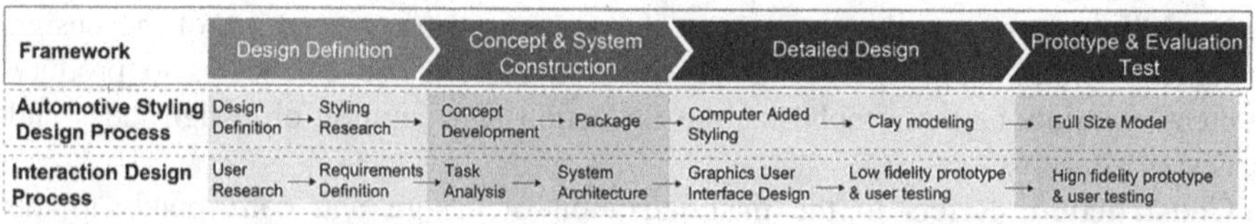

Framework	Design Definition	Concept & System Construction	Detailed Design	Prototype & Evaluation Test
Automotive Styling Design Process	Design Definition → Styling Research →	Concept Development → Package →	Computer Aided Styling → Clay modeling →	Full Size Model
Interaction Design Process	User Research → Requirements Definition →	Task Analysis → System Architecture →	Graphics User Interface Design → Low fidelity prototype & user testing →	High fidelity prototype & user testing

Fig. 2. Sequential structure of integrated design process of automotive human-machine interaction

- **Design definition:** In the integrated design framework, design definition refers to the design goal, positioning, and design direction of automobile human-machine interaction software and hardware interface integration based on brand, user, benchmark, and design theme.
- **Concept and system construction:** In the integrated design framework, concept and system construction refers to the concept theme discussion and system architecture of software and hardware interface integration, and the design scheme of node delivery drives the integrated evaluation decision at this stage.
- **Detailed design:** In the integrated design framework, the detailed design is based on the integrated concept theme, is dominated by software and hardware interface differentiation design activities and reflects the details of component styling and interface effects.
- **Prototype and evaluation test:** The main model and high-fidelity prototype for the styling and interaction design process. In the integrated design framework, the prototype and evaluation test are based on integrated evaluation carriers and strategic design goals.

The integrated design process framework consisting of design definition, concept and system construction, detailed design, prototype and evaluation test is an organizational framework for the design stages and design activities of the styling and interaction design, indicating the sequential relationship of the software and hardware interface integrated design.

It is worth noting that the so-called logical clues of design and the study of sequential structure seem to be the same, which are both descriptions of the design process, but are completely different. Logical clues refer to the logical relationship of design problem solving, while sequential structure refers to the sequential relationship of design problem solving.

3.3   Element Analysis: Objects and Design Tasks of Automotive Human-Machine Interface Integrated Design

The study of design objects helps us to understand the form and connotation of the design process in depth and is the epistemological basis and premise for research in any specific design field. The design objects of the automotive human-machine interaction interfaces are a cross-domain problem of automobile interior design and interaction design. Therefore, based on the design tasks and sequential structure of the design process, this paper analyzes the design objects of automobile interior styling and interaction. Automobile interior styling includes corresponding design objects from the product definition to the main model; interaction design includes corresponding design objects from user research to high-fidelity prototypes. The so-called integrated design first refers to the integration of design objects is shown in Fig. 3.

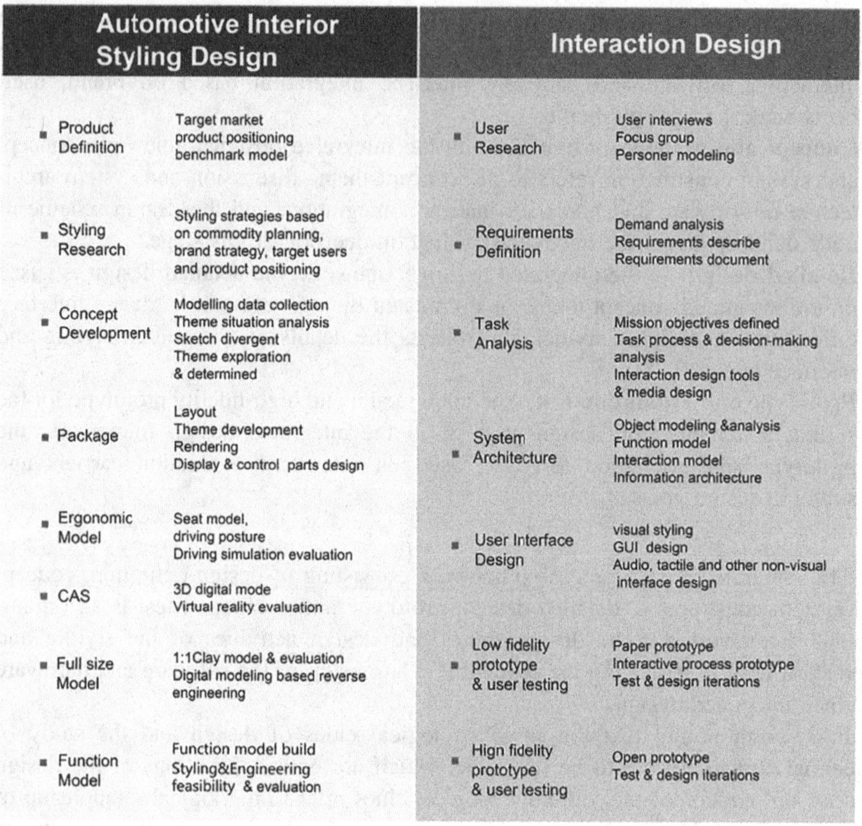

Automotive Interior Styling Design		Interaction Design	
▪ Product Definition	Target market product positioning benchmark model	▪ User Research	User interviews Focus group Personer modeling
▪ Styling Research	Styling strategies based on commodity planning, brand strategy, target users and product positioning	▪ Requirements Definition	Demand analysis Requirements describe Requirements document
▪ Concept Development	Modelling data collection Theme situation analysis Sketch divergent Theme exploration & determined	▪ Task Analysis	Mission objectives defined Task process & decision-making analysis Interaction design tools & media design
▪ Package	Layout Theme development Rendering Display & control parts design	▪ System Architecture	Object modeling &analysis Function model Interaction model Information architecture
▪ Ergonomic Model	Seat model, driving posture Driving simulation evaluation	▪ User Interface Design	visual styling GUI design Audio, tactile and other non-visual interface design
▪ CAS	3D digital mode Virtual reality evaluation		
▪ Full size Model	1:1Clay model & evaluation Digital modeling based reverse engineering	▪ Low fidelity prototype & user testing	Paper prototype Interactive process prototype Test & design iterations
▪ Function Model	Function model build Styling&Engineering feasibility & evaluation	▪ High fidelity prototype & user testing	Open prototype Test & design iterations

Fig. 3. The design objects of the automobile interior styling design and interaction design

In the integrated design process framework, design tasks have a sequential relationship, consisting of staged tasks and subtasks, and controlled by design nodes. This paper summarizes the relationship between design tasks and design objects of automotive human-machine interaction software and hardware interface integrated design. It is worth noting that the design objects in the integrated design process are deliverables of the design is shown in Fig. 4.

The design tasks defined in the design include user research, demand analysis, task analysis, and interface benchmarking; the design objects include user role models, and the human-machine interface design definition book.

The design tasks of concept and system construction mainly include system architecture, interaction paradigm exploration, the general layout design of human-machine interface, concept theme divergence, and visual style exploration; the design objects include the overall layout of man-machine interface, sketches of hardware man-machine interface, presentations (picture or animation) of software human-machine interface style, integrated system architecture (frame diagrams), and integrated concept theme performance (effect diagrams).

Design Process	Design Tasks	Design Objects
Design Definition	• User research • Needs analysis • Task analysis • Interface benchmarking	• Personer • Automotive HMI design brief
Concept & System Construction	• Concept theme • Interaction paradigm • System architecture • General layout of HMI • Visual style	• General layout design of HMI • Sketch of hardware HMI • Software HMI interface style demonstration (Renderings, animation) • Integrated system architecture • Integrate conceptual thematic representation
Detailed Design	• Styling and functional design of hardware HMI components • Software system GUI design • Flow & interaction design	• Hardware HMI digital model • Software GUI renderings • Multi-channel display, control design (prototype) • Software and hardware interface integration component design (renderings & prototype)
Prototype & Evaluation Test	• Low fidelity prototype • User test • High fidelity prototype • User test	• Hardware interface full size model • Interactive system low fidelity prototype • High fidelity prototype of interactive system • Integrated evaluation prototype

Fig. 4. Objects and design tasks of automotive human-machine interface integrated design

The detailed design tasks include the styling and function design of the hardware human-machine interface components, the graphical user interface design of the software system, process and interaction design, and multi-channel user interface design; the design objects include the hardware human-machine interface digital model, software graphical user interface effect diagrams, multi-channel interface displays, control designs (prototypes), and software and hardware interface integration component designs (effect diagrams and prototypes).

The main design tasks for prototype and evaluation tests include prototype construction and test evaluation; the design objects include the full-scale model of hardware interface, low-fidelity prototypes of interactive systems, the main model of human-machine interfaces, the high-fidelity model of interactive systems, and the integrated evaluation prototype.

It is worth noting that the integration of design tasks and design objects is the basis for design process integration.

3.4   Integrated Design Process

Integrated design process of automotive human-machine interaction software and hardware interfaces is shown in Fig. 5.

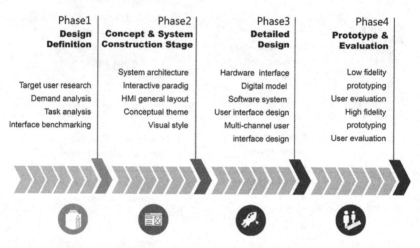

Fig. 5. Integrated design process of automotive human-machine interaction software and hardware interfaces

The core tasks in the definition stage of the design are (1) user research, i.e. identifying the target user group; and (2) benchmarking, i.e. identifying the design target. User goals and product goals constitute a unified understanding. The inputs in the definition stage of the design are the product definition and merchandise definition, and the output is the design definition book.

The inputs in the concept and system construction stage mainly include the design brief, engineering information, and automotive styling theme. The design brief inputs the product definition and design goals; the engineering information inputs the engineering hard points and geometric constraints, including the occupant layout and the human-machine size; and the automotive styling theme inputs appearance, interior styling, and styling features. The deliverable of the concept and system construction stage is a design scheme.

The detailed design is the stage of interface effect shaping and component refinement, mainly including the internal iterative design of software and hardware interface design. The core design tasks of the detailed design stage are (1) verification of the digital model of hardware interface and the engineering feasibility and (2) design of the graphical user interface and technical verification of the interaction design.

The prototype and evaluation test stage comprise a process of evaluating the usability, ease of use, and user experience of the product by means of testing combining factors such as technology and engineering.

4 Case Study of Human-Machine Interface Design for Electrical Vehicles

This case is based on an independent research and development project. The author verified the integrated design process by participating in the practice of interactive design of the interior styling and HMI system of electrical vehicles. The development process is shown in Fig. 6.

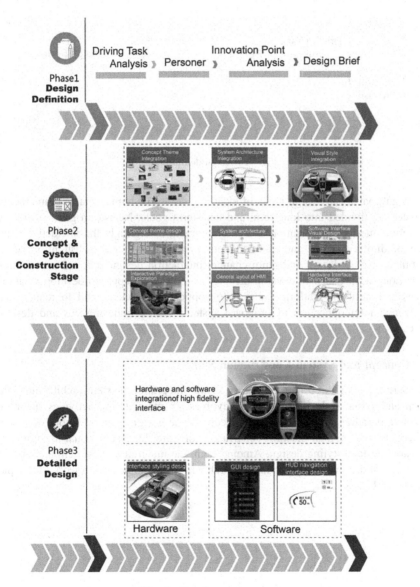

Fig. 6. Development process

4.1 Design Definition

Based on the previous research, the design definition of human-machine interaction interfaces for electric vehicles was given. The specific research included the following aspects: driving task analysis, user role creation, demand analysis, desktop research, and design innovation point analysis. The design deliverable is a design brief is shown in Fig. 7.

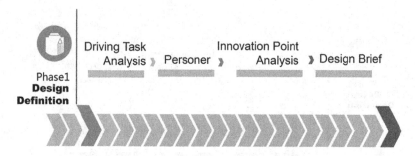

Fig. 7. Design definition

Design goals: The design goals of electric automotive human-machine interaction interfaces are divided into long-term and near-term goals. Near-term goals: to realize automotive interior digitalization and entertainment, to highlight the interactive experience of digital devices and entertainment systems, and to establish information-distributed display design and multi-channel interaction design centered on the main driver. Long-term goals: to develop driving-related mobile apps, to develop wearable devices and network platforms related to application services, and to realize data sharing and interconnection of on-board systems with mobile devices and desktop devices.

4.2 Concept and System Construction Stage

This stage includes three parts: Concept theme integration, system architecture integration and visual style integration. It involves six main design activities including interactive paradigm exploration and concept theme design, general layout of system architecture and human-machine interface, software interface visual design, and hardware interface styling design. Among them, the integration of system architecture is the focus of design. The following research will focus on the design work of this part is shown in Fig. 8.

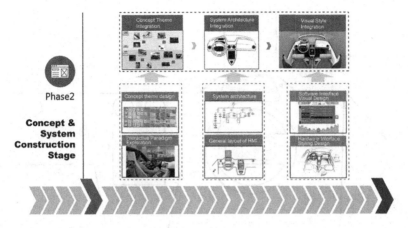

Fig. 8. Concept and system construction stage

The overall layout of the human-machine interaction interfaces is the design of interface architecture based on driving tasks, engineering constraints and human-machine hard points. The overall layout of the human-machine interaction interfaces is based on the design input of the software and hardware interfaces, involving passenger layout and human-machine size, and relevant interaction technology parameters. The design activities include (1) layout of display and control interfaces based on driving tasks and (2) layout of human-machine interaction interfaces.

The overall layout of the human-machine interaction interfaces and the software system architecture has an interdependent and mutually restrictive relationship. On the one hand, the display and control interfaces are the physical carrier of the system architecture; on the other hand, the system's function is an interactive technical parameter for the layout of the display and control interfaces.

The overall layout of the man-machine interface: The engineering input and interactive technical parameters of the electric vehicle show the general layout size of the interior and the technical requirements of the Ardunio sensor. The integrated input of the above information constitutes the design boundary of the overall layout of the human-machine interaction interfaces is shown in Fig. 9.

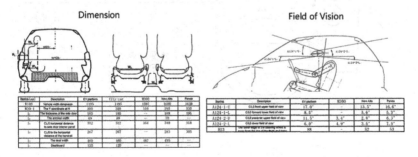

Fig. 9. The general layout size of the interior (part)

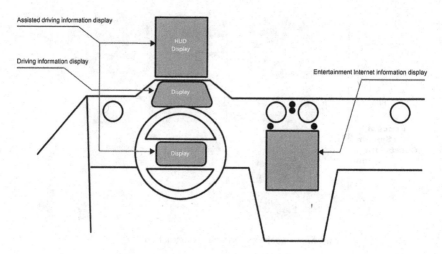

Fig. 10. Electric vehicle display interface

First, the layout of the display and control interfaces was designed. During the design process, the styling and interaction designers jointly completed the integrated design of the software and hardware interfaces such as the interface display position and display content, sensor position and control components. According to the content of information, the driving information is displayed through the main instrument interface; the driving assistance information is displayed through the head-up display (HUD) and the embedded interface in the steering wheel; and the entertainment and Internet information is displayed through the Surface Pro in the central control area, forming a distributed information display interface layout centered on the main driver. Figure 10 is a layout diagram of an electric vehicle display interface.

According to the driving tasks and technical requirements for gesture interaction, the steering wheel is arranged at the main driving task control area. Figure 11 is a layout diagram of an electric vehicle control interface.

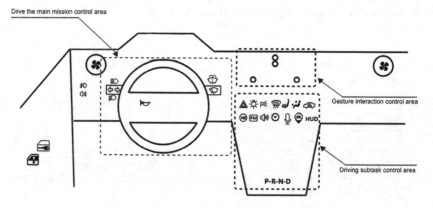

Fig. 11. Electric vehicle control interface.

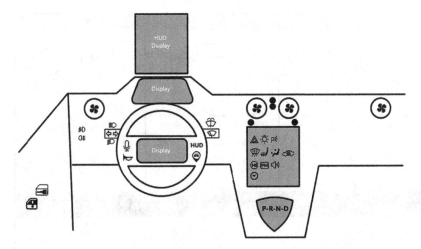

Fig. 12. General layout of human-machine interaction interfaces

The general layout of the human-machine interaction interfaces. Through multiple rounds of communication between the styling and interaction designers on the layout scheme, it was determined to design the shift lever as a knob and integrate it with the central control panel. For riding comfort, the spacing between the main driver and co-driver seats was optimized; for smooth gesture interaction, ample space for hand movement of the main driver was ensured is shown in Fig. 12.

The general layout of human-machine interaction interfaces based on driving tasks realizes partitioned integration of software and hardware, is a design idea of integration according to the function levels and reflects the integrated arrangement and design coordination of the interaction interface.

The interactive system architecture and the design of the overall layout of human-machine interface were synchronized. The main design tasks included ensuring functional architecture, information architecture, and interaction processes. First, based on the integrated input of driving tasks and the demand analysis and the design opportunity points, the functional architecture of the system was designed. Second, the information architecture and gesture interaction process were designed. Finally, with the core semantics, {simple: smart, agile}, {technology: smart, elegant}, as the design theme, the visual style of the software and hardware interfaces was designed is shown in Fig. 13.

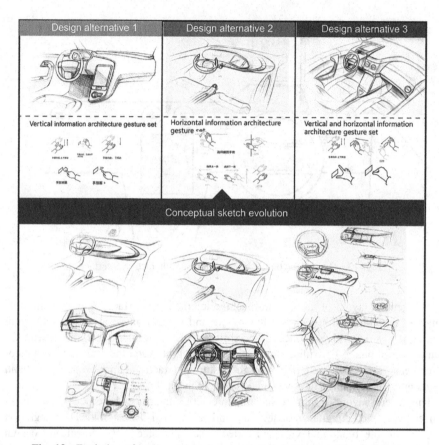

Fig. 13. Evolution of hardware interface concept sketch and styling exploration

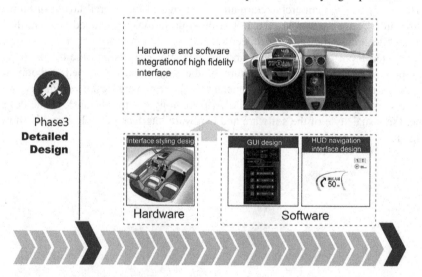

Fig. 14. Detailed design steps for the human-machine interface of an electric vehicle

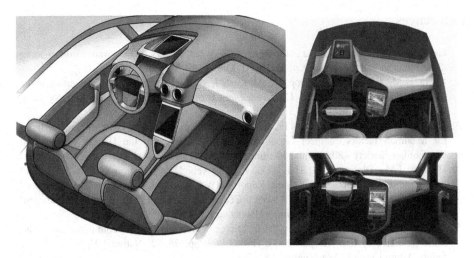

Fig. 15. Human-machine interface styling scheme of hardware (team works)

4.3   Detailed Design

The main design tasks of the detailed design include (1) to deepen the human-machine interface styling scheme of hardware based on a digital model and (2) to conduct information organization and visual design of the navigation system head-up display (HUD). The deepening of the human-machine interface styling scheme of hardware based on a digital model is the key link in the design is shown in Figs. 14 and 15.

5   Conclusion

This paper studies the design stages, design tasks and design objects of automotive human-machine interaction interfaces and constructs the integrated design process of automotive human-machine interaction software and hardware interfaces. Using the case analysis method, the electric vehicle, a typical complex industrial product, is used as the research entry point for design practice. In consideration of the trends of industrial design and interaction design, this paper has a forward-looking focus on the design and development of automotive and intelligent products and is an innovative contribution to the investigation of their research and development systems.

Acknowledgement. This research is supported by Humanities and Social Sciences Research Youth Fund of the Ministry of Education of the People's Republic of China (19C10288009), Ministry of Education of the People's Republic of China Industry-University Cooperation and Education Project (201801116001), Nanjing University of Science and Technology Independent Research Program (30917013111). We also gratefully acknowledge their financial support.

References

1. Gkouskos, D., Normark, C.J., Lundgren, S.: What drivers really want: investigating dimensions in automobile user needs. Int. J. Des. **8**, 59–71 (2014)
2. Krum, D.M., Faenger, J., Lathrop, B.: All roads lead to CHI interaction in the auto-mobile. In: Proceeding of ACM CHI Conference on Human Factors in Computing Systems, Florence Italy, pp. 2387–2390 (2008)
3. Bhise, V.D., Hammouded, R.: A PC based model for prediction of visibility and legibility for a human factors engineer's tool box. In: Proceedings of the Human Factors and Ergonomics Society 48th Annual Meeting, pp. 110–115 (2004)
4. Hankey, J.M., Dingus, T.A., Hanowski, R.J.: In vehicle information systems behavioral model and design support: final report. Report FHWA-RD-00-135, pp. 145–150. Sponsored by the Turner-Fairbank Highway Research Center of the Federal Highway Administration: Virginia Tech Transportation Institute, Blacksburg, VA (2001)
5. Tijerina, L., Parmer, E., Goodman, M.J.: Driver distraction with telecommunications and route guidance systems. Report DOT HS809-069, pp. 78–82. National Highway Traffic Safety Administration, Washington, DC (2000)
6. Hankey, J.M., Dingus, T.A., Hanowski, R.J.: In vehicle information systems behavioral model and design support, pp. 145–150. Virginia Tech Transportation Institute, Blacksburg, VA (2001)
7. Owens, J.M., Mclaughlin, S.B., Sudweeks, J.: On-road comparison of driving performance measures when using handheld and voice-control interface for cell phone and MP3 players. Presented at the 2010 SAE World Congress, Detroit, MI, SAE Paper. 2010-01-1036 (2010)
8. Drews, F., Yazdani, H., Godfrey, G.N., Cooper, J.M.: Text messaging during simulated driving. Hum. Fact. **51**, 762–770 (2009)
9. Bhise, V.D., Dowd, J.D.: Driving with the traditional viewed-through-the-steering wheel cluster vs the forward-center mounted instrument cluster. In: Proceedings of the Human Factors and Ergonomic Society 48th Annual Meeting, New Orleans, LA, pp. 49–53 (2004)
10. SAE Paper 2009-01-0562. Presented at the SAE World Congress, Detroit, MI (2009)
11. Van Cott, H.P., Kinkade, R.G. (eds.): Human Engineering Guide to Equipment Design, p. 41. Sponsored by the Joint Army-Navy-Air Force Steering Committee, McGraw–Hill Inc./U.S. Government Printing Press, New York City (1972)
12. Clarkson, J., Eckert, C.: Design Process Improvement: A Review of Current Practice, pp. 57–58. Springer, London (2005). https://doi.org/10.1007/978-1-84628-061-0
13. Payre, W., Diels, C.: Human-machine interface design development for connected and cooperative vehicle features. In: 8th International Conference on Applied Human Factors and Ergonomics (AHFE 2017), Los Angeles, USA, 17–21 July 2017, pp. 145–152 (2017)
14. Schmidt, A., Spiess, W., Kern, D.: Driving automotive user interface research. IEEE Pervasive Comput. **9**(1), 85–88 (2010)
15. Tan, H., Zhao, J., Wang, W.: Vehicle human machine interface design research. Chin. J. Autom. Eng. **9**(12), 315–320 (2012)
16. Sun, X., Li, T.: Survey of studies supporting the use of in-air gesture in car HMI. In: User Friendly 2014 UXPA the 11th Annual Conference of User Experience Industry in China, pp. 67–80 (2014)
17. Thomas, L.E.: Digital transformation of industries: automotive industry. World Econ. Forum Collab. Accenture **1**(4), 125–138 (2013)
18. Zeng, Q.: A integrated design study of automotive soft and hard human- machine interface. Ph.D. thesis, Hunan University (2016)

19. Cross N.: Creativity in design: not leaping but bridging. In: Creativity and Cognition. Proceedings of the Second International Symposium, Loughborough, pp. 115–120 (1996)
20. Lawson, B.: How Designers Think, vol. 115, 4th edn. The Architectural Press, Oxford (2005)
21. Zhao, J., Tan, H., Tan, Z.: Car Styling: Theory, Research and Application, vol. 47, 1st edn. Beijing Institute of Technology Press, Beijing (2011)

Culture-Based Design

Suspending Space and Time: The Body Under the Lens of the Japanese Concept of *Ma*

Cristina Elias[1]([✉]) and Priscila Arantes[1,2,3]

[1] Department of Design, University Anhembi Morumbi, São Paulo, Brazil
cristinaelias09@gmail.com,
priscila.a.c.arantes@gmail.com
[2] Museum Paço das Artes, State of Culture of São Paulo, São Paulo, Brazil
[3] Department of Art: History, Critics and Curatorship, PUC/SP Pontifícia
Universidade Católica, São Paulo, Brazil

Abstract. *Ma* means emptiness, space, time or pause and its origin is correlated to the ideas of transience and incompleteness characteristic of Zen-Buddhist aesthetics. However, more than a concept, *Ma* is a *modus operandi* in Japanese daily life, which illustrates a place available for the materialization of potential events. It is an inter-space of connection through which people, actions, objects can pass and that, precisely for this reason, is the place of the present time. In this article, we will address the application of *Ma* as the guiding principle of the process of creation in the arts of the body. The body will be treated as a *Ma*-body, that is, a body-in-process, in constant movement and total availability for interaction with various media and technologies in the production of meaning and creation of different art objects.

Keywords: Body · Performance · Animation · Ma · Buddhist aesthetic · Interaction · Creative process · Improvisation

1 Introduction: Considerations About *Ma*

1.1 What Is *Ma*?

Rhythm provokes an expectation, arouses a yearning. If it is interrupted we feel a shock. Something has been broken. If it continues, we expect something that we cannot identify precisely. It puts us in an attitude of waiting (Octavio Paz, *The bow and the lyre*).

"Inside burning. Outside, nothing."[1]. This directive of Tetsuro Fukuhara, second-generation *Butoh* artist[2], illustrates this state in which the body is ready to create,

---

[1] Oral source: Workshop, Studio Duncan 3.0, Rome, 2012.

[2] Danced with Tatsumi Hijikata, Kazuo Ohno and Akira Kazai, from whom he learned his *Aikido* based method. Since 2012, I have been accompanying Fukuhara in his *Space Dance* Workshop-Performances which he brings to various countries of the globe spreading his view of "International *Butoh*". In 2016, we offered together a *Butoh* based performace workshop at the Faculty of Dance of the University Anhembi Morumbi and a performance/installation experience at SESC Vila Mariana São Paulo.

© Springer Nature Switzerland AG 2019
P.-L. P. Rau (Ed.): HCII 2019, LNCS 11576, pp. 127–143, 2019.
https://doi.org/10.1007/978-3-030-22577-3_9

available, and open to grasp the impulses of the present moment, internalize them and put them out again in the form of art. Nothing. Empty. In reality, this suspended place is a void full of possibilities, a nothingness that can be everything. It is a body available for diverse associations, which responds to the external stimuli of each moment, combining itself with varied elements and creating new and unexpected results.

In Japan, there is a term, or a semantic universe, that represents this state of openness to events called *Ma*.[3] Literally, *Ma* signifies space, place, time or pause [1]. Several expressions, such as "empty space", "time-space interval", "silence", "non-action", "border" [2], "passage", "gate" [3], "negative space-time" [4], have been used to refer to what *Ma* means but they never seem to be enough to illustrate all of its meanings. The definition of *Ma* in words is controversial as it embraces a complex set of meanings with no specific word in other languages that matches this complexity. Besides, according to Japanese tradition, it should rather be felt than verbally explained. Fletcher [5] (p. 370) offers a negative definition of *Ma* as a form of artistic *non-place*:

> Space is substance. Cézanne painted and modeled space. Giacometti sculpted by *"taking the fat off space"*. Mallarmé conceived poems with absences as well as words. Ralph Richardson asserted that acting lay in pauses... Isaac Stern described music as *that little bit between each note - silences which give the form...* The Japanese have a word (*Ma*) for this interval, which gives shape to the whole. In the west we have neither word nor term. A serious omission.

Ma is actually a mode of perception, which underlies various layers of collective everyday life in Japan, from the relation between people, to *ikebana*, gardening, in the temples, dance, theatre and visual arts [3]. Its original meaning is intrinsically associated with time and space, or more specifically, with the fusion of both through phenomena or events that may occur at some point in a specific place:

> The idea of *Ma*, originally, is related to the empty mythological space, demarcated by pilasters, that can be tied by a rope, where the divine would appear in the created territory. It is an empty territory in which an event can occur, and can be correlated to zero of the possibility of birth, but not to that of death [6] (p. 178).

In Architecture, *Ma* indicates a room in the houses containing only a tatami floor and no furniture. An empty space that transforms into different spaces depending on the intended use and the organization of objects and actions within it: There is a kitchen when one sets a table to eat, a sleeping room when a *futon* is unfolded, an altar when a Buddha statue placed for meditation.

---

[3] As a practical part of my Masters in Movement Studies at the Royal Central School of Speech and Drama (London), I participated, as trainee direction assistant, in creation of the opera Matsukaze (2011, Sasha Walz and Toshio Hosokawa), inspired by Zeami's classic Noh Japanese theater. Besides, between 2012 and 2014, in Berlin and Rome, I had the opportunity to train and learn Butoh with second and third generation masters working in Europe: Minako Seki, Yuko Kaseki and Tetsuro Fukuhara. Also in Berlin, I became aware of and followed the *Aikido* based physical training taught by Prof. Martin Gruber at the Ernst Busch School of Performing Arts in Berlin. Nowadays, I am training Aikido in Sao Paulo at *Kizuna Aikido* with Sensei Ênio Kato. Some of the principles that guide these genres of Japanese origin have ultimately been the key to my reading of a creative body, through a translation and adaptation bias to my cultural and individual constellation.

In everyday language, the traditional enclosure in Japan receives a generic name of *Ma* - a tatami space usually devoid of furniture, hence "empty" in the physical dimension, waiting for objects and people, with the possibility of transforming into various environments, and determined by the established connection: a continuous space [2] (p. 81).

Greiner [3] defines *Ma* as a "between-where-when" as opposed to "nothing", referring to the metaphor of a "gate" to illustrate it. *Ma* here assumes the role of a connecting element that enables communication and transformation. A kind of portal available for the passage of objects and people, a place that *connects* one side to the other belonging concomitantly to both of them − something similar to the role played by the skin which, at the same time, separates and binds the body to the outside environment.

This idea is expressed in the Japanese ideogram of *Ma*, which consists of "two gates through which the sun can be seen in its inter-space" [2] (p. 26) (Fig. 1).

Fig. 1. *Ma* ideogram

The sun here indicating the possibility of an event, potential actions to be undertaken inside the borders of this demarcated territory. In this sense, the potentiality of meaning within *Ma* is infinite despite its limited dimensions and duration: "*Ma* is an empty space where various phenomena appear and disappear, giving birth to signs that are arranged and combined freely, in infinite ways" [2] (p. 53).

Therefore, "*Ma* presupposes division and intermediation, as well as relation and connection, instances in which the notion of border becomes a constant" [2] (p. 26). Here *Ma* acquires an ambiguous value, functioning both as a separation and as a junction of diverse territories, belonging both to one side and the other and configuring a "zone of coexistence, translation and dialogue" [2] (p. 27).

1.2 *Ma* and the Buddhist Aesthetic of Fragmented Time

Ma is a place where diverse arrangements of meanings can take place, where signs might combined in diverse ways, so that its inner content is always in process. This fragmentation, discontinuity, and nonlinear syntax in *Ma* is, according to Okano [2] (pp. 33–34), grounded in the aesthetics of Zen Buddhism, in what concerns the notions of "transience" and "incompleteness": "the fact that one appreciates the residual element in art, that is, the vestige that lies on the threshold between form and non-form, or between sound and silence, has this origin"[4] (Fig. 2).

---

[4] Here Okano makes reference to MINAMI, Hiroshi.: Ma no kenkyû: nihonjin no biteki hyôgen (Researching Ma: the aesthetic expression of the Japanese − In Japanese). Kodansha, Tokyo (1983).

Fig. 2. Wheel of Life [7] (p. 21)

The outermost layer of the "Wheel of Life" in Buddhism, a metaphor of the cyclical experience, represents the twelve links of "Interdependent Origination", that is, "how the mind constructs all movements (birth, duration and cessation or past, present, and future)" [7] (p. 37).

The first link of this layer of the wheel, *avidya*, is illustrated by a blind man walking with a stick. According to Samten [7] (p. 41), it means "loss of sight" and indicates a "narrowness of vision", more precisely, a cut made by the mind in the infinite space: images appear "at the same time that options of experiences are hidden by the experience of the images arisen". This concealment is also not noticed, that is, the said cut in infinity is not conscious. *Avydia* allows, therefore, the "concealment of the concealment" operating always through "delusion", an error that passes on the idea that what we can see is all that exists.

Avydia lives in this zone of duality, manifesting, at the same time, the "ability to manifest" and the "ability to conceal" [7] (p. 42): it allows the experience of a certain form that rests within its contours, while hiding others that are external. The ability to manifest, according to Buddhism, characterizes the "creative mind" and is called "luminosity".

Manifestation here would be the realization of the experience of one of the several forms that hover in space as potentiality, possibility; the lighting of a part of the infinite, leaving all its rest in the darkness. It is precisely this narrowness of vision, the focus of light created by the lantern of perception, which allows the individual to create. Therefore, creation is equivalent to operating a cut in the whole, with the inevitable concealment of the area external to the limits of that cut. This allows us to see the individual understanding of the world as a space-time cut in the cycle of eternity, a fragment or vestige of totality – a totality represented by a great emptiness.

Returning to *Ma*, as a cut or interval in infinite space-time, it can be said that *Ma* is the place of creativity, that is, the area delimited by perception, which although being a cut in the endless space (and precisely because of this), allows manifestation. *Ma* "is not the linear time, of the counting clock, nor the scenic time that is part of a universe of its own. It is a kind of interruption, a time-space of discontinuity" [8] (p. 45). In its transient construction, *Ma* is something that happens, which is constructed according to the arrangement that occurs at the moment of its own process, while the time of the event, of the phenomenon: of the experience of a hovering form.

2   My Practice/Research: A *Ma*-Body

All the works I created since 2010, such as *Here and There [or Somewhere Inbetween]* (Radialsystem and Festival Plataforma Berlin, 2011 | studio K77, Berlin, 2012 | Boddinale, Loophole Berlin, 2013 | Festival Dança em Foco, Rio de Janeiro, 2016), PAI (Midrash, Rio de Janeiro, 2012), *Phonetic Fragments of one (Self)* (Prize FUNARTE Women in Visual Arts 2013 | MIS and MAM São Paulo 2014 | Museu Casa Guilherme de Almeida, Festival *Transfusão*, São Paulo, 2015), *Performarsi: action as perception* (MAXXI, Roma, 2016), *Music Box* (Prize Season of Projects Paço das Artes, São Paulo, 2017 | Studio Stefania Miscetti, Roma, 2017), *Oggetti della Vita Cotidiana*[5] (Women Video Art Festival *She Devil*, Rome, 2017), among others[6], followed a similar procedural form: the focus was the construction a body that functions as a border station, interconnection space, passage or tunnel - "a zone of coexistence, translation and dialogue", in the words of Okano [2] (p. 27). A body that combines with various signs, sometimes focusing on specific ones, leaving others in the dark, and creating results whose prediction at a stage prior to its action or *interaction* is impossible.

My starting point for creation – whether in performances or for the production of objects, installations, video or photography – is the consecution of a *ma*-body: a body-in-process, in constant transformation and motion, completely available for interaction, whether with other plastic materials, with objects, with other people, with the specificities of the space in which the work is to take place (site specific), with other artistic languages (painting, sculpture, installation, writing) and media, including here the body's ability to interact with new technologies in the production of meaning.

---

[5] In collaboration with Sergio Nesteriuk.

[6] For further information about these works: http://www.cristinaelias.eu/works .

A *Ma*-body is a body that functions as a tunnel, through which stories, people, objects, events... may pass. My work embraces this phenomenological idea of *Ma*, as a space-time interval in which the event (action, movement) may emerge.

Actually, this process starts from making the *body-mind* available to feel stimuli offered by the space. This corresponds to freeing the body from excessive tensions and the mind from expectations and anxieties. Of course this is not always possible, maybe never. The human being will always be full of thoughts, fears, feelings... But it is possible to acknowledge these tensions and anxieties, to look at them with some objectivity and to deal with them in a different way than one would do if reacting automatically. According to Tetsuro Fukuhara:

> In my Space Dance, we can organize the body as the object, not as the subject, into *Ma*. Into *Ma* we can get a big energy from the environment. Also, into "MA" the surplus dimension will appear.[7]

Through continuous training, it is possible to, voluntarily, look at what one sees as his *actual real*, from a suspended perspective. It is also possible to learn how to change the quality of one's inner tension to a soft receptive energy, which can be used for creativity. It is in this state of soft receptive energy, of almost detachment of the self that the *Ma* space is created.

This state of soft receptive energy is present in the concept of *Zanshin*, which is a guiding principle of Japanese martial arts such as *Kendô*[8] and *Aikido*[9], translated as "remaining mind" or "alertness remaining-form" [9]. It is a "state of passive alertness and awareness" [9] in relaxation, in which one is prepared for the defense of possible attacks by the opponent. In *Aikido*, *Zanshin*'s training consists of a mental and physical attitude, the focus on the opponent, the alert and relaxed waiting for a form of action [10]. It is the state of mind that characterizes *Ma*.

It is not by chance that the whole of *Aikido*'s interplay happens around the notion of *Maai*. *Maai* is the space or interval between two opponents [10] (p. 13)[10]. It goes beyond a uniquely spatial configuration, which would refer only to the distance between two opponents, indicating also the time interval needed to cross this space and reach the other. Moreover, with the association of *Ma* and *Ai*, term which signifies harmonization or combination, *Ma*'s indissociability of a context of exchange, inter-section, frontier or space of coexistence between diverse or opposing elements becomes clear. The movement or action of the body in this context is a connecting element.

---

[7] Source: e-mail exchange of 08.01.2019.

[8] Japanese martial art descending from fighting techniques with samurai swords and being practiced with bamboo cables. In general terms means "the way of the sword'.

[9] Martial art that was born in Japan through Morihei Ueshiba between 1920 and 1930 and whose name is usually translated as "way to unify with vital energy".

[10] Here it is relevant to point out that, although the thought about *Ma* was present in writings on *Sakuteiki* (gardening), *Jubokushô* (calligraphy) and *Ikebana*, as well as on Zeami's *Fûshikaden*, there was no concern on the part of the authors to define a denomination for this idea . *Ma* was named in this way in the martial arts of the Êdo Era: "The strategy adopted for the fight was to rob the other's *Ma*, that is, that interval of carelessness of the adversary, in which he allows the entrance of the sword without having time to defend himself ." [2] (p. 33).

According to Martin Gruber[11], *Maai* is the "right distance to keep a simulated or a real situation at the height of the game. That is to say, at the level of exchange, where mutual actions become an experience that involves the body as a whole (body-mind) and which, in its outcome and effects, are neither predictable nor calculable"[12]. *Maai* is a territory where the *kinespheres* of both participants merge into a neutral space of exchange.

Eugenio Barba[13] [11] (p. 216) explains an idea of *Ma* associating it with the quality of *Noh* actors of being present, of making themselves visible even before beginning to act, even if they are in apparent immobility.

This moment of non-action of the actors that connects one movement to the next in *Noh* pieces is named by Zeami[14] as *Senu-hima*, which means exactly *Ma* [12]. Here the maintenance of silence is the very presentation. The essence of acting in the *Noh* context lies precisely in finding *Ma*: "Be careful to be conscious of your mind and associate it with the next mind (*kakyo*)." – said Zeami [12] (p. 90)[15]. Although the actor is in a non-action moment, attention must be maintained, he must be ready or available to start the next cycle of movement.

It is "a grammatically paradoxical expression, in which a passive form assumes an active meaning, and in which an indication of energized availability for action is presented as a form of passivity" [13] (p. 33). For Barba, *Ma* is associated with the creation of new connections with elements that are generally perceived by the body as automatisms, such as breathing. This means

---

[11] Director and choreographer, disciple of Kazuo Ohno, who took up Aikido as a basic training technique for performers. Currently, Head of the Movement Department of the *Ernst Busch University* of Performing Arts in Berlin, Germany.

[12] From the German "*Maai (Mae)* ist der jeweils richtige Abstand um in einer simulierten, oder echten Situation auf Spielhöhe zu bleiben. Das heißt auf einer Höhe des Austausches, auf der die gegenseitigen Handlungen zu einer ganzkörperlichen (bodymind) Erfahrung werden und im Ergebnis und in der Wirkung nicht vorhersehbar und berechenbar sind.". From e-mail exchange of 1 September 2018.

[13] Between 2010 and 2011, I concluded a Masters degree in Movement Studies at the *Royal Central School of Speech and Drama* (*University of London*, UK). During this research period, I became familiar with Eugenio Barba's theories on *Theatre Anthropology*, where he searches for essential principles for creating scenic presence in different movement/dance techniques that might be "translated" into the each performer's individual constellation.

[14] Zeami Motokiyo (c.1363 – c.1443), the best-known writer, actor, and theater director of the *Noh* genre. Zeami wrote nine treatises on this genre: "Teachings on Style and the Flower" (*Fushikaden*), "The True Path to the Flower" (*Shikado*), "A Mirror held to the Flower" (*Kakyo*), "Disciplines for the Joy of Art" (*Yugaku Shudo Fuken*), "Notes on the Nine Levels" (*Kyui*), "Finding Gems and Gaining the Flower" (*Shugyoku tokka*), "The Three Elements in Composing a Play" (*Sando* or *Nosakusho*), "Learning the way" (*Shudosho*), "An account of Zeami's reflection on art" (*Sarugaku dangi*). (Information taken from Masakazu, Y. On The Art of the Noh Drama: The major treatises of Zeami. Princeton University Press, Princeton (1984)).

[15] Zeami's quotes by Morioka were taken from the 36 notes that make up the *Densyo* ("descended book"), which was not published until the mid-nineteenth century.

to be aware of the tendency to automatically link gesture to the rhythm of breathing, speaking, and music and to break this link. The opposite of linking automatically is consciously to create a new connection [13] (p. 32).

The breakdown of automatic connection takes place in the actor's bodily universe through the action of to "kill the breathing. Kill the rhythm" [13] (p. 33). To "kill", in this context, means to be aware of the automatic tendencies that direct the activity of the body and to develop the capacity to look at these automatisms with a certain objectivity, in order to be able to change them, creating new ways of dealing with them.

Here, one can make a link to the "dead body" proposed in the *Butoh* of Tatsumi Hijikata, which changes of state through a process of deterioration:

> Observing a corpse in degradation, one can still see a series of movements of the deterioration of the body, under the action of the bacteria, of nature, in the end. There is no more action of the brain commanding the movements. But they exist and are visible (…) [3] (p. 27).

The *Butoh*'s dead body is actually an extremely live body that acts outside the sphere of automatisms of the individual, beyond the logical-rational command, "in the border between consciousness to non-consciousness" [3] (p. 70). Here, there is no detailed strategy of action, or more specifically, the only strategy is the reaction to what materializes in the present moment.

So, the process of consecution of this state of mind, a process that takes place continuously and methodically in my every day as an artist, is the first strand where *Ma* reflects in my creative process. Such as a musician has to train continuously to play an instrument (even after having mastered its technique), I train my body-mind to know how to reach this state of openness and availability necessary for artistic creation, in contexts where improvisation and chance play an essential role. This individual training or preparation *pathway*[16], I adapt from techniques and systems of movement such as *Butoh*, *Aikido* and some strands of contemporary dance. It involves *Ma* mainly as a form of cognition, where the whole body is involved: a synesthetic perception mode in which verbal communication does not play a central role[17].

As a second strand of radiation of *Ma* in my work, it operates as a guiding principle of the creative moment itself: while I am doing a performance, shooting a video or a photographic series, drawing on a canvas… From the organization of the space and the choice of elements, which will be present in this place, to the decisions I take within every interval of creation, all of these issues keep a blank space for chance and

---

[16] Regarding performance and forms of creation involving the body and chance, I consider the term pathway, which refers to the Japanese *Dô*, more appropriate for the semantic universe that I approach in this research. Method can direct the mind to a complex collection of fixed and immutable rules, which is not the matter discussed at all in this study. The pathway has an end, an objective, but it is traced in the unfolding of each action, as one walks - it is malleable method, open to the stimuli that emerge along the way.

[17] We will return to the theme of perception in the next section of this article.

actuality. I never know mathematically what specific material results will come out, but I trust the interaction of the outside (space, materials, participants, objects, tools) with the inside (cognition and expression), allowing them to act.

In a third front, *Ma* also influences my conceptual and formal choices: what I am talking about and how I will be doing it. My preference for transforming themes, the moving body, meanings deriving from compositions of images or symbols formed by chance, long silences in-between sounds, materials that may not be fixed, ephemerality in general; a certain tendency for the repetition of gestures and actions that, in fact, are never the same; the creation of synaesthetic atmospheres... all of these come from this same root.

3   Applying *Ma* as a Creation Pathway: Concrete Cases

Breathing is an automatic activity. Walking is an automatic activity. This is why these actions are the base of major Zen Buddhist meditation techniques:

Take my hand.
We will walk.
We will only walk.
We will enjoy our walk
without thinking of arriving anywhere.
(...)
Each step brings a fresh breeze.
Each step makes a flower bloom under our feet.
(...)

These are fragments of the poem *Walking Meditation* by the Zen master Nhat Hanh [15]. The basic principle of walking meditation is simply to be aware when one is walking. Thoughts and feelings will come and go. The aim is not to erase nor forbid the activity of the mind (prohibition which is a source of thoughts in itself) but only to acknowledge them: "I am thinking", "I am planning", "I am expecting"... To be aware of the present moment is the aim and means of this technique. When one is walking, they can "turn on the automatic pilot" of the motor coordination and just "enjoy" their walk. To nowhere. In a non-automatic manner. This is a completely new way of dealing with the action of walking than the one generally used in contemporary life: people are always rushing everywhere, even if they don't know what this somewhere is about. Being aware of the walk creates a new connection, the one with the self, and *kills* the automatism of walking without even noticing one is moving their feet.

Handwriting for me is an automatic activity. I do not have to think of which movement of my hand will result in the letter "A" or the letter "B". I think of a concept and immediately put it out on paper. One letter after the other, one word after the other, one sentence after the other... I do it in such an automatic way that it took long for me to notice how I have to move my arms and hands to write a word or to draw a letter.

However, once, during a *Butoh* workshop, I was told to dance blindfolded. With the eyes closed, intuition and touch turn into guiding senses. Hearing seems to become stronger. Turning off vision is a way of noticing how other senses also contribute to the perception of space. In this state, I decided to start writing or to recreate for me the movement of handwriting. First of all, I created an imaginary wall: a delimited space within the endless darkness coming from the blindfold. My *Ma* space. Then, I started writing any thoughts and feelings that would come into my mind – in a state inbetween being conscious and unconscious. Words being drawn in the air like events, phenomena.

The cognition characteristic of *Ma* is that of the "non-verbal text", although words here might appear as "residual signs" [14] (p. 15). The non-verbal text is a "daily experience", a "language without code", marked by "sign fragmentation" [14] (p. 14):

> (…) sounds, words, colors, strokes, sizes, textures, smells - the emanations of the five senses, which, as a rule, are abstracted, arise in the non-verbal together and simultaneously, but disintegrated, since immediately there is no convention, there is no syntax that relates them: their association is implicit, or rather needs to be produced" [12] (p. 15).

Therefore *Ma* as a cognitive operator offers an alternative way of comprehension of the world based on perceptual means [2] (p. 15) where meaning is something in construction, in progress.

In the first moments, I drew small sized letters. But it was not like writing on my notebook. Here, I was aware of the complex movements of the hands combined with the wrists. There is a kind of choreography of writing or form of writing. Then, I started to raise the size of the letters until they became huge ones. Changing their qualities and surprising my body-mind. The movement of the body has to change radically depending on the size of the font: in order to draw large letters, I have to move my whole body, in connection. I experienced the movement and forms created by the act of writing even if the material result, the written text, was not there – only the process of writing it.

From this abstract, ephemeral piece of writing that took place on an imaginary wall, I developed several works: from performance, to canvases, video and animation. All of them writing-based. However, not on imaginary walls: on tangible platforms. Charcoal sticks as extensions of fingers and hands so that the material result of the moving body could be seen. The body placed in relation, in interaction. The final object configuring a procedural object.

In *Music Box* (performance /installation, 2017)[18], I write a diary in real time on a large canvas that becomes my inhabitable space. I write in different languages, with charcoal sticks, non-stop for aprox. 2 h. The canvas as a suspended space within the exhibition room (Fig. 3).

When there is no space left on the canvas anymore, when I have filled in my first page, I start erasing the whole text with my own body. The charcoal words get stamped on my skin. When I have managed to blur everything, I start writing a new page. And then I blur it again, and start writing again… This for successive times, until an abstract image appears on the canvas inbetween the fragmentation of the text (Fig. 4).

---

[18] *Music Box* at Studio Stefania Miscetti (Rome, November 2017): https://vimeo.com/302341049; *Music Box* at Paço das Artes (São Paulo, September 2017): https://vimeo.com/233109413 .

Fig. 3. Cristina Elias in *Music Box*, Studio Stefania Miscetti (Rome), November 2017

Fig. 4. Cristina Elias in *Music Box*, Paço das Artes (São Paulo), September 2017

An image that incorporates all my narratives and that is the objective and material result of my body-mind actions during that specific period of time. This is when I stop. The canvas remains in the exhibition space, a work in itself, without my presence but whose process reminds of it.

In the animation-performance *Oggetti della vita cotidiana*[19] (2017), a body rotates as if it were the hands of a clock. A live clock that moves according to an irreversible and unpredictable flow of events, where each hour of the fictive day represents a feeling, a sensation or, according to Charles S. Peirce, a "quality of feeling" promoted by a "feeling consciousness" [17]. The text is drawn under the landscape of the body in two ways: as written and spoken words (Fig. 5).

Fig. 5. *Oggetti della Vita Cotidiana* (animation-performance, 2017), Cristina Elias with Sérgio Nesteriuk

Words appear progressively, creating, together, a spiral image that forms and deforms, which is constructed and deconstructed, which is written and erased in an endless cycle that always departs from and returns to a supposed emptiness. The *Ma* space.

Here, however, unlike the process of creation of *Music Box*, which involves real-time presence, the writer-meaning-reader relationship is built upon additional layers of mediation through the use of technology; the present time of the experience of the work is moved to another space, different from that of the present time of the artist's action.

In *Oggetti...*, during the moment of action, of performance, the viewer is a camera. Phenomena are suspended for another point in the timeline. The space is also suspended for another dimension. Later, this video will be watched on a screen of a telephone, a tablet, a computer... there will be no live presence. Exchange and interaction in this context happen through mediation of technological tools and effects.

---

[19] work available at: https://vimeo.com/235768035 .

The use of the *loop* allows, every time the body finishes its circular movement, the eternal return to the initial white screen, where the action began and where it ends. It also allows the appearance and disappearance of the text, its withdrawal from and re-approaching the centre: a metaphor of the passage from moments of deep inner awareness to the mechanical, automatic external life (and vice versa) within the same fragment of space-time of a particular individual.

In what regards to the movement of the body, *Oggetti...* was made through the *pixilation* technique, where various still photographs of the movement of the body are taken and afterwards reedited by technological tools in order to recreate movement (Fig. 6).

In other words, first movement is made still by technology to be subsequently recreated, under a different language, as movement. In this context, choreography and movement planning also change radically when compared to a live happening context. In *Oggetti...*, choreography was a fusion of prefixed elements and improvised actions.

Fig. 6. Set of pictures taken for *Oggetti della Vita Cotidiana*

The positions, which coincided with the hours of the day, were fixed based on pres-elected words, which were then translated into a bodily language, but still in a phase that preceded the shooting (Fig. 7).

Fig. 7. Words representing hours of the day in *Oggetti della Vita Cotidiana* – written notes by the artist.

Passing from one position to the next was improvised, so that between each hour (the five minutes or seconds between each number in the clock), there were four stills of non-controlled actions, chosen according to the needs of the actual context. Transforming, improvised, non-planed positions happening inside the fixed ticks of the clock, a reference to the phenomenology of *Ma*. The space inbetween the numbers as a passing station.

With regards to the acoustic landscape, which accompanies both of the visual layers of this work, it was also constructed as a binary structure. One layer of sound contained the repetitive pronunciation of the words being written, within a fixed structure. The second layer, where I was speaking in a flow of consciousness/unconsciousness (in that border stage characteristic of the *Butoh* dead body) with no prewritten text, was recorded within a fully improvised situation: listening to the words chosen as meta-phors for the hours of the day, I spoke freely, aiming at giving external form to the internal impressions they caused at the moment of recording. Both of these sound layers were superposed in the sound edition phase, so that words are pronounced, concomitantly, sometimes coinciding with each other, happening one on top of the other. Besides, this confusion is highlighted by the use of different languages at the same time such as in *Music Box*. The viewer/reader/listener, in this way, also participates in the work: filtering and choosing what he can understand, making a *cut* within the work that will be the *everything* to be experienced. Their *Ma* space.

4 Conclusion: The *Ma*-Body as Zone of *Inter-action* Between Inside and Outside

The action in these works starts from being aware of my feelings and thoughts. Such as in Zen Buddhist meditation, I am accessing my inner content without switching off from the outside, from non-self. The skin as the boundary between the self and the others, functioning both as a separation and as a junction of diverse territories, belonging both to one side and the other. The body available for the passing of information from the outside to the inside and vice versa.

> The function of every boundary and pellicule (from the membrane of a living cell to the biosphere while - according to Vernadski - pellicule covering our planet and the frontier of the semiosphere) consists of limiting the penetration of the external into the internal, filtering the external messages and translating them into a language of their own, as well as the conversion of external non-messages into messages, that is, the semiotization of what comes from outside and its conversion into information [18] (pp. 13–14).

This notion of frontier as a space that belongs to the inside and the outside concomitantly refers to the Japanese concept of *aida*[20]. *Aida* bases the construction of relations in Japanese society and means "space between men" [2]. In the context of *aida*, in which *Ma*'s shared space is inserted, "the self is not under its own control, but in the 'intermediate space between me and the other'" [2] (p. 76). Here, established relations acquire a determining function in the configuration of what can be perceived.

In her analysis of the representation of space in Japanese culture, Okano [2] also brings the concept of *fûdo*[21] as "the established relation between society, space and nature" (p. 67) and whose ideogram is the junction of "wind and earth" (p. 66). From the definition of space by Santos [19] while an "indivisible set of systems of objects and of systems of actions" (p. 19), so that "fixed and interacting flows express geographic reality (p. 50), it can be said that the wind represents what passes through a certain space, its "flows", and that the earth points out to the "fixed", the preexisting structure: the contours of *Ma*.

Berque [20] translates *fûdo* as *milieu* (medium) while the complex of relations that fundament the existence of men as subjects, as opposed to *environment* (environment),

---

[20] Concept adopted by KIMURA, Bin in the study *Hito to hito to no aida* (*The space between men*, in Japanese). 29 ed. Tokyo: Kôbundô, 2000 (1. Ed. 1972) and quoted by OKANO [2] (p. 76).

[21] Concept originally presented by Watsuji Tetsurô in *Fûdo: Ningenteki Kôsatsu* (*Fûdo: Philosofic reflection*, in Japanese), 1935.

which refers to the set of relations between objects. Berque defines the concept of *médiance* (mediation, from the Japanese *fûdosei*) as a "structural occasion of human existence". This existence "as subjects" (*subjectité*, from the Japanese *Shutaisei*, while the fact of being a subject and not *subjectivité*, in Japanese *Shukansei*, while the fact of being subjective) "is not made up of objects, but of things insofar as they are taken in their relation to this existence: in other words, as medium". Here again the universe of *Ma* as a place available for the establishment of relations, for the *inter-action* is put into play, while structural pillar of human existence. Mediation as a structural "occasion" brings forth the phenomelogical character of existence, and in the concrete case of art creation, of the materialization, the material productions of the work as well as its root in potentiality.

Yushufû ("internalization") is the word used by Zeami to indicate one of the *Noh* performer's essential qualities: through this "intense concentration", the "actor's mind" can "fully penetrate his body" so that he is able to recognize "the nature of the differences between external skill and interior understanding" [16] (pp. 141–142). The continuous practice of this form of **internalization, still in the "pre-expressive"** moment (BARBA, 2006) of the action, allows the development of an ability to access feelings and thoughts and to immediately express this internal material, already at the moment of expressiveness or communication (the moment of action), as movement, as text and as image. The *ma*-body as a tunnel, which connects the self and the non-self, that serves as *medium* (*milieu*) for the coexistence and exchange between diverse realities.

References

1. Free Online Dictionary. https://www.freedict.com/onldict/jap.html. Accessed 24 Jan 2018
2. Okano, M.: MA: interspace of art and communication in Japan (in Portuguese). Annablume, São Paulo (2012)
3. Greiner, C.: The art of living inbetween (In Portuguese) preface. In: Okano, M. (ed.) MA: Interspace of Art and Communication in Japan (in Portuguese). Annablume, São Paulo (2012)
4. Komparu, K.: The Noh Theatre: Principles and Perpsectives. Wheatherhill, New York (1983)
5. Fletcher, A.: The Art of Looking Sideways, p. 370. Phaidon, London (2001)
6. Okano, M.: MA space and Hélio Oiticica (in Portuguese). In: Greiner, C., Muniz Fernandes, R. (eds.) Tokyogaqui: An imagined Japan (in Portuguese), pp. 176–187. SESC, São Paulo (2008)
7. Samten, L.: The Wheel of Life (In Portuguese). Peirópolis, São Paulo (2010)
8. Greiner, C.: Butô: Thought in Evolution (in Portuguese). Escrituras, São Paulo (1998)
9. Mann, J.: When Buddhists Attack. Tuttle Publishing, Vermont (2012)
10. Shioda, G.: Dynamic Aikido. Kodansha International, Tokyo (1977)
11. Barba, E., Savarese, N.: A Dictionary of Theatre Anthropology. Routledge, New York (2006)
12. Morioka, M.: How to create Ma – the living pause. Int. J. Dialogical Sci. **9**(1), 81–95 (2015)
13. Barba, E.: The Paper Canoe. Routledge, New York (1995)
14. Ferrara, L.: Leitura Sem Palavras. Ática, São Paulo (2002)

15. Nhat Hanh, T.: Call me by My True Names – The Collected Poems of Thich Nhat Hanh. Parallax Press, Berkeley (2005)
16. Wylie-Marques, K.: Opening the actor's spiritual heart: the Zen influence on Noh training and performance. J. Dramatic Theor. Criticism, **XVIII**(1), 131–160 (2003). Fall 2003
17. Ibri, I.A.: Kósmos Noetós: The metaphysical architecture of Charles S. Peirce (In Portuguese). Paulus, São Paulo (2015)
18. Lotman, I.M.: La semiosfera I - Semiótica dela Cultura e del Testo. Ediciones Cátedra, S.A., Madrid (1996)
19. Santos, M.: A natureza e o espaço: técnica e tempo, razão e emoção. 4 edn. EDUSP, São Paulo (2002)
20. Berque, A.: Milieu e Logique du Milieu chez Watsugi. Revue Philosophique de Louvain, pp. 495–507 (1994). https://www.persee.fr/doc/phlou_0035-3841_1994_num_92_4_6876? q=fudo. Accessed 13 Feb 2019

The New Approach of Chinese Animation: Exploring the Developing Strategies of Monkey King - Hero Is Back

Wen Ting Fang[1,2]([⊠]), Mei-Ling Hsu[2], Po-Hsien Lin[2], and Rungtai Lin[2]

[1] School of Design and Innovation,
Changzhou Vocational Institute of Mechatronic Technology,
Changzhou, Jiangsu, People's Republic of China
f_wenting@163.com
[2] Graduate School of Creative Industry Design,
National Taiwan University of Arts, New Taipei City, Taiwan
g910504@gmail.com, t0131@ntua.edu.tw,
rtlin@mail.ntua.edu.tw

Abstract. The Chinese animation 'Monkey King: Hero is Back' had remarkable box office success and earned a good reputation for Chinese animated films, indicating a resurgence in Chinese animation, and that the successful marketing strategy is worth exploring. This study uses literature analysis and SWOT analysis to explore this animation's marketing strategies. The purpose of this research is to: (1) dissect the contents of the marketing strategy of this animation; (2) explore the developing strategies of the sequel to this animation; (3) provide this animation's developing strategies as reference for the development plan of Chinese animated films. Through SWOT analysis, this study pinpoints the developing strategies for Chinese animation. Firstly, animation designers ought to design the artwork incorporating elements of Chinese traditional culture and animation companies should specially train marketing personnel to promote the marketing model. Secondly, managers should improve the spin-off products, and the country vigorously support the animation industry. Thirdly, the film must meet the psychological needs of consumers and play a part in closing the distance between designers and audiences, and also help consumers choose conveniently. Fourthly, companies ought to introduce relevant personnel to improve the production technologies of animation films. Finally, designers should adopt innovative principles to retain their exquisite market advantages. The marketing ideas and promotion methods of Chinese animation films are still in their infancy and in the future, Chinese animation marketing must follow the principles combining with tradition and innovation.

Keywords: Monkey King - Hero is Back · Chinese animation · Marketing strategy · SWOT analysis

P.-L. P. Rau (Ed.): HCII 2019, LNCS 11576, pp. 144–155, 2019.
https://doi.org/10.1007/978-3-030-22577-3_10

1   Introduction

There is a huge gap between the box office receipts of animated films and the disproportionate of inputs and outputs, particularly against the background of the booming market for Chinese animation. The quality of animated films is important, but the role of advertising and promotion in box-office success becomes increasingly evident in the ever-expanding influence of new media. How to increase the influence without compromising the quality and attractiveness to audiences has been becoming a problem that every filmmaker should pay attention to it.

The growth momentum of Chinese animation has been swift in recent years. At present, the marketing strategies of animation focus on the individual consumers' attention and the best marketing methods are online marketing, event marketing and the best promotion platforms are website, BBS and email subscription (Yu 2012). At the stage of initial interest, companies design entertainment and interactive topics in microblogs or BBS, which are the direct marketing and emotional marketing approaches. At the search stage, the focus is mainly on the principles of interaction and interest activities which releases information through a variety of channels (including search engines, official websites, professional websites and online communities) as well as effectively monitoring online commentary. At the stage of operation and purchase, the methods adopted are a combination of visual marketing and promotion for use on the net. At the stage of sharing and word of mouth, the companies focus on customer interaction and use a combination of viral marketing and word-of-mouth marketing to spread their message on industry websites and microblogs (Liu 2013) (Fig. 1).

Fig. 1. Monkey King - Hero is Back

Monkey King - Hero is Back combines the features of artistry, technicality and peculiarity and is representative of Chinese animation, showning the artistic charm of Chinese animation and winning approval from the market and film critics. This film is based on the traditional story of Journey to the West and applies Chinese elements to the whole film production while utilizing the technology of Hollywood animation films to present a comprehensive and novel movie concept for Chinese audiences. Actually, this animation film is the first animation of Journey to the West to use 3D technology and garnered 955 million box office within two months in 2015 (Jiang 2016). Meanwhile, it has also won best art film at both the 13th Golden Rooster and the 7th China International Film & Television "Golden Dragon Award" (Qing 2016). This success represented a win-win aspect of economic and social benefits and set a new record in the history of Chinese animation film, becoming the champion of the current Chinese box office. Consequently, there have been few researches on the marketing strategies of Chinese animation and the phenomenon of the box office of Monkey King - Hero is Back is worthy of researching. This study uses literature analysis and SWOT analysis to discuss the marketing strategies of Monkey King - Hero is Back. The aim of this research includes: (1) analyze the marketing strategies of Monkey King - Hero is Back; (2) explore the developing strategies of the sequel of Monkey King - Hero is Back; (3) provide the strategies as the reference of the development plan of Chinese animation.

2 Literature Review

2.1 Marketing Strategy

Marketing is a means to an end and the ultimate goal is to make consumers recognize and understand the goods so as to trigger their desire to buy. The 4Cs of marketing strategies Consumer, Cost, Convenience and Communication were provided (Lauterborn 1990). This theory emphasizes that enterprises not only focus on the marketing model from the perspective of companies while carrying out the marketing strategies, but also pay attention to consumers' desire and pursue customers' satisfaction. Meanwhile, companies should effectively communicate with consumers to adjust their strategies and guide public opinion. The main contents of marketing methods include target market strategy, positioning strategy, marketing mix strategies and competition strategy (Ricky 2016). (1) The target market strategy consists of two parts, market segmentation and target market selection. Some factors must be considered when company choose their target market: the company's resources, current market position, the potential and competitors' target strategies and strengths. (2) Positioning strategy is to make every marketing plan combine closely to send customers those messages and images which they want to convey through the marketing mix. (3) Marketing mix strategies refers to various marketing activities that are to satisfy customer needs. There are many strategies companies can be used, but the most of them are marketing mix strategies, i.e., product, price, place, and promotion (McCarthy 1964). The enterprise can adjust the content of marketing mix strategies according to the different target markets so as to maximize the marketing method and achieve the marketing goal. (4) Competitive strategy means enterprises need to develop a competitive strategy in order to effectively compete with competitors and maintain their long-term competitive advantages.

2.2   Strategy Analysis

SWOT analysis is a frequently used tool for analyzing an organization's external and internal environments concurrently in order to provide a systematic approach and support for decision-making (Kurttila et al. 2000; Kangas et al. 2003; Yüksel 2007; Kotler 1988). SWOT analysis includes four factors such as strengths, weaknesses, opportunities and threats (Hill and Westbrook 1997). The SWOT analysis refers to systematic thinking and comprehensive diagnosis of factors relating to a new product, technology, management, or planning (Weihrich 1982). The SWOT analysis framework shows how SWOT analysis explains the environment scan as shown in Fig. 2 (Kahraman et al. 2008). The SWOT analysis constructs the framework to systematically study the SWOT factors, and there is a hierarchical structure of the SWOT matrix as shown in Fig. 2 (Gallego-Ayala and Juízo 2011), which is separated in three phases: the goal, SWOT group and SWOT factors (Görener et al. 2012).

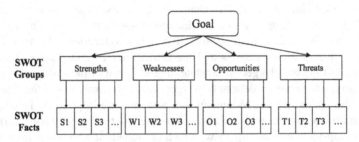

Fig. 2. Hierarchical structure of the SWOT matrix (Gallego-Ayala and Juízo 2011)

The analysis mainly considers whether the internal advantages and disadvantages of the enterprise are conducive to competing within the industry. Opportunities and threats are to explore the external environment of the enterprise and the evolution of the future of the industry so as to understand the impact of change for enterprises (Lee 1998). SWOT analysis is used to explore the cognitive level of the competitive environment; external and internal factors form four groups of strategic orientation. (1) The strategies of strengths and opportunities (SO) - this strategy is to actively integrate the external environment and internal conditions forming the niche; that is to maximize the effect of strengths and opportunities. (2) The strategies of taking advantages and avoiding threats (ST) - this strategy means enterprises can overcome the external threats; that is maximize the strength and minimize the threats. (3) The strategies of modifying weaknesses and grasping opportunities (WO) - this strategy is to use external opportunities to modify weaknesses, that is to improve the occasion. (4) The strategies of modifying weaknesses and avoiding threats (WT) - this strategy is to minimize the threats and weaknesses by organizations so as to achieve the goals of organizational development.

3 Results and Discussions

3.1 Marketing Strategy Analysis of Monkey King - Hero Is Back

Strengths
At the aspect of product, Monkey King - Hero is Back has a unique artistic charm from its own advantages and this research is to explore the film's internal advantages from the technical, semantic and effectiveness level, as shown in Table 1. Some researchers have constructed the animation research model which combines communication theory with animation evaluation factors as shown in Fig. 2. A visual and acoustic communication of animation is a process of coding through the artists' creation and then letting the audience decode. To discuss the differences between different times and places of the animation through image, color, lens, music and artistry on technical level; performance, atmosphere, plot, narrative and rhythm on semantic level and audience, theme, story, motif and connotation on effectiveness level (Fang et al. 2017).

The analysis of technical level. The characters in this film are innovative and distinctive. The Monkey King is no longer dressed in gold armor and with eye-catching eyes but has well-muscled limbs, appealing to people's conceptions of a hero. The style of the dragon draws on the classics of Nine-Dragon Screen and Western Han Totem and the shape of the four-legged little white dragon is that of the classic dragon of the Ming Dynasty, which moves delicately and precisely. The character of the demon king is drawn from animals of the Mountains and Seas and are inspired by Beijing Opera masks. The film is colorful with a classical Chinese charm. The viewpoint varies from magnificent top-view to close-up view, which confounds the common impression of Chinese animation by audiences. The music of this film is sublime and the animators selected different voice actors according to personality traits to make the characters lively. For example, Jiang, Liuer's voice is cute and demon king's voice is bewitching. Finally, the 3D artistry is of world-class standard.

The analysis of semantic level. Character performance is vivid which brings the role's personality to life. The atmosphere of this film is mysterious and dreamlike, presented in a distinctively Chinese manner. The narrative of this film is multiplex with boldly arranged and combined story elements from the Journey to the West used to establish the new narrative perspective and character relations. The rhythm of this film varies as the plot develops and is dramatic and attractive.

The analysis of effectiveness level. This film aimed at multi-age audiences, breaks the routine and attempts to become an international animated film which also arouses the confidence of Chinese audiences, and the audience no longer regarded it as young children's animated cartoon. The theme of this film is traditional Chinese aesthetics where the classic tale is remodeled for modern audiences. The structure of this story is clear and understandable. The motif of this film fully exploits the national culture classics and almost completely reconstructs the story of Journey to the West but does not violate the most classic elements and the favorite perspective of the audiences (Yang 2015). The film shows a profound cultural connotation and references the spirit of Chinese aesthetics.

Table 1. Product advantages of *Monkey King - Hero is Back*

Strengths	Technical level	Semantic level	Effectiveness level
Monkey King - Hero is Back	Image: innovative, unique	Performance: individual, lively	Audience: diverse
	Color: colorful	Atmosphere: Chinese manner	Theme: traditional
	Lens: various	Narrative: multiplex	Story: clear
	Music: sublime, anthropomorphic	Rhythm: variant	Motif: moral
	Artistry: excellent	Plot: dramatic	Connotation: cultural

At the aspect of promotion, Monkey King - Hero is Back is a painstaking work that took eight years to complete. It was made without the participation of well-known actors and due to its low budget is also hard-pressed to advertise, but effective promotional strategies create a strong word-of-mouth effect.

The aspect of attention. The promotional video is well-made and contains character introduction, narrative plot and story arcs to attract people's attention so as to promote the film. The videos are put on Youku, bilibili and other video sites with prominent social influence. (2) The aspect of interest. The ending song, Former Me, became a hit song even before the film came out which helped audiences enter the story before they watched it. That Monkey King - Hero is Back debuted in Cannes was a good basis for Chinese overseas sales and won it a good reputation, which attracted a new group of fans. (3) The aspect of desire. The universal promotion on social platforms such as microblog and WeChat was an effective means, with movie-related topics appeared frequently during the release period: for example, the original painting of Monkey King - Hero is Back was widely disseminated on WeChat. There were some effective continuing measures such as, the book dealing with behind-the-scenes of Monkey King - Hero is Back which triggered the audience's expectations of the sequel.

At the aspect of place, this film was released in most cities in China with wide coverage after triggering a hot discussion. The film became the most popular Chinese animation film in the American film market through screening at the annual meeting of the American film market and unveiling the poster there.

At the aspect of price, Monkey King - Hero is Back and other films have the same price. The audiences can choose to watch the film in a variety of formats such as 2D, 3D, China's giant screen and IMAX (Table 2).

Table 2. The SWOT analysis of *Monkey King - Hero is Back*

	Strengths (S)	Weaknesses (W)
Internal environment	S1: there are excellent design works from technical level, semantic level and effectiveness level S2: there are multiple marketing methods. For example, the promotional video is well-made; it won a good reputation through the debut of international film festival S3: this film was released around the most cities in China with wide coverage after triggering a hot discussion S4: The audiences can choose watch the film with different movie specifications such as 2D, 3D and IMAX	W1: there are several other movies based on Journey to the West on the market W2: the production company of this film is a small-scale enterprise with many unstable factors and is easily affected by the market W3: this film lacks funds and advertising investment and hasn't well-known actors involved W4: there are few films released at cinemas for this movie initially
External environment	**Opportunities (O)** O1: the country has supported the animation industry with the establishment of National Animation Base O2: the country has trained up some people to be the animation talent O3: the company can strive for the investment of other large enterprises to carry advertisements O4: the releasing rate of this film is higher than other Chinese animation films in various regions of China O5: social media has possessed platforms for sharing information, expressing opinions and exchanging ideas O6: the subject consciousness of audiences is stronger nowadays	**Threats (T)** T1: there is a huge gap between China and Hollywood, which has an impact by high-quality Hollywood at the same period T2: the reputation of 3d animation in China is poor in recent years T3: there are some animation films, most consumers just say "yes" instead of taking advantages, which has led to stereotypes that Chinese animation films have the poor quality T4: there is a phenomenon of over-marketing of domestic films T5: the idea of "marketing that is bigger than films" has quietly entered the hearts of moviegoers

Weaknesses

Firstly, At the aspect of product, there are other movies based on Journey to the West on the market. The production company of Monkey King - Hero is Back is a small-scale enterprise with many unstable factors and is easily affected by the market. Excellent 3d animation films must be designed over a long period; whether the sequel can build on the success of the first part is unknown. Secondly, at the aspect of promotion, this film lacks funds and advertising investment and there are no well-known actors involved, unlike domestic movies have the star effect. Finally, at the aspect of price, there are few films released at cinemas for this movie initially.

Opportunities

At Political aspects, the country has supported the animation industry with the establishment of National Animation Base and trained up some people with animation talent. Outstanding young animators have been placed at the forefront of the animation industry; therefore, there are some remarkable results from the Ministry of Education's support in the past decade and graduates from universities can come to the industry and join the team to create success. At economic aspects, the company can strive for the investment from other large enterprises to carry advertisements. The release rate of this film is higher than other Chinese animation films in various regions of China. At technological aspects, social media possesses platforms for sharing information, expressing opinions and exchanging ideas including social networking sites, Weibo, WeChat and forums (Wang 2016). At social culture, the subject consciousness of audiences is stronger nowadays and they have more space for consideration of the choice of cultural products, which heralds an opportunity to boost traditional Chinese culture.

Threats

Firstly, this is a phenomenon-level animated movie and there is a huge gap between China and Hollywood, which was emphasized by high-quality Hollywood animations in the same period. Secondly, the reputation of 3d animation in China has been poor in recent years. There are some animation films, most consumers just say "yes" instead of taking advantages, which leads stereotypes that Chinese animation films have the poor quality. Finally, there has been a phenomenon of over-marketing of domestic films, and the idea of "marketing that is bigger than films" has quietly entered the minds of moviegoers in this era of well-developed media.

3.2   Developing Strategy Analysis of the Sequel of Monkey King - Hero Is Back

SO Strategy

Firstly, creative script, story construction and character design are the basis for the development of the Chinese animation film industry. Animators seek a balance between Chinese elements and animation techniques, which was achieved in the interface between the adult's child psychology and the children's adult world and heralded the development trend of Chinese animated films. Secondly, Monkey King - Hero is Back must continue the design concept of Chinese traditional culture. Monkey King has always been a big hero in people's heart and the company should take advantage of people's love for Monkey King to present it as the return of childhood idol, arouse the enthusiasm and encourage innovative means to interpret it. Chinese animation films can regain their competitiveness to achieve sustainable development under the precondition of taking root in the national culture. Thirdly, it is necessary to train professional marketing talents in film promotion. Essentially, what we want to cultivate is traditional marketing talents who have the marketing capability in hot news, the premiere ceremony, and momentum as well as new media talents who can use network platforms to promote films. Finally, there are box office marketing strategies and non-box office marketing strategies in the diversified marketing model which are the important and diversified strategies to promote the development of the movie industry. The method of game and comic promotion can add movie characters into new versions of video games to achieve the aim of generalization. The cooperation between films and comics not only can expand the popularity of both, but also brings greater benefits. Award-winning promotion can enhance the visibility of the film, and brand promotion with their own huge membership base and high-quality media promotion are effective activities for the film.

WO Strategy

Firstly, companies must focus on the development of merchandise. There are various kinds of film derived merchandise including books, posters, audio-visual products, toys, souvenirs, daily necessities, collectibles, etc. and their industrial chains are intertwined. The company uses the development of merchandise to attract people's attention during early release of the movie, so that the image can be deeply engrained in the public consciousness. The development and management of merchandise is an important method of stimulating and maintaining the audience's attention and merchandise is released before the film. Secondly, the state must vigorously support the animation industry and strive to provide more financial subsidies to film-makers. In recent years, the state started to implement policies to support the animation industry and a large number of companies emerged under the encouragement of various measures which produce a rapidly-growing number of animation movies. Companies coordinate their resources to increase the flexibility with which they can respond to the market impact. Thirdly, the core principle of animation movies is that the plot meets the audience's psychological needs. In addition to entertaining young children, the animation companies should exploit their market consumption potential by also catering to other audiences' tastes. The emotional elements of the films can resonate with audiences and successfully break the bottleneck of focus on young people under the consumer-centric principle. Finally, it is important to schedule release to maximize opportunities for consumers. The company should choose the right time to release, such as winter and summer vacations so as to take advantage of large market demand (Table 3).

ST Strategy

Firstly, the company enhances consumers' participation through interaction with them which increases their affection for the movie, and prompts audiences to become loyal fans of the movie who contribute spontaneous publicity on the internet. Together with a good image the company has created, the folk reputation spreads rapidly and consumers virtually become advertisers for the company. Secondly, companies should introduce the relevant talents to improve the production technology of animation film. The production team ought to strengthen technology development to make animation works more excellent. For example, to make special effects and picture quality more beautiful and realistic, the animators must highlight the details of figures and backgrounds so as to touch the audience. Finally, companies must adopt marketing approaches with green health. The film company should abandon negative publicity such as excessive speculation and gimmicks and instead actively make use of diversified media platforms to establish a positive industry brand and image. Though

Table 3. Developing strategy analysis of the sequel of *Monkey King - Hero is Back*

Internal/external environment	Strengths (S)	Weaknesses (W)
Opportunities (O)	SO Strategy 1: Creative script, story construction and character design are the basis for the development of Chinese animation industry 2: Continue the design concept of Chinese traditional culture 3: It is necessary to train professional marketing talents in film advertising 4: There are box office marketing strategies and non-box office marketing strategies in the diversified marketing model and they are the important and diversified strategies to promote the development of the movie industry	WO Strategy 1: Companies must focus on the development of derived merchandise 2: The state must vigorously support the animation industry and strive for more financial subsidies to the company 3: The core value of animation movies is that the plot can appeal to the consumers' psychological needs 4: It is important to schedule for consumer's convenience
Threats (T)	ST Strategy 1: The company enhances consumers' participation through interaction with them and this increases their affection for the movie 2: Companies should introduce the relevant talents to improve production technology of animation film 3: Companies must adopt the marketing approach with green health	WT Strategy 1: The sequel needs to continue the 3D visual effects and excellent production to form the quality advantage 2: Innovation is the core power of continuous development of enterprises 3: The producers ought to define the movie market positioning

companies can get the attention of media and audience through the marketing methods of hype and scandal they will eventually be abandoned by the audience. Therefore, only by adopting a green health marketing strategy can they win the reputation.

WT Strategy

Firstly, the sequel needs to continue using the 3D visual effects and excellent production values to create a quality advantage. The sequel production still takes a realistic style, which sets a mysterious scene with beautiful pictures. Secondly, innovation is the core power behind the continuous development of enterprises. Innovation is not merely about the technology and content but also the marketing concept and brand development strategy for producers of Chinese original animation films. Finally, the producers ought to define their movies' market positioning. The original animation films intended to grab the opportunity in the full-year audience market must possess sufficient quality, attractive features and interesting topics. Essentially, the producers must not only rely solely on formal Chinese elements, but also need to highlight distinctive features from the story, the world outlook, emotions and other internal factors. Specifically, the producer should gain insight into their audiences and incorporate these into the story and characters in order to arouse the audiences' the emotional resonance.

4 Summary

Through SWOT analysis, this study reclaims the developing strategies for Chinese animation. Firstly, animation designers shall design the artwork with elements of Chinese traditional culture and the animation company shall train the specialized marketing personnel to develop the marketing model multifariously. Secondly, managers should strengthen the research of derived merchandise, and the country must support the animation industry vigorously. Thirdly, the film should meet the psychological needs of consumers and use interactive advantage to close the distance between designers and audiences, and also be scheduled conveniently for consumers. Fourthly, the company ought to introduce relevant personnel to improve the production values of animated films. Finally, designers should adopt innovative principles to extend their exquisite advantages and enhance their market position. The marketing ideas and promotion methods of Chinese animation films are still in their infancy. In the future, Chinese animation marketing must follow the principles while combining with tradition and innovation.

Actually, Chinese animation films as niche products in the Chinese movie industry are still in their infancy in terms of marketing ideas and promotion methods, and show the characteristics of design with blindness, innovation with tradition and promotion with interaction. The success of Monkey King - Hero is Back at the box office and its subsequent reputation means that the Chinese animation industry has begun to think deeply about its marketing model. Accordingly, marketing is the concept that shows throughout the whole process of animation creative, production and publication. Meanwhile, changes in marketing concepts and executive thinking will inevitably affect the mode of transmission. There is more space for Chinese animation to advertise in the new media environment, but consumers also have more voice, which will bring more interference. Therefore, if Chinese animation chooses a reasonable route of transmission and methods aiming at the target audiences under the overall marketing strategy, it will exceed the expected marketing goals.

Acknowledgements. The authors would like to thank my professors' valuable suggestions. The authors also wish to thank those who contributed to the research.

References

Fang, W.T., Lin, P.-H., Lin, R.: Western vs. Eastern: a reflective research on the development of Chinese animation. In: Rau, P.-L.P. (ed.) CCD 2017. LNCS, vol. 10281, pp. 25–36. Springer, Cham (2017). https://doi.org/10.1007/978-3-319-57931-3_3

Jiang, J.: Analysis of Chinese marketing model Monkey King - Hero is Back. Manag. J. **31**(29), 287 (2016)

Lee, T.H.: The key success factors to the metropolitan development: a case study of kaihsiung area. Master dissertation. National Chung Hsing University (1998)

Liu, T.: Analysis of new media marketing of Chinese animation movies. News World **24**(10), 260–262 (2013)

Qing, F.: Research on topic marketing strategy of Chinese movies in social media environment by Monkey King - Hero is Back. Master dissertation. Guangxi University (2016)

Ricky, W.G.: Management. South-Western College Publishing, Nashville (2016)

Wang, Z.C.: The trend of China's movie industry under the background of "Internet Plus" - a Case Study of Monkey King - Hero is Back and Little Door Gods. China Radio TV Acad. J. **29**(9), 85–88 (2016)

Yang, X.Y.: A phenomenon movie: a new chapter by pure China. In: The Symposium on Monkey King - Hero is Back. Contemporary Cinema **31**(9), 198–200 (2015)

Yu, X.Q.: New ideas for anime and manga marketing research. Master dissertation. China Academy of Art (2012)

Kurttila, M., Pesonen, J., Kangas, M., Kajanus, M.: Utilizing the analytic hierarchy process (AHP) in SWOT analysis a hybrid method and its application to a forest-certification case. Forest Policy Econ. **1**, 41–52 (2000)

Kangas, J., Kurttila, M., Kajanus, M., Kangas, A.: Evaluating the management strategies of a forestland estate-the SO-S approach. J. Environ. Manag. **69**, 349–358 (2003)

Yüksel, İ., Dagdeviren, M.: Using the analytic network process (ANP) in a SWOT analysis a case study for a textile firm. Inf. Sci. **177**, 3364–3382 (2007)

Hill, T., Westbrook, R.: SWOT analysis: it's time for a product recall. Long Range Plann. **30**, 46–52 (1997)

Kotler, P.: Marketing Management: Analysis, Planning, Implementation and Control. Prentice-Hall, New Jersey (1988)

Kahraman, C., Demirel, N.Ç., Demirel, T., Ateş, N.Y.: A SWOT-AHP application using fuzzy concept: e-government in Turkey. In: Kahraman, C. (ed.) Fuzzy Multi-Criteria Decision Making. Springer Optimization and Its Applications, vol. 16. Springer, Boston (2008). https://doi.org/10.1007/978-0-387-76813-7_4

Weihrich, H.: The TOWS matrix–a tool for situation analysis. Long Range Plann. **15**(2), 54–66 (1982)

Görener, A., Toker, K., Uluçay, K.: Application of combined SWOT and AHP: a case study for a manufacturing firm. Procedia – Soc. Behav. Sci. **58**, 1525–1534 (2012)

Gallego-Ayala, J., Juízo, D.: Strategic implementation of integrated water resources management in Mozambique: an A'WOT analysis. Phys. Chem. Earth Parts A/B/C **36**(14–15), 1103–1111 (2011)

McCarthy, E.J.: Basic Marketing. Richard D. Irwin, Homewood (1964)

Lauterborn, B.: New marketing litany: four P's passe: C-words take over. Advertising Age **61**(41), 26 (1990)

How to Preserve Taiwanese Cultural Food Heritage Through Everyday HCI: A Proposal for Mobile Implementation

Kuan-Yi Huang[1], Yu-Hsuan Ling[1], and Chung-Ching Huang[2(✉)]

[1] Therefore Ed, Taipei 11510, Taiwan
[2] National Taiwan University, Taipei 10617, Taiwan
ts245@st.thsh.tp.edu.tw

Abstract. We explore how cultural heritage can be preserved via human-computer interaction applications with a focus on food heritage in Taiwan. The contribution of this paper is its explanation of the existing and potential design space for HCI in the area of human-food interaction and is a step further in preserving the food culture in Taiwan. This paper represents a new step in this direction whereby all people can participate in the preservation prerevision of their own family recipes and the cultural meanings embodied in them by making a record of their daily meals. By highlighting the use of HCI's irreplaceable role in the relationship features function, recording culture, and celebratory technology [31], we hope to encourage a more comprehensive research agenda within HCI to design technologies pertaining to the preservation of food heritage.

Keywords: Mobile interaction · Design for aging ·
Context awareness for universal access · Design for preservation ·
Fabrication methods and tools · Taiwanese food heritage

1 Introduction

Taiwan has been separated from China for more than a decade [28]. Furthermore, significant Taiwanese cultural traits have emerged since WWII [26, 28, 29]. In comparison to other societies, the complexity of Taiwanese food culture cannot be understood as merely the array of foods and food activities of which it is composed [23]. Instead, it is found in the extremely subtle ways in which these foods and activities embody political and social implications.

Due to its position near the Pacific Ocean, Taiwan has an abundance of civilizations that have rich backgrounds of aboriginal culture, the traces of which are still visible today [31]. After WWII, many immigrants who came from Taiwan began to make a living by selling authentic Chinese food. As time passed, Taiwan, as an island in Southern Asia, began to develop its own flavors and cuisine (tai-chi) [2, 6]. When political issues became more extreme, the food became representative of self-awareness and self-identity for the Taiwanese [3, 27] (Table 1).

© Springer Nature Switzerland AG 2019
P.-L. P. Rau (Ed.): HCII 2019, LNCS 11576, pp. 156–169, 2019.
https://doi.org/10.1007/978-3-030-22577-3_11

Table 1. Population composition (source: Ministry of the Interior R.O.C).

Ethnic group	Percentage
Hoklo Taiwanese	67.93
Hakkanese	14.25
Taiwanese Aborigines	2.37
Mainlanders	12.35
New Immigration	3.1
Total	100

For the elderly generation, food is a key element in bonding with their families. For example, during the Chinese New Year's Eve, many families gather to share their grandparents' or ancestors' home cooking. Not only is the food delicious, there is also a moral lesson embodied in the meals [2, 10, 17]. Such explicit symbolic meaning can easily been illustrated by the shape of dumplings, which resemble gold nuggets, and represent good fortune; the stickier the dumpling, the more meat it can contain. Dumplings also represent the family's need to be united to overcome difficulties [2, 10, 21, 27].

The embodiment of a particularly rich and varied cultural heritage in food is important, ranging from the Beijing roast duck to Taiwanese beef noodles and Taiwanese meatballs (also known as Tonghua Bawan). Thus, we envisioned a simple and subtle HCI application capturing the richness of food heritage in everyday life. However, conveying all these different aspects within a single application using text, visuals, and audio has raised many different issues about the planning and production of cultural content for mobile use. In addition to usability, aspects regarding the design and distribution of a mobile application have increased the awareness of the Taiwanese culture and historical background, as well as illustrating the evolution of Taiwanese history; please refer to Fig. 1.

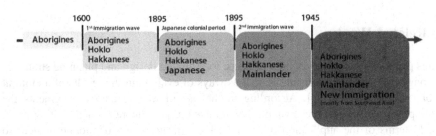

Fig. 1. Major immigration in Taiwan at different period (The latest adding indicated the newly arrived at the certain in the bottoms [1, 11])

According to the official census, the Taiwanese people consist of four major ethnicities: the Aboriginals, the Hakka, the Holo (the first three groups to settle on the island, all arriving before the Second World War) and the Mainlanders (who arrived from China after the Second World War). Strife among Taiwan's ethnicities is notorious because each different ethnic group has an uneven political status that entails varying degrees of access to economic resources.

The contribution of this paper is its explanation of the existing and potential design space for HCI in the area of human-food interaction and is a step further in preserving the food culture in Taiwan. According to Weiser [35], due to the exposure to the ubiquitous interaction with and use of computer and mobile technology, it is critical to understand how HCI is attempting to empower and enhance the experiences of all users.

This paper the preservation of their own family recipes and the cultural meanings embodied in them by making a record of their daily meals. By highlighting the use of HCI's irreplaceable role in the relationship features function, recording culture, and celebratory technology [31], we hope to encourage a more comprehensive research agenda within HCI to design technologies pertaining to the preservation of food heritage.

We structured the paper as follows: In the overview of existing projects in HCI and literature about HCI that preserve or record the cultural reviews [15, 17] and social science discoveries [7, 17], we reveal the positive ways that people enjoy cooking and sharing food [12, 28]. Furthermore, we provide a brief description of some characteristics of Taiwanese food, as this is practical for the study in our paper. Based on these findings, we present ideas for future work in designing a technology to preserve cultural heritage via human-food interaction. We also discuss the differing perspectives on food's place in people's lives that resulted from the diversity of cultural backgrounds that was revealed during the design of the study, [15], and suggest how this case study in Taiwan could be transferred to other places populated by different Chinese immigrants in relation to their historic backgrounds in Asia, such as Hong Kong [20], and Singapore [8, 15, 17]. We will conclude by describing the challenges that we encountered when designing a cultural technology in the realm of human-food interactions.

2   Related Work

In this paper, we outline all of these aspects, focusing on design and planning strategies for long-term user commitment, as well as ways of evaluating the results of a cultural mobile application [7, 17]. According to the use of mobile devices augments the development of cultural preservation and attracts tourists' interest when visiting [6, 7, 17]. In terms of the application of the HCI [7, 35], the ability of mobile devices to capture images via engagement and connection with mobile technology reinforces the memory of the tourist spots [20].

We include all the steps involved in developing a mobile application, and information that is of possible benefit to other application developers in the cultural sector. This proposal also discusses the development of a smartphone application that is context-aware. Pervasive computing has been used over the last decade to guarantee positive health outcomes for the aged population. Such applications have appeared in the form of remote monitoring [28], and the management of diseases such as Alzheimer's [24].

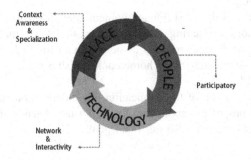

Fig. 2. Core domains of interest for user engagement

However, this proposed application will allow the user to capture the steps in the preparation of a meal, and to share those steps with family members across geographical boundaries; please refer to Fig. 2. According to the implications of HCI with regard to cultural behavior can be conceptualized as three separate, yet intersecting spheres of people, place, and technology [16].

Based on related work in cultural mobile applications, together with the consideration of users' behavior, we developed practical applications for context awareness. Building on the knowledge of HCI, we found that Taiwan has an exceptionally rich historical background, particularly with regard to food and cuisine, which made the island an appropriate case study for our research. Thus, we adopted Taiwanese users as our sample to examine how to implement mobile technology to integrate the cultural background with HCI practices in daily life.

3 Components of the Design Process

3.1 Users Behavior Characteristics

We conducted individual interviews with 15 elderly people aged between 58 and 73; two of them had three offspring, six of them had four offspring, four of them had five offspring, and three of them had six offspring. The interviews included eight questions. In order to obtain a comprehensive understanding of our target users, we also interviewed 15 younger adults aged between 18 and 30, none of whom lived with their parents or grandparents. The interviews included six questions.

From the user interviews, we found some of interesting findings. First, both the elderly and the younger adults placed emphasis on family time; however, distance prevented them from meeting often. They were eager to maintain their intergenerational relationships [30, 32]. Second, the elderly were usually proud of having their own family traditional family food taste, but few of them had written down and kept the recipes. The main reason was that they did not realize the importance of preserving the recipes. Third, all of the younger interviewees missed at least one home-cooked dish, but only four of them had learned how to cook the dish from their family members and can reproduce it successfully on their own. These findings show the demand for preserving the home recipes.

Furthermore, some of the most frequently mentioned elements of the home-cooked dish were the memory of sharing the same taste, the flavor that cannot be found anywhere else, and the life experiences associated with the dish. That is to say, the sense of belonging associated with the home-cooked dish is an irreplaceable element of the taste of the food [33].

When discussing the use of the application, the elderly thought that the complex interfaces and functions of the application were not user-friendly for them. Ways of addressing these problems was also our main goal.

3.2 Sensory and Cognitive Interaction

Cognitive psychology has shown that a decline in working memory capacity has a significant influence on the cognitive abilities of the elderly [34, 35], such as linguistic ability. When accomplishing a task that demands more working memory resources, older people may experience more difficulty [2]. However, they often develop strategies that can reduce the effects of the decline on interaction. The elderly needs ample time to process the information received [30], which can help them decrease the demand on their working memory. Moreover, the decline of higher order processes has a more serious impact on aging people due to the slowing of sensory-motor processes [2, 35], as cognitive psychologists have found that movement becomes less precise and slower as one ages [30, 32]. Therefore, it is important to ensure that the functions are simple and accessible to facilitate elderly people's use of technology via a suitable design.

3.3 Design for Fluency, Flexibility, Originality, and Elaboration

With regard to our mobile technology design approach, the four creative processes that we considered specifically were fluency, flexibility [16], originality [31], and elaboration, which were all identified as difficulties by the Taiwanese users across all generations [25]. First, design for fluency was identified as one of the most important elements mentioned by Guilford [34], who stated that creative thinkers are flexible thinkers, and have the ability to produce a great variety of ideas. With the inclusion of fluent and flexible design as a feature, adaptive interaction with mobile technology could assist not only the younger groups to use and understand the ideas of the mobile application that we developed easily, but also those active older users who eager to pass down their family recipes to prevent them from being lost. Building further on these design approaches, when designing for originality [4, 25, 34], the boundary between the original concept and creativity is so small that it can be stated: "[I]t may be an "easy" step in originality; that certain kinds of information in the problem data may spur similar 'creative' concepts" [14]. With regard to the last point, design for elaboration, the rapid development of the technology industry provides users with high participation by offering users high-quality interaction experiences [34]; according to Puerta [30], the implementation of an elaboration on the HCI model would foster users' attachment behavior and would allow them to detect problems when using it.

4 Mobile Implementation and Taiwanese Food Heritage

The application views each family as a unit, helping Taiwanese users to record videos of their home recipes and to share them with other family members. Figure 3 outlines an overview of the flow of our design process. It begins by clarifying the general requirements (such as video implementation and language function) for the system to be designed. Following this, it addresses the series of activities to be supported by the implementation of our application (such as the recipe category, the historical background, and the family blog), the domain (personal contextual learning), and any general constraints (such as publishers, naming, outlining the steps, and the budget available for the system design).

Based on the abovementioned processes, two parallel studies were mentioned explicitly in this example: a cultural mobile application under the cognitive approach, and the social cultural context-awareness structure. The result of our mobile application was an experimental construction of a Task Model [30] with the aim of illustrating the interaction within HCI.

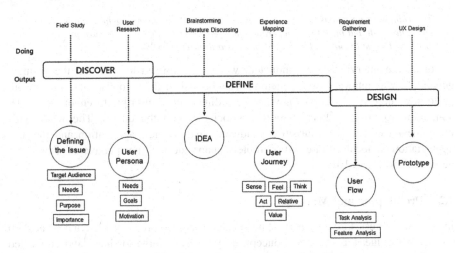

Fig. 3. Overview of the flow and main products of the design process.

An unavoidable problem that the design concept must solve is how to present a fluent, coherent, and appropriate, attractive system image, particularly when targeting older groups of Taiwanese people. With regard to the design guidelines [30], the appropriate system image must explain itself and be recognizable immediately by the users. Based on the users' journey presented and researched in the above, the color of our design for the older groups omitted colors with negative connotations that might trigger negative reactions [30] for older Taiwanese people. Another issue that could be taken into consideration is how these recipes and the cuisine could represent Taiwanese identities in a simulated environment by including their familiar locations or places. For example, the memory triggered by items such as "Taiwanese beef noodles" represents older people's respect [28] for the 'age of the farmer', or the agricultural era. Therefore, the prototype for our study will always be the history of the recipe at the beginning of the description with the aim of the cultural meaning being passed down successfully by anyone who shares a delicious recipe.

4.1   Integration with Taiwanese Food Heritage

In recent years [10], Taiwan has come rapidly and widely recognized as a "food paradise"; the statistics from the Taiwan Tourism Bureau Ministry of Transportation and Communication in 2009 showed that 52% of international tourists visit Taiwan for the main purpose of tasting "fine food" [5, 8]. The entire menu for the 2000 Inaugural Banquet of the tenth-term president of Taiwan is presented in Appendix 1 as an example of the famous foods and even those regarded as everyday food: Tainan Style

With regard to rice cakes, the so-called Tsai-Lai rice paste originated in the capital Tainan where the Taiwanese were under colonial rule. The historical background is that rice cakes were originally prepared for laborers and soldiers because the cakes were easy to carry in their pockets. These cakes were always stuffed with fragrant mush-rooms and small dried shrimp; during the survey, one of the interviewees mentioned:

> "The Tainan-style rice cake is so easy to make that people of the new generation might even neglect this dish, but back to my generation, the year of 1944, that was the most precious and tasty food for me to survive for the following two to three days.[1]"

In all the interviews we conducted, we were surprised to find that the younger generation was unaware of the memories embodied in these foods, therefore, in our prototype, there is a column for voice recordings and transcripts to enable the older generation to provide their memories associated with the dishes. The world-wide phenomenon of culinary tourism [8] indicates that the new application and the new appreciation of local culture will definitely shape the new perspective of Taiwanese heritage food [2, 9, 10].

4.2   Prototyping and Mockups

In order to address all the issues that have been discussed properly, we concentrated on the following ideas as our core concept: easy to use, simple to share, and connected strongly to the users. First, with regard to ease of use, consider the interface: We designed just three main function buttons, namely the buttons for the home page, the discovery page, and the works-you-like page. Users can operate our application easily. With regard to being simple to share, we considered the elderly, and attempted to ensure that every icon on the interface was direct, simple, and clear, so that the user

---

[1] In October 2018, I interviewed ten people at Garden Night Market, Tainan. Texts are translated from Taiwanese and have been paraphrased.

would not need to use too many cognitive resources to understand the instructions, thereby increasing the willingness to use our design. the following details can be illustrated by the Fig. 4 below.

Fig. 4. The mockups for the front page and sorting of family recipe. The users see a list of the family recipe (left one) and the details of it (middle one) along with the note by the older (right) They can leave comments that, in turn, are projected onto the pages

We chose not to have a specific platform on which the elders could post. This was because elders' profiles on platforms at present may include their travels, what they had for breakfast that day, and so on. Hence, they cannot classify their projects immediately. When using our application, elders do not need to spend a significant amount of time mastering the platform, since its design is similar to that of previous platforms. Furthermore, users are provided with a clear way of classifying their skills, thus enabling them to categorize their records.

Most importantly, when the elderly Taiwanese users record their recipes, there is a feature called the "Family Letter" that allows them to record messages for their family members. This feature is particularly useful for allowing the recorder to explain the symbolic meaning behind each item of cuisine, as this special message will be sent separately at the end of the recipe. Lastly, the application will allow elderly people in Taiwan to bond with their offspring and to share their lifestyles and values through unique and delicious recipes despite geographical boundaries (Fig. 5).

Fig. 5. The family letter bottom. (a) Left panel: general sorting box for all the message. (b) Letter panel: while following the recipe, there is a family letter function canvas where users can write their story behind the recipe, and traditional meaning of the recipe to their offspring. (c) Replying function panel: a replying note in edit recipe and pictures and voice, or in-text message.

5 Discussion

Since we conducted this research via a qualitative users' study, based on our users' journeys, we attempted to establish the extent to which our interactive design using mobile technology could succeed. With regard to the outcome, we were interested in determining whether the collection and preservation of recipes could connect and create bonds among users from generation to generation. We also wanted to identify whether users felt positively about understanding the background to their cuisine, and its role in trying to find their self-identity. From our research, we observed that a greater number of older people engaged in this survey, but the unfamiliarity of using the mobile technology tended to decrease their attachment to the mobile application; please refer to the questions in Appendix 1.

Overall, there were two main conclusions: the dynamic recipe collection, and the implications for design for preservation.

5.1 Dynamic Recipe Collection

When analyzing the field survey, we conducted, the aim was to determine whether users felt positively about understanding the background to their cuisine, and whether it was useful for identifying their self-identity. From our research, we observed that a greater number of older people engaged in this survey, but the unfamiliarity of using the mobile technology tended to decrease their attachment to the mobile application; please refer to the questions in Appendix 1. The application we designed also provides the "Family Letter" as a chat function linked to each recipe collection and family group. However, the 'family' button might not reflect their emotions accurately, as 40% of the messages were read but did not receive replies; please refer to the chart in the table provided below.

The 'collections' button thus became 'places' in the information space. We could have chosen to make the message show as "read", but this would have violated the users' privacy [18].

5.2 The Implications for Design for Preservation

The implementation of our application allows users to share their recipes, records, and even their messages, but we decided to disable this functionality in the users' study in order for the effects of awareness to be studied, and to avoid issues concerning the privacy of personal letters and relationships. Finally, the sharing of chats containing homemade recipes was even more identifiable in terms of implementation rate. However, as two users pointed out, instead of being one of the on-line social media applications, they generally associated this with one of the diary-based [18] mobile applications. In general, we employed an innovative approach by adapting HCI theories to provide Taiwanese people with an E-diary [30] application that allowed them to preserve a historical record through their everyday cuisine.

6 Conclusion

Therefore, the proposed application focuses on building an on-line social media application based on the Taiwanese family. The application emphasizes the importance of Taiwanese family relationships and the gratitude experienced when coming together to enjoy delicious cuisine. Making use of the minimalistic user interface features enhances the usability of smartphones greatly in order to adapt them to the aging generation's user behavior, such as having a specific button and clear instructions for each step.

By using the existing features on smartphones and emerging technologies such as speech recognition, the application makes it easier for Taiwanese users to archive their heritage recipes; moreover, it makes it easier for them to send letters to each other, allowing them to share and preserve recipes across generations and boundaries. These recipes will remain in each family and will fulfill the elderly Taiwanese people's dream of passing down their experiences, their lifestyles, and their family values at the end of their lifelong journeys.

This research demonstrates our exploratory work on preserving the cultural food heritage in Taiwan. The food culture is sufficiently unique and pervasive in people's everyday lives that the current approach to capturing this type of legacy might be outdated. Ordinary HCI implication might have had its day. We dream of an interactive, digital-humanity oriented approach to archive our cultural heritage, which is situated in a real context. We invite discussion from the HCI society regarding the implications of cultural richness.

Acknowledgements. We would like to address our thanks to Chung-Ching Huang for he opened an Elective Course: User Experiences Research of National Taiwan University. We thank Chung-Ching for his valuable input during the earliest stages of the project, and Yu-Huan for her endurable works of the paper. The authors wish to thank the PERSONA project members, and those subjects who took part in the case study for the valuable input and discussion.

Appendixes

Appendix 1

Q1	How often do you share meal times with your family?
Q2	Which dish made by you is your family's favorite?
Q3	Which dish made by your parents or grandparents is your favorite? Can you make it now?
Q4	Have you taught your children or grandchildren your signature dish?
Q5	Are you used to keeping the recipes for your signature dishes? If yes, how did you do? If not, would you like to do so?
Q6	What are the essential elements in your home taste?
Q7	What are the problems that you may experience when you want to keep recipe?
Q8	What are the problems that you may experience when you want to be following the recipe to cook?
Q9	What kinds of difficulties have you encountered when using mobile applications?
Q10	If there are going to have an app for keeping Taiwanese cultural food, what function included might interest you?

Appendix 2

Q1	How often do you share meal times with your family?
Q2	What would you do when you miss your family?
Q3	Which dish made by your parents or grandparents is your favorite? Can you make it?
Q4	Have you learned how to make your favorite family recipe from your parents or grandparents?
Q5	What would you do if you wanted to eat your family recipes?
Q6	What are the essential elements in your family recipe?
Q7	What are the problems that you may experience when you want to keep recipe?
Q8	What are the problems that you may experience when you want to follow the recipe to cook?
Q9	What kinds of difficulties have you encountered when using mobile applications?
Q10	If there are going to have an app for keeping Taiwanese cultural food, what function included might interest you?

Appendix 3

2000 Inaugural Banquet of the Tenth-term President of Taiwan
A. Spring Burgeoning:
1. Salmon, Scallops and Salmon Eggs Salmon (Origin: Deep sea fishing); Scallops.
(Origin: Deep sea fishing); Salmon eggs (Origin: Deep sea fishing).
B. Summer Nurturing:
2. Milkfish Ball Soup Milkfish paste (Origin: Tainan/Natural taste: sweet/
Character: moderate); STUFFING Bamboo Shoots (Origin: Chiayi, Yunlin).
3. Tainan Style Rice Cake Tsai-Lai rice paste (Origin: Taiwan); STUFFING
Fragrant Mushrooms (Origin: Taiwan); Small dried shrimp (Origin: Taiwan.).
C. Autumn Grace:
4. Steamed Lobster with Spring Onions and Ginger Lobster (Origin: Auti)
5. Smoked Cod Fish Cod fish(Origin: Deep sea fishing).
6. Mutton chop Roast Mutton Chop (Origin:Kangshan).
D. Winter Nourishment:
7. Taro & Sweet Potato Sponge Taro. (Origin: Shiahsien, Taiwan); Sweet potato
(Origin: Chinshan, Taiwan); Tsailai rice powder (Origin: Chianan Plain).
8. Glutinous Longan Gongee Chinese Jujube (Origin: Miaoli, Taiwan); Longan
(Origin: Chianan); Lotus seed (Origin: Tainan's Paiho); Glutinous rice (Origin:
Chianan).

References

1. Aygun, H.: The relationship between pre-service teachers' cognitive flexibility and interpersonal problem-solving skills. Eurasian J. Educ. Res. **18**(77), 1–24 (2018). https://doi.org/10.14689/ejer.2018.77.6
2. Barsocchi, P., Cimino, M., Ferro, E., Lazzeri, A., Palumbo, F., Vaglini, G.: Monitoring elderly behavior via indoor position-based stigmergy. Pervasive Mob. Comput. **23**, 26–42 (2015). https://doi.org/10.1016/j.pmcj.2015.04.003
3. Burrus, J.: Book reviews: CSIKSZENTMIHALYI, MIHALY (1996). Creativity: flow and the psychology of discovery and invention. New York: Harper Collins. Gifted Child Q. **41** (3), 114–116 (1997). https://doi.org/10.1177/001698629704100309
4. Henderson, J.C.: Food and culture: in search of a Singapore cuisine. Br. Food J. **116**(6), 904–917 (2014). https://doi.org/10.1108/bfj-12-2012-0291
5. Chan, S.: Food, memories, and identities in Hong Kong. Identities **17**(2–3), 204–227 (2010). https://doi.org/10.1080/10702891003733492
6. Pendit, U.C., Zaibon, S.B., Bakar, J.A.A.: Mobile augmented reality for enjoyable informal learning in cultural heritage site. Int. J. Comput. Appl. **92**(14), 19–26 (2014). https://doi.org/10.5120/16077-5286
7. Chen, G.: Digitalcommons.uri.edu (2019). http://digitalcommons.uri.edu/cgi/viewcontent.cgi?article=1006&context=com_facpubs
8. Cheung, S., Wu, D.: The Globalisation of Chinese Food. Taylor and Francis, Hoboken (2014)

9. Lien, C.-Y.: Establishing a consumption experience scale model for Taiwanese fine foods culture. Afr. J. Bus. Manag. **6**, 10 (2012). https://doi.org/10.5897/ajbm11.1718

10. Chuang, H.: The rise of culinary tourism and its transformation of food cultures: the national cuisine of Taiwan. Copenhagen J. Asian Stud. **27**(2), 84 (2009). https://doi.org/10.22439/cjas.v27i2.2542

11. Dorst, K., Cross, N.: Creativity in the design process: co-evolution of problem–solution. Des. Stud. **22**(5), 425–437 (2001). https://doi.org/10.1016/s0142-694x(01)00009-6

12. Dubois, E., Scapin, D.L., Charfi, S., Bortolaso, C.: Usability recommendations for mixed interactive systems: extraction and integration in a design process. In: Huang, W., Alem, L., Livingston, M. (eds.) Human Factors in Augmented Reality Environments. Springer, New York (2013). https://doi.org/10.1007/978-1-4614-4205-9_8

13. Economou, D., Gavalas, D., Kenteris, M., Tsekouras, G.: Cultural applications for mobile devices: Issues and requirements for authoring tools and development platforms. ACM SIGMOBILE Mob. Comput. Commun. Rev. **12**(3), 18 (2008). https://doi.org/10.1145/1462141.1462145

14. Grimes, A., Harper, R.: Ccs.neu.edu (2008). http://www.ccs.neu.edu/home/andrea/docs/grimes_food_chi08.pdf

15. Henderson, J.: Food as a tourism resource: a view from Singapore. Tourism Recreation Res. **29**(3), 69–74 (2004). https://doi.org/10.1080/02508281.2004.11081459

16. Hochheiser, H., Lazar, J.: HCI and societal issues: a framework for engagement. Int. J. Hum.-Comput. Interact. **23**(3), 339–374 (2007). https://doi.org/10.1080/10447310701702717

17. Irvine, D., Zemke, A., Pusateri, G., Gerlach, L., Chun, R., Jay, W.: Tablet and smartphone accessibility features in the low vision rehabilitation. Neuro-Ophthalmol. **38**(2), 53–59 (2014). https://doi.org/10.3109/01658107.2013.874448

18. Jacob, E., Stinson, J., Duran, J., et al.: Usability testing of a smartphone for accessing a web-based e-diary for self-monitoring of pain and symptoms in sickle cell disease. J. Pediatr. Hematol. Oncol. **34**(5), 326–335 (2012). https://doi.org/10.1097/mph.0b013e318257a13c

19. Lin, Y., Pearson, T., Cai, L.: Food as a form of destination identity: a tourism destination brand perspective. Tourism Hospitality Res. **11**(1), 30–48 (2010). https://doi.org/10.1057/thr.2010.22

20. Lombardo, V., Damiano, R.: Storytelling on mobile devices for cultural heritage. New Rev. Hypermedia Multimedia **18**(1–2), 11–35 (2012). https://doi.org/10.1080/13614568.2012.617846

21. Long, J.: Some celebratory HCI reflections on a celebratory HCI festschrift. Interact. Comput. **22**(1), 68–71 (2010). https://doi.org/10.1016/j.intcom.2009.11.006

22. Lopes, A., Marques, A., Junqueira Barbosa, S., Conte, T.: (2019) https://www.researchgate.net/publication/276206519_Evaluating_HCI_Design_with_Interaction_Modeling_and_Mockups_A_Case_Study

23. Lyons, B., Austin, D., Seelye, A., et al.: Pervasive computing technologies to continuously assess Alzheimer's disease progression and intervention efficacy. Front. Aging Neurosci. **7** (2015). http://dx.doi.org/10.3389/fnagi.2015.00102

24. Ma, C., Chen, M., Hong, G.: Energy conservation status in Taiwanese food industry. Energy Policy **50**, 458–463 (2012). https://doi.org/10.1016/j.enpol.2012.07.043

25. Othman, A.K., Mahmud, Z., Noranee, S., Noordin, F.: Measuring employee happiness: analyzing the dimensionality of employee engagement. KEER 2018. AISC, vol. 739, pp. 863–869. Springer, Singapore (2018). https://doi.org/10.1007/978-981-10-8612-0_90

26. Park, I., Hannafin, M.: Empirically-based guidelines for the design of interactive multimedia. Educ. Technol. Res. Dev. **41**(3), 63–85 (1993). https://doi.org/10.1007/bf02297358

27. Puerta, A.: A model-based interface development environment. IEEE Softw. **14**(4), 40–47 (1997). https://doi.org/10.1109/52.595902

28. Rockower, P.: Recipes for gastrodiplomacy. Place Brand. Public Dipl. **8**(3), 235–246 (2012). https://doi.org/10.1057/pb.2012.17
29. Sato, M., Ballinger, S.: Raising language awareness in peer interaction: a cross-context, cross-methodology examination. Lang. Aware. **21**(1–2), 157–179 (2012). https://doi.org/10.1080/09658416.2011.639884
30. Sharples, M., Corlett, D., Westmancott, O.: The design and implementation of a mobile learning resource. Pers. Ubiquit. Comput. **6**(3), 220–234 (2002). https://doi.org/10.1007/s007790200021
31. Sustar, H., Jones, S., Dearden, A.: Older people as equal partners in creative design. In: Holzinger, A., Ziefle, M., Hitz, M., Debevc, M. (eds.) SouthCHI 2013. LNCS, vol. 7946, pp. 649–656. Springer, Heidelberg (2013). https://doi.org/10.1007/978-3-642-39062-3_45
32. Sharples, M., Corlett, D., Westmancott, O.: Pers. Ubiquit. Comput. **6**, 220 (2002). https://doi.org/10.1007/s007790200021
33. Weiser, M.: Lri.fr (2019). https://www.lri.fr/~mbl/Stanford/CS477/papers/Weiser-SciAm.pdf
34. Welsh, G.: Creativity and intelligence. Institute for Research in Social Science, University of North Carolina at Chapel Hill, Chapel Hill, N.C. (1975)
35. Wolff, A., Mulholland, P., Zdrahal, Z.: Using machine-learning and visualization to facilitate learner interpretation of source material. Interact. Learn. Environ. **22**(6), 771–788 (2012). https://doi.org/10.1080/10494820.2012.731003

A Study of Cultural Ergonomics
in Atayal Weaving Box

John Kreifeld[1]([envelope]), Yajuan Gao[2]([envelope]), Gao Yang[3]([envelope]),
Hui-Yun Yen[4]([envelope]), Yuma Taru[3], and Rungtai Lin[3]([envelope])

[1] Tufts University, Medford, MA, USA
john.Kreifeldt@tufts.edu
[2] School of Fine Arts and Design, Guangzho University,
Guangzhou, People's Republic of China
78343821@qq.com
[3] Graduate School of Creative Industry Design,
National Taiwan University of Arts, New Taipei City, Taiwan
Lukegao1991@gmail.com, rtlin@mail.ntua.edu.tw
[4] Department of Advertising, Chinese Culture University, Taipei, Taiwan
pccu.yhy@gmail.com

Abstract. The purpose of this study is to explore the meaning of cultural objects and to extract their cultural features from Taiwanese aboriginal cultures. Atayal is a tribe of Taiwanese aborigines whose culture is disappearing rapidly due to a hundred years of colonization. The gungu, literally "weaving box" in the Atayal aboriginal language, is the subject of this study. Based on the previous studies, this study proposes a cultural ergonomic research model to provide designers with a valuable reference for designing a successful cross-cultural product as well as the interwoven experience of design and culture in the design process. This study attempts to illustrate how by enhancing the original meaning and images of Taiwan aboriginal culture features they may be transformed into modern products by taking advantage of new production technology and so fulfill the needs of the contemporary consumer market.

Keywords: Ergonomics · Cultural ergonomics · Atayal loom ·
Taiwan aboriginal culture

1 Introduction

Taiwan is a multi-culture from a variation of Southern China culture with significant East Asian influences including Japanese and such Western influences as American, Spanish and Dutch. Over time, Taiwan gradually developed its own distinct culture [23]. Hence, the prospect of Taiwan's local cultures will become crucial elements in cultural design applications [24]. For example, Taiwanese aboriginals have distinct and abundant cultures. With their beautiful, primitive, and spiritually motived visual arts and crafts, Taiwan's aboriginal cultures should have great potential for enhancing design value and being recognized in the global market [12]. Among the aboriginal tribes, Atayal which is composed of several subgroups is one of the best weaving tribes

© Springer Nature Switzerland AG 2019
P.-L. P. Rau (Ed.): HCII 2019, LNCS 11576, pp. 170–183, 2019.
https://doi.org/10.1007/978-3-030-22577-3_12

in Taiwan famous for the variety and sophistication of their textiles. In their traditional society, Atayal men did the hunting, fighting, farming and house building, while Atayal women were known for the artistry of their handwoven artifacts [2, 34]. The weaving art of the Atayal in Taiwan has developed rapidly over the past decade. Women's weavings have performed outstandingly in various textiles exhibitions through combining traditional textiles with modern weaving techniques [20, 35].

Having suffered from their traditions being nearly extinguished in the past colonial periods, the Atayal tribe members are now trying to retrieve their textile traditions and they have already achieved fruitful innovations rooted in their ancestors' wisdom [35, 36]. For example, Yuma Taru [31] has spent years "reverse engineering" many old woven tribal patterns by encoding them in modern weaving notation to preserve the knowledge of how to weave them, a knowledge that was formerly passed from mother to daughter. She also runs and is trying to improve a school for the children of a poor village in the hills above Miaoli; has built a cultural center called lihang workshop; and promotes interest in Atayal culture (https://www.facebook.com/lihangworkshop). Figure 1 shows some of Yuma's works.

Fig. 1. Some works of Atayal weaver Yuma Taru

Such spirituality characterizes much tribal design giving it an immediacy which even outsiders can feel deeply and respond to without knowing much, if anything, about the culture of the peoples who produced it. Such feeling can transcend cultural differences. By using a cultural ergonomic approach, the *gungu*, literally "weaving box" in the Atayal aboriginal language, was chosen as the cultural object for discussion in this study [17, 31]. A framework is proposed for examining the way designers communicate across cultures as well as the interwoven experience of ergonomic design and culture meaning in the design process. Using the framework, this study attempts to illustrate how, by enhancing the original meaning and images of Taiwan aboriginal culture features, and taking advantage of new production technology, they may be transformed into modern products and so fulfill the needs of the contemporary consumer market [23, 24].

2 A Cultural Product Design of the Atayal Loom

The Atayal loom is a type of horizontal ground or foot-braced backstrap loom which is the older of the looms of Ancient Egypt [4, 7, 32] although the date of the first loom or even what it looked like is unknown. As a weaving tool in one form or another it dates back at least to the ancient Egyptians and Greeks [29, 30]. The earliest example (201 B.C. – 8 A.D.) of a backstrap loom in eastern Asia is found at a site in Shizhaishan, Yunnan Province [1]. The gungu (weaving box) as shown in Fig. 2 [17, 31] is a seemingly simple user "product" designed long ago for the art of weaving as practiced by Taiwan's aboriginal Atayal weavers.

Fig. 2. Atayal gungu, ground loom and weaver

The Atayal woven crafts played a large role in the tribe's social customs, spiritual life and organization. These textiles were woven on a type of loom called a "backstrap" loom which is the subject of this study. "Backstrap" refers to the strap behind the weaver's back as in Fig. 2. The Atayal loom is one of the original types of simple movable backstrap and foot braced type looms [1, 17, 31]. That is, the weaver controlled the tension of the warp threads by pushing with her feet against a brace. The foot brace could be a simple bar but in the Atayal loom it is the culturally important "box". By changing the arrangement of the warping bench and one's way of weaving, the Atayal's own characteristic complex patterns can be woven [31]. With a simple bar for the foot brace of a backstrap loom, the total length of the warp (the "stationary" threads on the loom) is limited to about twice the leg length of the weaver. Among its other advantages the gungu increases the total warp length significantly. A desirable feature when such length is needed.

Traditional Atayal looms were composed of many parts, with one of the most important being the Weaving Box, made of tough woods like beech or Formosan michelia. The weaving box was not only an important part, but could also be used for storage when weaving wasn't taking place [1, 17, 31]. In the days long ago when head hunting was practiced, the hollow box could be struck to make a loud drum sound as a signal to the village that a warrior had returned with a head [17]. For a clear understanding of the Atayal loom, the features of all parts of the Atayal loom must be understood. Diagrams of their parts are included in Fig. 3 [31]. The "weaving art" consists of choosing the colors for the warp threads and the complexity of the lacing of the weft thread (the "moving" thread which also may change colors) as it goes over some warp threads and under others. The weaves used by the Atayal and patterns produced with them are technically interesting and aesthetically pleasing [20]. Creativity comes in designing aesthetically pleasing combinations. It is the particular lacing plan in combination with the coloring of the warp threads which makes the pattern. Practically infinite combinations of colors and lacings (i.e., patterns) exist [31].

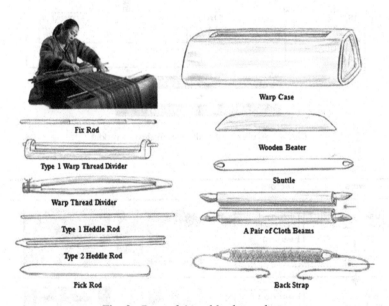

Fig. 3. Parts of Atayal backstrap loom

3 A Framework for Studying the Atayal Loom

For the human system design, Kreifeldt and Hill [16] proposed a user-tool-task system design model (Fig. 4) that integrates ergonomics into product design for producing aesthetically pleasing and functionally superior products [22]. The user-tool-task model is designed to solve the problem of completing a task with a tool; it focuses first on the manipulation interface between the user and the tool and then on the engagement interface between the tool and the task. Finally, for the global market, adding a cultural dimension to ergonomics has become an important issue for exploring interaction and experience in product design [19]. Along with technological progress, while product design has been transferred from being manufacturing-based to marketing driven to user centered for some time, there is now greater emphasis specifically on user experience, with ergonomics being increasingly considered in interactional design for marketing. By combining the user-tool-task model with the scenario, a framework which facilitates an understanding of cultural ergonomics in product design is shown in Fig. 5 [22].

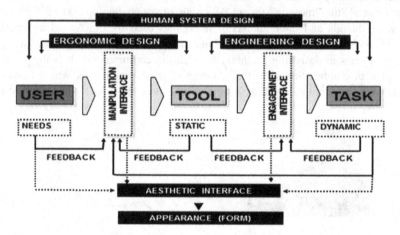

Fig. 4. A user-tool-task system design model

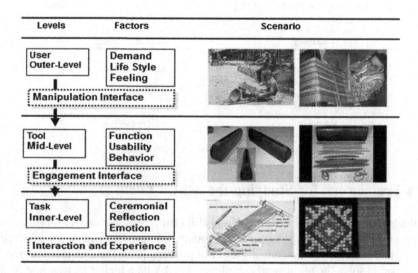

Fig. 5. Cultural ergonomics in product design with the scenario

For example, the ergonomic bench in Piegorsch's research [28] provides a culturally, environmentally, and economically viable alternative to traditional methods of working with the backstrap loom. Piegorsch [28] studied how an ergonomic bench was designed for indigenous weavers in Guatemala that is a typical example of cultural ergonomics. The ergonomic bench helps weavers enhance their productivity and improve textile quality, while also preventing cumulative trauma to their health. The bench focused on user-centered ergonomic design and also stimulated self-awareness in traditional weaving. The benefits of cultural ergonomics can be represented as a cycle with five stages: health, productivity, quality, culture and self-esteem [28]. Based on Piegorsch's study [28], a framework is shown in Fig. 6 for combining cultural features with ergonomic design which facilitates an understanding of cultural ergonomics in product design shown as the inner triangular factors. It is likely to be a never-ending process and can be applied universally, strengthening the connection between designers and their cultural heritage as shown as the outer circular factors [31].

Fig. 6. A never-ending process for studying cultural ergonomics [31]

For the cultural ergonomics approach [14, 18, 19], the framework consists of two main parts that function to explore the cultural ergonomics issues of the cultural object and to study problems related to human factors. To accomplish the outer circular factors: health, productivity, quality, culture and self-esteem, the inner triangular factors must be considered in practical ergonomic design [28]. This study proposes a cultural ergonomic research model to provide designers with a valuable reference for designing a successful cross-cultural product as shown in Fig. 7 [17]. The model consists of four main parts: conceptual model, research method, human system design, and cultural ergonomic approach. The conceptual model focuses on how to extract cultural features from cultural ergonomics and then transfer those features to the design transformation model in order to design cultural products. Thus, Fig. 7 details the various influences and interactions in a user-tool system and emphasizes the threefold nature of the design: user, tool, and task. The specific task illustrated here is "weaving" which produces a woven product as the system "output". Among the user-tool-task, there are the two interfaces of the user-tool manipulation interface (ergonomics) and the tool-task engagement interface (technology); and the various interactions between user needs and design requirements in the practical design process (marketing) [17].

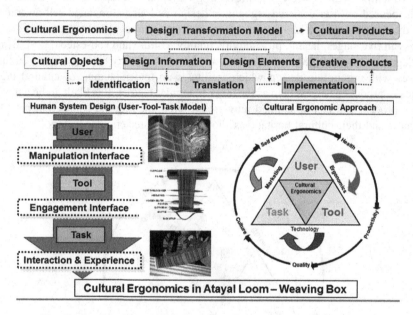

Fig. 7. A cultural ergonomic research model for the Atayal loom [31]

4   From Box to Box: A Case Study of the Atayal Loom

Based on the cultural ergonomic approach in Fig. 7, the purpose of the human system design approach focuses on and analyzes the weaving box's appearance, usability, cultural meaning, operational interface, and the scenario in which it is used. The approach consists of three parts: the study of cultural objects of "cultural ergonomics", "design transformation" (from cultural object to design elements to design elements), and "cultural products" (design creative products). For the practice, three stages are identified are: (1) extracting cultural features from original cultural objects (identification), (2) translating these features into design information and design elements (translation), and (3) designing a cultural product (implementation) [17, 31].

The subject of this study is the weaving box (gungu) used for the Atayal loom. Based on the approach (Fig. 7), the weaving box could be employed for a systematized and scientific method to study the three aspects of cultural ergonomics. First, ergonomic study of the weaving box across user operational situations needs to be analyzed to study the manipulation interface (ergonomics) between users and the weaving box. Then, based on that analysis, the engagement interface (technology) is studied to identify the relationship between the weaving box and the task. Finally, based on the cultural-feature transformation model, the weaving box is identified with three levels of cultural ergonomics and used to demonstrate how to design cultural products (marketing) [11, 21]. There are social meanings, ergonomic concerns and the functional achievement associated with this cultural object. To develop an ideal loom, both the cultural and operational interfaces of the "weaning box" need to be well-studied using a user-tool-task approach [16, 22].

4.1   Study of the Cultural Ergonomics of Atayal Loom

Considered from the perspective of ergonomics, to develop an ideal loom in the form of the Atayal loom (weaving box), both the social and operational interfaces of the weaving box need to be well designed using a user-tool-task approach [22]. To use the loom, the weaver braces her feet against the gungu around which the continuous warp threads pass completing their circuit around the breast beam held near her body by a strap fastened at each end and passing behind her back: hence the name "backstrap". Thus, many studies were made to evaluate the prevalence of low back pain among the handloom weavers [3, 5, 6, 25]. The weaver would alternately tighten and loosen the warp threads as part of the weaving process. She did this by pushing with her feet against the box creating a strain against the strap against her back to tighten the thread tension as she "beat" a new weft (cross) thread down and then relaxed to loosen the tension so that she could insert the next weft thread as shown in Fig. 8. She continued this basic process until the weaving was completed [2]. Figure 8 shows many ergonomic issues, so the studies suggested the need for further research regarding the postural strain of weavers and also emphasized the implementation of ergonomic design into the weaver's loom [10, 13, 15, 32].

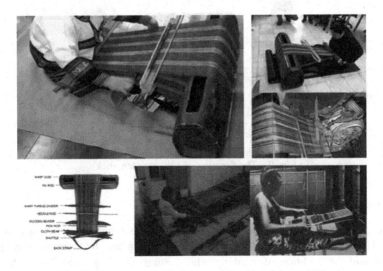

Fig. 8. Some ergonomic issues of the Atayal loom [32]

Considered from the perspective of technology, many tools were needed in traditional Atayal weaving as shown in Fig. 3. There are mainly two tools for the Atayal women to do the weaving; the Warping Post and the Loom, as shown in Fig. 9. A warping post is composed of two wooden sticks and one "Y" wooden middle stick as shown at the upper middle in Fig. 9. In ancient times, the warping posts were beaten into the ground so the set made of just the posts was enough to do the warping. However due to the change of living conditions, people started to live in houses with floors instead of living on the ground. The Atayal people therefore created a base made of a long and thick wooden base with several holes. The combination of the base and warping posts became the one which is commonly seen in the Atayal's Warping Post. After warp setting, the warping post is laid on its side (Fig. 9) and the sticks unpegged from the base. Then the fix rod is inserted in the left most opening behind the warp threads "crossing"; the thread divider in placed in the opening on the other side of the crossing one part of the cloth beam is inserted at the right most post; and the heddle positioned to receive the warping thread formed during the warping process. After all the weaving tools are put in place the warping posts are removed and the heddle closed to prevent the threads from sliding off. This process is shown at the right column in Fig. 9 [15, 31].

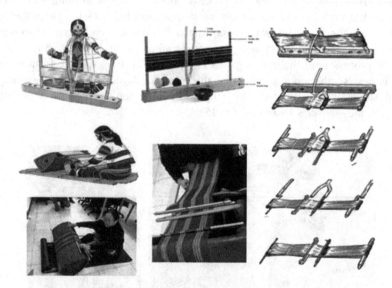

Fig. 9. The function of "Y" wooden stick

4.2   Modern Weaving Art of Atayal Loom

Women produced beautiful cloth relying on their professional and aboriginal weaving skills [34] but their tools are inconvenient for fetching due to their overweight and numbers, and the tradition of weaving while sitting on the ground. Meanwhile, the reintroduction of weaving not only required the Atayal weavers to retrace their weaving history and to reconstruct and revive lost skills but also opened up a new opportunity to create new motifs with the Atayal loom [2, 36]. In recent years Atayal people has been seeking creative and alternative ways. A new type of loom called a desktop inkle loom has been devised. Inkle weaving is a type of warp-faced weaving where the shed (the opening under the set of raised warp threads above the unraised ones) is created by manually raising or lowering the warp yarns [27] some of which are held in place by fixed heddles. The inkle loom is useful for weaving belts and narrow bands. The term "Inkle" simply means "ribbon" or "tape" and probably refers to a similarly structured woven good that could have been made on different types of looms, such as a box-loom shown as in Fig. 10 [10, 13, 15]. Inkle weaving is commonly used for narrow work such as trims, straps and belts. (https://en.wikipedia.org/wiki/Inkle_weaving).

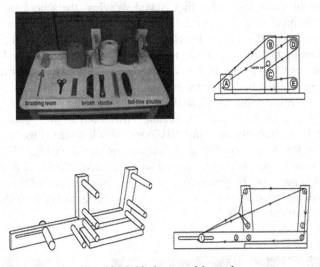

Fig. 10. Inkle loom and its tools

For the cultural and creative industry in Taiwan, aboriginal cultural products that tourists purchase as souvenirs are often actually imitations of the original products, and sold without authorization from the aboriginal group [8]. Atayal textiles are now handwoven by some aboriginal women in Wulai who weave primarily for the Wulai Atayal Museum. Weaving exhibitions are the main purpose of the Wulai Atayal museum since it opened in 2005 [34, 35]. Other than displaying materials, techniques and final works, the museum arranges to have weavers do live demonstrations on weekends to attract tourism. For the marketing, the museum also sells the works by the members in the weaving association and invites them to be the seed teachers to design promotional activities such as do-it-yourself for user experience, and promote traditional weaving through the flourishing tourism [33].

4.3   From Box to Box – Modern Atayal Weaving Box

The Atayal tribe members are now trying to retrieve their textile traditions and rooted in their ancestors' wisdom [36] as for example, Mrs. Yuma Taru [31] in Miaoli County.

Many of the aboriginal patterns which would otherwise be lost have now been pre-served in modern weavers' notation so that they can be woven again. Mrs. Taru is trying to improve a school for the children of a poor village in the hills above Miaoli and has built a cultural center called Lihang workshop (https://www.facebook.com/lihangworkshop). While teaching Atayal loom weaving at Lihang workshop in Miaoli, a few children wanted to know how to weave. Weaving need not be an expensive undertaking unsuitable for the classroom situation. Children, as well as novice crafts persons, can be treated to a fairly inexpensive and easily-learned introduction to this useful, cultural, and enjoyable art craft.

The basic procedures of traditional Atayal weaving are: spinning → thread poaching → dye → vertical thread sorting → weaving [13, 15, 31]. Because these take much time, in the courses on inheriting Atayal weaving, the school usually teaches students only the procedures of vertical thread sorting and weaving. The inkle, a simple loom, was suited to teach weaving in school, therefore, after studying the ergonomics of the Atayal loom, this study is trying to re-design an inkle loom – modern weaving box [11]. Based on the approach in Fig. 7, some questions need to be considered before using the research model to explore the weaving box of the Atayal loom. For example, Taru et al. [31] identified the main questions: for the user and ergonomics, for the tool and technology, and for the task and marketing. After study of the ergonomic issues, a desktop inkle loom (modern weaving box/loom) which replaces the vertical thread sorting shelf of the Atayal loom was re-designed as shown in Fig. 11. The modern weaving box used to beat horizontal thread so as to make it connect tightly; used to shove the shuttle into cloth by generating a gap. The main function of the shuttle which is chiseled and shaved from bamboo or wooden pieces is to insert to the horizontal thread into the vertical threads.

Fig. 11. Modern Atayal weaving box/loom and practice by children

5 Conclusions and Suggestions

It is strange that as these cultures diminish or vanish altogether their old traditional art pieces become more and more sought by museums and private collectors and consequently become more and more valuable. Beauty is the soul of the artist expressed in her art. Based in strong religious beliefs, tribal arts express that soul very strongly. As others begin to see the beauty of the art and are moved by it, they wish to possess it even without understanding or even knowing the culture behind the art. There are many parallels to these questions and problems everywhere that native cultures are disappearing and their arts and crafts along with them [17].

Such cross cultural attraction with consequent desire for possession is what designers of products for the international market should hope to have their products evoke. Recently, the reintroduction of weaving has had multiple effects on the Atayal community. Now the Atayal proudly claim their weaving culture as a part of their ethnic identity. It has become an ethnic symbol and a tourism product. It expressed feelings of modernity but in the tradition of the Atayal women's people. Continuing studies of what makes tribal arts such as the weavings of the Atayal, or even a "tool" like the weaving box, so attractive cross culturally can definitely aid in designing successful cross cultural products. This research suggests that the communication matrix approach will be validated in more testing and evaluating of product design in further study to improve its completeness. Moreover, we hope that this study will encourage more researches to inspect the connection between design and cross-cultural communication in the near future.

In the past, each tribe could be distinguished by the unique types and patterns of its weavings. Recently, with the rapidly changing social trends and progress in technology, tribes or individual studios weaving textiles hope to see this field embracing both tradition and originality in order to create different possibilities for future development. Furthermore, new Atayal weavers work closely with tourism marketing channels to balance the production and marketing of textiles. Therefore, the future of weaving art is full of hope and potential. The Atayal loom is apparently unique and deserves in-depth study.

Results presented herein have helped us create an approach to examine the framework in which designers apply and embody the idea of cultural products as well as the interwoven experience of cultural ergonomics in the design process. In addition, this study proposed a paradigm to integrate ergonomic considerations into human performance in "feeling" for cultural products. Finally, it is hoped that the notions of cultural ergonomics in "feeling" and cultural product design in "function" manifested through the case study of "from box to box" will be validated through more testing and evaluating in further studies.

Acknowledgments. This research based on the previous research [17, 31]. The authors gratefully acknowledge the support for this research provided by the Ministry of Science and Technology, Taiwan under Grants MOST 105-2221-E-144-001-MY2. The authors also wish to thank those who contributed to the research.

References

1. Broudy, E.: The Book of Looms: A History of the Handloom from Ancient Times to the Present. UPNE, New York (1979)
2. Chang, J., Wall, G., Chang, C.L.: Perception of the authenticity of Atayal woven handicrafts in Wulai, Taiwan. J. Hospitality Leisure Mark. **16**(4), 385–409 (2008)
3. Chaman, R., et al.: Psychosocial factors and musculoskeletal pain among rural hand-woven carpet weavers in Iran. Saf. Health Work **6**(2), 120–127 (2015)
4. Crowfoot, G.M.: Of the warp-weighted loom. Ann. Br. Sch. Athens **37**, 36–47 (1937)
5. Donohue, N.: The Weaver's Idea Book: Creative Cloth on a Rigid Heddle Loom (2010)
6. Durlov, S., et al.: Prevalence of low back pain among handloom weavers in West Bengal, India. Int. J. Occup. Environ. Health **20**(4), 333–339 (2014)
7. Faxon, H.: A model of an ancient Greek loom. Bull. Metropolitan Museum Art **27**, 70–71 (1932)
8. Guttentag, D.: The legal protection of indigenous souvenir products. Tourism Recreation Res. **34**(1), 23–34 (2009)
9. Johnson, H.: Reflections on 40 years. Part 3. Am. Indian Art Mag. **40**(3), 23 (2015)
10. Holland, N.: Inkle loom weaving. Design **77**(1), 20–23 (1975). https://doi.org/10.1080/00119253.1975.9934474
11. Hsu, C.-H., Lin, C.-L., Lin, R.: A study of framework and process development for cultural product design. In: Rau, P. (ed.) IDGD 2011. LNCS, vol. 6775, pp. 55–64. Springer, Heidelberg (2011). https://doi.org/10.1007/978-3-642-21660-2_7
12. Hsu, C.-H., Chang, S.-H., Lin, R.: A design strategy for turning local culture into global market products. Int. J. Affect. Eng. **12**, 275–283 (2013)
13. Aitken, I.A.: Weaving with inkle and with cards. Design **43**(9), 14–16 (1942). https://doi.org/10.1080/00119253.1942.10741988
14. Kaplan, M.: Introduction: adding a cultural dimension to human factors. In: Advances in Human Performance and Cognitive Engineering Research, vol. 4, pp. XI–XVII (2004)
15. Koster, J.B.: From spindle to loom: weaving in the Southern Argolid. Expedition: Mag. Univ. Pennsylvania **19**(1), 29–39 (1976)
16. Kreifeldt, J.G., Hill, P.H.: Toward a theory of man-tool system design applications to the consumer product area. In: Proceedings of the Human Factors and Ergonomics Society Annual Meeting (1974)
17. Kreifeldt, J., Taru, Y., Sun, M.-X., Lin, R.: Cultural ergonomics beyond culture - the collector as consumer in cultural product design. In: Rau, P.-L.P. (ed.) CCD 2016. LNCS, vol. 9741, pp. 355–364. Springer, Cham (2016). https://doi.org/10.1007/978-3-319-40093-8_36
18. Kring, J., Morgan Jr., B.B., Kaplan, M.: Cultural Ergonomics. In: Karwowski, W. (ed.). International Encyclopedia of Ergonomics and Human Factors, 2nd edn, vol. 3. CRC Press (2006)
19. Lin, C.L., Chen, S.J., Hsiao, W.H., Lin, R.: Cultural ergonomics in interactional and experiential design: Conceptual framework and case study of the Taiwanese twin cup. Appl. Ergon. **52**, 242–252 (2016)
20. Lin, R., Kreifeldt, J.: Do Not Touch – A Conversation Between Dechnology to Humart. NTUA, New Taipei City (2014)
21. Lin, R., Kreifeldt, J., Hung, P.H., Chen, J.L.: From dechnology to humart – a case study of Taiwan design development. In: Rau, P.L.P. (ed.) CCD 2015. LNCS, vol. 9181, pp. 263–273. Springer, Heidelberg (2015). https://doi.org/10.1007/978-3-319-20934-0_25

22. Lin, R., Kreifeldt, J.G.: Ergonomics in wearable computer design. Int. J. Ind. Ergon. **27**, 259–269 (2001)
23. Lin, R.: Transforming Taiwan aboriginal cultural features into modern product design: a case study of a cross-cultural product design model. Int. J. Des. **1**, 45–53 (2007)
24. Lin, R.: Designing friendship into modern products. In: Toller, J.C. (ed.) Friendships: Types, Cultural, Psychological and Social, pp. 1–24. Nova Science Publishers, New York (2009)
25. Motamedzade, M., Afshari, D., Soltanian, A.: The impact of ergonomically designed workstations on shoulder EMG activity during carpet weaving. Health Promot. Perspect. **4** (2), 144–150 (2014)
26. Nettleship, M.A.: A unique South-East Asian loom. Man New Ser. **5**(4), 686–698 (1970)
27. Patrick, J.: The Weaver's Idea Book: Creative Cloth on a Rigid Heddle Loom. F+W Media, Inc. (2010)
28. Piegorsch, K.: An ergonomic bench for indigenous weavers. Ergon. Des.: Q. Hum. Factors Appl. **17**(4), 7–11 (2009)
29. Roth, H.L.: Ancient Egyptian and Greek Looms. Library of Alexandria (1913)
30. Roth, H.L.: Studies in primitive looms. J. Anthropol. Inst. Great Britain Ireland **48**, 103–144 (1918)
31. Taru, Y., Kreifeldt, J., Sun, M.X., Lin, R.: Thoughts on studying cultural ergonomics for the atayal loom. In: Rau, P.L. (ed.) CCD 2016. LNCS, vol. 9741, pp. 377–388. Springer, Cham (2016). https://doi.org/10.1007/978-3-319-40093-8_38
32. Turnau, I., Broudy, E.: The Book of Looms. A History of the Hand-Loom from Ancient Times to the Present. Eric Broudy, New York (1981)
33. Varutti, M.: Crafting heritage: artisans and the making of Indigenous heritage in contemporary Taiwan. Int. J. Heritage Stud. **21**(10), 1036–1049 (2015)
34. Wu, S.H.: The characteristics of Taiyal weaving as an art form. Doctoral dissertation, Durham University, UK (1998). http://etheses.dur.ac.uk/5054/
35. Yoshimura, M.: Weaving and identity of the atayal in Wulai, Taiwan. Master thesis, University of Waterloo, Canada (2007)
36. Yoshimura, M., Wall, G.: Weaving as an identity marker: atayal women in Wulai, Taiwan. J. Res. Gender Stud. **2**, 171–182 (2014)

Designing Gardenia-Inspired Cultural Products

Shin Ling Kuo[✉]

Graduate School of Creative Industry Design, National Taiwan University of
Arts, New Taipei City, Taiwan
kssuling@gmail.com

Abstract. Recently, Taiwan's community development has shifted toward emphasizing local cultural characteristics, where local handicrafts and agricultural products have been the primary drivers of the development of local specialty industries. From 1920s to 1940s, many residents of the Fuzhou area of Banqiao in what is now New Taipei City relied on the fragrant flower industry (i.e., growing gardenia, *Gardenia jasminoides*) as their primary source of income. This study used gardenia as a basis to transfer local culture into cultural codes before designing a series of gardenia-inspired cultural products. Finally, this study performed questionnaire analysis to determine perceptions of the cultural products; the results may serve as a reference for future design studies.

Keywords: Local culture · Fuzhou area · Gardenia · Cultural products · Cultural codes

1 Introduction

Taiwan has undergone substantial community development in the past half century. In 1968, it promulgated the Regulations on Community Development Work. In 1994, the Council for Cultural Affairs (now Ministry of Culture) introduced the concept of comprehensive community development. In 2002, the Executive Yuan introduced the Challenge 2008: National Development Plan, which was later developed into the New Hometown Community Building Project. Similarly, Taiwan launched the Taiwan Cultural Life Brand Internationalization Project, in which local cultural elements were utilized for industrial development, produce value enhancement, and brand internationalization. These endeavors have enabled nonprofit organizations in Taiwan's cultural and creative industry to prosper while developing into local specialty industries that feature unique products such as handicrafts and agricultural products. In 1989, industries and products with local characteristics were selected from the 319 townships in Taiwan for the One Town One Product project, aiming to enhance the value of such products through branding and creative marketing, transforming local characteristics to knowledge economy-based cultural and creative industries.

© Springer Nature Switzerland AG 2019
P.-L. P. Rau (Ed.): HCII 2019, LNCS 11576, pp. 184–202, 2019.
https://doi.org/10.1007/978-3-030-22577-3_13

1.1   Study Motivation

From the 1920s to 1940s, many residents of the Fuzhou area of Banqiao in what is now New Taipei City grew gardenia (*Gardenia jasminoides*) as their primary source of income. Sales of gardenias dominated the scented tea market in China and even spread to Southeast Asia. However, the decline of the fragrant flower economy caused gardenia farming to slowly disappear in Fuzhou; this decline combined with the increasing number of small-scale processing plants that changed the focus of local industry and rendered gardenias mostly irrelevant to local people's lives. This study browsed ancient literature for gardenia- and *zhi*-related (*zhi* is an ancient drinking vessel used for ceremonial purposes and namesake of the gardenia) historical records to determine the possibility for *zhi* and gardenia to transfer, transit, and transform cultural codes, on the basis of which cultural and creative products are developed. The objective was to help industrialize the local culture of Fuzhou and combine the knowledge economy with culture, art, aesthetics, and creation-oriented cultural and creative industries to meet diversified global consumer demands to drive the area's economic growth.

1.2   Research Objectives

1. Use two orders of signification, a core theory proposed by Barthes for applying semiotics to cultural studies as the design methodology to develop a procedure for transforming the cultural code gardenia into cultural and creative products.
2. Obtain the semic codes of Fuzhou's local cultural characteristics and gardenia, analyze the denotations of connotations of these codes to decipher their meanings, translate the meanings into design elements to be applied in cultural product designs, and implement deductive reasoning using experimental design projects as references for subsequent design creations.
3. Utilize local cultural assets in product designs to preserve characteristics of local culture, promote local industry transformation, and facilitate cultural industrialization as well as industrial culturalization.

1.3   Research Methods

This study conducted document analysis and used grounded theory, case analysis, and semiotic methods to interpret and analyze data. A quantitative research method was adopted for case verification.

Qualitative Research

This study used the semiotic analysis framework proposed by Fiske and Hartley (1978) as an extension of Barthes' theories on signs. The framework integrates and distinguishes three levels of meanings, denotation (the first level), connotation and myth (the second level), and symbol (the third level). Denotation comprises signifier and signified, and connotation and myth illustrate the broad principles of culture used to organize and explain phenomena. This framework was used to establish a mechanism for transferring the cultural code gardenia as well as a system for related cultural product design.

Quantitative Research

This study referenced transfer, transit, and transform, the three levels of cultural creative product transform (Lin), and adopted instinctive design, behavioral design, and reflective design, the three dimensions of such a transfer process, to design a questionnaire, which was then used to investigate the designs of gardenia-inspired cultural products. The questionnaire design solicited perceptions regarding three aspects—appearance, function, and emotion—and viewer and consumer perceptions were identified from survey results to design related cultural products. The questionnaire design is shown in Table 1.

Table 1. Questionnaire design for gardenia-inspired cultural products

Dimension	Operational aspect	Question
External level	Perceptions of appearance	Q1. Does this product appropriately use the appearance of the gardenia to form its overall appearance? Q2. Does this product appropriately use the appearance of *zhi* to form its overall appearance? Q3. Does this product appropriately use the decorative elements of *zhi* to form its overall appearance?
Behavioral level	Perceptions of function	Q4. Does this product look beautiful and unpretentious? Q5. Is this product convenient to use? Q6. Do the functions of this product meet the needs of modern people?
Psychological level	Perceptions of emotions	Q7. Does this product show the fun of history? Q8. Can this product display cultural meanings? Q9. Does this product touch you emotionally?
Assessment level	Overall perceptions	Q10. Do you find this product creative and ingenious? Q11. Are you fond of this product?

This study conducted a quantitative questionnaire survey and analyzed participant data using the SPSS 20 software package and descriptive statistical methods. The analysis of reliability in this study calculated internal consistency reliability by using Cronbach's coefficient. According to Sapp (2002), reliabilities of .80–.90 for standardized tests may be acceptable. The alpha values of .934, .954, and .950 reflected excellent reliability in the whole scale for each of three products. Subsequently, this study performed factor analysis to determine the factors influencing aspects of each scale.

1.4 Research Framework

The design process was divided into five steps according to the design transfer model proposed by Lin (2014). The process is as follows: (1) analyze cultural characteristics, (2) link to product context, (3) select suitable concepts, (4) design and develop, and

(5) decide the final products to be produced. The three levels of design transform namely transfer, transit, and transform, are used to help designers design cultural products. Figures 1 and 2 show the three design models and levels of gardenia-inspired cultural products, respectively.

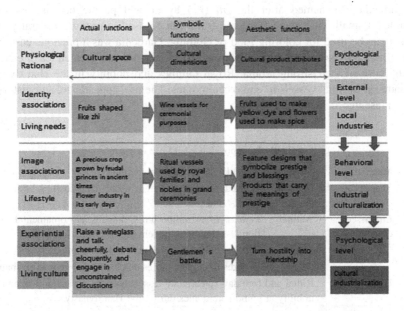

Fig. 1. Design model of gardenia-inspired cultural products

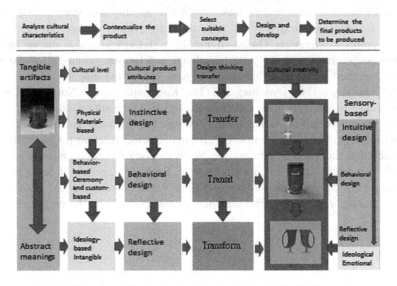

Fig. 2. Three-level design level of gardenia-inspired cultural products

2 Related Theories and Literature Review

2.1 Ancient Books and Literature

Naming of the Gardenia

The gardenia was named after the *zhi* (卮) by ancient people because its fruits resembled a small wine glass. Gardenia fruits can be used to produce natural yellow dye that can be used for coloring food or clothing. Gardenia was a precious cash crop during the Han dynasty, and gardenia flowers were used to make scented tea or eaten as food because of their strong aroma. Royal families and nobility in the Han dynasty used jade *zhi* as ritual vessels in grand ceremonies. The use, appearance, and history of *zhi* are presented in Table 2.

Table 2. Appearance and use of *zhi*

Zhi	Material	Silver, copper, jade, stone, lacquer, ceramic	
	Shape	Capped, cylindrical, featuring straight walls, deep "bellies," flat "bottoms," "ears," and three "feet"	
	Embossed ornaments	Animal	Patterns of vermilion birds, dragons, *chi* ornamental hornless dragons), phoenixes, or bears
		Plant	Patterns of grasses, peaches and persimmons
		Other	Patterns of clouds, fairies on clouds, and geometric shapes
	Use	Ritual and birthday celebration vessels used by royal families and nobility at grand ceremonies during the Han dynasty	

Origin of Yellow as the Color of Emperors

In ancient Chinese culture, yellow was a symbol of nobility and power, and the color was used for emperors' dragon robes. After the Tang dynasty, yellow was the favorite color of emperors. Emperor Gaozu of the Tang dynasty issued a decree banning common people from wearing yellow clothing, and Emperor Gaozong of the same dynasty amended the decree, banning everyone except the emperor from wearing yellow. During the Five Dynasties and Ten Kingdoms period, Northern Han and Khitan people invaded the south, and Zhao Kuangyin led a northern military expedition to pacify the rebels. In 960, when a mutiny occurred at Chenqiao Town, soldiers wore yellow robes and cheered for Zhao to become the emperor. After his return to Bianjing, Zhao ascended the throne, founding the Northern Song dynasty. Yellow robes thus officially became a symbol of imperial power. Emperor Renzong of Song issued a decree banning common people from wearing yellow robes or robes with yellow patterns, making yellow robes and the color yellow exclusive to the emperor.

2.2 Culture, Signs, and Cultural Codes and Products

Signs

From a semiotics perspective (as opposed to a positivism perspective), all cultural phenomena in the world can be viewed as sign systems. All forms of expression (e.g., languages, words, and culture) can be viewed as combinations of signs, and the meanings of these signs are based on cultural conventions and relationships (Fiske 1997). Barthes divided sign meaning into two levels; in addition to the first level of meaning, or denotation, the second level of meaning can be generated in the forms of connotation, myth, and symbol. All three forms exhibit the interaction between sign-generated meaning and social culture. Connotations are derived from traditions or culture and illustrate how signs interact with users' feelings, emotions, and cultural values (Fiske 1990). Barthes (1972) separated denotation from connotation, explaining that denotation refers to the apparent meaning of a sign, and connotation refers to the meanings given by social culture. When signs carry cultural value, their connotations can explain how their interpreters' perceptions, emotions, or cultural values influence the way they interpret the signs. Specifically, myth is a major principle for a certain culture to interact with and interpret external reality; that is, it is a culture-specific way of thinking.

Culture

Geertz introduced culture from a semiotics perspective, indicating that culture comprises meanings (presented in the form of signs) that have survived the course of history and is based on human exchanges and the preservation and development of knowledge about and attitude toward life (translated by Han 1999). Culture also refers to various forms of human activities and the symbolic structure these activities display (Leong and Clark 2003). Barthes (1992) mentioned that culture is a language and added a second level (i.e., signification) to the equation (i.e., signifier/signified = signs) proposed by Saussure, transforming primary sign meanings into secondary sign meanings (Storey 2001). Product semantics, which studies the subtle relationships between signs and products, enables sign semantics to be applied to product designs in practice and allows the appearance of technological products to be related to people's daily activities (Hjelm 2002; Krippendorff 2006).

Cultural Codes

Barthes used the term "cultural code" in his book *S/Z: An Essay*, where he performed structural analysis of a narrative work and defined five functional codes with textual implications, one of which was cultural code. Silverman (1983) stated that cultural codes offer a connotative structure, and each code is associated with a cluster of symbolic attributes. Clotaire Rapaille, author of *The Culture Code*, introduced the concept of cultural unconsciousness, arguing that cultural codes are meanings we attach to objects subconsciously through the culture from which we grow up (Clotaire 2006). Rapaille (2006) suggested that products establish a deep emotional bonding (an imprint) with their consumers, and favorable products must have the ability to "activate" consumers' cultural codes. Cultural code has also been discussed in marketing studies. Schroeder (2009) contended that cultural and historical contexts, moral ethics, and traditional customs must be addressed when creating brand value. From a design perspective, cultural codes are the symbolic meanings or the story of image symbols; cultural codes are not only the smallest elements constituting the meanings of material signs (sounds, images), but can also be adopted to investigate the principles governing how these elements should be combined as well as the meanings of these elements after they have been combined in relevant culture.

Cultural Products The United Nations Educational, Scientific and Cultural Organization defined cultural product generally refers to consumer goods that convey opinions, symbols and lifestyles. Through informing or entertaining, they build collective identity and influence cultural activities. The results of individual or collective creativity are reproduced on the basis of copyright through industrial processes and global distribution, thus promoting the exchange of cultural objects through books, magazines, multimedia products, software, records, movies, videotapes, sound and light entertainment, crafts and fashion design. Ultimately, they offer the public diversified cultural options. Chen and Chuang (2008) remarked that products should be manufactured from a consumer-centric perspective and expounded that consumers do not need all aspects of a product to be optimal to purchase it; all they need is a satisfying product with emotional value. This means that when consumers purchase cultural products, they expect the products to meet their spiritual needs in addition to providing basic functions. Accordingly, product sign value has become a factor influencing consumer purchase decisions. People buy cultural products not merely for their functions, but also to possess their symbolic meanings (Goldman and Papson 1996).

Cultural products are created through reviewing and reflecting on the cultural elements originally contained in specific objects, using design techniques to generate a modern look of such cultural elements, and exploring the spiritual satisfaction that can be achieved through object use; these characteristics differentiate cultural products from ordinary products (Ho et al. 1996). The design renders cultural products subtler and more appealing to consumers (Folkes and Matta 2013). Often serving as an extension of everyday-life culture and memories, cultural and creative products involve the creation cultural context and the passing down of culture and art. The combination of creativity and design as well as the emphasis on qualia characteristics are the key factors that Taiwan's cultural and creative products can strengthen the cultural and creative industry (Yen et al. 2014). From a business model perspective, cultural creativity entails using culture to manufacture products used in people's daily lives, creating product brands in the process. From a daily life perspective, companies use business models to make culture a part of people's lives. In other words, through designing, culture can be transformed into products used in daily life, creating a life culture in the process (Lin 2014).

3 Applying Semiotics to Design Cultural Products

3.1 Translating Model for the Cultural Implications of Gardenia

The focus of cultural design is imbuing products with cultural depth. When designing and developing cultural products, designers must consider the relevance of the products to the cultural elements they embody as well as ensure the completeness of the cultural presentation techniques. Thus, designers must first understand the culture, and develop cultural attributes according to target consumer groups. Additionally, they should use a combination of forms, colors, materials, and structure to present these attributes.

The translation from the first level of meaning, denotation, to the second level of meaning, the connotation, myth, and symbolic meaning as indicated by Barthes, involves an analysis of the interaction between a cultural code and the social culture. For the first level of meaning (connotation), sign translation refers to the relationship between the signifier and its signified. A literature review revealed that the gardenia earned its name because its fruits shared a similar shape with *zhi*. During the Han dynasty, families with a thousand *dan* (an ancient measure word meaning 100 L) of gardenia (a cash crop with high economic value) rivaled those with a thousand horses in wealth. Additionally, the color (i.e., yellow) of the dye extracted from gardenia was favored and used during the Tang and Song dynasty exclusively by emperors, respectively. In terms of denotations gardenia generated considerable profits, had fruits shaped like *zhi*, and produced dye with a color associated with nobles.

Table 3. Translating model of gardenia's cultural meanings

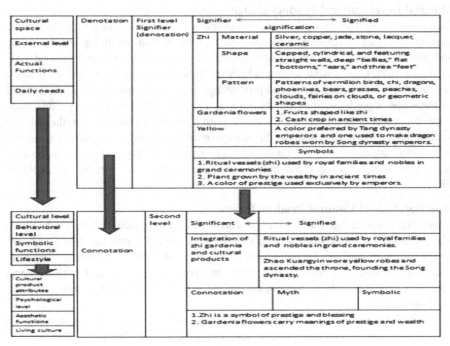

Connotations are cultural meanings given by societies. The connotations of *zhi* came from China's important national, traditional cultural ceremonies. The use of *zhi* as ritual vessels in ceremonies, an interaction between the object and cultural values, made *zhi* a symbol of prestige and blessing. Historical records showed that yellow was the color used exclusively by the emperor, making yellow the color of nobility. The custom of using yellow for emperors led to the color becoming a symbol of prestige. As a cash crop with high economic value that could be used to create dye used by emperors and contained fruits that shared a similar shape with *zhi*, gardenia carries a cultural meaning of prestige and wealth. Table 3 presents the translating model of gardenia's cultural meanings.

3.2   Cultural Characteristics of Gardenias and Product Design Concepts

Three-Level Design Concepts Involving Gardenias

This study drew its design inspirations from Lin (2005c, 2010) and examined the types and forms of gardenia-inspired cultural products. The cultural characteristics and design concepts of the products were analyzed, and the cultural characteristics of *zhi* and gardenias described in ancient books and literature were presented. The design levels of transfer, transit, and transform were used to obtain the cultural and symbolic meanings of *zhi* and gardenia, showing how historical culture and classical literature were integrated into modern culture product designs (Table 4).

Material Level Cultural Product Design

Regarding the design concept transfer proposed by Lin (2014), design transfer on the material level can be achieved by employing various methods including understanding and utilizing colors and ornamentation, using and matching materials innovatively, capturing overall or partial styling characteristics, enhancing or simplifying lines, engaging or not engaging in detailed processing, and restructuring the product. Inspired by the shape of gardenia fruits and their use as a source of bright yellow dye, this study created a gardenia fruit-shaped light fixture with a powerful visual design; the color of yellow was utilized to stimulate the senses, evoke a sense of warmth, and attract consumers' attention. The design of this light fixture also focused on the functional perspective aiming to spark consumers' purchase intention. The product is shown in Fig. 3.

Behavioral Level Cultural Product Design

Behavioral level design transfer can be classified as the transit of cultural characteristics. Lin (2014) proposed transiting cultural characteristics into use behavior-based designs through methods including preserving and extending functions; maintaining operation actions and forms; providing intuitive, convenient, and safe designs; observing object trajectory changes, and trying various forms of structuring and their combinations.

A literature review revealed that in ancient times, *zhi* was a ritual vessel as well as a wine vessel used in ceremonies. This study adopted the two-level sign transfer presented by Barthes to consider *zhi* a symbol of prestige and blessings. The color yellow and gardenia, which symbolized prestige and wealth in the Han dynasty, respectively, were employed. The aforementioned cultural characteristics were combined to design a product, in which qualia and user experience were considered. In other words, the functions of *zhi* as ritual vessels and their shapes and ornamentation were extended and

Table 4. Three-level design concepts involving gardenia

Compila-tion and analysis of cultural characteris-tics	Classification: Han dynasty		Name of artifact	*Zhi*
	Image		Artifact category	Ritual and wine vessels
			Material	Silver, copper, jade, stone, lacquer, ceramic
			Shape	Capped, cylindrical, and featuring straight walls, deep "bellies," flat "bottoms," "ears," and three "feet"
			Embossed ornament	
			Animal	Patterns of vermilion birds, *chi*, dragons, phoenixes, or bears
			Plant	Patterns of grasses, peaches, and persimmons
			Human	Patterns of fairies on clouds
			Other	Patterns of clouds or geo-metric shapes
	Usage		*Zhi* were used as wine vessels for rituals	
	"Grammar" and configu-ration of the shapes	Appearance	• *Zhi* and gardenia fruits share a similar shape • Gardenia fruits can be used to make yellow dye	
		Connota-tions	• A *zhi* is a round wine vessel • Yellow was the color used exclusively by em-perors	
		Cultural significance	• The use of *zhi* as ritual vessels in ancient times subsequently made *zhi* a symbol of prestige and blessings • Tang and Song dynasty emperors' love for yellow resulted in the color becoming a symbol of prestige • Literature has shown that growing gardenias was a sign of wealth	

(Continued)

Table 4. *(Continued)*

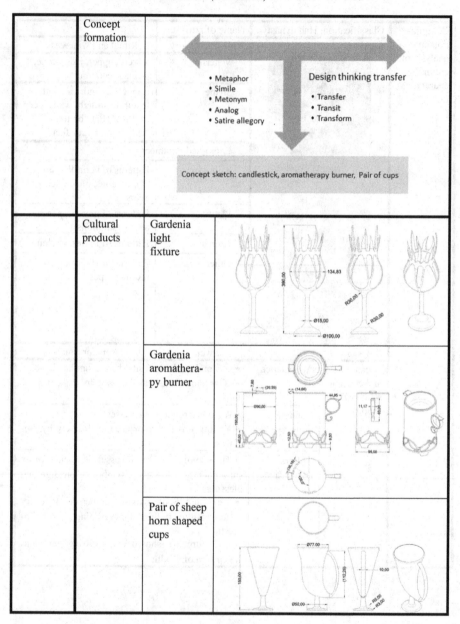

Concept formation		
		• Metaphor • Simile • Metonym • Analog • Satire allegory Design thinking transfer • Transfer • Transit • Transform Concept sketch: candlestick, aromatherapy burner, Pair of cups
Cultural products	Gardenia light fixture	
	Gardenia aromatherapy burner	
	Pair of sheep horn shaped cups	

transited, the purposes (i.e., serving as ritual vessels and a symbol of blessings) of *zhi* in important ceremonies were retained, and the safety and convenience of use were considered. The structural form of *zhi* was transited to design an aromatherapy burner filled with the cultural meaning of *zhi*.

Fig. 3. Gardenia light fixture (Color figure online)

The product materials used mainly comprised transparent glass with metal at the bottom. The shape of gardenia fruits, embossed ornamentation found on *zhi* in ancient times, and a dragon-pattern handle derived from transiting *chi* (a mythical creature resembling dragon) were incorporated into the design of the burner to elicit a sense of prestige. Essential oil could be added to the upper layer of the burner for aromatherapy, and a candle with gardenia essential oil could be placed inside. The color yellow, used exclusively by emperors, echoed with the dragon-shaped handle to evoke a sense of prestige. This design transferred cultural implications into a cultural product to evoke thoughts of the past. The product is shown in Fig. 4.

Fig. 4. Gardenia-inspired aromatherapy burner (Color figure online)

Cultural Product Design Conveying Intangible Ideas

Lin (2014) suggested designing cultural products by highlighting the special meanings, stories, and cultural characteristics of the products, transforming these special meanings, records, and legends of culture to evoke users' feelings, present lifestyles, and reflect on related matters. In this way, intangible ideas are conveyed in the form of tangible elements.

Zhuangzi described "*zhi* talk" as words spoken unintentionally, which are natural displays of thought. The so called "utterances produced on a daily basis," or "utterances renewing on a daily basis," constitute a creative language that evolves continuously. This suggests that *zhi* and language have a metaphorical relationship, where *zhi*, which possesses a physical form, facilitates the natural and endless conveyance of intangible ideas through language as men talk joyfully and enthusiastically during wine-drinking.

The *Analects* mentions fights between gentlemen. Gentlemen exhibit modesty and avoid picking up fights with others in most occasions. Even in archery competitions, they compete politely, and winners offer wine to losers to show their etiquette. The archery competition may be extended to mean verbal battles or ideological exchanges, in which gentlemen display a sense of humility. Even when they gentlemen are involved in arguments, they use wine (served in *zhi*) after the verbal arguments to turn hostility into friendship and demonstrate broad-mindedness. This study designed *zhi* to transform abstract meanings (i.e., utterances renewing on a daily basis) into tangible objects. Sheep horns, bows, and arrows served as the sources of inspiration for the product design; the sheep horn and bow-shaped handle of the product indicated conflict and archery competition, respectively, and fights between gentlemen were transformed into a pair of cups. The core value of the product design was its emphasis on users' feelings, making it a design transfer on the psychological level. The products are shown in Fig. 5.

Fig. 5. Pair of sheep horn–shaped cups

3.3   Quantitative Research and Analysis

In the 1920s through 1940s, gardenias were a crucial cash crop in the Fuzhou area and a major source of yellow dye and essential oils. The gardenia earned its Chinese name (*huangzihua*) because its fruits resemble *zhi*, a ritual vessel used in ancient times. Eloquently debating, exchanging thoughts, and talking joyfully with zest and gusto during wine-drinking sessions were all part of the daily lives of scholars and literati in the past. This study used local cultural characteristics to design three cultural products: a gardenia light fixture, a gardenia aromatherapy burner, and a pair of sheep horn–shaped cups. The study used a questionnaire to analyze and compare perceptions and feelings regarding the gardenia-inspired cultural product designs. The questionnaire results may serve as a reference for future studies in designing related products.

Descriptive Statistical Analysis

The questionnaire survey was conducted in November and December of 2018, and the participants consisted of university students, teachers, artists, designers, and others without an art background. The questionnaires were presented in Google Forms, where the participants completed the questionnaires based on their understanding of the questions. The questionnaire measured four dimensions; each dimension contained two or three questions, for which the answers were scored from 1, *complete disagreement*, to 5, *complete agreement*. All 137 questionnaires completed were valid, yielding a valid response rate of 100%. The 137 questionnaires subsequently underwent a basic descriptive statistical analysis.

An analysis of the questionnaire participants demonstrated the following distributions. (a) Regarding gender, 101 participants (73.7%) were women, and 36 (26.3%) were men. (b) Regarding age, 60 participants were (43.8%) aged 41–50 years, 35 (25.5%) were aged 31–40 years, 22 (16.1%) were aged 51 years or older, and 20 (14.6%) were aged 30 years or younger. (c) In terms of education, 68 (49.6%) had graduated from graduate schools, 60 (43.8%) had graduated from colleges or universities, and 9 (6.6%) had other education levels. (d) Regarding their professional backgrounds, 25 people (18.2%) had an art-related background, 17 (12.4%) had a design-related background, and 95 people (69.3%) had other learning backgrounds.

The participants' opinions about the gardenia-inspired cultural products were as follows.

1. Gardenia light fixture: In terms of appearance, 91.2% of the participants agreed that the product used the appearance of the gardenia appropriately to form its overall appearance; 51.1% and 40.1% gave scores of 5 and 4, respectively. Additionally, 57% of the participants agreed that the product used the appearance of *zhi* to form its overall appearance appropriately, and 59.1% of the participants agreed that the product used the ornamental elements of *zhi* to form its overall appearance appropriately. Concerning function, 82.5% of the participants agreed that the product looked beautiful and unpretentious, with 46.7% and 35.8% of the participants giving scores of 5 and 4, respectively; 56.9% of the participants agreed that the product was convenient to use; and 60.6% of the participants agreed that the functions of the product met the needs of modern people. Regarding emotional perceptions, 59.1% of the participants agreed that the product demonstrated the fun of history, 73.7% of the participants agreed that the product displayed cultural meanings, and 59.8% of the participants agreed that the product touched them emotionally. With respect to overall assessment, 59.1% of the participants agreed that the product was creative and ingenious, and 60.6% of the participants agreed that they were fond of the product.

2. Gardenia aromatherapy burner: In terms of appearance, 48.2% of the participants agreed that the product used the appearance of the gardenia appropriately to form its overall appearance, 75.9% of the participants agreed that the product used the appearance of *zhi* appropriately to form its overall appearance, and 70.1% of the participants agreed that the product used the ornamental elements of *zhi* appropriately to form its overall appearance. Concerning function, 69.3% of the participants agreed that the product looked beautiful and unpretentious, 70.8% of the participants agreed that the product was convenient to use, and 62.8% of the participants agreed that the functions of the product met the needs of modern people. Regarding emotional perceptions, 55.4% of the participants agreed that the product demonstrated the fun of history, 62% of the participants agreed that the product displayed cultural meanings, and 55.5% of the participants agreed that the product touched them emotionally. With respect to overall assessment, 66.4% of the participants agreed that the product was creative and ingenious, and 59.2% of the participants agreed that they were fond of the product.

3. Pair of sheep horn–shaped cups: In terms of appearance, 46.7% of the participants agreed that the product used the appearance of the gardenia appropriately to form its overall appearance, 59.9% of the participants agreed that the product used the appearance of *zhi* appropriately to form its overall appearance, and 45.3% of the participants agreed that the product used the ornamental elements of *zhi* appropriately to form its overall appearance. Concerning function, 84% of the participants agreed that the product looked beautiful and unpretentious, 70.8% of the participants agreed that the product was convenient to use, and 67.9% of the participants agreed that the functions of the product met the needs of modern people. Regarding emotional perceptions, 67.9% of the participants agreed that the product demonstrated the fun of history, 64.2% of the participants agreed that the product displayed cultural meanings, and 76.6% of the participants agreed that the product touched them emotionally. With respect to overall assessment, 75.2% of the participants agreed that the product was creative and ingenious, and 63.5% of the participants agreed that they were fond of the product.

Research and Analysis

This study performed statistical analysis on the results of four aspects of perceptions, namely appearance, function, emotion, and overall assessment determined by the questionnaire, and various statistical data were investigated to determine their effects on how creative and ingenious the participants thought the products to be and how fond the participants were of the products. Results showed that gender, age, and academic background influenced how creative and ingenious the participants thought the products to be and how fond they were of the products, and participants' perceptions of the products' functions and emotions had an effect on their overall assessment of the product. The data were generalized to serve as a reference for future design studies (Table 8).

Table 5. Results of t test for the effect of gender on overall product assessment ($N = 137$)

Product	Item	Gender	Mean	SD	t value	Sig.
Gardenia light fixture	Q10	Male	3.72	1.085	−2.471*	0.015
		Female	4.18	0.899		
Gardenia aromatherapy burner	Q10	Male	3.53	1.055	−2.057*	0.042
		Female	3.93	0.993		
	Q11	Male	3.33	1.171	−2.167*	0.032
		Female	3.79	1.061		

P < .05*

Table 6. Mean analysis on the effect of age on perceived product function ($N = 137$)

Product	Aspect	Age group	N	Mean	F test	Sig.
Gardenia light fixture	Function	-30	20	3.35	3.567*	0.016
		41–50	60	4.01		

*P < .05

Table 7. ANOVA for the effect of age on perceived product function ($N = 137$)

Product	Aspect	SS		df	MS	F test	Sig.
Gardenia light fixture	Function	Between groups	7.836	3	2.61	3.567*	0.016
		Within group	97.37	133	0.73		
		Sum	105.21	136			

*P < .05

Table 8. Effect of design-related background on overall product assessment ($N = 137$)

Cultural product	Item	N	Mean
Gardenia	Q10	17	3.41
light fixture	Q11	17	3.12
Gardenia	Q10	17	3.12
Aromatherapy burner	Q11	17	2.82
Pair of sheep horn-shaped cups	Q10	17	3.12
	Q11	17	3.06

Table 9. ANOVA on the effect of background on overall product assessment ($N = 137$)

Product	Item	SS		df	MS	F test	Sig.
Gardenia light fixture	Q10	Between groups	8.497	2	4.24	4.783*	0.010
		Within group	119.03	134	0.88		
		Sum	127.53	136			
	Q11	Between groups	11.153	2	5.57	5.214**	0.007
		Within group	143.31	134	1.07		
		Sum	154.46	136			
Gardenia aromatherapy burner	Q10	Between groups	19.460	2	9.73	10.65***	0.000
		Within group	122.33	134	0.91		
		Sum	141.79	136			
	Q11	Between groups	14.477	2	7.23	6.392**	0.002
		Within group	151.74	134	1.13		
		Sum	166.21	136			
Pair of sheep horn-shaped cups	Q10	Between groups	13.810	2	6.90	7.360**	0.001
		Within group	125.72	134	0.93		
		Sum	139.53	136			
	Q11	Between groups	9.808	2	4.90	4.247*	0.016
		Within group	154.71	134	1.15		
		Sum	164.52	136			

*P < .05, **P < .01, ***P < .001

Table 10. Regression analysis on the effects of participants' perceptions of product functions and emotions on how creative and ingenious they thought the products to be ($N = 137$)

Product	Aspect	B	β	t value	Sig.
Gardenia light fixture	Functional	0.373	0.339	4.897***	0.000
	Emotional	0.493	0.464	5.454***	0.000
Gardenia aromatherapy burner	Functional	0.291	0.259	0.004**	0.004
	Emotional	0.610	0.543	0.000***	0.000
Pair of sheep horn-shaped cups	Functional	0.485	0.424	5.967***	0.000
	Emotional	0.534	0.503	6.386***	0.000

*P < .05, **P < .01, ***P < .001

Table 11. Regression analysis on the effects of participants' perceptions of product functions and emotions on how they were fond of the products ($N = 137$)

Product	Aspect	B	β	t value	Sig.
Gardenia light fixture	Functional	0.563	0.464	6.563***	0.000
	Emotional	0.562	0.480	5.524***	0.000
Gardenia aromatherapy burner	Functional	0.457	0.376	4.559***	0.000
	Emotional	0.554	0.456	5.622***	0.000
Pair of sheep horn-shaped cups	Functional	0.530	0.427	6.636***	0.000
	Emotional	0.497	0.432	6.055***	0.000

*P < .05, **P < .01, ***P < .001

Table 5 shows the t-test results for the effect of gender on overall product assessment, revealing significant differences in overall assessment between male and female participants for the gardenia light fixture and gardenia aromatherapy burner. Compared with the male participants, the female participants thought the products were more creative and ingenious, and they were fonder of the products. Table 6 shows the mean analysis results for the effect of age on perceived function ($N = 137$), indicating significant differences between participants of different ages for the gardenia aromatherapy burner. The difference between perceived function for participants aged 41–50 years and for those 30 years or younger was significant at the 0.016 level. Tables 7 and 9 correspondingly show the effect of design-related background on overall assessment ($N = 137$) and one-way analysis of variance results on the effect of background on overall assessment ($N = 137$), revealing that the participants with design-related backgrounds gave the three cultural products lower overall assessment scores than those with other backgrounds (including those with art-related background). Tables 10 and 11 demonstrate that perceptions of both functions and emotions exhibited a significant effect on participants' overall assessment of the cultural products. These analysis results and the opinions of design experts can be incorporated and used as a reference when designing cultural products in the future.

4 Conclusion and Recommendations

This study demonstrated that both the functions and cultural meanings of cultural products as well as the feelings they evoke in consumers influence consumers' overall assessments of products. Chris Chang, manager of Prada Taiwan, once said that what Prada sells is a lifestyle, or a taste. Today, consumers no longer purchase products solely for their practical value; they also pay attention to the symbolic meanings of the products. Consumers will continue to purchase products if they can see cultural meanings in the products, have feelings toward them, and receive joy from them.

This study adopted a core theory of semiotics (i.e., the two orders of signification) proposed by Barthes and investigated the intangible cultural codes of, a cash crop grown in the Fuzhou area in what is now New Taipei City in the 1920s through 1940s. Subsequently, three levels of design thinking were used to translate gardenia and design cultural products based on it. Unlike the traditional design approach, which highlights physical and functional design, this study imbued the products with local cultural meanings. The study results and recommendations for future research directions are as follows.

(1) This study incorporated cultural code design methods and the three levels of design thinking to develop cultural product designs. Empirical results verified that by decoding intangible culture and transferring, transiting, and transforming cultural elements into design, cultural products with intangible meaning could be designed and developed.

(2) Future studies can reference this study to devise a procedure to design their cultural product, and apply the procedure in the creative design of cultural assets of intangible value in Taiwan, such as local operas, historical buildings, and unique local ceremonies. Such endeavors will preserve Taiwan's traditional culture, enable the development of cultural products, and facilitate local industry development, driving the regional economy.

References

Barthes, R.: Writing Degree Zero. China Times Publishing Company, Taipei (1991)

Barthes, R.: Element of Semiology. Shinning Culture Publishing Co., Taipei (1992)

Chiang, L.: Sustainable Urban Village with Infrastructure Landscape-A Case Study of Fu-Chou Area in Banquio (2013)

Chinese Text Project. https://ctext.org/zh

Clotaire, R.: The Culture Code. Broadway Books, New York (2006)

David, H.: The Cultural Industries. A Sage Publications Company, London (2002)

Edles, L.D.: Cultural Sociology in Practice. Blackwell Publishers Inc., Massachusetts (2002). P.1

Gilmore, J.H.: The Experience Economy: Work is Theatre & Every Business a Stage. Harvard Business School Press, Boston (1999)

Hsu, C.H., Chang, S.H., Lin, R.: A design strategy for turning local culture into global market products. Int. J. Affective Eng. 12, 275–283 (2013)

Kreifeldt, J., Taru, Y., Sun, M.X., Lin, R.: Cultural ergonomics beyond culture-the collector as consumer in cultural product design. In: Rau, P.L. (ed.) CCD 2016, vol. 9741, pp. 355–364. Springer, Cham (2016). https://doi.org/10.1007/978-3-319-40093-8_36

Lin, R., Kreifeldt, J.: Do Not Touch – A Conversation Between Dechnology to Humart. NTUA, New Taipei City (2014)

Lin, R., Kreifeldt, J., Hung, P.H., Chen, J.L.: From dechnology to humart – a case study of Taiwan design development. In: Rau, P.L.P. (ed.) CCD 2015. LNCS, vol. 9181, pp. 263–273. Springer, Heidelberg (2015). https://doi.org/10.1007/978-3-319-20934-0_25

Lin, R., Kreifeldt, J.G.: Ergonomics in wearable computer design. Int. J. Ind. Ergon. 27, 259–269 (2001)

Lin, R.: Transforming Taiwan aboriginal cultural features into modern product design: a case study of a cross-cultural product design model. Int. J. Des. 1, 45–53 (2007)

Lin, R.: Designing friendship into modern products. In: Toller, J.C. (ed.) Friendships: Types, Cultural, Psychological and Social, pp. 1–24. Nova Science Publishers, New York (2009)

Hsiao, M.Y.: Case study on cultural creativity and design transformation. J. Chaoyang Univ. Technol. 16, 69–90 (2011)

Ho, M.C., Lin, C.H., Liu, Y.C.: Some speculations on developing cultural commodities. J. Des. 1 (1), 1–15 (1996)

Ministry of Culture. https://www.moc.gov.tw/informationlist_285.html

National Palace Museum. https://www.npm.gov.tw/

National Cultural Heritage Database Management System. https://nchdb.boch.gov.tw/

Smith, P.: Cultural Theory: An Introduction. Massachusetts, p. 153. Blackwell Publishers Inc., Massachusetts (2001)

Patton, M.Q.: Qualitative Evaluation & Research Methods. Sage Publications, Thousand Oaks (2003)

Strauss, A., Corbin, J.: Grounded Theory in Practice. Sage, Thousand Oaks (1997)

Somekh, B., Lewin, C.: Research Methods in the Social Sciences. Sage, London (2005)

Schmitt, B.H.: Experiential Marketing: How to Get Customer to Sense, Feel, Think, Act, and Relate to Your Company and Brands. The Free Press, New York (1999)

Sapp, M.: Psychological and Educational Test Scores. Charles C Thomas Publisher, Ltd., Springfield (2002)

Taru, Y., Kreifeldt, J., Sun, M.X., Lin, R.: Thoughts on studying cultural ergonomics for the atayal loom. In: Rau, P.L. (ed.) CCD 2016. LNCS, vol. 9741, pp. 377–388. Springer, Cham (2016). https://doi.org/10.1007/978-3-319-40093-8_38

A Study on Productive Preservation and Design Innovation of Taoyuan Wood Carving

Mingxiang Shi[✉] and Simin Ren

School of Fine Arts, Hunan Normal University,
36, Lushan Street, Changsha 410081, Hunan, China
64149555@qq.com

Abstract. Taoyuan wood carving—a gem among intangible cultural heritages in Hunan Province—is deeply important to the region's folk culture. However, it is one of the folk arts that faces an urgent risk of extinction due to a sharp decline in sales, lack of a new generation of "Taoyuan artisans," and a decline in teaching skills to younger generations. Once it is lost, we will not be able to revive it. Hence, its study should facilitate its revitalization through social innovations and assist its adaptation to contemporary society, as well as integration into modern life. This article adopts the perspective of "productive preservation" in the study of Taoyuan wood carving, building a Taoyuan wood carving intangible cultural heritage knowledge platform through social innovation to digitalize and preserve intangible cultural heritage resources while also helping Taoyuan wood carving continue to shine in the modern commercial environment as a form of art by commercializing its achievements.

Keywords: Taoyuan wood carving · Productive preservation · Design innovation introduction

1 Introduction

Taoyuan woodcarving (TWC) is a form of folk wood carving rooted in the Yuan River and Li River basin, located at the tail end of the Wuling mountain range. The craft was named for the fact that most of its artisans are Taoyuan artisans from Taoyuan County. Taoyuan wood carving—a gem among intangible cultural heritages in Hunan Province—is deeply important to the region's folk culture, because it bears a rich cultural memory, as well as the sentiments, life, and faith of this region's people. However, it is one of the folk arts that faces an urgent risk of extinction due to a sharp decline in sales, lack of a new generation of "Taoyuan artisans," abandoned workshops, and decline in teaching skills to younger generations. Previous research indicates that in the 1950s, there were more than 100 wood carving artisans in Shejiaping Village alone; however, there are now less than 30 in all of Taoyuan County. Wood carving requires both physical and mental labor. According to surveys [1–4], the majority of the artisans are in their sixties. Their declining physical strength and eyesight make it difficult for them to continue their work.

© Springer Nature Switzerland AG 2019
P.-L. P. Rau (Ed.): HCII 2019, LNCS 11576, pp. 203–214, 2019.
https://doi.org/10.1007/978-3-030-22577-3_14

Taoyuan wood carving, as an intangible cultural heritage, is continuously carried forward by humans. Once it is lost, we will not be able to revive it. Hence, its study should facilitate its revitalization through social innovations and assist it in adapting to the time changes, as well as integrating it into modern life.

2 Related Work

Current studies on TWC focus on two main aspects: its history and artistic style—namely, the origins and connotations of forms and patterns in wood carving articles—and its culture. The former focuses primarily on studying and analyzing forms and pattern designs, as well as their potential use in furniture and other home applications, substantiated by fruitful results of connotation analyses of wood carving patterns. The latter mainly focuses on history, sociology, and literature. There are several notable studies on the historical origins and artistic styles of this craft: Wenchao Du studied and explored the cultural origins of wood carving and its artistic characteristics by analyzing different themes, proposing methods for its application in interior design [5]; Boxiong Lu studied the origins and developmental course of TWC, specifically exploring the themes, techniques, and connotations of representative works [6]; and Xiaoli Xie studied sculptural styles based on the materials and forms of Taoyuan wood carving, as well as its historical and cultural backgrounds [7]. The cultural aspect of research on Taoyuan wood carving has been explored by Yuehui Qi, who believed that TWC is a crucial folk-art resource and source of power for the construction of Changde's unique city culture [8]. Ping Liang adopted socio-anthropological methodology and studied 52 TWC artisans from 10 counties and urban districts in Changde City, Hunan Province through field research [9]. He researched their basic information, trajectory and mode of inheriting skills, current conditions of their artworks, current income levels, and other social activities, aiming to analyze TWC artisans' living conditions and forms of skill inheritance; this study intended to propose plans to pass on the intangible cultural heritage of this craft. Xiong Zhao compared the subject matters and techniques of Taoyuan and Huxiang wood carvings [10]. Through the lens of a shared origin between Xiang and Chu cultures, he studied the distinct cultural connotations of Huxiang wood carving.

TWC has over two thousand years of history as a folk art rooted in the Yuan River basin in northwestern Hunan Province. Nevertheless, under the pressure of market economy and modern industry, this art has been gradually declining for two primary reasons: First, the wood carving culture that accompanies the traditional agricultural lifestyle can neither keep up with the changing times, nor integrate into modern life; second, methods by which artisans pass on these skills are very fragile. It mostly relies on one-on-one teaching from masters to apprentices or among family members, with high risks of interruption or variation. Moreover, it is passed down through family lines as a marketable skill. Targeting the problems identified above, this study has two implications. First, from the prospective of the productive protection of an intangible cultural heritage, TWC must adapt to the needs of modern time, generate profit, and develop into an industry to promote its continuity and development. Therefore, there is theoretical significance for research that contributes to a knowledge platform and sharing database for TWC and encourages the sustainable development of local cultural resources through design and social innovation. Second, on the basis of preserving the original culture and unique artistic characteristics of TWC, it is of value to research to effectively transform the craft from an intangible cultural heritage into products and services through business model innovation and support for the preservation, promotion, innovation, and industrialization of traditional culture in northwest Hunan.

The research presented above mainly focused on the artistic achievement and survival status of TWC without deeply exploring how to protect this craft. Hence, this article adopts the perspective of "productive preservation" in its study of Taoyuan wood carving, building a Taoyuan wood carving intangible cultural heritage knowledge platform through social innovation to digitalize and preserve intangible cultural heritage resources while also helping this craft shine in the modern commercial environment as a form of art.

3 Research on the Intangible Cultural Heritage (ICH) of the Taoyuan Woodcarving Craft (TWC) from the Perspective of Productive Protection

This study adopted an artistic anthropological method when dealing with the issue of TWC's productive protection. In the early stage of the study, substantial research of print literature and actual artifacts were conducted. The findings obtained from these processes comprise the basis of our research. These were supplemented by field investigation methods adapted from anthropological research, such as direct and participatory observations, as well as structured and non-structured interviews. Research group members conducted systematic field investigations on the ICH of TWC to understand the population structure, production methods, consumption patterns, and social organization of the target villages. The researchers also explored the subject matter together with villagers of Taoyuan County and local TWC artisans who are non-familial inheritors of the craft to ensure that the designers identified problems with the inner perspective of the cultural holders and to find effective ways of innovating within that specific cultural ecosystem. Figure 1 shows the TWC field investigation site.

3.1 Field Investigation of the TWC Artisans

More than 50 inheritors of TWC skills from 10 county areas in Changde City were surveyed; data were gathered on their general circumstances, apprentice pedigree, method of learning the craft, current status of their craft, income, and social activities. From the findings, the first issue identified was the small number of practicing craftsmen [11]. They are advanced in age and rich in work experience, but the structure of their teams lacks rationality. In the 1950s, there were more than 100 woodcarvers in the Shejiaping Township of Taoyuan County alone; now, the entire county has fewer than 30 artisans. The average age of the artisans interviewed was 54.7 years old, 17 of which (32.7%) were over 60 years old. Of the 4 under 40 years old, 3 had left to work as migrant workers elsewhere [12]. Woodcarving involves both physical and mental

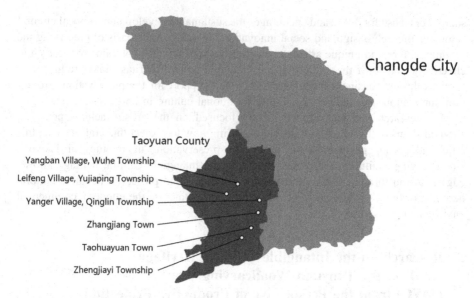

Fig. 1. Map of the TWC field investigation site

work and demands meticulous attention to details. Generally, craftsmen over 60 years old lacked the competence required for the work due to weakening physical strength, declining faculty of memory, and blurred eyesight. Most of them began learning the craft early in their lives: 13.5% of them had been in the trade for more than four decades, while 71% of them had worked for more than three decades. Despite their weakening physical states and their meager incomes, they struggled and persisted out of their deep passion for woodcarving.

The second issue was the collapse of the apprentice system through which the masters passed down their skills. There were very few apprentices. It was difficult to pass down interpretations of skills, and team succession was not implemented. During the agricultural era when transportation was inconvenient and information was lacking, the main method of passing down folk arts was the father-son relationship at home or the master-apprentice relationship in the workshop. In the age of informatization, the population's level of integration and mobility had accelerated. People's lifestyles, production methods, consumption awareness, and attitudes toward life had also changed. These had severely affected the system of passing down handicraft skills among blood relatives, family members, in-laws, or locals from the same village. Among the interviewed artisans, only a few had taken over the trade from their father. Of the woodcarvers, 75% had not trained any apprentice in the past two decades, and only three of them had apprentices over the past 15 years [13]. This was because the general population believed that they could not earn much from learning a craft and that future prospects of the trade were bleak. Young people preferred to select their own careers and be migrant workers elsewhere. Another reason was that the artisans felt that "the process of training apprentices is time-consuming and laborious, and they would leave after mastering the skills." Separately, some artisans insisted that apprentices must be family members who are related by blood, as they did not want the skills to be passed to outsiders. Various factors had led to the severe shortage of young people engaged in the folk art of TWC, leading to a situation in which there was no team succession planned. There is a worrying trend that the craft would disappear in the future if it is not passed down continuously.

The third issue identified was the sluggish market demand and the resulting lack of business, meager incomes, and team instability. During the Qing Dynasty and the era of the Republic of China, whenever the people of the Yuanli Watershed or their children got married, they would commission TWC artisans to carve decorations for the house and prepare dowry items. These included the qiangongchuang (千工床), a marital bed that requires thousands of craftsmen to make; wanggongjiao (万工轿), a bridal sedan that takes craftsmen tens of thousands of hours to complete; and shilihong jiazhuang (十里红嫁妆), which refers to the bride having so many dowry items that the procession carrying these stretches for several kilometers. Even those from lower-income families would hire the artisans to make simpler items with less ornate carvings. In the industrial age, furniture items that are mass produced by machines on a large scale have multiple design options and varieties. These items quickly monopolized the market with their low prices, causing TWC—which relies on the patronage of locals from the rural villages—to lose its unique niche and avenue of survival.

A survey conducted at Huangfengping Village in Qihe Town of Taoyuan County revealed that in the 1960s, 90% of the approximately 80 households owned furniture with decorative carved patterns. The village has 132 households today, but none had engaged a woodcarver for nearly 30 years [14]. Only one household owns a wooden carved bed. Among the interviewed craftsmen, nine had switched careers since there were no woodcarving jobs available. Another eight were in semi-retirement due to the lack of business. Those who were still clinging on to the trade were mainly creating replicas of ancient wood carvings for parks, scenic spots, temples, ancestral halls, or furniture stores (Fig. 2).

Fig. 2. Taoyuangong studio artisans (the author photographed at the field study site)

In summary, TWC artisans are presently facing a bottleneck that is difficult to break through: finding ways to innovate and develop the traditional and local culture in the context of urbanization of rural areas. The ages of permanent residents living in Taoyuan's villages are extremely polarized. Many adults have left to be migrant workers elsewhere. Psychologically, they have a blind obedience to urban modernized culture and have denied or deliberately forgotten about TWC and its representation of the traditional and local culture. These mindsets and behaviors have caused them to refrain from participating in folk cultural activities and be unwilling to accept folk arts, such that there is no one to whom the artisans could pass on their skills. At the same time, the artisans' enthusiasm to engage in and develop the craft had been seriously undermined, and they were not motivated to innovate. From the perspective of productive protection, it is necessary to encourage the artisans to actively participate in design innovation. This will transform them from being pure manual laborers to owners and co-producers of ICH, thereby making them actors and internal forces driving innovation.

3.2   Research on the TWC's Artistic Forms and Characteristics

The subjects and themes of TWC are varied and include characters, landscapes, flowers and birds, antique utensils, and decorative patterns. Character-related themes can be subdivided into historical figures (e.g., Jiang Ziya fishing, Zhang Liang formally became an apprentice to a master), operatic figures (e.g., Pan Jinlian flirting with Wu Song, poet Li Bai drunk), and religious/mythological figures (e.g., the Eight Immortals crossing the sea). Items with religious themes account for a large proportion of the works. Religions make use of folk art to convey messages, and the contents generally reflect parables that people are familiar with. Religions are a social phenomenon: ordinary people often seek a form of spiritual comfort and solace in the fantasy world of religions to extricate themselves from their own difficulties and pains [15]. This has led to the creation of many themes that represent people's desires for beauty and happiness, such as "the Eight Immortals crossing the sea," "Liu Hai playing with the golden toad," and "Guanyin carrying a child." Most TWC works embodying such themes come in complete sets, are realistically carved, and vividly depict the characters' facial expressions, movements, and even the patterns on their clothes [16].

Another considerable proportion of TWC works are small articles that reflect local customs, such as zither, Go (a chess-like game), calligraphy, and painting, which are considered to be the four arts that Chinese scholars must master; children at play; farmers cultivating the land, and abundant harvests of grains and food crops. The theme of flowering plants and fruits include plum blossoms, Chinese roses, peonies, lotuses, peaches, and pomegranates [17]. The animal theme commonly includes dragons, phoenixes, lions, bats, mandarin ducks, and butterflies. Some items depict patterns found on porcelain objects such as bottles and pots, presenting a form of antique charm. These are usually motifs of abstract geometric shapes and serve as thematic border decorations.

For the animal theme, carvings of bats and lions leave the deepest impressions. The latter represents power, dignity, and majesty; the former is bianfu (蝙蝠) in Chinese, with the second character being the homonym of good blessing and fortune (福), so it is commonly used in TWC as an auspicious symbol [18]. In the past, artisans would spend time being creative and thinking about the designs and layouts of bats, leading to a multitude of representations being showcased. Some would carve the bats' heads into that of dragons', which added a touch of mythical magic; others transformed the heads into the shape of ruyi (如意), a ceremonial scepter representing auspiciousness; some carved bats in the shape of butterflies, making the scene lively and interesting while others used abstract techniques to present decorative beauty, such that those who looked at the carvings could not help but admire the artisans' originality and ingenuity.

Hand-crafted items that are most closely related to the people's lives are often the most succinctly designed for purpose of convenience and ease of use. However, it is precisely these items that manifest the artisans' level of craftsmanship. In general, artistic creations by artisans are the materialization of beauty found in local quaint customs. It is not about the flaunting one's power or showing off one's mastery of brilliant technical skills; rather, the aim is to express meaning in a simple and straightforward way and to achieve a decorative effect that is simple and down to earth. Most of these woodcarving works are coarse, unrefined, wild, and uncouth, with some even bearing the marks of axes and carving knives. Yet, such seemingly rough qualities are actually manifestations of the artisans' true skills. There is an impeccable natural beauty about these works: coarse but not botched, unrefined but not mediocre, wild but not untamed, and uncouth but not inelegant. Folk wood carvings are precious exactly due to their being coarse, unrefined, wild, and uncouth.

The traditional approach of shifting perspective and mobile focal points are adopted in the composition, with the carved objects arranged in an orderly and proportionate manner depending on the scale of the scene portrayed, with the juxtaposition of real and imaginary situations. The main subjects, birds, and flowers are usually placed at the center of the scene for prominence with magnified forms, while the sizes of the secondary characters would be reduced to complement the main theme. This approach creates a clear distinction between the main and supporting subjects, resulting in a fast, rhythmic effect. The artisans may not deeply understand the theories of composition such, as juxtaposing the real and imaginary, matching black and white, or dense versus sparse arrangements. However, their carvings are densely packed and visually overwhelming, with the entire scene filled with details. Some scenes are even completely filled with various characters and patterns, leaving no empty space. Although the finished products look unrefined, these reveal an abundant, simple, and genuine artistic conception. These give people a sense of satiation and actuality compared to the ethereal beauty of Western paintings and modern art. Figure 3 shows the TWC works.

Fig. 3. The TWC works (the author photographed in the Taoyuangong studio)

In summary, although TWC has its unique artistic value, integrating it into modern living to achieve economic benefits is a difficult process. For productive protection, the key issue is establishing the means to effectively transform ICH outputs into products and services through business model innovations, while preserving TWC's inherent cultural and artistic features. The next step was to study and propose an appropriate productive protection strategy.

4 Productive Protection Strategy for TWC

4.1 Establishing an ICH Knowledge Platform for the TWC's Productive Protection

The core of the entire digital preservation project was the establishment of the ICH knowledge database for TWC, which is connected to the Web via computers. In his book Big Data, Viktor Mayer-Schönberger pointed out that "data has become a form of commercial capital that can create new economic benefits. With a change in mindset, data can be ingeniously used to inspire new products and types of services [19]." The digitization work being undertaken currently will bring about unlimited potential for the subsequent design innovation and application of TWC. The applications of the craft are limited to traditional furniture and building supplies, and the scope of development for the industrial model of traditional woodcarving is similarly limited. The short-comings are reflected in several areas. First, the mechanism for diversified and innovative development—evolving from handicrafts to products of traditional arts and crafts, and finally to contemporary products with innovative designs—has not been formed. Second, there is no public service platform that strikes a balance between the preservation of the original cultural ecology and the internationalization of innovative designs and industrial transformation. Third, TWC artisans have limited abilities for independent innovation and market expansion and have yet to form an influential brand and production base.

The establishment of the ICH knowledge platform for TWC was guided by the industrial needs of woodcarving. It provides important information support for related industries to undertake digitization, informatization, and product design, as well as a comprehensive, rich, and diversified industrial chain. These support existing artisans in establishing and developing their brands and will help to groom a new batch of talents with an innovative spirit to undertake design innovation and carry on the TWC tradition. The digitized platform—based in Hunan to provide the entire industry with localized services—will contribute by promoting development of the local economy and culture.

4.2 Details on the ICH Knowledge Platform for TWC

The establishment of the ICH knowledge platform for TWC involved three main aspects. The first was the establishment of a TWC basic database, with the aim of it being a unique thematic database for knowledge sharing. The vision was to create a professional knowledge database that integrates TWC culture and techniques, based on information retrieved from literature searches and collected from field investigations. Next was the establishment of a resource database of case samples. It was determined that the structure for the development of TWC applications required multiple domains and diversified data; then, information technology was used to collect, store, and organize the resources. The specifications for establishing a shared data resource library and related designs were then finalized to ensure that the case samples can be reused indefinitely. This will address the lack of a resource library for the design and development of derivative products from woodcarving, as well as a thematic case resource library oriented towards domain applications [20]. The last was the setting up of a TWC portal website that acts as the social portal for the digital platform. is shown in Fig. 4.

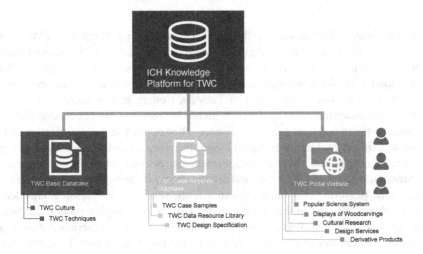

Fig. 4. Details on the ICH knowledge platform

4.3 Steps for Establishing the ICH Knowledge Platform for TWC

- **Analysis of the platform's orientation.** The target vision for the ICH knowledge platform for TWC was to integrate the various main modules, including a popular science system, displays of woodcarvings, cultural research, systems for derivative products, design services, and innovation promotion. The database combines the dual functions of a digital museum and a library of industrial application materials, thereby becoming a platform for sharing of cultural resources, improving the efficiency of design applications, and catalyzing rational innovation.
- **Functions of the platform.** The platform for propagating and promoting woodcarving was built upon a public application framework and oriented toward the industry. It provides a source platform for obtaining resources and inspirations, promoting cultural integration, displaying of products, and facilitating business cooperation. This helps to create a digital brand for TWC. At the same time, the business model and operational activities of the users' website could be explored while taking into account its developmental stage and users' characteristics. is shown in Fig. 5.

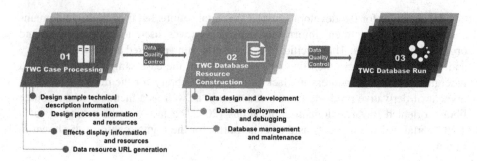

Fig. 5. Framework of the ICH knowledge platform

- **Design innovation based on the ICH knowledge platform for TWC.** The databases to be built include a digital museum for TWC's case samples and a library of materials used in the craft. Considering the current crisis of the decline of TWC, an important topic of cultural preservation is to ensure that the woodcarving craft culture goes beyond the confines of Taoyuan County so that more people know about and understand it. The digital museum is crucial to the knowledge dissemination platform and is of great significance when applied to the preservation of the woodcarving craft. First, it is digital-based, therefore it has the advantages of large storage capacity and diverse storage methods. Second, there is no longer any restriction in terms of regionality and distance because the collection is displayed on an online platform. This infinitely expands the scope for propagating knowledge and culture. This is further enhanced by the various display modes, including pictorial, textual, audio, and video. This will allow users to experience the collection in a comprehensive, multi-perspective, and in-depth manner. Last, the museum's system for derivative products can provide new ideas for the innovative development of woodcarving.

The library of woodcarving materials serves as an application platform for related industries and can be considered a general resource sharing platform. Users can search for resources matching their needs and then download and use them. Its existence can greatly improve the work efficiency of related industries. It aims to realistically and completely vectorize traditional woodcarving patterns and standardize the traditional style of the patterns, thereby establishing a cultural framework for the reuse of patterns and prevention of deviation when the graphics are used. This is also one of the ways that the platform is participating in design. Moreover, with the integration of CAM technology, the downloaded materials are in formats that can be directly used in production, which greatly reduces the gap between culture and the market. This reduction in the distance between culture and products will further promote the propagation of culture to a great extent is shown in Fig. 6.

Systematic research on Taoyuan wood carving (TWC) and its social innovation is conducted by combining the study of art works and literature review through a cultural anthropology perspective. The craft may be combined with modern design methodology, and its application will be attempted in real life based on the results of theoretical studies. The detailed methodology is as follows: Study the functions and forms

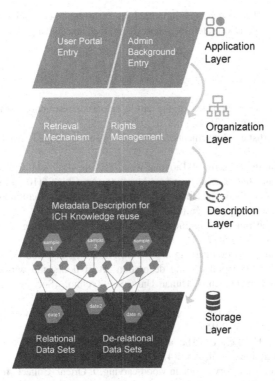

Fig. 6. Framework of digital museum for TWC's case samples conclusion

of TWC in furniture, interior design, and other goods through a literature review to gather explicit knowledge on the local culture, folk customs, and lifestyles; adopt methodologies from anthropological research and conduct field studies at TWC markets and workshops to discover and learn about the techniques and skills involved in TWC; gather tacit knowledge, including idea generation, subject matter selection, and creating process by conducting structured and unstructured interviews or participatory observation with artisans. On this basis, the building of a TWC knowledge platform includes two parts: Building a TWC database through methods such as literature sorting, on-site data collection, and normalized data centralization to integrate knowledge resources on the craft such as its subjects, sculpting styles, techniques, and categories. This process yields an extraction of intangible cultural heritage knowledge from cultural and technical perspectives. Building a TWC digital database using 3D scanning, 3D modeling, and photography is a study on the preservation and inheritance of intangible cultural heritage knowledge using digital tools. Future research is necessary to understand the essence of Taoyuan intangible cultural heritage knowledge by using distinct methods such as image scaling, semantic space, adjective extraction, and context paneling to determine the design components of TWC through symbolic ambiguity mechanisms and help them conform to modern design culture and aesthetic notion. This also includes building a symbol system for TWC works and using it as a foundation to achieve design transformation.

Acknowledgement. This research is supported by National Social Science Fund of China program (17BG149). We also gratefully acknowledge the financial support.

References

1. Qi, Y.: Changed characteristics of the city's cultural construction of folk-art resources. J. Wuling **6**(37), 65–69 (2012)
2. Zhao, X.: The artistic achievements of Taoyuan wood carving. J. Art China **3**(7), 82–90 (2014)
3. Lu, B.: Study on the art form of Taoyuan wood carving. J. Orient. Collect., 30–46 (2011)
4. Xie, X.: Aesthetic study of Taoyuan wood carving. Art China **5**(10), 113–120
5. Jing Zheng, D.: A study on the Hunan folk furniture. PhD thesis, Central South University of Forestry and Technology, Hunan (2006)
6. Wang, X.: On the practical significance of Huxiang wood carving. J. Hunan Univ. Sci. Technol. (Soc. Sci. Ed.) **5**(17), 166–175 (2014)
7. Chen, X.: Hunan folk wood carving art. J. Nat. Art **2**(20), 176–185 (1994)
8. Ying, J., Xie, R.: On wood carving decoration art of doors and windows of traditional dwellings in southern Hunan. J. Hunan Univ. Sci. Technol. (Soc. Sci. Ed.) **9**(18), 99–109 (2008)
9. Liang, P.: Study on the current situation of Taoyuan wood carving artists. J. Mingsu Mingfeng **7**(11), 59–65 (2015)
10. Tang, L., Wen, H., Lei, F.: The application of Taoyuan wood carving art in visual communication design. J. Lit. Art **2**(4), 170–177 (2012)
11. Yi, M.: The theme and story of hunan wood carving. J. Orient. Collect. **4**(10), 78–87 (2013)
12. Xiang, R.: Hunan folk woodcarving regional artistic characteristics. J. Lit. Art Res. **5**(10), 161–168 (2012)
13. Zhou, J.: Hunan Woodcarving, 1st edn. Hunan Fine Arts Publishing House, Changsha (2000)
14. Zhu, Y.: Study on wood carving decoration of folk architecture. J. Inter. Des. **1**(10), 35–44 (2014)
15. Li, J., Ying, J.: Taoyuan folk wood carving art. J. Central South Univ. (Soc. Sci. Ed.) **4**(2), 84–90 (2003)
16. Zhang, D., Ji, T.: Collaborative design "Trigger" revival of traditional community. J. Zhuangshi **12**(284), 26–28 (2016)
17. Sanders, N., Stappers, P.: Co-creation and the new landscapes of design. J. CoDesign **4**(1), 5–18 (2014)
18. Qiu, C.: Productive protection: 'self-hematopoiesis' of intangible cultural heritage. J. China Cult. Daily **2**(21), 15–18 (2012)
19. Manzini, E., Zhong, F.: Design, When Everybody Designs, 1st edn. Electronic Industry Press, Beijing (2016)
20. Luo, S., Dong, Y.: Integration and management method of cultural artifacts knowledge for cultural creative design. J. Comput. Integr. Manuf. Syst. **4**(24), 964–977 (2018)

Research on the Audience's Cognition and Preference of the Styles of Chinese Landscape Paintings

Jun Wu[1,2]([⊠]), Jiede Wu[1,2], and Po-Hsien Lin[2]

[1] Department of Animation, School of Journalism and Communication,
Anhui Normal University, Wuhu 22058, People's Republic of China
junwu2006@hotmail.com, 125082357@qq.com
[2] Graduate School of Creative Industry Design,
National Taiwan University of Arts, Xinpei 22058, Taiwan
to131@ntua.edu.tw

Abstract. The main purpose of the research is to explore the audience's cognition of the styles of Chinese landscape paintings through a case study of Chinese landscape paintings. Taking five landscape paintings of different styles created by the author at Hongcun Town of Huangshan as samples of the research, 127 respondents from the online community were invited to take part in the research. Eight styles were selected such as elegant and primitive, composed and powerful, ethereal, vigorous and smooth, wild and cold to describe the styles of Chinese landscape paintings and evaluate the ordinary audience's cognition of these styles. The results indicate: 1. The twelve styles introduced in the ancient theory of painting can be used as evaluation criteria for the contemporary Chinese landscape paintings, which are positively related with the preference of the works. 2. The twelve styles show certain clustering effects, which can generally be divided into two categories. 3. The artistic conception of the works is highly related with the preference of the works.

Keywords: Chinese landscape paintings · Cognition of styles ·
Difference of preference

1 Introduction

As a sentence in the Analects of Confucius goes, "The benevolent like mountains and the wise like waters". Chinese landscape paintings have secured a special position in the world's history of arts for their profound artistic conception, unique painting language, delicate and diversified styles and charm, image-based expression. They are either grand and marvelous, elegant and lofty, luxuriant and mild, silent and peaceful, or as vibrant as a surge of cloud, or as quiet and tranquil as a mirror. Bing Zong, a painter of Song of the Southern dynasties said, "One can comprehend the Tao when his mind is quiet and peaceful, one's mind can travel far when he is appreciating paintings while sitting or lying". Xi Guo of Song Dynasty said in his works The Elegance of the Bamboo and Spring, "The people of the world have reached a conclusion that we can walk, observe from a height, enjoy sightseeing or find habitat in mountains and

© Springer Nature Switzerland AG 2019
P.-L. P. Rau (Ed.): HCII 2019, LNCS 11576, pp. 215–225, 2019.
https://doi.org/10.1007/978-3-030-22577-3_15

waters." Chinese landscape paintings feature an elegant and attractive style, which are not only artistic creations full of aesthetic appeal, but also a carrier for men of literature and writing to express their feelings and aspirations. As a unique product of ancient civilization, Chinese paintings carry the spiritual characteristics and aesthetic kernel of Chinese culture and manifest the humankind's cognition of the nature, society and other associated areas such as philosophy, literature and arts. However, in terms of international propagation, the spreading and exporting of Chinese painting works have been emphasized, while the promotion of the spirit of Chinese paintings has been neglected. It is insufficient in width and depth [1, 2]. Chinese paintings convey feelings and ideas, with which scholars and literati express their feelings, pursue aesthetic appeal, emphasize "artistic conception" and "romantic charm", manifest certain personality charm and humanistic spirit, and the heart and feelings of the painters [3]. In different periods, influenced by the social culture, the aesthetic connotation unique to Chinese paintings have found different expressions and comprehensions [4]. The audience of Chinese paintings are mainly scholars and literati who emphasize romantic charm and even advocate that romantic charm can be comprehended but cannot be explained. This seriously limits its propagation. As time passes, Chinese paintings are not so popularized among the common audience. Wu [5] pointed out that, due to the unique way of creation, elegant aesthetics system and limited means of Chinese paintings propagation, the general public has fallen into an aesthetic dilemma of Chinese paintings as global digitization is speeding up. We should carry on the efforts on aesthetic education of Chinese paintings and further their promotion and spreading. Therefore, Chinese landscape paintings are known as a symbol of elegance for their high artistic and cultural value. Besides, most of them are an expression of images, pursuing a realm of a vivid artistic conception, emphasizing resemblance in spirit but neglecting the forms. This has caused certain difficulty to the common audience in appreciating the works. While aesthetics is being promoted among all people, how should we make the common audience better appreciate and spread the traditional culture? There are many factors influencing the audience's perception and cognition of artworks, of which style is a key one and an important and complex topic. On the cognition of the styles of Chinese landscape paintings, the current research mainly covers the following aspects.

a. Twelve styles were selected from the *Twenty-four Styles of Chinese Paintings* to evaluate the audience's cognition of the styles of Chinese landscape paintings;
b. The audience's preference and cognition of different styles of Chinese landscape paintings.

2 Literature Review

2.1 Inheritance of Painting Theories

He Xie of South Qi Dynasty proposed in Six Principles of Chinese Painting (around 490 AD), "There are six techniques of Chinese painting, which are lively spirit and charm, brush using techniques, shaping in resemblance to real objects, use of colors according to the category, management of positions and imitation of existing works." These six techniques, as important principles for the evaluation and commenting of Chinese paintings, have been carried on and developed by theorists and authors of later generations and times. Huaiguan Zhang of Tang Dynasty proposed in the Notes on Evaluation of Painting Works (around 725 AD) that like the beauty of a person, the beauty of Chinese paintings is reflected in three levels, namely, spirit, bone and flesh. Xiufu Huang of Song Dynasty proposed in Four Qualities (1006 AD) that Chinese paintings have four qualities, "elegance, spirit, wonderfulness and vigor". Daochun Liu of Song Dynasty proposed six requirements and six advantages in *Comments on Famous Paintings of Song Dynasty* (around 1080 AD), "The so-called requirements are sufficient spirit and charm, mature pattern and system, rational changes, smooth and glossy colors, natural and smooth transition and absorbing the merits and abandoning the shortcomings. The so-called six advantages are being rough but following the law of brush and ink applying, being uncomplicated in brush applying techniques but conveying talent, being exquisite and smart but displaying force and strength, being wild and bizarre but showing rationality, applying no ink but achieving a dyeing effect, flat painting to display length." Yue Huang of Qing Dynasty proposed in Twenty-four Styles of Chinese Painting (around 1,800 AD), "The so-called twenty-four styles of Chinese paintings are spirit and charm, ingenious, elegant and primitive, vigorous and smooth, composed and powerful, harmonious, tranquil and far-reaching, simple, unconventional, odd, free, incisive, wild and cold, clear and open, spiritual, natural, secluded, clear and bright, robust and straight, brief, prudent, refreshing, ethereal and graceful" [5]. The aforesaid indicate that the principles of ancient China for the commenting and evaluation of paintings kept changing, enriching and growing and reached the peak in Qing Dynasty. Other than these painting theories, there are also many arguments of other painters and scholars which will not be stated here due to the limitation of space. The arguments on landscape paintings include *Preface to Landscape Paintings* by Zong Bing of Song of Southern and Northern Dynasties, *Narration on Paintings* by Wei Wang of Song of Southern and Northern Dynasties and *Notes on Brush Applying Techniques* by Jing Hao of the Five Dynasties. Considering that the research is mainly focused on the styles of landscape paintings, the *Twenty-four Styles of Paintings* by Yue Huang of Qing Dynasty is selected.

2.2 Inheritance of Cultural Implications

Nowadays the demands of customers in products have shifted from attention to pragmatic functions and appearances to a pursuit of the meanings and recognition behind the products, or the ideas and concepts, lifestyle or spiritual resonance conveyed by the works [7]. Liao [8] pointed out that the ultimate purpose of designing products is to provide customers with material functions, and more importantly a sense of security. Cultural information is infused into design to meet the spiritual demands of customers and highlight the cultural meanings of the works and carry forward cultural aesthetics. Cultural meanings and aesthetics are important attributes of products. Cultural meanings are expressed by applying cultural symbols (cultural elements) [9]. Barthes [10] pointed out, "cultural code" or "cultural symbol" is one of the functional codes of narrative texts. Chen and Yang [11] argued that by creating and applying cultural codes, we can promote the renewal and regeneration of culture and achieve differentiation and hierarchy. Such kind of differentiation can continue to be created in the use of codes and promote the cultural level. Cultural meanings are transformed and applied and turned into various concrete manifestations, which are well received by the audience and strengthen the recognition by customers or increase the added value. This is the application of cultural industry as well as where the values of knowledge economy lie. Creating cultural values is itself a process of digesting knowledge, creating forms, defining audience and cultural marketing, which requires a foundation of broad and deep cultural background [12].

2.3 Presentation of Styles

Lin [13] pointed out that only works with distinctive styles can be competitive in the market. In terms of artistic creation, different intentions of the authors will create different characteristics. Such kind of difference is classified as some feature or image based on its characteristics, which is also known as "style" [14]. The works with the same style display some common elements in external representations or techniques, carry on some common rules and share some common characteristics and image perception [15]. Arts are a manifestation of culture, while style is the most distinctive characteristic of the culture [16]. The research of styles is an exploration of the similarity and difference of works [17]. After a group of people encodes the external forms of styles and images, the internal feelings and meanings of styles and images are interpreted by a systematic mechanism analysis and summary [18]. The judging of styles is a process of categorizing. After each example of the categories undergoes the action of paradigm effect, the best paradigm will be taken as the prototype. By exploring the paradigm and prototype of styles, it helps us understand the logic behind the construction of styles and images [14, 19, 20]. The designers encode the meanings on the basis of external forms, materialize the cultural characteristics and meanings and create the cultural images and identification of the products. Customers experience the symbolic significance and culture by perceiving and decoding the external forms [21]. Lin and Lee [22] pointed out that artists express their creative concepts by internal transformation and external forms and the artists and the audience establish a positive exchange as the works are appreciated and understood by the audience.

3 Methodology

3.1 Research Subject

The author has created 24 Chinese landscape paintings of Hongcun, Huangshan, Anhui, which display traditional and modern styles. Experts were invited to classify these works into five categories based on their styles. Experts were invited to vote on the works of each style. The works that got more votes than others were selected to represent the style. So 5 landscape paintings were selected, which were labeled as P1 to P5.

3.2   Questionnarire Design

The *Twenty-four Styles of Chinese Paintings* by Huang Yue were adopted, which include spirit and charm, ingenious, elegant and primitive, vigorous and smooth, composed and powerful, harmonious, tranquil and far-reaching, simple, unconventional, odd, free, incisive, wild and cold, clear and open, spiritual, natural, secluded, clear and bright, robust and straight, brief, prudent, refreshing, ethereal and graceful. 12 experts (3 professors, 6 associate professors, 3 doctoral students) were invited to select 12 styles considered by them as the most important. A total of 13 styles were selected by more than 6 of the experts, which were in sequence: style and charm, simple, ingenious, unconventional, secluded, ethereal, vigorous and smooth, tranquil and far-reaching, spiritual, clear and bright, elegant and primitive, prudent and refreshing. Based on the interpretation of each principle given in the painting theory, the above principles were explained with words which are easy to be understood by the common audience and retain the original meaning. Common respondents were invited to perform a test to further correct and modify those difficult to understand. So the following results were obtained in the end, disposition and charm, simple and naive, creativity and ingenuity, extraordinary and refined, deep and profound, concise and smart, heavy and smooth, modest and foresighted, natural, clear and bright, classical and elegant, prudent and particular, realistic and imitated.

Since disposition and charm is a general evaluation of the works, the other 12 descriptions were taken as the evaluation criteria for the styles of landscape paintings and labeled in sequence as f1 to f12. The respondents were asked to score the five landscape paintings on a five-point scale. They could score 5 if they believed that the works were most consistent with the evaluation criteria, and score 1 for the works that were most inconsistent with the evaluation criteria. Finally, the respondents were asked to pick a favorite one from the works.

3.3   Respondents

127 valid questionnaires were obtained, including 38 males (29.9%) and 89 females (70.1%). 43 of them aged between 20 and 29 (33.9%), 33 aged below 19 (26%), 21 of them aged more than 50 (16.5%), and 15 respondents aged between 30 and 39 and another 15 aged between 40 and 49. Their professional backgrounds: 67 in arts and design related majors (52.8%), 20 from other majors (15.7%), 17 from the majors of calligraphy and painting (13.4%), 13 studied liberal arts (10.2%), 10 studied science and engineering related majors (7.9%). Their education level: 63 were undergraduates (49.6%), 23 with other education levels (18.1%), 22 masters (17.3%) and 19 doctors (15%).

4   Research Results and Discussion

4.1   Reliability and Validity Analysis

The validity analysis reveals that the KMO coefficient is .921, a relatively high value, Sig value is .000, highly significant, the eigenvalue is 7.11, which can interpret

60.404% of the variances of predefined purpose. The factor loading of each question ranges from .387 to .799 and the communality ranges from .150 to .638. The questionnaire presents a good construct validity. The reliability analysis of the questionnaire is made to evaluate the internal consistency of each perspective of the questionnaire and the reduction of Cronbach's α in each dimension after a single question is deleted, which is used as a reference standard for the selection of questions and evaluating the reliability of the questionnaire. The analysis of the questionnaire reveals: the Cronbach's α is .916. The total correlation between each perspective of styles and characteristics and the correction of a single question ranges from .358 to .742. The Cronbach's α after the deletion of a single question ranges from .906 to .913, which indicates that the internal consistency of the questions is rather high and the choice of questions is reasonable.

4.2   Analysis of Styles of Works

A matrix was established with the original data. The mean score of the five landscape paintings in 12 different styles was worked out. Through MDS analysis (Fig. 1), our purpose was to analyze their distribution by employing the perceptual mapping and study the cognitive space of five landscape paintings and 12 styles. The results of MDS analysis reveal that the stress coefficient is .02431, less than 0.25, which indicates that the stress coefficient and adaptability are very good. The determination coefficient RSQ is .98801, near 1.0. Therefore, in assigning the original attribute data, it shows a rather high conformity, indicating that two dimensions are suitable for depicting the spatial relation between the five works and 12 styles [23].

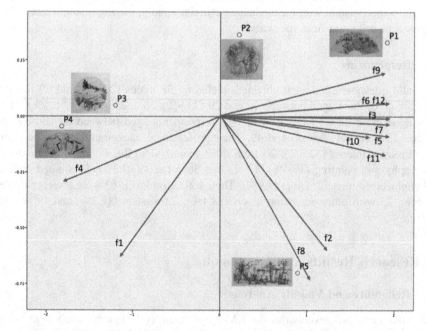

Fig. 1. MDS spatial distribution map of 5 landscape paintings and 12 styles

The two-dimension spatial axial diagram of the five works is shown as Fig. 1. The included angle of the axial diagram of each style was analyzed with multiple regression to obtain the cognitive spatial maps of 12 styles. It reveals: (1) The 12 styles are distributed in the first, third and fourth quadrants, of which f6 (vigorous and smooth) overlays with f12 (realistic and imitated). (2) P3 and P4 rest in the second and third quadrants and form a cluster, which shows similar attributes in styles. (3) P1 and P2 rest in the first quadrant, sharing some common attributes. However, their spatial distribution indicates that their styles are different to a certain extent. (4) P5 stands in the fourth quadrant alone, whose style is distinctively different from that of the other works.

After drawing a spatial map of attributes, the degree of style attributes of each landscape painting was further explored. The distance between the vector projection point from landscape paintings to the attributes and the original point was worked out. The OD distance in the MSD map is the distance from landscape paintings to the level of attributes. The formula for working out OD distance is shown in Fig. 2. The value of b2/b1 is the slope of the vector. The vector projection of D on the original point shows the strength of characteristic, with the vector contributing to the attributes of the works [24].

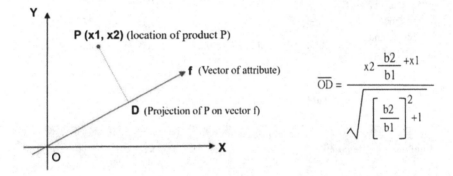

$$\overline{OD} = \frac{x2 \dfrac{b2}{b1} + x1}{\sqrt{\left[\dfrac{b2}{b1}\right]^2 + 1}}$$

Fig. 2. OD distance formula function

Table 1 shows the OD distance value of each of the 9 landscape paintings in the 8 vectors of style attributes. Taking vigorous and smooth (f6) as an example, P1 is the highest and its distance is largest in the twelve style attributes f1 to f12 and is highest in simple (f1), unconventional (f3), secluded (f4), ethereal (f5), modest and foresighted (f7), clear and bright (f9), classical and elegant (f10), prudent (f11) and realistic and imitated (f12). In the ingenious (f2), P4 and P5 are the highest and the distance is the same. In spiritual (f8), P5 is the highest.

The exploratory factor analysis was employed to test the relations between the potential variances and twelve style attributes. The eigenvalue of the two factors is bigger than 1 and the total variance is 77.887, shown in Table 2. Two clusters are formed, one being f7, f5, f12, f6, f10, f3, f9, f11 and f4, corresponding to the works P1; the other being f8, f1, f2, corresponding to the works P5. The styles of the two clusters display internal correlation. The works most prominent in each style attribute and their average score are also listed in Table 4, which indicates that P1 is highest in f1, f3, f4, f5, f6, f7, f9, f10, f11 and f2, P5 is highest in f2 and f8, but lowest in f1, which means that this style is stronger.

Table 1. Distance between projection point from five landscape paintings to style attribute vectors and the original point

		P1	P2	P3	P4	P5
Simple	f1	1.39	0.42	-0.66	-1.10	-0.04
Ingenious	f2	0.94	-0.15	-0.79	-1.11	1.11
Unconventional	f3	1.91	0.21	-1.20	-1.82	0.91
Secluded	f4	1.89	0.34	-1.09	-1.70	0.56
Ethereal	f5	1.85	0.17	-1.20	-1.80	0.98
Vigorous and smooth	f6	1.93	0.24	-1.19	-1.82	0.85
Modest and fore-sighted	f7	1.89	0.20	-1.20	-1.82	0.93
Spiritual	f8	0.63	-0.22	-0.62	-0.84	1.04
Clear and bright	f9	1.93	0.30	-1.15	-1.78	0.69
Classical and ele-gant	f10	1.84	0.16	-1.19	-1.80	0.99
Prudent	f11	1.79	0.13	-1.18	-1.77	1.03
Realistic and imi-tated	f12	1.93	0.24	-1.19	-1.82	0.85

Table 2. Factor analysis of the 12 styles

Fundamental Relations	Factor Loading		Works	Style Attributes
	Factor1	Factor2		
Modest and foresighted(f7)	.997	.032		Modest and fore-sighted
Ethereal(f5)	.992	.097		Ethereal
Realistic and imitated(f12)	.991	-.070		Realistic and imi-tated
Vigorous and smooth(f6)	.989	-.068		Vigorous and smooth
Classical and elegant(f10)	.983	.110	P1	Classical and elegant
Unconventional(f3)	.982	.013		Unconventional
Clear and bright(f9)	.948	-.261		Clear and bright
Prudent(f11)	.946	.180		Prudent
Secluded(f4)	-.892	.419		Secluded
Spiritual(f8)	.407	.823		Spiritual
Simple(f1)	-.585	.777		Simple
Ingenious(f2)	.614	.746	P5	Ingenious
Eigenvalues	9.346	2.145		
% of Variance	77.887	17.877		
Cumulative %	77.887	95.764		

4.3   General Evaluation of the Works

The general evaluation of the spirit and charm of every work is shown in Table 3. The comparison of the average values indicates that P1 > P5 > P2 > P3 > P4, the average scores of P1 and P5 being the highest. The respondents were asked to select a favorite one from the five works. The result is shown in Table 4, which indicates P1 > P5 > P3 > P2 > P4. The popularity of the works is relatively consistent with the ranking of the scores of spirit and charm in Table 3, which indicates that the evaluation of the spirit and charm of works by the respondents is correlated with their preference of landscape paintings to a certain extent.

Table 3. The Ranking of the Degree of style and charm

Rank	1	2	3	4	5
No	P1>	P5>	P2>	P3>	P4
Product					
Mean Scores	4.024	3.740	3.598	3.449	3.370

Table 4. The favorite one from the works

Rank	1	2	3	4	5
No	P1>	P5>	P3>	P2>	P4
Product					
N (%)	35 (27.6)	33 (26)	25 (19.7)	21 (16.5)	13 (10.2)

5   Research Conclusion and Suggestions

Only The evaluation results of five landscape paintings by the 127 respondents reveal that:

a. The twelve styles show certain clustering effects, of which the styles modest and foresighted, ethereal, realistic and imitated, vigorous and smooth, classical and elegant, unconventional, clear and bright, prudent and secluded are classified in a category, while spiritual, simple and ingenious are classified in the other category;

b. The twelve styles are effective for the evaluation of the styles of landscape paintings. The works most popular among the audience got higher scores in the aforesaid twelve styles, which show positive correlation;

c. The styles spiritual, clear and bright are two typical styles. Their scores are correlated with the preference of the audience in landscape paintings;
d. The audience's evaluation of the spirit and charm of works is highly correlated with
their preference in the works. The top evaluation criteria which have been carried on
for thousands of years from the ancient theories on painting are still applicable in
the contemporary era.

Suggestions: The evaluation criteria for works in the ancient painting theories of
China are mostly straightforward evaluation and cannot cover all style aspects, which
still need to be further explored to perfect the evaluation criteria of the styles of Chinese
landscape paintings. Besides, the current research is only an exploration into the
audience's cognition of the styles. More researches need to be done on how the twelve
styles contribute to the overall cognitive difference of the respondents and how
respondents with different backgrounds perceive the styles of landscape paintings.

References

1. Chen, Y.: Inheritance and spreading of Chinese paintings and innovative application
research. Guangxi Soc. Sci. **258**(12), 209–211 (2016)
2. Zhang, W.: Research on the strategy for spreading Chinese Paintings under the China-
ASEAN background. Hundred Sch. Art **9**, 222–224 (2017)
3. Liang, Y.: Exploration on appreciation and spreading of Chinese Paintings under multiple
cultural backgrounds. J. Mudanjiang Educ. Coll. **147**(5), 115–136 (2014)
4. Mo, J.: Get out of the swamp of "Chinese Painting". Art Observation **3**, 20 (2012)
5. Wu, J.: Dilemma, opportunities and breakthrough of public aesthetics of Chinese Paintings
in contemporary era–taking water-and-ink animation as an example. Paint. Calligr. World
(2), 77–78 (2017)
6. Yu, K.: Collection of Chinese Painting Theories. Huazheng Book Company, Taipei (1975)
7. Yan, H.Y., Lin, P.H., Lin, R.T.: Exploration of perceptual features of cultural and creative
products. J. Percept. **1**, 34–61 (2014)
8. Liao, J.H.: Cultural code and its application in product design. Packag. Eng. **28**(7), 145–147
(2007)
9. Hung, P.H., Lin, P.H.: Exploration of the styles of cultural and creative products in Taiwan.
J. Arts (101), 79–105 (2017)
10. Barthes, R.: S/Z: An Essay. (Trans. Richard Miller). Hill & Wang, New York (1974)
11. Chen, H.F., Yang, Y.Z.: From collection of cultural relics to value creation of cultural and
creative products–taking the cooperation between the imperial palace and Wanshi. Book Inf.
J. **14**(1), 115–149 (2016)
12. Hsieh, P.H., Fan, L.C.: Exploring the design thinking of cultural creative products on visual
arts segment. J. Des. Sci. **10**(1), 69–89 (2007)
13. Lin, R.T.: Exploration of perception experience design from innovative thinking of service.
Des. Res. **14**(S), 13–31 (2011)
14. Chen, J.Z.: Exploring cognition and judgement of chinese and western design styles taking
chair design as an example. J. Des. **6**(2) (2001)
15. Chen, C.C.: The application of grey multiple attribute decision-making method on style
typicality evaluation-using modern loop chair designs as examples. J. Des. **8**(1), 65–82
(2003)

16. Chen, C.H., Cheng, Y.P.: A study on side and arm chairs of ming dynasty using the theory of style. J. Des. **10**(4), 87–105 (2005)
17. Ross, S.D.: A Theory of Art. State University of New York, New York (1982)
18. Kao, C.H.: Exploring the relationship between the style and image and the goggles feature - from the style of prototype. J. Des. **7**(1), 33–47 (2002)
19. Jansson, D.G., Condoor, S.S., Brock, H.R.: Cognition in design: viewing the hidden side of the design process. Environ. Plan. B: Plan. Des. **19**, 257–271 (1992)
20. Rosch, E.: Cognitive reference points. Cogn. Psychol. **7**, 535–547 (1975)
21. Chen, J.Z., Shen, Z.X.: Research on the preference of customers in innovative design of traditional culture–taking the design of cultural dolls as an example. J. Arts (89), 127–150 (2011)
22. Lin, R.T., Lee, S.: Poetic and Picturesque–Sharing of Working Experience of Beauty of Xianyun. Yuchen Business Corporation (2015)
23. Lin, Z.Y.: Multivariate Analysis. Best-WisePublishingCo., Ltd., Taipei (2007)
24. Lin, P.-H., Yeh, M.-L.: The construction of cultural impressions for the idea of cultural products. In: Rau, P.-L.P. (ed.) CCD 2018. LNCS, vol. 10912, pp. 212–224. Springer, Cham (2018). https://doi.org/10.1007/978-3-319-92252-2_16

Cross-Cultural User Experience

UsabEU: Online Platform for Translation, Validation and Native Use of Usability Questionnaires with Multilingual User Groups

Bojan Blažica(✉) and Tome Eftimov

Computer Systems Department, Jožef Stefan Institute, 1000 Ljubljana, Slovenia
{bojan.blazica,tome.eftimov}@ijs.si
http://cs.ijs.si/

Abstract. The goal of UsabEU is to provide a starting point for usability evaluations with questionnaires in native or mother tongue. The platform supports online collaborative translation of usability questionnaires and their validation. Additionally, it serves as a repository for all validated questionnaires and a tool to perform statistically sound usability evaluations. The current proof-of-concept platform supports the translation and validation of the System Usability Scale questionnaire and statistical assistance for sample size estimation and data summarization.

Keywords: Cross-cultural product and service design ·
Cultural differences ·
Developing HCI expertise and capability worldwide ·
International usability evaluation ·
Translation and technical documentation · Usability testing

1 Introduction

The goal of UsabEU is to provide common multilingual resources for usability testing with multilingual user groups (e.g. the unified European market). Usability questionnaires are basic building block of usability research [17] and are designed to reliably and precisely measure the usability of different types of products and services. As they are sensitive to cultural and language differences [11,30], questionnaires must be translated in a rigorous way to retain their validity. Of the most commonly used usability questionnaires (SUS, SUMI, WAMMI, QUIS, UEQ ...) only few of them have adequately been translated into other languages (e.g. SUS is available 12 of the 24 official languages of the EU, UEQ in 14 languages, 22 in total). This lack of tools makes usability testing with multilingual user groups at best unreliable (using an English questionnaire with non-native speakers) or even impossible (with children or those who dont speak English). Additionally, user studies often suffer from inadequate application of statistics [6] (although the appropriate use of statistics in HCI is under consideration lately [9,15,16]).

© Springer Nature Switzerland AG 2019
P.-L. P. Rau (Ed.): HCII 2019, LNCS 11576, pp. 229–238, 2019.
https://doi.org/10.1007/978-3-030-22577-3_16

As a proof of concept, the UsabEU platform supports the translation of the System Usability Scale (SUS) questionnaire. The SUS was selected due to its wide-spread use. The SUS was created in the 1980s by John Brooke at DEC and published in 1996 [5]. Since then usability practitioners have used it to evaluate the perceived usability of different types of systems including websites, hardware products, and consumer software. It has even been used to assess systems based on technologies that did not exist when it was developed [1]. Sauro and Lewis [27] reported that in a collection of 90 unpublished usability studies, the SUS was the most commonly used standardized usability questionnaire, accounting for 43% of post-test questionnaire usage. It has been cited in nearly 7000 times and incorporated into commercial usability toolkits [1,4,27].

Besides the translation of the SUS questionnaire, UsabEU supports also the validation of translated questionnaires, their use as an online tool for usability testing and statistical assistance for usability testing, e.g. sample size estimation, data summarizing, and computation of confidence intervals (Fig. 1).

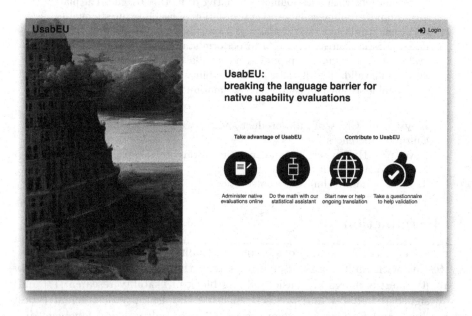

Fig. 1. Anyone can either contribute to UsabEU by helping in the translation process or in the validation of existing translations or exploit the platform using it to perform an online usability evaluation in mother tongue and easily compute statistics relevant to the study s/he is performing.

2   Research Approach

The UsabEU platform supports collaborative translation and validation of questionnaires based on a protocol adopted from [2] and outlined in Fig. 2. The protocol consists of a 3-step translation process and a final validation step where the translation is used to evaluate a well-known tool and compare the results with existing benchmarks.

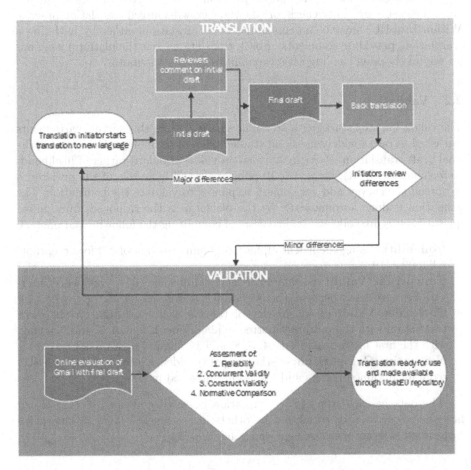

Fig. 2. Collaborative translation and validation of questionnaires protocol adopted by the UsabEU platform.

2.1 Translation

Translation is a three-stage process. First, the initiator of the translation process prepares a first draft translation. S/he then invites at least 10 reviewers to individually review the draft translation. Second, s/he incorporates their comments in the final draft of the translation. The third stage is to perform a back-translation. In this step, at least three independent translators, without reference to the original, translate the final draft back into the original language - English. The initiator of the translation then reviews the back translations. If there are great differences between the original questionnaire and the back-translations, s/he can start the process of translation all over again. If the differences are minor, the final draft of the translation goes into validation.

Validating the final draft and its psychometric properties is also a quality control measure or sanity check for the whole crowd-sourced translation process. Within UsabEU, anyone can contribute to a translation, either by initiating a translation, providing comments or back translations, but the platform itself has no way of checking the linguistic capabilities of the contributor.

2.2   Validation

The validation step starts with an online survey [18]. In this survey, participants are asked to rate a widely used and studied piece of technology, Gmail, using the final draft translation. Participants also provide a standard rating of likelihood-to-recommend (LTR), using a 0–10 point scale [29]. The role of the initiator is to spread the survey and get enough responses to validate the translation. The validation is done automatically by the platform as the responses from online questionnaires are collected and consists of computing the following parameters:

- **Reliability:** using coefficient alpha, minimum criterion of .70 for acceptable reliability [19, 25].
- **Concurrent Validity:** using statistical significance (95% confidence interval) for correlation between the overall SUS score and LTR.
- **Construct Validity:** consistency of the two-factor solution for the draft translation with the pattern reported in [28], items 1, 2, 3, 5, 7, and 9 aligned with the first factor, and items 4, 6, 8, and 10 aligned with the second.
- **Normative Comparison:** overlapping of confidence intervals for mean SUS score for obtained results and the norm published in [18].

The data at each step of the translation is stored and open so that is can later be reviewed and reanalyzed by others increasing the body of knowledge regarding construct measurement and validation [24].

2.3   Online Use of Questionnaires

When a questionnaire is validated it becomes available for use as an online survey offering similar functionalities as other online surveys, e.g. Google Forms, SurveyMonkey or Typeforms.

A user can start a usability evaluation for a product or service s/he is offering to the public by first choose among the available languages, so that the evaluation can be performed across different languages. Next, for each language, s/he can add a short introductory text explaining what is being tested and some other relevant info as well as a short text that will appear after someone completes the questionnaire on a thank you page (Fig. 3). In the future, well add support for additional questions both free form and some standardized demographic questions or frequency of use questions.

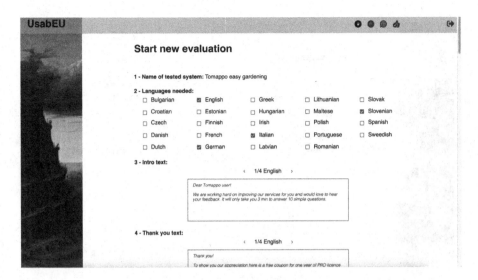

Fig. 3. Starting a new evaluation with UsabEU: after entering the name of the system tested and desired language for testing, the practitioner add some intro and thank you text. After that the links are ready to be sent to participants.

After the survey is created, the user gets a link for each language s/he is testing in and a universal link that lets the recipient decide which language s/he wants to answer in (for cases where we dont know in advance the mother tongue of the recipient, e.g. when sharing a questionnaire over a social media channel with an international audience). After the questionnaire is out, the user will have the options to view the results in the platform (Fig. 4), already converted in SUS scores and optionally download the raw data to do some additional offline analysis or simply for archiving.

This data is also anonymized and stored for future reference and research about validity, correlation, sensitivity etc. of usability questionnaires and usability measures.

2.4 Statistical Assistance

UasbEU provides statistical analyses that can help HCI practitioners to produce more valid results. This is a crucial task for usability testing because only an appropriate selection of participants and tasks can lead to successful usability evaluation.

The statistical analyses provided by the UsabEU can be split into three groups:

– Descriptive statistics,
– Confidence intervals,
– Sample size estimation.

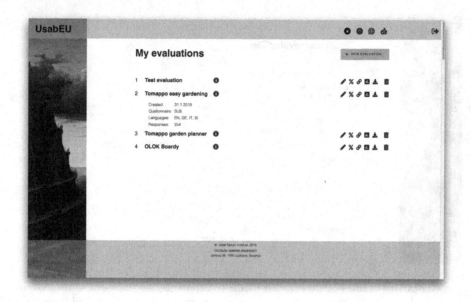

Fig. 4. A list of the practitioner's evaluations with the available options to edit and delete the evaluation, compute sample size estimation, retrieve links for different languages or a universal link, view results and download raw data for additional analysis.

Descriptive statistics aims to summarize the data sample, while it is not used to learn about the population from where the sample is taken [10]. It includes a distribution of single ranodm variable, measures of central tendency (i.e. mean, median, and mode), and measures of variability (i.e. standard deviation, variance, and the minimum and maximum value). The *distribution* of a single random variable represents every value of the variable and the number of how many times the value appears in the data sample. To compute the *mean* we sum all the values in our data sample and then divide the sum by the sample size. The *median* can be assumed as the middle value of an ordered data sample, while the *mode* is the value from the data sample that appears with the highest frequency. The variability of a distribution refers to the spread of the data values around the central tendency. The *minimum* and the *maximum* value are the minimum and the maximum value that appear in the data sample. *Standard deviation* quantifies the amount of variation or dispersion of a set of data values. A low standard deviation indicates that the data values are close to the mean, while a high standard deviation indicates that the data values are spread out over a wider range of values. The *variance* is the square of the standard deviation.

The second part is for calculating confidence intervals (CIs) [3]. In some experiments, the distribution of the data is known, but the parameters that describe the distribution are unknown and must be estimated from the data sample. One way to estimate them is to use the $(1 - \alpha)$ 100% CI. A CI is a type of interval estimate of an unknown parameter, which is calculated using the collected experimental data and it potentially includes the unobserved parameter of interest. The parameter that indicates how frequently the interval contains the true parameter is the confidence level (α). For example, a 95% CI indicates there is 95% probability that the calculated CI contains the true value of the population parameter, but it does not mean that for a given interval there is a 95% probability that the population parameter lies within the interval. UsabEU supports two approaches for CI calculating. The first one is for CI constructed around the mean and it is based on *t-scores*, while the second one is *binomial* CIs that are used for calculating CIs for proportions or percentages computed from count data rather than means.

The last part is focused on sample size estimation for different scenarios including hypothesis testing for one or two samples, problem discovery studies, and parameter estimation and comparative studies for one or two samples. Sample size estimation for population parameter estimation and comparative studies depends on having an estimate of the variance of the dependent measure of interest and an idea of how precise the measurement must be. In this scenario, UsabEU allows users to perform a sample size estimation for one sample or a situation in which users plan to compare scores from two independent groups, which have the same sample size. Hypothesis testing involves two hypotheses: a null hypothesis (H_0) and an alternative hypothesis (H_A) [31]. The null hypothesis is a statement of no effect or no difference, while the alternative hypothesis is a statement indicating the presence of an effect or a difference. To test the null hypothesis, we need to apply an appropriate statistical test. Each statistical test has its power, which is the probability that the test will reject a false null hypothesis. In the case of sample size estimation for hypothesis testing, additionally to the parameters that need to be specified for population parameter estimation and comparative studies, the power of a statistical test should be specified. UsabEU allows users to calculate the sample size estimation for hypothesis testing in the case of one and two samples.

The last scenario that is covered by the UsabEU is estimating sample sizes for tests that have the primary purpose of discovering the problems in an interface depends on having an estimate of p, characterized as the average likelihood of problem occurrence or, alternatively, the problem discovery rate.

Examples and more details for the statistical approaches supported by the UsabEU can be found in [21].

3   Conclusion and Future Work

The main contributions of this work are two, one more practical and the other scientific. From a practical point of view, UsabEU enables native usability evaluations in multilingual environments and helps practitioners with statistical analysis. The first is especially important when evaluating international products, e.g. online tools used globally like UsabEU itself or when the evaluation is done for smaller, but linguistically fragmented markets like the EU or even countries with multiple official languages, e.g. Belgium, Switzerland etc.

On a scientific level, UsabEU contributes to the creation of design knowledge that helps us to develop platforms for translation and validation of measurement items. First and foremost, it is intended to be used for usability evaluation questionnaires, but could also be extended to other fields where questionnaires are heavily used, need to be psychometrically evaluated and can be administered online. Examples include nutrition questionnaires and quality of life questionnaires which are often used with people not fluent in English (children or elderly). Furthermore, the data gathered by the platform will enable research related to local and linguistic differences, such as the understanding of terms and differences in responses based on target population.

Once the platform is live, the next steps will be to promote its use. One of the objectives is to have at least the SUS questionnaire translated and validated in all official languages of the European Union making native usability evaluation possible in the unified EU market. The next step is to have SUS available in all world languages which includes adapting USabEU interface to support right to left languages as well as other localizations.

Finally, the development of UsabEU will go towards incorporating other questionnaires such as the technology acceptance model TAM [7,8,13], Usability metric for user experience UMUX [12] and its shortened version UMUX Lite (with both 5- and 7-point scales) [22], User experience questionnaire UEQ [20] and its shorter version UEQ-S and others (depending also on licensing options). Collecting data in various languages for various questionnaire will open research possibilities to explore correlations among questionnaires, usability measures and their sensitivity [14,26], prediction of results of a certain questionnaire from the results of another one as in [22] or large scale validation of such formulas [23].

Acknowledgments. This work was supported by the project from the Slovenian Research Agency (research core funding No. P2-0098).

References

1. Bangor, A., Kortum, P.T., Miller, J.T.: An empirical evaluation of the system usability scale. Int. J. Hum.-Comput. Interact. **24**(6), 574–594 (2008)
2. Blažica, B., Lewis, J.R.: A Slovene translation of the system usability scale: the SUS-SI. Int. J. Hum.-Comput. Interact. **31**(2), 112–117 (2015)
3. Box, G.E., Hunter, J.S., Hunter, W.G.: Statistics for Experimenters: Design, Innovation, and Discovery, vol. 2. Wiley, New York (2005)
4. Brooke, J.: SUS: a retrospective. J. Usability Stud. **8**(2), 29–40 (2013)
5. Brooke, J., et al.: SUS - a quick and dirty usability scale. Usability Eval. Ind. **189**(194), 4–7 (1996)
6. Cairns, P.: HCI... not as it should be: inferential statistics in HCI research. In: Proceedings of the 21st British HCI Group Annual Conference on People and Computers: HCI... but not as we know it, vol. 1, pp. 195–201. British Computer Society (2007)
7. Davis, F.D.: Perceived usefulness, perceived ease of use, and user acceptance of information technology. MIS Q. **13**, 319–340 (1989)

8. Davis, F.D., Bagozzi, R.P., Warshaw, P.R.: User acceptance of computer technology: a comparison of two theoretical models. Manag. Sci. **35**(8), 982–1003 (1989)

9. Dix, A.: Making sense of statistics in HCI: from P to Bayes and beyond. In: Proceedings of the 2017 CHI Conference Extended Abstracts on Human Factors in Computing Systems, pp. 1236–1239. ACM (2017)

10. Eftimov, T., Korošec, P., Potočnik, D., Ogrinc, N., Heath, D., Koroušić Seljak, B.: How to perform properly statistical analysis on food data? An e-learning tool: advanced statistics in natural sciences and technologies. Up-to-date Advances on Research and Educational Ideas, Book Chapter-Science within Food (2017)

11. Finstad, K.: The system usability scale and non-native English speakers. J. Usability Stud. **1**(4), 185–188 (2006)

12. Finstad, K.: The usability metric for user experience. Interact. Comput. **22**(5), 323–327 (2010)

13. Van der Heijden, H.: User acceptance of hedonic information systems. MIS Q. **28**, 695–704 (2004)

14. Hornbæk, K., Law, E.L.C.: Meta-analysis of correlations among usability measures. In: Proceedings of the SIGCHI Conference on Human Factors in Computing Systems, pp. 617–626. ACM (2007)

15. Kaptein, M., Robertson, J.: Rethinking statistical analysis methods for CHI. In: Proceedings of the SIGCHI Conference on Human Factors in Computing Systems, pp. 1105–1114. ACM (2012)

16. Kay, M., Haroz, S., Guha, S., Dragicevic, P., Wacharamanotham, C.: Moving transparent statistics forward at CHI. In: Proceedings of the 2017 CHI Conference Extended Abstracts on Human Factors in Computing Systems, pp. 534–541. ACM (2017)

17. Kirakowski, J., Murphy, R.: A comparison of current approaches to usability measurement. In: UPA 2009 Workshop: Comparative Usability Task Measurement (CUE-8) (2009)

18. Kortum, P.T., Bangor, A.: Usability ratings for everyday products measured with the system usability scale. Int. J. Hum.-Comput. Interact. **29**(2), 67–76 (2013)

19. Landauer, T.K.: Behavioral research methods in human-computer interaction. In: Handbook of Human-Computer Interaction. 2nd edn, pp. 203–227. Elsevier, Amsterdam (1997)

20. Laugwitz, B., Held, T., Schrepp, M.: Construction and evaluation of a user experience questionnaire. In: Holzinger, A. (ed.) USAB 2008. LNCS, vol. 5298, pp. 63–76. Springer, Heidelberg (2008). https://doi.org/10.1007/978-3-540-89350-9_6

21. Lewis, J.R.: Usability testing. Handb. Hum. Factors Ergon. **12**, e30 (2006)

22. Lewis, J.R., Utesch, B.S., Maher, D.E.: UMUX-LITE: when there's no time for the SUS. In: Proceedings of the SIGCHI Conference on Human Factors in Computing Systems, pp. 2099–2102. ACM (2013)

23. Lewis, J.R., Utesch, B.S., Maher, D.E.: Investigating the correspondence between UMUX-LITE and SUS scores. In: Marcus, A. (ed.) DUXU 2015. LNCS, vol. 9186, pp. 204–211. Springer, Cham (2015). https://doi.org/10.1007/978-3-319-20886-2_20

24. MacKenzie, S.B., Podsakoff, P.M., Podsakoff, N.P.: Construct measurement and validation procedures in MIS and behavioral research: integrating new and existing techniques. MIS Q. **35**(2), 293–334 (2011)

25. Nunnally, J.C., Bernstein, I.H., et al.: Psychometric Theory, vol. 226. McGraw-Hill, New York (1967)

26. Sauro, J., Dumas, J.S.: Comparison of three one-question, post-task usability questionnaires. In: Proceedings of the SIGCHI Conference on Human Factors in Computing Systems, pp. 1599–1608. ACM (2009)

27. Sauro, J., Lewis, J.R.: Correlations among prototypical usability metrics: evidence for the construct of usability. In: Proceedings of the SIGCHI Conference on Human Factors in Computing Systems, pp. 1609–1618. ACM (2009)

28. Sauro, J., Lewis, J.R.: When designing usability questionnaires, does it hurt to be positive? In: Proceedings of the SIGCHI Conference on Human Factors in Computing Systems, pp. 2215–2224. ACM (2011)

29. Sauro, J., Lewis, J.R.: Quantifying the User Experience: Practical Statistics for User Research. Morgan Kaufmann, Burlington (2016)

30. Van de Vijver, F., Leung, K.: Personality in cultural context: methodological issues. J. Pers. **69**(6), 1007–1031 (2001)

31. William, L.T.: Null hypothesis testing: problems, prevalence, and an alternative. J. Wildl. Manage **64**(4), 912–923 (2000)

Design for Bilingual Information in a Cross-Cultural Context—Design Strategy and Conceptualization in Branding Tongji Design Week

Qin Du[(⊠)]

Tongji University, Shanghai 200442, China
duqin@tongji.edu.cn

Abstract. The Tongji Design Week held since 2012 in Shanghai by Tongji University College of Design and Media, presents a classic case study of cross-cultural design. By analyzing the problems and challenges faced by this recurring design project, this paper examines the strategy and approaches taken by the design team of Tongji Design Week, and the specific design solutions, guidelines and rules in relation to the design strategy and concept set forth by the designer. This paper also examines how innovative contemporary communication design concepts and approaches could be combined with the needs of cross-cultural design to shape an up-to-date design language in a bilingual and cross-cultural context.

Keywords: Communication design · Branding · Typography · Bilingual design

1 The Tongji Design Week Presents a Classic Example of Cross-Cultural Design and Calls for a Modern Design Language

1.1 The Brief

Tongji Design Week (abbreviated as TJDW hereafter) is an academic event held since 2012 in Shanghai, China, hosted by Tongji University College of Design and Innovation mainly located on the campus. The way TDJW is organized and developed over the years present a unique model as the College of Design and acts not only as the organizer of the event, its professors, lecturers and students all work together initiating and participating in the sub-events, but it also plays the role of uniting the academics, businesses, professionals, educators and students to come together in a two-week long forum of innovative design education, research and social practices.

Although under the umbrella of a design school and named after the university above the school, TJDW is organized not only within the realm of the university but also far beyond that—it connects different forces and aspects of design and invites contributions from all over the world and a vast spectrum of professional fields. Therefore designing for the Tongji Design Week is an endeavor which involves

P.-L. P. Rau (Ed.): HCII 2019, LNCS 11576, pp. 239–247, 2019.
https://doi.org/10.1007/978-3-030-22577-3_17

multiple stakeholders, relates to a variety of audiences of different nations, and reflects the complex nature of cross-cultural design today.

TDJW is normally comprised of one major academic conference, the EPC (Emerging Practices Conference), and more than 20 sub-events including exhibitions, forums, seminars, workshops, and performances, mostly initiated by professors and lecturers of the school. Some of the events are hosted on-site with a few at satellite venues. The mission of TJDW is developing a platform for cross-border communication in innovative design education, research and social practices, which aims at enhancing design-driven innovation capabilities, and the development in design not only in and around the university but the city of Shanghai as well.

1.2 Defining the Design Problems and Challenges

The Demand of Bilingual Information. For such an event involving both local and international audiences, it is mandatory to run both English and Chinese in parallel for the nature of the event. And the practical consideration of combining information of both languages in one layout in most scenarios presents a classic problem in designing with two languages/scripts.

First to be noted is the complex relationships existing between different types of glyphs from a typographic point of view—Chinese characters, Latin letters, Arabic numbers, punctuations marks of both languages which are visually and proportionally different. The heights, widths, visual weight, contours and counters, and how they are constructed fundamentally, are all different between Chinese characters and Latin letters [1]. The ways how they are aligned horizontally are also different (See Fig. 1).

Fig. 1. Chinese character and Latin letters compared.

This is typically understood as a problem of bilingual design or typography, however in the case of TJDW in addition to that it is more closely linked with a fundamental approach to the development of the visual identity.

Aesthetics and Style. Designing for such ambitious and pioneering event which covers a vast array of topics under innovation and design calls for a visual style and aesthetic that matches the spirit and vision of the organizers, a design that is vibrant and versatile, but not excessive, impactful yet disciplined, understandable but also well pronounced with a distinct visual voice. At its best, the design is hoped to reflect the cutting edge of contemporary visual communication design both visually and conceptually.

Limitations and Opportunities. Budgetary and time limitations have to be taken into consideration as the TJDW is largely self-funded by the college. Due to those reasons and a flexible planning strategy, it is impossible to predict each year how many and what events will be and it is typically not possible to have all materials in place before design and production. As improvised projects are also accepted as long as there is a meaningful contribution, even after the editing and designing of information have begun. All these require the design solutions to be flexible and respond to unexpected adding or canceling of events. However, this requirement of super flexibility also makes it possible to devise a system that is lightweight and easy to execute.

2   Brand Strategy and Design Concepts

2.1   Establishing the Overall Structure and the Basic Brand Guidelines

Given the basic needs of a large-scale design event such as TJDW, when dealing with the materials of TJDW a formulaic solution and overall structure naturally emerge and recurs annually. This covers the theme, program, map(s), and introductions to the sub-events with illustrations. With the intention of condensing all the information in the format of an ephemeral piece participants can take with them and check whenever they like, the TJDW poster is printed on the back of a foldable leaflet, to give both context and contrast to the dense blocks of information on the front (See Fig. 2).

Fig. 2. TJDW brand guidelines, different combinations of English and Chinese logotypes.

2.2 Bilingual Typography

Due to the very different visual qualities and construction, as a strategy the typography system is simplified to avoid as much as possible undesirable juxtapositions between the Latin letters and Chinese characters, This could be done by separating the informations of the two languages, to put them on different pages, or in different blocks created for more convenient placement and layout work.

2.3 Icons and Funny Flags

In an earlier stage of the design process, icon font was mixed with Latin letters, and Chinese characters to create a cacophony of visual elements echoing the theme of TJDW 2018. The concept of flags as containers of information was added along the process, together with the color scheme of three basic colors, the flags reflect the international nature of the event, and embedded icons were a metaphor for the New Communities theme (See Fig. 3).

Fig. 3. TJDW 2018 – new communities, design concept with flags in which icons are embedded to create meanings in relation to the theme. (Color figure online)

2.4 Creating a Lightweight, Versatile Visual Language

Over the years of designing for TJDW, it has been experimented and solidified as a design and brand strategy to use a lightweight visual system that is flexible and versatile enough to create vibrant visuals and compositions. The simplicity of basic graphics and type is contrasted with the colorful and rich visuals, strengthening the concept of design even more.

2.5 Designing Rules for Systems

Also to be noted is that the design of TJDW is closely linked to a set of clearly defined rules which are simple enough to carry out by the design team. The concept of creating rules for design systems, although not digital, is especially important as in the age when computers are becoming more and more advanced, the designer's job therefore is more and more about making rules for systems to carry out without mistake rather than competing with machine. To create simple but smart rules which lead to maximum outcome matters in both digital systems and print mediums.

3 The Design Solutions

3.1 Resolving the Problems with Two Scripts

Choice and Matching of Fonts. Several typefaces have been experimented, Neuzeit S Grotesk, Theinhardt, Helvetica Neue, Graphik, and Calibre, to test with a few Chinese equivalents—the formal quality of the Neo-grotesque typefaces were meticulously balanced with contemporary Chinese Heiti, at first LanTing Hei and Hiragino Sans GB, then PingFang SC, later on Source Han Sans when it came out.

It's extremely difficult to match typefaces of different scripts, especially those of Chinese and Latin, which are almost diametrically different comparing them visually. Chinese characters are mostly mono-width, mono-height, and mono-spaced, its typography based on a grid system in which the square-shaped character frames are the most basic units. Latin letters in contrast are non-lining, proportional, and the spacing between letters, known as kerning, varies. For the two scripts to coexist in one system requires a great deal of effort and the result is often not ideal [2].

To the untrained eye, the subtle variations make very little difference however through these usages, the design team arrived at the combination of Source Han Sans and Graphik, and later Calibre, for the text face, and Theinhardt for the flexible logotype. Graphik, and later Calibre, were favored due to their geometric construction, short ascenders and descenders, and pronounced counter, which being placed next to Chinese characters create less visual fluctuation, thus maintain a more comfortable reading line.

A Disciplined Use of Typefaces. To avoid complicating the visual relationships between the two scripts, it is advisable to stick to one or two weights and giving maximum presentation of the sub-events to reflect and respond to the broad and deep topics the design week accommodates each year and its sub-events. A certain level of abstraction is required to make this possible.

Due to an interest in typography and faced with the need of bilingual information, the designer and his team started with the most fundamental aspect of communication design to respond to the brief of TJDW, the design is focused on contrasting Latin letters and Chinese characters and balancing the information of both languages. Given that

3.2   Design with Brand Behavior

Brand Behavior vs Logo-Centered Design. Brand behavior from the angle of design is how the visual identity, be it logo, logotype, or combination(s) of them, 'behaves' in a given design scenario. Contrary to the classic logo-centered design approach, in which logo or logotype is carefully placed to create an authoritative and refined look, in recent years the way logos are used have become more and more important. Many companies start to simplify their logos with a very long history, to have something as simple as possible, often resulting in a minimal 'flat' 2D logo, with brand name next to it. The emphasis is gradually being placed on how this logo performs in all kinds of mediums, digital and analog, online and offline. The most famous example of this may be Google's logo which is only 305 Bytes allowing for super dynamic and responsive applications, brand behavior.

In the case of TJDW, from the very beginning, the design team tried to stay way from a logo-centered design ideology. This is especially because in the context of TJDW, where dynamism and confrontation of ideas are often the main spirit which is reflected in the branding of TJDW.

Basic brand guidelines were established during the 2017 TJDW, in which spaced letters of T, J, D, and W are spaced as if the other letters of TJDW have been taken out, creating gaps that force the viewer to complete the whole name. No graphic is used in it, but the name appears again under T, J, D, W for those who have no clue, but in certain scenarios the full name underneath will be taken off, to have a succinct look of the identity.

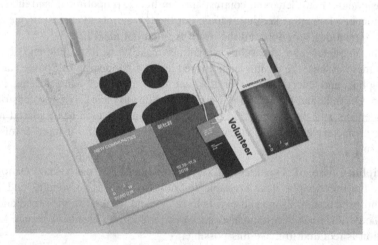

Fig. 4. TJDW 2018 tote bag, staff badge and brochure.

3.3   Visual Devices

Squares as Containers of Information. Instances from the icon font are embedded in the flags which serve as containers of information, and by cropping and scaling, creating contrast, meanings, and a kind of interaction in-between. Squares as basic units of those information containers, contain different types of info. Therefore content of both languages are separated and placed in different squares. This 'avoids' the necessity of bilingual typography and in so creates a visual order and intense style (See Fig. 4).

4   The Design Language

4.1   Visual Identity System Without a Logo

The key to the design language of TJDW 2018 is that there's not a key-visual or logo for the theme New Communities. Instead, the Chinese and English titles of the theme are being distributed on different parts of any given layout, but always aligned to the edges, in this way constructing the simple rules aforementioned. In this case, typeface plays the role of a visual identity to some extent, as the form of bold text is visually intense, its proportion and thick thin contrast etc. all communicating to the viewer a brand personality while sending the message (See Fig. 5).

Fig. 5.   TJDW 2017 poster.

4.2   Creating Meanings with Icons and Flags

Using Google's material design icon font [3] sets up a large base of symbols for meanings to emerge when they are embedded in the flags. This is a simple and fun game to be played by the designers with pleasing results.

Icons and flags as a visual device are also easily linked with a symbolic language of embracing the international audiences and topics to address the challenges brought about by the cross-cultural activities.

4.3   Blurring Between the Digital and Analog

From Digital Screen Back to the Physical World. The design for TJDW is an experimentation to blur the boundaries of online and offline worlds. In 2016, the New York based design studio 2x4 designed the visual identity and environmental graphics for Google SPAN [4] conference in which 2x4 made bold use of the pre-fabricated symbols of Google's own icon font, as an appropriation of the "ready-made". Through an exaggerated way of contrasting the macro and the micro by changing the scale of elements.

Fig. 6. TJDW 2017 banner at Tongji University College of Design and Innovation. (Color figure online)

Icons, symbols, even emojis are being more and more used in newer generations of designs. In the instance of TJDW 2018, the use of icons is in close connection with the invented flags concept. Fake and funny flags were composed to form a template and container of color fields, icons and informations. Real flags are also made in addition to the representations of flags in both digital and physical/print mediums, thus blurring even more between the digital and physical, the real flags and the representations of them, creating a kind of 'in-between' visual language. Meaning and interpretations may emerge through such manipulations (See Fig. 6).

5   Conclusion

This paper examines visual identities developed for TJDW and its overall branding, from the angle of designing in a cross-cultural setting, but also from its core design concept and methodologies such as brand behavior, analog and digital media, rule-based design, and bilingual typography, which together contribute to a design that is modern, vibrant and responds to the design problems risen from this context.

In developing the visual identity for TJDW 2018 under the theme New Communities, by reorganizing different types of texts in the flags, information in both Chinese and English are well balanced by very simple rules. This may serve as an example and starting point for further research of how immensely different types of information and languages can coexist using the creation and force of design.

References

1. Du, Q.: 现代中文版面肌理与排版学规范研究 [A study on modern Chinese text image and typography norms]. Central Academy of Fine Arts, Beijing, pp. 130–131 (2014)
2. Tam, K.C.H.: A descriptive framework for Chinese-English bilingual typography. Typographische Monatsblätter 4(5), 38–46 (2012)
3. Material Design website. https://material.io/tools/icons/
4. 2x4 website. https://2x4.org/work/google-span/. Accessed 21 Nov 2019

How People Browse Mobile News Feed?
A Study for Mobile News Feed Design

Hui Li[✉], Nan Chen, Minjuan Zhou, Chenyi He, Jingbo Li,
and Yujie Shi

Baidu Content Ecosystem User Experience Department,
Beijing, People's Republic of China
lihui15@baidu.com

Abstract. With the widespread emergence of "feed" in mobile Internet products, their competition for users and their usage time has become increasingly fierce, which makes improving the feed reading experience important. This research focuses on the news feed of Chinese news applications (apps) and attempts to provide an integrated picture of user experience with mobile news feed. The research was conducted in two phases. In the first stage, we explored users' demands on mobile news feed and extracted important factors affecting users' preference for products through in-depth interviews. Excluding the influence of news contents, the graphic layout and image quality, ancillary information, and template combination play important roles in users' preference for products. On this basis, the template combination was further studied with an eye-tracking experiment. Results of eye-tracking data and subjective evaluation of six combinations show that templates and their combination influence users' browsing behaviors and their subjective evaluation. It is a good choice to combine large-picture template with consecutive single-picture templates or consecutive three-picture ones since it can be well integrated. When consecutive three-picture templates work with one single-picture template, the score on users' satisfaction of "good organization" is low, and the single-picture template is more likely to be ignored by the user, which greatly weakens the value of this piece of news. The research results provide design suggestions for the news feed of mobile news apps.

Keywords: News feed · Mobile news apps · User experience ·
Interface design · Eye tracking

1 Introduction

In the era of mobile Internet, the information explosion is characterized by a higher degree of fragmentation. There are two main ways to connect user and information: search and feed. Feed is a simple and efficient way to help users get information, and recommends content for users based on their interests provided by the personalized algorithm. As a typical representative of the human-machine interactive recommendation system in the field of mobile Internet, feed has been increasingly appearing in social media, news, short video, and other mobile phone apps. In China, almost all mobile phone news apps adopt the form of feed to recommend users rich and

© Springer Nature Switzerland AG 2019
P.-L. P. Rau (Ed.): HCII 2019, LNCS 11576, pp. 248–265, 2019.
https://doi.org/10.1007/978-3-030-22577-3_18

diversified content that interests them. In the huge competition among news apps for users and their usage time, it is particularly important to optimize product's user experience. Besides continuous efforts to improve the quality of content sources and recommendation algorithms, proper interface design is also essential.

Overseas researches on the reading experience of feed mainly focused on social media products (e.g., the feed of Facebook), studying users' browsing behavior and their attention to information [1, 2]. In recent years, with the fast emergence of mobile news apps in China, Chinese scholars have begun to study the design of mobile news apps [3] and the impact of layout design on users' visual browsing [4, 5]. Due to the limited research topics concerning news feed of mobile news apps, a comprehensive understanding of the reading experience of mobile news feed is needed, including how users browse mobile news feed, what demands they have for mobile news feed, what key factors affect users' reading experience, as well as what should be done to improve the design.

Therefore, this research focuses on the reading experience of mobile news feed and conducts researches in two stages. Study 1 explores information that users pay attention to when browsing the news feed and reasons concerning users' preference for products, and then draws a conclusion on critical factors affecting the reading experience of mobile news feed. Study 2 focuses on the specific design of one of the critical factors found in study 1. The research results provide design suggestions for mobile news feed products.

2 Related Work

When browsing through news feed, users are faced with an information-rich page composed of text and graphics and they pay different attention to the text and graphics. A joint study by Poynter Institute and Stanford University on online news on computer screens found that news readers started with the text, instead of graphics, after opening the website [6]. Based on an eye tracking research on the news feed of Facebook, Vraga, Bode, and Troller-Renfree [1] found that the style of the post matters for attention patterns, with richer content (e.g., pictures, links) enhancing attention especially for social and news posts. Sülflow, Schäfer, and Winter [2] studied what drives attention to content within the news feed of Facebook and what influences the selection of news posts. Their eye tracking measurement showed that users preferred to select news posts with content reinforcing their attitudes and they spent more time with news posts from sources with high credibility and selected them more frequently.

A good news product needs to achieve the goal of improving users' reading efficiency and promote their immersive experience [3]. In recent years, as news apps in the Chinese market are extensively using feed to recommend content to users, Chinese researchers have begun their research work on the graphic layout design of news feed, in an attempt to enhance the reading efficiency and experience of users.

Currently, there are three typical templates of graphic layout designs among news apps in the Chinese market, namely the single-picture template, the three-picture template, and the large-picture template. Among them, the single-picture template has two forms, the text left and picture right type and the picture left and text right type, while in the large-picture template, a video snapshot or merely a picture is presented (see Table 1).

Table 1. Typical templates of graphic layout designs of news apps in the Chinese market

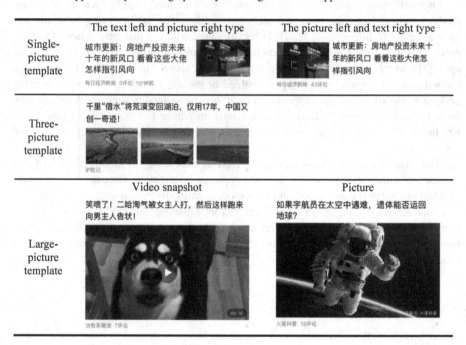

Liu and Hou [4] studied the impact of graphic layout of mobile news feed with single-picture and three-picture template structures on users' reading efficiency. They found that users presented the text-oriented visual browsing rule and their hot spots were on the text. That is to say, users tend to look at the text and choose content that they are interested in, and then browse the corresponding picture. Therefore, for most right-handed users, the text left and picture right type of single-picture template is less prone to block the text than the picture left and text right type. Lv et al. [5] further tested eye movement of right-handed and left-handed users when browsing news in the text left and picture right type and the picture left and text right type. Their research results confirmed the impact of the position of fingers on the hot spot. When fingers and pictures were on the same side, users had a larger browsing scope, which enabled them to explore more information on the page. However, in terms of fixation duration, both right-handed and left-handed users had longer fixation duration on news headlines under the condition of the picture left and text right type, i.e., this type made it easier to allow users to pay more attention to news headlines.

On the whole, past researches on the reading experience of mobile news feed mainly focus on social media platforms (e.g., Facebook) and news platforms (e.g., computer news websites and mobile news apps). On the one hand, it is not proper to directly apply results of researches on the news feed of social media platforms to the feed design of mobile news apps, because of their difference in both the product attribute and the form of the feed. On the other hand, current researches on the news feed of mobile news apps only focus on the graphic layout, and their design schemes are all with the single-picture template or with the three-picture template, which is much different from news feed with mixed templates in real products. As a result, past researches can only provide limited guidance on the actual feed design of mobile news apps.

Given limitations above and the broad usage of mobile news feed products in China, it is necessary to conduct more comprehensive and in-depth research on factors affecting users' reading experience, so as to sharpen the understanding of experience of news feed users and provide design suggestions for products. To this end, this research studies news feed of mobile news apps and deeply probes into factors mattering the reading experience of mobile news feed and related design principles. The research was conducted in two phases. Study 1 examined critical factors influencing users' reading experience of mobile news feed at first.

3   Study 1: On Factors Mattering Users' Reading Experience of Mobile News Feed

3.1   Tasks

The task consisted of a free-viewing paradigm of three typical news feed of mobile news apps in the Chinese market, and followed by an in-depth interview. Free-viewing refers to the behavior of users when they view information freely without explicit search targets. As news feed is a typical product for users to kill time, free-viewing is the most important scenario in its daily use.

In the interview, participants were asked to browse the news feed of three typical mobile news apps in a given order, and then ranked them according to their preference and explained their reasons.

3.2   Participants

54 Chinese participants (27 males and 27 females) were recruited to participate the interview. They were all workers aged between 18–34 years old. To control the impact of past experience of using mobile news apps on users' preference, it was set that each news app to be tested had 18 current users, and participants should use only one news app to be tested in the past month, with a frequency of 4 times a week or higher. Participants received a reward for their participation after the interview.

3.3 Stimulus

Materials were long screenshots of the news feed of three typical mobile news apps, namely A, B, and C (see Fig. 1). There were 25 pieces of news in each long screenshot, which was set according to the average number of pieces of news read by users every day. With the online proportion of product A as a reference, 6, 12, and 7 pieces of news were presented with the single-picture template, the three-picture template, and the large-picture template respectively. Detailed design principles of materials are as follows:

- To avoid the impact of news headlines on users' preference. News content shared by the three products was chosen. All schemes had the same news headline and source.
- To avoid the impact of brand on users' preference. Brand names and specific colors were removed, and icons at the bottom were replaced with generic ones.
- To reproduce the online schemes of products. Templates (the single-picture template, the three-picture template, or the large-picture template), pictures, release time, number of comments, text font, font size, line spacing, spacing between paragraphs, margins on both sides, and spacing between pictures of every piece of news were as same as elements outlined in specifications of online news of the three products.

3.4 Apparatus

Three iPhone 6plus were used in the experiment (screen size: 5.5 in., resolution: 1920 × 1080). Each device presented a long screenshot of the news feed of one news app so that participants could simultaneously compare the three products at the end of the interview. In consideration of the impact of mobile phone background color and contracts on the reading experiences of participants, the screen brightness was set the same among three iPhone 6plus devices. The experiment was carried out indoors with fluorescent lamps.

3.5 Procedure

Before the experiment began, participants were told about the experimental procedures in detail. Then they were asked to browse through three news feeds marked with A, B, and C in a given order. After it, they would have a one-on-one interview with the staff, and rank the three schemes according to their preference and explain their reasons (comparing the three schemes presented on the three mobile phones was allowed). To avoid the effect of sequence on user's preference, Latin square design was used for the order.

Fig. 1. Materials used in study 1 (part of the long screenshots)

3.6   Results

User's ranking of the three schemes was measured (see Table 2). 24% of users liked A most, while 56% preferred B and 20% preferred C.

Table 2. User's ranking of three schemes

	A	B	C
1st	24%	56%	20%
2nd	35%	24%	41%
3rd	41%	20%	39%

After analyzing reasons why users preferred the news feed that ranked in the first place, we found three critical factors mattering their choices, namely graphic layout and image quality, ancillary information, and template combination.

Graphic Layout and Image Quality

- Graphic layout

42.6% of participants mentioned that they preferred a scheme because of its graphic layout of the single-picture template (the text left and picture right type or the picture left and text right type). Their reading habits influenced their choices. Until now, there has no clear research conclusions on the superiority of the two types, and the results of two relevant studies showed that the two schemes had their strong points and weaknesses in the hotspot and fixation duration [4, 5].

> "I prefer B. The text left and picture right type is more appropriate to my reading habit for I usually start with the text, and then move to the picture. If the picture is on the left, the page will look top-heavy and make me uncomfortable."

> "I prefer A. With the picture on the left, it is seemingly more straightforward than the text. The picture is the best information."

- Image quality

Image quality includes three aspects: information content, color, and cropping.
31.5% of participants mentioned that extracted pictures needed to concur with the topic in the news and convey as much information as possible.

> "If the picture is attractive or well presented, it will increase my reading interest. I will click on it to see what it is about. Only the text is not that attractive."

> "In the news about "Six Walnuts" (the second news in the test material), the second graph (in scheme C) is proper, more realistic, and is more consistent with the headline, while pictures in the other two schemes look like advertisements."

What is more, 3.7% of participants mentioned the color and cropping of pictures, and they hoped that pictures would have a comfortable color and be properly cropped.

> "I like A in which pictures look warm, bright, clear, real but not glaring."

> "I don't like B. Some pictures are not well cropped so that some words are missing."

Ancillary Information

Ancillary information includes the source, release time, and number of comments. Since this study chooses news headlines that appear on all three products, there is no difference in the news source among three schemes. The release time and number of comments are consistent with the online designs of each product, so the three schemes are different in terms of these two elements.

31.5% of participants mentioned that they preferred a scheme because of it shows the release time and that they judged the timeliness of the news from this.

> *"I prefer B because it shows that the news was updated a few minutes ago and I know that this is the latest news."*

24.1% of participants mentioned the number of comments is quite important and they believed that it was one of the key messages to help them judge the quality of the news and whether it is clickbait.

> *"I like the scheme that displays the number of comments. The more comments the news has, the more eager I am to read it. If there is no comment, I will think it is unpopular and will not click on it."*

Template Combination

13.0% of participants mentioned the template combination in reasons of preference. They hoped that template combination would follow a certain rule that makes the page neat, orderly and more comfortable to read.

> *"I prefer the template combination in which a piece of news with one picture (single-picture template) is followed by two ones with three pictures (the three-picture template) so the overall page does not look so messy."*

> *"Horizontal (the three-picture template or the large-picture template) and vertical (the single-picture template) patterns should appear alternately in a transitional way. If a vertical pattern suddenly appears after horizontal ones, the page will look messy and make it painful to read."*

Based on analysis of users' ranking and reference reasons, we extracted critical factors mattering the reading experience of news feed of mobile news apps:

- Graphic layout and image quality. Graphic layout should be appropriate to users' reading habits and image quality should be high (e.g., concurrence with the topic, deliver rich and straightforward information, and has proper brightness and cropping).
- Ancillary information. Provide complete ancillary information about the news (including its release time and number of comments) to help users judge its timeliness and quality and decide whether to click on it for further reading.
- Template combination. A neat and orderly template combinations that creates a good reading pace.

4 Study 2: The Effect of Template Combination on Reading Experience of Mobile News Feed

Study 1 shows that template combination is a critical factor that affects users' preference for news feed of mobile news apps. What is the "neat and orderly" template combination that users prefer? Based on the three typical design templates (the single-picture template, the three-picture template, and the large-picture template), study 2 probes into the combination of these three templates, and measures the viewing paradigm of users under the condition of different template combination with the eye tracking methodology to find the "neat and orderly" template combination.

4.1 Tasks

The experiment followed a free-viewing paradigm. Participants were required to browse six news feeds with different template combinations in a given order, and then scored their satisfaction for each feed.

4.2 Participants

32 Chinese users were recruited to participate the eye tracking experiment. There were 17 males and 15 females, 26 workers and 6 students. All participants were aged between 18 and 24 and used mobile news apps more than 4 times a week in the past month. Their vision or corrected visual acuity were normal. They received a reward for their participation after the experiment.

4.3 Design of Experiment

The within-subject design was adopted for the experiment, with template combination as the independent variable. Given the fact that about four pieces of news appear on a single screen of mainstream mobile phones, templates were combined and designed for four pieces of news as a basic unit in the experiment. Based on the single-picture template and the three-picture template, the "3+1" combination was chosen to produce six combinations: A. All single-picture templates; B. Three single-picture templates and one three-picture template; C. Three single-picture templates and one large-picture template; D. All three-picture templates; E. Three three-picture templates and one single-picture template; and F. Three three-picture templates and one large-picture template. Figure 2 shows the smallest unit in each combination.

The dependent variables included both objective and subjective measurements. Objective measurements were from eye-tracking data, including users' sequence of gaze point, heat map, and fixation duration. Because of high sampling frequency, high precision and low interference to users, the eye-tracking technology is widely used to emulate real human-computer interaction for the test [7], and serve as an important objective indicator to measure users' experience of mobile apps [8]. Sequence of gaze point shows the browsing order of the interest area with a visible ratio greater than 50%. The heat map shows the attention aroused stimuli from participants with different colors and visualizes the tendency of fixation for analysis; red indicates more attention while green means less attention. Fixation duration corresponds to how long the fixation on a point in the region of interest last for and is used to analyze users' attention on a specific region. The longer the fixation duration is, the more attractive the region is. In this experiment, with one piece of news as a region of interest, each participant's overall fixation duration on all pieces of contents of each piece of news was calculated, and the

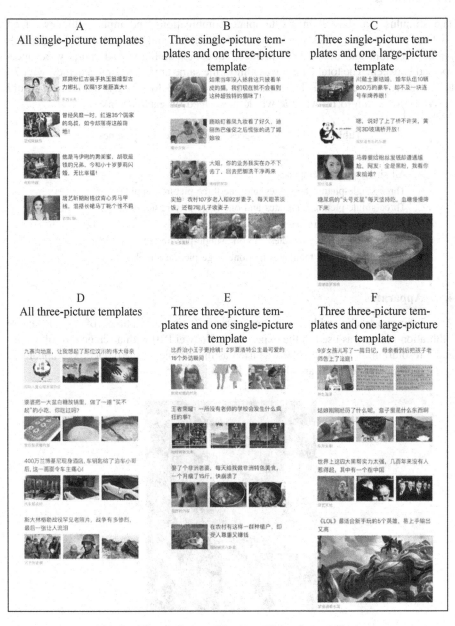

Fig. 2. Six template combinations (Color figure online)

average value of all participants was calculated. Subjective measurements were from questionnaires with three items, including "good organization", "ease of reading", and "overall satisfaction." Likert Scale was used (1 = very unsatisfied, 3 = neutral, 5 = very satisfied). The higher the score was, the more satisfied the user was with the item.

4.4   Stimulus

The stimulus was based on six template combinations and input with news feed content. Most of the news were about entertainment and life which received much public attention, and news about finance, education, military, and sports were interspersed between. The total length was almost the same among testing schemes, with 70 to 100 pieces of news varied by schemes (see Table 3 for details). Participate would spend 1.5 to 2 min to browse the whole news feed on each scheme.

Table 3. Number of pieces of news in testing schemes

Testing schemes		Pieces of news
A.	All single-picture templates	100
B.	Three single-picture templates and one three-picture template	99
C.	Three single-picture templates and one large-picture template	86
D.	All three-picture templates	83
E.	Three three-picture templates and one single-picture template	89
F.	Three three-picture templates and one large-picture template	71

4.5   Apparatus

A desktop eye tracker with a sampling rate of 30 Hz, an accuracy of 0.5°–1° and 9 calibration points was used in the experiment. Huawei P10 with a screen size of 5.1 in. and a resolution of 1920 × 1080 was used as the mobile phone device. The apparatus and experimental scenario are shown in Fig. 3.

Fig. 3. Apparatus and experimental scenario

4.6   Procedure

Before the experiment, participants were told about the entire experimental procedures in detail. Then, they sit down in front of the eye tracker for the program running, eye tracker connection and calibration. In the pilot after calibration, participants were guided to familiarize themselves with the interface and operation of the mobile phone and browse the news feed according to their habits. After the above tasks, the formal experiment began. Participants needed to browse through six schemes of news feed according to a given order, schemes A and D first (in random order) and then B, C, E, and F (also in random order). Each time when they finished one scheme, they scored their satisfaction.

The experimental process was controlled by participants. After browsing one news feed, participants were required to fill in a questionnaire asking for their satisfaction about this scheme, and then they clicked the next button and moved to the next one. To prevent the fatigue, participants could take a break after finishing two schemes. When all six schemes were browsed through, and the questionnaires were complete, participants were asked to tell their preferences for the six schemes and reasons.

4.7   Results

Eye Tracking Results of Different Template Combinations

How Users Browse Mobile News Feed?
Figures 4 and 5 show the average fixation duration on news at different positions in schemes with mainly single-picture templates and three-picture templates respectively. The overall zigzag tendency indicates that instead of the one by one manner, participants browse news feed selectively, namely, in the way of skimming.

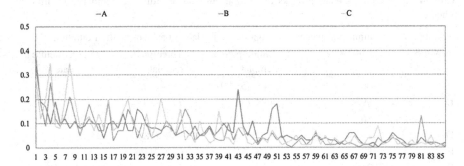

Fig. 4. Distribution of fixation duration on each piece of news in three schemes with mainly single-picture templates (unit: second)

The type and combination of templates affect users' behaviors of browsing the news feed. Table 4 shows the results about relative peaks of fixation duration of individual templates in different template combinations. The relative peak means that for two consecutive pieces of news if the fixation duration of the second one is longer

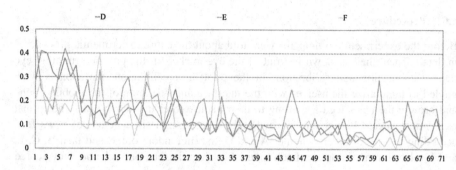

Fig. 5. Distribution of fixation duration on each piece of news in three schemes with mainly three-picture templates (unit: second)

than that of the first one, the second one is marked as a relative peak. As can be seen from Table 4, the proportion of relative peaks of fixation duration of the large-picture template, whether it was combined with the single-picture template (scheme C) or three-picture template (scheme F), was higher, which indicated that participants were unconsciously attracted more by the large picture. When a three-picture template was mixed with consecutive single-picture templates (scheme B), participants paid more attention to the three-picture template and focused less on the single-picture template. As for the case in which a single-picture template was mixed with consecutive three-picture templates (scheme E), only 5 of the 21 single-picture templates had the relative peak (accounting for 24%), which suggested that participants obviously paid more attention to the three-picture template, and single-picture template was less attracted and even be ignored.

Table 4. Proportion of relative peaks of fixation duration of individual templates in different schemes

Testing schemes	Number of pieces of news	Proportion of relative peaks of fixation duration		
		Single-picture template	Three-picture template	Large-picture template
A	100	54% (53/99)	–	–
B	99	46% (34/74)	79% (19/24)	–
C	86	42% (27/65)	–	95% (19/20)
D	83	–	46% (38/82)	–
E	89	24% (5/21)	64% (43/67)	–
F	71	–	36% (19/53)	88% (15/17)

Browsing Behaviors under Schemes Mainly Based on Single-picture Templates
Figure 6 shows the sequence of gaze point and heat map of schemes A, B, and C. When consecutive single-picture templates were mixed with either three-picture template or large-picture template, participants had a relatively good reading pace.

In the sequence of gaze point, compared with scheme A with all single-picture templates, the scan path of participants under the condition of the scheme C with three single-picture-templates and one large-picture template, remained nearly linear, with few movements or zigzags. When three single-picture templates were mixed with one three-picture template (scheme B), there was no specific rule in the scan path, and the gaze point of participants alternated between the text and the picture, which would cause a frequent switching between "text analysis" and "picture analysis" in the area of brain cognition.

The classic "F"-shaped reading pattern was not shown in the heat maps of schemes B and C, instead, the "1"-shaped pattern with a bulge from the middle to the two sides was distinct; when combined with the three-picture template, the "bulge" was more apparent.

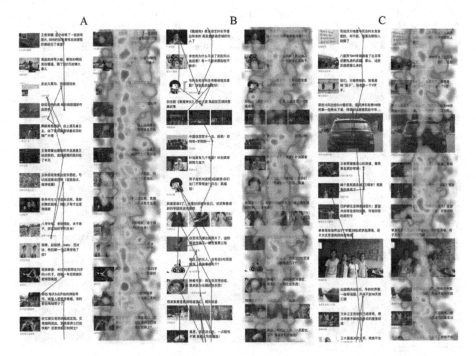

Fig. 6. The sequence of gaze point and heat map of schemes A, B, and C mainly based on single-picture templates

Browsing Behaviors under Schemes Mainly Based on Three-picture Templates

Figure 7 shows the sequence of gaze point and heat map of schemes D, E, and F. When consecutive three-picture templates were mixed with single-picture template (scheme E), the reading pace was poor, but when mixed with the large-picture template (scheme F), there were fewer changes in the reading pattern, the reading pace was better.

Compared with scheme D, scheme E showed the "F"-shaped reading pattern concave from the middle to the right because of the difference in structure between the three-picture template and the single-picture template. In the case of scheme F with three-picture template combined with large-picture template, both of the two templates have a top-bottom structure, few changes in the reading pattern was shown when compared with scheme D, and thus this combination is relatively balanced for the large-picture harmonizes with the three-picture ones.

In addition, from the sequence of gaze point and heat map, within the three-picture template, participants' attention to pictures was concentrated on the first two pictures, especially the first one, and the third one was ignored. Therefore, when such template is used, the order of pictures is critical, and the most high-quality picture should be put in the first place to increase users' attention to the news.

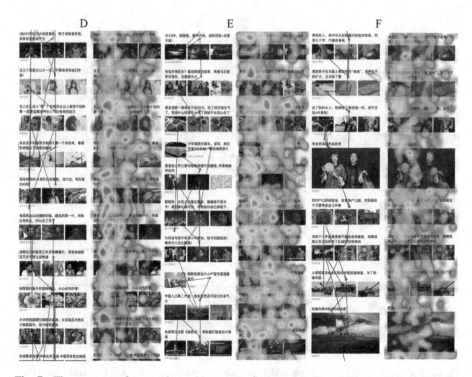

Fig. 7. The sequence of gaze point and heat map of schemes D, E, and F mainly based on three-picture templates

Subjective Evaluation of Different Template Combinations

From the subjective evaluation of participants, the effect of template combination on the evaluation of "good organization" was marginally significant, while its effect on "ease of reading" and "overall satisfaction" was not significant (see Table 5). In pairwise comparisons (see Table 6), the score of scheme E with three three-picture templates and one single-picture template was much lower than that of scheme A with all single-picture templates, which indicated that participants believed that the combination in scheme E did not look that neat and orderly when compared with scheme A.

Table 5. The effect of template combination on users' satisfaction

Dependent variable	Mean value						F (5,162)	p
	A	B	C	D	E	F		
Good organization	4.21	3.82	3.79	3.86	3.61	4.00	1.983	0.084
Ease of reading	3.79	3.82	3.82	3.75	3.50	3.71	0.611	0.692
Overall satisfaction	3.82	3.71	3.57	3.79	3.43	3.64	0.843	0.521

Table 6. Pairwise comparisons of template combinations in terms of "good organization" (Tukey's test)

	B	C	D	E	F
A	.410	.311	.520	.045*	.906
B		1.000	1.000	.906	.955
C			.999	.955	.906
D				.834	.983
E					.410

*$p < .05$

5 Discussion

Study 1 explores users' demands on the news feed of mobile apps and summarizes critical factors mattering user's reading experience through the qualitative research method that combines free viewing paradigm and interview session together. Excluding the influence of news contents (i.e., headlines and sources), the graphic layout (whether it is appropriate to users' reading habits) and image quality (whether it is concurrence with the topic, deliver rich and straightforward information, has proper brightness and cropping), the ancillary information (whether the release time and number of comments are complete), as well as the template combination (whether it is neat and orderly) will greatly affect users' reading experience of the mobile news feed.

Based on the findings of study 1, study 2 further investigated what kind of template combination is neat and orderly to identify the better combination according to users' eye-tracking data and subjective evaluation of six combinations. The results show that templates and their combination influence the browsing behavior of users and that there are differences in gaze behavior among different templates and even among different regions in the same template. The large-picture template is generally more attractive to users, with higher proportion of relative peaks of fixation duration. With the three-picture template, users usually focus their attention on the first two pictures and barely see the third one. As for different combinations, the main findings are as follows:

- When consecutive single-picture templates are combined with large-picture template, the scan path remained nearly linear, with few movements or zigzags. Such scheme did not interrupt the pace of scanning.
- When consecutive single-picture templates are combined with three-picture template, there was no specific rule in the scan path, and the gaze point of users alternated between the text and the picture, which would cause a frequent switching between "text analysis" and "picture analysis" in the area of brain cognition.
- When consecutive three-picture templates are combined with single-picture template, because of the difference in structure between the two templates, users would think the page looked messy and unorganized, and the single-picture template was less attracted and more likely to be ignored by users, which greatly weakened the value of this piece of news.
- When consecutive three-picture templates are combined with large-picture template, the two forms of templates had a top-bottom structure, few changes in the reading pattern was shown when compared with all three-pictures, and thus this combination was relatively balanced for the large-picture template harmonizes with the three-picture ones.

Based on the findings above, we propose the following design suggestions for the news feed of mobile news apps:

1. The combination of consecutive three-picture templates with single-picture template should be avoided as much as possible.
2. The large-picture template is a good choice to be combined with consecutive single-picture templates or consecutive three-picture templates since it can be well integrated. It should be noted that since the large picture receives much more attention, its quality has a significant impact on user experience and therefore high quality should be guaranteed. However, the quality of large pictures in current news feed vary, some of them are not appealing or have poor resolution, which greatly harms the reading experience.
3. When using three-picture template, put the high-quality picture in the first place could increase users' attention to the news.

6 Conclusion and Future Work

This research studied users' browsing behavior and demands on news feed of the mobile news apps. Two studies were conducted to find critical factors affecting users' reading experience and investigated the influence of template combination to find out appropriate combinations for mobile news feed. Based on research results, proposals were put forward to guide the design of mobile news feed. The approach of this paper is based on current mainstream products in the Chinese market, with specific and limited choices in the value range of independent variables, user groups, and mobile devices. In the future, more work should be done to explore more diversified template combinations, broaden the scope of participants' ages as well as the mobile devices of different sizes, so as to provide a whole guidance on the experience design of mobile news feed.

References

1. Vraga, E., Bode, L., Troller-Renfree, S.: Beyond self-reports: using eye tracking to measure topic and style differences in attention to social media content. Commun. Methods Meas. **10** (2–3), 149–164 (2016)
2. Sülflow, M., Schäfer, S., Winter, S.: Selective attention in the news feed: an eye-tracking study on the perception and selection of political news posts on Facebook. New Media Soc. **21**(1), 168–190 (2019)
3. Wang, H.Y.: The research of navigation design of mobile news client based on cognitive psychology. Mater thesis. Jiangnan University, Nanjing, China (2015)
4. Liu, T., Hou, W.J.: Graphic layout design study of mobile news app based on visual behavior. J. Beijing Univ. Post Telecommun. (Soc. Sci. Ed.) **18**(3), 6–13 (2016)
5. Lv, M.S., Lv, B., Wu, T.N.: Research on user visual browsing pattern under different layout design of mobile news app. Chin. J. Ergon. **23**(5), 34–38 (2017)
6. O'Toole, K.: Eye movement research points to importance of text over graphics on websites. Stanford report (2010). https://news.stanford.edu/news/2000/may10/eyetrack-55.html. Accessed 14 Feb 2019
7. Bol, N., Boerman, S.C., Romano Bergstrom, J.C., Kruikemeier, S.: An overview of how eye tracking is used in communication research. In: Antona, M., Stephanidis, C. (eds.) UAHCI 2016. LNCS, vol. 9737, pp. 421–429. Springer, Cham (2016). https://doi.org/10.1007/978-3-319-40250-5_40
8. Qu, Q.X., Zhang, L., Chao, W.Y., Duffy, V.: User experience design based on eye-tracking technology: a case study on smartphone apps. In: Duffy, V.G. (ed.) Advances in Applied Digital Human Modeling and Simulation. AISC, vol. 481, pp. 303–315. Springer, Cham (2017). https://doi.org/10.1007/978-3-319-41627-4_27

3D Gesture Interface: Japan-Brazil Perceptions

Anna Carolina Soares Medeiros[1(✉)], Photchara Ratsamee[1], Yuki Uranishi[1], Tomohiro Mashita[1], Haruo Takemura[1], and Tatiana Aires Tavares[2]

[1] Osaka University, Osaka, Japan
anna@lab.ime.cmc.osaka-u.ac.jp
{photchara,uranishi,mashita}@ime.cmc.osaka-u.ac.jp
takemura@cmc.osaka-u.ac.jp
[2] Federal University of Pelotas, Pelotas, Brazil
tatiana@inf.ufpel.edu.br

Abstract. Gestures are used naturally in communication, and use with modern computer systems is becoming increasingly feasible and applicable for interaction. Analyzing how gesture interfaces are perceived in different parts of the world can help in understanding possible weak and strong points, allowing for different improvements to the interfaces. This study aims to analyze how different technological familiarization levels impacts the user experience of gestural interfaces. Our work describes the findings of an experiment that was replicated in two countries: Brazil and Japan. In each experiment, 20 subjects tested two applications; one had a mouse-based interface and the other a gesture-based interface. User experience was measured using questionnaires from AttrakDiff. Subjectivity and abstract concepts largely differed, but major agreement was found regarding room for improvement of the pragmatist quality of the gestural interface in order to be embraced by the average user.

Keywords: Natural language interfaces · Gesture interface · Graphical user interface

1 Introduction

Human body language is a key aspect of human interaction. Whether used to give support or as a main tool [1, 2], gestures are a crucial factor in interpersonal communication [3]. During the last decade, it has become easier to explore gesture interface paradigms thanks to available, off-the-shelf, and affordable devices like Kinect [4] and Leap Motion [5]. These technologies are not limited to only image-based devices but can also rely on different aspects of gestural perception, like the electromyography-based Myo [6] or radar-based Project Soli [7].

As devices improve and diversify and the range of ideas for gesture-based interfaces increases [8–10], interaction paradigms that started appearing about three decades ago have been further explored. One challenge that arises as this

P.-L. P. Rau (Ed.): HCII 2019, LNCS 11576, pp. 266–279, 2019.
https://doi.org/10.1007/978-3-030-22577-3_19

investigation continues comes from the fact that humanity deals in abstract concepts, whereas the computers typically require clear, definite, and pragmatic data. A holistic metric that can be used to measure the different aspects of the user experience when using such interfaces is therefore complex to define. Effort [11,12] seems to be an often-chosen metric, but it alone cannot encompass all facets of gestures as a means of interaction.

Evaluating gestural interfaces is a complex task because it involves many nuances of perceptions that can easily change from user to user. This work proposes an investigation and discussion about how to improve gestural interfaces by presenting a user experience evaluation where opinions about a mouse interface and a gesture interface were compared using metrics that tried to capture the abstract perceptions of the subjects. The gesture interface application's strong and weak qualities were identified and analyzed by volunteer participants in Brazil and Japan. Understanding how gesture interfaces are perceived in different cultures can be helpful to contribute to the effectiveness of this type of interface.

2 Overview of Experiment

Gestural interfaces should ideally have the ability to always determine when the user was moving naturally, just scratching his nose, waving to a friend, or really intended to access a function of the system. It should be able to adapt its recognition algorithm to every different person in order to provide accuracy and better anticipate each user's needs. Gestural interfaces should be able to seamlessly blend into our lives to facilitate tasks, assist in daily life, or even encourage healthier pastimes.

In order to achieve this level of perception, challenges have to be addressed both on the human side and on the technological side. This paper focuses on exploring the user's perception of gestural interfaces and comparing it to those of a conventional mouse interface. In order to do that, we set up an experiment using two applications: one with a gestural interface using leap motion, the other using a mouse and keyboard. Both applications had the same system functions; users could Select, Rotate, Translate, Scale and Deselect a red cube on the screen, the only difference was the input mode. Subjects could test both applications, sometimes making remarks about the interaction. To try to capture more abstract nuances of user's perceptions about both systems, subjects were asked to answer questionnaires provided the AttrakDiff tool [13].

The AttrakDiff is a 28-item semantic differential tool used measure the perception of two broad qualities: Hedonic quality and pragmatic quality [14,15]. Hedonic quality refers to the fulfillment of psychological needs and is represented by two subdivisions: Identification and Stimulation. Pragmatic quality refers to a product's perceived potential to support relevant task achievement. In addition, AttrakDiff also measures general appeal. Appeal is encapsulated as the consequences of pragmatic and hedonic quality perception.

Two universities provided available resources to carry out the study: the Federal University of Paraíba in Brazil and Osaka University in Japan. The choice of places for the experiments was motivated due to the different access levels of the general population regarding technology in daily life. Japan was placed 10th in a global ranking that assesses nations on their level of development in information and communication technology [16], as a result of high levels of investment in ICT infrastructure, high-quality networks, and high levels of take-up of services by consumers. The same study places Brazil on the 66th position, showing a considerable gap between both countries, which is also true in previous assessments [17]. Universities are a place were individuals from various financial backgrounds, beliefs, and views can meet and socialize with each other; this environment seemed beneficial to analyze how different technological familiarization levels impacts the user experience of gestural interfaces.

The following sections describe the experiment procedures, participant groups, and data collection in detail and then analyze the results obtained from the study. Confidence intervals and a 2-tailed Student's Paired T-test were conducted on the average results for each word pair from the questionnaires.

3   Materials and Human Resources

The following text describes the participants that volunteered for the experiment, the applications, equipment, and questionnaires that were used, and how the experiment was setup.

3.1   Participants

For each country, 20 subjects took part in the experiment. In Brazil (age: min = 19, max = 43, $\bar{x}$ = 23.45, SD = 5.5), the subjects were Brazilian students of the Federal University of Paraíba. No one had previous experience with gesture interfaces or knew about them. In Japan (age: min = 21, max = 51, $\bar{x}$ = 25.95, SD = 7.3), the participants were Japanese students and staff of Osaka University. Only one participant had previous experience with gesture interfaces, but 33% knew about it. In both countries half of the participants were female. The experiment was conducted individually with each participant.

3.2   Applications

Two applications were used: CubeNI (Natural Interaction) and CubeMK (Mouse and Keyboard). The gesture set for CubeNI was defined using a previously researched gesture-development methodology [18], and they can be observed in Fig. 1. The experiment in Brazil was originally executed with the objective of verifying and validating this methodology. In CubeNI and CubeMK, the user could interact with a red 3D cube on the screen. After selecting it, the cube could be rotated, translated, or scaled. Additionally, all the interaction with the cube could be stopped by deselecting the cube. Figure 2 shows all possible interactions with the red cube on both applications. CubeNI utilized a gestural interface through Leap Motion, while CubeMK utilized a mouse and keyboard interface. The keyboard was only used to deselect the cube.

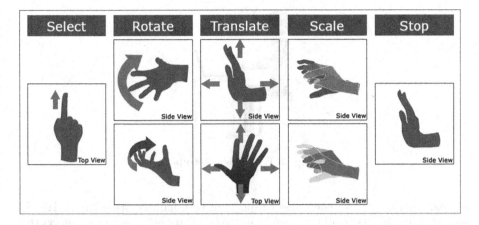

Fig. 1. CubeNI's gestures

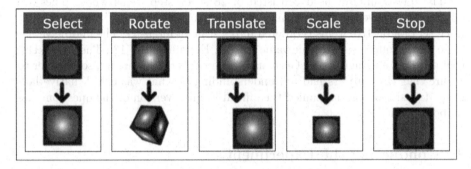

Fig. 2. CubeNI and CubeMK's possible interactions with the red cube. (Color figure online)

3.3 Tangible Resources

The Leap Motion controller was chosen as the gesture capture device. A wireless mouse and a laptop with a 14-in. display at a 1920 × 1080 resolution was used to conduct the experiment. All participants completed the experiment sitting on a table with the devices adjusted at a comfortable distance in front of them, as shown in Fig. 3. The provided questionnaires were obtained using the AttrakDiff tool.

3.4 Questionnaires

The AttrakDiff questionnaire gauges how attractive a product is in terms of usability and appearance [13]. The theoretical work model has been researched and tested in several studies [19–22]. These studies showed that Hedonic (HQ) and Pragmatic Qualities (PQ) are perceived consistently and independently of one another. Both contribute equally to the rating of Attractiveness (ATT), and

Fig. 3. Experiment set-up

a separation of the two constituent aspects of HQ, namely Stimulation (HQ-S) and Identity (HQ-I), would be preferable. AttrakDiff optimizes and supports the distinction between the sub-qualities, S and I, within the HQ rating.

The questionnaires used consisted of 28 seven-step items whose poles are opposing adjectives (e.g. "confusing - clear", "unusual - ordinary", "good - bad"). Each set of adjective items is ordered into a scale of intensity. The middle values of an item group create a scale value for PQ, HQ and ATT [13]. The AttrakDiff tool provides an English and German version of its questionnaire, so in order to ensure that the subjects had full understanding of what was asked, native language translations accompanied the official English version of the questionnaire on both countries.

4   Conducting the Experiment

The experiment described here explores what users' preferences and perceptions were when using different interfaces for performing the same tasks.

4.1   Routine

One of the two applications (CubeNI or CubeMK) was chosen at random to start the experiment. The participant was then asked to Select, Rotate, Translate, Scale, and Deselect the cube. After all tasks were completed, the remaining application was then started and the same tasks repeated (Fig. 4).

In both countries, half of the subjects started the experiment with the gesture application, CubeNI, and the other half with the mouse application, CubeMK, to offset effects introduced by the order of the procedures. After testing both applications the participants were given two copies of the AttrakDiff questionnaire; one for each application.

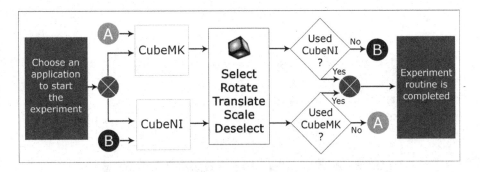

Fig. 4. Experiment's routine

4.2 Results

In order to capture users' perception of the product, AttrakDiff uses pairs of opposite adjectives as a method of investigation. These adjective-pairs make a collation of the evaluation dimensions possible. The following product dimensions are evaluated: The Pragmatic Quality (PQ) describes the usability of a product and indicates how successful users are in achieving their goals using the product. The Hedonic Quality - Stimulation (HQ-S) dimension indicates to what extent the product is novel and interesting, considering stimulating functions, content, interaction, and presentation styles. The Hedonic Quality-Identity (HQ-I) dimension indicates to what extent the product allows the user to identify with it. The Attractiveness (ATT) dimension describes a global value of the product based on the quality perception. Hedonic and pragmatic qualities are independent of one another, and contribute equally to the rating of attractiveness.

Those four dimensions are depicted in three graphics: Diagram of Average Values, Description of Word-Pairs, and Portfolio of Results. The Diagram of Average Values combines the means for each of the four dimensions evaluated. In both countries' Diagram of Average Values (Figs. 5 and 6) it can be observed that Brazil's and Japan's perceptions of both types of interface were similar: CubeMK was considered more pragmatic, meaning that it permitted the user to achieve his objectives more easily, while the CubeNI was deemed more stimulating, attractive, and the user could identify himself/herself more easily with the product when using this type of interface.

The Description of Word-Pairs shows the average of the questionnaire answers by the 20 volunteers for each word pairs, in each country. In Brazil (Fig. 7), the biggest differences between CubeMK and CubeNI results were that the mouse application was considered much more Practical and Straightforward whereas gesture application was regarded as much more Human and Innovative. However, both applications were considered to be equally Good and Professional to the Brazilian subjects.

In Japan (Fig. 8), considering all major divergence points between both applications' average scores, CubeNI's marks were closer to the best possible scores than CubeMK's. Also, CubeNI was especially considered to be highly Innovative

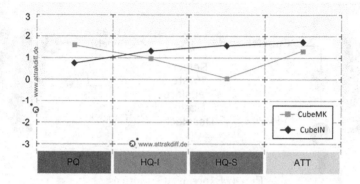

Fig. 5. Brazilian experiment's diagram of average values

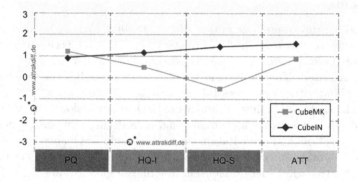

Fig. 6. Japanese experiment's diagram of average values

and a Novelty (as opposed to Ordinary). As for the converging points, CubeMK and CubeNI were regarded as equally Pleasant and Simple.

When comparing CubeMK's results between both countries the greatest significant difference found was that in Brazil, it was judged to be Creative whereas in Japan it was considered Unimaginative. On both countries it was found to be similarly Pleasant, Simple, Predictable, and Manageable.

When comparing CubeNI's scores in Brazil and Japan, a big difference in opinion was that the Brazilian subjects found the gesture application to be Human, whereas in Japan it was deemed Technical; Another diverging point was that Japanese subjects found the gestural interface to be Undemanding, whereas Brazilians thought it Challenging. The common opinion was that CubeNI was considered equally Attractive and similarly Integrating and Simple.

In the Portfolio of Results, the values of HQ are represented on the vertical axis (low values at the bottom). The horizontal axis represents the value of the PQ (low values at the left). Depending on the dimension's values, the product will lie in one or more of these presented regions. The bigger the confidence rectangle, the less sure one can be to which region it belongs. A small confidence

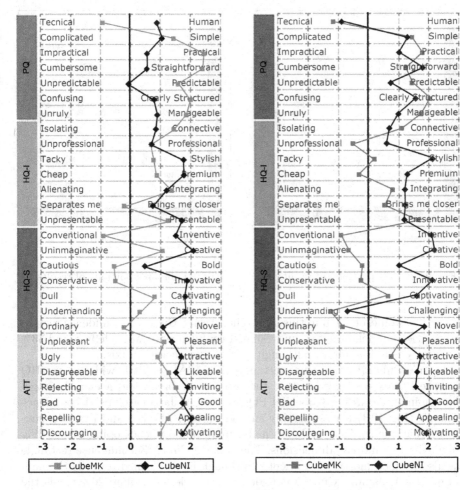

Fig. 7. Brazil's description of word-pairs

Fig. 8. Japan's description of word-pairs

rectangle is more informative since investigation results in that area are less coincidental, making them more reliable. The confidence rectangle essentially shows if the users are in agreement in their evaluation of the product. The bigger the confidence rectangle, the more variable the evaluation ratings.

By analyzing both countries' portfolios of results, we observed that the Brazil's CubeMK confidence rectangle (Fig. 9A) is wider on the HQ than the PQ axis, suggesting that the subjects in Brazil had a more homogeneous opinion regarding CubeNI's PQ dimension. As for Brazil's CubeNI confidence rectangle (Fig. 9B), the opposite occurred; it was wider on the PQ axis than the HQ axis, suggesting that the subjects in Brazil had a more homogeneous opinion regarding CubeNI's HQ dimension. This portfolio considers the balance between self-oriented and task-oriented features; the quadrant marked "desired" represents

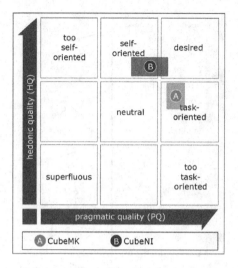

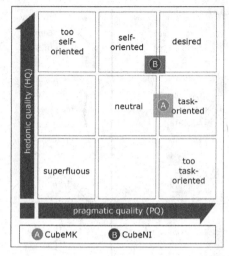

Fig. 9. Brazil's portfolio of results   **Fig. 10.** Japan's portfolio of results

values that would be ideal in this case. The Brazil's CubeMK confidence rectangle was deemed task-oriented, and CubeNI confidence rectangle fell around 33% inside the desired quadrant, although on its most uncertain axis.

Japan's CubeMK confidence rectangle (Fig. 10A) is a little wider on the HQ than the PQ axis, suggesting that the subjects in Japan had a more homogeneous opinion regarding CubeNI's PQ dimension. Japan's CubeNI confidence rectangle (Fig. 10B) is considerably smaller on both the HQ and PQ axis, suggesting that the subjects in Japan had a more homogeneous opinion regarding CubeMK's PQ and HQ dimensions. The Japan's CubeMK confidence rectangle was also deemed mostly task-oriented although it also leaned towards the neutral quadrant. Japan's CubeNI confidence rectangle fell around 20% inside the desired quadrant, where the opinions of the Japanese subjects were clearly more homogeneous than the Brazilian subjects.

A 2-tailed Student's Paired T-test (Fig. 11) was conducted on the results obtained from the questionnaires. A significance level of 5% was considered. In Brazil, CubeMK and CubeNI were compared (p = 0.10, t-critical = 1.70) and no statistically significant differences were found. Additionally, a 2-tailed Student's Paired T-test between the results of each of the 4 qualities groups (PQ, HQ-I, HQ-S, ATT) was also conducted (Fig. 12). For PQ (p = 0.14, t-critical = 2.44) and HQ-I (p = 0.19, t-critical = 2.44) there were no statistically significant differences found, but for HQ-S (p = 0.0006, t-critical = 2.44) and ATT (p = 0.009, t-critical = 2.44) there were statistically significant differences between subjective metrics for both applications in Brazil.

In Japan, a statistically significant difference was found between CubeMK and CubeNI's results (p = 0.0009, t-critical = 2.05). The results for each quality group was compared between both applications; here it was observed that in the

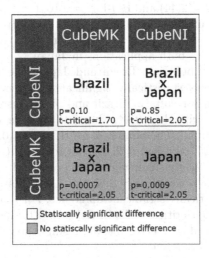

Fig. 11. Student's Paired T-test overall results between Brazil and Japan.

	Brazil	Japan	CubeMK	CubeNI
PQ	CubeMK x CubeNI p=0.14 t-critical=2.44	CubeMK x CubeNI p=0.20 t-critical=2.44	Brazil x Japan p=0.08 t-critical=2.44	Brazil x Japan p=0.57 t-critical=2.44
HQ-I	CubeMK x CubeNI p=0.19 t-critical=2.44	CubeMK x CubeNI p=0.10 t-critical=2.44	Brazil x Japan p=0.16 t-critical=2.44	Brazil x Japan p=0.49 t-critical=2.44
HQ-S	CubeMK x CubeNI p=0.0006 t-critical=2.44	CubeMK x CubeNI p=0.002 t-critical=2.44	Brazil x Japan p=0.15 t-critical=2.44	Brazil x Japan p=0.84 t-critical=2.44
ATT	CubeMK x CubeNI p=0.009 t-critical=2.44	CubeMK x CubeNI p=0.004 t-critical=2.44	Brazil x Japan p=0.02 t-critical=2.44	Brazil x Japan p=0.47 t-critical=2.44

☐ Statiscally significant difference
▨ No statiscally significant difference

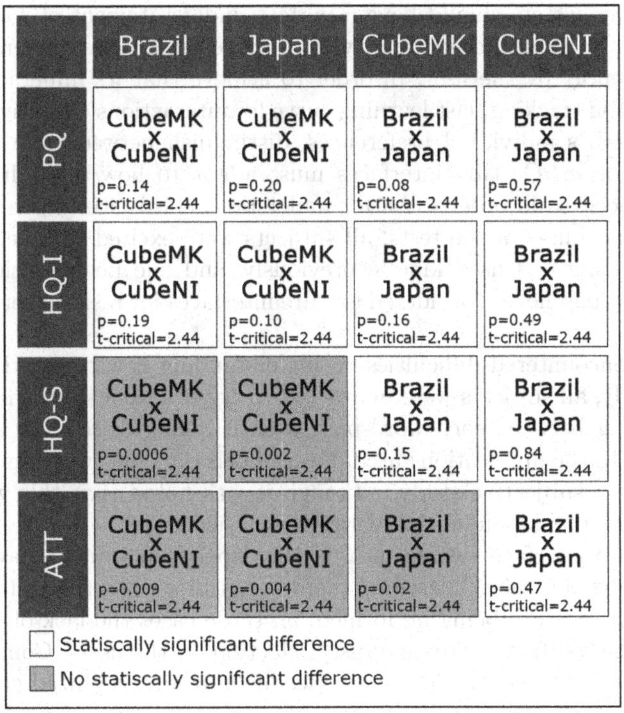

Fig. 12. Student's Paired T-test results between Brazil and Japan, considering every possible comparison regarding the four qualities (PQ, HQ-I, HQ-S and ATT).

PQ (p = 0.20, t-critical = 2.44) and HQ-I (p = 0.10, t-critical = 2.44) there were no statistically significant differences, but for the HQ-S (p = 0.002, t-critical = 2.44) and ATT (p = 0.004, t-critical = 2.44) there were statistically significant differences found between both applications in Japan.

When comparing CubeMK in Brazil and Japan, the results (p = 0.0007, t-critical = 2.05) show a statistically significant difference. For the group of qualities PQ, CubeMK's results in Brazil and Japan were compared and the outcome (p = 0.08, t-critical = 2.44) shows that there were no statistically significant differences found. The same goes for HQ-I (p = 0.16, t-critical = 2.44) and the HQ-S (p = 0.15, t-critical = 2.44), but for ATT (p = 0.02, t-critical = 2.44) there was a statistically significant difference found.

The scores (p = 0.85, t-critical = 2.05) for CubeNI's results in Brazil and Japan showed no statistically significant difference. For PQ (p = 0.57, t-critical = 2.44), HQ-I (p = 0.49, t-critical = 2.44), HQ-S (p = 0.84, t-critical = 2.44) and ATT (p = 0.47, t-critical = 2.44) CubeNI's results shows that no statistically significant differences were found.

5   Discussion

Utopically, any system should have a perfect understatement of what its users want, when they want and how they would like to get it done, preferably requiring minimal effort by the user. In order to achieve that its imperative to have accurate motion tracking, fast learning curve for interactions (intuitive gestures), understand user's individual preferences, distinguish between idle and action-requesting motion. Gesture interfaces must adapt to how individuals express unique practices, so in order to better understand it this study was conducted.

During the course of the tests, all subjects were excited to take part in the experiment, some had used kinetic previously, and one Leap Motion, but the great majority had never considered gesture interfaces for tasks other then entertainment.

Subjects encountered difficulties on understanding how to use the questionnaires properly, all subjects were instructed to try to give a spontaneous answer when matching between each word-pair, even if failing to see how some word-pairs applied to the applications used. Overall this difficulty was expected, given that this was a subjective study, although it was noted that this was a much bigger issue for the Japanese than Brazilian subjects.

The gesture interface system used in the experiments didn't have a perfect motion tracking accuracy. Therefore, there were times when the system couldn't understand the gesture being performed, on those cases the lack of satisfactory feedback promoted frustration and dissatisfaction on the users. Comments were made that the interface should try give feedback to unrecognized gestures (e.g. "gesturing too fast, losing track of hands") in order to improve user satisfaction when better accuracy on gesture recognition is not possible.

One interesting result was that the application with gestural interaction was deemed more "Technical" than "Human" in Japan (Fig. 8, Technical-Human):

Japan's result for the mouse interface was very close together to its gestural one. The 95% confidence interval for all 20 Japanese answers for the Human-Technical word pair is as follows: for the CubeNI it varies from 2.2 to 4.0, for the CubeMK from 2.0 to 3.6. According to studies [16,17], Japanese people are more familiarized with technology, compared to Brazilians, and while on the questionnaires those words are considered complete opposites, it seems that the perception in Japan was that they weren't. The perception of CubeNI being more "Technical" could come from the simple fact that both Leap Motion and Mouse are devices, therefore technical.

Overall, all subjects from both countries seemed very excited to try the gestural interface, but once this novelty wears off we need to think about building realistic standards for gestural interfaces. One very apparent challenge on this study was the metrics; how to choose or build a metric than can balance the scales when users from different backgrounds, preferences, interests, behaviors have different expectations and demands from a system. Subjectivity and abstract concepts are challenging, but on this study a point where there was major agreement was that the pragmatist quality of the gestural interface has a lot of room to improve in order to be embraced by the average user.

6 Conclusion

The aim of this work was to analyze how different technological familiarization levels impacts the perceived user experience of gestural interfaces. In order to do that, we set up an experiment to compare a gestural interface (CubeNI) with a mouse interface (CubeMK). This experiment took place in Brazil and Japan, inside university environments. The AttrakDiff questionnaire was used to evaluate user experiences of both products.

As shown before, statistically significant differences were found only in two situations: between Brazil and Japan regarding CubeMK's results, and between CubeNI and CubeMK's results in Japan (Fig. 11). As for the four qualities group (Fig. 12), in Brazil, the comparison between CubeNI's and CubeMK's HQ-S and ATT qualities had statistically significant results. In Japan, the same goes for the comparison between CubeNI's and CubeMK's HQ-S and ATT qualities. Additionally, the comparison between Brazil-CubeMK's and Japan-CubeMK's ATT qualities also had statistically significant results.

In both countries the major advantage of the gestural interface was that it was considered much more stimulating to the users' senses than the mouse-based interface. The disadvantage was that the pragmatic qualities of the gesture interface has yet to match the mouse's objectiveness. This suggests that there is still a need to improve the ease of use of gesture interfaces, so that the users' attention can focus entirely on task completion and not on interface usage. To that end it is recommended improving feedback when system cant recognize user's gestures.

Regarding gestural interfaces many paths could be taken to contribute to its development: Researching how to improve metrics for evaluating this type of interface would be welcomed, more studies in different countries can be beneficial to better understand what is globally expected from this type of interface, and research on gesture precision enhancement for future gestural interfaces could help to increase this type of interface's pragmatic qualities. To that end, during the course of tests, improvement on feedback was suggested when the system failed to recognize the gestures. Other possible continuation to this investigation course is measuring how users perform (time, effort, accuracy) when given more complex test routines, in addition to perception investigation, in order to balance subjectiveness with objectiveness.

Additionally, the usage experience of this type of interface relies not only on the gesture-detection precision of the device chosen but also on the gesture used; to that end it is also a concern to notice that the gesture-development process can be very expensive and time-consuming due to the fact that it often needs to rely on human subjects to define new gestures.

References

1. Galloway, G., Fant, L.: AMESLAN - an introduction to American sign language. Am. Ann. Deaf **116**(6), 658–658 (1973). Accessed http://www.jstor.org/stable/44387803
2. Goldin-Meadow, S., Morford, M.: Gesture in early child language: studies of deaf and hearing children. Merrill-Palmer Q. 145–176 (1985)
3. Lund, K.: The importance of gaze and gesture in interactive multimodal explanation. Lang. Resour. Eval. **41**(3–4), 289–303 (2007)
4. Kinect   Homepage.   https://developer.microsoft.com/en-us/windows/kinect. Accessed Jan 2019
5. Leap Motion Homepage. https://www.leapmotion.com/. Accessed 31 Jan 2019
6. Myo Homepage. https://support.getmyo.com/hc/en-us. Accessed 30 Jan 2019
7. Project Soli. https://atap.google.com/soli/. Accessed 31 Jan 2019
8. Imura, S., Hosobe, H.: Biometric authentication using the motion of a hand. In: Proceedings of the 2016 Symposium on Spatial User Interaction, pp. 221–221. ACM (2016)
9. Babic, T., Reiterer, H., Haller, M.: GestureDrawer: one-handed interaction technique for spatial user-defined imaginary interfaces. In: Proceedings of the 5th Symposium on Spatial User Interaction, pp. 128–137. ACM (2017)
10. Kytö, M., Dhinakaran, K., Martikainen, A., Hämäläinen, P.: Improving 3D character posing with a gestural interface. IEEE Comput. Graph. Appl. **37**(1), 70–78 (2017)
11. Schwaller, M., Lalanne, D.: Pointing in the air: measuring the effect of hand selection strategies on performance and effort. In: Holzinger, A., Ziefle, M., Hitz, M., Debevc, M. (eds.) SouthCHI 2013. LNCS, vol. 7946, pp. 732–747. Springer, Heidelberg (2013). https://doi.org/10.1007/978-3-642-39062-3_53
12. Liu, X., Thomas, G.W.: Gesture interfaces: minor change in effort, major impact on appeal. In: Proceedings of the 2017 CHI Conference on Human Factors in Computing Systems, pp. 4278–4283. ACM (2017)
13. AttrakDiff Homepage. http://www.attrakdiff.de/sience-en.html. Accessed 31 Jan 2019

14. Hassenzahl, M.: The thing and I: understanding the relationship between user and product. In: Blythe, M., Monk, A. (eds.) Funology 2. HIS, pp. 301–313. Springer, Cham (2018). https://doi.org/10.1007/978-3-319-68213-6_19

15. Hassenzahl, M.: Experience design: technology for all the right reasons. Synth. Lect. Hum.-Cent. Inform. **3**(1), 1–95 (2010)

16. ITU: Measuring the Information Society Report 2017: Volume 1 and 2. ITU, Geneva (2017). http://handle.itu.int/11.1002/pub/80f52533-en

17. ITU: Measuring the Information Society 2016. ITU, Geneva (2016). http://handle.itu.int/11.1002/pub/80de56e8-en

18. Medeiros, A.C.S., Tavares, T.A., da Fonseca, I.E.: How to design an user interface based on gestures? In: Marcus, A. (ed.) DUXU 2015. LNCS, vol. 9186, pp. 63–74. Springer, Cham (2015). https://doi.org/10.1007/978-3-319-20886-2_7

19. Hassenzahl, M.: Beautiful objects as an extension of the self: a reply. Hum.-Comput. Interact. **19**(4), 377–386 (2004)

20. Hassenzahl, M.: Hedonic, emotional, and experiential perspectives on product quality. In: Encyclopedia of Human Computer Interaction, pp. 266–272. IGI Global (2006)

21. Hassenzahl, M., Tractinsky, N.: User experience-a research agenda. Behav. Inf. Technol. **25**(2), 91–97 (2006)

22. Tractinsky, N., Hassenzahl, M.: Arguing for aesthetics in human-computer interaction. I-com **4**(3), 66–68 (2005)

Scenario-Based User Experience Differences of Human-Device Interaction at Different Levels of Proactivity

Hao Tan[1] and Min Zhu[2(✉)]

[1] State Key Laboratory of Advanced Design and Manufacturing
for Vehicle Body, Hunan University, Changsha 414000, China
[2] School of Design, Hunan University, Changsha 414000, China
15895829528@163.com

Abstract. In this paper, it mainly studied the satisfaction and mental comfort of people interacting with intelligent devices at different levels of proactivity. Three models were proposed corresponding to 3 levels of proactive interaction: L1 - "arouse and wait", L2 - "arouse and output", and L3 - "output directly". The experiment was conducted with 6 short video sequences divided into two contexts where intelligent devices proactively initiated interaction with people at the three levels mentioned above. The short video sequences in each scenario were designed under the three models. In addition, the discovered subjective scores of participants' satisfaction and comfort were presented, together with participants' opinions on different levels of the devices' proactive interaction. The analysis of the data revealed that people showed various levels of satisfaction and comfort towards the models under different contexts. Furthermore, this study also discussed the reasons behind the subjective scores and the benefits of the proactive interaction models. This research is aimed at offering some guidance in choosing interaction models to proactive interaction design.

Keywords: Proactive interaction · Human-device interaction ·
Proactive interaction models · User study

1 Introduction

1.1 Human-Device Interaction

With the development of technology, intelligent devices can interact with humans directly through speech output, serving as a conversation companion [1, 2], or interacting with humans as a mediator between humans [3, 4]. The interactions between humans and devices are increasingly similar to human communication, and devices are becoming more and more proactive [5, 6]. However, currently, there is only limited research on devices' degree of proactivity. Originating from Asimov's Three Laws of Robotics, social acceptance of human-device interaction has become an increasingly emerging research topic [7]. The purpose of this paper is to explore the level of the devices' proactivity in direct interactions between devices and humans with high user satisfaction under specific scenarios.

© Springer Nature Switzerland AG 2019
P.-L. P. Rau (Ed.): HCII 2019, LNCS 11576, pp. 280–290, 2019.
https://doi.org/10.1007/978-3-030-22577-3_20

The relationship between humans and devices are becoming closer, and the interaction between them is called interspecific interaction (between two different species) [3]. In the traditional human-device interaction, devices mostly play the role of humans' tools [8–10]. Previously, some studies focused on these tools' different levels of automation [10]. In recent years, Mäkitalo and his colleagues have proposed that there has been a new kind of socio-digital system between humans and proactive context sensing mobile devices, where the mobile devices work as active participants and can initiate interactions between devices and humans [5] (Fig. 1).

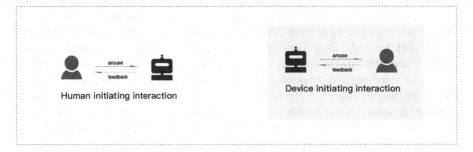

Human initiating interaction

Device initiating interaction

Fig. 1. Comparison of human initiating interaction and device initiating interaction.

In humans' face-to-face interaction, stimuli to initiate a conversation is essential when people are not familiar with each other, which is called "ticket to talk" according to Sacks [11], such as "hello" or some other casual topics. Among most of the previous research, when humans interact with devices, they need to first "wake up" devices using input devices such as radio or buttons, which will then respond to humans [12]. The development of artificial intelligence technology promotes the exchange of active roles between people and devices [13]. Up to now, a lot of research has been done on social applications of smart device, and consequently, research on social features of smart devices has become a hot topic [4, 14–16]. Compared with humans' face-to-face interaction, the stimuli to initiate human-device interaction is essential.

1.2 Proactivity and Social Device

The theory of proxemics indicates that the increased proximity between people may indicate an intention to interact [17]. Tennenhouse proposed that the majority of computers would be proactive [18]. Pradthana created a sense of proactivity of the technology and allowed an intuitive way of interacting with mobile technology in a social situation [13]. Mäkitalo and Pääkkö introduced the concept of social devices and its implementation, which focused on enriching local interaction by means of technology [5]. Paasovaara designed an application called Next2You which aims to inform users of opportune connections and encourage face-to-face interaction between people [6]. Jarusriboonchai developed Who's Next, a multiplayer quiz-based mobile game, which was intended to break the ice within a group of strangers [19]. However, most of the research on SD is about the role of devices in human interaction. In this thesis, three models are proposed to represent the intelligent devices' different levels of proactivity, with the aim of studying users' experience on devices' proactively initiating the interaction with humans at different levels of proactivity.

1.3 Scenarios

According to Bonarini, many intelligent devices like vacuum cleaners, automatic doors and cars are called "non-bio-inspired robots" [20]. Our research object is the intelligent device with active interaction function, so we will combine the usage scenarios of robots with the usage scenarios of social devices to be the usage scenarios of intelligent devices. There have been a lot of studies on social robots on the home scene [14, 21, 22], and some studies have found that the home scene is a suitable scene for robot research [23]. Recently, there have been a lot of research focusing on active interaction in public environment, but some research suggested that active interaction in public could cause some negative emotions, such as embarrassment [4]. Thus, how to handle this problem has become a key research point. In this paper, it will study the differences of user experience with different active interaction degrees in two scenarios: home environment and office environment, so as to obtain a more appropriate interaction degree under different contexts.

2 User Study

2.1 Participants

The experiment with 6 short video sequences was conducted, in which two actors were invited to carry out some tasks in each scenario. There has been some research using video sequences to match the dog videos to the robot videos with emotional states [3]. In addition, Zwinderman and his colleagues compared the experiment with videos recorded by actors to the direct experiment, finding that as a medium, video could draw attention to what users do with technology instead of technical workings [24].

30 participants were involved in this study (16 male, 14 female), aged from 22 to 65 with an average age of 33 years old. The participants were recruited by means of a questionnaire survey, which consisted of two parts: the demographic characteristics, and the questions designed for dividing different types of groups. The total participants were divided into two groups: home group and office group, according to the experiences of each scenario. Most participants' highest level of education was a four-year college degree or higher (66.7%, n = 20), which was followed by a junior college degree (16.7%, n = 5) and then a high school diploma or below (16.6%, n = 5).

2.2 The Proactive Interaction Models

Paasovaara studied social devices with three levels of interaction: automatic, technology-mediated and face-to-face, which was aimed to inform users of the opportune connections and encourage face-to-face interactions between people [6]. However, there is almost no division on devices' degree of proactivity when devices interact with people. According to the degrees of proactivity, three proactive interaction models were presented (Fig. 2):

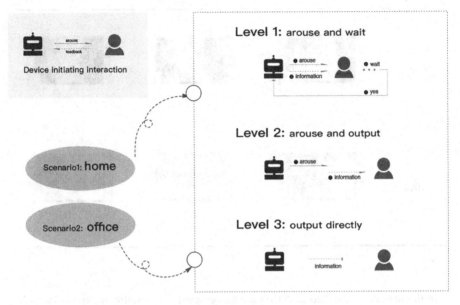

Fig. 2. Three levels of proactive interaction.

L1 - "arouse and wait". The L1 model was the least active one among the three models, which represented a pattern that the device aroused people proactively with a beep or other forms of sound (sparkling, motion, graph or voice) and then waited for people's feedback.

L2 - "arouse and output". The L2 model was designed for the moderate level. It outputted its intention after arousing the people without the feedback from human beings.

L3 - "output directly". The L3 model was the most active model in which the device outputted its intention directly without arousing people.

2.3   Preparation of the Video Materials

Classification of Contexts. The contexts were divided into two categories: home scene and office scene. People usually feel relaxed at home as home is a private space. Hence, the home scene possesses the feature of ease. In contrast, the office is a public place where no noise is needed, so people always keep quiet on the office scene.

Video Producing. In this research, a total of 6 short video sequences were studied, which were made by applying the three proactive interaction models to the two contexts with an intelligent device in each scenario (seen Table 1).

Table 1. Classification of 6 video sequences

Scenario	L1- "arouse and wait"	L2- "arouse and output"	L3- "output directly"
A: Home	A1	A2	A3
B: Office	B1	B2	B3

In the first video marked as A1 on the home scene, the intelligent device swung its head to arouse the man and waited for a feedback, which then expressed a request that it want to play music after getting verbal feedback from the man, and then it played music, otherwise, the device wouldn't play music if the man didn't give feedback. In the second video marked as A2, it aroused the man first and enhanced its intensity until the man noticed it and then outputted its intention directly without human's verbal feedback. Furthermore, the intelligent device greeted the man with voice proactively and directly without any arousing once the man came back from outside and went through the door in the video marked as A3.

On the office scene, the intelligent device aroused the woman in the B1 video and waited for a feedback, and once getting verbal feedback it outputted its intention. In the B2 video, it aroused the woman first and enhanced the intensity of arousing and then outputted its intention directly without verbal feedback. The intelligent device outputted the sound of the phone ringing directly without any arousing in the B3 video.

2.4 Experiment

The study was composed of three parts: (1) pilot experiment, in which the participants were presented with three prepared short video sequences to explain the three proactive interaction models before the main experiment was conducted; (2) the main experiment, including 6 short video sequences which were divided into 2 scenarios, where the participants were presented with 3 sequences of the same scenario every time in a random order, and they were asked to rate each model in the video with subjective scale concerning satisfaction and mental comfort levels (Table 2); (3) a semi-structured interview, after three videos of a single scenario, the participants were asked about the reasons for the scores through verbal expressions. To keep a quiet environment, the study was carried out in a laboratory in School of Design, Hunan University, China.

Table 2. Subjective scale on satisfaction and mental comfort level.

(1) Were you satisfied with the model in video?				
1	2	3	4	5
Unsatisfied			Very satisfied	
(2) Did you feel comfortable with the model in video?				
1	2	3	4	5
Not comfortable			Very comfortable	

In the main experiment, the participants were presented with three video clips representing the three models every time, which were depicted in the same scenario, and then were asked to rate each model under the context of 5-Point-Likert scale concerning satisfaction and mental comfort. This was followed by a semi-structured interview, where the participants were required to explain the reasons behind the scores, describe their subjective experiences in imaging themselves in the depicted stories and give some advice on these models.

2.5   Data Analysis Methods

In this study, two types of data were produced: (1) subjective scores of participants' levels of satisfaction and mental comfort were measured on a numerical scale ranging from 1 to 5; (2) notes and audio recordings obtained from the semi-structured interview. The data analysis consisted of two phases: quantitative analysis and qualitative analysis.

Effects of the levels of proactive interaction on dependent variables (satisfaction and comfort) were tested separately by means of repeated measurement analyses of variance (ANOVAs), with an alpha level of .05 involved in all statistical tests. If an interaction effect between the factors was found, a univariate ANOVA and a Scheffé post hoc test would be performed to figure out which level or levels of the factor differed from others in their effects on dependent variables.

The qualitative data were recorded by experimenters on the spot while the other experimenters were given an interview. The data were analyzed based on clustering analysis, thus producing a bottom-up hierarchy of themes. The purpose of the qualitative analysis was to account for the participants' subjective scores and help us better understand their subjective experiences and opinions towards the concept as well as the application of the models.

3 Results

3.1 Satisfaction Level

On the home scene, the main effect of the level of proactive interaction on satisfaction was statistically significant, $F (2,29) = 3.527$, $p = .034$. As was shown, the participants were mostly satisfied with the L3 - "output directly" model with a mean rating of 4.33 followed by the L1 - "arouse and wait" model (mean = 3.80) and the L2 - "arouse and output" model (mean = 3.76). On the office scene, the main effect of the level of proactive interaction on satisfaction was statistically significant, $F (2,29) = 7.169$, $p = .001$. As was shown, the participants were more satisfied with the L1 - "arouse and wait" model with a mean rating of 4.10 compared with the L3 - "output directly" model (mean = 3.00) (Fig. 3).

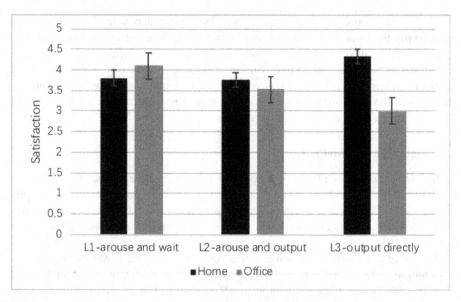

Fig. 3. Mean subjective satisfaction evaluation of the three models.

When considering the entire types of scenarios, the effects of participants' demographic characteristics on satisfaction would be discovered. The participants classified into the office group were more unsatisfied with the L3 model compared with the home group, and the participants classified into the home group were more satisfied with the L1 model compared with the office group. In addition, no significant difference was found in terms of gender. Only one significant difference was manifested in age when it came to satisfaction ratings. The users aged 36 to 45 were more satisfied with L1 model compared with those aged 18 to 25.

3.2   Comfort Level

The main effect of the level of proactive interaction on comfort on the home scene was statistically significant, F (2,29) = 3.508, p = .034. The most comfortable model on the home scene was the L3 - output directly model with a mean rating of 4.27 followed by the L1 and L2 model, 3.90 and 3.53 respectively. On the office scene, A test for the effect of the level of proactive interaction on comfort showed significant effects, F (2,29) = 14.630, p = .000. A post hoc test showed that the comfort rating of the L3 model was significantly lower than that of the other two models (Fig. 4).

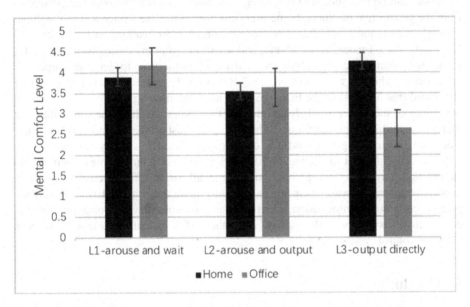

Fig. 4. Mean subjective mental comfort evaluation of the three models.

4   Discussion

4.1   Home Scenario

On the home scene, the participants were mostly satisfied with the L3 - output directly model, considering the L3 was the most comfortable choice on the home scene, which was mainly because they regarded home as a private place where they could do what they wanted without bothering anyone. One of the subjects named U10 said, "the L3 model is pretty good as it can remind me to do something directly and I think it very practical." User U8 said, "the L3 can timely remind me." From this perspective, the direct output model (L3) is quite functional. User U20 said, "I always feel very tired when coming back home after working for a long time, but the device interacts proactively with me, which can ease my loneliness like a pet." "It is very warm-hearted for the device to talk to me actively when I come back" said user U20. Therefore, most subjects think of their homes as their own space, as a result, tending to have the intelligent device that can initiatively care about them at home. Therefore, the output directly model is suitable for the home scene, and the reasons may include both its practical function and warm-hearted role at home.

4.2 Office Scenario

The most satisfactory and comfortable model in on the office scene is the "arouse and wait" model. As the office scene was a public place, the participants argued that the device should keep quiet so as not to disturb others. The reasons for subjects' choice of L1 model can be classified into two categories: from subjects' personal perspective or from the perspective of others. Some users considered that the device's output without human's permission would interrupt the thoughts of those working in the office. The U18 said, "the L3 model is too abrupt, and it will interrupt my thoughts, while the L1 model will remind me with a prompt, and I can set the time to get it to output the information, which is more comfortable." Based on the user's explanation, it can be concluded that for most of the time, the users are concentrating on the office scene, so the output of the device is likely to interrupt their work. At the same time, users are afraid of disturbing their colleagues. The U11 said, "just a little reminder, otherwise it would be embarrassing to disturb my colleagues." "The L1 is pretty suitable for the office, because it is not too active, but is practical enough to remind me or help me do something after getting my permission." All in all, in an office scenario, the users expect the device to wake them up in a slightly proactive way and waited for their permission to output information, which is mainly because they are concerned that the device may disturb both themselves and others if it outputs information without human's control.

5 Conclusion

According to the results, in different scenarios, people's choices of the proactive levels of smart devices are quite different. As to personal space like homes, people are more inclined to choose L3 active interaction degree model. However, in order to avoid disturbing others in public space, people tend to use the L1 active degree model to get rid of embarrassment. Meanwhile, people in public space usually concentrate on dealing with the matters at hand, so choosing L1 model can guarantee practicality without disturbing their thoughts.

As a future evolution of the present work, the research will be focused on more detailed division of proactivity degrees and external events such as tasks that affect the active interaction in specific scenarios. Furthermore, the state of users will also be one of the effects to be taken into consideration.

6 Limitations

One limitation in this work is that we did not measure user's experience from more experience dimensions, instead, we measure user's experience through satisfaction and comfort. Other limitation is all of our subjects were from a second-tier cities in China. In the future, we will study the influence of different tasks and different state of users on model selection.

Funding. The paper was supported by Newton Fund of United Kingdom (AHRC project No. AH/S003401/1) and Baidu AI Interaction Design Lab.

References

1. Konok, V., Korcsok, B., Miklósi, Á., Gácsi, M.: Should we love robots? – the most liked qualities of companion dogs and how they can be implemented in social robots. Comput. Hum. Behav. **80**, 132–142 (2018)
2. Friedman, B., Kahn Jr., P.H., Hagman, J.: Hardware companions?: what online AIBO discussion forums reveal about the human-robotic relationship. In: Proceedings of the SIGCHI Conference on Human Factors in Computing Systems, pp. 273–280. ACM (2003)
3. Gácsi, M., Kis, A., Faragó, T., Janiak, M., Muszyński, R., Miklósi, Á.: Humans attribute emotions to a robot that shows simple behavioral patterns borrowed from dog behavior. Comput. Hum. Behav. **59**, 411–419 (2016)
4. Väänänen-vainio-mattila, K.: Social devices as a new type of social system: enjoyable or embarrassing experiences? In: Workshop on Experiencing Interactivity in Public Spaces (EIPS), in Conjunction with CHI 2013, pp. 1–5 (2013)
5. Mäkitalo, N., Raatikainen, M., Aaltonen, T., et al.: Social devices: collaborative co-located interactions in a mobile cloud. In: International Conference on Mobile and Ubiquitous Multimedia, pp. 1–10 (2012)
6. Paasovaara, S., Olshannikova, E., Jarusriboonchai, P., et al.: Next2You: a social application for nearby strangers. In: The International Conference, pp. 339–341 (2016)
7. Koay, K.L., Dautenhahn, K., Woods, S.N., et al.: Empirical results from using a comfort level device in human-robot interaction studies. In: ACM SIGCHI/SIGART Conference on Human-Robot Interaction, pp. 194–201. ACM (2006)
8. Du, Y., Qin, J., Zhang, S., Cao, S., Dou, J.: Voice user interface interaction design research based on user mental model in autonomous vehicle. In: Kurosu, M. (ed.) HCI 2018. LNCS, vol. 10903, pp. 117–132. Springer, Cham (2018). https://doi.org/10.1007/978-3-319-91250-9_10
9. Song, Y., Liu, Y., Yan, Y.: The effects of center of mass on comfort of soft belts virtual reality devices. In: Rebelo, F., Soares, Marcelo M. (eds.) AHFE 2018. AISC, vol. 777, pp. 312–321. Springer, Cham (2019). https://doi.org/10.1007/978-3-319-94706-8_35
10. Dibitonto, M., Medaglia, C.M.: Improving user performance in a smart surveillance scenario through different levels of automation. In: Kurosu, M. (ed.) HCI 2015. LNCS, vol. 9170, pp. 706–716. Springer, Cham (2015). https://doi.org/10.1007/978-3-319-20916-6_65
11. Sacks H.: Lectures on Conversation, vol. I, II (2010)
12. Farhad, M., MacKenzie, I.S.: Evaluating tap-and-drag: a single-handed zooming method. In: Kurosu, M. (ed.) HCI 2018. LNCS, vol. 10903, pp. 233–246. Springer, Cham (2018). https://doi.org/10.1007/978-3-319-91250-9_18

13. Jarusriboonchai, P., Olsson, T.: User experience of proactive audio-based social devices: a wizard-of-oz study. In: Mobile & Ubiquitous Multimedia, pp. 98–106 (2014)
14. De Graaf, M.M.A., Ben Allouch, S., Van Dijk, J.A.G.M.: Long-term evaluation of a social robot in real homes. In: AISB Workshop on New Frontier in Human-Robot Interaction, p. 54 (2014)
15. Miklósi, A., Gácsi, M.: On the utilization of social animals as a model for social robotics. Front. Psychol. **3**, 75 (2012)
16. Jarusriboonchai, P., Olsson, T.: Roles, scenarios and challenges of social devices. In: ACM Conference on Pervasive and Ubiquitous Computing Adjunct Publication, pp. 1575–1578. ACM (2013)
17. Hall, E.: The Hidden Dimension. Anchor Books, New York City (1990)
18. Tennenhouse, D.: Proactive computing. Commun. ACM **43**, 43–50 (2000)
19. Jarusriboonchai, P., Malapaschas, A., Olsson, T.: Design and evaluation of a multi-player mobile game for icebreaking activity, pp. 4366–4377 (2016)
20. Bonarini, A.: Can my robotic home cleaner be happy? Issues about emotional expression in non-bio-inspired robots. Adapt. Behav. **24**, 335–349 (2016)
21. Mcginn, C., Sena, A., Kelly, K.: Controlling robots in the home: factors that affect the performance of novice robot operators. Appl. Ergon. **65**, 23–32 (2017)
22. Porcheron, M., Fischer, J.E., Reeves, S., et al.: Voice interfaces in everyday life. In: ACM CHI Conference on Human Factors in Computing Systems. ACM (2018)
23. Forlizzi, J.: How robotic products become social products: an ethnographic study of cleaning in the home. In: ACM/IEEE International Conference on Human-Robot Interaction, pp. 129–136. IEEE (2007)
24. Zwinderman, M., et al.: Using video prototypes for evaluating design concepts with users: a comparison to usability testing. In: Kotzé, P., Marsden, G., Lindgaard, G., Wesson, J., Winckler, M. (eds.) INTERACT 2013. LNCS, vol. 8118, pp. 774–781. Springer, Heidelberg (2013). https://doi.org/10.1007/978-3-642-40480-1_55

Effect of Vibrotactile Feedback on Simulator Sickness, Performance, and User Satisfaction with Virtual Reality Glasses

Bingcheng Wang and Pei-Luen Patrick Rau[⊠]

Tsinghua University, Beijing, China
rpl@tsinghua.edu.cn

Abstract. This study investigated the effects of vibrotactile feedback on simulator sickness, human performance, and user satisfaction when wearing virtual reality glasses. A total of 36 participants were recruited and 30 of them finished the experiments. They were asked to wear virtual reality glasses to play a car race game with a vibrotactile vest and a vibrotactile gamepad. The vest and gamepad provided vibration feedback, which was turned on in one task and turned off in the other task. The performance was measured during the tasks and simulator sickness and satisfaction were measured through questionnaires. The results showed that the participants suffered severe simulator sickness without vibrotactile feedback and they were more satisfied with vibrotactile feedback. However, there was no significant difference observed in terms of performance. This study suggested that virtual reality glasses with vibrotactile feedback would improve the user experience. The result can help VR developers to choose proper vibrotactile feedback in VR applications.

Keywords: Virtual reality · Simulator sickness · Vibrotactile feedback

1 Introduction

The development of display technology and smart devices has enabled people to experience virtual reality at a very low cost. Many virtual reality glasses have been introduced in the market, but the design of most of these products lacks careful consideration of ergonomics, which results in poor usability and unpleasant user experience [1–3]. Though the creators of the virtual reality glasses have provided many suggestions for both developers and users, there are still many complaints about the many discomforts experienced when using virtual reality glasses. Most of the discomforts were caused by simulator sickness.

Simulator sickness is one of the major obstacles that hinder the popularity of virtual reality glasses. To solve this problem, one of the options is to simulate the human perception of the real world in virtual reality, which includes visual sense, auditory sense, tactile sense etc. Since most of the virtual reality glasses only provide visual and auditory feedback, the effects of tactile feedback, especially vibrotactile feedback, have received less attention. Hence, it is important to study the influence of vibrotactile feedback on simulator sickness, the performance of the glasses, and user satisfaction.

© Springer Nature Switzerland AG 2019
P.-L. P. Rau (Ed.): HCII 2019, LNCS 11576, pp. 291–302, 2019.
https://doi.org/10.1007/978-3-030-22577-3_21

The aim of this study was to investigate the effects of vibrotactile feedback on simulator sickness, performance, and user satisfaction when a user wears virtual reality glasses. In addition, the study will validate the sensory conflict theory and postural instability theory since there is some conflict between these two theories. Based on the result of the experiments, this study will provide some suggestions and recommendations on the design of virtual reality glasses.

2   Literature Review

The primary cause of discomfort experienced with virtual reality glasses is simulator sickness. Though viewed as a syndrome different from motion sickness, simulator sickness is treated as a related phenomenon by many researchers because the two syndromes share many symptoms such as fatigue, headache, visual strain, sweating, nausea, etc. [4]. There are mainly four theories that explain this syndrome: sensory conflict theory, postural instability theory, eye movement theory and evolutionary theory [2]. Sensory conflict theory, the most widely accepted theory, explains that motion sickness is caused by the conflict between the visual and vestibular perceptions of human beings [5]. Virtual reality glasses cannot provide the accelerations and amplitudes equivalent to those experienced during real motion. Thus, users are likely to suffer simulator sickness in this situation. However, there is another theory explaining the cause of simulator sickness. Postural instability theory suggests that human beings, like other animals, tend to maintain their postural stability. When they are not able to balance their body posture, they are very likely to get sick [6]. In a virtual environment, human beings must learn a new strategy to control their bodies. Before they acquire the ability to maintain the balance in this new environment, they may suffer from simulator sickness. This was proved by many studies [7, 8] and this theory can also explain the adaption to the simulator as well. In eye movement theory, Ebenholtz [9, 10] suggested that two specific eye movements, optokinetic nystagmus, and vestibular ocular response, might induce some errors and thus result in motion sickness and simulator sickness. In the view of evolutionary theory, the brain of a human being regards sensory conflict as being equivalent to poisoning. The motion sickness and simulator sickness are mechanisms of self-protection, which will lead to vomiting of the poisoned food [11].

According to sensory conflict theory, providing additional motion stimulus will reduce simulator sickness. One of the options is to provide vibrotactile feedback to users wearing virtual reality glasses because it can provide more motion information, especially with respect to the amplitudes of the motion. In this way, the conflict between visual and vestibular perceptions can be reduced. However, because the vibrotactile feedback is different from real motion, from the perspective of postural instability theory, human beings cannot avoid the learning process of balancing their body in virtual reality with vibrotactile feedback. So, providing additional vibrotactile feedback cannot ensure the reduction of simulator sickness. Therefore, it is very interesting to investigate the effect of vibrotactile feedback on simulator sickness.

Hypothesis 1: Vibrotactile feedback will reduce simulator sickness of a user who is wearing virtual reality glasses.

Some other factors may also influence simulator sickness. The field of view influences simulator sickness. The field of view (FOV) of a single eye has a range of approximately 200° in the horizontal direction and approximately 135° in the vertical direction [12]. In the monocular system of Head-Mounted Displays (HMDs), the FOV is related to the screen size, lens size, eye relief distance, exit pupil size, and focal length. A very large FOV will lead to simulator sickness [12]. However, a narrow FOV may decrease the immersion of the user. A previous study [13] suggests that the field of view should be between 85° and 120° for virtual reality glasses. Lag and latency are other factors that may induce simulator sickness. There are three sources of lag that may influence a virtual reality system. The first source is the system lag that is influenced mainly by the speed of the central processing unit and the graphics processing unit. The second source of lag is the latency between the input device and the processor. The third source of lag is the latency between the processor and the output device. High delays may hamper the performance of the user and induce simulator sickness.

Vibrotactile feedback is mainly used in smartphones and gaming consoles. It provides users with vibrotactile information at a very low cost. The current virtual reality glasses provide visual feedback and audio feedback. Vibrotactile feedback has rarely been used in products till now. If providing vibrotactile can reduce simulator sickness, the human performance and user satisfaction may improve because users would feel more comfortable wearing virtual reality glasses. In addition, many studies suggest the positive effect of vibrotactile feedback on task performance and satisfaction. Vibrotactile cues are employed for alert, direction, spatial orientation and communication because they decrease the users' reaction time and improve their situation awareness [14]. Studies have also shown that with vibrotactile feedback, users can enjoy a higher level of realism and immersion [15]. Based on the literature above, we can speculate that vibrotactile feedback would improve users' performance and satisfaction. In addition, many studies have explored the usage of vibrotactile feedback in virtual reality [16, 17]. However, very few studies look into the effect of vibrotactile feedback on user experience in virtual reality, especially on simulator sickness, performance, and user satisfaction.

Hypothesis 2: Vibrotactile feedback will improve the users' performance when they wear virtual reality glasses.
Hypothesis 3: Vibrotactile feedback will improve the users' satisfaction when they wear virtual reality glasses.

3 Methodology

3.1 Experiment Design

The experiments were conducted on a group of participants, who received two treatments. In one treatment, the participants were asked to finish the tasks without vibrotactile feedback and in the other treatment, participants finished the tasks with vibrotactile feedback. Both treatments had visual feedback and audio feedback. To negate the learning effect, the order of the two treatments was randomized. In the experiments, participants were asked to wear virtual reality glasses and vibration vests. They used a controller that could provide vibrotactile feedback as well to play a car race game. In the game, they were asked to drive along the road as fast as they can and avoid a collision. During the experiments, the performance was recorded. After each experiment, the participants were asked to fill a simulator sickness questionnaire to assess their severity of simulator sickness. They were also asked to fill a satisfaction questionnaire to know their feelings about the virtual reality experience and vibration. After all the experiments, they were asked to fill a questionnaire to compare their relative experience in the two scenarios of vibration and no vibration.

To reduce the effect of the participants' familiarity with the controller in the experiment, it was ensured that the task was simple. A car race game, Project CARS, was chosen. This game was of high graphic quality and compatible with virtual reality. Figure 1 shows a driving scene in the games. In the experiment, the participants were required to drive for 10 min in the game. The track in the game is 12 miles long with 95 turns.

Fig. 1. Driving scene in the games

3.2   Apparatus

The VR system in the experiment requires five components: virtual reality glasses, a high-performance PC, an earphone, two controllers and a vibration vest. Figure 2 shows the set-up of the experiment including the environment and equipment. The virtual reality glasses used were Oculus Rift DK2 with a resolution of 960 × 1080 per eye.

The configuration of the PC used for the experiment was I7 4970k and NVIDIA GTX 970, which ensured high fraps and clear image in the experiments. The controllers were two Xbox One controllers. The wires of vibration motors in one controller were cut off to remove the vibrotactile feedback because there was no such option in the game. The controller would vibrate on three occasions: speeding up, running on different grounds, and crashing with other objects. The vibration vest in the experiments was KOR-FX that vibrated according to the sound of the game. The vest would generate strong vibrations in case of loud sounds in the game, such as collisions. In one treatment, the vibrations of the vest and controller were turned on and in another treatment, the vibrations were turned off.

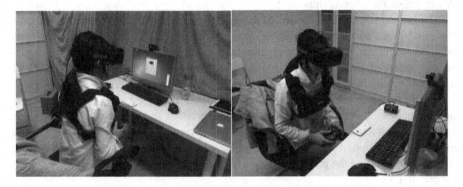

Fig. 2. Set-up of experiment environment and equipment

3.3 Measurement

There are mainly three approaches to measure simulator sickness: motion sickness checklist questionnaires, rapid self-report questionnaires, and psychophysiological measurements. Motion sickness checklist questionnaires are the most popular method to measure motion sickness. Participants are asked to assess their overall state and fill the checklist before and after the experiments. But the questionnaires usually have a long checklist that makes it difficult to fill during the experiment. Thus, rapid self-report questionnaires are developed to record the state of the participants in the process of experiments. Rapid self-report questionnaires usually have much fewer questions, but each question has more levels than checklist questionnaires. The limitation is that the data is not normally distributed, which complicates statistical analysis. Psychophysiological measurements seem preferable and objective to measure the states of participants because these methods can record the real-time information without requiring participants to pause during the experiment to report. But Lawson (2014) pointed out that psychophysiological measurements are not ideal for measurement of severity of motion sickness because: (1) the correlations between physiological data and motion sickness self-reports are usually weak and inconsistent, (2) many factors other than motion sickness can affect the nervous system, (3) physiological effects of movement or exercise can also influence the data collected in some experiments involving head movement. Hence, psychophysiological measurements are not common in studies conducted to measure the simulator sickness.

In this experiment, we use a Simulator Sickness Questionnaire (SSQ) to measure the severity of simulator sickness of the participants. SSQ is one of most popular motion sickness checklist questionnaires. It was developed by Kennedy et al. [4] and consists of 16 questions, which are related to 16 symptoms of simulator sickness. Participants usually fill out the questionnaire before and after the experiment to compare the effects of the virtual environment on the human body. However, Kennedy recommended using the post-exposure questionnaire as the index of simulator sickness instead of the difference between the pre-exposure questionnaire and the post-exposure questionnaire. The pre-exposure questionnaire can be used to test if the subjects are able to finish the experiments.

The performance was recorded based on two parameters: distance the participants drive in 10 min and the total number of errors in 10 min. In this experiment, errors included collisions, pull-ups, and retrogrades. During the experiment, the experimenters watched the screen and recorded each error. But if there was a series of collisions caused by one collision, it would be recorded as one error.

Satisfaction was measured by the questionnaire. Because there was no questionnaire to measure the satisfaction of virtual reality glasses and vibrotactile feedback, we formulated a questionnaire that covered five aspects: physical comfort, visual and auditory satisfaction, interaction, and immersion. Each aspect was assessed using several questions and the participants were asked to choose their level of satisfaction on a score of 1 to 7.

3.4   Participants

36 participants (17 males and 19 female) were recruited through social platforms but only 30 (13 males and 17 females) of them accomplished the experiment. The rest of them became too sick to finish the task. The participants were students with a bachelor's degree or higher educational qualifications and they did not have any eye disease. The average age of the participants was 22.7 years with SD = 1.37. Among those who had the experiment, eight participants had prior experience of using virtual reality glasses, primarily for games and videos.

3.5   Procedure

This research was carried out in the Laboratory of Human Factors. The total time of the experiment was around 60 min. The participants were told the purpose of the experiments. They were asked to sign the informed consent and fill in a chart about their personal background including name, age, gender, physical condition and the previous experience using virtual reality. Then the participants were asked to wear the virtual reality glasses and vibration vest. They were taught to use the controller. They could drive in the games for a while to get used to the virtual reality scenes and operation.

According to the experiment design, the order of the two treatments for each participant was randomly disrupted. The participants put on the virtual reality glasses to finish the first task. During the task, the experimenters record the performance of the participants. After the tasks are finished, subject take off the virtual reality glasses and fill the simulator sickness questionnaire and satisfaction questionnaire. Then, they can rest for 10–20 min, which depends on their own preference. If the participants feel adequately recovered they can put on the virtual reality glasses to finish the second task. After the experiments, the subjects are interviewed.

4   Result and Analysis

The effect of vibrotactile feedback on simulator sickness was analyzed. The three sub-scores of simulator sickness were compared. Then, we examined the influence of vibrotactile feedback in virtual reality on human performance, taking the rate of error into account. The satisfaction of the participants was presented to examine the impact of vibrotactile feedback on the satisfaction. To ensure the appropriate outcome of the SSQ and Satisfaction Questionnaire, its reliability and validity should be checked. The Cronbach's Alpha values of all the items are higher than 0.8, which ensures the reliability and validity of the questionnaire result.

SSQ scores were calculated by three sub-scores: nausea, oculomotor, and disorientation. Nausea included general discomfort, increased salivation, sweating, nausea, difficulty concentrating, stomach awareness and burping. Oculomotor included general discomfort, fatigue, headache, eye strain, difficulty focusing, difficulty concentrating and blurred vision. Disorientation included difficulty focusing, nausea, fullness of head, blurred vision, dizziness, and vertigo.

4.1   Descriptive Statistics

First, we compared the simulator sickness scores with and without vibrotactile feedback, which also included a comparison between the three sub-scores. From Fig. 3, it can be observed that nausea, oculomotor, disorientation, and simulator sickness is all higher without vibrotactile feedback. Similar comparisons were made in terms of satisfaction, as depicted in Fig. 4. However, the difference the between two treatments is not obvious. On the other hand, considering the individual difference between simulator sickness, performance, and satisfaction, a better way to compare the results is by comparing the result to themselves. Thus, we used a paired t-test in the following analysis.

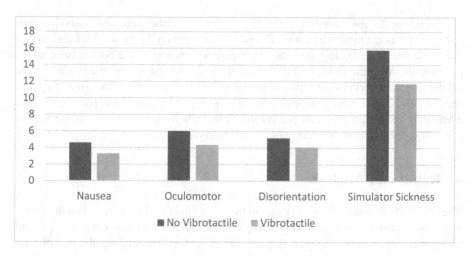

Fig. 3. Comparison of simulator sickness scores with and without vibrotactile feedback

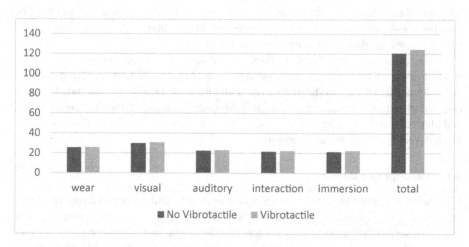

Fig. 4. Comparison of satisfaction scores with and without vibrotactile feedback

4.2 Effect of Vibrotactile Feedback on Simulator Sickness

To compare the mean SSQ scores obtained from the two treatments, a paired T-test is used. As shown in Table 1, simulator sickness without vibrotactile feedback (M = 15.77, SD = 8.597) is higher than with vibrotactile feedback (M = 11.73, SD = 6.992, t(30) = 3.946, p < 0.001). Three sub-scores were also investigated. Nausea was significantly higher without vibrotactile feedback (M = 4.60, SD = 2.908) than with vibrotactile feedback (M = 3.30, SD = 2.322, t(30) = 2.956, p = 0.006). Oculomotor was also significantly higher without vibrotactile feedback (M = 6.00, SD = 3.206) than with vibrotactile feedback (M = 4.33, SD = 2.893, t(30) = 3.893, p = 0.001). Disorientation was also higher without vibrotactile feedback (M = 5.17, SD = 3.445) than with vibrotactile feedback (M = 4.10, SD = 2.833, t(30) = 2.874, p = 0.008).

Table 1. Paired t-test of simulator sickness between no vibrotactile feedback and vibrotactile feedback

Measure	Treatment	Mean	N	SD	t	p
Nausea	No vibrotactile	4.60	30	2.908	2.956	0.006*
	Vibrotactile	3.30	30	2.322		
Oculomotor	No vibrotactile	6.00	30	3.206	3.854	0.001*
	Vibrotactile	4.33	30	2.893		
Disorientation	No vibrotactile	5.17	30	3.445	2.874	0.008*
	Vibrotactile	4.10	30	2.833		
Simulator sickness	No vibrotactile	15.77	30	8.597	3.946	0.000*
	Vibrotactile	11.73	30	6.992		

*Significant difference at the level of .05

4.3   Effect of Vibrotactile Feedback on Task Performance

We measured the performance in terms of the distance the participants drove and the number of errors they committed in 10 min. The distance was given in the form of percentages because the game only provided the percentage of distance covered in the total track. As is shown in Table 2, there is not a significant difference in the performance between no vibrotactile and vibrotactile feedback scenarios.

Table 2. Paired t-test of performance between no vibrotactile feedback and vibrotactile feedback

Measure	Treatment	Mean	N	SD	t	p
Distance	No vibrotactile	0.8877	30	0.1345	−1.606	0.119
	Vibrotactile	0.9267	30	0.1365		
Error	No vibrotactile	19.83	30	11.724	0.095	0.925
	Vibrotactile	19.67	30	9.956		

*Significant difference at the level of .05

4.4   Effect of Vibrotactile Feedback on Satisfaction

The satisfaction is measured in five aspects: wearing satisfaction, visual satisfaction, auditory satisfaction, interaction satisfaction and immersion. To compare the difference between the mean of satisfaction scores of the two treatments, a paired T-test is used. As shown in Table 3, the total score was significantly higher with vibrotactile feedback (M = 124.43, SD = 20.025) than without vibrotactile feedback (M = 120.57, SD = 20.668, $t_{(30)}$ = 3.147, p = 0.004). It is also suggested that interaction satisfaction with vibrotactile feedback (M = 22.37, SD = 3.917) is higher than without vibrotactile feedback (M = 21.57, SD = 4.099, $t_{(30)}$ = 2.658, p = 0.013). The immersion with vibrotactile feedback (M = 22.60, SD = 4.031) is significant higher than without vibrotactile feedback (M = 21.40, SD = 4.031, $t_{(30)}$ = 3.095, p = 0.004). No significant difference was found in wearing satisfaction, visual satisfaction, and auditory satisfaction when using virtual reality glasses without vibrotactile feedback and with vibrotactile feedback.

Table 3. Paired t-test of satisfaction between no vibrotactile feedback and vibrotactile feedback

Measure	Treatment	Mean	N	SD	t	p
Total satisfaction	No vibrotactile	120.57	30	20.668	−3.147	0.004*
	Vibrotactile	124.43	30	20.025		
Wearing satisfaction	No vibrotactile	25.40	30	5.184	−.764	0.451
	Vibrotactile	25.67	30	5.142		
Visual satisfaction	No vibrotactile	29.77	30	6.740	−1.324	0.196
	Vibrotactile	30.77	30	6.078		
Auditory satisfaction	No vibrotactile	22.43	30	3.866	−1.831	0.077
	Vibrotactile	23.00	30	4.283		
Interaction satisfaction	No vibrotactile	21.57	30	4.099	−2.658	0.013*
	Vibrotactile	22.37	30	3.917		
Immersion satisfaction	No vibrotactile	21.40	30	4.048	−3.095	0.004
	Vibrotactile	22.60	30	4.031		

*Significant difference at the level of .05

5 Discussion

Vibrotactile feedback can significantly reduce simulator sickness. It can be explained by Sensory conflict theory. From the literature review, we can see that the simulator sickness is caused by a mismatch between visual information and body movement. The body movement is sensed by a vestibule in the inner ear, which is the balance tense's acceptor. Its nerve adjust function decides the balance ability. When users use virtual reality glasses, they are usually in a still position. The vestibule will inform the central nervous system that the body is still. However, the visual information suggests that the body is moving. This contradictory information will induce many symptoms. The vibrotactile feedback will reduce these symptoms by providing the movement stimulus. It may deceive the vestibule into believing that the body is in motion and thus reduce the disparity between visual information and movement information. In this way, the simulator sickness is reduced. In our experiment, the participants drove very fast in a car as their sense of their surrounding changed very fast. So, the visual information told them that they are moving fast. However, in reality, they just sit still in a chair. Without vibrotactile feedback, the participants would feel very sick. So, if we give the participants some vibrotactile feedback that would give them the perception of being in a real car, this sickness will be significantly reduced.

On the other hand, from the view of postural instability theory, this stimulus of vibration may increase of postural instability, which may, in turn, increase the simulator sickness. But the experiment result does not support this idea and it can be explained by two aspects. First, the participants were actually in a stable position and do not need to maintain the stability of posture. Second, the vibrotactile feedback only gave haptic feedback which did not affect the participant's sense of motion.

Vibrotactile feedback can significantly improve users' satisfaction, especially audio satisfaction, and interaction satisfaction. The vibrotactile feedback can provide users with information that cannot be offered by visual feedback and audio feedback. In other words, vibrotactile feedback will make virtual reality more real. With vibrotactile feedback, the user can feel the virtual world in a more detailed way. Due to the more information obtained by the feedback, the interaction appears more precise and interesting. In our experiment, different roads will lead to different feedbacks. For example, a grass road will generate a stronger feedback than a normal road because the grass road is rougher. But it is very difficult to see roughness on a visual system; it can only be felt from vibrotactile feedback. In the experiments, the participants are frequently made to run against a wall or other obstacles. With vibrotactile feedback, the users can feel real force when they hit something rather than just seeing it.

The performance is not significantly influenced by vibrotactile feedback. It may be the result of learning effect. The interval between the two experiments is too short and the participants usually performed much better in the second experiment. It may be much better if the participants get enough rest. In addition, some participants were not familiar with the controller operation, which also could have influenced their performance.

It was inferred from the interview after the experiment that almost all the participants preferred the vibrotactile feedback. Only one participant thought otherwise. He thought that vibrotactile feedback did not have much positive effect on him. Given that he was the participant who had the highest experience of virtual reality among our participants, this may be a very interesting finding, suggesting that the preference of virtual reality may have something to do with the extent of experience.

Another interesting finding is about the six participants who were unable to finish the task. Five of them had finished the first task but were unable to finish the second task after a rest of 20 min. According to their response, they felt more sickness, nausea, and headache in the second task than in the first task, which may suggest that the time interval between two exposures to the virtual environment may have some effect on simulator sickness and experience. It is also important to know how long it takes to recover after using virtual reality glasses.

6 Conclusion

This study examined the effect of vibrotactile feedback on simulator sickness, performance, and users' satisfaction by conducting multiple experiments within a group of participants. The participants were asked to play a car race game in a virtual reality environment with and without vibrotactile feedback. By comparing the result of the two experiments, we arrived at two major findings: vibrotactile feedback can reduce simulator sickness in virtual reality and vibrotactile feedback can improve users' satisfaction of virtual reality glasses. So, it is recommended to provide vibrotactile feedback during the usage of virtual reality glasses.

The major limitation of this study lies in the experiment design. The learning effect is obvious even though the participants have enough rest to reduce the symptoms of simulator sickness. Many participants performed much better in the second experiment. It should be also noted that participants in the experiments were Tsinghua University students. Their preference and acceptance of virtual reality may differ from ordinary people. Despite these limitations, we believe that this study can contribute to the design of virtual reality glasses. The simulator sickness is one of the obstacles that prevents ordinary people from accepting this new technology. Providing vibrotactile feedback may have a positive effect on simulator sickness and satisfaction. Adding a new dimension of feedback will benefit a lot of users and open a huge market for virtual reality glasses.

Acknowledgments. This study was funded by National Science Foundation of China, grant #71188001.

References

1. Sharples, S., Cobb, S., Moody, A., Wilson, J.R.: Virtual reality induced symptoms and effects (VRISE): Comparison of head mounted display (HMD), desktop and projection display systems. Displays **29**, 58–69 (2008)
2. Brooks, J.O., et al.: Simulator sickness during driving simulation studies. Accid. Anal. Prev. **42**, 788–796 (2010)
3. Serge, S.R., Moss, J.D.: Simulator sickness and the oculus rift: a first look. In: Proceedings of the Human Factors and Ergonomics Society Annual Meeting, vol. 59, pp. 761–765 (2015)
4. Kennedy, R.S., Lane, N.E., Berbaum, K.S., Lilienthal, M.G.: Simulator sickness questionnaire: an enhanced method for quantifying simulator sickness. Int. J. Aviat. Psychol. **3**, 203–220 (1993)
5. Bles, W., Bos, J.E., de Graaf, B., Groen, E., Wertheim, A.H.: Motion sickness: only one provocative conflict? Brain Res. Bull. **47**, 481–487 (1998)
6. Riccio, G.E., Stoffregen, T.A.: An ecological theory of motion sickness and postural instability. Ecol. Psychol. **3**, 195–240 (1991)
7. Stoffregen, T.A., Smart, L.J.: Postural instability precedes motion sickness. Brain Res. Bull. **47**, 437–448 (1998)
8. Duh, H.B., Parker, D.E., Furness, T.A.: An independent visual background reduced simulator sickness in a driving simulator. Presence **13**, 578–588 (2004)
9. Ebenholtz, S.M.: Motion sickness and oculomotor systems in virtual environments. Presence: Teleop. Virt. Environ. **1**, 302–305 (1992)
10. Ebenholtz, S.M.: Oculomotor Systems and Perception. Cambridge University Press, New York (2001)
11. Treisman, M.: Motion sickness: an evolutionary hypothesis. Science **197**, 493–495 (1977)
12. Arthur, K.W.: Effects of field of view on performance with head-mounted displays (2000)
13. Taha, Z., Soewardi, H., Dawal, S.Z.M.: Axiomatic design principles in analysing the ergonomics design parameter of a virtual environment. Int. J. Ind. Ergon. **44**, 368–373 (2014)
14. van Erp, J.B.F.: University Utrecht: Tactile displays for navigation and orientation: perception and behaviour (2007). http://dspace.library.uu.nl/handle/1874/21442
15. Kim, S.-Y., Kim, K.-Y.: Interactive racing game with graphic and haptic feedback. In: Oakley, I., Brewster, S. (eds.) HAID 2007. LNCS, vol. 4813, pp. 69–77. Springer, Heidelberg (2007). https://doi.org/10.1007/978-3-540-76702-2_8
16. Yang, U., Jang, Y., Kim, G.J.: Designing a VibroTactile wear for close range interaction for VR-based motion training. In: ICAT 2002, pp. 4–9 (2002)
17. Kim, S., Kim, K.Y., Soh, B.S., Yang, G., Kim, S.R.: Vibrotactile rendering for simulating virtual environment in a mobile game. IEEE Trans. Consum. Electron. **52**, 1340–1347 (2006)

A Study on the Auditory-Visual Fatigue Classification Validation Based on the Working Memory Task

Xin Wang[✉], Zhen Liao, Jin Liang, Zhiqiang Tian, Tuoyang Zhou,
Shuang Liu, Lei Liu, Chi Zhang, and Zhanshuo Zhang

Lab of Human Factor Engineering,
China Institute of Marine Technology and Economy, Beijing 100081, China
xinwang_thu@126.com

Abstract. In this research, three experiments were conducted to investigate the consistency of information processing in visual and auditory working memory tasks. On this basis, the comprehensive exploration and verification for the fatigue classification were carried out in the visual and auditory channels. It is shown from the experiments that: (1) Similar accuracy can be obtained in information processing of visual and auditory channels, however, processing time of auditory channel was longer than that of visual channel when the working memory capacity is 3 (for the N-back test); (2) the working memory task with the duration of 5 min, 30 min and 60 min can be utilized to induce low-level, medium-level and high-level fatigue respectively, which has been verified through the experiment III comprehensively; (3) there were some differences in information processing between visual channel and auditory channel, and it is more likely to accumulate fatigue for visual channel than that for auditory channel.

Keywords: Working memory · Fatigue classification ·
Auditory and visual channel

1 Introduction

Mental fatigue has been becoming one of the most important factors perplexing people's work due to the fast-paced and high-pressure work in modern society. Mental fatigue is often caused by excessive mental or physical activity, resulting in the decline of psychological and cognitive function [1]. It is manifested in the inability of individuals to maintain a certain level of psychological operation, which usually was caused by short-term high-intensity work and long-term monotonous repetitive work [2]. Besides affecting the individual's work efficiency, mental fatigue also may lead to life-threatening accidents for some professions related to safety in production. Therefore, effective monitoring of mental fatigue is of great significance to reduce the adverse impact of mental fatigue on work and life, and scientific classification of mental fatigue is the key to effectively monitor the state of mental fatigue.

Psychological fatigue, whether caused by short-term high-intensity work or long-term monotonous repetitive work, is mainly due to the overload of information

© Springer Nature Switzerland AG 2019
P.-L. P. Rau (Ed.): HCII 2019, LNCS 11576, pp. 303–322, 2019.
https://doi.org/10.1007/978-3-030-22577-3_22

processing process under the condition of limited cognitive resources [1–6]. Therefore, psychological fatigue caused by visual information processing may be different from that caused by auditory information processing, due to the difference of information processing process and mechanism between visual and auditory channels [7–9]. Hence, this study intended to explore the consistency of visual and auditory information processing, and based on which the classification and validation of visual and auditory fatigue is carried out.

Working memory, as one of the important links in information processing, is a psychological process in which people process and store information at the same time [10, 11]. It is shown that the capacity of working memory, which is the amount of information processed simultaneously by working memory system, can reflect the load level of information processing [12–14]. It is assumed that the fatigue state of short-time high strength and long-time low strength can be simulated through adjusting the information processing intensity and time, which can induce different levels of fatigue, and ultimately achieve the classification and verification of fatigue.

2   Experiment I: Cognitive Processing Consistency Test Between Audio and Visual Information

2.1   Method

2.1.1   Experimental Material

Visual Material

Ten meaningless pictures were evaluated and screened out from multiple pictures collected on the internet through multi-round expert evaluation method. Ten pictures were evaluated by six subjects from the same group described in Sect. 2.1.1 from six aspects: the difference between pictures, aesthetics, easy association, likability, meaning (whether it has special meaning), and pleasure. Picture materials were assessed with a 10-level score of 0–9. The smaller the number, the smaller the difference between the two pictures/the less beautiful the picture/the less easy it was for the subjects to associate/the less they liked the evaluated pictures/the less they felt the pictures had specific meanings/the unhappier they felt when they saw the pictures. After several-round evaluation, nine pictures were selected as visual stimulus materials in this experiment according to the scores on different dimensions and the results of cluster analysis.

Auditory Material

Under the condition of the same total energy, nine sounds were generated by changing the frequency, line spectrum and attenuation. Then, nine sounds were evaluated by seven subjects from the same group described in Sect. 2.1.1 from six aspects: the difference between sounds, loudness, sharpness, pleasure, associativity and enjoyment. The smaller the number, the smaller the difference between the two sounds/the smaller the loudness/the lower the voice/the less easy it is for the subjects to produce associations/the unhappier it sounds. According to the results of cluster analysis, the frequency, broadband spectrum, attenuation and energy of nine sound were adjusted, which, finally, were selected as the auditory stimulus materials in this experiment.

2.1.2   Experimental Procedure

The experiment was conducted in a quiet environment with sound insulation, room temperature of about 20 °C, as well as suitable humidity and lighting. Visual and auditory working memory tasks were used to examine the consistency of information processing between visual and auditory channels. The experimental procedure was shown in Fig. 1.

Visual Working Memory Task

2-back: As the experiment starts, a "×" mark with duration of 200 ms will appear in the center of the screen, reminding the subjects to start the task immediately. After that, a "+" mark with duration of 1000 ms will appear in the center of the screen, then a picture, as the visual stimulus, will show 500 ms. The subjects need to judge whether the picture is the same as the previous second picture. If the same, please press the "F" button, if not, press the "J" button. For example, assuming that the stimulus presented as "Picture 1, Picture 2, Picture 3, Picture 4...". When the third picture appears, the subjects press the "F" button if it is the same as the first picture, and press the "J" button otherwise. There are 64 trials, including 22 trail for exercise and 42 trails for test. The first two numbers after the beginning of the experiment do not need to be judged by the subjects, and the correct rate of the exercises must reach 60% before the formal experiment can start. Before the experiment, the subjects were told to react as quickly and accurately as possible. It takes about 5–6 min to complete all the exercises and formal experiments.

3-back: The experimental procedure was basically the same as the visual 2-back working memory task, but the difference was whether the current picture is the same as the previous third one.

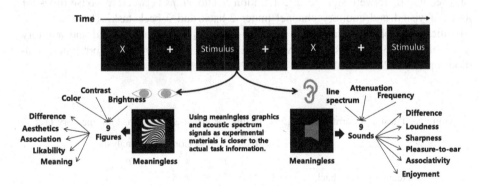

Fig. 1. Experimental procedure for working memory task

Auditory Working Memory

2-back: As the experiment starts, a "×" mark with duration of 200 ms will appear in the center of the screen, reminding the subjects to start the task immediately. After that, a "+" mark with duration of 1000 ms will appear in the center of the screen, then a sound, as the auditory stimulus, will be played 500 ms. The subjects need to judge whether the sound is the same as the previous second sound. If the same, please press the "F" button, if not, press the "J" button. There are 64 trials, including 22 trail for exercise and 42 trails for test. The first two sounds after the beginning of the experiment do not need to be judged by the subjects, and the correct rate of the exercises must reach 60% before the formal experiment can start. Before the experiment, the subjects were told to react as quickly and accurately as possible. It takes about 5–6 min to complete all the exercises and formal experiments.

3-back: The program is basically the same as the 2-auditory 3-back working memory task. The difference is that the subjects need to respond to whether the current playing voice is the same as the previous third voice.

2.2   Results

The response time and correct rate of 11 subjects who completed visual and auditory working memory tasks are shown in Figs. 2 and 3.

Intra-group variance analysis was used to test the data with response time and accuracy as dependent variables, working memory capacity and channel type as independent variable. The results showed in Table 1 that:

In terms of accuracy, the main effect of capacity is significant, ($F(1, 11) = 15.03$, $p < 0.05$, $\eta^2 = 0.60$). The analysis shows that the accuracy of subjects under 2-back condition is significantly higher than that under 3-back condition; the main effect of channel and the interaction between them are not significant.

Using response time and accuracy as dependent variables and information channel as self-adaptability, paired T-test and correlation analysis were carried out. The results showed that there were significant correlation relationships between response times for both of visual and auditory channel under 2-back and 3-back task. There was also significant correlation relationship between accuracy for both of visual and auditory channel under 3-back task, however, there was no such significant correlation relationship under 2-back task.

Table 1. T-test and correlation analysis results for visual-auditory working memory task

	T-test			Correlation analysis	
	T	df	p	R	p
Accuracy for 2-back	−0.57	10	0.58	0.55	0.082
Response time for 2-back	−1.29	10	0.23	0.89	<0.001
Accuracy for 3-back	0.78	10	0.45	0.63	<0.05
Response time for 3-back	−2.27	10	<0.05	0.72	<0.05

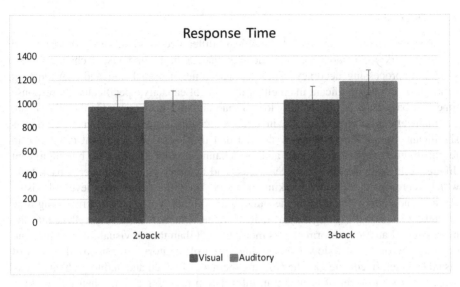

Fig. 2. Response time for visual and auditory working memory

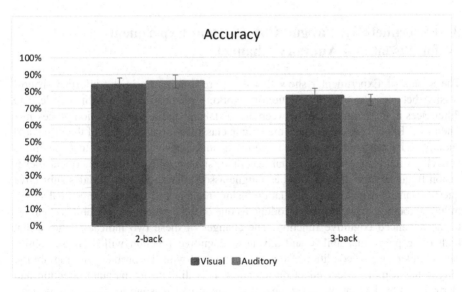

Fig. 3. Accuracy for visual and auditory working memory

2.3   Discussion

At the same capacity, there was no significant difference in the accuracy of visual and auditory working memory tasks, indicating that auditory and visual channels were similar in processing accuracy. The response time of visual and auditory working memory tasks has significant main effect in terms of capacity, specifically the response time of 3-back tasks is significantly longer than that of 2-back tasks. On the other hand, the main effect is not significant in terms of channels, and the interaction edge is significant. Simple effect analysis showed that there was no significant difference in response time between visual and auditory channels under 2-back task, but significant difference in response time between visual and auditory channels under 3-back task, which represented at lower working memory load, the processing level of visual channel and auditory channel is the same, but at higher workload, the processing time of auditory channel is longer than that of visual channel. This may reflect that the processing of auditory information is more difficult than that of visual information, and may also be due to the slower processing speed of auditory information than that of visual channel. In conclusion, the working memory of visual and auditory channels can achieve the same level of accuracy in information processing, but when the working memory load is high, the processing time of auditory channels is longer than that of visual channels.

3   Experiment II: Fatigue Classification Experiment for Visual and Auditory Channel

The results of Experiment I show that there are differences in the information processing between the visual and auditory working memory tasks, which may lead to differences in the fatigue trend between the visual and auditory information processing. Therefore, Experiment II explores the fatigue classification parameters of the visual and auditory channels respectively. Previous studies have confirmed that cognitive behavioral indicators such as digital decoding, short-term memory and critical flicker fusion frequency can also be used as fatigue assessment indicators, besides subjective questionnaires [15]. Critical scintillation fusion frequency is the basic perceptual ability of human beings, while digital decoding, as one of the problem solving ability, belongs to the advanced cognitive function. The changes of these two indicators shows that both basic perceptual ability and advanced cognitive function will decrease significantly under fatigue condition. However, compared with the problem-solving ability, fatigue has a more direct effect on attention. It is difficult to maintain attention and alertness under fatigue, which is one of the important reasons for many safety accidents. Therefore, in experiment 2, subjective scale combined with alertness and basic reaction time were selected as the criteria of fatigue classification.

3.1   Method

3.1.1   Subjects

Eleven healthy male adults, with an average age of 24 (SD = 3.12), were right-handed and had normal vision or corrected visual acuity. They were paid a certain amount after the experiment.

3.1.2   Experimental Procedure

The experiment was conducted in a quiet environment with sound insulation, room temperature of about 20 °C, as well as suitable humidity and lighting. Visual and auditory working memory tasks were used to induce visual and auditory cognitive fatigue, respectively. The fatigue self-assessment questionnaire and attention-alert tasks were used as fatigue criteria. The NASA load scale was utilized as work load evaluation index to test the validity of the fatigue classification and its relevant parameter. Specific fatigue classification and related task parameters determination procedures are as follows:

Classification of Fatigue Grade and Preliminary Determination of Task Parameters
Assuming that the relationship between fatigue level and cognitive task performance may follow a growth curve model. In order to better distinguish the different fatigue levels, the lower limit inflection point value, the middle value and the upper limit inflection point value of the curve model can be selected as the low, middle and high three fatigue level values, which has been represented as "red points" in Fig. 4. Then, the working memory task parameters, inducing different fatigue levels, has been determined preliminarily, which includes the number of memory targets, task duration, task trial number, see Table 2.

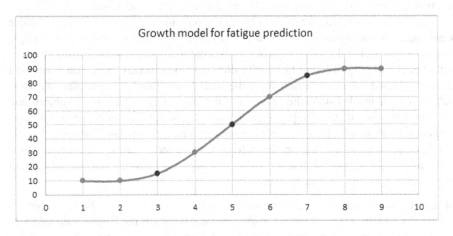

Fig. 4. Growth model for fatigue prediction (Color figure online)

Table 2. Working memory task parameters corresponding to different fatigue levels

Level	Workload	Time/min	Channel
Low	2-back	5	Visual
		5	Auditory
	3-back	5	Visual
		5	Auditory
Medium	2-back	30	Visual
		30	Auditory
	3-back	30	Visual
		30	Auditory
High	2-back	60	Visual
		60	Auditory
	3-back	60	Visual
		60	Auditory

Hierarchical Design Experiment

Since it is not yet possible to determine whether the fatigue levels, induced by the working memory task levels corresponding to the low, middle and high fatigue levels described in Table 2, can fit the lower, middle and upper inflection points in the prediction model, the experiment is carried out by using the method of hierarchical experimental design to determine the task parameters corresponding to different fatigue levels.

Stage I: Using the working memory task parameters of middle and low levels described in Table 2, the fatigue scores induced by the corresponding tasks were obtained, and the levels of fatigue at different times, loads and channels were determined.

The fatigue grade was determined by taking polynomial response time, subjective scale and attention alertness test as fatigue criterion. We used the method of multiple measurements within the subjects to obtain the criterion data of the same subject before and after completing different tasks with different experimental time, load levels and channels. Based on the criterion data, the model was fitted to determine the task-induced fatigue level. Taking the time cost of the test, the endurance of the subjects and the cumulative fatigue that the pre-test may cause to the subsequent experimental tasks into consideration, we did not collect the pre-test data for each task, but took the pre-test data before all task as the pre-test reference value for all tasks. Adequate rest was given to reduce the possible impact of fatigue caused by previous tests on subsequent tests, due to multiple tests in the same day.

Stage II: According to the experimental results of the Stage I, the experimental parameters of three kinds of fatigue grades are determined. If the fatigue induced by 5-min task in Stage I is low-grade fatigue and that induced by 30-min task is medium-grade fatigue, 45 min or 60 min would be used as the experimental task parameters of high-level fatigue induction. Based on the experimental results of Stage I, the fatigue grade can be determined. Selected experimental parameters are shown in Table 3.

Table 3. Optional set of fatigue classification test parameters based on the Stage I

Time/min	Fatigue	Undetermined fatigue level in Stage II	Optional set/min
5	Low	High	45/60
30	Medium		
5	Low	Medium	15
30	High		
5	Medium	Low	2
30	High		
5	Low	Medium/High	45/60
30	Low		
5	Medium	Low/High	2/45
30	Medium		
5	High	Low/Medium	1/3
30	High		

3.2   Results

3.2.1   Results for Working Memory Task

The response time of the visual and auditory working memory tasks with the duration of 5 min and 30 min have been shown in Fig. 5. Response time for fatigue classification experiment and Fig. 6. Intra-group variance analysis was used by taking response time and accuracy as dependent variables, task duration, working memory load and channel type as independent variables. The analysis results showed that the main effect of channel was significant in terms of response time, ($F(1, 10) = 24.22$, $p < 0.001$, $\eta^2 = 0.71$). Other main effects and interactions were not significant, as

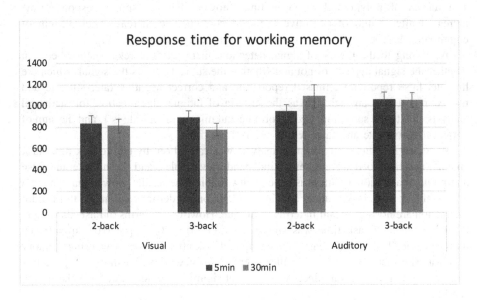

Fig. 5. Response time for fatigue classification experiment

shown in Fig. 5. On the other hand, in terms of accuracy, the main effect of load is significant ($F(1, 10) = 14.65$, $p < 0.01$, $\eta^2 = 0.59$), and the interaction between time and channel is significant ($F(1, 10) = 10.27$, $p < 0.01$, $\eta^2 = 0.51$), however, the main effect of channel and the interaction related to them were not significant.

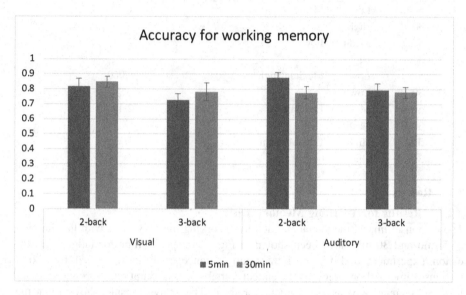

Fig. 6. Accuracy for fatigue classification experiment

3.2.2   Results for Cognitive Behavior Performance

The results of polynomial response time showed that the simple response time increased after 5 min of cognitive task and continued to increase after 30 min of cognitive task. The results were consistent with the hypothesis, see Fig. 7.

According to the theory of signal detection, there are four relationships between whether the signal appears or not and whether the subject detects the signal, which are hit rate, false report rate, missed report rate and correct negative rate. Hit rate and missed report rate are selected as the criteria of fatigue classification for statistical analysis, due to the sum of missed report rate and missed report rate is 1, and the sum of correct negative rate and false report rate is 1.

Repeated measurement variance analysis was carried out by taking task time, task channel and task load were taken as independent variables, and the hit rate and false alarm rate of attention alertness as dependent variable. The results showed that the main effects of task time, task channel and task load, second-order interaction and third-order interaction are not significant in terms of hit rate. However, in terms of false alarm rate, the main effect of task time was significant ($F(1, 5) = 20.61$, $p < 0.01$, $\eta^2 = 0.81$), more specifically, the false alarm rate of vigilant task after 30 min of working memory task was significantly higher than that after 5 min of working memory task, the rest main effect and interaction effects were are not significant in terms of false alarm rate, see Fig. 8.

The results above showed that the alertness of the subjects gradually decreased with the increase of fatigue level, which showed that the false alarm rate of completing 5-min working memory task was higher than that of baseline level, and the false alarm rate of completing 30-min working memory task was higher than that of completing 5-min working memory task.

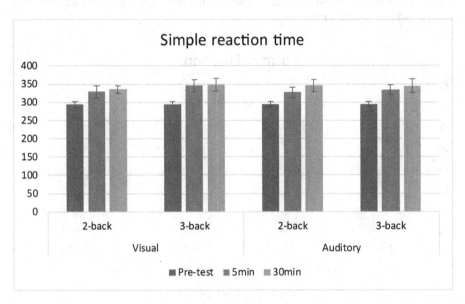

Fig. 7. Simple reaction time under different fatigue condition

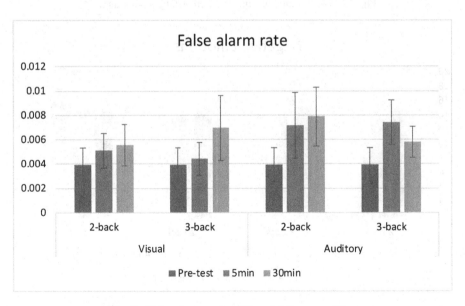

Fig. 8. False alarm under different fatigue condition

3.2.3 Results for Cognitive Behavior Performance

The results showed that after 5 min of working memory task, the positive emotions from the PASSS Emotion Scale decreased. After 30 min of working memory task, the positive emotions were lower than the baseline level and that for 5-min condition, which accorded with the research hypothesis, see Fig. 9. Negative emotions have no significant difference between 5-min working memory task and 30-min working memory task, as shown in Fig. 10.

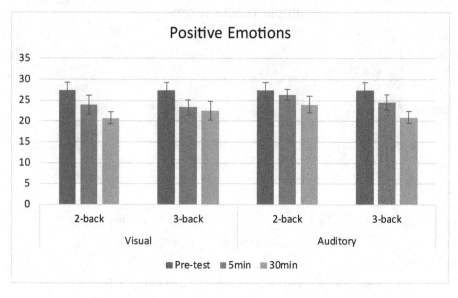

Fig. 9. Positive emotions under different fatigue condition

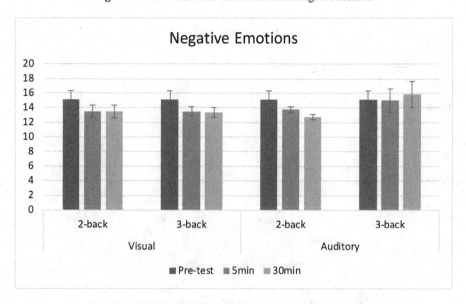

Fig. 10. Negative emotions under different fatigue condition

The Fatigue Scale score (see Fig. 11) showed that the fatigue induced by 30-min working memory task was significantly greater than that induced by 5-min working memory task, especially for the auditory channel. However, the 5-min working memory task induced less fatigue than the baseline level.

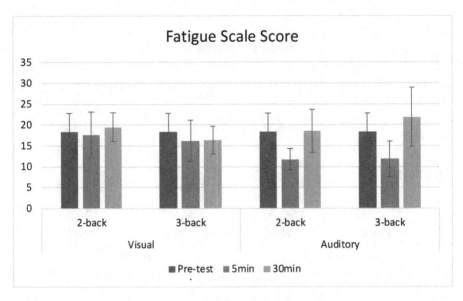

Fig. 11. Fatigue scale score

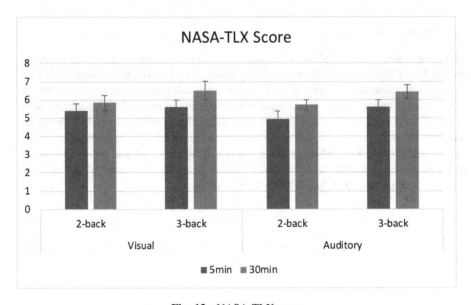

Fig. 12. NASA-TLX score

The experimental results show that the workload of 30-min working memory task is greater than that of 5-min working memory task (Fig. 12), and the main difference is mental workload (Fig. 13). This shows that working memory task mainly induces mental workload, and with the increase of task time, the workload increases, which is consistent with the research expectations.

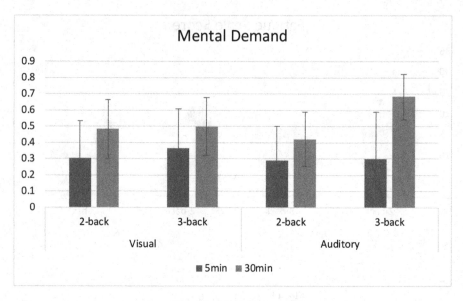

Fig. 13. Mental demand

3.3   Discussion

The false alarm rate of vigilant tasks after 30-min working memory tasks was significantly lower than that after 5-min working memory tasks, which represented that the vigilance of subjects after 30-min working memory tasks was lower than that after 5-min working memory tasks. It is indicated that the fatigue induced by 30-min working memory tasks was significantly greater than that induced by 5-min tasks. Therefore, working memory tasks with different duration can be used as fatigue-inducing tasks. According to the scores of fatigue scale and workload scale, 30 min working memory task can induce moderate level fatigue. Hence, 60 min is determined as the working memory task parameter induced by high-level fatigue.

4 Experiment III: Comprehensive Verification of Fatigue Classification

4.1 Method

4.1.1 Subjects

Five healthy male adults, with an average age of 24.40 (SD = 5.51), were right-handed and had normal vision or corrected visual acuity. They were paid a certain amount after the experiment.

4.1.2 Experimental Procedure

Based on the results of fatigue grading experiment, visual and auditory 2-back working memory task with the duration of 60 min were selected to induce fatigue. Subjects did working memory tasks in visual and auditory channels respectively, between which interval was at least one day. The subjects were asked to ensure adequate rest one day before the experiment. The order of visual and auditory tasks was balanced among the subjects.

In order to monitor and evaluate the subjects' subjective fatigue state in real time during the experiment, the 60-min working memory task was divided into 10 blocks. After each block, they were asked to score their fatigue state, and then the next Block experiment was conducted immediately without any rest for the subjects. The state score is 0–9, 0 represents very unhappy/no fatigue at all, 9 represents very happy or extreme fatigue, the closer to 0 the score is, the less unhappy or fatigue, and the closer to 9 the score is, the happier or fatigue is. The experimental process is shown in Fig. 14.

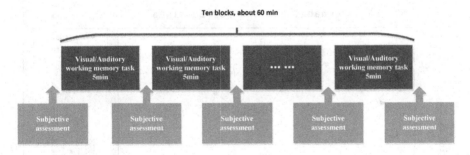

Fig. 14. Fatigue comprehensive verification of audiovisual channel

4.2 Results

4.2.1 Subjective Evaluation Result

Subjective Fatigue Score

The subjects were asked to score their subjective fatigue status with 0-9 data every five minutes. The results showed that the subjective fatigue evaluation score increased gradually with the working memory time, as shown in Fig. 15.

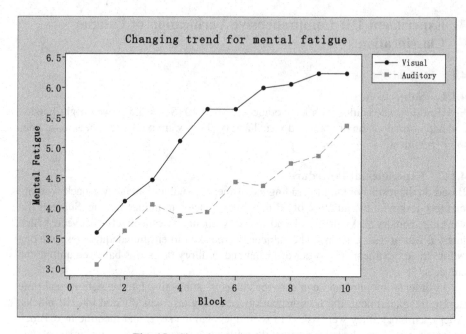

Fig. 15. Changing trend for mental fatigue

Subjective Emotion Score
Whether in visual or auditory channels, the subjective emotions showed a gradual downward trend with the increase of working time, see Fig. 16.

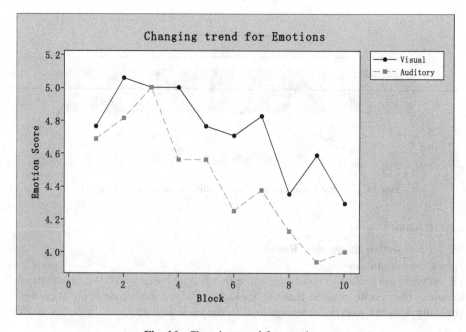

Fig. 16. Changing trend for emotions

4.2.2 Results for Cognitive Behavior

Response Time

The experimental results showed that the working memory response time of the subjects on the visual channel decreases continuously with the elapse of the task time, while that on the auditory channel decreases first with the elapse of the task time, then maintains a relatively stable level after the third time period, and declines again at the sixth time period, and then increases slowly, as shown in Fig. 17.

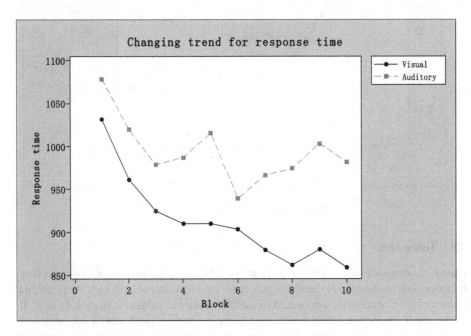

Fig. 17. Changing trend for response time

Accuracy Rate

Whether visual or auditory, the accuracy of the working memory task decreased gradually with the task time, and presented a stepwise downward trend, as shown in Fig. 18. In terms of the auditory channel, the accuracy rate is relatively high in the first and second time periods (5–10 min). In the fourth and sixth time periods (20–30 min), it decreases and stabilizes to a certain level, and reach the lowest point in the eighth time period. In the ninth and tenth time periods, the accuracy rate of the subjects slightly increases. In terms of the visual channel, the change trend of working memory task accuracy is similar to that of auditory channel, but there are some differences between the results of Gergelyfi's research [12]. Gergelyfi's 120-min working memory task using visual channel showed that the accuracy of 24–48 min increased, even exceeded the average accuracy of 0–24 min, and then continued to decrease. However, in this study, although the accuracy rate of the subjects also increased during 25–30 min, the average accuracy rate of 25–45 min was not significantly higher than the average accuracy rate of 0–25 min.

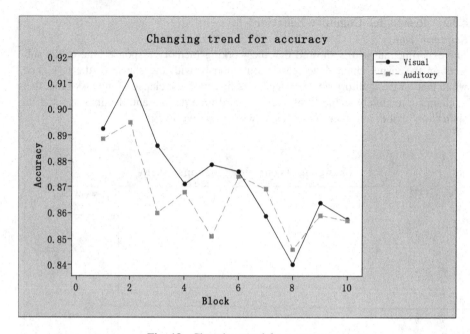

Fig. 18. Changing trend for accuracy

4.3 Discussion

Based on research above, this study utilized 5-min, 30-min and 60-min working memory task to induce low-level fatigue, medium-level fatigue and high-level fatigue respectively. The subjects were asked to use 0–9 score to evaluate subjective fatigue. If 0–9 score is divided into five grades, 0–1 score is the first level, which can represent almost no fatigue or low fatigue, 2–3 score is the second level, which can represent lower fatigue, 4–5 score is the third level, which can represent middle fatigue, 6–7 score is the fourth level, which can represent high fatigue, 8–9 is the fifth level, can represent extreme high fatigue:

At the beginning of the working memory experiment including visual and auditory channel, the fatigue was at lower level. When the task lasted for about 30 min, i.e. the 5th and 6th periods, the fatigue was at a moderate level. At the end of the experiment, the fatigue was at a higher level. The change trend of subjective fatigue of the visual channel was in line with the expectation.

5 General Discussion

This study explored the consistency of visual and auditory information processing through visual and auditory working memory tasks. On this basis, the fatigue classification and validation of visual and auditory channels were carried out. The results of Experiment 1 showed that there was no significant difference in the accuracy of working memory tasks between visual and auditory channels, which indicated that the information processing of visual and auditory channels could achieve similar accuracy. In terms of processing time, when the workload is low, there is no significant difference between visual channel and auditory channel in processing time, but when the workload level is high, the working memory response time of auditory channel is significantly longer than that of visual channel, which indicates that there is a certain difference in processing time between visual channel and auditory channel. The longer processing time on the auditory channel may reflect that the processing of auditory presentation information is more difficult than that of visual presentation information, or the processing speed of auditory information is slower, which needs further study and discussion.

In experiment 2, it was determined that low, medium and high levels of fatigue could be induced by 2-back tasks of 5 min, 30 min and 60 min, and the fatigue-induced tasks were comprehensively validated in experiment 3. At the same time, the experimental results also show that the fatigue caused by visual information processing is different from that caused by auditory information processing. Visual channel is easier to accumulate fatigue than auditory channel, which may be related to the differences in the characteristics and ways of information processing between visual channel and auditory channel.

Mental fatigue, whether it is caused by short-term high-intensity work or long-term monotonous repetitive work, mainly comes from people's overloaded information processing process. 2-back working memory task is a low-difficulty task, hence the lower, middle and higher levels of fatigue, induced in experiment 2 and Experiment 3, were similar with the fatigue caused by monotonous repetitive mental work. Researchers generally believe that 3-back tasks are more difficult than 2-back tasks [13, 16]. However, in experiment 2, there is no significant difference between 2-back tasks and 3-back tasks in response time, but the accuracy of 2-back tasks is significantly lower than that of 3-back tasks (Note: The average correct rate of 3-back tasks in different channels and time is more than 72.9%, which is consistent with previous studies [12]). However, there was no significant difference between the fatigue induced by 3-back task and 2-back task, no mater the task time was 5 min or 30 min, which indicated that although 3-back task was more difficult than 2-back task, the fatigue caused by 3-back task was similar to that caused by 2-back task. Thus, 3-back can not be used as a fatigue-induced task to simulate short-time high-intensity work. If it is necessary, the difficulty of work can further be increased, such as choosing 4-back working memory task. However, there may be a risk that the participants will not be able to complete the task well or even give up the task because of the significant decline in the quality of task completion [17]. This risk exists not only in the use of working memory tasks, but also in the use of other difficult tasks to induce fatigue. Therefore, in future studies, in order to avoid the risk of completing tasks or even giving up tasks, it better choose low intensity and long duration task during fatigue induction.

6 Conclusion

(1) There are difference in information processing between visual channel and auditory channel. The processing accuracy of the two channels is similar, but the

processing time of auditory channel is longer than that of visual channel at higher workload level.

(2) 2-back tasks with duration of 5 min, 30 min and 60 min can be used as low, medium and high levels of fatigue induction tasks.

(3) When 2-back working memory task with duration of 60 min is used to induce fatigue caused by long-term low-intensity repetitive work, visual task is more likely to accumulate fatigue than auditory channel.

References

1. Meijman, T.F.: Mental fatigue and the efficiency of information processing in relation to work times. Int. J. Ind. Ergon. **20**(1), 31–38 (1997)
2. Martin, K., et al.: Mental fatigue impairs endurance performance: a physiological explanation. Sports Med. **48**, 2041–2051 (2018)
3. Gergelyfi, M., et al.: Dissociation between mental fatigue and motivational state during prolonged mental activity. Front. Behav. Neurosci. **9**, 176 (2015)
4. Davranche, K., et al.: Impact of physical and cognitive exertion on cognitive control. Front. Psychol. **9**, 2369 (2018)
5. Marcora, S.M., Staiano, W., Manning, V.: Mental fatigue impairs physical performance in humans. J. Appl. Physiol. (1985) **106**(3), 857–864 (2009)
6. Borragan, G., et al.: Cognitive fatigue: a time-based resource-sharing account. Cortex **89**, 71–84 (2017)
7. Cowan, N., et al.: Development of the ability to combine visual and acoustic information in working memory. Dev. Sci. **21**(5), e12635 (2018)
8. Carrasco, M., Kinchla, R.A., Figueroa, J.G.: Visual letter-matching and the time course of visual and acoustic codes. Acta Physiol. (Oxf) **69**(1), 1–17 (1988)
9. Kaminski, M., et al.: Coupling between brain structures during visual and auditory working memory tasks. Int. J. Neural Syst. **29**, 1850046 (2018)
10. Baddeley, A.: The episodic buffer: a new component of working memory? Trends Cogn. Sci. **4**(11), 417–423 (2000)
11. Baddeley, A.: Working memory: looking back and looking forward. Nat. Rev. Neurosci. **4**(10), 829–839 (2003)
12. Oberauer, K., Lange, E., Engle, R.W.: Working memory capacity and resistance to interference. J. Mem. Lang. **51**(1), 80–96 (2004)
13. Unsworth, N., et al.: Complex working memory span tasks and higher-order cognition: a latent-variable analysis of the relationship between processing and storage. Memory **17**(6), 635–654 (2009)
14. Botto, M., Palladino, P.: Time and interference: effects on working memory. Br. J. Psychol. **107**(2), 239–258 (2016)
15. Duan, T., et al.: Study on the preferred application-oriented index for mental fatigue detection. Int. J. Environ. Res. Public Health **15**(11), 2555 (2018)
16. Jansen, R.J., et al.: Hysteresis in mental workload and task performance: the influence of demand transitions and task prioritization. Hum. Factors **58**(8), 1143–1157 (2016)
17. Boardman, J.M., et al.: The ability to self-monitor cognitive performance during 60 h total sleep deprivation and following 2 nights recovery sleep. J. Sleep Res. **27**(4), e12633 (2018)

Using Psychophysiological Techniques to Evaluate User Experience of Touchscreen Protectors

Man Wu, Bingcheng Wang, Qin Gao[(✉)], and Pei-Luen Patrick Rau

Department of Industrial Engineering, Tsinghua University,
Beijing, People's Republic of China
gaoqin@tsinghua.edu.cn

Abstract. Since touchscreens were introduced into mobile devices, interaction directly on the touchscreen replaced interaction with the keyboard. In order to protect touchscreens and improve user experience, touchscreen protectors are widely used. This study selected three different designs of touchscreen protectors with three different levels of friction, and a touchscreen without a protector as a control group. The experiment was divided into two tasks, namely the moving task (including horizontal movement and vertical movement) and the circling tasks (including clockwise movement and counter-clockwise movement). User experience was measured through performance, questionnaires and psychophysiological techniques including electromyography (EMG) and electroencephalography (EEG) measurements. Results reflected that a touchscreen without a protector was most suitable for gesture control to improve performance. Among various types of protectors, the protector with the same friction as a touchscreen, was more suitable to improve performance. Results suggested that protectors with excessive or too little friction cannot improve performance.

Keywords: Psychophysiological techniques · User experience · Touchscreen protectors

1 Introduction

With the development of the Internet and mobile technology, mobile devices were rapidly developing, and significantly changed our lives and behavior. For its convenience and flexibility, mobile devices are currently reaching a mass audience. Since touchscreens were introduced into mobile devices, interaction directly on the touchscreen replaced interaction with the keyboard. Although touchscreens clearly enhance the user's experience by offering an even more user-friendly interface than tactile keypads, there is also a need to improve the input performance for the use [1]. Direct touch interaction allows a variety of gesture control, such as clicking, dragging, zooming and rotating [2]. Recently, many mobile applications use gesture control as an input method, especially mobile games, a video game played on mobile devices. Mobile device users can play a great variety of mobile games anytime and anywhere. However, long-term large number of gesture control on touchscreens also causes some harm, such as muscle fatigue, and even muscle pain.

© Springer Nature Switzerland AG 2019
P.-L. P. Rau (Ed.): HCII 2019, LNCS 11576, pp. 323–337, 2019.
https://doi.org/10.1007/978-3-030-22577-3_23

In order to protect touchscreens and improve user experience, touchscreen protectors are widely used. Many people buy a specific screen protector designed for mobile games to improve performance. Retailers of these protectors claim that protectors can reduce the resistance of touchscreens and improve the smoothness of touchscreens. However, there are various kinds of protectors. The materials, surface and manufacturing process of these protectors are different, resulting in difference in physical parameters such as friction, thickness, and hardness. Liu et al. [3] studied the factors affecting the usability of smartphone screen protectors for the elderly. The protectors were classified according to functions such as anti-smudge and anti-glare. But relationships between physical parameters of protectors and user experience are unclear. Among physical parameters of protectors, the coefficient of friction, which influences the smoothness of a protector, has the greatest impact on user experience. To date, there have been few studies on the friction of touchscreens or protectors.

Evaluation of user experience of touchscreens or protectors on previous research is mainly through subjective self-reports such as questionnaires and interviews. In a usability study of touchscreen protectors for the elderly, touchscreen protectors were scored with a usability evaluation questionnaire [3]. Likert Scales were used to evaluate the level of errors, efficiency, learnability, memorability, and satisfaction. Page [4] conducted a usability studied on touchscreen mobile devices for older adults. He used pre-interview to understand participants' current perceptions of touchscreen technologies and post-interview to obtain thoughts and attitudes towards the touchscreen mobile devices. However, since user experience of touchscreens or protectors is greatly affected by the task, subjective self-reports such as questionnaires and interviews cannot separate the feeling of touchscreens or protectors from the feeling of the task. Xiong and Muraki [1] used psychophysiological techniques to investigate relationships between thumb muscle activity and thumb operating tasks on a smartphone touchscreen. Compared with subjective self-reports, psychophysiological techniques can be used to obtain objective physiological data and help understand the state of participants during the task. Electromyography (EMG) measures muscle activity by detecting surface voltages that occur when a muscle is contracted [5]. EMG data can be used to evaluate muscle effort and fatigue of muscles during the experiment.

The current study aims to explore relationships between the coefficient of friction and user experience. This study selected three different designs of touchscreen protectors, and a touchscreen without a protector as a control group. Compared with the touchscreen without a protector, the three protectors selected contained three different levels of friction, which were smaller than the touchscreen, larger than the touchscreen and equal to the touchscreen. User experience in this study was measured through performance, questionnaires and psychophysiological including EMG and electroencephalography (EEG) measurements. This study should provide a better understanding of protectors' friction and its connection to user experience, and offer a knowledge base for the better design of touchscreen protectors.

2 Methodology

2.1 Participants

Fifteen students (11 males, 4 females) at Tsinghua University ages 22 to 27 (M = 23.81, SD = 1.22) were invited to participate in the experiment. The dominant hands of all the participants were right-handed. None of the participants reported a musculoskeletal disorder or pain, nor any motor disorders or symptoms. All the participants owned touchscreen smartphones for daily use and they all had extensive experience in mobile games. Recruitment priority was given to the participants who took a long time to play mobile games.

2.2 Experimental Sample

This study selected three types of touchscreen protectors with different levels of friction, which were smaller than the touchscreen, larger than the touchscreen and equal to the touchscreen. This study selected two typical materials of touchscreen protectors that were widely used in the market, namely TPU and PET materials. The coefficient of friction of TPU protector was the same as the touchscreen, ranging from 0.15–0.20. Especially, there were two kinds of protectors made of PET material, which were normal PET protector and special PET protector. The coefficient of friction of normal PET protector was the largest among three types of protectors, ranging from 0.20 to 0.25. Special PET protector was manufactured using a special processing technology and had a special composite coating. As a result, its coefficient of friction, ranging from 0.10 to 0.15, was the smallest, even smaller than a touchscreen without a protector. Table 1 shows materials, surface, features, visual characteristics, and physical parameters of three types of protectors and a touchscreen without a protector.

Table 1. Characteristics of three types of protectors and the touchscreen without a protector

Name	TPU protector	Normal PET protector	Special PET protector	Touchscreen without a protector
Material	TPU	PET	PET	Glass
Surface (coating)	AF	AF	AG and AR	AF
Visual characteristics	Glossy	Glossy	Matte	Glossy
Features	Anti-smudge	Anti-smudge	Anti-smudge, anti-glare and anti-reflection	Anti-smudge
Coefficient of friction	0.15–0.20	0.20–0.25	0.10–0.15	0.15–0.20
Thickness	0.15–0.2 mm	0.13–0.16 mm	0.13–0.16 mm	\
Hardness	HB	H	H	\

2.3   Design of Experiment

Two experiments were conducted to investigate user experience associated with the line movement and the circle movement. The effects of the type of protectors (TPU protector, normal PET protector, special PET protector, and a touchscreen without a protector) and the type of thumb (left thumb and right thumb) were examined in the experiment (See Table 2). The type of protectors and the type of thumb were both within-subject factors. The participants completed tasks on different types of protectors in a random order in order to balance the impact of the sequence of experiments. Since there were several subtasks in an experiment of a protector, the participants completed subtasks in a fixed order, which was an alternating sequence starting with the left thumb.

Table 2. Design of experiment

		Type of thumb	
		Left thumb	Right thumb
Type of protectors	TPU protector	A	B
	Normal PET protector	C	D
	Special PET protector	E	F
	Touchscreen without a protector	G	H

2.4   Tasks

The experiment was divided into two tasks, namely the moving task and the circling tasks. Each task contained two subtasks, which were horizontal movement and vertical movement in the moving task, and clockwise movement and counter-clockwise movement in the circling task (See Fig. 1). The participants were required to slide along the specified trajectory as accurately as possible, but there was no need to be too slow to pursue accuracy, allowing the participants to maintain normal speed.

The specified trajectory in the moving task was a line with two dots, namely A and B. The diameter of the dots was 60 px and distance between the target dots was 600 px. In the moving task, movement back and forth (A-B-A) was recorded as one time. The participants were required to repeat line movement ten times for each subtask. There was a display of the remaining number of times on the experimental smartphone as a reminder. The specified trajectory in the circling task was a circle with a dot, namely A. The diameter of the dot was 60 px and diameter of the circle trajectory were 600 px. In the circling task, movement along a circle (A-A) was recorded as one time. The participants were required to repeat circling movement ten times for each subtask.

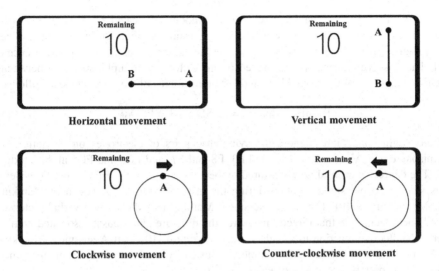

Fig. 1. The specified trajectory (taking the right hand as an example)

2.5   Measurements

Task Performance. Performance was measured by accuracy and time to complete the task. Accuracy refers to the proximity between the actual trajectory of the movement and the specified trajectory. The software records the coordinates of the track during the experiment and distance between the actual trajectory and the specified trajectory can be obtained. This study used the standard deviation of the distance of all ten times movement as the measurement of performance accuracy. Time to complete the task can reflect the speed of movement. This study used the duration of all ten times movement as the measurement of time to complete the task.

Thumb Muscle Activity. Abductor pollicis brevis (APB) in right and left thumb were targeted in this study. In APB, the electrodes were placed over the muscle belly between the metacarpophalangeal (MCP I) and carpometacarpal (CMC I) joints [6]. EMG data were used to evaluate muscle effort on a touchscreen protector, as well as fatigue of thumb movement. This study used the root mean square (RMS) amplitude at APB in right and left thumb as the measurement of muscle effort. When muscles are fatigued, the spectrum shifts from high frequency to low frequency and the median frequency (MF) value also decreases. The greater difference in decline reveals higher levels of muscle fatigue. In this study, the difference between the median frequency (MF) of APB in the first 20% of the time period and the median frequency (MF) of APB in the last 20% of the time was used as the measurement of muscle fatigue.

Subjective Usability Evaluation. To measure usability evaluation, protectors were scored with a questionnaire completed immediately after tasks of each protector. Three items were related to thumb muscle activity, including perceived effort of thumb muscles, perceived fatigue of thumb muscles and perceived comfort of thumb muscles. Three items were related to touchscreens or protectors, including user satisfaction, frustration, and perceived response speed. One item was related to the task, which was difficulty of the task. Each subjective variable was measured with a single item with 7-point Likert scale.

Emotion. Two-dimensional Arousal-Valence model advocated by Russell [7] was used in this study. EEG data was used to measure emotion during the task. The asymmetrical frontal EEG activity may reflect the valence level of emotion experienced [8]. The positive valence was measured by the difference in alpha spectrum between right hemispheres of the frontal lobe and left hemispheres of the frontal lobe as follows.

$$\text{Positive valence} = \alpha\,\text{PSD}_{right} - \alpha\,\text{PSD}_{left} \tag{1}$$

where "right" and "left" denote the symmetric pairs of electrodes on the left/right hemisphere, i.e. AF4 and AF3, F4 and F3, F8 and F7, and FC6 and FC5 in this study.

The degree of arousal was measured by beta spectrum on the frontal lobe. Besides, this study also measured emotion during the task through Self-Assessment Manikin (SAM) instrument [9]. The Self-Assessment Manikin (SAM) is a non-verbal pictorial assessment technique that directly measures the pleasure and arousal associated with a person's affective reaction to a wide variety of stimuli [10]. Self-Assessment Manikin (SAM) instrument was added to subjective usability evaluation questionnaire completed immediately after tasks of each protector.

2.6   Apparatus and System

A testing system was developed to present the tasks and collect performance data during the task execution (See Fig. 2). All the participants used the same five-inch screen Android smartphone to maintain a level of experimental consistency.

Delsys wireless system was used to collect EMG data in this study. Two wireless EMG electrodes were placed on abductor pollicis brevis (APB) muscles in right and left thumb (See Fig. 2). Before mounting the electrodes, the skin was cleansed with alcohol pads to remove skin debris and improve the electrical contact with the electrodes.

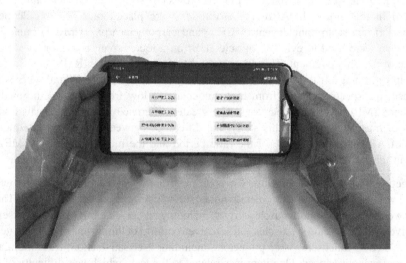

Fig. 2. EMG equipment and Android smartphones used in the experiment

Emotiv was used to collect EEG data in this study. Emotiv device has 14 electrodes locating at AF3, F7, F3, FC5, T7, P7, O1, O2, P8, T8, FC6, F4, F8, AF4. The sampling rate of the Emotiv headset is 128 Hz. The bandwidth of the device is 0.2–45 Hz, and digital notch filters are at 50 Hz and 60 Hz. The A/D converter is with 16 bits resolution.

2.7 Procedure

The participants signed an informed consent agreement at first. The sequence of three types of protectors and a touchscreen was randomized for the participants. Experimental content and process were introduced at the beginning. The participants were allowed to practice before the formal test. Once the participants had sufficient practice, Delsys wireless system and Emotiv wireless system were worn. In each experiment of touchscreen protectors, the participants clicked "Start" to enter the formal test. The moving task with four subtasks (horizontal movement with the left thumb, horizontal movement with the right thumb, vertical movement with the left thumb, and vertical movement with the right thumb) was completed at first. After completing the moving task, the participants were given the subjective evaluation form to complete. Then the circling task with four subtasks (clockwise movement with the left thumb, clockwise movement with the right thumb, counter-clockwise movement with the left thumb, and counter-clockwise movement with the right thumb) was completed, followed by the subjective evaluation form to complete. A rest period (at least five minutes) was provided for the participants when an experiment of a protector was completed. Upon completion of all of the experiments, the participants were interviewed about the difference that they found between protectors and the touchscreen.

3 Results

Two-way ANOVAs were used to determine the main and interaction effects of the type of protectors (TPU protector, normal PET protector, special PET protector, the touchscreen without a protector) and the type of thumb (left thumb, right thumb) on user experience in the moving task and the circling task independently. Statistical significance was accepted at p-values less than 0.05.

3.1 Task Performance

Accuracy. As shown in Fig. 3, in the moving task, the main effect of type of protectors and its interaction with the type of thumb were not significant for performance accuracy. The main effect of the type of thumb was significant for performance accuracy ($P < 0.001$). The performance accuracy of right thumb was significantly better than that of left thumb. As shown in Fig. 4, in the circling task, the main effect of the type of protectors ($P = 0.023$) and the type of thumb ($P < 0.001$) were significant. The interaction effect of them was not significant. The performance accuracy of right thumb was significantly better than that of left thumb. The post hoc tests using BH method showed that the standard deviation of moving distance on the touchscreen without a protector (M = 18.68, SD = 5.58) was significantly less than normal PET protector (M = 20.88, SD = 6.87) and special PET protector (M = 20.31, SD = 7.13), and marginally significantly less than TPU protector (M = 19.61, SD = 5.89). The TPU protector was significantly less than normal PET protector.

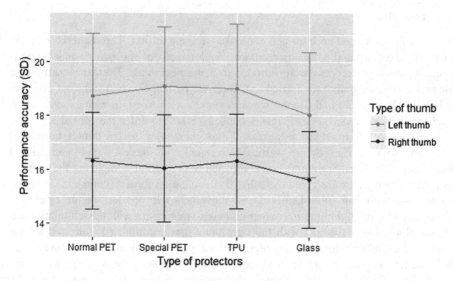

Fig. 3. Accuracy in the moving task

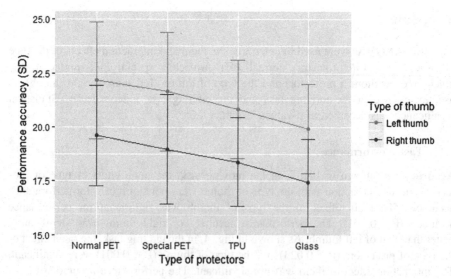

Fig. 4. Accuracy in the circling task

Time to Complete the Task. No significant difference between the type of protectors and its interaction with the type of thumb were obtained in both the moving task and the circling task. The main effect of the type of thumb was significant in time to complete the task in both the moving task (P = 0.012) and the circling task (P = 0.012). Right thumb used significantly less time to complete the task than left thumb.

3.2 Thumb Muscle Activity

Muscle Effort. As shown in Fig. 5, in the moving task, although there seemed to be a difference between types of protectors, the main effect of the type of protectors and its interaction with the type of thumb were not significant for muscle effort of APB. The main effect of the type of thumb was significant for muscle effort of APB (P < 0.001). The muscle effort in right thumb was significantly more than effort in left thumb. Paired t-tests were used to further explore the difference between types of protectors. Results showed that muscle effort of special PET protector (M = 124, SD = 105) was significantly less than TPU protector (M = 169, SD = 213), and marginally significantly less than touchscreen without a protector (M = 166, SD = 250). In the circling task, the main effect of the type of protectors and the type of thumb and their interaction were not significant.

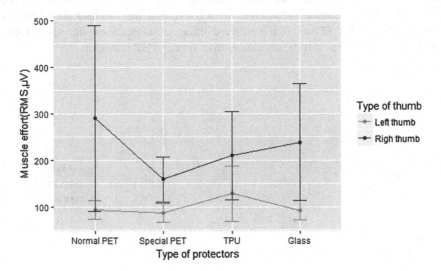

Fig. 5. Muscle effort in the moving task

Muscle Fatigue. In the moving task, the main effect of the type of protectors and its interaction with the type of thumb were not significant for muscle fatigue of APB. The main effect of the type of thumb was significant for muscle fatigue of APB (P = 0.023). The muscle fatigue in right thumb was significantly more than that in left thumb. In the circling task, the main effect of the type of protectors and the type of thumb and their interaction were not significant.

3.3   Subjective Usability Evaluation

Perceived Effort of Thumb Muscles. Perceived effort of thumb muscles was measured by 7-point Likert scale (1 represented too small, 7 represented too large). As shown in Fig. 6, in the moving task, the main effect of the type of protectors was significant (P = 0.015). There was no significant difference between types of thumb in perceived effort of thumb muscles. The post hoc tests using BH method showed that the perceived effort of thumb muscles on special PET protector (M = 3.43, SD = 1.10) was significantly less than normal PET protector (M = 4.23, SD = 0.90), TPU protector (M = 4.00, SD = 0.79), and the touchscreen without a protector (M = 4.30, SD = 0.75). As shown in Fig. 7, in the circling task, the main effect of the type of protectors was significant (P < 0.001). There was no significant difference between types of thumb in perceived effort of thumb muscles. The post hoc tests using BH method showed that the perceived effort of thumb muscles on normal PET protector (M = 4.80, SD = 0.96) was significantly more than special PET protector (M = 3.80, SD = 0.85), TPU protector (M = 4.03, SD = 0.93), and the touchscreen without a protector (M = 4.30, SD = 0.92). Perceived effort of muscles on the touchscreen without a protector was significantly more than special PET protector.

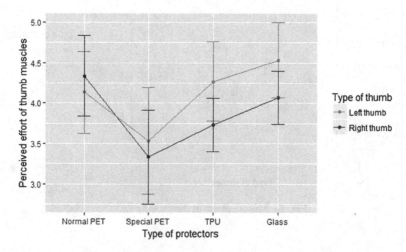

Fig. 6. Perceived effort of thumb muscles in the moving task

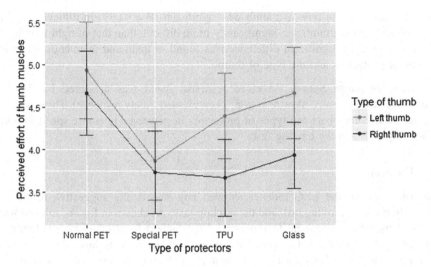

Fig. 7. Perceived effort of thumb muscles in the circling task

Perceived Fatigue of Thumb Muscles. Perceived fatigue of thumb muscles was measured by 7-point Likert scale (1 represented not fatigue at all, 7 represented much fatigue). The main effect of the type of protectors and the type of thumb and their interaction were not significant in both the moving task and the circling task.

Perceived Comfort of Thumb Muscles. Perceived comfort of thumb muscles was measured by 7-point Likert scale (1 represented not comfortable at all, 7 represented very comfortable). In the moving task, the main effect of the type of protectors (P = 0.026) and the type of thumb (P = 0.049) were significant. The perceived comfort of thumb muscles of right thumb was significantly better than that of left thumb. The post hoc tests using BH method showed that perceived comfort of thumb muscles on normal PET protector (M = 4.20, SD = 1.32) was significantly more than special PET protector (M = 5.20, SD = 1.45), TPU protector (M = 5.27, SD = 1.34), and the touchscreen without a protector (M = 5.10, SD = 1.21). In the circling task, no significant difference was found in main and interaction effect of the type of protectors and the type of thumb.

User Satisfaction. User satisfaction was measured by 7-point Likert scale (1 represented not satisfied at all, 7 represented very satisfied). There was no significant difference between types of protectors in user satisfaction in both the moving task and the circling task.

Frustration. Frustration was measured by 7-point Likert scale (1 represented not frustrated at all, 7 represented very frustrated). There was no significant difference between types of protectors in frustration in both the moving task and the circling task.

Difficulty of the Task. Difficulty of the task was measured by 7-point Likert scale (1 represented very easy, 7 represented very difficult). In the moving task, the main effect of the type of protectors and its interaction with the type of thumb were not significant.

The main effect of the type of thumb was significant (P = 0.039) in difficulty of the task. The task of left thumb was significantly more difficult than that of right thumb. In the circling task, no significant difference was found in main and interaction effect of the type of protectors and the type of thumb.

Perceived Response Speed. Perceived response speed was measured by 7-point Likert scale (1 represented slow response, 7 represented timely response). There was no significant difference between types of protectors in perceived response speed in both the moving task and the circling task.

3.4   Emotion

Valence. None of the EEG indexes showed any statistically suggestive results in valence in both the moving task and the circling task. As shown in Fig. 8, valence was measured by SAM instrument (1 represented the highest level of positive valence, 9 represented the lowest level of positive valence). In the moving task, no significant difference was found between types of protectors. In the circling task, a significant difference was found between types of protectors (P = 0.001). The post hoc tests using BH method showed that the valence of the touchscreen without a protector (M = 2.33, SD = 0.98) was significantly more positive than special PET protector (M = 3.13, SD = 1.19) and normal PET protector (M = 3.67, SD = 1.23). The valence of TPU protector (M = 2.53, SD = 0.83) was significantly more positive than normal PET protector (M = 3.67, SD = 1.23).

Arousal. None of the EEG indexes showed any statistically suggestive results in arousal in both the moving task and the circling task. Arousal was measured by SAM instrument (1 represented the highest level of arousal, 9 represented the lowest level of arousal). No significant difference was found between types of protectors in both the moving task and the circling task.

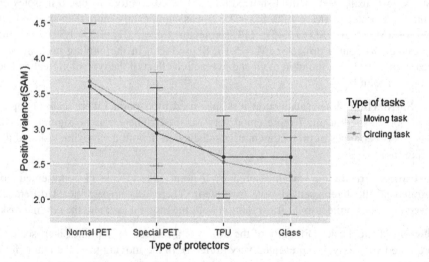

Fig. 8. Valence measurement using SAM instrument

4 General Discussion

Results of task performance revealed that the circling movement was more susceptible to the type of protectors than the line movement. In the moving task, no significant difference in accuracy was found between types of protectors. But there was a significant difference in accuracy in the circling task. Besides, no significant difference between types of protectors was found in time to complete the task. It suggested that difference in accuracy was not due to the speed of movement, but due to the type of protectors itself. Among different types of protectors, special PET protector had the smallest friction and normal PET protector had the largest friction. But performance of them in the circling task was worse than TPU protector and the touchscreen. It reflected that a protector with excessive or too little friction could not improve performance. A protector with the same friction as the touchscreen had the best performance compared with other types of protectors. However, performance of the touchscreen was better than three types of protectors, even better than the protector with the same friction as the touchscreen. Therefore, the touchscreen without a protector was most suitable for gesture control to improve performance. Among various types of protectors, TPU protector, which has the same friction as the touchscreen, was more suitable for gesture control to improve performance.

Thumb muscle activity was measured through EMG at APB in right and left thumb and the item perceived effort of thumb muscles in subjective usability evaluation. The subjective self-reports found a significant difference in perceived effort of thumb muscles between types of protectors in both the moving task and the circling task. In the moving task, perceived effort of thumb muscles on special PET protector was significantly less than other types of protectors and the touchscreen. Compared with results of subjective self-reports, the mean value ordering of EMG measurement in the moving task was consistent with it. Paired t-tests showed that muscle effort on special PET protector was significantly less than TPU protector and the touchscreen. The reason that the results of EMG measurement were not significant may be a too large variance of EMG measurement. In the circling task, perceived effort of thumb muscles on normal PET protector was significantly more than other types of protectors and the touchscreen. It reflected the relationship between friction and muscle effort. Thumb movement on special PET protector with the smallest friction used the least muscle effort. Thumb movement on normal PET protector with the largest friction used the most muscle effort. For muscle fatigue, no significant difference between types of protectors was found in both EMG measurement and subjective self-reports. The reason may be that each subtask lasted less than thirty seconds during the experiment and the short-term thumb movement could not cause obvious muscle fatigue.

Except for the item perceived effort of thumb muscles, there were six items in subjective usability evaluation. However, only one item, perceived comfort of thumb muscles, was significant in the moving task. Perceived comfort of thumb muscles on normal PET protector was significantly more than other types of protectors and the touchscreen.

Emotion during the task was measured through EEG and subjective SAM instrument using two-dimensional Arousal-Valence model. No significant difference between types of protectors was found in EEG indexes in valence and arousal dimensions in both the moving task and the circling task. But using the SAM instrument, a significant difference in valence was found in the circling task. The valence of the touchscreen without a protector was significantly more positive than special PET protector and normal PET protector. The valence of TPU protector was significantly more positive than normal PET protector. Results of subjective valence measurement were in accordance with performance. In the circling task, the best performance on the touchscreen led to the highest level of positive valence, and worst performance on normal PET protector led to the lowest level of positive valence.

Therefore, the touchscreen without a protector had the best performance and the highest level of positive valence, followed by TPU protector with the same friction as the touchscreen. Special PET protector, which had smaller friction than the touchscreen, had the smallest muscle effort. But performance of special PET protector was worse than the touchscreen and the level of the positive valence of special PET protector was also lower than the touchscreen. Normal PET protector had the largest friction and the largest muscle effort among types of protectors. It had the worst performance and the lowest level of positive valence.

In addition, this study also compared right thumb with left thumb. The dominant hands of all the participants were right-handed. Results showed that right thumb performed better and used less time than left thumb in both the moving task and the circling task. EMG measurement showed that right thumb had more muscle effort and a higher level of fatigue during the moving task. Results of subjective usability evaluation showed that participants felt more comfortable and easier in the moving task using right thumb.

The limitation of the current study is that this study only selected three types of protectors. These three types of protectors contained different materials, manufacturing process and different physical parameters such as coefficient of friction, thickness, and hardness. This study mainly compared protectors with three different levels of friction but did not control other physical parameters. Further research could conduct an experimental design with different types of physical parameters to explore relationships between these physical parameters and user experience.

Acknowledgments. This study was supported by Huawei Device Co., Ltd.

References

1. Xiong, J., Muraki, S.: An ergonomics study of thumb movements on smartphone touch screen. Ergonomics **57**, 943–955 (2014)
2. Brandl, P., Forlines, C., Wigdor, D., Haller, M., Shen, C.: Combining and measuring the benefits of bimanual pen and direct-touch interaction on horizontal interfaces. In: Proceedings of the Working Conference on Advanced Visual Interfaces, pp. 154–161. ACM, New York (2008)

3. Liu, S.-F., Chang, C.-F., Wang, M.-H., Lai, H.-H.: A study of the factors affecting the usability of smart phone screen protectors for the elderly. In: Zhou, J., Salvendy, G. (eds.) ITAP 2016. LNCS, vol. 9754, pp. 457–465. Springer, Cham (2016). https://doi.org/10.1007/978-3-319-39943-0_44

4. Page, T.: Touchscreen mobile devices and older adults: a usability study. Int. J. Hum. Factors Ergon. **3**, 65 (2014)

5. Stern, R.M., Stern, R.M., Ray, W.J., Quigley, K.S.: Psychophysiological Recording. Oxford University Press, Oxford (2001)

6. Seror, P., Maisonobe, T., Bouche, P.: A new electrode placement for recording the compound motor action potential of the first dorsal interosseous muscle. Neurophysiol. Clin./Clin. Neurophysiol. **41**, 173–180 (2011)

7. Russell, J.: Affective space is bipolar. J. Pers. Soc. Psychol. **37**, 345 (1979)

8. Liu, Y., Sourina, O., Nguyen, M.K.: Real-time EEG-based emotion recognition and its applications. In: Gavrilova, Marina L., Tan, C.J.K., Sourin, A., Sourina, O. (eds.) Transactions on Computational Science XII. LNCS, vol. 6670, pp. 256–277. Springer, Heidelberg (2011). https://doi.org/10.1007/978-3-642-22336-5_13

9. Hodes, R.L., Cook, E.W., Lang, P.J.: Individual differences in autonomic response: conditioned association or conditioned fear? Psychophysiology **22**, 545–560 (1985)

10. Bradley, M.M., Lang, P.J.: Measuring emotion: the self-assessment manikin and the semantic differential. J. Behav. Ther. Exp. Psychiatry **25**, 49–59 (1994)

Is SERVQUAL Reliable and Valid?
A Review from the Perspective of Dimensions
in Different Typical Service Industries

Quan Yuan[✉] and Qin Gao

Department of Industrial Engineering,
Tsinghua University, Beijing 100084, China
yuan-q15@mails.tsinghua.edu.cn, gaoqin@tsinghua.edu.cn

Abstract. SERVQUAL is the best known and most commonly used scale measuring service quality in a wide variety of service environments. But several researchers have identified potential difficulties with the reliability and validity of the scale when it is used in a specific service environment. The purpose of this study is to review the scales measuring service quality in researches, comparing with SERVQUAL from the perspective of research method and dimensionality, and to investigate whether SERVQUAL are still suitable for measuring quality of typical service industries. We chose four well-studied service industries as key domains, and reviewed related researches about developing scales of measuring service quality in those four domains in the past 30 years. The four industries are retail banking, transportation, higher education and online shopping. Results showed that, even though the quality of most typical service industries cannot be completely measured by using SERVQUAL, the dimensionalities of scales in typical industries are associated to SERVQUAL's five dimensions. SERVQUAL is still valuable for service quality scale development.

Keywords: Perceived service quality · Dimensionality · Research method · Typical service industry · SERVQUAL

1 Introduction

Over the past three decades, a great deal of studies has researched various aspects of service quality. In much of these studies, researchers were devoted to developing reliable and valid scales for measuring the service quality. Some of the scales can be applied to the whole service industries, and the best known and most commonly used instruments now is called "SERVQUAL" scale, which was originally developed by Parasuraman et al. (1985) and Parasuraman et al. (1988). The SERVQUAL scale was originally applied in five service domains. Later on, it has been used to measure service quality in a wide variety of service industries.

While SERVQUAL has been widely applied into specific service fields, such as banking, hotel, website service and education, and valued by scholars and service managers alike, many researchers have identified potential difficulties with the conceptual foundation and empirical operationalization of the scale. In particular, researchers have questioned whether the five dimensions of the scale, and its

© Springer Nature Switzerland AG 2019
P.-L. P. Rau (Ed.): HCII 2019, LNCS 11576, pp. 338–351, 2019.
https://doi.org/10.1007/978-3-030-22577-3_24

psychometric properties, are generically applicable in all service industries (Ladhari 2009). As a result, many researches adapted SERVQUAL for measuring service quality in specific industries, while others were willing to develop brand new scales for different domains. Researches began to use several research methods rather than just use SERVQUAL during development in order to ensure the reliability and validity of their instruments.

Against this background, the aim of ours study is to provide a review of service quality scales development in different typical service industries. We summarized the research methods of those scales and compared their dimensions with SERVQUAL to study the similarities between the scales. Sequentially, we can get a simple understanding about SERVQUAL's application and reliability and validity in typical industries.

2 The SERVQUAL Scale

Parasuraman et al. (1985) considered that service quality was subjectively perceived by customers, and it was the gap between customer expectations and service performance. They chose retail banking, credit card, securities brokerage, and product repair and maintenance as investigated service industries, conducted several focus groups and in-depth interviews as research method, and built a multidimensional service quality model with ten dimensions. Sequentially, Parasuraman et al. (1988) developed the SERVQUAL scale which consists of 22 items representing following five dimensions:

- Tangibles (measured by four items): the appearance of physical facilities, equipment, and personnel;
- Reliability (five items): the ability to perform the promised service dependably and accurately;
- Responsiveness (four items): the willingness to help customers and provide prompt service;
- Assurance (four items): the knowledge and courtesy of employees and their ability to inspire trust and confidence; and
- Empathy (five items): the level of caring and individualized attention the firm provides to its customers.

SERVQUAL has been used widely to measure service quality in a variety of service industries and applied in several countries (Ladhari 2009), while there have been debates about various aspects of the scale, including:

1. Reliability and validity problem in specific service environment. Ladhari (2009) reviewed twenty years of SERVQUAL research and considered that the applicability of SERVQUAL in different culture context and different service settings were debated in the reliability, convergent validity, discriminant validity and predictive validity by both service managers and academics;

2. The applicability of SERVQUAL to the online environment. Parasuraman et al. (2005) claimed that the development of the Internet deeply changed service industrial in both environments and service mode, thus the SERVQUAL scale were hard to be used to measure the service quality related to the Internet;
3. The uncertainty of detailed target to which the dimensions point. Brady and Cronin (2001) considered that if service quality perceptions represent a latent variable, something specific must be reliable, responsive, empathetic, assured, and tangible. And they suggested that identifying "something" was critical in the literature.

3 Methodology

According to the development of studies in measuring service quality in different service industries, we summarized four types of service industries: (1) traditional industries that are investigated during the development of the SERVQUAL scale; (2) traditional industries but are not the sample industries for developing SERVQUAL; (3) complex industries which are ignored by researchers in early stage; (4) industries directly related to the Internet. We respectively chose retail banking, transportation, higher education and online shopping as four typical service industries, and reviewed the relative studies about developing scales of measuring service quality in these four service industries.

We use "service quality", "measure", and each industry as keywords, searching the keywords on Google scholar. Studies in recent thirty years and focusing on developing a complete instrument for measuring service quality are included and are subjected to a comprehensive in-depth content. 31 literature including a complete instrument developing procedure and a final scale were reviewed in this study.

We then integrated the research method used in scale development and final dimensions of scales, comparing with SERVQUAL to understand the applicability of SERVQUAL in different typical service industries.

4 SERVQUAL and Other Scales in Retail Banking

Retail banking service is one of the sample services for developing SERVQUAL. There are two tendency of service domains when researchers study the quality measurement in retail banking. One is traditional offline retail banking service, and the other is online banking service. SERVQUAL are widely used in both offline banking and online banking. We reviewed eight studies related to retail banking, including 4 studies about offline banking and 4 studies about online banking. Table 1 shows the details of reviewed studies about retail banking. Each dimension in the final scale and its related dimensions in SERVQUAL are also listed in the table.

Table 1. Selected studies on service quality scale development in retail banking.

Study	Domains of measurement	Research methods for identify dimensions	Final number of dimensions and items	Final dimensions (* refers the dimension is the same as it in SERVQUAL)	Related dimensions in SERVQUAL
Kemal Avkiran (1994)	Retail banking	Adapted from SERVQUAL	4 dimensions with 17 items	Staff conduct Credibility Communication Access to teller services	Reliability/Responsiveness/ Assurance/Empathy Reliability/Assurance Responsiveness Tangibles/Reliability/Responsiveness
Bahia and Nantel (2016)	Retail banking	Adapted from SERVQUAL	6 dimensions with 31 items	Effectiveness and assurance Access Price *Tangible service Portfolio *Reliability	Reliability/Assurance Tangibles/Reliability/Responsiveness Assurance Tangibles Tangibles/Empathy Reliability
Aldlaigan and Buttle (2002)	Retail banking	According to technical and functional quality (Grönroos 1984)	4 dimensions with 21 items	System quality Behavioral service quality Service transactional accuracy Machine service quality	Tangibles/Reliability/Responsiveness Reliability/Responsiveness/Empathy Reliability/Assurance Reliability/Responsiveness/Assurance
Jabnoun and Hassan Al-Tamimi (2003)	Retail banking	Adapted from SERVQUAL	3 dimensions with 22 items	Human skills *Tangibles *Empathy	Reliability/Responsiveness/Assurance Tangibles Empathy
Jayawardhena (2004)	Online banking	Adapted from SERVQUAL	5 dimensions with 21 items	Access Website interface Trust Attention Credibility	Tangibles/Reliability/Responsiveness Tangibles Assurance Responsiveness Reliability
Yang et al. (2004)	Online banking	Adapted from SERVQUAL	6 dimensions with 20 items	*Reliability *Responsiveness Competence Ease of use Security Product portfolio	Reliability Responsiveness Assurance Tangibles/Responsiveness Reliability Tangibles/Empathy
Sohn and Tadisina (2008)	Online banking	Adapted from SERVQUAL	6 dimensions with 25 items	Trust Customised communications Ease of use Website content and functionality *Reliability Speed of delivery	Reliability/Assurance Empathy Tangibles/Responsiveness Tangibles/Responsiveness Reliability Responsiveness
Ho and Lin (2010)	Online banking	Literature and user interview	5 dimensions with 17 items	Customer service Web design *Assurance Preferential treatment Information provision	Reliability/Responsiveness/Assurance Tangibles Assurance Tangibles Tangibles

From research method aspect, there are six in eight studies adapted SERVQUAL to a new scale. When studying offline banking, researchers add few dimensions and modify many items. When it comes to online banking, dimensionality of SERVQUAL is not enough, and researchers tend to add more dimensions and items to adapt SERVQUAL.

From final scale aspect, the final number of dimensions (M = 4.9, SD = 1.1) and items (M = 21.8, SD = 4.3) in the scales are both close to that in SERVQUAL. As we can see in Table 1, dimensions in offline and online banking have several properties. Dimensions in offline banking are more similar to dimensions of SERVQUAL, which proved the fitness of SERVQUAL in offline banking service. Tangibles, reliability and assurance are frequently contained in the scales, and refer to the demands from customers. However, since SERVQUAL did not claim "something" must be tangible, reliable, and assured, the items classification in new scales are not consistent as SERVQUAL in factor analysis, and consequently the name of dimensions in final scales are different from each other. For example, staff (Aldlaigan and Buttle 2002; Jabnoun and Hassan Al-Tamimi 2003; Kemal Avkiran 1994) is an independent dimension, which actually identify the "something". Dimensions in online banking are modified on the basis of SERVQUAL, and many dimensions and items are changed. Because of offering similar service as offline banking, online banking also focuses on tangibles, reliability and assurance, and dimensions tend to identify what they describe. However, because of the differences in procedure of service, the describing objects are different between offline and online banking. For example, new dimensions in online banking are web design (Ho and Lin 2010; Jayawardhena 2004; Sohn and Tadisina 2008) and ease of use (Sohn and Tadisina 2008; Yang et al. 2004), which can be classified into tangibles as website is the tangible equipment; Security and competence (Yang et al. 2004) is similar as reliability and assurance. These conditions stated that customers pay attention to the security of online banking, and proved the applicability of SERVQUAL in online banking.

In reviewed studies, there are a number of scales adapted from SERVQUAL, and the final scales are similar in both size and dimensionality to SERVQUAL, which proved the applicability of SERVQUAL in retail banking. When the describing objects are identified in SERVQUAL, the scale do better. Both offline and online banking focus on tangibles, reliability and assurance, but the objects are little different because of procedure difference.

5 SERVQUAL and Other Scales in Transportations

Transportations is an old service industry. Even if SERVQUAL was not based on transportations, SERVQUAL is used in a variety of domains of the industry. We reviewed ten studies about measuring service quality of airline, railway, city bus and so on. Table 2 shows the details of reviewed studies about transportations.

Table 2. Selected studies on service quality scale development in transportations.

Study	Domains of measurement	Research methods for identify dimensions	Final number of dimensions and items	Final dimensions (* refers the dimension is the same as it in SERVQUAL)	Related dimensions in SERVQUAL
Hu and Jen (2006)	City buses	Adapted from SERVQUAL	4 dimensions with 20 items	Interaction with passengers *Tangible service equipment Convenience of service Operational management support	Reliability/Responsiveness Tangibles Reliability/Responsiveness Reliability/Assurance/Empathy
Liou et al. (2007)	Airline service	Expert research	6 dimensions with 12 items	Employee's service Safety and reliability On board service Schedule On time performance Frequent flyer program	Reliability/Responsiveness Reliability/Assurance Reliability/Responsiveness/ Assurance/Empathy Assurance Reliability Assurance
Sánchez Pérez et al. (2007)	Public-sector transport	Adapted from SERVQUAL	5 dimensions with 21 items	*Tangibility *Reliability Receptivity *Assurance *Empathy	Tangibles Reliability Responsiveness Assurance Empathy
Pakdil and Aydın (2007)	Airline service	Adapted from SERVQUAL	8 dimensions with 34 items	Employees *Tangibles *Responsiveness *Reliability and assurance Flight patterns Availability Image *Empathy	Reliability/Responsiveness/ Assurance Tangibles Responsiveness Reliability/Assurance Reliability/Responsiveness/ Assurance/Empathy Responsiveness Reliability Empathy
Prasad et al. (2010)	Railways	Adapted from SERVQUAL	7 dimensions with 26 items	Comfort Convenience *Tangibility *Reliability *Assurance *Responsiveness *Empathy	Tangibles Reliability/Responsiveness Tangibles Reliability Responsiveness Assurance Empathy
Mishra (2013)	Public transportation services	Adapted from SERVQUAL	6 dimensions with 24 items	Security *Tangibility *Reliability *Responsiveness *Assurances *Empathy	Reliability Tangibles Reliability Responsiveness Assurance Empathy
Randheer et al. (2011)	Public transportation services	Adapted from SERVQUAL	5 dimensions with 23 items	Culture *Reliability *Responsiveness *Assurances *Empathy	Tangibles Reliability Responsiveness Assurance Empathy

(*continued*)

Table 2. (*continued*)

Study	Domains of measurement	Research methods for identify dimensions	Final number of dimensions and items	Final dimensions (* refers the dimension is the same as it in SERVQUAL)	Related dimensions in SERVQUAL
Irfan et al. (2012)	Rail transport	Adapted from SERVQUAL	8 dimensions with 29 items	*Tangible	Tangibles
				*Empathy	Empathy
				*Assurance	Assurance
				Safety	Reliability
				Information	Tangibles
				Food	Tangibles
				*Responsiveness	Responsiveness
				Timeliness	Assurance
Barabino et al. (2012)	Urban bus transport	Adapted from SERVQUAL	4 dimensions with 15 items	*Tangible	Tangibles
				*Reliability	Reliability
				*Assurance	Responsiveness
				*Responsiveness	Assurance
Bakti and Sumaedi (2015)	Public land transport	Survey	4 dimensions with 18 items	Comfort	Tangibles
				*Tangible	Tangibles
				Personnel	Reliability/Responsiveness
				*Reliability	Reliability

From research method aspect, there are eight in ten studies adapted SERVQUAL to a new scale. And in seven studies, researchers use only dimensions of SERVQUAL but not items, and then add items according to other literatures. While the only different one is the study of Sánchez Pérez et al. (2007) about public-sector transport. They used only items but not dimensions of SERVQUAL, and then divided items into new dimensions by factor analysis.

From final scale aspect, the final number of dimensions (M = 5.7, SD = 1.5) and items (M = 22.2, SD = 6.2) in the scales are mostly close to that in SERVQUAL, and the name of dimensions are similar to the name in SERVQUAL. More than half of dimensions in eight studies are the same as dimension of SERVQUAL. Specifically, Sánchez Pérez et al. (2007) use only items, and the dimensions of final scale is still similar to SERVQUAL dimension. Moreover, Bakti and Sumaedi (2015) did not consider SERVQUAL in their research methods, but the final scale is also similar to SERVQUAL. These cases proved the applicability of SERVQUAL in transportation industry. As we can see in Table 2, eight in ten final scales contained reliability dimension. The most important goal of transportation service is sending customers to destination according to the schedule, consequently, reliability dimension is important in transportation.

In reviewed studies, there are a number of scales adapted from SERVQUAL, and the final scales followed the name of SERVQUAL dimension, and the scales not adapted from SERVQUAL are also similar to SERVQUAL, which proved the applicability of SERVQUAL in retail banking. Reliability is important in transportation service.

6   SERVQUAL and Other Scales in Higher Education

Even though higher education is an old service, it is complex and ignored by researchers in early stage. Research about measuring higher education service quality were conducted a little late. We review eight related studies between year 1996 and year 2010. Five in eight studies finished a whole procedure of scale development, one studies directly use SERVQUAL to measure higher education quality, and other two studies did a comparison between different higher education quality scales. Table 3 shows the details of five reviewed studies about developing higher education quality scales.

Table 3.   Selected studies on service quality scale development in higher education.

Study	Domains of measurement	Research methods for identify dimensions	Final number of dimensions and items	Final dimensions (* refers the dimension is the same as it in SERVQUAL)	Related dimensions in SERVQUAL
Soutar and McNeil (1996)	Higher education	Adapted from SERVQUAL	2 dimensions, 14 sub-dimensions with 52 items	1. Academic aspects: *Reliability *Tangibles *Responsiveness *Assurance *Empathy Knowledge Communication 2. Non-academic aspects: *Reliability *Tangibles *Responsiveness *Assurance *Empathy Communication Systems	1. Academic aspects: Tangibles Reliability Responsiveness Assurance Empathy NONE NONE 2. Non-academic aspects: Tangibles Reliability Responsiveness Assurance Empathy NONE Reliability/Responsiveness/Assurance
Abdullah (2006a)	Higher education	Focus group	HEdPERF 6 dimensions with 45 items	Non-academic aspects Academic aspects Reputation Access Programme issues Understanding	Reliability/Responsiveness/Assurance Reliability/Responsiveness/Assurance Reliability NONE Reliability/Assurance Empathy
Nadiri et al. (2009)	Higher education	Adapted from SERVQUAL	2 dimensions with 22 items	Intangibles Tangibles	Reliability/Responsiveness/ Assurance/Empathy Tangibles

(*continued*)

Table 3. (*continued*)

Study	Domains of measurement	Research methods for identify dimensions	Final number of dimensions and items	Final dimensions (* refers the dimension is the same as it in SERVQUAL)	Related dimensions in SERVQUAL
Lagrosen et al. (2004)	Higher education	Adapted from SERVQUAL	11 dimensions with 31 items	Corporate collaboration Information and responsiveness Courses offered *Campus facilities Teaching practices Internal evaluations External evaluations Computer facilities Collaboration and comparisons Post-study factors Library resources	NONE Responsiveness Tangibles/Reliability/Empathy Tangibles Reliability Reliability NONE Tangibles Credibility NONE Tangibles
De Jager and Gbadamosi (2010)	Higher education	Literature	13 dimensions with 48 items	Internationalisation Marketing and support Access and approachableness of service International students and staff Academic reputation Student focused Academic quality Variety and reach Location and logistics Accommodation and scholarship Sports reputation and facilities Safety and Security Parking	NONE Reliability/Assurance NONE NONE Reliability Reliability Assurance Empathy Tangibles Tangibles Tangibles Reliability Tangibles
Tsinidou et al. (2010)	Higher education	Survey	7 dimensions with 40 items	Academic staff Administration service Library's service Curriculum structure Location Facilities Career prospects	NONE Reliability Tangibles Tangibles Tangibles Tangibles Reliability

From research method aspect, there are two in five studies adapted SERVQUAL to a new scale. And other three studies chose to develop completely new scales with no referring to SERVQUAL. Since higher education is a big and complex service, in order to better understanding the service quality of the industry, in scale developing stage, researchers tend to obtain a huge number of dimensions and items about higher education through many research methods such as literature reviews and interviews. Among these studies, Abdullah (2006a) developed a scale called HEdPERF without referring SERVQUAL, which had a profound impact on higher education service quality measurement. In the two studies based on SERVQUAL, researchers still added many dimensions and items to the new scales. These facts show that researchers widely believed the dimensions and items can not totally cover the service quality model of higher education.

From final scale aspect, the final number of dimensions (M = 10.2, SD = 3.2) and items (M = 43.2, SD = 7.2) in the scales are much more than the number in SERVQUAL. As we can see in Table 3, the dimensions of scales in studies based on SERVQUAL kept several properties of SERVQUAL, while the dimensions in studies without SERVQUAL have no properties in common with dimensions of SERVQUAL. According to researches, SERVQUAL performed worse in practice compared with HEdPERF (Abdullah 2006a; Brochado 2009). Due to the complex and big system of higher education, the dimensions of SERVQUAL can not cover the whole service quality, but they can still represent a small part of quality. Among the final dimensions, reputation (Abdullah 2006b; De Jager and Gbadamosi 2010), internal evaluations (Lagrosen et al. 2004) and career prospects (Tsinidou et al. 2010) are all related to the reliability dimension, while library's service (Lagrosen et al. 2004; Tsinidou et al. 2010), facilities (De Jager and Gbadamosi 2010; Lagrosen et al. 2004; Tsinidou et al. 2010), and accommodation and scholarship (De Jager and Gbadamosi 2010) are related to the tangibles dimension.

In reviewed studies, because of the complex system of higher education, the content of final scales is commonly much more than SERVQUAL. SERVQUAL cannot measure the complete service quality in higher education, but the dimensions of SERVQUAL can still represent part of quality, among which reliability and tangibles are important. In studies about measuring higher education quality, SERVQUAL can be part of reference for researchers, but cannot be the main theoretical model. Researchers need to conducted surveys to collect more dimensions and items for modify the scale.

7 SERVQUAL and Other Scales in Online Shopping

As a completely new service industry based on the Internet, online shopping services have already created a huge market and played an important role in the whole service industry. We reviewed five representative studies about measuring online shopping service quality. Four in five studies finished a whole procedure of scale development, and the other study did a comparison between different higher education quality scales. Table 4 shows the details of four reviewed studies about developing online shopping quality scales.

Table 4. Selected studies on service quality scale development in online shopping

Study	Domains of measurement	Research methods for identify dimensions	Final number of dimensions and items	Final dimensions (* refers the dimension is the same as it in SERVQUAL)	Related dimensions in SERVQUAL
Lee and Lin (2005)	Online shopping	Adapted from SERVQUAL	4 dimensions with 12 items	Web site design *Reliability *Responsiveness Personalization	Tangibles Reliability Responsiveness Assurance/Empathy
Yoo and Donthu (2001)	Online shopping	Survey	SITEQUAL 4 dimensions with 18 items	Ease of use Aesthetic design Processing speed Security	Tangibles/Responsiveness Tangibles Responsiveness Reliability
Feng et al. (2007)	Online shopping	Survey	6 dimensions with 24 items	Timeliness Personal contact quality Order quality Order discrepancy handling Order condition Convenience	Reliability/Responsiveness Reliability Reliability Assurance Tangibles Reliability/Responsiveness
Ananthanarayanan Parasuraman et al. (2005)	Online shopping	Survey	E-S-QUAL: 4 dimensions with 22 items; E-RecS-QUAL (salient only to customers who had nonroutine encounters with the sites): 3 dimensions with 11 items	1. E-S-QUAL scale: Efficiency Fulfillment System availability Privacy 2. E-RecS-QUAL: *Responsiveness Compensation Contact	1. E-S-QUAL量表: Reliability Assurance Tangibles/Responsiveness Reliability 2. E-RecS-QUAL量表 Responsiveness Tangibles/Assurance Responsiveness

From research method aspect, there are one in four studies adapted SERVQUAL to a new scale. And other three studies chose to develop completely new scales with no referring to SERVQUAL. The authors of SERVQUAL referred in their later studies the impact on service industry brought by the development of the Internet, and the necessity of developing a replacement of SERVQUAL to adapt online environments (Parasuraman et al. 2005). Even though there still exist researches trying to adapt SEVQUAL to measure the service quality of online shopping, other two scales without referring SERVQUAL influence more hardly on the quality measurement: the SITEQUAL scale (Yoo and Donthu 2001) and the E-S-QUAL scale (Parasuraman et al. 2005). Most researchers tend to develop completely new scales for measuring online shopping service quality.

From final scale aspect, when we just consider the quality of online shopping platform, the final number of dimensions (M = 4.5, SD = 0.9) and items (M = 19.0, SD = 4.6) in the scales are a little less than the number in SERVQUAL. As we can see in Table 4, the dimensions of scales in studies based on SERVQUAL are close to the dimensions of SERVQUAL (Lee and Lin 2005), and the dimensions in studies without SERVQUAL have several properties in common with dimensions of SERVQUAL. For example, ease of use with tangibles, processing speed with responsiveness, security with reliability in SITEQUAL (Yoo and Donthu 2001), and efficiency and privacy with reliability, fulfillment with assurance, system availability with tangibles in E-S-QUAL (Parasuraman et al. 2005). Although the dimensions are not the same in these two significant scales, they more or less contained part of the items of SERVQUAL. Similar to the dimensions in online banking, dimensions in online shopping, such as website design (Lee and Lin 2005), privacy (Parasuraman et al. 2005) and security (Yoo and Donthu 2001), reflected the demand of website usability and security from customer, which are tangibles and reliability in SERVQUAL.

In reviewed studies, most of researchers chose to develop a completely new scale replacing the SERVQUAL scale. However, although online shopping is different from traditional offline service, after adaptation, the dimensions of SERVUQAL are still suitable for measuring part of online shopping service quality. But SERVQUAL cannot cover all the service quality. In studies about measuring online shopping quality, website can be seen as tangibles in SERVQUAL, and items of SERVQUAL can be adapted to describing online shopping service, but researchers still need to add new dimensions and items to develop a complete scale rather than directly use SERVQUAL.

8 Conclusion

As the best known and most commonly used scale for measuring service quality, SERVQUAL was used widely in a variety of service industries. However, the applicability of SERVQUAL in different industries are not the same. In traditional offline service industries, such as retail banking service and transportation service, the applicability of SERVQUAL is great, although the lack of object identification cause the name of dimensions are different in different studies. When it comes to complex and big service domain, such as higher education, the dimensions of SERVQUAL can just represent part of service quality. Even if researchers try to adapt SERVQUAL to a new scale, they need to add much more new dimensions and items, the content of final scales is much more than that of SERVQUAL. Consequently, it is inadvisable to use SERVQUAL as a main theoretical basis to develop scales. In the online service, such as online banking and online shopping, when identifying the objects of every dimension, researchers can adapt SERVQUAL to measure part of service quality, while they need to use some other research method to obtain new dimensions and items to develop a complete scale.

In summary, SERVQUAL can be used to measuring the complete or part of service quality in specific service industry. It is still the necessary reference in developing a new service quality measuring scale. When conducting a new study for measuring service quality, researchers need to refer the dimensions of SERVUQAL, identify describing objects of each dimension, and use other research methods to obtain new dimensions and items, thus they can get a reliable and valid service quality model.

Acknowledgement. This study was supported by National Key Research and Development Plan grant 2016YFF0204102.

References

Abdullah, F.: The development of HEdPERF: a new measuring instrument of service quality for the higher education sector. Int. J. Consum. Stud. **30**(6), 569–581 (2006a)

Abdullah, F.: Measuring service quality in higher education: HEdPERF versus SERVPERF. Mark. Intell. Plan. **24**(1), 31–47 (2006b)

Aldlaigan, A.H., Buttle, F.A.: SYSTRA-SQ: a new measure of bank service quality. Int. J. Serv. Ind. Manag. **13**(4), 362–381 (2002)

Bahia, K., Nantel, J.: A reliable and valid measurement scale for the perceived service quality of banks. Int. J. Bank Mark. **18**(2), 84–91 (2016)

Bakti, I.G.M.Y., Sumaedi, S.: P-TRANSQUAL: a service quality model of public land transport services. Int. J. Qual. Reliab. Manag. **32**(6), 534–558 (2015)

Barabino, B., Deiana, E., Tilocca, P.: Measuring service quality in urban bus transport: a modified SERVQUAL approach. Int. J. Qual. Serv. Sci. **4**(3), 238–252 (2012)

Brady, M.K., Cronin Jr., J.J.: Some new thoughts on conceptualizing perceived service quality: a hierarchical approach. J. Mark. **65**(3), 34–49 (2001)

Brochado, A.: Comparing alternative instruments to measure service quality in higher education. Qual. Assur. Educ. **17**(2), 174–190 (2009)

De Jager, J., Gbadamosi, G.: Specific remedy for specific problem: measuring service quality in South African higher education. High. Educ. **60**(3), 251–267 (2010)

Feng, Y.X., Zheng, B., Tan, J.R.: Exploratory study of logistics service quality scale based on online shopping malls. J. Zhejiang Univ. **8**(6), 926–931 (2007)

Grönroos, C.: A service quality model and its marketing implications. Eur. J. Mark. **18**(4), 36–44 (1984)

Ho, C.-T.B., Lin, W.-C.: Measuring the service quality of internet banking: scale development and validation. Eur. Bus. Rev. **22**(1), 5–24 (2010)

Hu, K.C., Jen, W.: Passengers' perceived service quality of city buses in Taipei: scale development and measurement. Transp. Rev. **26**(5), 645–662 (2006)

Irfan, S.M., Kee, D.M.H., Shahbaz, S.: Service quality and rail transport in Pakistan: a passenger perspective. World Appl. Sci. J. **18**(3), 361–369 (2012)

Jabnoun, N., Hassan Al-Tamimi, H.A.: Measuring perceived service quality at UAE commercial banks. Int. J. Qual. Reliab. Manag. **20**(4), 458–472 (2003)

Jayawardhena, C.: Measurement of service quality in internet banking: the development of an instrument. J. Mark. Manag. **20**(1–2), 185–207 (2004)

Kemal Avkiran, N.: Developing an instrument to measure customer service quality in branch banking. Int. J. Bank Mark. **12**(6), 10–18 (1994)

Ladhari, R.: A review of twenty years of SERVQUAL research. Int. J. Qual. Serv. Sci. **1**(2), 172–198 (2009)

Lagrosen, S., Seyyed-Hashemi, R., Leitner, M.: Examination of the dimensions of quality in higher education. Qual. Assur. Educ. **12**(2), 61–69 (2004)

Lee, G.G., Lin, H.F.: Customer perceptions of e-service quality in online shopping. Int. J. Retail Distrib. Manag. **33**(2), 161–176 (2005)

Liou, J.J., Tzeng, G.H., Chang, H.C.: Airline safety measurement using a hybrid model. J. Air Transp. Manag. **13**(4), 243–249 (2007)

Mishra, A.K.: Measuring Commuters' Perception on Service Quality Using SERVQUAL in Delhi Metro (2013)

Nadiri, H., Kandampully, J., Hussain, K.: Students' perceptions of service quality in higher education. Total Qual. Manag. 20(5), 523–535 (2009)

Pakdil, F., Aydın, Ö.: Expectations and perceptions in airline services: an analysis using weighted SERVQUAL scores. J. Air Transp. Manag. 13(4), 229–237 (2007)

Parasuraman, A., Zeithaml, V.A., Berry, L.L.: SERVQUAL: a multiple-item scale for measuring consumer perc. J. Retail. 64(1), 12 (1988)

Parasuraman, A., Zeithaml, V.A., Berry, L.L.: A conceptual model of service quality and its implications for future research. J. Mark. 49(4), 41–50 (1985)

Parasuraman, A., Zeithaml, V.A., Malhotra, A.: ES-QUAL: a multiple-item scale for assessing electronic service quality. J. Serv. Res. 7(3), 213–233 (2005)

Prasad, M.D., Shekhar, B.R.: Impact of service quality management (SQM) practices on Indian railways: study of South Central Railways (2010)

Randheer, K., Al-Motawa, A.A., Vijay, P.J.: Measuring commuters' perception on service quality using SERVQUAL in public transportation. Int. J. Mark. Stud. 3(1), 21 (2011)

Sánchez Pérez, M., Carlos Gázquez Abad, J., María Marín Carrillo, G., Sánchez Fernández, R.: Effects of service quality dimensions on behavioural purchase intentions: a study in public-sector transport. Manag. Serv. Qual.: Int. J. 17(2), 134–151 (2007)

Sohn, C., Tadisina, S.K.: Development of e-service quality measure for internet-based financial institutions. Total Qual. Manag. 19(9), 903–918 (2008)

Soutar, G., McNeil, M.: Measuring service quality in a tertiary institution. J. Educ. Adm. 34(1), 72–82 (1996)

Tsinidou, M., Gerogiannis, V., Fitsilis, P.: Evaluation of the factors that determine quality in higher education: an empirical study. Qual. Assur. Educ. 18(3), 227–244 (2010)

Yang, Z., Jun, M., Peterson, R.T.: Measuring customer perceived online service quality: scale development and managerial implications. Int. J. Oper. Prod. Manag. 24(11), 1149–1174 (2004)

Yoo, B., Donthu, N.: Developing a scale to measure the perceived quality of an Internet shopping site (SITEQUAL). Q. J. Electron. Commer. 2(1), 31–45 (2001)

Reliability and Validity of Measurement Scale for Perceived Service Quality in Internet Bank: A Review

Quan Yuan[✉] and Qin Gao

Department of Industrial Engineering, Tsinghua University,
Beijing 100084, China
yuan-q15@mails.tsinghua.edu.cn,
gaoqin@tsinghua.edu.cn

Abstract. Internet banking is a new service related to both traditional retailing banking and the Internet. This study reviews the literatures on service quality measurement of Internet bank, with an emphasis on the methodological issues involved in developing measurement scales and issues related to the reliability and validity of service quality. We selected some studies on Internet bank service quality measurement instruments in recent five years from Web of Science, and subjected them to a thorough content analysis. The study identifies several conceptual and methodological limitations associated with developing Internet banking service quality measurement such as the lack of a rigorous validation process, the problematic sample size and composition, the focus on functional aspects, and the use of a data-driven approach. The study undertakes an elaborate literature review of research on the development of Internet bank scales, and summarizes guidelines for developed a reliable and valid scales measuring Internet banking service quality. The findings should be valuable to academics and practitioners alike.

Keywords: Internet bank · Perceived service quality · Scale development · Five years review · Reliability and validity

1 Introduction

Over the past three decades, numerous scholars efforted to develop reliable and valid scales for measuring customers' perceived quality of service industry. Among those scales the best known one is called SERVQUAL, which was developed by Parasuraman et al. (1988; 1985). SERVQUAL is based on a multidimensional model including five dimensions and 22 items. And the model has a far-reaching impact on later studies about measuring service quality. However, Parasuraman et al. (2005) found that judging online service quality differed from judging traditional service quality, and developed two new scales for online service quality measurement. Ladhari (2009) reviewed numerous scholars about e-service quality and found that dimensions of e-service quality tended to be contingent on the service industry. Therefore, scales of measuring online service quality of a specify service industry need to be studied independently.

© Springer Nature Switzerland AG 2019
P.-L. P. Rau (Ed.): HCII 2019, LNCS 11576, pp. 352–362, 2019.
https://doi.org/10.1007/978-3-030-22577-3_25

Retail banking is one of the sample service industries for developing SERVQUAL. Since Internet banking service have been offered by a lot of banks, a large number of customers enjoy retail banking services online. Recently, there are two obvious changes occurring in the Internet bank industry for retail customers. Firstly, with the rise of the Internet and smart phones, mobile applications and even mobile payment are easy to use and become more and more popular among people, and banks launched their mobile applications for retail customers one after another, in order to offer more convenient service to customers. Secondly, since many mobile payment companies launched online financial products to attract individuals, so that individuals would like to save money in their applications rather than in bank, and the role of service quality in fostering the growth of online financial services has received much attention in the academic and practitioner communities. In order to restore the loss of customers, many banks also offered individual wealth management service as a new online service to customers, which now is one of the hottest services in online retail banking. Consequently, recent online service quality has a significant changing influence on many important aspects of retail banking service. An understanding of how consumers evaluate Internet bank now is thus of the utmost importance for scholars and practitioners alike.

The purpose of this study is to review reliability and validity of scales measuring Internet banking service quality in recent studies, and to summarize guidelines for developed a reliable and valid scales measuring Internet banking service quality. We reviewed the literature on Internet bank, with an emphasis on the methodological issues involved in developing measurement scales and issues related to the reliability and validity of the Internet banking service quality construct. We selected some studies on Internet bank in recent five years from Web of Science, and subjected them to a thorough content analysis.

2 Issues of Internet Banking Service

Internet banking began in the 1990s. In 1992, some American banks launching their e-banking services (Sikdar et al. 2015). Since then, e-banking service became more and more important and more and more popular for both bank and customers (Keskar and Pandey 2018). Today, banks are almost being replaced by mobile phones, tablets, and laptops. Customers use Internet banking services to finish the deposits, remittances, transfers, payments, securities orders, insurance services, and interest rate inquiries, and even do some investment recently, by using electronic devices at any time and place without personally attending a bank.

Previous studies agreed that service quality was a multidimensional construct but there was no firm agreement regarding the generic dimensions (Peng and Moghavvemi 2015). And the key dimensions to the service quality of Internet bank still need to be explored today (Dharmavaram and Nittala 2018), because of the everchanging needs of customers and the addition of new Internet banking services. Previously, customers were concerned only with the safety and ease of operating Internet banking interfaces. As Internet banking evolved, websites were user-centered designing, mobile service were opened, and new money arrangement services were offered, customers began focusing on other factors such as the information content and professionalism and attitudes of customer service personnel in online banking. Thus, previous scales of measuring Internet banking service quality are likely to be inappropriate for measurement now. We need to pay attention to new studies about measuring Internet banking service quality in recent years.

3   Methodological Issues in Developing Service Quality Scales of Internet Bank

We use "Online", "Bank", "Service quality", "Measure" as keywords, searching the keywords on web of science. Only studies in recent five years and focusing on developing a complete instrument for measuring Internet banking service quality are

Table 1. Selected studies on Internet banking service quality scale development.

Study	Domains of measure	Sample	Original items battery	Data analysis procedure for assessing factor structure	Final items battery	Final number of dimensions (number of items)	Internal reliability coefficient alpha / Composite construct reliability
(Raza et al. 2015)	Internet banking in Pakistan	400 users Internet banking of different banks located in Karachi city	25 items	Exploratory factor analysis	25 items	5 dimensions: assurance (5), empathy (5), reliability (5), responsiveness (5), tangibility (5)	Ranges from 0.651 to 0.983
(Roy and Balaji 2015)	Online financial service	630 users who have had experience of using online financial services in the last 12 months	44 items, five-point Likert scale, offline administration	Exploratory and confirmatory factor analysis	25 items	5 dimensions: convenience quality (4), functionality (4), interaction quality (7), information quality (5), image quality (5)	Ranges from 0.88 to 0.91
(Amin 2016)	Internet banking	520 users	14 items, five-point Likert scale, offline administration	Confirmatory factor analysis and the squared multiple correlation	14 items	4 dimensions: personal need (3), site organization (4), user friendliness (4), and efficiency of website (3)	Ranges from 0.851 to 0.916
(Jovovic et al. 2016)	Electronic Banking	135 users from more than 7 banks	29 items, five-point Likert scale	Exploratory factor analysis	28 items	3 dimensions: website design and reliability (13), effectiveness (8), communication and empathy (7)	Ranges from 0.898 to 0.970
(Arcand et al. 2017)	Mobile banking	375 users, all accustomed to conducting banking activities on mobile platforms	16 items, seven-point Likert scale	Structural equation model	16 items	5 dimensions: security/privacy (3), practicality (5), design/aesthetics (3), sociality (2), enjoyment (3)	Ranges from 0.83 to 0.96

included and are subjected to a comprehensive in-depth content. Only five literature including a complete instrument developing procedure and a final scale were found, and other thirteen incomplete studies were also reviewed in this study. Table 1 shows the complete studies we found.

The general complete method for developing scales measuring perceived Internet banking service quality can be concluded from literatures as eight steps: (1) Define construct of service quality; (2) Identify dimensions; (3) Generate items on all dimensions and design a scale according to items; (4) Collect data; (5) Purify scale; (6) Collect fresh data from a new sample on a set of items to emerge from the previous step; (7) Further purify scale and get the final version of the scale; (8) Evaluate reliability and validity of the scale. During the first three steps, researchers designed an original version of service quality scale with some methods to ensure the reliability and validity of the scale. In the next four steps, the original scale was purified for better reliability and validity by factor analysis. In the last step, a final version of scale had been completed and researchers measured the reliability and validity of the final version to proof the usability and effectivity of the scale.

The methodological issues identified in this review can be summarized as follows: research methods for identify dimensions; research methods for generation of items; sampling methods; assessment and purification of scale; scale reliability and validity.

3.1 Research Methods for Identify Dimensions

All of the studies we reviewed used one or more qualitative methods to identify dimensions of Internet banking service quality. Full literature reviews were conducted by all the studies.

Raza et al. (2015) finally decided to use five dimensions in SERVQUAL model directly. Amin (2016) use the scales from (Herington and Weaven 2009) and (Ho and Lin 2010). Arcand et al. (2017) intergraded all the literatures they reviewed and finally got five dimensions including security/privacy, practicality, design/aesthetics, sociality and enjoyment. However, the three studies did not explain why they choose these dimensions.

Jovovic et al. (2016) stated the theoretical model applied in their study was ES-QUAL/E-Rec S-QUAL, developed by Parasuraman et al. (2005), modified for measuring the quality of online banking services. They considered quality dimensions of e-banking services consisted of efficiency, privacy, readiness to provide answers/contact, as well as dimensions of security, empathy, and website design. Effectiveness, privacy and responsiveness had been taken from ES-QUAL/E-Rec S-QUAL, which served as the basis, while the rest of dimensions had been taken from other similar models in accordance with the needs of e-banking services in Montenegro. However, although Parasuraman et al. (2005) considered ES-QUAL/E-Rec were suitable for measuring all online services, they in fact just chose electronic commerce industry as research sample, which was extremely different from Internet banking service.

Only Roy and Balaji (2015) used more than one method to identify dimensions. Their study based on the Grönroos's (1984) service quality model and Delone and McLean's (2003) Information system success model. And moreover, three focus group interviews consisting of eight participants each, and eight depth interviews exploring participants' insights on their evaluation of the quality of online financial services were carried out to design original scales. Each of the focus groups lasted for about 90 min and moderated by an experienced moderator. And they finally identify for dimensions including system quality, information quality, interaction quality and image quality.

Due to the big changes of new platform and new service mode in recent Internet banking service, new dimensions may be included in service quality. Thus, re-searcher should use qualitative research at the earliest stage, using more than one method rather than use only literature reviews. Using only literature review method is inadvisable. One method that researchers seldom use in complete scale design study is the critical incident technique (CIT), a qualitative interview method to study significant processes, incidents and events identified by respondents (Chell 2004). Jun and Palacios (2016) use CIT to identify the dimensions of mobile banking service quality, and a total of 17 dimensions were successfully found, five of which considered as the main sources of customer satisfaction, which proved that the dimensionality of recent Internet banking service quality is far more complex than that in past service because of business and platform changes. CIT is suitable for finding new dimensions of quality in new service, but is more effortful at the same time, so researchers can selectively use CIT, or refer the outcomes by other studies based on CIT.

3.2   Research Methods for Generation of Items

Because that scale items are specific in different context of Internet banking service, they are generated using both inductive methods (such as literature reviews) and deductive methods (such as exploratory research).

Researchers are more active in doing research to generate items than identify dimensions, and the descriptions of procedure in generation are more detailed in their articles. But still part of researches came through deductive methods. Raza et al. (2015) only did literature review, and even did not explain the literature source of items. Jovovic et al. (2016) also did literature review only to gather items. Arcand et al. (2017) gathered items in literature review and modified some items by themselves to fit for local Internet banking service.

Roy and Balaji (2015) did both literature reviews and offline interviews with experts to generate items. They referred the measurement scales from the previous research studies and additional items identified in the interviews and focus group discussions were used to identify an initial pool of measurement items for the dimensions. And then, five administrators of online financial service providers in India were interviewed to obtain clarity on the constructs' composition. These items were then adjusted per the interviewee's perceptions of the importance of each of the dimensions.

Amin (2016) did an offline questionnaire research after literature review to generate items. The questionnaire was written in both Bahasa Malaysia and English language to ensure clarity, and their content validity (wording and meaning) was checked carefully by two Malaysians experts. A convenience sampling approach was used, and respondents were selected among those customers who visited the sampled banks during day time and at various days for a week or a month. Ten commercial banks and forty branches were selected in four different cities in Peninsula Malaysia. Finally, 25 respondents participated the research.

In several studies, items generated are based on literatures and qualitative research such as expert interviews and focus groups, but are based solely on literatures in other studies. Future research should develop a more specific theoretical framework to identify scale-items.

3.3 Sampling Methods

The samples for purifying scale of measuring Internet banking service quality are drawn from a variety of populations. Most studies use convenience sampling and random sampling methods. Raza et al. (2015) collected the data of 400 users of Internet banking of different banks located in Karachi city of Pakistan. Roy and Balaji (2015) collected the data of 630 customers who have had experience of using online financial services in the last 12 months. Arcand et al. (2017) cooperated with the marketing research firm tasked with randomly sending invitations to panelists, and finally collected the data of 375 users, all accustomed to conducting banking activities on mobile platforms. While Amin (2016) and Jovovic et al. (2016) did not introduce specific sampling methods.

In convenience sampling, the reasons for Internet use and the behavior of these participants may differ from those in other places. The literature on traditional service quality shows that dimensions of service quality differ from one country to another (Ladhari 2008). Therefore, future studies should use more diversified samples.

3.4 Assessment and Purification of Scale

The dimensionality and items of the scale are commonly assessed using exploratory factor analysis (EFA) and/or confirmatory factor analysis (CFA, belonging to structural equation model). Factor analysis is used to reduce the items whose factor loading are low, and to confirm the number of dimensions.

Some researcher directly used factor analysis to purify the original version of scale. Raza et al. (2015) and Jovovic et al. (2016) did EFA after collecting data. In the study of Raza et al. (2015), the 25 questions related to the Internet banking and customer satisfaction have been categorized into five overlapping groupings of items. Factor loading were all over 0.5, except one item, which factor loading was negative, author thought question of the item is required to be interpreted in an opposed direction from the actual way it is written for that factor. The outcome of EFA were satisfactory, since dimensions and items had no changes, which proved the reliability and validity of SERVQUAL. Jovovic et al. (2016) did EFA and the analysis has provided results of three dimensions, and a rejection of one item because of its equal factor loadings with two dimensions.

Moreover, other researchers did some pre-tests to assess the scale before doing the factor analysis. Roy and Balaji (2015) finished pilot studies in two steps for assessing the scale. First step is student evaluation. 30 students were asked to comment on general design of the questionnaire and clarity of individual measurement items. Second step is interviewing real users by CATI telephone data collection methodology.

the actual users of online financial services, final usable response is 190. Then they did both EFA and CFA, finally obtained a 5-dimension model with 25 items, cutting off 19 items whose factor loadings were below 0.5. Amin (2016) conducted a pre-test to improve questionnaire structure and content before using CFA in the study, but details about the pre-test is not described in the article. The outcome of CFA was good, and a 4-dimension model with 14 items was confirmed with no original items being dropped. Arcand et al. (2017) stated that the questionnaire in their study was developed by the research team and pretested twice to validate the measures and ensure that the questions/statements were clear and well understood. And then they did structural equation model to assess the scale, and finally get a 5-dimension model with 16 items. No origin items were dropped.

EFA and CFA are suitable for purification of scales, and pre-test to modify some descriptions of items or develop a clear questionnaire is also important for avoiding bias from respondents' understanding of scales, so that researchers can get better outcome of factor analysis.

3.5 Scale Reliability and Validity

The reliability of scales (that is, the internal homogeneity of a set of items) is usually assessed by Cronbach's α coefficient. All the scales in the present review exhibit good reliability in terms of Cronbach's α coefficient, with values greater than 0.70, the minimum standard according to Nunnally's work (1978). The good outcome of Cronbach's α coefficient in all the five studies indicates that the scales in recent study of measuring Internet banking service quality provides a good estimate of internal consistency.

Validity of scale is more complex and more neglected than reliability by researchers in Internet banking service quality study. Raza et al. (2015) and Jovovic et al. (2016) even only measured the reliability in their study and did not use any method to assess the validity of final scale.

Other researchers measured construct validity of the scales, including discriminant validity (that is, the extent to which measures of theoretically unrelated constructs do not correlate with one another) and convergent validity (that is, the extent to which a set of items assumed to represent a construct does in fact converge on the same construct). Convergent validity can be ascertained if the factor loadings in factor analysis are greater than 0.5 (Fornell and Larcker 1981), composite reliability (CR) greater than 0.7 (Hair et al. 2011) and the average variance extracted (AVE) is greater than 0.5 (Fornell and Larcker 1981). Discriminant validity can be ascertained by comparing the AVE values with the corresponding inter-factor squared correlation values. Roy and Balaji (2015) used factor loading and the AVE values to confirm the convergent and discriminant validity. Amin (2016) used factor loading, CR and the AVE values to assess the convergent validity. Arcand et al. (2017) used factor loading and the AVE values to assess the validity.

Predictive/nomological validity (that is, the extent to which the scores of one construct are empirically related to the scores of other conceptually related constructs), belonging to criterion-related validity, were measured by structural equation modeled in several studies (Amin 2016; Arcand et al. 2017; Roy and Balaji 2015). However, all of the studies did not measure the overall service quality during data collection, so they cannot measure the correlation between scale outcome and overall service quality, which referred to content validity and concurrent validity, other type of criterion-related validity.

The good reliability and ignoring content and concurrent validity mean that, the recent scales of measuring Internet banking service quality are accurately for measuring a concept, but the concept may not be the service quality, or not be the whole service quality. Since the big changes happened in Internet bank recently, the possibility of bad validity is high. Researchers should consider the validation process a major issue. Future studies addressing the measurement of Internet banking service quality scale should rigorously test and report on the psychometric properties of the newly developed scales.

4 Conclusion

Even though the reliability of new scale is great according to our review, there are three obvious problems about validity in recent Internet banking service quality scales studies:

Firstly, when identifying dimensions and generating items, researchers mostly refer literature without considering the changes of Internet banking service, and even some of researchers developed the scale according only to literatures. No new dimensions and items can be found during the procedure of scale development, which are the cause of low content validity to new service quality measurement;

Secondly, convenience sampling method and lack of pre-test before factor analysis, and the brief descriptions about the preparations of sampling and pre-testing work in articles, are both terrible for validity of the scale;

Thirdly, researchers paid more concern on the relationship between service quality and other concepts such as customer satisfaction and loyalty, but not the relationships between the outcome of scale and overall service quality. Few recent studies measured the overall service quality during data collection, which means they cannot measure the correlation between scale outcome and overall service quality. Thus, they cannot confirm the validity of their new scale.

Since there are many big and important changes in Internet banking services as we mentioned before, new scales are need to be developed at the beginning of the whole development procedure. But current status of researches is unsatisfactory. We considered integrated guidelines to help future studies, hoping researchers can develop a reliable and valid new scale for measuring the new Internet banking service quality. Guidelines for the reliability and validity of scales were summarized as follow:

4.1 Ways to Ensure Reliability and Validity

We summarized ways to ensure the reliability and validity of a service quality scale during designing and developing process.

There were many ways can be used by researchers to ensure the original scales' reliability and validity during designing process. Researchers firstly identify critical factors or determinants of service quality, build a service quality model containing several dimensions and many items belonging to each dimension through literature reviewing. A draft scale measuring service quality need to be designed according to the service quality model. Because some of the dimensions and items come from other service quality models or scales from other service industries or with other range of application, modification need to be done for better content validity, construct validity and internal consistency reliability. Experts or customers are invited to participate in interviews, in-depth interview, focus groups, CIT or pre-testing to comment on any perceived ambiguities, omissions or errors concerning the dimensions and items in the draft scales, and consequently changes are made accordingly, and the original scale can be built.

Iterative questionnaire researches and Exploratory Factor Analysis are the common ways to purify original scales for better validity and reliability. Researchers send the original scales as a questionnaire to target customers, collecting data from them. Customers sampling are important for representative reliability, so balance of age, gender, sites and so on were considered in most questionnaire survey. The data need to be analyzed by Exploratory Factor Analysis. Before factor analysis, Kaiser–Meyer–Olkin and Bartlett's tests should be done to check sampling adequacy. The dimensions and items of the scales are modified according to the outcome of EFA, which was called scale purifying. The original scale is purified several times to be developed to the final version. Factor loadings in EFA, exceed the recommended level of 0.5, are the assurance of the construct validity and internal consistency reliability of the scales.

4.2   Measurement of Reliability and Validity

We summarized methods to measuring the reliability and validity of a service quality scale.

Reliability. The internal consistency of scales has been demonstrated in numerous studies of the application of the measure. Most researchers have used Cronbach's alpha to evaluate the reliability of scales, which is necessary. Moreover, there are three advice for researchers to evaluate to scale reliability. Firstly, the test-retest method can measure the coefficient of stability, supporting for the test-retest reliability. Secondly, messing up the item order to measure the coefficient of equivalence, supporting for the alternative form reliability. Thirdly, although most researchers have traditionally used Cronbach's alpha, Spearman–Brown formula or item-to-total correlation to evaluate the reliability has been increasing criticism of this practice in the past ten years. Several authors have suggested that Cronbach's alpha might not be the most appropriate measure of psychometric quality and recommend Spearman–Brown formula or item-to-total correlation.

Validity. Content validity is ensured by quality model constructing and pretesting. Construct validity is classified into two types, convergent validity and discriminant validity. Convergent validity is supported by the factor loadings for all constructs exceed the recommended level of 0.7, indicating acceptable item convergence on the intended constructs. Discriminant validity ss supported by the correlation between constructs, with the correlations of no pair of measures exceeding the criterion (0.9 and above). The total construct validity can be measured by structural equation model such as confirmatory factor analysis, regression model, correlations between dimensions and Fornell and Larcker's discriminant validity test. Criterion-related validity is tested by the correlations between the scales' score and criterion score. The common criterions are customers' overall perceived service quality, recommendation intention, complaint level, satisfaction or other service quality scale.

This study reviewed the development of scales measuring service quality of Internet bank in recent five years, and offered guidelines for getting reliable and valid scales of measuring Internet banking service quality. The findings should be valuable to academics and practitioners alike.

Acknowledgement. This study was supported by National Key Research and Development Plan grant 2016YFF0204102.

References

Amin, M.: Internet banking service quality and its implication on e-customer satisfaction and e-customer loyalty. Int. J. Bank Mark. **34**(3), 280–306 (2016)

Arcand, M., PromTep, S., Brun, I., Rajaobelina, L.: Mobile banking service quality and customer relationships. Int. J. Bank Mark. **35**(7), 1068–1089 (2017)

Chell, E.: Critical incident technique. In: Cassell, C., Symon, G. (eds.) Essential Guide to Qualitative Methods in Organizational Research, pp. 45–60. Sage, London (2004)

Delone, W.H., McLean, E.R.: The DeLone and McLean model of information systems success: a ten-year update. J. Manag. Inf. Syst. **19**(4), 9–30 (2003)

Dharmavaram, V., Nittala, R.: Service quality and customer satisfaction in online banking. Int. J. Online Mark. **8**(2), 45–56 (2018)

Fornell, C., Larcker, D.F.: Evaluating structural equation models with unobservable variables and measurement error. J. Mark. Res. **18**(1), 39–50 (1981)

Grönroos, C.: A service quality model and its marketing implications. Eur. J. Mark. **18**(4), 36–44 (1984)

Hair, J.F., Ringle, C.M., Sarstedt, M.: PLS-SEM: indeed a silver bullet. J. Mark. Theory Pract. **19**(2), 139–152 (2011)

Herington, C., Weaven, S.: E-retailing by banks: e-service quality and its importance to customer satisfaction. Eur. J. Mark. **43**(9/10), 1220–1231 (2009)

Ho, C.T.B., Lin, W.C.: Measuring the service quality of internet banking: scale development and validation. Eur. Bus. Rev. **22**(1), 5–24 (2010)

Jovovic, R., Lekic, E., Jovovic, M.: Monitoring the quality of services in electronic banking. J. Cent. Bank. Theory Pract. **5**(3), 99–119 (2016)

Jun, M., Palacios, S.: Examining the key dimensions of mobile banking service quality: an exploratory study. Int. J. Bank Mark. **34**(3), 307–326 (2016)

Keskar, M.Y., Pandey, N.: Internet banking: a review (2002–2016). J. Internet Commer. **17**(3), 310–323 (2018)

Ladhari, R.: Alternative measures of service quality: a review. Manag. Serv. Qual. Int. J. **18**(1), 65–86 (2008)

Ladhari, R.: A review of twenty years of SERVQUAL research. Int. J. Qual. Serv. Sci. **1**(2), 172–198 (2009)

Peng, L.S., Moghavvemi, S.: The dimension of service quality and its impact on customer satisfaction, trust, and loyalty: a case of Malaysian banks. Asian J. Bus. Acc. **8**(2), 32 (2015)

Nunnally, J.: Psychometric Methods. McGraw-Hill Book Co., New York (1978)

Parasuraman, A., Zeithaml, V.A., Berry, L.L.: Servqual: a multiple-item scale for measuring consumer perc. J. Retail. **64**(1), 12 (1988)

Parasuraman, A., Zeithaml, V.A., Berry, L.L.: A conceptual model of service quality and its implications for future research. J. Mark. **49**(4), 41–50 (1985)

Parasuraman, A., Zeithaml, V.A., Malhotra, A.: ES-QUAL: a multiple-item scale for assessing electronic service quality. J. Serv. Res. **7**(3), 213–233 (2005)

Raza, S.A., Jawaid, S.T., Hassan, A.: Internet banking and customer satisfaction in Pakistan. Qual. Res. Financ. Mark. **7**(1), 24–36 (2015)

Roy, S.K., Balaji, M.S.: Measurement and validation of online financial service quality (OFSQ). Mark. Intell. Plann. **33**(7), 1004–1026 (2015)

Sikdar, P., Kumar, A., Makkad, M.: Online banking adoption: a factor validation and satisfaction causation study in the context of Indian banking customers. Int. J. Bank Market. **33**(6), 760–785 (2015)

Cultural Differences, Usability and Design

Inferring Human Feelings and Desires for Human-Robot Trust Promotion

Xingzhi Guo[1], Yu-Cian Huang[1], Edwinn Gamborino[2], Shih-Huan Tseng[3], Li-Chen Fu[1,2(✉)], and Su-Ling Yeh[1,2]

[1] National Taiwan University, Taipei 10617, Taiwan
lichen@ntu.edu.tw
[2] NTU Research Center for AI and Advanced Robotics, Taipei 10617, Taiwan
[3] National Kaohsiung University of Science and Technology,
Kaohsiung 82445, Taiwan
http://robotlab.csie.ntu.edu.tw/, http://ai.robo.ntu.edu.tw/

Abstract. Trust is a key component in developing successful interpersonal relationships. In this paper, we posit that the same is true for Human-Robot Interaction (HRI), since human trust toward robots can facilitate HRI in terms of comfort and usability. We investigated the ability of a socially assistive robot to promote trust in the social relationship with its user by inducing self-disclosure of the user's negative experiences and offering coping mechanisms to deal with these. To achieve this purpose, our system is equipped with deep learning techniques to detect the user's negative facial expressions, which in turn can be used as cues for the robot to proactively induce self-disclosure. Once triggered, using a conversational model, the robot engages the user to determine the cause of their negative mood. Then, it infers the user's internal feelings by applying Markov Chain Monte Carlo (MCMC) inference over a Bayesian Network on the user's utterance. Combining the information gathered from the concept inferencing process and the self-disclosure content, the system is able to estimate a set of desires from the Bayesian Network. Experiments show that our proposed work can correctly infer the user's feelings and desires from their utterances, as well as generate an appropriate response, resulting in the improvement of human's trust toward the robot.

Keywords: Human-Robot trust · Social robot companion ·
Bayesian network · Reinforcement learning ·
Commonsense knowledge graph

This research was supported in part by the Joint Research Center for AI Technology and All Vista Healthcare under Ministry of Science and Technology of Taiwan (MOST grants 107-2218-E-002-009, 107-2634-F-002-019 and 108-2634-F-002-016) and Center for Artificial Intelligence & Advanced Robotics, National Taiwan University.

P.-L. P. Rau (Ed.): HCII 2019, LNCS 11576, pp. 365–375, 2019.
https://doi.org/10.1007/978-3-030-22577-3_26

1   Introduction

In recent years, service robots have become ubiquitous in several aspects of our daily lives. Furthermore, they are expected to have long-term social interactions with their users. In these social tasks, one of the robot's pro-social factors—trust—plays an extremely important role. As a corner stone of Human-Robot Interaction, trust between humans and robots has been explored frequently by researchers from different disciplines (psychology and computer science). Researchers [12] believe that (1) a trustful relationship between humans and robots can prevent misusage or overuse of the robot, and that (2) Human-Robot trust can enhance human's reliance on robots.

According to one of the most accepted definitions in the literature [15], trust is the willingness to expose one's own vulnerabilities. Generally speaking, the vulnerabilities of people are related to negative life experiences. If a robot companion is able to properly induce a person to self-disclose said vulnerabilities and initiate a meaningful interaction, a chance for human-robot trust promotion can be created. Previous research in the fields of robotics [3,8,16] and psychology [4,9] suggest that for a social robot to be able to deal with a person's vulnerabilities and promote trust, it should display the following features in interaction: (1) empathy, (2) goodwill, and (3) awareness of personal preference. Empathy, a feature of social interaction present in humans and other animals, is the ability to understand and internalize the experience of others into oneself through means of verbal and non-verbal communication. Goodwill is defined as a generally friendly, helpful or cooperative attitude, which can be reflected in an agent's behavior. Finally, awareness of personal preference refers to the realization that different individuals, due to a variety of unknown factors, differ in their preferred objects, persons, environments, etc.

Studies on human vulnerability as well as the three factors mentioned above inspired the development of this work. In order to address the problem of human-robot trust promotion, we designed an interactive conversation system for a robot companion to induce a person to self-disclose their vulnerabilities and infer the user's emotional feelings and desires given what has happened to them through a commonsense knowledge graph. By adopting these two factors, the robot companion is able to appropriately handle its user's vulnerabilities by generating an appropriate response and ultimately promote trust through social interaction.

The remainder of this paper is organized as follows: Sect. 2 provides a survey on the related literature that inspired the present work. Section 3 further details the contributions of this work, which surround the development of the interaction system for Human-Robot Trust promotion: The vision module (Sect. 3.2) must be able to capture the user's facial expression and discriminate when the mood of the user is negative in real time, using this information as a cue to engage the user. Once in interaction, in order to induce self-disclosure, we built an inference model and a causal commonsense knowledge base based on ConceptNet [17]; with this information on hand, the robot has the capability of understanding human's common sense and therefore, the internal desires and causes for their negative outlook (Sects. 3.3 and 3.4). In Sect. 4 we present an experiment designed to evaluate the user experience when interacting with our system as well as the self-reported perceived trust towards the robot. In Sect. 5, we finalize the document with a few closing remarks.

2   Related Works

In order to establish a firm theoretical background for the proposed idea, we review the literature from the research fields of Social Psychology and Human-Robot Interaction related to trust. In fact, psychologists have investigated interpersonal trust and presented several different trust models, as shown in Sect. 2.1. For HRI researchers, these interpersonal trust models involve factors of cognition, emotion and individual preference.

2.1   Interpersonal Trust and Human-Robot Trust

Interpersonal trust refers to trust between two or more individuals, a common phenomenon in our daily lives. One foundation of the interpersonal trust is cognition. Baier [1] suggested trust is accepted vulnerability to another's possible but not expected ill will (or lack of good will) toward one". In other words, the formation of cognition-based trust is taking into account the central elements: partners' competence, responsibility and goodwill. Besides cognition-based trust, Lewis and Wiegert [11] claimed that affective foundations for trust also exist, consisting of the emotional bonds between individuals. In addition, Lewicki *et al.* [10] also proposed an evolutionary interpersonal trust model. In this proposed model, the highest level of trust can be built only when a partner can fully understand another's value and preference and, therefore, take actions in favor of their partners. Thus, our papers explore the factors of empathy, goodwill and personal preference in the formation of Human-Robot Trust.

Lee [7] investigated the effects of robot's nonverbal behaviors on Human's trust during social interactions. Their experiments manipulated robot's gestures during Human-Robot Interaction (HRI), and afterwards, a trust game was conducted in order to measure the person's trust level towards the robot with different gestures during the prior interactions. The results of the experiments showed three positive gestural cues of robot for developing trust as follows: leaning-forward, having-arms-in-lap and open-arms.

Martelaro et al. [13] investigated human's trust and sense of companionship in HRI by manipulating robot's vulnerability and expressivity. The vulnerability of the robot was displayed via a personalized conversation. The expressivity was displayed by multimodal interaction (*i.e.* verbal and non-verbal behaviors). Their results showed that participants reported more trust and feelings of companionship with a vulnerable robot, and reported disclosing more of their internal feelings and vulnerabilities with an expressive robot when compared to a non-expressive robot.

Mota et al. [14] presented a pilot study about how people judge trustworthiness of a robot during social Human-Robot Interaction. They examined this phenomenon using 'Trust Game', a common scenario in behavioral economics. Qualitative results suggested that participants may follow a human-robot trust model which is quite similar to the interpersonal trust model. In addition, they also found that people try to interact socially with robots, but due to lack of common social cues, they draw from prior interpersonal social experience, or create new experiences by actively exploring the robot's behaviors.

In summary, most of the existing works exploring human-robot trust focused on cognition-based trust by manipulating the robot's performance during the tasks.

2.2 Emotional Feeling Inference

Among the crucial factors for trust promotion explored earlier (i.e. empathy, goodwill and personal preference), empathy is the only factor that involves building an affective bond with one's peers. From the definition of Paivio et al. [2], empathy is strongly related to one's ability to understand the emotional feelings of others. For example, a person can easily understand that losing money may cause feelings of sadness, anger and disappointment. Furthermore, a person with a strong sense of empathy may then display an appropriate response, based on the inferred emotional feelings of their partner. In other words, the inference of emotional feelings is the first step toward displaying empathy.

There are some existing works addressing the emotion inference tasks from the perspective of Natural Language Processing (NLP). Most of the research in this field considers this task as a multi-class classification problem where the classes are the human's emotions and the observed input data is the human's utterance (i.e. the text content of the speech).

3 Human Emotional Feeling and Desire Inference System

As mentioned earlier in this paper, the scope of this project is to build this system into a social robot companion that is able to promote trust with its user by interaction. Towards meeting this goal, in this paper we describe in detail a method by which a computer interface is able to detect a negative mood in the user based on their facial expression and then, using natural language, communicate with the user to expose these vulnerabilities and inferring the internal feelings and desire that cause their emotional distress. In the following subsections, the visual module and desire and feeling inference module are discussed.

3.1 Visual Module

Advanced service robots must integrate capabilities to detect human's presence in their vicinity and interpret human facial expressions. Therefore, facial expression recognition is a crucial capability for social robots, especially in the context of HRI.

Deep Temporal Appearance-geometry network (DTAGN) [5] is a deep learning model for human's facial expression recognition, which combines two deep networks: the deep temporal appearance network (DTAN) and the deep temporal geometry network (DTGN). As shown in Fig. 1, the DTAN, CNN-based model, is used to extract the temporal appearance feature for facial expression recognition. Meanwhile, the DTGN, a fully-connected DNN, is used to capture geometrical information about the motion of the facial landmark points. These two models are integrated in order to boost the performance of the facial expression recognition. In this paper, we apply the same architecture of DTAGN model and train it on Radboud Faces Database [6].

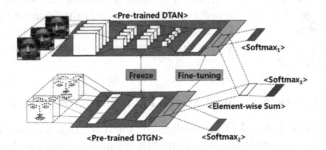

Fig. 1. The joint fine-tune architecture in face expression recognition.

3.2 Causal Commonsense Knowledge Graph

In order to display empathy and goodwill, the robot should be able to infer human's feelings and desires. In our system, we build a causal commonsense knowledge module, based on ConceptNet [17]. ConceptNet is the largest public commonsense knowledge base. It is composed of: (1) nodes: a natural language words/phrases; (2) edges: the relationships between two nodes; (3) weights: the level of intensity of each edge. The following sub-section will describe the feeling inference and desire inference modules separately.

Human Feeling Knowledge Graph. While ConceptNet contains a large variety of edges describing several types of relations between concepts, in this paper we set up two criteria to construct the human feeling knowledge graph: (1) The type of edge should be one of the causal relations shown in Table 1. (2) The end node should be an adjective phrase. Because of the characteristics of Concept-Net, most of the end nodes in a causal relation and containing adjective phrases is designed to describe human's feelings.

Human Desire Knowledge Graph. Similar to previous Human Feeling Knowledge Graph, the Human Desire Knowledge Graph can be constructed by applying two necessary criteria to screen certain nodes in the ConceptNet

Table 1. The causal relations in the ConceptNet and the examples of sentence patterns.

Relation	Sentence pattern
Causes	The effect of *VP* is *NP VP*
MotivatedByGoal	You would *VP* because you want *VP*
Desires	*NP* wants to *VP*
CausesDesire	*NP* makes you want to *VP*

and adding the valid node pairs to the knowledge graph. The first criterion is exactly the same as the first criterion in Human Feeling Knowledge Graph as described in the previous sub-section. For the second criterion, the ending node should be a verb phrase. This is because the objective of the desire inference module is to predict a probable action the user may want to do based on what they previously said.

3.3 Probabilistic Graphical Model for Inferring Feeling and Desire

We used Bayesian Networks to formulate the inference task as a maximum posterior problem, and applied Gibbs Sampling approximation algorithm to infer the posterior probability given the observed evidence. In our case, the observed evidence is the keywords extracted from the user's disclosure content, which are then mapped to the nodes in the pre-built commonsense knowledge graph as observed nodes.

Model Construction. In order to construct the Bayesian Network from the knowledge graph to model the dependencies among human's feelings, we retain the topological structure of the knowledge graph, and derive the conditional probability tables based on the raw weights of each edge.

We define the following concepts to help introduce our way to build the Bayesian network as shown in Fig. 2.

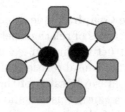

Fig. 2. An example of a constructed Bayesian network. Black nodes are seed nodes, square nodes represent feelings and circle nodes represent desires.

Seed: Seed is an observed node from which the Bayesian network starts to grow. The observations are all from the human's utterance. All the child nodes will be pulled out from the human's causal knowledge graph and become the structure of the resulting Bayesian network. There are two types of nodes in a causal knowledge graph — feelings and desires. Moreover, the Bayesian network could have more than one seed, depending on the content richness of the user's self-disclosure. All the child nodes of the seed nodes will be queried from the knowledge graph to construct the Bayesian network.

Width: Width refers to the maximum number of child nodes that are queried from the knowledge graph of each seed node. The definition of width can prevent useless data from the knowledge graph entering the Bayesian network. The candidate child nodes are first sorted by the corresponding weight, then only the top-N nodes, where N = width, can be added into the Bayesian network.

Depth: Depth is defined as the longest distance from the root, seed node in this case, to the corresponding queried child nodes. In this paper, depth is always set to be one under the assumption that human's desire or feeling is directly related to life events.

Conditional Probability Table. By querying the seed nodes and completing the topological structure of the Bayesian Network, we build the conditional probability table for each nodes based on the weights from the knowledge graph. The conditional probability table is set individually for each node in the Bayesian network as the CPT Builder algorithm shown in Fig. 3.

Function CPT_Builder(G) returns a complete conditional probability table $CPT(X)$

  Local variables: X, all the nodes in the graph G.

          W, the weights of the directional edges in the graph G.

  for each x_i **in** X **do**

    set $C = parents(x_i)$, the parent nodes of x_i

    if $C = Null$ **then continue**

    for each a_{ij} in the binary combinations in the length of C **do**

$$\text{set the value CPT}(x_i) = \begin{cases} sigmoid\left(\sum_c a_{ij} w_{c_j \to x_i}\right), x_i = True \\ 1 - sigmoid\left(\sum_c a_{ij} w_{c_j \to x_i}\right), x_i = False \end{cases}$$

      where $w_{c_j \to x_i}$ is the weight from the parent node x_j to node x_i

  return CPT(X)

Fig. 3. The algorithm for building the conditional probability table (CPT).

The algorithm assigns the conditional probability to each node x_i, except the seed nodes, by carrying out the calculation $CPT(x_i)$. The conditional probability of x_i is defined by a sigmoid based function, whose value range is [0.5, 1]. The lower-bound of the CPT function is set to be 0.5 since the existence of the causal relations means at least someone think the edge is valid; Moreover, the weights are all positive, therefore the result of sigmoid function can not be a negative value. The upper bound of the function is 1 since that is the natural characteristic of the sigmoid function.

Model Inference. The goal of the inference task is to find the feelings and desires in the user's mind given the observations.

As mentioned before, the evidence nodes are the observed life events in the human's self-disclosure. We use Gibbs Sampling approximation inference algorithm to infer the full joint probability of all nodes in the Bayesian Network, then the sampling results can be converted into the conditional probability by fixing the states of the observed nodes.

In this way, the posterior probability for all the nodes can be obtained. The larger the probability, the more likely it is the human's feeling or desire. Therefore, the unobserved nodes, feelings and desires, are ranked according to their values of posterior probability respectively, resulting in two ranked list for further usage.

4   Experiments

In order to evaluate the modules in the proposed system, an HRI experiment was designed to measure the system performance. Different from the explicit and direct evaluation for classification tasks with a testing or validation dataset, the proposed modules are in a human-in-loop system, involving human's subjective judgement; Thus, the evaluation for the proposed system is based on the ratings from human participants, using questionnaires or interviews.

Followed by this experimental paradigm, an HRI experiment is designed to measure the performance of Human Feeling Inference Module, Human Desire Inference Module and the overall Trust Promotion system. Participants were asked to interact with the robots with different configurations, as shown in Table 4-3, for two days, 30 mins per day and 12 interaction sessions in total. Also, Participants were asked to fill out questionnaires before and after the experiments based on their experience and observations in order to do the a temporal evaluation of the system.

In the following sections, the materials (Stimuli scenarios and questionnaires) used in the experiment are described. Afterwards, the results and discussions of each module and the overall system are presented.

4.1   Feeling Inference Evaluation

For this experiment, participants were asked to rate the performance of the system to infer human feelings. Participants were 23 males and 4 females ranging from 22 to 48 years old (average = 25.0, stdev = 5.7). During an experiment session, a story describing a virtual character's negative life experience is presented to the participant. The purpose of the storytelling is to let the participant become immersed into the environment of the story, and substitute themselves into the role of the main character of the story.

The four stimuli scenarios were related to (1) Study Pressure; (2) Personal Affair; (3) Working Pressure and (4) Loneliness. The corresponding story descriptions were shown to the participants in order to encourage the feeling of character substitution.

Afterwards, the robot started to induce the participant's self-disclosure. The participant would reply with the description about what happened to them (in the role of the virtual character) in natural language. Then, the human feeling inference module calculated the probability of each node in the constructed human's feeling knowledge graph. The inferred nodes were sorted with respect to the inferred probability. The top-5 nodes were shown to the participants, and rated by them using a Five-Point Likert scale. The score reflects the extent as to which the participant judged the inferred feelings as reasonable or correct given the scenario.

As show in Fig. 4(a), the overall average score for the inferred human's feeling was 4.25 with a standard deviation of 0.94. This score is significantly higher than average 3-pt (neither agree nor disagree), which can be interpreted as the participants agreeing that the inferred feelings are reasonable. Therefore, we can conclude that the system is able to leverage its human feeling inference module to display its empathy—that is, to show its ability to understand human's emotional feelings given what recently happened to them.

4.2 Desire Inference Evaluation

The participants and procedure are similar to the previous experiment but we only show the top-10 nodes to the participants for rating in a Five-Point Likert scale.

The overall average score for the inferred human's desire is 3.76 while the standard deviation is 1.4. Compared with the score of the previously inferred human's feelings, the overall average score of inferred desire is much lower and has greater variation. This can be interpreted as the result of individual's difference. While the personal variance exists, the inferred desires are generally reasonable since the average score for each inferred desire is greater than average, as shown in Fig. 4(b). While these results may vary according to the individual preferences of each person, we believe this effect may be mitigated by learning the individual preference of a user through continuous, long-term interaction.

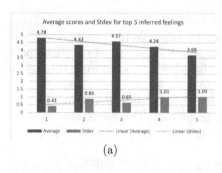

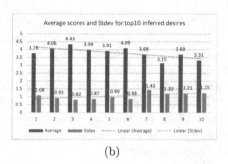

(a)   (b)

Fig. 4. (a) The rating statistics about the inferred feelings; (b) The rating statistics about the inferred desires.

5   Conclusions

We proposed an interactive human-robot trust promotion system, which endows a robot companion with the ability to correctly understand human's feelings and desires from their self-disclosure, showing empathy, goodwill and awareness of personal preferences. Our experimental results on human-robot interaction show that the proposed system outperform lesser system configurations and can promote the human's trust toward the robot companion.

References

1. Baier, A.: Trust and antitrust. Ethics **96**(2), 231–260 (1986)
2. Paivio, S.C., Laurent, C.: Empathy and emotion regulation: reprocessing memories of childhood abuse. J. Clin. Psychol. **57**, 213–226 (2001)
3. Cramer, H.S.M., Goddijn, J., Wielinga, B.J., Evers, V.: Effects of (in)accurate empathy and situational valence on attitudes towards robots. In: Proceedings of the 5th ACM/IEEE International Conference on Human Robot Interaction (HRI), pp. 141–142 (2010)
4. Feng, J., Lazar, J., Preece, J.: Empathy and online interpersonal trust: a fragile relationship. Behav. Inf. Technol. **23**(2), 97–106 (2004)
5. Jung, H., Lee, S., Park, S., Lee, I., Ahn, C., Kim, J.: Deep temporal appearance-geometry network for facial expression recognition (2015)
6. Langner, O., Dotsch, R., Bijlstra, G., Wigboldus, D.H., Hawk, S.T., van Knippenberg, A.: Presentation and validation of the Radboud Faces Database. Cogn. Emot. **24**(8), 1377–1388 (2010)
7. Lee, J.J., et al.: Computationally modeling interpersonal trust. Front. Psychol. **4**, 893 (2013)
8. Leite, I., Pereira, A., Mascarenhas, S., Martinho, C., Prada, R., Paiva, A.: The influence of empathy in human-robot relations. Int. J. Hum Comput Stud. **71**(3), 250–260 (2013)
9. Lewicki, R., Wiethoff, C.: Trust, trust development, and trust repair. In: The Handbook of Conflict Resolution: Theory and Practice, pp. 86–107, January 2000

10. Lewicki, R.J., Tomlinson, E.C., Gillespie, N.: Models of interpersonal trust development: theoretical approaches, empirical evidence, and future directions. J. Manag. **32**(6), 991–1022 (2006)
11. Lewis, J.D., Weigert, A.: Trust as a social reality. Soc. Forces **63**(4), 967–985 (1985)
12. Lewis, M., Sycara, K., Walker, P.: The role of trust in human-robot interaction. In: Abbass, H.A., Scholz, J., Reid, D.J. (eds.) Foundations of Trusted Autonomy. SSDC, vol. 117, pp. 135–159. Springer, Cham (2018). https://doi.org/10.1007/978-3-319-64816-3_8
13. Martelaro, N., et al.: Tell me more: designing HRI to encourage more trust, disclosure, and companionship. In: The Eleventh ACM/IEEE International Conference on Human Robot Interaction (2016)
14. Mota, R.C.R., et al.: Playing the 'trust game' with robots: social strategies and experiences. In: 2016 25th IEEE International Symposium on Robot and Human Interactive Communication (RO-MAN) (2016)
15. Nienaber, A.M., Hofeditz, M., Romeike, P.D.: Vulnerability and trust in leader-follower relationships. Pers. Rev. **44**(4), 567–591 (2015)
16. Oestreicher, L., Eklundh, K.S.: User expectations on human-robot co-operation. In: Proceedings of the 15th IEEE International Symposium on Robot and Human Interactive Communication, pp. 91–96 (2006)
17. Speer, R., Chin, J., Havasi, C.: ConceptNet 5.5: an open multilingual graph of general knowledge. In: Proceedings of the Thirty-First AAAI Conference on Artificial Intelligence, pp. 4444–4451 (2017)

Effect of Layout on User Performance and Subjective Evaluation in an Augmented-Reality Environment

Xin Lei, Yueh-Lin Tsai, and Pei-Luen Patrick Rau[✉]

Department of Industrial Engineering, Tsinghua University, Beijing, China
rpl@mail.tsinghua.edu.cn

Abstract. In this study, the effect of layout on user performance and subjective evaluation in an augmented-reality (AR) environment was investigated. A scenario where participants had to work on three windows simultaneously was used. Three basic layouts of these windows have been examined, i.e., a horizontal layout, a vertical layout, and a diagonal layout. Additionally, two experimental tasks had to be completed; one was a reading comprehension task requiring a low switching frequency (LSF), and the other was a classification task requiring a high switching frequency (HSF). The results revealed that first, participants performed best in the diagonal layout in the LSF task, whereas they performed best in the vertical layout in the HSF task. Second, no significant differences were found in the disorientation between different layouts. Third, participants were significantly less satisfied with the diagonal layout in the HSF task. In conclusion, a horizontal layout is first recommended for general tasks and a vertical layout is recommended for HSF tasks. The switching distance and switching path are two important factors to be considered in the layout design in an AR environment.

Keywords: Multi-window · Layout · Augmented reality · Switching

1 Introduction

People often work with several computer applications simultaneously; however, the size of the computer screen limits the display of multiple windows. Most windowing systems follow the independent overlapping windows approach; thus, the oldest window is always overlapped by the new active one. Owing to the current manner of interaction, frequent switching can cause users to easily lose location awareness and operation awareness, thus leading to a limited sense of perceived control [1]. Finally, the performance and work satisfaction of users can be negatively affected.

The advent of augmented reality (AR) has broken the limitations of current information display modes. For example, the AR head-mounted display (HMD), such as HoloLens, frees users from the computer screen and makes all environment space into users' "desktops". Users can divide the environment space into several regions; then, they may combine relevant windows and separate irrelevant windows. This enables users to configure a certain group of windows into a specific spatial region.

© Springer Nature Switzerland AG 2019
P.-L. P. Rau (Ed.): HCII 2019, LNCS 11576, pp. 376–385, 2019.
https://doi.org/10.1007/978-3-030-22577-3_27

Moreover, this changes the manner of interaction when users switch between multiple windows. Therefore, users may easily and conveniently access a window just by turning their heads.

The multiple-window layout displayed in one environment space has an important influence on the information processing of users. Although there are few studies that are focused on augmented-reality-based layouts, layouts have been investigated and they have been proved to be significant in traditional visual information presentation. For example, the Web page layout has been considered to be a major influencing factor on performance, orientation, and subjective satisfaction [2–5]. Thus, we suspect that the layout of multiple windows is highly important in the augmented-reality environment as well. The aim of this study is to examine the influence of several basic layouts on the user performance and the subjective evaluation, and then to identify the appropriate layouts for different tasks.

2 Related Work

Layouts have been proved to be significant in visual information presentation in numerous fields. First, layouts are important in website designs; placing web objects at expected locations and designing their appearance according to user expectations facilitates orientation; therefore, users can perform faster searches and remember more easily [6]. Second, layouts have influence on graph readability. Three layouts (i.e., force-directed, hierarchical, and orthogonal layout) have different levels of readability in different tasks; the force-directed layout outperformed the other layouts in certain tasks; however, all three layouts performed equally well in certain other tasks [7]. Moreover, in several research works, it has been shown that the graph layout affects the readability as well as the understanding of the underlying data [8]. Third, layouts are important in tag clouds as well, which have become a popular visualization and navigation interface on the Web. The layout of a tag cloud influences its perception; tags in the upper left quadrant are better recalled and can be noticed more quickly, whereas tags in the middle of the cloud attract more user attention than tags near the borders [9].

2.1 Performance

The overall screen layout is considered to have a major impact on task performance [5]. Horizontal menus (left and right) cause a significantly quicker reaction time than vertical menus (top and bottom) for both hits and correct rejections for the visual search task [10]. Moreover, a different study shows the same effect of layout both on accuracy and speed measures, with frames located at the top or left of the screen leading to better performance. Furthermore, layouts and tasks have an interaction effect on performance. For example, the force-directed layout outperformed other layouts in certain tasks; however, all layouts performed equally well in certain other tasks [7].

2.2   Disorientation

Disorientation has been defined as the tendency to lose one's sense of location and direction in a nonlinear document [11, 12]. It can cause users to become frustrated, lose interest, and experience a measurable decline in efficiency [13]; however, it can be minimized via the improvement of navigation design [14]. Therefore, disorientation can serve as an additional tool to evaluate information technology. However, it is not easy to measure disorientation; two fundamental approaches exist regarding disorientation: one that claims a link between the actions of the users and disorientation, and another that claims that user disorientation can only be measured by asking users about their perceptions [11, 15]. Furthermore, it has been investigated that perceived disorientation is predictive of task performance in an interactive search task; however, the actions of the users are not [11]. Moreover, there are differences in the perceived disorientation of the same system that are linked to the sex of the user because certain sex differences have been identified in spatial abilities, including spatial navigation, object location, and spatial rotation [16].

2.3   Perceived Satisfaction

User satisfaction has been recognized as the most dominant criterion of website success. Muylle et al. [17] empirically validated a standard instrument for measuring website user satisfaction that consisted of three components, i.e., information, connection, and layout. Similarly, a different website quality assessment considers the usefulness and the layout as the two most important criteria [18]. Furthermore, it has been found that layouts have great effect on the perceived satisfaction of users [17, 19–21].

3   Design and Evaluation of Different Layouts

3.1   Design of Multi-window Layouts

In this study, a scenario is considered in which users work using three windows simultaneously. Users have to collect and process information from these windows, and then respond accordingly. Multitasking in user behavior can be represented along a continuum in terms of the time spent on one task before switching to another [22]. Thus, three types of windows are defined in this study owing to the total time allocated on a window while multitasking. Window A represents the core task, which consumes most of the user time, window B represents the secondary task, and window C represents the auxiliary task, which consumes the least time. According to previous studies, people tend to concentrate more on the center and upper-left areas; thus, important windows (namely A and B) should be located in the two most appropriate areas. Therefore, we propose three common layouts for the three windows, i.e., the horizontal layout (H), the vertical layout (V), and the diagonal layout (D) (Fig. 1).

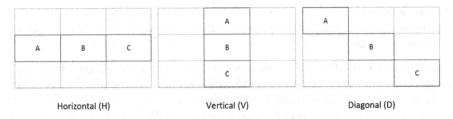

Horizontal (H)   Vertical (V)   Diagonal (D)

Fig. 1. Three layouts examined in this study

3.2   Evaluation Experiment

Experimental Scene. We used Unity 3D to design our experimental scenes and conducted the experiments on the AR HMD HoloLens. Each layout consisted of three windows, which was set 100 cm in front of users. Three windows were in the equal sizes of 50 × 30 cm, and the font size of the information shown in each window was 10 pt.

Experimental Task. There were two types of tasks, namely one with a low switching frequency (LSF) and the other with a high switching frequency (HSF).

The LSF task was reading comprehension. Participants had to read an article and complete three multiple-choice questions in 5 min. The articles and questions used in this study were all extracted from the College English Test-6 in China, and they are in the same difficulty level. The LSF task involved three windows. A window presented the English article. A window presented three multiple choice questions. The last window presented the Chinese meaning of the English words in the article that users might not understand, but users may not frequently look at this window. According to the time length that users spent on each window, the article window was type-A window, the question window was type-B window, and the dictionary window was type-C window. In the LSF task, participants had five minutes to finish the questions. When the time was up, the correct answer would appear automatically. At this time, participants could not continue answering the questions and we counted the number of their correct answers.

HSF task was data classification. Participants had to classify twelve events into four categories according to their degree of importance and degree of urgency. A window was the description window that presented the degree of importance and urgency of all events, and users had to get necessary information from this window. A window was the working window where participants labeled events in each category. The last window presented the classification rule, but participants may not frequently look at this window because they should be able to remember the classification rule. They might only occasionally refer to this window to check the rule. According to the time length that users spent on each window, the description window was type-A window, the working window was the type-B window, and the rule window was the type-C window. In the HSF task, the timer would automatically stop when the participant would correctly complete the task and the completion time was recorded. However, if the participant would not succeed in completing the task in one trial, the data were not used for analysis because this completion time would be significantly longer than that of the one-time success.

Experimental Procedure. The experiment consisted of three phrases. In the first phase, the experimenters introduced the experimental tasks and rules to the participant. Then, the participant had to practice the data classification task on paper, no less than three times in order to become familiar with the task. In addition, the participant had to practice the "select" operation on the HoloLens because it would be heavily used in the formal experiment. The practice prior to the testing was aimed toward avoiding the effect of inexperience on the completion time in the formal experiment. In the second phase, participants had to complete LSF tasks and HSF tasks on the HoloLens, and they had to fill in a short questionnaire every time they completed a task. In the third phase, participants were interviewed about their preferences and they had to comment on the different layouts.

Measurements. Three dependent variables were measured in this study, i.e., the performance, the disorientation, and the perceived satisfaction. The performance consisted of accuracy and efficiency; the accuracy was measured in the LSF task, which was the number of correct answers, whereas the efficiency was measured in the HSF task, which was the completion time. The disorientation and the satisfaction were measured through a five-point Likert scale. A larger value of disorientation indicated that it was easier for participants to become confused in this layout. A higher value of satisfaction indicated that participants were more satisfied with this layout.

Participants. Twenty-four participants from Tsinghua University took part in the experiment. Their average age was 23.4 (SD = 1.39). All participants signed an informed consent agreement prior to testing.

Data Analysis. All dependent variables did not obey the normal distribution; thus, non-parametric analysis was used. The Friedman test was used to examine the main effect of the layout on the performance, the switching times, the disorientation, and the satisfaction. Then, the Wilcoxon signed rank test was used to perform the pairwise comparison between different layouts.

4   Results

4.1   Performance

Table 1 lists the descriptive statistics of the performance under different layouts as well as the results of the Friedman test and of the pairwise comparison. Regarding the LSF task, the performance is the number of correct answers; therefore, a higher value corresponds to a better performance. Regarding the HSF task, the performance is the completion time; therefore, a higher value corresponds to a worse performance.

In the LSF task, the statistical difference in accuracy was marginally significant, namely, $\chi_2^2 = 4.78$ and p $= .091$. As the post-hoc analysis showed, the accuracy of the participants was significantly higher in the diagonal layout than that in the horizontal layout, and the effect size was considerable, namely, $V = 64.5, p = .042,$ and $r = .41$. Although the difference between the horizontal layout and the vertical layout was not statistically significant, the effect size was medium, namely, $V = 66.5, p = .124$, and $r = .31$. Hence, the diagonal layout was the best and the vertical layout was the worst.

In the HSF task, the layout had a significant effect on the completion time, namely, $\chi_2^2 = 20.08$ and $p < .001$. The vertical layout led to the shortest completion time; the difference between the vertical layout and the remaining two layouts was large, both yielded $r > .55$. The diagonal layout resulted in the longest completion time and the difference between the diagonal layout and the horizontal layout was not significant; however, the effect size was medium, namely, $V = 205, p = .121,$ and $r = .32$. Therefore, the diagonal layout was the worst; however, the vertical layout was the best. This result contradicted the results of the LSF task.

Table 1. The main effect of layout on user performance

Layout	LSF task: reading comprehension				HSF task: classification			
	Mean	SD	χ_2^2	p-value	Mean	SD	χ_2^2	p-value
Horizontal	1.75	0.85	4.78	.091	92.13	33.47	20.08	<.001
Vertical	1.46	0.88			84.12	25.51		
Diagonal	1.92	0.72			96.27	25.98		
Post-hoc Analysis								
	V	p-value	r		V	p-value	r	
H-V	66.5	.124	.31		242	.007	.55	
D-H	50.5	.356	.19		205	.121	.32	
D-V	64.5	.042	.41		300	<.001	.87	

4.2   Disorientation

Table 2 lists the descriptive statistics of disorientation under different layouts as well as the results of the Friedman test and those of the pairwise comparison. A higher value means higher disorientation; therefore, a lower value is preferred instead of a higher one. However, no statistically significant differences were found in the disorientation for different layouts in both LSF and HSF tasks. In the HSF task, the perceived disorientation was greater in the vertical layout than in the horizontal layout and diagonal layout; although the p-values were higher than .05 and the effect sizes were medium, namely, they were both $rs = .30$.

Table 2. The main effect of layout on disorientation

Layout	LSF task: reading comprehension				HSF task: classification			
	Mean	SD	χ_2^2	p-value	Mean	SD	χ_2^2	p-value
Horizontal	2.75	0.99	0.24	.888	2.08	0.65	2.63	.268
Vertical	2.79	0.98			2.50	0.98		
Diagonal	2.83	0.76			2.46	1.06		
Post-hoc analysis								
H-V	76	1		0	40	.144		.30
D-H	32.5	.738		.10	42	.145		.30
D-V	56	.847		.04	73.5	.903		.02

4.3 Perceived Satisfaction

Table 3 lists the descriptive statistics of perceived satisfaction under different layouts as well as the results of the Friedman test and those of the pairwise comparison. A higher value indicates higher satisfaction; therefore, a higher value is preferred instead of a lower one. No statistically significant differences were found in satisfaction of different layouts in both LSF and HSF tasks. However, in the HSF task, participants were more satisfied with the horizontal and vertical layouts than they were with the diagonal layout, both $ps < .077$ and $rs > .36$. The differences were marginally significant and the effect sizes were large.

Table 3. The main effect of layout on user satisfaction

Layout	LSF task: reading comprehension				HSF task: classification			
	Mean	SD	χ_2^2	p-value	Mean	SD	χ_2^2	p-value
Horizontal	3.13	0.95	0.70	.703	3.25	1.22	3.09	.213
Vertical	3.29	1.04			3.25	1.11		
Diagonal	3.42	1.02			2.63	0.97		
Post-hoc analysis								
	V	p-value		r	V	p-value		r
H-V	62	.489		.14	123	.803		.05
D-H	87	.324		.20	72	.071		.37
D-V	87.5	.609		.10	58.5	.077		.36

5 Discussion

The experimental results showed that the layout of multiple windows has a significant effect on the user performance and the subjective evaluation in the AR environment. According to the short post-experiment interviews with participants, two major factors were identified as the ones that influenced user performance and evaluations toward different layouts: the switching distance and the switching path. The two factors can explain the experimental results at a certain extent.

The most important factor is the switching distance, namely, the distance that the heads of the participants moved when participants switched from one window to another. The diagonal layout presented the longest switching distance, followed by the horizontal layout, and then the vertical layout. This can explain why participants were significantly less satisfied with the diagonal layout in the HSF task but not in the LSF task. In the HSF task, users had to frequently switch between windows, thus the influence of the switching distance was more evident. In the LSF task, however, users did not need to frequently switch; therefore, the complaints of the users about the long switching distance was not particularly evident. This could also explain why users performed best in the vertical layout in the HSF task. The classification task was focused on the completion time of the users. The shortest switching distance was observed in the vertical layout, namely, the shortest switching time, where the shortest completion time was observed as well.

The second factor was the switching path, namely, the direction toward people had to turn their heads during switching. In the horizontal layout, users turned their heads left and right; in the vertical layout, users turned their heads up and down; in the diagonal layout, users turned their heads in two sets of directions, namely left–right and up–down. The left–right movement was the most natural for human users, followed by the vertical layout, which was followed by the diagonal layout. This can also explain why participants were significantly less satisfied with the diagonal layout in the HSF task but not in the LSF task. The influence of the head-moving direction was more evident when users had to frequently turn their heads.

6 Conclusion

In this study, the effect of the layout on the user performance and the subjective evaluation in the AR environment was examined. In the experiment, participants had to work on three windows simultaneously. Two experimental tasks were required to be completed; one was a reading comprehension task, which required a low switching frequency, and the other was a classification task, which required a high switching frequency. According to the experimental results, the average number of switching times in the LSF tasks was approximately 4 per minute, whereas the average number in the HSF tasks was approximately 16 per minute. In the LSF tasks, participants performed better in the diagonal layout and the horizontal layout than in the vertical layout. In addition, participants switched less frequently in the diagonal layout than in the horizontal layout, and they switched most frequently in the vertical layout. In the HSF tasks, participants performed significantly better in the vertical layout than in the horizontal layout. Moreover, participants performed worst in the diagonal layout. Additionally, participants were less satisfied with the diagonal layout than with the horizontal and vertical layouts. Two important factors that influenced user performance and evaluations toward different layouts were the switching distance and the switching path.

In conclusion, certain AR-based layout design suggestions should be proposed. First, the switching distance and the switching path should be strongly considered in AR-based multi-screen layout designs. Short switching distances and natural switching paths were preferred. Second, the horizontal layout would be recommended first. Its switching distance was moderate, and the switching path was left and right, which is natural and in line with the daily habits of people. User performance and perceived satisfaction were both acceptable for the horizontal layout. Third, the vertical layout is recommended for tasks requiring frequent switching and emphasizing efficiency. The switching distance of this layout is short; however, its switching path is up and down, which is not as comfortable as the horizontal layout. Finally, the designers should avoid locating a window that would require user operation in the left region.

References

1. Zhang, Y., Mao, M., Rau, P.-L.P., Choe, P., Bela, L., Wang, F.: Exploring factors influencing multitasking interaction with multiple smart devices. Comput. Hum. Behav. **29**, 2579–2588 (2013)
2. Brinck, T., Gergle, D., Wood, S.D.: Usability for the Web: Designing Web Sites that Work. Elsevier, Amsterdam (2001)
3. Deaton, M.: The Elements of User Experience: User-Centered Design for the Web. Interactions **10**, 49–51 (2003)
4. Krug, S.: Don't Make Me Think! A Common Sense Approach to Web Usability. Pearson Education India (2000)
5. Parush, A., Shwarts, Y., Shtub, A., Chandra, M.J.: The impact of visual layout factors on performance in Web pages: a cross-language study. Hum. Factors **47**, 141–157 (2005)
6. Roth, S.P., Tuch, A.N., Mekler, E.D., Bargas-Avila, J.A., Opwis, K.: Location matters, especially for non-salient features–an eye-tracking study on the effects of web object placement on different types of websites. Int. J. Hum.-Comput. Stud. **71**, 228–235 (2013)
7. Pohl, M., Schmitt, M., Diehl, S.: Comparing the readability of graph layouts using eyetracking and task-oriented analysis. In: Computational Aesthetics, pp. 49–56 (2009)
8. Huang, W.: Using eye tracking to investigate graph layout effects. In: 2007 6th International Asia-Pacific Symposium on Visualization, APVIS 2007, pp. 97–100. IEEE (2007)
9. Lohmann, S., Ziegler, J., Tetzlaff, L.: Comparison of tag cloud layouts: task-related performance and visual exploration. In: Gross, T., Gulliksen, J., Kotzé, P., Oestreicher, L., Palanque, P., Prates, R.O., Winckler, M. (eds.) INTERACT 2009. LNCS, vol. 5726, pp. 392–404. Springer, Heidelberg (2009). https://doi.org/10.1007/978-3-642-03655-2_43
10. Pearson, R., van Schaik, P.: The effect of spatial layout of and link colour in web pages on performance in a visual search task and an interactive search task. Int. J. Hum.-Comput. Stud. **59**, 327–353 (2003)
11. Ahuja, J.S., Webster, J.: Perceived disorientation: an examination of a new measure to assess web design effectiveness. Interact. Comput. **14**, 15–29 (2001)
12. Head, M., Archer, N., Yuan, Y.: World wide web navigation aid. Int. J. Hum.-Comput. Stud. **53**, 301–330 (2000)
13. McDonald, S., Stevenson, R.J.: Effects of text structure and prior knowledge of the learner on navigation in hypertext. Hum. Factors **40**, 18–27 (1998)
14. Webster, J., Ahuja, J.S.: Enhancing the design of web navigation systems: the influence of user disorientation on engagement and performance. MIS Q. **30**, 661–678 (2006)

15. Santa-Maria, L., Dyson, M.C.: The effect of violating visual conventions of a website on user performance and disorientation: how bad can it be? In: Proceedings of the 26th Annual ACM International Conference on Design of Communication, pp. 47–54. ACM (2008)
16. Stenstrom, E., Stenstrom, P., Saad, G., Cheikhrouhou, S.: Online hunting and gathering: an evolutionary perspective on sex differences in website preferences and navigation. IEEE Trans. Prof. Commun. **51**, 155–168 (2008)
17. Muylle, S., Moenaert, R., Despontin, M.: The conceptualization and empirical validation of web site user satisfaction. Inf. Manag. **41**, 543–560 (2004)
18. Grigoroudis, E., Litos, C., Moustakis, V.A., Politis, Y., Tsironis, L.: The assessment of user-perceived web quality: application of a satisfaction benchmarking approach. Eur. J. Oper. Res. **187**, 1346–1357 (2008)
19. Cyr, D.: Modeling web site design across cultures: relationships to trust, satisfaction, and e-loyalty. J. Manag. Inf. Syst. **24**, 47–72 (2008)
20. Eighmey, J.: Profiling user responses to commercial web sites. J. Advertising Res. **37**, 59–67 (1997)
21. Eighmey, J., McCord, L.: Adding value in the information age: uses and gratifications of sites on the World Wide Web. J. Bus. Res. **41**, 187–194 (1998)
22. Salvucci, D.D., Taatgen, N.A., Borst, J.P.: Toward a unified theory of the multitasking continuum: from concurrent performance to task switching, interruption, and resumption. In: Proceedings of the SIGCHI Conference on Human Factors in Computing Systems, pp. 1819–1828. ACM (2009)

User Requirements Gathering in mHealth: Perspective from Ghanaian End Users

Eric Owusu[(⊠)] and Joyram Chakraborty[(⊠)]

Department of Computer and Information Sciences, Towson University,
7800 York Road, Towson, MD 21252, USA
{eowusu, jchakraborty}@towson.edu

Abstract. Understanding user requirements is a fundamental part of information systems design and is key to the success of interactive systems. Factors such as ease of use, cross-cultural interface design are crucial to building usable products that will gain high acceptance among users. Developing a utilizable mobile health application involves applying human-centered design methodologies. However, mHealth applications face usability challenges in terms of their usefulness due to lack of end user inclusion during the design process. In order to investigate usability impact on the end user, this paper examines the challenges and findings from Ghanaian migrant communities in the United States. This paper seeks to contribute to the requirement gathering process by highlighting the needs and noting the challenges in the collection of user requirement data needed to design and develop a targeted mHealth application. The results of gathered user requirements will contribute to informing the design of mobile health interventions tailored for Ghanaian migrants.

Keywords: Cross-cultural design · Usability · User requirements

1 Introduction

Developing a utilizable mobile health application involves human-centered design. ISO 9241-210:2010 defines Human-centered design as an approach to interactive systems developments that aims to make systems usable and useful [1]. This is achievable by focusing on the users, their needs and requirements, and by applying human factors, and usability knowledge and techniques. This paper examines the findings and challenges from a user requirement gathering among Ghanaian migrant communities in the United States.

Health Information Technology (HIT) is increasingly being used by healthcare providers to improve patient care and can possibly transform all facets of the healthcare industry by addressing existing challenges [2]. Health disparities have long been established within the United States, and Ghanaian migrants fall within the category of people described as underserved by the healthcare industry [2]. With the advance in technology, and increase in usage of smartphones and mobile devices, mobile health applications offer great potential in bridging the healthcare disparity gap. For mobile mHealth applications to become an instrumental social innovation of benefit to people from all walks of life, it is expedient to study the sociocultural heterogeneity of the user

© Springer Nature Switzerland AG 2019
P.-L. P. Rau (Ed.): HCII 2019, LNCS 11576, pp. 386–396, 2019.
https://doi.org/10.1007/978-3-030-22577-3_28

base, and integrate this in mHealth services delivery, taking cognizance of user behavior and cultural preferences. To increase satisfaction and generate positive user experience, it is important to involve the end user in the initial stages of the development process. Barriers between product developers with technical backgrounds and end users need to be overcome. This is possible by gathering information on user contexts and user needs and translating them into user requirements for product development. The user requirements gathering process goes beyond user interfaces by focusing on end users and eliciting useful information on user needs necessary to inform product design. Information from user requirements gathering directly affects the process of developing usable systems.

Specifically, the aim of this paper is to gain insight from Ghanaian users on their perception of mHealth applications, understand their needs, know their objectives and motivations and also find out how Ghanaian users interact with mHealth technology.

2 Background of the Study

Overall, the literature review establishes that there are opportunities for mobile applications to address healthcare needs relative to prevention and living a healthy life style among migrants in developed countries. mHealth technology provides the platform for Ghanaian migrants to be empowered to manage their health and adopt healthy lifestyle behaviors [3, 4]. Although there are few examples of mHealth tools that are quite popular in the United States, the use of mHealth tools is variant from community to community and are usually dependent on simplicity of use [2].

To develop useful and usable applications it is necessary to comprehend user needs and contexts, and subsequently translate these into user requirements with a focus on users throughout the development process [5]. Analysis of user requirements have not typically been performed prior to the design of such mobile applications [6]. To acknowledge the potential of mHealth applications, there is a need to investigate how these applications are perceived by end users in the aspect of its perceived usefulness, preferences and as a cross-cultural interface design impact. The objective is to gather useful information and enhance the design of mobile health tools tailored for Ghanaian migrants through user requirement gathering conducted within the targeted end users [5, 6].

Empirical research studies have confirmed that there is potential to improve health services delivery among communities with disparities by use of mHealth technology applications [2]. As such, understanding what motivates users from different cultures is important for positioning brands in different markets [7]. Such implicit cultural values need to be considered when designing mobile applications intended to reach end users from all cultural backgrounds [8]. This paper focuses on the challenges of user requirement gathering from Ghanaian migrants as end users. Investigating the usability of mobile health technology among migrant communities will highlight behavioural patterns and provide useful data to improve the design and utilization of mobile health interventions.

2.1   User Requirements

A requirement is a statement that defines what a system should do. According to Withall, the requirements specify the flaws of a system and outlines the steps needed to solve the problem [9]. Withall further explains that a requirement is a single measurable objective that must be satisfied by a system. In other words, they must be precise and unambiguous. A challenge in the past has been how to present requirements in a way that is understandable to both technical system designers or developers and formal and informal users. User needs and contexts need to be translated into user requirements in a structured way for product designers but must be understandable by users as they must verify them [10].

Rombach divides the more formal description of requirements into two, technical requirements and user requirements [11]. Technical requirements outline how a product will be implemented to meet user requirements. User requirements on the other hand are from the user perspective and describe the functions, constraints and other features that must be provided to satisfy user needs [11, 12]. Gathering user needs is a necessary step to develop a usable product. There is a need for real data on users and their needs. Use cases can still be used on a regular basis to determine users' way of task execution. However, these implicit assumptions risk the mutual understanding between users and designers [5].

The requirements gathering process is encumbered with several challenges including users and designers thinking along the same lines and reflecting current system and processes, rather than being innovative, and users being unsure or not knowing what they want from a future system [1].

Measuring user requirement will position Ghanaian users to drive the design of systems that are tailored for them. To that effect, incorporating behavioral and cultural preferences with emphasis on user satisfaction, ease of use, and accessibility, will advance the use of mHealth applications within the Ghanaian migrant communities. User interface designers will also benefit as they design for the global market with cognition of the specific requirements of ethnic minorities.

2.2   User Centered Design

In our homes, offices and on our phones, we find ourselves inundated with systems and applications that are redundant because we find them difficult to understand, navigate or operate. These can range from the high-tech photocopier in the office to the newest healthcare application on your phone. Computer-based systems need to be designed with an understanding of the users they are intended for. User centered design (UCD) is a design approach that is aimed at increasing the usability of systems by active involvement of users at all phases of the design process. According to Johnson et al., the use of fundamental principles of good design at the start and throughout the design life cycle results in systems that are easy to learn, increase user productivity and satisfaction, increase user acceptance, decrease user errors, and decrease user training time [13]. User-centered design has become an important concept in the design of interactive systems that is primarily concerned with the design of sociotechnical systems that focus on users, and the use of technologies by users in their daily routines [14].

Research has indicated that human resources and economic resources are wasted by numerous health care systems that are designed without consideration of user centered guidelines, resulting in dissatisfied users and abandoned systems [13]. Johnson et al., emphasizes that a major goal in the design of usable health care software should be to design systems that takes the characteristics of users and their environments into account and matches user capabilities.

Health information technology is a very promising area that is facing expectation challenges due to design flaws that are unable to meet user requirements [15]. Despite the continued proliferation and popularity of mHealth applications, evidence shows that more than 95% have not been tested [16]. There is limited research on the effectiveness and little support for understanding how best to design mHealth applications [17]. mHealth applications also fail to live up to their expectations due to lack of end-user feedback in the design process [18]. Growing research highlights the above shortfalls and emphasizes the need for further research to ensure that mHealth technologies are appropriately designed based on a user-centered approach [17, 19–21].

2.3 User Interface (UI)

An interface is the part of a system through which a user interacts with a system. Head describe an interface as the visible piece of a system that a user sees, hears or touches [22]. Whether you get in your car and drive from one point to another, switch on the vacuum cleaner, operate a treadmill, browse on your computer or use an application on your phone, you get the task done by interacting with the systems interface. A good interface effectively communicates with users on how to get tasks done. Inadequately designed interfaces on the other hand, are difficult to navigate and often leave users frustrated. Irrespective of how trivial, incidental or artful the design might be, good design interfaces are reliable and effective intermediaries that are based on solid design principles that enhance use [22].

A usable interface is a vital element in the software development process. Users are diverse and as such interact with systems in different ways. Understanding users and their behavior is key to the development of usable interfaces [23]. System designers who understand users and think from the perspective of users, are able to translate their knowledge about users into developing systems with good interface design that support user interaction without difficulties [22]. Galtiz indicated that most applications in the market today appear to be generalized and unusable, but proper interface design incorporates a fusion of well-designed input and output mechanism that satisfy a user's needs, capabilities, and limitations in the most effective way [24].

2.4 Cultural Components in UI Development

Culture is an element that cannot be overlooked in the interface design process. Within one locality you may find users from different cultures. As user interface designers strive to develop more usable systems, there is a need to be cognizant of their own cultures and the culture of the intended users. Attention to their own cultural orientation and knowledge of the preferred structures and processes of other cultures, positions interface designers to achieve more desirable localized and customized designs [25]. Only a limited number of published classical theories on culture are known in the interface design community. Hofstede explains culture to be essential patterns of thinking, feeling, and acting that are well established in individuals at childhood, and are evident in a person's choices of symbols, heroes/heroines, rituals and values [26]. Hofstede's work establishes 5 dimensions of culture that affect user interface design, namely: Power distance, Collectivism vs individualism, Femininity vs masculinity, Uncertainty avoidance, and Long vs short term orientation. Based on a user's culture they may exhibit several characteristic including being active or passive, expressive or less expressive, easy going and relaxed, or aggressive with strong emotions [26]. All these subtle or distinct cultural nuances largely influence a user's choice and affect what they expect or require from an interface. In order not to be culturally biased, it is expected that designers be cognizant of all these factors when designing user interfaces. According to Marcus, several questions remain unanswered about the consideration of cultural dimensions in user interface design [25]. Examples include: What cost effective tools are needed to support multicultural UI design? How can the success of multi-cultural UIs be measured so that templates can be developed for appropriate content delivery?

3 Methodology

A preliminary study was conducted to gather user requirements from Ghanaian end users. The study was developed using qualitative data collection techniques. The goal of this approach was to gather and better understand Ghanaian end user requirements. To this end a qualitative questionnaire was developed with open-ended questions, closed questions and Likert scales. The study was carried out over a 5-month period. A stratified random sampling approach was used in selecting participants comprising of migrants in one specific geographical location in Frederick, Maryland, U.S.A. Partic-ipants were chosen by recommendations and word of mouth. All participants agreed to be interviewed on a one-on-one basis at a convenient location of their choice. The purpose of the study was explained including the participants rights, and the right to terminate the participation at any time.

The facilities used for the interviews were Frederick community center and a local shopping mall. Each interview lasted 10–15 min. Data was collected from 30 Ghanaians comprising of 12 males and 18 females. All participants were interviewed face-to-face. The selected age groups that participated were within the ranges of age 30 to 55 and above. During each interview, the interviewer explained the purpose of the study to the participants and assured them of confidentiality. A questionnaire was given to the participants to follow after the interviewer's questions, which allowed for con-sistency of responses relevant for the study. Data was captured directly by marking or writing responses on the questionnaire for the different question types. The data obtained from the interview was cleaned, analyzed and relevant patterns recorded and then analyzed.

3.1 Data Collection Instrument

User requirements Gathering Questionnaire
   Circle Value:

1. Identify your age from the ranges listed below.

   18–29 30–35 36–40 41–45 46–50 51–55

2. Gender

   Male Female

3. What mobile device do you currently use?

a. iPhone
b. Android
c. Windows

4. How long have you owned/been using this mobile device?

a. 0–6 months
b. 6 months – 1 year
c. 1–3 years
d. Over 3 years

5. How would rate yourself about mobile technology usage?

a. Novice
b. Moderate
c. Advanced

6. How often do you use mobile applications?

a. 0–30 min per day
b. 1 h per day
c. More than 2 h per day
d. Other, ...

7. What mobile application(s) do you currently use regarding health?

   ....

8. What specifically do you like most about the application that you use, in terms of functionality and features?

   Why? ....

9. What specifically do you not like about the application that you use?

   Why? ....

10. Does the application help you to fulfil the health reason for which the application is intended?

    If yes, how...
    If no, why? ....

11. As a Ghanaian, would you use an application that is specifically designed to address health issues for Ghanaians currently living in the USA?

If yes, why? ....

If no, why? ....

12. What specific features and functionalities would you expect the application to have to help you achieve your health goals?

....

4 Results

Detailed analysis of the questionnaire revealed the following findings:

All participants had smartphones with 56.7% (17) having iPhones and the remaining 43.3% (13) having android phones. 56% of participants rated themselves as advanced mobile technology users, whiles 43.3 rated themselves as moderate mobile technology users. 80% (24) of participants already had mobile applications on their phones that they used to manage their health. Main features participants did not like about the applications they were currently using included its complexity (36.7%), lack of accuracy (13.3%), limited options (10%) and security concerns (10%). 66% of participants indicated that they would be interested in a mHealth application specifically designed for Ghanaians. 27% declined to answer. 7% said no, with the reason being security/trust issues. With regards to the question on what specific features and functionalities participants would need in an application designed to help them achieve their health goals, answers obtained have been grouped into functional and nonfunctional requirements and represented in the chart (Table 1) below.

Table 1. User needs categorized into functional and nonfunctional requirements.

Functional requirements	Percent (%)	CI* (95%)	Different from zero
Diet management /Ghanaian foods	20.5	6.05% to 34.95%	Yes
Fitness management	6.8	−2.21% to 15.81%	No
Health management	22.7	7.71% to 37.69%	Yes
General wellness information	27.3	7.71% to 37.69%	Yes
Voice command function	2.3	−3.06% to 7.66%	No
Nonfunctional requirements			
Privacy	2.3	−3.06% to 7.66%	No
Availability	4.5	−2.92% to 11.92%	No
Ease of Use	11.4	0.03% to 22.77%	Yes
Performance	2.3	−3.06% to 7.66%	No
Total	100		

*CI: Confidence interval

5 Discussion

The results obtained indicated that 100% of participants used smart phones. This is promising in light of the potential benefits of smartphones. Smartphones are comparable to computers and they stand to potentially transform the face of the healthcare industry as they have the capacity to support eHealth applications and also afford all the benefits and uses of traditional computers with the added benefit of affordability and mobility. The impact of smartphones on medicine has been noted to be very significant [27]. Other factors that make smartphones an easy source for access to health information and communication is their widespread distribution, the relative cheapness, small size and homogeneity of products [28].

80% of participants had mHealth application on their phones, with the most popular apps being Apple health and Samsung health. With the advent of smartphones there has been an increase in the mobile phone applications. In 2010 there were more than 7000 smartphone applications dedicated to health, with estimates indicating 300 million applications downloaded in 2009, and 5 million downloaded in 2010 [28]. This high usage of applications among participants is very encouraging due to the fact that applications play an essential role in patient education, disease self-management, remote monitoring of patients, and collection of dietary data [29]. However, despite the large numbers of mobile phone ownership, the surge in electronic health advances, the high usage of health applications, and the promising prospects of mobile health technology within the healthcare industry, the lack of evidence of clinical effectiveness and lack of formal evaluation and review are key limitations that need to be addressed [29].

Participants were very elaborate on what they needed in an application tailored for Ghanaian migrants. The list of functionalities needed include Diet management, health management, ease of use, fitness management, General wellness information, privacy, good performance and availability. The most significant of the needed functionalities, with high confidence intervals (Table 1), were general wellness information, health management, diet management, and ease of use. A noteworthy point is that when indicating their needs all participants specified the need for the functionalities to be delivered in the Ghanaian context where possible. For example, a diet management application in this context, should include the Ghanaian cuisine repertoire with its emphasis on starchy vegetables and legumes, and should also provide users with dietary information such as caloric contents for Ghanaian specific foods. Although general messages have been shown to have an impact on behavior change, evidence indicates that tailored messages stimulate greater cognitive ability in its audience [30]. In this respect making health, wellness, fitness and diet information relevant in context to the Ghanaian audience will be key in increasing uptake, acceptability and adoption within this group.

These findings are key foundational points that should inform the design when tailoring an application for Ghanaian migrants, however subsequent studies with larger data sets might be needed to substantiate the findings.

There were several challenges with this study. Identifying the features users would like in a tailored application was difficult as users had limited knowledge of specific functionalities that can be tailored in an application. Other problems included, insufficient information, unclear statements, and contradicting requirements. As such, data collection incorporating a larger sample size might be needed to clarify or substantiate findings in this study. Gathering requirements from the older participants (51–55 years) was a challenge. The older participants did not use their smart phones to their full capacity. They indicated that they mainly used their phones for making calls and texting. However, they rated themselves as moderate and advanced users of mobile technology. Surprisingly, although these participants used smartphones and had a health application installed on their mobile phones, they were less likely to use an application for healthcare monitoring and relied on their healthcare practitioner for tracking their healthcare needs. One participant stated that "My health is a priority to me, however, I don't trust a machine to tell me what to do when it comes to improving my healthcare or giving me advice on steps to take, but if a trusted friend or colleague recommends it, I will be willing to give it a try." The willingness to accept a mobile health application if it is recommended by friends brings up the issue of trust. In other words, if an application has been tried and tested by someone a user can associate with, they are more likely to accept it. The challenge is how to interpret this perception into a workable solution for such users.

Inconsistencies in answers was another challenge. Some participants indicated they already had a mobile application but were interested in a mobile health application that was tailored to meet their needs. However, they refused to answer follow up questions on what they liked about the applications they currently had on their phones and what specific features and functionalities they needed in a mobile health application.

Some participants had limited knowledge about the features and functionalities of mobile health applications, or they were just unable to articulate the actual needs they wanted to address. They were interested in an application tailored to meet their needs and liked the fact that it would provide them the avenue to access information from a wearable gadget, or something that was already compatible with their phones. However, they were unable to clearly express their needs, and this resulted in unclear statements that presented a challenge for the researcher to code when analyzing the data.

Contradicting or conflicting requirements was another issue that was noticed. Participants wanted an easy to use, uncomplicated health application. However, they wanted the applications to have several functionalities and features, such as diet management fitness management and health and general wellbeing management all in one.

Another challenge was participants who were unwilling to accept new technology. These participants indicated that in their opinion physical doctors and hospitals were the right way to access healthcare information and did not think having a shortcut to monitor their health via smart phones would work for them. They were not interested in a healthcare application and answered NA (no answer) for most questions.

It is anticipated that embracing and engaging participants with all their varied perceptions in the requirement gathering process and making provision for feedback during the iterative design process of a system will build confidence and acceptability and promote a sense of ownership in users.

6 Conclusion

User requirement gathering is an important step needed to provide information for developing guidelines for iterative prototype design, necessary for developing acceptable applications for specific audiences. This paper makes a contribution to the field of cross-cultural usability studies by providing a preliminary understanding from a user perspective, the needs of Ghanaians in terms of content and features, of a tailored mHealth application. Measuring usability requirement augments the Ghanaian user to drive the design. To that effect, incorporating user requirements with emphasis on tailored information on general wellness, health management, and diet management, will go a long way to advance the use of mHealth applications within Ghanaian migrant communities. User interface designers will also benefit as they design for the global market with cognition of ethnic minorities. There is a need for further exploratory studies in migrant groups in mHealth technology and the potential to engage and empower all users to be in control of, and to manage their health.

References

1. Maguire, M., Bevan, N.: User requirements analysis. In: Hammond, J., Gross, T., Wesson, J. (eds.) Usability. ITIFIP, vol. 99, pp. 133–148. Springer, Boston, MA (2002). https://doi.org/10.1007/978-0-387-35610-5_9
2. Owusu, E., Chakraborty, J.: Usability impact of user perceptions in mHealth—the case of ghanaian migrants. In: Karwowski, W., Ahram, T. (eds.) IHSI 2019. AISC, vol. 903, pp. 557–562. Springer, Cham (2019). https://doi.org/10.1007/978-3-030-11051-2_84
3. Latif, S., Rana, R., Qadir, J., Imran, M., Younis, S.: Mobile health in the developing world: review of literature and lessons from a case study. IEEE Access 5, 11540–11556 (2017)
4. Luxton, D.D., McCann, R.A., Bush, N.E., Mishkind, M.C., Reger, G.M.: mHealth for mental health: integrating smartphone technology in behavioral healthcare. Prof. Psychol.: Res. Pract. 42, 505 (2011)
5. Kujala, S., Kauppinen, M., Rekola, S.: Bridging the gap between user needs and user requirements. In: Advances in Human-Computer Interaction I (Proceedings of the Panhellenic Conference with International Participation in Human-Computer Interaction PC-HCI 2001), pp. 45–50. Typorama Publications (2001)
6. Zhang, H., Zhang, H., Wang, X., Yang, Z., Zhao, Y.: Analysis of requirements for developing an mHealth-based health management platform. JMIR mHealth and uHealth 5, e117 (2017)
7. De Mooij, M., Hofstede, G.: Cross-cultural consumer behavior: a review of research findings. J. Int. Consum. Mark. 23, 181–192 (2011)
8. Leidner, D.E., Kayworth, T.: A review of culture in information systems research: toward a theory of information technology culture conflict. MIS Q. 30, 357–399 (2006)
9. Withall, S.: Software Requirement Patterns. Pearson Education, London (2007)
10. Rumbaugh, J.: Getting started. J. Object-Oriented Program. 7 (1994)
11. Rombach, H.D.: Software specifications: a framework. SEI curriculum module. Technical report SEI-CM-11-2.1, Software Engineering Institute, Carnegie (1990)
12. Abbott, R.J.: An Integrated Approach to Software Development. Wiley, New York (1986)
13. Johnson, C.M., Johnson, T.R., Zhang, J.: A user-centered framework for redesigning health care interfaces. J. Biomed. Inf. 38, 75–87 (2005)

14. Issa, T., Isaias, P.: Sustainable Design. Springer, Heidelberg (2015)
15. Kellermann, A.L., Jones, S.S.: What it will take to achieve the as-yet-unfulfilled promises of health information technology. Health Aff. **32**, 63–68 (2013)
16. Furlow, B.: mHealth apps may make chronic disease management easier (2012). Accessed 10 Jan 2013
17. Kumar, S., et al.: Mobile health technology evaluation: the mHealth evidence workshop. Am. J. Prev. Med. **45**, 228–236 (2013)
18. Schnall, R., et al.: A user-centered model for designing consumer mobile health (mHealth) applications (apps). J. Biomed. Inf. **60**, 243–251 (2016)
19. Wolf, J.A., et al.: Diagnostic inaccuracy of smartphone applications for melanoma detection. JAMA Dermatol. **149**, 422–426 (2013)
20. Brown III, W., Yen, P.-Y., Rojas, M., Schnall, R.: Assessment of the health IT usability evaluation model (Health-ITUEM) for evaluating mobile health (mHealth) technology. J. Biomed. Inf. **46**, 1080–1087 (2013)
21. Norman, D.A.: Design principles for cognitive artifacts. Res. Eng. Des. **4**, 43–50 (1992)
22. Head, A.J.: Design wise. Thomas H Hogan Sr, Medford Google Scholar (1999)
23. Stone, D., Jarrett, C., Woodroffe, M., Minocha, S.: User interface design and evaluation. Inf. Vis. **5**, 77–78 (2006)
24. Galitzum, W.O.: The Essential Guide to User Interface Design: An Introduction to GUI Design Principles and Techniques. Wiley, Hoboken (2007)
25. Marcus, A.: Global/Intercultural User Interface Design. Lawrence Erlbaum Associates (2003)
26. Hofstede, G., Bond, M.H.: Hofstede's culture dimensions: An independent validation using Rokeach's value survey. J. Cross-Cult. Psychol. **15**, 417–433 (1984)
27. Ozdalga, E., Ozdalga, A., Ahuja, N.: The smartphone in medicine: a review of current and potential use among physicians and students. J. Med. Internet Res. **14**, e128 (2012)
28. Bert, F., Giacometti, M., Gualano, M.R., Siliquini, R.: Smartphones and health promotion: a review of the evidence. J. Med. Syst. **38**, 9995 (2014)
29. Carroll, J.K., Moorhead, A., Bond, R., LeBlanc, W.G., Petrella, R.J., Fiscella, K.: Who uses mobile phone health apps and does use matter? A secondary data analytics approach. J. Med. Internet Res. **19**, e125 (2017)
30. Kreuter, M.W., Wray, R.J.: Tailored and targeted health communication: strategies for enhancing information relevance. Am. J. Health Behav. **27**, S227–S232 (2003)

User Experience of Tactile Feedback on a Smartphone: Effects of Vibration Intensity, Times and Interval

Jun Tan[1,2], Yan Ge[1,2(✉)], Xianghong Sun[1,2], Yubo Zhang[3], and Yanfang Liu[3]

[1] CAS Key Laboratory of Behavioral Science,
Institute of Psychology, Beijing, China
gey@psych.ac.cn
[2] Department of Psychology,
University of Chinese Academy of Sciences, Beijing, China
[3] Huawei Technologies Co., Ltd., Beijing, China
liuyanfang2@huawei.com

Abstract. Tactile feedback has been widely used in smartphones in recent years. To explore the factors impacting the user experience of smartphone tactile feedback, the current study tested three aspects of these factors: the intensity of vibration (weak, moderate and strong), feedback times (once or twice) and the interval between two vibrations (100 ms, 230 ms, 370 ms and 500 ms). Twenty-six participants evaluated their tactile experience after finishing each touch task under different conditions on a model phone with three gestures. The results showed that satisfaction with tactile feedback increased along with the increasing intensity of vibration. However, such tactile satisfaction decreased as the interval between two vibrations increased. There was a significant interaction between the intensity and interval of vibrations. The results of the current study can provide guidance for product design in the related field of touchscreen products.

Keywords: Vibration intensity · Vibration interval · Tactile feedback · User experience

1 Introduction

Tactile feedback of a touchscreen is an important aspect of smartphone design. As touchscreens became the main operation interface of smartphones, researchers had to pay much more attention to this issue during the preceding decade [1–4]. Researchers confirmed that tactile feedback could improve the effectiveness of interaction. For example, Fukumoto and Sugimura found that tactile feedback can reduce the operation time by approximately 5% to 15% in different situations [1]. Hoggan *et al.* [5] conducted two experiments to investigate the effects of vibration feedback on a physical keyboard, a touchscreen without feedback, and a touchscreen with tactile feedback in both lab settings and mobile environments; they observed that touchscreens with tactile feedback produce greater speeds and fewer text entry errors than those of standard touchscreen keyboards without tactile feedback in two experimental conditions.

© Springer Nature Switzerland AG 2019
P.-L. P. Rau (Ed.): HCII 2019, LNCS 11576, pp. 397–406, 2019.
https://doi.org/10.1007/978-3-030-22577-3_29

Altinsoy and Merchel investigated the differences in several aspects, including execution time, error rate, and subjective satisfaction with tactile and auditory feedback on a touchscreen. The results showed that a touchscreen with tactile feedback had a more positive effect than a touchscreen without feedback on the quality, error rate, and satisfaction [6]. Tactile feedback could not only provide simple information but also could present sophisticated information, such as spatial and temporal information [7, 8], to interface users.

Tactile feedback was useful for providing support to special (e.g., blind or elderly) users of mobile phones [9, 10]. With advancing age, cognitive ability, comprehension ability, learning ability and memory will decline, especially in the elderly. For example, Hertzum *et al.* [11] recruited three groups of subjects, consisting of young (12–14 years old), adult (25–33 years old), and elderly (61–69 years old) individuals, to investigate their performance of operating a touchpad. The results showed that young participants made fewer errors and completed tasks more quickly than did elderly participants. The elderly participants cannot adapt to new technologies such as smartphones and touchscreens. Vibration feedback can, to a certain extent, compensate for the deficiencies of the elderly users when using smartphones.

There are many factors that could influence the user experience of tactile feedback. Previous studies have explored some basic issues during the interaction, including operation mode, activation mechanism, button size, etc.[2]. Additionally, the gesture was another factor that could influence the efficiency of tactile feedback [12, 13]. To understand the relationship between usability and user experience, researchers also explored several parameters of vibration, such as the latency of tactile feedback after the user pressed on the touchscreen. Kaaresoja *et al.* [3] performed three experiments to investigate how tactile feedback latencies impacted the user performance and satisfaction. The researchers manipulated the time between the button press and tactile feedback from 18 ms to 118 ms in their experiment. The results showed that there were no significant differences in performance between these conditions. However, compared to other conditions, the shortest feedback latency was evaluated as being more pleasant to use. Hwang et al. proved that the perceived intensity of vibrotactile feedback for mobile devices was influenced by the direction, amplitude and frequency of motor vibration [14]. Hoggan and Brewster found that the waveform of vibration had a higher recognition rate than those of amplitude modulation and frequency for creating a texture [15]. Based on these studies, the physical parameter of vibration was the key factor of user experience of tactile feedback. To our knowledge, no research has explored the effect of vibration times and interval on user experience. Hence, we designed this study to investigate these new parameters of vibration design.

Evaluation of user experience of tactile feedback was also meaningful in optimizing interface design. Previous studies mainly focused on the usability of tactile feedback; however, few studies have focused specifically on evaluating the feeling of tactile feedback. Some studies involved this aspect but only considered the subjective satisfaction of vibration [3]. However, no research has explored the dimensions of users' vibrotactile experience. The general user experience questionnaire (UEQ) [16] could be used as a reference for the evaluation. The UEQ has been translated into many languages [17, 18] and used in different scenarios [19]. This scale was made up of 6 dimensions: Attractiveness, Perspicuity, Efficiency, Dependability, Simulation and Novelty. Another widely used experience scale, the Brand Experience Scale (BES) [20], was also considered for the vibrotactile experience questionnaire design. The BES included four dimensions: sensory, affective, intellectual, and behavioral. Compared to the UEQ, the BES considered more behavioral intentions. Both sets of dimensions are very important for a successful product. Hence, we developed a new questionnaire for evaluating user experience of tactile feedback based on these two scales.

In sum, the purpose of this study was to explore the effect of vibration intensity, vibration times and interval between two vibrations on users' experience of tactile feedback. We also developed a questionnaire to evaluate the user experience.

2 Methods

2.1 Participants

A total of twenty-six users (female: 10; male: 16) were recruited for participation in this experiment. Their ages ranged from 18 to 31 years old (Mean = 22.7, SD = 3.1). All of them had normal vision and were right-handed. All of them were users of smartphones with touchscreens.

2.2 Apparatus

The experiment was conducted on a prototype phone. The phone size was 145.3 mm × 69.3 mm × 6.98 mm; it had a 5.1-inch touchscreen. We designed 2 icons on the screen. One icon vibrated once when pressed, and the other vibrated twice when pressed. The interval between two vibrations could be manipulated. The intensity of vibration for both icons could also be adjusted.

2.3 Materials

The Vibrotactile Feedback Questionnaire was developed to measure the user experience of tactile feedback. The questionnaire included three dimensions: sensory, affective, and behavioral intention. The sensory experience focused on the sensory feeling of using tactile feedback, including the perceived intensity, location and timeliness of feedback. The affective experience referred to the emotional factors of using tactile feedback, such as immersion, preference and intimacy. The behavioral intention mainly concerns whether there is a willingness to buy the mobile phone it and whether one would recommend it to other users. There are 14 items in total in this scale. Each item described a kind of experience. The users needed to self-report if they agreed or disagreed with each description on a five-point Likert scale (1 = "strongly disagree", 5 = "strongly agree").

2.4   Experimental Design

A within-subjects design was used in this experiment, in which three within-subjects variables (the intensity of vibration, vibration times and vibration interval) were manipulated. The intensity of vibration had three levels (weak, moderate and strong). There were two choices of vibration times (once and twice). For the case of two vibrations, 4 intervals were established in the experiment (100 ms, 230 ms, 370 ms and 500 ms). These durations were determined by a pilot test. During the pilot test, five participants set the vibration interval first on the prototype phone and then clicked the icon to feel the vibration. Participants were asked to choose four level intervals that he/she liked best. Afterwards, we calculated the average of their choices.

2.5   Data Analysis

The General Linear Model with repeated measures was used to examine the main effects and interaction of each independent variable, using SPSS 24.0. As to post hoc analyses, the least significant difference (LSD) tests were performed on the significant main effects. In addition, the simple effect test was performed if a significant interaction existed.

3   Results

3.1   Effect of Vibration Intensity and Times

The descriptive results for the intensity of vibration and vibration times are displayed at Table 1.

Table 1. Descriptive statistics of TEQ for various vibration intensities and times (figures shown are mean values, with SD shown in parentheses)

Dimension	Times	Intensity		
		Weak	Moderate	Strong
Sensory	Once	3.15 (.85)	3.18 (.75)	3.78 (.86)
	Twice	3.28 (.69)	3.38 (.83)	3.51 (.72)
Affective	Once	3.13 (.71)	3.15 (.89)	3.45 (1.05)
	Twice	3.00 (.77)	3.08 (.84)	3.05 (.83)
Behavioral	Once	2.74 (.95)	2.88 (.98)	3.31 (1.13)
	Twice	2.84 (.89)	2.92 (.96)	2.93 (.91)

Sensory Experience. According to the results of the General Linear Model with repeated measures, the main effect of the intensity of vibration ($F_{(2, 50)} = 9.49$; $p < 0.001$) was significant. The LSD tests revealed that the sensory experience of strong vibration (M = 3.64) was better than that of moderate (M = 3.28) and weak (M = 3.21) conditions.

The interaction between the intensity of vibration and vibration times was significant ($F_{(2, 50)} = 4.53$; $p < 0.05$). The simple effect test revealed that when the vibration intensity was strong, the sensory experience of a single vibration was better than that of vibrating twice. However, when vibrations were weak or moderate, the sensory experience of a single vibration was worse than that of two vibrations (Fig. 1).

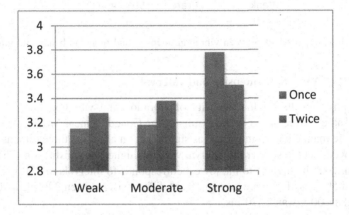

Fig. 1. Interaction effect between vibration intensity and times on sensory experience

Affective Experience. All the main effects of vibration intensity and times on affective experience are not significant, as are their interactions.

Behavioral Intention. According to the results of the General Linear Model with repeated measures, the main effect of the intensity of vibration ($F_{(2, 50)} = 3.35$; $p < 0.05$) on behavioral intention was significant. The LSD tests revealed that the willingness to use and recommend the strong vibration (M = 3.12) was higher than that in the weak (M = 2.79) condition.

The interaction between vibration intensity and vibration times ($F_{(2, 50)} = 3.68$; $p < 0.05$) was also significant. The simple effect test revealed that when the intensity of vibration was strong, the behavioral intention of a single vibration was higher than that of two vibrations. No significant simple effect was observed in weak and moderate conditions (Fig. 2).

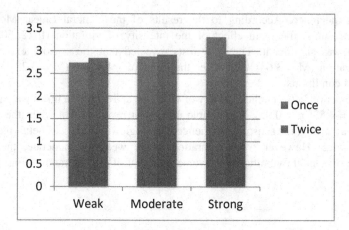

Fig. 2. Interaction effect between vibration intensity and times on behavioral intention

3.2 Effect of Vibration Intensity and Interval

The descriptive results for the intensity of vibration and vibration intervals are displayed in Table 2. According to the results of the General Linear Model with repeated measures, the main effect of interval was significant on all of the three dimensions. The results showed that the shorter the interval was, the higher the satisfaction. The trend of satisfaction from the highest to the lowest corresponds to intervals of 230 ms, 100 ms, 370 ms and 500 ms. There are no significant differences between 230 ms and 100 ms, also between 100 ms and 370 ms.

Sensory Experience. The main effect of interval (F (3, 75) = 17.71; p < 0.001) was significant. The LSD tests revealed that the sensory experience of the interval of 230 ms (M = 3.61) was significantly improved compared to that in 370 ms (M = 3.35) and 500 ms (M = 3.04) conditions. The satisfaction at the interval of 100 ms (M = 3.55) was significantly higher than that at the interval of 500 ms (M = 3.04). The satisfaction at the interval of 370 ms (M = 3.36) was significantly higher than that at the interval of 500 ms (M = 3.04). No interaction effect was observed.

Affective Experience. The main effect of interval (F (3, 75) = 17.18; p < 0.001) on the affective experience was significant at the level of 0.01. The LSD tests revealed that the affective experience of the interval of 100 ms (M = 3.24) was significantly higher than that of the intervals of 370 ms (M = 3.00) and the interval of 500 ms (M = 2.62). The affective experience of the interval of 370 ms (M = 3.00) was significantly improved compared to that of the interval of 500 ms (M = 2.62).

Table 2. Descriptive statistics of TEQ for various vibration intensities and intervals (figures shown are mean values, with SD shown in parentheses)

Interval	Sensory experience			Affective experience			Behavioral intention		
	Weak	Moderate	Strong	Weak	Moderate	Strong	Weak	Moderate	Strong
100 ms	3.39 (.70)	3.52 (.87)	3.73 (.91)	3.12 (.84)	3.27 (1.01)	3.32 (.97)	2.92 (.93)	3.17 (1.07)	3.14 (1.01)
230 ms	3.45 (.91)	3.56 (.75)	3.81 (.84)	3.30 (.89)	3.36 (.79)	3.28 (1.03)	3.14 (1.00)	3.14 (.98)	3.23 (1.16)
370 ms	3.37 (.77)	3.39 (.97)	3.30 (.78)	2.98 (.92)	3.14 (1.07)	2.88 (.90)	2.88 (1.11)	2.97 (1.24)	2.74 (.95)
500 ms	2.89 (.84)	3.05 (.98)	3.18 (.82)	2.59 (.94)	2.55 (.96)	2.71 (.90)	2.40 (.97)	2.38 (1.05)	2.62 (.97)

Behavioral Intention. The main effect of interval (F (3, 75) = 16.38; p < 0.001) was significant at the 0.01 significance level. The LSD tests revealed that the behavioral intention at the interval of 230 ms (M = 3.17) was significantly higher than that at the intervals of 370 ms (M = 2.87) and 500 ms (M = 2.47). The behavioral intention at the interval of 100 ms (M = 3.08) was significantly higher than that at the interval of 500 ms (M = 2.47). The behavioral intention at the interval of 370 ms (M = 2.87) was significantly higher than that at the interval of 500 ms (M = 2.47).

Suitability of Vibration Intensity. On the item of vibration strength being comfortable, the main effects of vibration's intensity (F(2, 50) = 3.83; p < 0.05) and interval (F(3, 75) = 5.89; p < 0.001) were significant. The LSD tests revealed that the intimacy of the strong condition (M = 3.60) was higher than that of the weak condition (M = 3.14). It was indicated that strong was the most comfortable intensity of vibration for users.

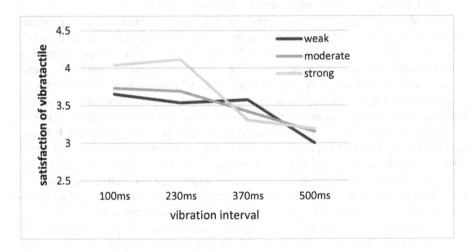

Fig. 3. Interaction effect between vibration intensity and intervals on timeliness of feedback

Timeliness of Feedback. On the item of timeliness of feedback, the main effect of vibration interval (F (3, 75) = 10.71; p < 0.001) was significant. The LSD tests revealed that users felt the timeliness of feedback with the interval of 230 ms

(M = 3.78) was significantly higher than that of intervals of 370 ms (M = 3.44) and 500 ms (M = 3.16). The timeliness of feedback with the interval of 100 ms (M = 3.81) was significantly higher than that of intervals of 370 ms (M = 3.44) and 500 ms (M = 3.16). The satisfaction at the interval of 370 ms (M = 3.44) was significantly higher than that at the interval of 500 ms (M = 3.16). The descriptive results for the vibration interval are displayed in Fig. 3. The difference between strong and weak intensities was larger at 100 ms and 230 ms than those at 370 ms and 500 ms.

4 Discussion

This paper investigated the effect of tactile feedback on user experience of touchscreen virtual button interaction. The vibration intensity, vibration times and the interval between two vibrations were compared under different conditions. The user experience was evaluated for three aspects. The results include several significant results that could be used in the future design of tactile feedback. In particular, vibration intensity was observed to have a significant effect on user experience, strong vibrations being significantly preferred to the other two intensity levels. Additionally, giving feedback only once was better than doing so twice when the intensity was strong. In the condition of giving feedback twice, the interval between two vibrations has a significant impact on user experience. Users preferred a shorter interval to longer intervals.

First, the user experience was enhanced by the increase of vibration intensity. This effect was significant on sensory experience, especially on the perceived suitability of vibration intensity and timeliness of feedback. These results confirmed the facts that perceived intensity was very important in vibration feedback.

Second, the effect of vibration times was affected by vibration intensity. When vibrations were strong, vibrating once was better than vibrating twice. However, when vibrations were weak or moderate, the effect was reversed. This phenomenon was clearly observed in sensory experience. The behavioral intention showed the same trend. These results implied that the satisfaction of vibration was a dynamic process. Perceived intensity was one of the main impact factors. When its level did not satisfy the need of users, other factors, such as vibration times, could compensate for its effect.

Finally, the user experience deteriorated with the increase of the interval between two vibrations. The best experience was observed at 230 ms in the strong vibration intensity condition. As a supplement of intensity, a shorter interval played a role, resulting in better sensory experience, affective experience and behavioral intension than those of longer intervals. The possible explanation was a long interval could be perceived as a response delay or stumbling. Hence, the user experience was poor.

Our research has some limitations. The main task of this experiment was to touch the icon and to feel the tactile feedback of the icon using distinct gestures. This task is simple and not involved in real-world tasks performed while using a smartphone. Hence, no performance could be recorded in this task. This limitation restricts the real-world applicability of the experiment. Future studies could design more realistic tasks to explore the effect of these parameters on users' experience and performance.

In a word, our experiment fills the research gap between the physical parameters of tactile feedback and the subjective user experience. The results of our study could provide some standards for vibration feedback design. The questionnaire for evaluating the tactile experience of vibration feedback could be used in future studies in this research field.

References

1. Fukumoto, M., Sugimura, T.: Active click: tactile feedback for touch panels. In: CHI 2001 Extended Abstracts on Human Factors in Computing Systems, pp. 121–122 (2001)
2. O'Sullivan, S.S., Evans, A.H., Lees, A.J.: Dopamine dysregulation syndrome an overview of its epidemiology, mechanisms and management. CNS Drugs 23(2), 157–170 (2009)
3. Kaaresoja, T., Anttila, E., Hoggan, E.: The effect of tactile feedback latency in touchscreen interaction. In: World Haptics Conference, pp. 65–70 (2011)
4. Schönauer, C., Mossel, A., Zaiţi, I.-A., Vatavu, R.-D.: Touch, movement and vibration: user perception of vibrotactile feedback for touch and mid-air gestures. In: Abascal, J., Barbosa, S., Fetter, M., Gross, T., Palanque, P., Winckler, M. (eds.) INTERACT 2015. LNCS, vol. 9299, pp. 165–172. Springer, Cham (2015). https://doi.org/10.1007/978-3-319-22723-8_14
5. Hoggan, E., Brewster, S.A., Johnston, J.: Investigating the effectiveness of tactile feedback for mobile touchscreens. In: CHI 2008: Conference Proceedings of 26th Annual Chi Conference on Human Factors in Computing Systems, vols. 1 and 2, pp. 1573–1582 (2008). (in English)
6. Altinsoy, M.E., Merchel, S.: Audiotactile feedback design for touch screens. In: Proceedings of Haptic and Audio Interaction Design, vol. 5763, pp. 136–144 (2009). (in English)
7. Lee, J.H., Spence, C.: Spatiotemporal visuotactile interaction. In: International Conference on Haptics: Perception, Devices and Scenarios, pp. 826–831 (2008)
8. Sahami, A., Holleis, P., Schmidt, A., Häkkilä, J.: Rich tactile output on mobile devices. In: Aarts, E., et al. (eds.) AmI 2008. LNCS, vol. 5355, pp. 210–221. Springer, Heidelberg (2008). https://doi.org/10.1007/978-3-540-89617-3_14
9. Ghiani, G., Leporini, B., Paternò, F.: Vibrotactile feedback to aid blind users of mobile guides. J. Vis. Lang. Comput. 20(5), 305–317 (2009)
10. Al-Razgan, M.S., Al-Khalifa, H.S., Al-Shahrani, M.D., AlAjmi, H.H.: Touch-based mobile phone interface guidelines and design recommendations for elderly people: a survey of the literature. In: Huang, T., Zeng, Z., Li, C., Leung, C.S. (eds.) ICONIP 2012. LNCS, vol. 7666, pp. 568–574. Springer, Heidelberg (2012). https://doi.org/10.1007/978-3-642-34478-7_69
11. Hertzum, M., Hornbaek, K.: How age affects pointing with mouse and touchpad: a comparison of young, adult, and elderly users. Int. J. Hum.-Comput. Interact. 26(7), 703–734 (2010). (in English)
12. Bragdon, A., Nelson, E., Li, Y., Hinckley, K.: Experimental analysis of touch-screen gesture designs in mobile environments. In: CHI 2011, pp. 403–412 (2011)
13. Azenkot, S., Zhai, S.: Touch behavior with different postures on soft smartphone keyboards. In: International Conference on Human-Computer Interaction with Mobile Devices and Services, pp. 251–260 (2012)
14. Hwang, I., Seo, J., Kim, M., Choi, S.: Vibrotactile perceived intensity for mobile devices as a function of direction, amplitude, and frequency. IEEE Trans. Haptics 6(3), 352–362 (2013)
15. Hoggan, E., Brewster, S.: New parameters for tacton design. In: CHI 2007 Extended Abstracts on Human Factors in Computing Systems, pp. 2417–2422 (2007)

16. Laugwitz, B., Held, T., Schrepp, M.: Construction and evaluation of a user experience questionnaire. In: Holzinger, A. (ed.) USAB 2008. LNCS, vol. 5298, pp. 63–76. Springer, Heidelberg (2008). https://doi.org/10.1007/978-3-540-89350-9_6
17. Rauschenberger, M., Schrepp, M., Cota, M.P., Olschner, S.: Efficient measurement of the user experience of interactive products. how to use the user experience questionnaire (UEQ). example: spanish language version. Int. J. Interact. Multimedia Artif. Intell. 2(1), 39–45 (2013)
18. Cota, M.P., Thomaschewski, J., Schrepp, M., Gonçalves, R.: Efficient measurement of the user experience. A Portuguese version. Procedia Comput. Sci. 27(1), 491–498 (2014)
19. Schrepp, M., Hinderks, A., Thomaschewski, J.: Applying the user experience questionnaire (UEQ) in different evaluation scenarios. In: Marcus, A. (ed.) DUXU 2014. LNCS, vol. 8517, pp. 383–392. Springer, Cham (2014). https://doi.org/10.1007/978-3-319-07668-3_37
20. Brakus, J.J., Schmitt, B.H., Zarantonello, L.: Brand experience: what is it? How is it measured? Does it affect loyalty? Soc. Sci. Electron. Publ. 73(3), 52–68 (2009)

Research on the Relationship Between Online Merchandise Display and Consumer Shopping Behavior

Yanyun Wang and Linong Dai[✉]

School of Design, Shanghai Jiao Tong University, Shanghai, China
wangyanyun_c@163.com, lndai@126.com

Abstract. With the continuous development of the times, online merchandise sales have become one of the more important shopping channels for consumers. But for online sales, consumers can't directly contact the goods, so online product display has an important impact on the shopping experience. In this study, eye tracking and subjective perception were used to explore the behavioral and perceived differences of consumers in different display modes. Under different display modes, consumers have different gaze duration, gaze trajectory and subjective perception. This study provides some suggestions and considerations for the follow-up study of online merchandise display.

Keywords: Online merchandise display · Shopping behavior · Eye tracking

1 Introduction

With the development of Internet technology, the sale of the online merchandises has gradually become one of the main ways for consumers to go shopping. The growth rate and scale of the Chinese market are superior to other countries. According to the report of China E-Commerce Research Center, online sales reached 6.6 trillion yuan in the period from October 2016 to September 2017. Compared to the previous cycle, it has increased by 38%, which is also the highest in the same period, and it is expected to grow to 750 million yuan in 2018. Online sale has also gone through the basic stage of development. Many fundamental issues, such as payment security and logistics have been gradually solved. In the future, more attention will be paid to the experience, emotion and other high-level needs to meet and segment the development of the field.

Unlike traditional offline sales, consumers are more difficult to interact with the actual physical space directly in the online sales scenario. Therefore, for online sales, the display mode of the product has a greater impact on the user's shopping experience. However, most of the merchants just pile up elements, and do not deeply study the brand image and consumer preferences. Some small-volume merchants have no ability to hire specialized designers. Therefore, the experience still needs to be improved in such circumstances.

There are few studies related to online merchandise display in academia, but scholars have more research on page usability and perception research. Liu disassembles the visual elements in the page [1]. Yuan did an experimental analysis of the

© Springer Nature Switzerland AG 2019
P.-L. P. Rau (Ed.): HCII 2019, LNCS 11576, pp. 407–421, 2019.
https://doi.org/10.1007/978-3-030-22577-3_30

shopping page based on the systematic layout planning model (SLP) and dynamic line analysis, and improved the design of the webpage according to the ECRS model [2]. Kun used the eye tracking method to evaluate the layout of the instrument panel of the aircraft [3].

2   Theoretical Framework

2.1   Online Merchandise Display

SLP Model. This experiment introduces the SLP model which Yuan used in her research [2]. The SLP model is a representative research method proposed by Richard Joseph of the United States in the 1960s. It is a methodical, step-by-step, and applicable method for layout of design projects. This model mainly includes four parts: determining location, overall differentiation, detailed arrangement, and implementation [4].

Online Merchandise Display. According to the 2017 online retail B2C market share of the e-commerce center, it can be seen that Jingdong and Tmall have occupied more than 80% of the market. Therefore, our research mainly takes the pages of Jingdong and Tmall as examples.

The merchandise display page mainly has three types (see Fig. 1): platform frame page, store display page, and detail page. The platform frame page has less flexible in design because of large consumer base. The detail page has higher design freedom and lower standardization due to different product categories and features. For the store display page, there are certain specifications and flexible adjustments. Therefore, the store display page is the object of this study.

Fig. 1. Platform frame page (left) store display page (middle) detail page (right)

The following picture (see Fig. 2) shows a screenshot of some pages. You can see that the store display page is more standardized, and the display layout of different product selections is different. In line with the previous inferences about the store display page, the page gives a certain degree of freedom on the basis of certain norms.

Fig. 2. The store pages

In the past, scholars have disassembled and analyzed the shopping website pages, but the definition is rather vague. In the research, Zhang mentioned the influence of online store page organization including graphic structure and presentation form, color matching and other related factors [5]. Some scholars have pointed out the influence of color on consumer sentiment and shopping behavior [6]. There are also scholars who study the impact of the hierarchical structure of the website on consumer shopping behavior [7].

Combined with the research of the above scholars, most scholars have mentioned the color, plate, structure and other factors in the page design, which is also corresponding to the two layers of the structural layer and the presentation layer element in the five elements of the user experience. Therefore, this study deconstructs the store display page into three sections (see Fig. 3): display layout, product information, and style atmosphere. The bottom layer is the display layout. Then the product information includes image, price, sales and other elements. Finally, the style atmosphere mainly consists of color and decorative elements.

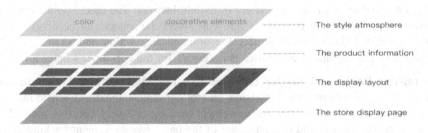

Fig. 3. Sections of the store display page

Ting Zhang's research shows that different styles of online stores have different influences on consumers' shopping intentions, and page design and the product information are the key factors affecting shopping intentions [5]. However, in her research, the definition of page design is relatively vague, which can roughly correspond to the display layout and the style atmosphere. Computer scientists Katharina Reinecke and other scholars have found that the color and visual of the website pages have a greater impact on the perception and preference of the website [8], thus proving the relevance of the style atmosphere to the consumer's shopping behavior. Based on previous researches, it has been proved that the style atmosphere layer and the product information layer have certain relevance to the consumer's shopping behavior, so this article will focus on the relation between the display layout layer and consumer shopping behavior.

The Display Layout. According to the framework analysis of a large number of store display pages, three typical display layout forms are abstracted. According to the degree of density, from the sparse to the dense, the three forms are named as the bar format, the field format, and the square format (see Fig. 4). The experiment will explore the correlation between different display layout and consumer shopping behavior.

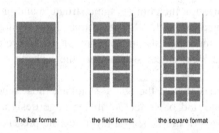

The bar format   the field format   the square format

Fig. 4. The three typical display layout forms

2.2   Online Merchandise Display

Consumer Shopping Behavior Theory. China Internet Monitoring Research Authority & Data Platform DCCI Internet Data Center proposed the behavioral model SICAS describing consumers in the era of mobile Internet. The model points out that consumers' behavior can be divided into consumers' behaviors can be divided into Sense, Interest & Interactive, Connect & Communicate, Action and Share. At each stage, the display of the merchandises is necessary for the consumer's behavior.

Quantifying Shopping Behavior Based on Eye Tracking. 80% of the information that people get is obtained through vision, and for consumers, the direct way to interact with the page is also vision, so eye movement tracking is a very effective method to evaluate the advantages and disadvantages of the page. Eye movement tracking is the tracking of people's eye movements. Many scholars have applied eye movement tracking to the usability research of web pages. However, there is not enough research on mobile terminal. This study mainly focuses on the subdivision of the merchandise display on mobile phone, which is commonly used by e-commerce consumers.

Eye movements are mainly composed of gaze and eye movement [9]. When you look at something, it is called gaze. The process of moving an eye from one point of fixation to another is called an eye jump. This process is very fast and the brain does not process the information for this process [10].

Some scholars have applied eye tracking indicators to the page research of shopping scenes, so based on previous research, this experimental index was formed (see Table 1). Eye movement indicators are divided into qualitative indicators and quantitative indicators. Common qualitative indicators are gaze plot map and eye movement heat map. In the research of page layout, researchers often use this result to explore the differences which the subjects pay attention to under different page conditions [11]. Common quantitative indicators of eye movement are fixation duration and fixation count. The fixation duration indicator reflects how long the subject stays in this area. Gazing for a long time indicates that the subject is interested in the content or confused with the content. For this experiment, there is no difficulty in understanding the product because we chose daily products. So, the long Fixation duration shows the degree of interest in the content. In the experiment, the count of subjects clicked on the pages was recorded at the same time. The count reflected the strong desire of subjects to purchase the product in this form.

Table 1. Eye tracking indicators.

Number	Indicators
1	Gaze plot
2	Hot map
3	Consumer click (the count of subject clicked on the page)
4	Fixation duration
5	Fixation count

Consumer Subjective Perception. Eye tracking can objectively describe the consumer's shopping behavior to a certain extent, but the judgment of the consumer's subjective shopping experience is not enough. Therefore, this study uses the in-depth interview and the questionnaire scale to evaluate the subjective perception of consumers.

In He's research, he measured the customer satisfaction with seven aspects based on ACSI theory [12]: perceived quality, perceived value, perceived convenience, online service, perceived risk, logistics and after-sales service. This study selected some indicators to establish subjective perception indicators: pleasure, security, convenience, quality and comfortability.

In order to ensure the integrity of the indicator system, the in-depth interview method is used to supplement the research on the perceived behavior of consumers.

3 Method

3.1 Research Methods and Hypothesis

The purpose of this experiment is to explore the impact of different product display methods on consumer shopping behavior. The experiment collects user data from both subjective and objective aspects. Through the eye movement experiment, the user's attention and operational behavior are observed. The questionnaire and in-depth interviews are used to understand the subjective perception of the page after the test.

Subjects Selection. In online sales, young people aged 18–25 are the main consumers of consumption. At the same time, the experiment was limited by the eye-moving field. The study population was scheduled for the 18–25 age.

Shopping Task. Combined with Zhang Ting [5] and Yong JW's [13] research methods, this experiment divides shopping behavior tasks into purposeful tasks and purposeless tasks. The purposeful task is to let the participants make purchase clicks of the specified category of goods, while the purposeless task is to allow the participants to browse at random, and to make purchase clicks for the products of interest.

The Display Layout. In this experiment, the store display page is divided into three groups: a, b, and c. Group a is the display page mainly for the bar format, Group b is the display page mainly for the field format, and Group c is the display page mainly for the square format. Through the survey of consumers' frequently purchased categories, the pages displayed in this experiment select daily-use items. The three groups of pages display the same products, and hide the sensitive factors such as price and sales volume.

Experimental Hypothesis. This experiment explores the relevance of online merchandise display and consumer shopping behavior. Based on relevant theoretical research, the following assumptions are proposed:

H1. In the purposeless task, consumers have different fixation duration for different display layout. The more arranged the page, the longer the fixation duration.
H2. In the purposeful task, consumers have different completion time for different display layout. The tighter the pages, the shorter the completion time.
H3. Under different display layout, consumers pay different attention to different areas of the page, and there are certain rules in the gaze.
H4. Under different display layout, consumers click different times.
H5. Under different display layout, consumers have different subjective cognition.

3.2 The Experimental Process

The Participants Recruited. There were 26 subjects aged 18–25 years old in this experiment. The ratio of male to female is 1:1. At the time of recruitment, users who have a certain online shopping experience and maintain a certain frequency are selected.

Content of the Experiment. This experiment uses a hybrid design of 3 (display layout: A, B, C) × 2 (shopping behavior: purposeful, purposeless). Each subject looked at three sets of randomly ordered pages and did purposeful (select a cup/bag/tableware) and purposeless browsing tasks for each group of pages. Subjects were required to fill out the questionnaire after browsing each group of pages. Then subjects were interviewed after all the three groups of pages have been browsed.

Experimental Instrument. This experiment was conducted using a portable eye tracker named Tobii pro glass2 and a mobile phone (Huawei P9). Tobii pro glass2 can accurately capture the measured eye movement behavior. After the test, the data was imported into the supporting analysis software Tobii pro lab for corresponding analysis.

4 Result

4.1 Eye Tracking Data Analysis

Fixation Duration. The subjects were statistically analyzed during the A.B.C three-group page browsing process. Since there are three groups in this experiment, one-way ANOVA is used when only one factor of gaze duration is considered. The degree of difference was judged by comparing the size of F with Fcrit. If F > Fcrit, there is a significant difference between the data between groups.

For purposeless tasks, descriptive statistical analysis and variance test analysis were performed (see Table 2). As can be seen from the analysis of Table 4, F = 6.33 > Fcrit = 3.11, indicating that the three sets of data have significant differences in the length of fixation. It can be seen from the data in the Table 3 that the average gaze duration between different groups is different. The length of gaze from group a to group c is decreasing. The more arranged the page, the longer the fixation duration. This result verifies the hypothesis H1. In the purposeless task, consumers have different fixation duration for different display layout. The more arranged the page, the longer the fixation duration.

Table 2. Fixation Duration (purposeless tasks)

Number	Group a	Group b	Group c
1	62.14	43.32	35.45
2	96.97	67.85	54.24
3	64.12	60.23	59.66
4	100.15	106.75	68.12
5	71.87	53.91	45.56
6	54.28	62.71	41.66
7	38.93	66.99	63.47
8	150.41	136.88	70.69
...	...	...	...
26	88.23	56.12	49.23

Table 3. Descriptive statistics of Fixation duration (purposeless tasks)

Group	Number	Summation	Average	Variance
a	26	1702.043726	65.46322023	865.9470194
b	26	1472.127436	56.62028634	637.1305291
c	26	1092.067009	42.00257727	224.545277

Table 4. Variance analysis of Fixation duration (purposeless tasks)

	SS	df	MS	F	P-value	F crit
Between groups	1910.1480	2	955.07403	3.8454635	0.0257115	3.1186421
Inside the group	18627.286	75	248.36382			
Total	20537.434	77				

For purposeful browsing, the subjects ended the experiment after selecting a product. It can be seen from the Table 6 that F = 3.84 > Fcrit = 3.11, indicating that the three groups of data also showed significant differences for purposeful browsing. It can be seen from the data in the Table 5 that the average gaze time is different between different groups, and the gaze duration from group a to group c decreases. This result verifies the hypothesis H2. In the purposeful task, consumers have different completion time for different display layout. The tighter the pages, the shorter the completion time.

Table 5. Descriptive statistics of Fixation duration (purposeful tasks)

Group	Number	Summation	Average	Variance
a	26	1041.420851	40.05464812	344.9798491
b	26	878.426948	33.78565185	239.8244062
c	26	726.320571	27.93540658	160.2872218

Table 6. Variance analysis of Fixation duration (purposeful tasks)

	SS	df	MS	F	P-value	F crit
Between groups	1910.1480	2	955.07403	3.8454635	0.0257115	3.1186421
Inside the group	18627.286	75	248.36382			
Total	20537.434	77				

Consumer Clicks. When browsing without purpose, the user can click on the item of interest without limiting the number of clicks. It can be seen from the Table 8 that F = 4.96 > Fcrit = 3.11, so there is a significant difference in the number of shopping clicks between the comparison groups. The three groups of pages present the same products, so the difference in the number of clicks proves the impact of different display methods on the number of clicks. As can be seen from the Table 7, from A to C, the number of clicked items is decremented. This result verifies the hypothesis H4. Under different display layout, consumers click different times. At the same time, it was found in the statistical data that the trend of the clicks of a small number of participants was different from the statistical results. From A to C, the trend of increasing the number of items was clicked, and in-depth interviews were conducted for these users to understand the reasons.

Table 7. Descriptive statistics of Consumer click

Group	Number	Summation	Average	Variance
a	26	116	4.461538462	5.218461538
b	26	95	3.653846154	4.235384615
c	26	70	2.692307692	2.861538462

Table 8. Variance analysis of Consumer click

	SS	df	MS	F	P-value	F crit
Between groups	40.794871	2	20.39743	4.9687695	0.009409	3.1186421
Inside the group	307.88461	75	4.1051282			
Total	348.67948	77				

Split the page into separate screens, and compared the fixation duration and count in the three groups of pages (see Fig. 5). Due to the different durations and counts of the gaze of the different subjects, the date is converted into the proportion of the statistics. It can be seen from the line graph that in the b and c groups, with the increase of the screen number, the fixation duration and count have a relatively obvious downward trend, but group a is more uniform. The distribution of the three groups of pages all showed an alternating polyline trend. If the previous screen was longer, the attention time of the next screen decreased significantly.

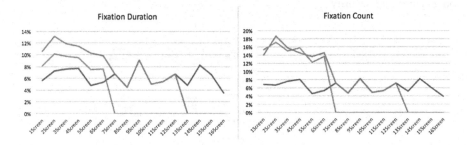

Fig. 5. Fixation duration (left) and Fixation count (right)

Gaze Plot and Hot Map. The gaze data of the three sets of pages is analyzed (see Fig. 6). The left image shows the gaze plot of the representative subject No. 4. The heat map on the right is a superposition of all the measured heat maps. For group a, the page is mainly composed of a column frame, and it is not easy to miss the page information. For group b, the page is mainly composed of a double-column frame. It is measured to display a zigzag browsing trajectory when browsing. After browsing an item, the probability of continuing to browse vertically is greater than that of horizontal browsing, so that it is easy to miss other products in the same row. For the group c, the page is mainly composed of a three-column frame. When viewed, it also shows a jagged browsing track, but the middle row of goods gets more attention than the left and right rows. This result proves H3. Under different display layout, consumers pay different attention to different areas of the page, and there are certain rules in the gaze.

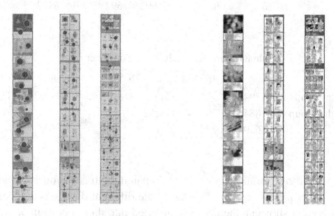

Fig. 6. Gaze Plot (a b c) and Hot map (a b c)

4.2 Subjective Perception Data Analysis

The subjective description keywords of the three groups of pages are extracted and cluster analysis is performed (see Fig. 7). The study found that the subject's description of subjective feelings can be clustered into five aspects: cognition, quality, comparison, convenience and security.

Cognition	Quality	Comparison	Convenience	Security
Large picture	high quality	Information explosion	Low efficiency	Brand
Small picture	advanced	Strong contrast	slow	Guaranteed
Attention to detail	expensive	close	Too long	Wholesaler
No details	confidence	Crowded	high efficiency	Small shop
see it clearly	Cheap	Unable to compare	high speed	Worried about
...	Good quality	Pressure	Look much more	quality
	Exquisite	Sense of control	at once	Gift
	...	tired	...	...
		Messy		
		...		

Fig. 7. Subjective perception

The loosely arranged (such as group a) display method will give the subject a higher sense of quality and security, but the convenience and contrast are lower. The arrangement of the more closely arranged (such as Group c) will give the subject a lower quality and security, but the convenience and contrast are higher. This result verifies the hypothesis H5. Under different display layout, consumers have different subjective cognition.

Questionnaire. After each group of users has finished browsing a group of pages, the subjective perception questionnaire is filled out. In the end, 26 subjects recovered 78 valid questionnaires. The reliability and validity of the questionnaire were analyzed. The reliability analysis was performed using the commonly used Cronbach α coefficient, and the value was $0.877 > 0.8$. The validity was KMO analysis, and the value was $0.85 > 0.8$. The reliability of this questionnaire was obtained. It has good validity and can be further analyzed.

The data in the table shows that the results of the interviews are mutually validated: the sense of quality and security are decreasing from group a to group c, while the convenience is increasing from group a to group c (see Table 9).

Table 9. Questionnaire

	Pleasure	Security	Convenience	Quality	Comfortability
a	0.92	0.76	0.36	1.24	1.08
b	0.56	0.6	0.56	0.56	1.01
c	0.19	0.5	0.81	0.52	0.31

5 Discussion

Online sales are different from offline, consumers can't really contact with goods, so how to display goods has a greater impact on consumers' behavior and experience. This study mainly explores the correlation between online merchandise display and consumer shopping behavior, and takes the shop page in the exhibition as an example for case study. The study uses eye tracking and subjective perception to explore the behavioral and perceived differences of consumers in different display modes. In the course of the experiment, the display frames were divided into three groups A, B, and C according to the arrangement and density, so that the subjects were browsed in a purposeful and purposeless background.

5.1 Different Display Modes for Different Shopping Motives

The experiment found that the more arranged the page, the longer the fixation duration in the purposeless task. First of all, under the premise of the same number of products, the longer the group page is, the longer the length of the group will be, and the time for browsing will increase. At the same time, because the page is too long, the possibility of the participant giving up reading will increase. However, during the experiment, it was found that for the display mode of the arrangement, most of the subjects not only finished the browsing of the page content, but also performed a detailed review of the slip back. Perhaps this suggests that the way to arrange the sparseness is more attractive to the participants and the degree of interest is higher. In a more closely arranged way, the details of the goods cannot be displayed, and the consumer has a shorter stay time with each item. Some participants mentioned in the interview that because they received information on multiple items at the same time, they could not choose which item to browse, so they gave up and quickly crossed.

On the contrary, when the subjects were given a specific task to select a certain product, the closer the arrangement was, the shorter the time required to complete the task. In the interview, the subjects mentioned that the tight arrangement can be used to compare multiple products at the same time, so the selection efficiency is high, while the page with sparse arrangement is relatively low, thus lengthening the task time.

Therefore, in different shopping motive scenarios, if the merchant provides different display methods, it may enhance the commercial effect. For example, in a highly targeted scenario, the merchant may choose a more closely arranged manner to improve efficiency. For the scene without purpose browsing, more sparse way can be selected to enhance the consumer's interest.

5.2   Different Display Methods Are Suitable for Different Product Placement Rules

For the bar format, there is almost no leakage of goods, but in the field of the field and the palace format, there are different levels of missing goods. After browsing an item, the possibility of vertical reading is greater than horizontal. According to previous research conclusions on the web page [14] [15], the subject's gaze time for the left part is longer than the right part. However, no obvious left-right tendency was observed in this experiment. For the three rows of exhibitions, the participants stayed in the middle row longer than the left and right sides. The reason may be related to the difference between the mobile terminal and the web terminal. For the square format, in each horizontal browsing, browsing to the middle will result in a high probability of vertical viewing, so that the overall middle stay is longer than the left and right. Therefore, merchants can make targeted choices when placing goods. For example, for the square format, the main push products can be placed in the middle row to get more attention.

In the previous research on the webpage [16], most of the consumers' gaze time stayed in the first two screens. However, the study found that although the gaze time is decreasing continuously with the increase of the number of screens, there is no case where the first two screens are dominant. This may have something to do with the characteristics of the mobile phone. The sliding cost of the mobile page is lower than the webpage. After years of training in mobile phone operating habits, the subjects have been accustomed to sliding operations. Instead, the data shows that consumers often stay longer on the second screen, and the first screen is less attractive to consumers, perhaps because consumers are more interested in the following display content, which leads to an increase in the exposure of the next few screens.

Among them, b, c two arrangement, the first four screens get higher exposure and more stable, so the first four screens are more valuable. For the more arranging methods, such as group a, it may be because the content is attractive to consumers, and the latter screens still get a low gaze duration. Therefore, the merchant can increase the attention to the 2–4 screen content when placing the product, instead of focusing only on the first screen content. If you want to get a certain exposure when you have more screens, consider more sparse way.

5.3 Different Display Methods Are Suitable for Different Industries and Consumers

The three groups of pages present the same products, so the difference in the number of clicks proves the impact of different display methods on the number of clicks. Some subjects mentioned that they found goods that were not found in group b and c in group a. But the reality is that the products in the three groups of pages are exactly the same. Participants ignored some of the items in the other two pages because of the different presentation formats.

During the experiment, it was also found that the selection trend of a very small number of subjects was different from that of most of the subjects. Researchers believe that it may be related to consumers' shopping habits. Different types of users are sensitive to perception factors. In the interviews, it was found that tests that are more sensitive to efficiency and comparative sensibility have a higher desire to purchase pages that are more closely aligned. Therefore, in the design of the future display, personalized display can be carried out according to the consumption habits of different users, thereby inspiring consumers to purchase more and increase business value.

The loosely arranged display method will give the subject a higher sense of quality and security. The arrangement of the more closely arranged will give the subject a lower quality and security. Therefore, when shops in different industries choose the display method, they can have a certain preference. For example, for the maternal and child industry with higher security requirements, more choices may be made. For fast-moving industries with higher convenience and higher requirements, more compact arrangements can be chosen.

5.4 Limitation

This experiment has certain limitations at the same time. The whole experiment is carried out in the experimental environment, which is different from the actual consumption scene of consumers. The sample is concentrated on young people aged 18–25, and different age groups may have an impact on the results of the experiment. In the selection of experimental samples, the selection of daily necessities products has certain representativeness, but different categories may still have certain differences.

6 Conclusion

This study mainly explores the correlation between online merchandise display and consumer shopping behavior. Through this research, it is found that different display methods will affect consumers' fixation duration, gaze plot and subjective perception during shopping:

1. In the purposeless task, the more arranged the page, the longer the fixation duration. In the purposeful task, the tighter the pages, the shorter the completion time.
2. Different ways of displaying goods can affect the number of clicks by consumers. For most people, the more the product arrangement, the more consumers click.
3. Under different display layout, consumers pay different attention to different areas of the page, and there are certain rules in the gaze. For a three-column palace format, the middle row gets more gaze time than the left and right sides.
4. As the number of display screens increases, consumer gaze time shows a downward trend. The exposure of the 2–4 screens of Groups b and c is higher and stable, but for the bar frame, the downward trend is slower, and the number of screens behind can also be obtained for a longer gaze duration.

This research provides some basis and suggestions for merchants to choose the way of displaying goods, and provides some thoughts and ideas for the design and research of mobile terminal display.

References

1. Liu, H.L., Ma, F.M.: Research on visual elements of web UI design. IEEE International Conference on Computer-aided Industrial Design & Conceptual Design. IEEE (2011)
2. Yuan, Y.J., Ye, C.Y., Sun, J.H.: Study on mobile shopping website design based on moving line observation and SLP. Chin. J. Ergon. (2016)
3. Yang, K., Gao, W.C., Bai, J.: Research on the evaluation of flight instruments layout based on eye movement indices. Chin. J. Ergon. (2016)
4. Suhardini, D., Septiani, W., Fauziah, S.: Design and simulation plant layout using systematic layout planning. In: IOP Conference Series: Materials Science and Engineering, vol. 277, p. 012051 (2017)
5. Zhang, T., Ning, D.H., Zhang, J.M.: The effect of the online shop style on consumers shopping intention: an eye movement study. Chin. J. Ergon. (2015)
6. Wu, C.S., Cheng, F.F., Yen, D.C.: The atmospheric factors of online storefront environment design: an empirical experiment in Taiwan. Inf. Manag. **45**(7), 493–498 (2008)
7. Griffith, D.A.: An examination of the influences of store layout in online retailing. J. Bus. Res. **58**(10), 1391–1396 (2005)
8. Harrison, L., Reinecke, K., Chang, R.: Infographic aesthetics: designing for the first impression. In: ACM Conference on Human Factors in Computing Systems (2015)
9. Strandvall, T.: Eye tracking in human-computer interaction and usability research. In: Gross, T., et al. (eds.) INTERACT 2009. LNCS, vol. 5727, pp. 936–937. Springer, Heidelberg (2009). https://doi.org/10.1007/978-3-642-03658-3_119
10. Andrews, T.J., Coppola, D.M.: Idiosyncratic characteristics of saccadic eye movements when viewing different visual environments. Vis. Res. **39**(17), 53–2947 (1999)
11. Sheng, P.: The difference of IPO financing cost of Chinese enterprises. Southwest Jiaotong University (2017)
12. Anderson, E.W., Fornell, C.: Foundations of the American customer satisfaction index. Total Qual. Manag. **11**(7), 869–882 (2000)
13. Yong, J.W., Hernandez, M.D., Minor, M.S.: Web aesthetics effects on perceived online service quality and satisfaction in an e-tail environment: the moderating role of purchase task. J. Bus. Res. **63**(9–10), 935–942 (2010)

14. Djamasbi, S., Siegel, M., Tullis, T.: Visual hierarchy and viewing behavior: an eye tracking study. In: Jacko, J.A. (ed.) HCI 2011. LNCS, vol. 6761, pp. 331–340. Springer, Heidelberg (2011). https://doi.org/10.1007/978-3-642-21602-2_36
15. Matsuda, Y., Uwano, H., Ohira, M., Matsumoto, K.: An analysis of eye movements during browsing multiple search results pages. In: Jacko, J.A. (ed.) HCI 2009. LNCS, vol. 5610, pp. 121–130. Springer, Heidelberg (2009). https://doi.org/10.1007/978-3-642-02574-7_14
16. Solman, G.J.F., Cheyne, J., Smilek, D.: Memory load affects visual search processes without influencing search efficiency. Vis. Res. 51(10), 1185–1191 (2011)

"Big Screen Is Watching Me?": A Study on the Attractiveness and Reading Efficiency of a Rotating Screen

Yuan Yao[1(✉)], Chao Wang[2], Minghao He[3], Chuyi Yan[4], Robert Elder[1], Chen Zhao[5], and Haipeng Mi[1]

[1] Tsinghua University, Beijing, China
`yaoyuan18@mails.tsinghua.edu.cn`
[2] Northeastern University, Boston, USA
[3] Colby College, Waterville, USA
[4] Beijing Forestry University, Beijing, China
[5] Alibaba Group, DAMO Natural HCI Lab, Sunnyvale, USA

Abstract. Interactive public displays are often deemed to be more effective and engaging in delivering information to people. This paper presents three studies on directive displays — a type of display that rotates in response to a passerby's movement direction and their effectiveness in drawing the attention of a single nearby passerby. The studies build progressively on each other, using three iterations of rotating directive displays, with evaluations of their performance compared with a static screen. Our results demonstrate a rotating screen that adapts to a passerby's movement in real-time is more effective in both attracting passerby attention and improving screen reading efficiency. These results may provide a reference for future designs of public displays.

Keywords: Directive display · Rotating screen · Reading efficiency · Attractiveness · Visual focus area

1 Introduction

Public TV screen displays have become a very common sight. These screens show content from a variety of information sources. As people increasingly get adapted with the display as a medium to obtain information, it is a well known problem that passersby generally do not notice [1,2], or pay sufficient attention to such displays [3]. Interactive techniques been added to many displays as a means to attract user attention. Digital displays can show diverse content in different situations, and have distinct effects on specific passersby, and on groups of passersby, according to the viewers' intentions [4]. Dr. Muller has conducted detailed research of Audience Funnel [5] and how the display should respond differently for viewers at different intention-phases [6]. In this research, we investigate how to manipulate display screens and the content on it for a

© Springer Nature Switzerland AG 2019
P.-L. P. Rau (Ed.): HCII 2019, LNCS 11576, pp. 422–439, 2019.
https://doi.org/10.1007/978-3-030-22577-3_31

Fig. 1. A directive display can track and adapt its rotating angle to directly face passersby as they approach and walk past the screen.

single passerby at a close distance in order to provide a more efficient method for presenting information (Fig. 1).

Simply showing rich content on display is not sufficient since not all passersby will look at the screen with strong intent, particularly at different distances from the screen. Furthermore, people who pass by may not turn their heads to look at the display in the first place, in which case the content on the screen has little impact on attracting a passersby attention. To solve this problem, this research proposes a novel public display with physical movement: a rotating screen that always faces the passerby through real-time adaption.

There is a significant amount of related works in the field of robotics research relevant to the subject of public displays [7]. In this paper, we discuss the user-screen interaction relationship between passersby and directive displays in public environments. A directive display has directional and rotational functions, and can respond to and guide a passerby by facing, turning away, and retracting itself to be visible or hidden, from them.

We investigated the impact of directive displays on users in three multi-level experiments. The first experiment intended to quantify the influence of different types of screens on participants' reading efficiency. The second experiment analyzed the impact of both directive and static screens on passersby's visual focus on the screen. The third experiment investigated the effect of a rotating screen on passerby behavior.

Each experiment tests a hypothesis that exists independently of the others, yet they have a progressive relationship. The first level of hypothesis is that the directive screen can enhance user attention; the second level is that user's visual focus area is more concentrated when using directive screens; the third and highest level is that a rotating screen helps to improve the reading efficiency of the passersby. The results of these experiments point out that a directive display has a positive impact on the passersby in terms of improving passerby focus on the screen.

2   Related Works

2.1   Proxemics and Public Displays

Anthropologist Hall [8] coined the term "proxemics" in 1966 when proposing the concept of proxemic zones involving a relationship between interpersonal distance and social interaction. Nowadays, with the explosive growth of digital devices, proxemic interactions have great potential to inform the implementation of natural user interfaces, particularly with consideration of the position, identity, movement, and orientation of nearby people and other devices [9]. Vogel and Balakrishnan [4] designed a framework that characterized how people interact with public displays into four phases: Ambient Display, Implicit Interaction, Subtle Interaction, and Personal Interaction. Meanwhile, a gradual engagement design pattern by Marquardt et al. [9] describe the three stages of how a device can gradually engage a user. In this paper, we apply proxemics from ambient displays to subtle interaction in order to adapt content to user's location, distance, and orientation.

2.2   Display Forms

There are different types of screens nowadays [10]. In addition to screen type, the placement of the display within the broader environmental space is also important to consider. A screen can be placed in myriad places within a room: on the wall [11], the ground [12], and even the ceiling [13]. At the same time, screen designs come in different shapes, to fit different viewing situations [14]. Additionally, there are methods of adapting the display to achieve a desired effects for users [15]. For instance, perspective-corrected displays can increase user's reading speed in a meeting room by adapting content orthogonally to the user's perspective. Schmidt et al. [16] discuss a large perspective-corrected display in public space in passerby scenarios. Additionally, Ardito [17] summarized the interaction modes between users and various kinds of screens of different sizes, angles, and combinations. These previous works provide the theoretical foundation and reference for comparative analysis for the rotating screen proposed in this paper.

2.3   Perception Area and Watch-Parameters

Previous research discusses methods of watching the screen, including the perception area and interaction distance. Ball claimed that the useful field of vision (UFOV) angle is around 60-degrees [18]. Furthermore, Schmidt proposed the watching angle of the screen should be less than 86-degrees [16]. Mayer et al. [19] discussed that the distance from player-player and player-display. Moreover, according to Dostal et al. [20], the distance from the screen can make some difference in the object that is being displayed. This impact can measured according to "visualization type, detail level, and zoom level."

Our research investigates the impact of the screen on users. Previous research works [21] have explored and evaluated audience behavior [1,22], user experience [4], user acceptance [23], user performance [24], effectiveness [3,25], privacy [26] and social impact [27] with lab and field studies. Existing research has also been conducted on how external factors can contribute to the failure of a public display, e.g., by making it less visible to passersby [28]. These parameters discussed in previous works provide a backdrop for the environmental design of the experiments in our study.

In summary, our research builds on proxemics by using the position and direction of a passerby to create a novel interaction between passersby and a directive display. Although there are many existing interaction techniques for large displays, these techniques generally do not pay attention to (1) directive displays, (2) user's perceptions of the screen in different directions, and (3) legibility of content for different types of display.

3 Technical Setup

Both Study 1 and Study 2 are conducted in a laboratory environment where we are capable of controlling several variables and parameters, including the TV size, participants' position, distance, walking speed, angle of turn, task form and difficulty, and others, as introduced before. In order to study how various display types affect audiences, we chose three types of display-designs that are all based on the same screen. Two pilot studies determined the most natural path of the experiment area, consisting of the distance between the participants and the screen and the range of the angle in which passersby walk pass the display.

In this research, we chose a 48-in. LCD TV as the test device. The display area of the screen is between 1 m and 2 m tall, in line with the normal user's height range (1.6 m − 1.85 m). Study 1 and Study 2 use a horizontal screen, while Study 3 selected a vertical screen to better fit the content shown on the screen. We created three types of displays, all built using the same TV model. The angle and speed of rotation of the display were adjusted manually by the experimenter according to participant's position.

1. **Static screen:** Static content is presented on a static screen, as the display does not respond to participants' movement.
2. **Static screen with transformable content:** Dynamic content presented on a static screen, the angle of the content is actively adjusted according to the passerby's perspective, such that content appears to be constantly facing the passerby regardless of their position.
3. **Rotating screen:** Static content is presented on a dynamic screen, and the screen rotates smoothly according to participant's head position. The line determined by the participant's head and center of the screen remains orthogonal with the plane of the screen throughout the entire interaction experience.

Two crucial parameters for the reading path, distance to screen, and the starting position were determined to enable a natural and comfortable reading experience. According to Schmidt's model, every pixel of 0.03 m can be recognized from 103 m when standing orthogonally (0° right-angle) to the screen, and from 73 m at from a 45° vantage point [16]. Meanwhile, Ball's theory of UFOV maintains that human's comfortable vision angle is within 55°. From these two theories, we can narrow down the parameters for a comfortable viewing angle, but the range (0.26 m to 73 m; 0° to 55°) is still too broad for the task-path design. Therefore, a pilot study was conducted to refine the parameters.

Via a pilot study, we determined a comfortable distance based on the size of the TV screen. This pilot study asked 10 participants to stand in their most comfortable position in front the screen, with the screen showing images that would be used later in the experiments. The mean distance at which participants stood is approximately 2 m. In an open area, a further pilot study asks participants to walk by the static screen on a straight path 2 m away from the screen. Based on the result of the pilot study. We determined the reading path as 2 m away and 6 m long.

In this paper, we abstract all factors that may influence legibility, and simply assume that distance and angle are highly influential. We use the same screen in three studies. Because of this, the test area used in this research is not universal, but is adapted to the certain specifications of the display size of the TV screen used and the experiment location's physical environment.

4   STUDY 1: Reading-Efficiency of Rotating Display

The purpose of this study is to evaluate the legibility performance of a rotating screen. Schmidt et al. showed that a static screen with transformable content has better performance than a static screen [16]. In order to know whether a rotating screen outperforms both a static screen and a static screen with transformable content, we conducted three sets of experiments comparing the legibility of three types of screens: a static screen, a static screen with transformable content, and a rotating screen. In the experiments, the time taken to read the content and the accuracy of reading were measured to quantify the reading efficiency.

4.1   Parameters

The experiment was conducted in a controlled laboratory environment. A 48-in. LCD TV was chosen to deliver three types of display. The angle and speed of rotation are adjusted manually by experimenter according to participant's position. In addition, referencing Larson's research, there is almost no impact on legibility for screen rotations up to 55° for a static screen with transformable content [29]. We conducted a pilot experiment in order to specify this angle for a rotating content. Five experts were asked to stand at specified start and end points. The initial angle of the transformable content was set at 55°, and we asked the user adjust it to their most comfortable viewing angle. The path with a perspective transformable angle within 40°.

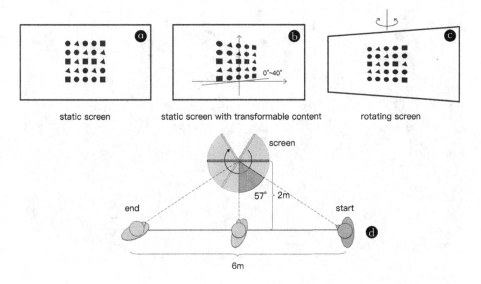

Fig. 2. (a) (b) (c) Differences in three experimental stimuli; (d) Task path.

4.2 Task and Stimulus

A 5*5 grid is presented at the center of the screen, with either a square, a triangle or a circle in each grid (Fig. 2). In each trial, one specific shape is assigned to the participant, whose task is to count the number of that shape in the grid. Participants have to observe the content while moving forward at a constant speed. Walking back or stopping in the process was not allowed. Three difficulty levels were chosen, each based upon the number of the target shapes shown (i.e. accurately count ten triangles would be harder than counting five). Each participants completed 27 trials in a three by three within-subject design, with three levels of difficulty (easy, medium, high) and the three types of displays (static screen, static screen with transformable content, rotating screen). The order of the trials were balanced with a Latin square.

4.3 Procedure

A total of 15 participants (40% female, *Mean* age = 27.6, *SD* = 10.1) were recruited to participate in the experiment. After a brief informed consent, participants were asked to walk by the screen from the right side to the left at a uniform speed (around 1 m/s) along the previously determined path (6 m long, 2 m away from the screen), while observing the content on the screen. As soon as the participant reached the end line, the content disappeared from the display and the participant was asked to orally report the number of the given shape to experimenters immediately. A GoPro camera was attached to the participant's head to keep track of their head direction. An additional camera recorded the

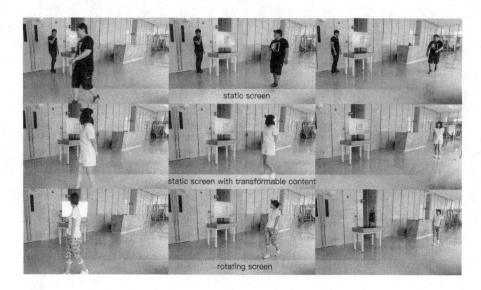

Fig. 3. Experiment procedure in Study 1

full scene to facilitate further analysis. After the trials were completed, participants were thanked and orally debriefed. The experiment took about 15 min for each participant (Figure 3).

4.4 Result

Reading Accuracy. To establish whether different types of dynamic display affect participants' reading efficiency, we coded participants' responses into a dichotomous variable based on correctness, and carried out an analysis of variance (ANOVA). The result shows that difficulty-level unsurprisingly influences accuracy, $F_{2,269} = 17.457$, $p < 0.001$, but a significant main effect of display types on reading accuracy was also found, $F_{2,269} = 6.010$, $p = 0.003$. Post-hoc LSD test further showed that reading accuracy for a rotating screen performed significantly better than for a static screen with transformable content ($p < 0.001$, 95% confidence interval $[-0.3751, -0.0843]$). A regular static screen has a medium accuracy, but still significantly better than rotating content ($p = 0.024$, 95% confidence interval $[-.2490, -.0177]$). Compared with a static screen, participants performed significantly better when interacting with a rotating screen, and significantly worse when the content is transformable (Figure 4).

Reading Time. To mitigate the possibility of discrepancies in reading accuracy performance arising because of differences in participants' reading time, an additional ANOVA test was conducted to examine the display's effect on reading time. The results, $F_{2,269} = 0.421$, $p = 0.657$, showed that there is no significant difference in reading time between the three displays (Figure 4).

4.5 Discussion

From this study, the rotating screen provides a higher average reading accuracy compared with other types of screen. This indicates a rotating screen can significantly improve reading efficiency for passersby, relative to both a static screen and a static screen with transformable content.

Our results showed that static screens with transformable content are less successful in conveying information to users, a finding that contradicts previous research [16, 30]. This suggests perspective-correction for transformable content does not offset the impact of screen direction for two-dimensional screens. Although the content has been perspective-corrected, users may perceive it to be facing away from them if the screen does not face them sufficiently.

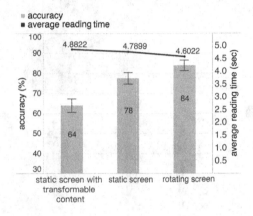

Fig. 4. Comparison of accuracy and average reading times.

5   STUDY 2: Visual Focus of the User

According to the first study, a rotating screen not only has no negative impact on reading efficiency, but also has better legibility than both the static screen and the static screen with transformable content. In contrast, the static screen with transformable content has the poorest performance on reading efficiency. Taking into consideration the low performance of the static screen with transformable content, we decided to proceed by only investigating the performance of the rotating screen compared with the static screen in the remaining studies in this paper.

This study examines a user's dynamic visual focus while passing by two types of screen. There were two hypotheses: The first one is that passerby's visual focus area on the rotating screen will be more concentrated than on a static screen; the second one is that the dynamic visual focus of a passerby follows a predictable pattern depending on the screen type. We did two sets of experiments comparing the static screen and the rotating screen. In these experiments, we recorded a

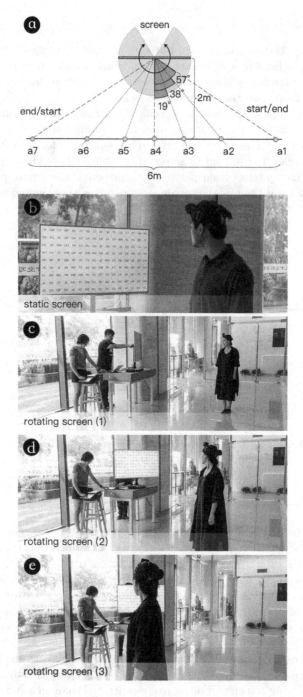

Fig. 5. (a) Seven position-points we marked on the ground. Each point recorded the coordinate of the user's visual focus area. (b) (c) (d) (e) The experiment content and process.

passerby's line of vision from different angles at multiple vantage points in a coordinate plane in order to quantify the user's visual focus area.

According to the observations from the previous study, a passerby could choose any position from which to start looking at the screen. We did not allow the passerby to walk continuously in a straight line, in order to mitigate a situation where participants look at a single fixed point from the beginning to end of the experiment. We asked the participant to stand in seven assigned positions on a designated walking path, then recorded the first group of letters that the user observed at each position. The positions on the ground were assigned depending on the range angles calculated from the results from study 1. We subdivided the angle by six, with each angle equaling approximately 19°, from the start to the end point of the walk-line. A total of six angles and seven position-points were set for the experiment (Figure 5).

5.1   Participants and Apparatus

There were 20 participants (35% female, *Mean* age = 27.75, *SD* = 8.61) in this experiment. A TV was used to project the stimulus. On top of the TV, a GoPro camera was used to track, time, and record passersby's behaviors. We marked the seven positions on the ground, two meters away from the TV.

5.2   Task and Stimulus

Participants were asked to step on each of the position from a1–a7, with their body position always facing towards the walking direction. At each position, participant glanced over the screen, which showed a 9*16 grid, with each grid containing two random capital letters. A Python program was used to ensure no letters were repeated within a grid. We asked participants to quickly read out the first letter pair they saw at first glance. Then we updated a new grid as the participant walked to next position.

5.3   Condition

The 9 * 16 grid of random letters took up full of the screen. If the participant did not speak out the combination in 2 s, the stimulus would change into a new 9 * 16 grid. For this experiment, each participant walked in front of the screen for four rounds, including two rounds of rotating screens, and two rounds of the static screen. For each round, the participant walked around each position two times: once forward, and once backward. In total, 28 different grids were used across the participants. Each grid provided 144 possible locations in the coordinate.

5.4   Result

Visual Focus Areas. Contrary to the static screen, the rotating screen provides a stable and concentrated visual focus area for passersby. Figure 6 shows the

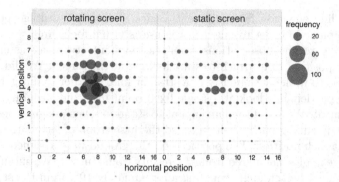

Fig. 6. The result shows that participants' line of vision was more focused on the rotating screen, compared with the static screen.

viewpoints of participants for each screen type while passing the display. The scatter diagram is drawn according to the coordinates of the letter pair first identified by the participant and the frequency at which each point was identified.

The diagram of the rotating screen (Fig. 7 shows that participants' line of vision was more focused on the rotating screen, compared with the static screen. This is shown by the size of the circular bubbles, which indicate the frequency at which participants looked at a particular point. In contrast, the view points on the static screen were more evenly distributed across the screen's coordinate-space, implying participants' visual focus shifts as they walk pass the screen.

The Trend of Visual Focus Area While Walking. It is also surprising that for static screens, the visual focus can change with the direction of motion. Figure 8 shows that as participants passed by the test area from right to left, the center of the corresponding chart also shifts from right to left. Similarly, comparing this chart to the rotating screen diagram, it is easy to find that the visual focus area of the static screen changes as the user moves, while the rotating screen stabilizes in a central area.

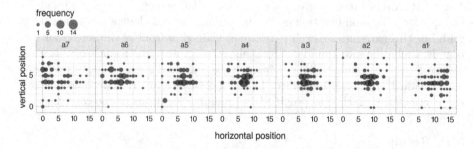

Fig. 7. The result shows that as participants passed by the test area from right to left, the center of the corresponding chart also shifts from right to left.

5.5   Discussion

Screen content, such as layout, color, font size, and etc., often has an impact on the user's visual focus area. To control for this variable and reduce the influence of screen content on participants' line of vision, we opted for black and white letter pairs placed at fixed blocks for the screen content in these experiments. Meanwhile, the size of the screen also limits the user's field of view. Accordingly, a larger display may have been more suitable for this study.

Our experiment shows that users' visual focus area changes significantly when passing by different types of screens. For future studies, we will consider designing a dynamic layout for on-screen content, which automatically adapts to a passerby's position.

Moreover, this experiment only used a rotating screen and a static screen as the objects of measurement. In future studies, it is possible to measure user's visual focus area on other types of screens, including movable screen, through a similar experimental setup and implementation.

6   FIELD STUDY: Attractiveness of Display

A rotating screen is designed to attract the attention of passersby and enable them to pay attention to content on the screen that they may not have otherwise noticed. The rotating screen was shown to be effective in improving both reading efficiency and visual focus area of passersby, according to the results of Study 1 and Study 2. However, Study 1 and Study 2 were conducted in a laboratory, which may not suitably represent a public environment.

Therefore, the purpose of this field study was to validate the effectiveness of a rotating display in a real-world environment, as well as the results of Study 1 and Study 2 by observing passersby reactions in a public space. To do this, the field study focused on the behavior of passersby and counted the number and proportion of passersby who paid attention to the screens. The experimenter would randomly choose a target passerby and adjust the screen's rotation manually to fit the participant's direction and speed.

6.1   Deployment

The rotating screen was installed in a well-frequented lobby of a university building. Its initial direction was oriented to the main walking path beside the building elevator. Passersby included students, faculty members, staff, and visitors of the university. A vertical TV was used because of content display and safety considerations: It can better accommodate the field of view of people of different heights, is more suitable for presenting movie posters, and people are less likely to accidentally bump into a vertical TV.

Fig. 8. Passersby look at the poster on a rotating screen.

6.2 Method

Our deployment was divided into two phases across two days. On Day 1, the screen-installation was set up in a position that could more easily be seen by passersby, who would had a clear line of vision to the screen without having to adjust their normal walking path. It was important to minimize the conspicuous of our installation to reduce the impact of passersby' attention being drawn by a change in their environment, rather than by the rotating screen. At the same time, we measured users' walking speed and recorded a suitable interactive range and angle for the rotating screen. When recording the flow of passersby, we selected the period of maximum human traffic, from 8: 00 am–10: 00 am and 11: 30 am–1: 30 pm, as the testing phase. On Day 2, the first testing phase was from, 8: 00 am–10: 00 am, during which the static screen was deployed. In the second period, from 11: 30 am–1: 30 pm, we deployed the rotating screen and observed passersby who walked into the interaction range randomly. Our results validated the results of Study 1 and Study 2.

6.3 Content

We chose to display commercial-free content that would be relevant to passersby. Given the experiment was conducted in the building of the art school, we chose to display movie posters. The screen presented 122 posters randomly at a rate of one poster every five seconds.

6.4 Data Collection

We collected videos from the three GoPro cameras and conducted continuous on-site observations, with two researchers on-site at all times. These researchers were at hand to oversee the safety of the experiment, and to conduct random interviews with participants.

6.5 Findings

Because this field study used a camera to count passersby, there is a risk of incompleteness in our statistics. Nevertheless, passersby who noticed the

Fig. 9. (a) The girl was exploring the technology. (b) Waving the arm and (c) Kicking leg to test the interaction. (d) Even detecting the edge of the screen.

screen accounted for 25.74% of the total number of passersby (130/505) during the static screen phase, and 48.46% during the phase of the rotating screen (205/423). These results verified our hypothesis: The directive display is relatively more effective in attracting the attention of passersby (Fig. 9).

Prior to this field study, a primary concern was whether the screen-installation would be able to influence passerby behavior significantly enough. For both types of screen, the content did not have an impact on passersby at a far distance, who did not stop or slow down. Passersby only read the screen content in some detail when they came close to the screen. During the static screen phase, most passersby focused on the content first, and then noticed that this was a new screen that had been installed in the space. One person stopped and tried to wave their arms and interact with the static screen.

For the rotating screen test, we observed two types of passersby based on their behavior. From our interviews, we learned that one type of passerby believed that the screen was rotating freely. Most passersby in this group were generally further from screen($>8\,$m); The second type, of whom most were at close distance($<4\,$m), recognized the screen was following them, even if the screen's movement was slightly delayed in response to their movements. Furthermore, some users attempted to interact with the rotating screen by waving their hands, kicking out their legs, and even touching the screen. If they attempted to interact with the screen, many users proceeded to further test the capabilities of the installation. For example, by moving around quickly, walking to the edges of the TV screen to explore maximum angle for the adaptive rotation. Groups of two people or more also walked in opposing directions to check which one of them the screen would track (Figure 10).

Fig. 10. Users further away from the screen do not pay much attention to the screen (blue area). Most Users close to the screen think that the screen is actively following them (orange area). (Color figure online)

7   Design Consideration

Compared with the static screen, the rotated screen includes a blind spot, which reduces the efficiency of information transmission. Therefore, the rotating screen may not be suitable for fast-moving or important information, and may be more suitable for leisure and entertainment information. In addition, this research only considers close interaction distances between passersby and displays. Furthermore, the range of motion of passersby was limited, as they were only observed from a close distance and at the same angle. It's possible that a combination of a rotating and static screen, which can be adapted to a wider set of user behaviors, would be a better way to implement a display passersby who haven't approached the interaction area.

Furthermore, the rotating screen we discussed only moves to directly face passersby in real-time. However, many more interaction motions for the display screen are possible. For example, the screen could mimic a "shy" interaction by hiding, turning away, and showing its back to users. Different interaction motions enable a wider variety of design application, like advertising, navigating in the public environment, or presenting private information to specific individuals. At the same time, multi-levelled information of content can be presented at one display.

8   Conclusion and Future Work

This paper presented a study on how a type of physically moving display, a rotating screen, can draw the attention of a single passerby at a close distance. Our work involved three experiments, in which we built a directive display used to track the visual focus of passersby as they approach the display. The experiments' results imply that a rotating screen can (1) improve reading efficiency, (2) help viewers develop a more concentrated visual focus than a static screen, and

(3) effectively attract passersby via rotating in real-time in response to passerby's movement. These findings can provide interaction designers and researchers with a reference for understanding the passerby-screen interaction relationship, which may help in designing content and displays that better attract user attention.

This research only pays attention to screen rotation, which is just one of various forms of physically moving displays. Future research can be extended to many other types of physical movement of displays, such as lateral, vertical, and back and forth movements, and even combinations of these. In addition to conducting research on physical screen movements, there is also potential to investigate content that moves on the screen, including investigating the design and layout of on-screen content that adapts to a passerby's shifting visual area of focus. In future studies, we will also continue to explore the interaction relationship between larger displays and users.

Acknowledgement. The authors would like to thank Junai Cai, Zichun Guo, Huining Qian and all volunteers for assistance.

References

1. Müller, J., et al.: Display blindness: the effect of expectations on attention towards digital signage. In: Tokuda, H., Beigl, M., Friday, A., Brush, A.J.B., Tobe, Y. (eds.) Pervasive 2009. LNCS, vol. 5538, pp. 1–8. Springer, Heidelberg (2009). https://doi.org/10.1007/978-3-642-01516-8_1
2. Dalton, N., Collins, E., Marshall, P.: Display blindness? Looking again at the visibility of situated displays using eye tracking, pp. 3889–3898 (2015)
3. Huang, E.M., Koster, A., Borchers, J.: Overcoming assumptions and uncovering practices: when does the public really look at public displays? In: Indulska, J., Patterson, D.J., Rodden, T., Ott, M. (eds.) Pervasive 2008. LNCS, vol. 5013, pp. 228–243. Springer, Heidelberg (2008). https://doi.org/10.1007/978-3-540-79576-6_14
4. Vogel, D., Balakrishnan, R.: Interactive public ambient displays: transitioning from implicit to explicit, public to personal, interaction with multiple users. In: ACM Symposium on User Interface Software & Technology. ACM (2004)
5. Michelis, D., Müller, J.: The audience funnel: observations of gesture based interaction with multiple large displays in a city center. Int. J. Hum.-Comput. Interact. **27**(6), 562–579 (2011)
6. Müller, J., Alt, F., Michelis, D., et al.: Requirements and design space for interactive public displays. In: International Conference on Multimedia, MM 2010. ACM (2010)
7. Rodriguez-Lizundia, E., Marcos, S., Zalama, E., et al.: A bellboy robot: study of the effects of robot behaviour on user engagement and comfort. Int. J. Hum.-Comput. Stud. **82**, 83–95 (2015)
8. Hall, E.T.: The Hidden Dimension. Leonardo (1966). 6(1)
9. Ballendat, T., Marquardt, N., Greenberg, S.: Proxemic interaction: designing for a proximity and orientation-aware environment. In: ACM International Conference on Interactive Tabletops and Surfaces, ITS 2010, Saarbrücken, Germany, 7–10 November 2010. ACM (2010)

10. Ojala, T., Kostakos, V., Kukka, H., et al.: Multipurpose interactive public displays in the wild: three years later. Computer **45**(5), 42–49 (2012)
11. Zhang, Y., Yang, C.J., Hudson, S.E., et al.: Wall++: room-scale interactive and context-aware sensing. In: Proceedings of the 2018 CHI Conference on Human Factors in Computing Systems, p. 273. ACM (2018)
12. Monastero, B., McGookin, D.K.: Traces: studying a public reactive floor-projection of walking trajectories to support social awareness. In: Proceedings of the 2018 CHI Conference on Human Factors in Computing Systems, p. 487. ACM (2018)
13. Petford, J., Nacenta, M.A., Gutwin, C.: Pointing all around you: selection performance of mouse and ray-cast pointing in full-coverage displays. In: Proceedings of the 2018 CHI Conference on Human Factors in Computing Systems, p. 533. ACM (2018)
14. Ten Koppel, M., Bailly, G., Müller, J., et al.: Chained displays: configurations of public displays can be used to influence actor-, audience-, and passer-by behavior. In: Proceedings of the SIGCHI Conference on Human Factors in Computing Systems, pp. 317–326. ACM (2012)
15. Kimura, N., Rekimoto, J.: ExtVision: augmentation of visual experiences with generation of context images for a peripheral vision using deep neural network. In: Proceedings of the 2018 CHI Conference on Human Factors in Computing Systems, p. 427. ACM (2018)
16. Schmidt, C., Müller, J., Bailly, G.: Screenfinity: extending the perception area of content on very large public displays. In: Proceedings of the SIGCHI Conference on Human Factors in Computing Systems, pp. 1719–1728. ACM (2013)
17. Ardito, C., Buono, P., Costabile, M.F., et al.: Interaction with large displays: a survey. ACM Comput. Surv. (CSUR) **47**(3), 46 (2015)
18. Ball, K.K., Beard, B.L., Roenker, D.L., et al.: Age and visual search: expanding the useful field of view. JOSA A **5**(12), 2210–2219 (1988)
19. Mayer, S., Lischke, L., Grønbæk, J.E., et al.: Pac-many: movement behavior when playing collaborative and competitive games on large displays. In: Proceedings of the 2018 CHI Conference on Human Factors in Computing Systems, p. 539. ACM (2018)
20. Dostal, J., Hinrichs, U., Kristensson, P.O., et al.: SpiderEyes: designing attention- and proximity-aware collaborative interfaces for wall-sized displays. In: Proceedings of the 19th International Conference on Intelligent User Interfaces, pp. 143–152. ACM (2014)
21. Alt, F., Schneegaß, S., Schmidt, A., et al.: How to evaluate public displays. In: Proceedings of the 2012 International Symposium on Pervasive Displays, p. 17. ACM (2012)
22. Müller, J., Walter, R., Bailly, G., et al.: Looking glass: a field study on noticing interactivity of a shop window. In: Proceedings of the SIGCHI Conference on Human Factors in Computing Systems, pp. 297–306. ACM (2012)
23. Kukka, H., Oja, H., Kostakos, V., et al.: What makes you click: exploring visual signals to entice interaction on public displays. In: Proceedings of the SIGCHI Conference on Human Factors in Computing Systems, pp. 1699–1708. ACM (2013)
24. Khan, A., Matejka, J., Fitzmaurice, G., et al.: Spotlight: directing users' attention on large displays. In: Proceedings of the SIGCHI Conference on Human Factors in Computing Systems, pp. 791–798. ACM (2005)
25. Kunze, K., Sanchez, S., Dingler, T., et al.: The augmented narrative: toward estimating reader engagement. In: Proceedings of the 6th Augmented Human International Conference, pp. 163–164. ACM (2015)

26. Alt, F., Kubitza, T., Bial, D., et al.: Digifieds: insights into deploying digital public notice areas in the wild. In: Proceedings of the 10th International Conference on Mobile and Ubiquitous Multimedia, pp. 165–174. ACM (2011)
27. Peltonen, P., Kurvinen, E., Salovaara, A., et al.: It's mine, don't touch! Interactions at a large multi-touch display in a city centre. In: Proceedings of the SIGCHI Conference on Human Factors in Computing Systems, pp. 1285–1294. ACM (2008)
28. Mäkelä, V., Sharma, S., Hakulinen, J., et al.: Challenges in public display deployments: a taxonomy of external factors. In: Proceedings of the 2017 CHI Conference on Human Factors in Computing Systems, pp. 3426–3475. ACM (2017)
29. Larson, K., van Dantzich, M., Czerwinski, M., et al.: Text in 3D: some legibility results. In: CHI 2000 Extended Abstracts on Human Factors in Computing Systems, pp. 145–146. ACM (2000)
30. Nacenta, M.A., Sakurai, S., Yamaguchi, T., et al.: E-conic: a perspective-aware interface for multi-display environments. In: Proceedings of the 20th Annual ACM Symposium on User Interface Software and Technology, pp. 279–288. ACM (2007)

Visual Symbol Attention and Cross-Cultural Communication

A Case Study of Catering Commercial Graphic Advertising

Huang Zhang[1(✉)] and Li Zhang[2]

[1] School of Art and Design, Wuhan University of Technology,
No.123 Luoshi Rd, Hongshan District, Wuhan 430070, China
664782154@qq.com
[2] Department of Art and Design, Purdue University,
552 W Wood St, West Lafayette, IN 47907, USA
Lzhang3@purdue.edu

Abstract. Taking the catering commercial graphic advertisement as the experimental material, this paper focuses on the Chinese and American subjects' attention to the graphic, color, composition, text and those visual symbols' categories in the advertisement. This study starts from the theory of cultural cognition and takes cultural cognitive differences as the premise. To explore the different ways in which the eastern and western communities deal with the visual information in commercial advertisements. Based on the principles of visual design in commercial advertising, this paper deconstructs the visual symbols in graphic advertising design and compares them one by one, so as to draw the difference of attention to visual symbols between Chinese and American subjects in commercial graphic advertising design. Finally, the evaluation results and relative weight values of various visual elements are obtained to form the priority results of attention of commercial graphic advertising design elements, so as to provide technical guidance for multinational enterprises and designers to design commercial advertisements more in line with consumer needs. The results of this experiment can be used for reference and inspiration in the application of the visual theory of cross-cultural cognition in the design of transnational advertisements.

Keywords: Visual symbol attention · Cross-cultural · Fussy-AHP ·
Multi criteria decision analysis · Graphic advertising design

1 Introduction

Now, we are live in a world of cross-cultural context. People who grow up with different cultural backgrounds may process and understand the same information very differently. Based on this phenomenon, starting from the processing mode of visual information in cross-cultural cognition, this paper takes catering commercial graphic advertisements as experimental materials to explore the similarities and differences

© Springer Nature Switzerland AG 2019
P.-L. P. Rau (Ed.): HCII 2019, LNCS 11576, pp. 440–457, 2019.
https://doi.org/10.1007/978-3-030-22577-3_32

between Chinese and Americans in the processing mode of visual information in graphic advertisements.

This study collected more than one hundred global cases of catering commercial advertising design, about 40 target users (20 subjects of American and 20 subjects of China) have carried on the questionnaire survey. Using Fussy-AHP (Analytic Hierarchy Process) to analyze the commercial ads visual symbol, to help multinational companies to find attention of visual symbols of commercials in different ethnic groups and design the optimal ads design solution.

2 Literature Review

2.1 Cross-Cultural Cognition and Communication Theory

At present, many scholars have carried out various experiments and analysis on the cross-cultural cognitive differences of visual patterns, especially the analysis of the differences between the East and the West. As McQuail's words, "The model that applies to all purposes and all levels of analysis is undoubtedly non-existent." To "select the right model for your own purposes [1]." Therefore, it is necessary to explore the differences in cognitive patterns among users of different ethnic groups in the East and West. However, the differences in cognitive tendencies between these two ethnic groups are also reflected in design and related fields. Gu [2], from the perspective of the transformation of cross-cultural cognition, through the methods of color theory and color psychology, objectively recognizes the color and image of "Sissi Yellow", then he made a brief analysis of the cross-cultural cognitive transformation of this color. Xu [3] analyzed the differences in cognitive orientation between Chinese and Western passengers when watching the subway guidance system through eye movement experiments and improved the general design level of the subway guidance system. Finally, it is concluded that Westerners are analytical cognitive tendencies. They pay more attention to the guidance information in the guidance environment. The Chinese are comprehensive cognitive orientations, pay more attention to background information, and encode the environment as a whole, which the guide information and background information are analyzed together. Lu [4] compared the aesthetic differences between Chinese and German users in car styling from a cross-cultural perspective. The conclusion is that Chinese users are moving horizontally in the process of observing the front face of the car. However, the eye movement trajectory of German users is more focused on the central area of the front face of the car. Nisbett [5] compared the influence of cognitive disparity on the expression of Eastern and Western paintings and quantified the horizontal and horizon positions in the paintings into statistical data and found that the horizon and horizontal lines in East Asian paintings were significantly higher. He supposed the difference in cognitive tendencies is reflected in the connotation and composition of painting space, and the aesthetic of the communication is also different. In addition, many scholars have also studied the cross-cultural differences in visual patterns in web design [6–11], Fan [12] analyzed the defects of the Xi'an Municipal Government's English website in constructing the city image from the perspective of cross-cultural communication, and started from the website image information and interaction, analyzed the problem and proposed a feasible solution. Juric [13] identified general questions about cross-cultural web design by defining a list of design elements related to the website and investigating culturally specific design elements through examples of Korean and UK web environments. The survey found that Korean websites use more icon/image sources on their websites than British websites, and the typical Korean website's main layout is "horizontal place-ment" (i.e. using the bottom scroll bar), while a typical UK website, more inclined to "vertical orientation" (i.e. using side scroll bars). There are also some theoretical models for cross-cultural cognitive differences. On the basis of demand and cross-cultural research, Zhang [14] conducted tests and interviews on Chinese users based on two service cases in Milan and Wuxi, and analyzed relevant indicators such as eval-uation indicators, influence dimensions, and willingness to participate. It can help designers understand the characteristics of cultural cognition of Chinese user groups and the differences between them and Western users. And put forward corresponding suggestions: that is, to fully understand the local background and understanding of users, pay attention to the evaluation of the benefits of the program, and combine the feasibility of implementation, ease of operation and the dissemination of relevant information.

However, these studies cannot indicate how cultural differences affect commercial graphic advertising design. Therefore, this study conducts an experimental analysis of the cognitive differences in visual symbols that appear in commercial advertising design to help multinational companies find more suitable commercial advertising design concerns.

2.2 Commercial Advertising Design and Cross-Cultural Marketing

The ever-increasing business internationalization and globalization are increasingly dependent on the cross-cultural, transnational cognitive, and perceived differences [15]. More and more marketers have begun to invest more manpower, financial resources, and material resources to try to understand the differences between markets and con-sumers around the world. Further, one of the most important issues in international business is how the implementation of international standards and localization adoption depends on the perceptions and preferences of consumers around the world [16]. Cross-cultural marketing is usually defined as when the actual consumer's own culture is different from the marketer's culture, including language, religion, beliefs, habits, etc., marketers need to adopt strategic marketing advertising methods [17]. Therefore, if marketers want to succeed in cross-cultural advertising, they need to find or create marketing strategies that match the perceptions of different cultural consumers. So, studying the cultural differences in the international market is undoubtedly very important. From the perspective of cross-cultural marketing advertising, commercial graphic advertising design is the most common and effective marketing tool.

The paper finds the commercial advertisement design in the specific international market as the research material. Based on the cognitive differences of the visual model, this paper proposes experimental methods to try to find the cross-cultural differences that may exist in the cognitive processing of such information.

3 Research Method

3.1 Analytic Hierarchy Process (AHP)

AHP was formally proposed by Professor Thomas L. Saaty of the University of Pittsburgh in 1971. Analytic hierarchy process is a simple, convenient, practical, and multi-criteria approach. It is a systematic and hierarchical analysis method combining qualitative and quantitative [18, 19]. It can simplify complex problems into system-level problems and then compare the importance of each element. Due to the flexibility and simplicity of its methods, it is rapidly used in various fields of social economy, including: economic management, resource allocation, optimal program decision-making, urban planning, system design, scientific research evaluation and other issues. In the field of design, researchers also use AHP's approach to analyze a large number of design decision problems. Calantone illustrates the use of the Analytic Hierarchy Process (AHP) as a decision support model to aid managers in selecting new product ideas to pursue. The need for flexible models that are highly customized to each firm's challenges (such as AHP) to support the screening decision and to generate knowledge that will be used as input for a firm's expert support system is emphasized [20]. Gülfem Işıklar applies AHP to evaluate the preference order of selected users of mobile phones, thus establishing the relative weight of evaluation criteria [21].

The core idea of the analytic hierarchy process is to serialize and quantify the problems to be solved. When the method is used to study the visual symbol attention of commercial advertisements, it is first necessary to determine the factors affecting the visual symbols of commercial advertisements and layer the design factors according to certain criteria. The basic process of operation is as follows:

(1) Establish a hierarchical structure model.
(2) Establish a judgment matrix to establish the priority between elements by one-to-one comparison those elements.
(3) Calculate the weight value and pass the consistency test (the consistency test passes are the valid reference value).
(4) Calculate the comprehensive weight value and do the comprehensive weight consistency test. After passing, the decision can be made according to the result displayed by the weight vector.

3.2 Fussy Analytic Hierarchy Process (FAHP)

AHP performs quantitative analysis on the basis of qualitative analysis and combines the two to propose a systematic analysis method. However, the analytic hierarchy process is also susceptible to extreme values, and the establishment of hierarchical relationships tends to be subjective. Participants may not understand the issues/elements involved in all rating factors. The fuzzy comprehensive evaluation method is based on the principle of fuzzy mathematics and is used to study mathematical methods with ambiguity. When people make decisions, they often make fuzzy judgment choices because of the ambiguity of the problem. Therefore, scholars proposed the Fuzzy Analytic Hierarchy Process (FAHP) based on the AHP method, which is a multi-criteria decision-making method that combines qualitative and quantitative analysis [22]. This study uses fuzzy analytic hierarchy process to evaluate the opinions of expert groups and interviewees, effectively solving the problem of inaccuracy in decision-making. Researchers also combined AHP with fuzzy number theory in early design concept assessments to address the ambiguity and subjectivity of expert assessments [23]. Yong use a new TOPSIS approach for selecting plant location under linguistic environments is presented, where the ratings of various alternative locations under various criteria, and the weights of various criteria are assessed in linguistic terms represented by fuzzy numbers [24]. In Geng's paper, a new integrated design concept evaluation approach based on vague sets is presented [25]. By integrating the strength of rough sets in handling vagueness and the merit of grey relation analysis in modeling multi-criteria decision-making, Zhai applied a rough number which enabled grey relation analysis (called rough-grey analysis) is proposed to evaluate design concepts [26]. In order to determinate the criteria weight in a fashion design scheme evaluation system, Lin use fuzzy analytic hierarchy process (FAHP) to find the criteria weight [27]. Shi has also applied the FAHP method to the innovative design of elderly walkers [28]. There are other scholars who have used the FAHP method extensively in the design and product design of the elderly [29, 30].

4 Case Study

4.1 Evaluation Process of Visual Symbol Attention in Catering Commercial Graphic Advertising Design Based on FAHP Method

(1) Collect samples and obtain the design elements and characteristics of commercial graphic ads. In this case, a total of 150 graphic image data were collected, and the basic principles of advertising design were taken as the basic considerations.

(2) Establish an indicator hierarchy, and the target layer is the visual symbol attention for commercial graphic ads. Through the group research method, the factor layer is finally divided into four design elements: graphics, color, composition, and text. The category layer refines each design element based on the collected graphic design sample.

(3) Select representative samples according to the classification of design elements and make a questionnaire for the attention of visual symbols in graphic advertising design.

(4) According to the results of the questionnaire, establish a judgment model of the visual symbol attention degree of the graphic advertisement design, then test and analyze the results.

(5) Calculate the relative weights, and finally draw conclusions, obtain the different weight values of each visual element of the commercial graphic ads design of the Chinese and American subjects, and give the designers the priority to find the visual elements of the commercial graphic ads design (Fig. 1).

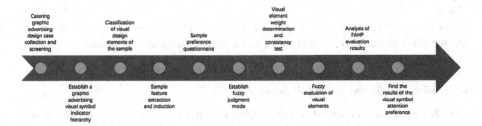

Fig. 1. Flow chart of visual elements of catering commercial graphic ads design.

4.2 Analysis of Visual Symbol Affecting Commercial Advertising Design

Graphic design refers to the creative combination of graphic images, texts, colors, layouts, etc. in a two-dimensional space to create a visual design activity that conveys ideas or messages. Graphic design has been widely used in the advertising industry. Through graphic design, people can intuitively accept the information to be transmitted by products, thus achieving the purpose of visual marketing and promotion. A good graphic advertising design depends on a large extent on the rational application of the aesthetic symbols in the visual image. The visual symbols may mean differently in the international markets.

Graphics

As the earliest tool for human beings to use for information transmission and emotional communication, graphics brought unique imagination, creativity and surreal free structure in displaying unique glamour in the visual image of advertising. Every graphic design work is inseparable from the use of graphics.

From the collection of advertisements, the elements of the graphics are reflected in the following aspects:

(1) *Photography*. Photography is the most direct way to capture the real world. In commercial graphic advertising, designers tend to use the product's photographic images directly as materials to help consumers quickly and intuitively understand the product.

(2) *Photography manipulation*. It is through the element addition, combination, reconstruction, etc. of the photographic picture, we call this mode "photography manipulation", using PS and other digital image technology to achieve the details of the photographic picture. Such as contoured images, image element replacement, and so on.

(3) *Artistic performance*. A large number of artistic expression techniques appear in more and more print advertisements. The most common methods are the direct display of painting art and the translation of artistic style.

(4) *Creative graphics*. The characteristics of this type of graphics are reflected in the designer's use of stimulating, agitating graphics to enhance the audience's association.

(5) *Information visualization graphics*. Such graphics tend to visualize the content of the product to the audience and have gained the realism of the product.

Color

Color is a subordinate symbol in a complete design system, which is directly related to the meaning of the work. The effect of color visual effects in commercial graphic ads can convey the theme of advertising and mobilize people's emotions, so its role is very important. Then, the color application reflected in the design of commercial graphic advertising is reflected in the following ways:

(1) *The harmonious color of the theme.* This kind of advertising design usually adopts some soft color matching methods. The main way is to extract the theme color of the advertising object and use the adjacent colors related to the theme to create a harmonious atmosphere.

(2) *Simple tones based on black, white and gray.* Designers began to add a variety of colors in the specific poster design process to capture the audience's eye, but sometimes it will cause the opposite effect, and affecting the reading and making it looks very messy. Therefore, more and more product advertisements have a simple color style, especially concentrated in the commercial works of Japan and South Korea, which black and white or gray as a means of color expression.

(3) *Strong contrasting colors.* Color psychology research shows that the color of strong visual expression can not only bring different feelings to the audience, but also influence the public emotions and leave a deep impression on the audience. Such works often break the theme color, use strong color contrast, and even use abnormal color effects to achieve a strong visual impact.

(4) *Warm tones.* In the graphic advertisement of the catering category, warm colors are often used in the design, because warm colors are more likely to cause appetite.

(5) *Cool tones.* In many advertising works, more and more cool colors have appeared which can bring consumers a calm feeling.

Composition

Reasonable use of layout design can achieve the purpose of transmitting advertising information and integrating advertising elements, which can effectively improve the visual art function of graphic ads and enhance the dissemination effect of graphic ads.

(1) *Center-style composition.* It is the most common form of composition in commercial graphic advertising. It uses the spotlight expression to highlight the main object and enlarge the contrast between the main body and the background.

(2) *Enclosing composition.*

(3) *Divergent composition.*

(4) *Diagonal composition.* The diagonal motion line is used to widen the sense of space and enhance the dynamics of the picture while enhancing the expressive power of the subject. This way of composing is also a common way in many advertising works.

Text

The text in graphic advertising design is one of the essential elements to convey information, which can help consumers get information quickly. According to the survey, in the current mainstream advertising design works, there are four main ways of expressing characters: *(1) text graphics (2) handwritten fonts (3) fonts collection (4) fonts collection manipulation.*

4.3 Catering Commercial Graphic Advertising Visual Symbol Attention Degree FAHP Model Construction and Establishment of Weight

(1) Establish an Indicator Hierarchy

The hierarchical structure model constructed according to the principle of graphic advertisement design is shown in Fig. 2. The first layer is the target layer P, which is the visual symbol attention of the catering graphic advertisement; the second layer is the factor layer, which is the four factors that affect the design of the catering graphic advertisement. The factors A–D are: graphics, color, composition, text; the third layer is the category layer, which is divided into A1–A5, B1–B5, C1–C4, D1–D4, the specific representation of each visual factor. The specific category is shown in Fig. 3. Among them, there are strong and weak differences in the influence of the category layer on the factor layer, and the difference between the strong and the weak is reflected by the questionnaire results.

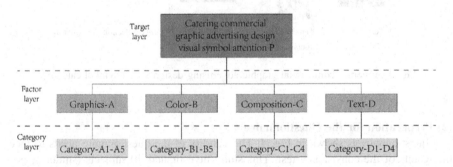

Fig. 2. Catering commercial graphic advertising design visual symbol attention degree hierarchy model diagram

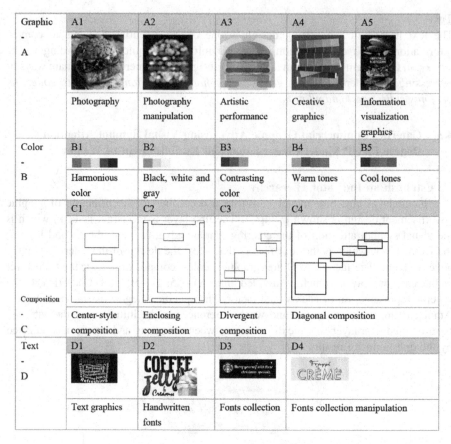

Graphic - A	A1	A2	A3	A4	A5
	Photography	Photography manipulation	Artistic performance	Creative graphics	Information visualization graphics
Color - B	B1	B2	B3	B4	B5
	Harmonious color	Black, white and gray	Contrasting color	Warm tones	Cool tones
Composition - C	C1	C2	C3	C4	
	Center-style composition	Enclosing composition	Divergent composition	Diagonal composition	
Text - D	D1	D2	D3	D4	
	Text graphics	Handwritten fonts	Fonts collection	Fonts collection manipulation	

Fig. 3. Catering commercial graphic advertising design visual symbol category

(2) Preparation for the Questionnaire

The questionnaire is shown in Fig. 4. The validity of the questionnaire needs to meet the results of the consistency test. This study investigated 40 subjects (students, professors, and design users) involved in commercial graphic design. Participants included 10 experts (5 Chinese and 5 Americans), 20 advertising design students (10 Chinese and 10 Americans), and 10 mass consumers (5 Chinese and 5 Americans).

Questionnaire content:

To understand the scoring items you value when reading commercial graphic ads, consider the relationship between the various ratings.

Which one is more important when considering the visual symbols of catering commercial graphic design?

Please compare them one by one, check the relationship between the two (1-9):

1: indicates that the two are equally important;

9: indicates the closer side, the factor is more important

Factor 1	relatively important						equally important						relatively important				Factor 2
	9	8	7	6	5	4	3	2	1	2	3	4	5	6	7	8	9	
Graphic							√											Color
			√															Composition
					√													Text
Color							√											Composition
						√												Text
Composition													√					Text

Category A-Graphic

Category1	relatively important						equally important						relatively important				Category 2
	9	8	7	6	5	4	3	2	1	2	3	4	5	6	7	8	9	
Photography			√															Photography manipulation
	9	8	7	6	5	4	3	2	1	2	3	4	5	6	7	8	9	

Fig. 4. Catering commercial graphic advertising design visual symbol attention degree questionnaire

(3) Construct a Fuzzy Judgment Matrix

The AHP method does not consider the ambiguity of people in making judgments when constructing the judgment matrix. Therefore, many scholars have proposed an analytical method called fuzzy AHP, which uses fuzzy numbers instead of the exact numbers in the AHP structural model to improve the scientificity of evaluation. The fuzzy numbers in the FAHP of this paper adopt the triangular fuzzy numbers, and the precise numbers are processed by the triangular fuzzy numbers, and finally the quantitative results are obtained. The 1–9 scale is used to indicate the degree of importance between indicators. The fuzzy quantized values are shown in Table 1:

Table 1. Semantic variables used in FAHP

Scale level	Semantic value	Fuzzy number
1	Equal important	$\tilde{1} = (1, 1, 2)$
3	Slightly important	$\tilde{3} = (2, 3, 4)$
5	Important	$\tilde{5} = (4, 5, 6)$
7	Very important	$\tilde{7} = (6, 7, 8)$
9	Extremely important	$\tilde{9} = (8, 9, 9)$
2,4,6,8	Intermediate value inserted between two continuous dimensions	$\tilde{2} = (1, 2, 3)$, $\tilde{4} = (3, 4, 5)$, $\tilde{6} = (5, 6, 7)$, $\tilde{8} = (7, 8, 9)$
1/3,1/5, 1/7,1/9	The ratio of the importance of elements i to j is aij, then the ratio of the importance of elements i to j aij = 1/aji	$\widetilde{1/3} = (1/4, 1/3, 1/2)$ $\widetilde{1/5} = (1/6, 1/5, 1/4)$ $\widetilde{1/7} = (1/8, 1/7, 1/6)$ $\widetilde{1/9} = (1/9, 1/9, 1/8)$

According to the hierarchical structure of the visual element attention degree index of the graphic advertisement design, the following triangular fuzzy number reciprocal judgment matrix is established by taking a group of questionnaires as an example:

$$\tilde{P} = \begin{bmatrix} \tilde{1} & \widetilde{1/3} & \tilde{3} & \tilde{2} \\ \tilde{3} & \tilde{1} & \tilde{4} & \tilde{3} \\ \widetilde{1/3} & \widetilde{1/4} & \tilde{1} & \widetilde{1/2} \\ \widetilde{1/2} & \widetilde{1/3} & \tilde{2} & \tilde{1} \end{bmatrix} \qquad \tilde{A} = \begin{bmatrix} \tilde{1} & \tilde{4} & \tilde{3} & \widetilde{1/2} & \widetilde{1/3} \\ \widetilde{1/4} & \tilde{1} & \tilde{3} & \widetilde{1/6} & \widetilde{1/2} \\ \widetilde{1/3} & \tilde{3} & \tilde{1} & \widetilde{1/4} & \widetilde{1/2} \\ \tilde{2} & \tilde{6} & \tilde{4} & \tilde{1} & \tilde{3} \\ \tilde{3} & \tilde{2} & \tilde{2} & \widetilde{1/3} & \tilde{1} \end{bmatrix}$$

$$\tilde{B} = \begin{bmatrix} \tilde{1} & \tilde{4} & \tilde{3} & \widetilde{1/2} & \tilde{2} \\ \widetilde{1/4} & \tilde{1} & \widetilde{1/2} & \widetilde{1/6} & \widetilde{1/2} \\ \widetilde{1/3} & \tilde{2} & \tilde{1} & \widetilde{1/5} & \widetilde{1/2} \\ \tilde{2} & \tilde{6} & \tilde{5} & \tilde{1} & \tilde{3} \\ \widetilde{1/2} & \tilde{3} & \tilde{2} & \widetilde{1/3} & \tilde{1} \end{bmatrix} \qquad \tilde{C} = \begin{bmatrix} \tilde{1} & \widetilde{1/2} & \tilde{2} & \tilde{4} \\ \tilde{2} & \tilde{1} & \tilde{3} & \tilde{4} \\ \widetilde{1/2} & \widetilde{1/3} & \tilde{1} & \tilde{2} \\ \widetilde{1/4} & \widetilde{1/4} & \widetilde{1/2} & \tilde{1} \end{bmatrix}$$

$$\tilde{D} = \begin{bmatrix} \tilde{1} & \widetilde{1/5} & \widetilde{1/3} & \widetilde{1/4} \\ \tilde{5} & \tilde{1} & \tilde{4} & \tilde{2} \\ \tilde{3} & \widetilde{1/4} & \tilde{1} & \widetilde{1/2} \\ \tilde{4} & \widetilde{1/2} & \tilde{2} & \tilde{1} \end{bmatrix}$$

(4) Calculate Feature Vector and Consistency Test

(1) *Calculate the comprehensive weight value of the evaluation element*
①Calculate the vector $\widetilde{W_\iota}$, the fuzzy weight of each column i at $\tilde{R}$

$$\tilde{Z_\iota} = (\widetilde{a_{\iota 1}} \otimes \widetilde{a_{\iota 2}} \otimes \ldots \otimes \widetilde{a_{1n}})^{1/n}, \; \forall i = 1, 2, \cdots, n$$

$$\widetilde{W_\iota} = \tilde{Z_\iota} \otimes (\widetilde{Z_1} \oplus \widetilde{Z_2} \oplus \ldots \oplus \widetilde{Z_n})^{-1}, \; \forall i = 1, 2, \cdots, n$$

②Calculating fuzzy values $\widetilde{W_\iota}$

$$\widehat{W_i} = \text{Defuzzy}(\widetilde{W_\iota})$$

③Calculate the relative weight W_i and perform normalization calculation.

$$W_i = \frac{\widehat{W_\iota}}{\sum_{i=1}^{n} \widehat{W_\iota}} \tag{1}$$

(2) *Consistency test*

In order to ensure the scientificity of the quantitative results, the final weight result needs to be tested for rationality, that is, the consistency test of the fuzzy judgment matrix.

Calculate the consistency index CI (consistency index):

$$CI = \lambda \text{max} - n/(n-1)$$

The consistency ratio CR (consistency ratio) is used as a criterion for the degree of consistency:

$$CR = CI/RI(\text{random index})$$

If CR < 0.1, the judgment matrix is reasonable, and vice versa, the judgment matrix needs to be adjusted appropriately. After calculation, the judgment matrix has consistency and the weight number is reasonable.

4.4   Catering Commercial Graphic Advertising Visual Symbol Attention Degree FAHP Evaluation Results

The weights of various visual factors can be obtained by analyzing the data results of FAHP, and the following results are obtained from the experimental data (Table 2):

Table 2. Catering commercial graphic advertising design visual symbol attention degree values

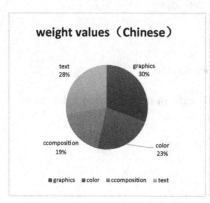 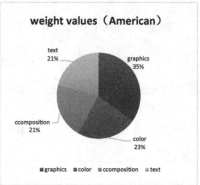

We divided the data into two parts: the test results of Chinese subjects and the test results of American subjects. From the chart, among the four visual symbols that affect commercial ads design, graphics are the most critical factor affecting the effectiveness of advertising, both for Chinese and American subjects. In Chinese subjects' view, words are more important than color, while American subjects think color is more important. And both Chinese and American participants believe that composition is the least important factor.

In addition, the weight values of the visual element categories obtained according to the FAHP method are as follows (Table 3):

According to the chart, among the graphical factors, Chinese subjects are most concerned with photography (0.34), while American subjects are most concerned with creative graphics (0.35). In the view of Chinese participants, for the graphic factors in commercial advertising, their priority is: photography (0.34), information visualization graphics (0.24), creative graphics (0.23), artistic performance (0.1), photography manipulation (0.09). In the view of American subjects, their priorities are: creative graphics (0.35), photography (0.24), information visualization (0.17), artistic expression (0.13), photography manipulation (0.12).

Table 3. Weight values of the visual element categories

Among the color factors, Chinese subjects tend to choose warm colors (0.37) as the main color of commercial graphic advertising, while Americans prefer harmonious color. The second factor category is harmonious color (0.35). For the five factors of color, Chinese and American subjects have different attention order. For Chinese, the order is warm color, harmonious color, black white and gray, contrasting color, and cool color. For American, the order is harmonious color, warm color, cool color, black white and gray, and contrasting color.

For composition factors. Chinese subjects prefer to choose diagonal composition (0.36), followed by central composition (0.25) and divergent composition (0.2) and finally enclosing composition (0.19). However, subjects in the United States are most concerned with central composition (0.39), followed by enclosing composition (0.27), divergent composition (0.2), and diagonal composition (0.15).

Chinese and American subjects almost have a consistent attention when choosing text factors. The prioritization of the text factor of Chinese is: handwritten fonts, fonts collection manipulation, fonts collection, text graphics. The order of American is handwritten fonts, fonts collection manipulation, text graphics, fonts collection.

Results. According to FAHP's result, we can get the relative weight of each visual symbols and the attention degree order of each visual element. (Tables 4 and 5):

Table 4. Relative weight and attention order of catering commercial graphic ads' each symbol (Chinese)

Visual symbol	Weight	Sub-category	Weight	Relative weight	Attention order
Graphic	0.30	Photography	0.34	0.102	2
		Photography manipulation	0.09	0.027	15
		Artistic performance	0.1	0.03	14
		Creative graphics	0.23	0.069	6
		Information visualization graphics	0.24	0.072	5
Color	0.23	Harmonious color	0.25	0.058	8
		Black, white and gray	0.21	0.048	9
		Contrasting color	0.1	0.023	16
		Warm color	0.37	0.085	4
		Cool color	0.08	0.018	18
Composition	0.19	Center-style composition	0.25	0.048	9
		Enclosing composition	0.19	0.036	12
		Divergent composition	0.2	0.038	11
		Diagonal composition	0.36	0.068	7
Text	0.28	Text graphics	0.08	0.022	17
		Handwritten fonts	0.45	0.126	1
		Fonts collection	0.13	0.036	12
		Fonts collection manipulation	0.34	0.095	3

Table 5. Relative weight and attention order of catering commercial graphic ads' each symbol (American)

Visual symbol	Weight	Sub-category	Weight	Relative weight	Attention order
Graphic	0.35	Photography	0.24	0.084	2
		Photography manipulation	0.12	0.042	11
		Artistic performance	0.13	0.045	10
		Creative graphics	0.35	0.123	1
		Information visualization graphics	0.17	0.060	7
Color	0.23	Harmonious color	0.35	0.081	5
		Black, white and gray	0.13	0.030	17
		Contrasting color	0.07	0.016	18
		Warm color	0.28	0.064	6
		Cool color	0.17	0.039	15
Composition	0.21	Center-style composition	0.39	0.082	3
		Enclosing composition	0.27	0.057	8
		Divergent composition	0.2	0.042	11
		Diagonal composition	0.15	0.032	16
Text	0.21	Text graphics	0.2	0.042	11
		Handwritten fonts	0.39	0.082	3
		Fonts collection	0.19	0.040	14
		Fonts collection manipulation	0.22	0.046	9

5 Conclusion

First of all, with the Fussy analytic hierarchy process, the visual symbols of commercial graphic design are taken as object in this paper. We combine the factors and fussy analysis which can provide designer a clear direction to meet consumers' needs. In addition, these data are quantified, making perceptual factors a quantitative result, connecting designers and consumers closely. We can also clearly see how we prioritize our attention to the visual elements that appear in commercial ads.

Second, this paper is based on cross-cultural research. By analyzing the weight values of each data, we can clearly compare the differences in the attention of Chinese and American subjects to visual symbols.

For Chinese subjects, they are more concerned with the photographic that appear in the advertisements. While American subjects are more concerned with creative graphics. These two results can also reflect that China pays more attention to image thinking, while Americans pay more attention to abstract thinking. In addition, this result more effectively guides the designer's design, and allows multinational companies to more accurately grasp the market of different nationalities when advertising.

References

1. McQuail, D.: Communication Models. Shanghai Translation Publishing House (1987). (Translated by Zhu, J.)
2. Gu, Y.: A Brief Analysis on Sissi Gelb and Cross-Culture Chromatic Cognitive Transformation. Shanghai Arts and Crafts (2012)
3. Xu, Z.: An empirical study on the cross-culture cognition of sign system based on eye tracking data. Packag. Eng. **39**, 117–122 (2018)
4. Lu, Z.: Comparative research on users' visual pattern recognition oriented to automotive styling features. Comput. Integr. Manuf. Syst. **21**(6), 1711–1718 (2015)
5. Nisbett, R.E., Masuda, T.: Culture and point of view. Proc. Nat. Acad. Sci. U.S.A. **100**(19), 11163–11170 (2003). (Author Abstract)
6. Calabrese, A., Capece, G.: Cross-cultural strategies for web design. In: Proceedings of World Academy of Science, Engineering and Technology, no. 71, p. 78 (2012)
7. Cyr, D., Trevor-Smith, H.: Localization of web design: an empirical comparison of German, Japanese, and United States web site characteristics. J. Am. Soc. Inform. Sci. Technol. **55**(13), 1199–1208 (2004)
8. Li, G., Li, Y., Zhang, J., Zhang, X.: A design feature and cross-culture based comparative evaluation of web maps. In: Proceedings of the Human Factors and Ergonomics Society Annual Meeting, vol. 61, no. 1, pp. 818–822 (2017)
9. Cyr, D., Bonanni, C., Bowes, J., Ilsever, J.: Beyond trust: website design preferences across cultures. J. Glob. Inf. Manag. **13**(4), 24–52 (2005)
10. Cyr, D.: Website design, trust and culture: An eight-country investigation. Electron. Commer. Res. Appl. **12**(6), 373–385 (2013)
11. Luna, D., Peracchio, L., Juan, A.: Cross-cultural and cognitive aspects of web site navigation. J. Acad. Mark. Sci. **30**(4), 397–410 (2002)
12. Fan, Z.: Urban image construction from the perspective of intercultural communication. New West. **33**, 39–40 (2018)
13. Juric, R., Kim, I., Kuljis, J.: Cross cultural web design: an experience of developing UK and Korean cultural markers. In: 2003 Proceedings of the 25th International Conference on Information Technology Interfaces. ITI 2003, pp. 309–313 (2003)
14. Zhang, L.: Cross-culture thinking in sustainable service design of social innovation: case comparison between Milan, IT and Wuxi, China, no. 03, pp. 66–70 (2015). (Creation and Design)
15. Weber, E., Hsee, C.: Culture and individual judgment and decision making. Appl. Psychol. **49**(1), 32–61 (2000)
16. Solberg, C.: Standardization or adaptation of the international marketing mix: the role of the local subsidiary/representative. J. Int. Mark. **8**(1), 78–98 (2000)
17. Tylor, E.B.: Primitive Culture: Researches into the Development of Mythology, Philosophy, Religion, Art, and Custom, 7th Edn. Brentano's, New York (1924/1874)
18. Thomas, L.S.: Fundamentals of Decision Making: The Analytic Hierarchy Process. RWS Publications, Pittsburgh (2006)
19. Belton, V., Gear, A.E.: On a shortcoming of Saaty's method of analytic hierarchies. Omega **13**, 143–144 (1983)
20. Calantone, R.J., Benedetto, A.D., Schmidt, J.B.: Using the analytic hierarchy process in new product screening. J. Prod. Innov. Manag. **16**, 65–76 (1999)
21. Işıklar, G., Büyüközkan, G.: Using a multi-criteria decision-making approach to evaluate mobile phone alternatives. Comput. Stan. Interfaces **29**(2), 265–274 (2007)

22. Bozbura, F.T., Beskese, A., Kahraman, C.: Prioritization of human capital measurement indicators using fuzzy AHP. Expert Syst. Appl. **32**(2), 1100–1112 (2007)
23. Wang, T.-C., Liang, L.-J., Ho, C.-Y.: Multi-criteria decision analysis by using fuzzy VIKOR. In: Proceedings of International Conference on Service Systems and Service Management, vol. 2, pp. 901–906 (2006)
24. Yong, D.: Plant location selection based on fuzzy TOPSIS. Int. J. Adv. Manuf. Technol. **28** (7), 839–844 (2006)
25. Geng, X., Chu, X., Zhang, Z.: A new integrated design concept evaluation approach based on vague sets. Expert Syst. Appl. **37**(9), 6629–6638 (2010)
26. Zhai, L.-Y., Khoo, L.-P., Zhong, Z.-W.: Design concept evaluation in product development using rough sets and grey relation analysis. Expert Syst. Appl. **36**(3), 7072–7079 (2009)
27. Lin, C.: Application of fuzzy Delphi method (FDM) and fuzzy analytic hierarchy process (FAHP) to criteria weights for fashion design scheme evaluation. Int. J. Clothing Sci. Technol. **25**(3), 171–183 (2013)
28. Shi, Y., Chen, W.: Innovation design of walking-aid robot for the elderly based on SET and FAHP. J. Mach. Des. **33**(10), 116–120 (2016)
29. Guo, Y., Yang, M.: Study on PSD model with FAHP method in the product design for older adults. In: Zhou, J., Salvendy, G. (eds.) ITAP 2017. LNCS, vol. 10297, pp. 223–232. Springer, Cham (2017). https://doi.org/10.1007/978-3-319-58530-7_16
30. Mastura, M.T., Sapuan, S.M., Mansor, M.R.: A framework for prioritizing customer requirements in product design: incorporation of FAHP with AHP. J. Mech. Eng. Sci. **9**, 1655–1670 (2015)

Comparative Analysis Comprehensibility of Healthcare Symbols Between USA and China

Chuanyu Zou[1(✉)] and Guangxin Wang[2]

[1] AQSIQ Key Laboratory of Human Factors and Ergonomics (CNIS),
Beijing, China
zouchy@cnis.gov.cn
[2] Department of Psychology, School of Humanities, Beijing Forestry University,
Beijing, China

Abstract. With the tide of globalization getting ever higher and stronger, the need grows rapidly to travel aboard in order to obtain better health care. Hospital normally consists of many clinical departments and medical technology departments. It is difficult for patients to obtain medical information. Graphical symbols are helpful for patients who have limited ability to understand medical environment. In this study, 10 USA healthcare symbols from SEGD and 10 Chinese healthcare symbols from GB/T 10001.6 were conducted comprehension test. It was found that Chinese participants' average comprehension level on Chinese healthcare symbols is higher than that of American healthcare symbols. The study showed that the understanding of words, characters, etc. is highly correlated with the cultural background. They are not applicable as main element of a public information symbol. Furthermore, the respondents with higher education level have less difficulty than those with lower education level in comprehending graphical symbols.

Keywords: Comprehensibility test · Public information guidance system · Wayfinding

1 Introduction

1.1 Background

Due to the gradual increase of patients, hospitals are in a period of continuous expansion. The medical technology and medical environment of many hospitals have gradually become complicated. All modern hospitals will encounter a cyclical process after are built. Hospitals will be constantly remodeling and expanding, and new buildings slowly integrated with the entire medical environment. They hope to resolve the contradiction between the advancement of medical technology and the original built environment.

Moreover, with the tide of globalization getting ever higher and stronger, the need grows rapidly to travel aboard in order to obtain better health care. As a special crowded public place, hospital normally consists of many clinical departments and

P.-L. P. Rau (Ed.): HCII 2019, LNCS 11576, pp. 458–467, 2019.
https://doi.org/10.1007/978-3-030-22577-3_33

medical technology departments, so the building structure is very complex. Under the pressure, anxiety and tension, it is difficult for patients to find their target floors or departments especially in a foreign hospital. A reasonable and effective wayfinding system becomes especially important.

Public information guidance system is an information system that guides people to locate in public places, understand their location, and be free to move. Its main role is the guiding role, that is, "guidance." The hospital public information guidance system is not only a supplementary explanation for the design content of the architectural environment, nor is it merely a symbolic semiotics and communication content in the visual communication discipline. It is an indispensable, irreplaceable important part in an environmental space. Belonging to a complicated marginal interdisciplinary subject, the public information guidance system contains the characteristics of the architectural engineering framework and the characteristics of artistic design in a complex environmental space. This requires strengthening the overall planning of the public information guidance system in the specific public environment of the hospital. The ultimate goal is to eliminate the barriers of language and culture through the effective guidance, and better promote the harmony between the public environment and people.

Among many wayfinding aids, graphical symbols are helpful for those patients who have limited ability to communicate in local language. Graphical symbol is a visually perceptible figure with a particular meaning used to transmit information independently of language.

1.2 Current Status of Relevant Standards

A national standard system on public information guidance systems has initially established in China. It consists of 26 standards in three categories, information element standard, guidance element design standard and system setting standard, namely GB/T 10001 "Public information graphic symbol" [1], GB/T 20501 "Public information guidance system– Design elements and requirements" [2], GB/T 15566 "Public information guidance system– Setting principles and requirements" [3]. Among them, GB/T 10001.6 "Public information graphical symbols for use on sign-Part 6: Symbols for medical treatment and health care", specified 43 medical and health-related standardized graphic symbols such as "emergency", "outpatient" and "pharmacy". According to the medical treatment process, GB/T 15566.6 "Public information guidance systems - Setting principles and requirements - Part 6: medical site" standardizes the setting of the guidance elements at the key nodes of the hospital's wayfinding system.

ISO/TC 145 has developed ISO 7001 "Public information graphic symbols" [4], which specifies 168 standardized graphical symbols. Among them, the medical related graphic symbols include "Hospital" and "Dentist". The organization has also developed ISO 28564 "Public information guidance systems" standard [5], giving design guidelines for guiding elements such as guiding signs and position signs.

1.3   Current Research Status

In October 2010, Society for Experiential Graphic Design (SEGD) proudly introduced a universal set of healthcare symbols, developed in collaboration with Hablamos Juntos [6], including 54 graphical symbols, e.g. "Inpatient", "Outpatient".

Yang et al. [7] conducted a satisfaction survey on 1060 outpatients and inpatients in the public information guidance system of the hospital. The study found that the patient was dissatisfied with the hospital's public information guidance system, the reasons related to the patients, the staff, the unreasonable design of the signs, the complexity of the content, and the lack of conspicuousness. The study suggests that the hospital's public information guidance system should be simple and easy to understand, and use graphical symbols to convey information directly, so that patients with low education background can understand it.

Hong et al. [8] conducted a study on the public information guidance system of hospitals in Taiwan. Taiwan's hospitals used a large number of simple and easy-to-understand images in the design of signs, which played a very good indication and conciseness. The systems design has the advantages of conciseness, standardization, artistry and humanity. The scientific concept, normative and people-oriented design concepts and measures of Taiwan hospital wayfinding systems are worth learning and promotion.

Lee et al. [9] tested universal healthcare symbols in the United States, South Korea, and Turkey to compare the comprehension of symbols cross-country and identify predictors of the correct comprehension.

2   Methods

2.1   Objects

ISO standardizes a series of standardized test methods for graphical symbols in ISO 9186, in which ISO 9186-1:2014 [10] specifies a method for testing graphical symbol comprehension, ISO 9186-2:2008 [11] specifies a graphical symbol for the perceptual quality test method. ISO 9186-3:2014 [12] specifies the symbol referent association test method. This paper uses the graphical symbol comprehension test method specified in ISO 9186-1:2014 [10], conducted comparative analysis on the comprehensibility of healthcare symbols between USA and China.

In this study, 10 USA healthcare symbols from SEGD were tested (Fig. 1 with black background), including Emergency, Pharmacy, Obstetrics and gynecology department, Pediatrics department, Pathology department, Operating room, Radiology department, Patient file room, Electrocardiographic room, Prevention and health protection department. 10 Chinese healthcare symbols (Fig. 1 with white background) with the same meaning were also tested. About 200 respondents were involved.

2.2   Participants

A paper questionnaire was used to conduct the comprehension test. 200 questionnaires were distributed and 164 valid questionnaires were collected, with a recovery rate of

Fig. 1. 20 healthcare symbols from SEGD and China

82%. Demographic variables are age, gender, and education, basic information of the participants is shown in Tables 1, 2 and 3. "Age" is divided into three categories, 15–30 years old, 31–50 years old, 51–70 years old (see Table 1). "Gender" is divided into two categories (see Table 2). Level of education is divided into four categories: primary or secondary, specialist or technical schools, universities (including reading), graduate students and above (see Table 3).

Table 1. Age distribution of participants

Age	Number	%
15–30	88	53.66
31–50	56	34.15
Above 50	20	15.19

Table 2. Gender distribution of participants

Gender	Number	%
Male	64	39.02
Female	100	60.98

2.3   Test

Test Questionnaire. The questionnaire includes comprehension tests for 10 USA healthcare graphic symbols and 10 Chinese medical graphic symbols. Each graphic symbol has one test page. Each page included a description of the expected location of

Table 3. Level of education distribution of participants

Category	Level of education	Number	%
1	Primary or secondary school	40	24.39
2	Specialist or technical school	30	18.29
3	University (including undergraduate)	86	52.44
4	Graduate and above	8	4.88

the graphical symbol, and the question to be respond, the graphical symbol itself and the actual application scenario of the graphical symbol to be tested. Each healthcare graphical symbol was set in 50 mm × 50 mm square. At the bottom of the entire page is the test respond area, marked with a rectangular frame. Participants were asked to fill their responds into the rectangular box below the graphical symbol (that is, the meaning of the graphical symbol). If participants did not know the responds, fill in the blank with "Don't know." In order to prevent the sequence effect, the whole set of questionnaires is not numbered and the order was set.

Test Procedure. The comprehensibility test of 20 healthcare graphical symbols was conducted in the Institute of Human Factors and Ergonomics lab in China National Institute of Standardization. After arriving at the laboratory, participants signed the informed consent and completed self-report page about their demographic information. Show an example page of a commonly known public information graphical symbol and confirm that all participants say that they understand their task. All participants were required to complete the test independently by reading and filling the test pages one by one.

Data Collection. All participants filled in the answers in the blank space below the graphic symbol. The scoring standards are shown in Table 4.

Table 4. Scoring standards

Category	Meaning
1a	Completely correct
1b	Approximate correct
2a	Wrong
2b	Wrong and opposite
3	Do not know
4	No response

Since the responses of the participants are all in text, first the answers with similar meanings should be classified, and then standardize the answers into relative categories. Take the first question as an example: fill in with "emergency", "emergency room", "emergency treatment" and "emergency first" and so on as "emergency", that is, completely correct, classified as category "1a"; fill in with "do not know" as category "3".

3 Test Result

According to ISO/TC 145, the criterion of acceptability on the comprehension test is that the percentage of responses in category 1 (correct, including complete correct and approximate correct) shall be 66% or over [13]. Cross tabulation of the results from comprehension test for 20 Chinese and USA healthcare graphical symbols was developed (Table 5).

Table 5. Cross tabulation of 20 healthcare graphical symbols comprehension (unit: % of correct responses reported).

	Emer	Phar	Obst	Pedi	Path	Oper	Radi	Pati	Elec	Prev
CHN	83.3	96.6	98.9	92.0	44.8	81.0	78.7	69.5	97.1	93.7
USA	58.7	53.9	95.2	89.2	41.3	71.3	79.6	47.9	95.2	85.6
Aver	71	75.25	97.05	90.6	43.05	76.15	79.15	58.7	96.15	89.65

9 out of 10 Chinese have comprehension rates higher than the criterion of acceptability by ISO standard (see Table 5). They are Emergency (83.3%), Pharmacy (96.6%), Obstetrics and gynecology department (98.9%), Pediatrics department (92.0%), Operating room (81.0%), Radiology department (78.7%), Patient file room (69.5%), Electrocardiographic room (97.1%), Prevention and health protection department (93.7%).

6 out of 10 USA healthcare symbols have comprehension rates higher than the criterion of acceptability by ISO standard (see Table 5). They are Obstetrics and gynecology department (95.2%), Pediatrics department (89.2%), Operating room (71.3%), Radiology department (79.6%), Electrocardiographic room (95.2%), Prevention and health protection department (85.6%).

It is shown that Chinese participants' average comprehension level of Chinese healthcare symbols (83.56%) is higher than that of American healthcare symbols (71.79%).

Among 20 graphical symbols, the comprehension test scores of six graphical symbols simultaneously reached the criterion of acceptability on the comprehension test of ISO. They are Obstetrics and gynecology department (average 97.05%), Pediatrics department (average 90.6%), Operating room (average 76.15%), Radiology department (average 79.15%), Electrocardiographic room (average 96.15%), Prevention and health protection department (average 89.65%). These graphical symbols have a common feature of the department: the functions and features of the diagnosis are widely understood and easily identifiable.

The graphic symbol with the lowest understanding score is "Pathology department" (average 43.05%). The Department of Pathology is one of the important departments of large-scale hospitals. Its main task is to undertake pathological diagnosis in the medical process, including through biopsy, exfoliation and puncture cytology to provide a clear pathological diagnosis for the clinic and determine the nature of the disease. In China, the patient or relative's contact with the pathology department is taking the pathology of the tissue specimen from the patient to the department, and then retrieving the pathological diagnosis report at the prescribed time. The patient does not understand the working environment of the pathology department or the main pathology work.

The design of the graphic symbols of the pathology department came from the main detection tool, microscope, of the pathology department. The symbolic element of the pathological slice added to the American graphic symbols. Since the participants do not understand the working environment of the pathology department or the main testing work, it is natural that the comprehension test score is the lowest.

The graphical symbols with the highest level of comprehension are Obstetrics and gynecology department (average 97.05%), Electrocardiographic room (average 96.15%). The designs of two graphic symbols "Obstetrics and gynecology" all come from the figure of a pregnant woman. Among them, the Chinese one uses the side view of pregnant women as symbolic elements, and the Americans one use the front view of pregnant women as symbolic elements. The designs of two graphical symbols "Electrocardiographic room" use the heart figure and the electric wave as the main symbol. The functions and features of the two departments are widely understood and easily identifiable, so the high scores of comprehension test are naturally.

4 Analysis and Discussion

4.1 Chi-Square Test in Chinese Healthcare Symbols

Chi-Square Test of Age Difference. The researchers conducted a chi-square test on the difference of Chinese healthcare symbols in terms of age. From the results of the chi-square test, the Chinese healthcare symbols did not have an age difference in comprehension.

Chi-Square Test of Education Level Difference. The researchers conducted a chi-square test on the difference of Chinese healthcare symbols in terms of educational level. From the results of the chi-square test, the test results of different healthcare symbols are quite different. 9 out of 10 Chinese healthcare symbols did not find any difference in education level in comprehension test. "Obstetrics and gynecology department" graphical symbol was found to be associated with education level. The chi-square value is 17.054, and the sig value is 0.009, which has reached a significant level of 0.01, indicating that the education level does have an impact on the understanding of "Obstetrics and gynecology department" graphical symbol. In category "1" (correct), the correct rate of comprehension with education level "3" and "4" was 88.3%. In category "2" (wrong), the error rate of comprehension with education level "2" is 9.5%, which is much higher than the average error rate 3.3%. In the "I don't know" answer, the rate with education level "1" and "2" was 10.2%, which was also higher than the average rate of 8.0%. Of course, the reason for the relationship between the graphical symbol and education level may also be influenced by the sample distribution, that is, the sample of error rate in the sample distribution is small, which may affect the chi-square test results.

4.2 Differences in Understanding of Chinese Participants on Two Sources of Healthcare Graphical Symbols

Chinese participants took part in the comprehension test on Chinese and USA healthcare graphical symbols. The comprehension test scores of two graphical symbols differed significantly (see Table 5), e.g. "Emergency" (CHN 83.3%, USA 58.7%), "Pharmacy" (CHN 96.6%, USA 53.9%). Checking response category data of 1–4 (see Table 6), it is found that the difference between the graphical symbol "Emergency" and the graphical symbol "Pharmacy" was mainly due to the fact that a large number of participants did not know the meaning of the graphical symbols (22.8% and 37.7%, respectively). The main reasons for "Don't know" filled by participants were "do not understand the meaning of words" and "do not understand the meaning of characters." The main symbolic element of the American graphic symbol "Emergency" is the cross and the English word "Emergency", while the main symbolic elements of the graphic symbol "Pharmacy" is transparent lid containers and English letters (P is the first letter of Pharmacy). ISO 22727:2007 [14] specifies the characters used in the design of graphic symbols: "Letters, numbers, punctuation marks, mathematical symbols, and other characters shall be used only as an element of a public information symbol." The reason is that the understanding of words, characters, etc. is highly correlated with the cultural background, and does not conform to the principle of graphic symbol design "understanding is not affected by language and cultural barriers."

Table 6. Comprehension test data of Emergency and Pharmacy

Category	Emer	Phar
1	58.7	53.9
2	18.6	8.4
3	22.8	37.7
Total	100	100

4.3 Relationship of Graphic Symbol Design and Comprehension

In ISO 22727:2007 [14], it is required that graphical symbols be readily associated with its intended meaning. The best way to design graphical symbols is based on objects, activities, etc., or a combination of these, which are reliably identifiable by the target audience. According to the design features, graphical symbols can be divided into two types: abstract symbols and concrete symbols.

The comprehension scores of those two types were listed in Tables 7 and 8. If both symbols (CHN and USA) are concrete symbols, the average correct response is used.

It is obvious that most symbols are concrete symbols (only one abstract symbol), design elements like objects and activities are used to form the figure.

Table 7. Cross tabulation of concrete symbols (unit: % of correct responses reported)

CHN-Emer	Aver-Phar	Aver-Obst	Aver-Pedi	Aver-Path	Aver-Oper	Aver-Radi	Aver-Pati	Aver-Elec	Aver-Prev	Total-Aver
83.3	75.25	97.05	90.6	43.05	76.15	79.15	58.7	96.15	89.65	78.91

Table 8. Cross tabulation of abstract symbols (unit: % of correct responses reported)

USA-Emer	Total-Aver
58.7	58.7

The average correct response of concrete symbols is 78.91%, which is much higher than that of abstract symbols (58.7%). By analyzing the design of abstract symbols and concrete symbols, the root causes of the differences between the comprehensibility scores of them can be further understood.

An abstract symbol is constituted by graphic elements unrelated to the apparent or activity characteristics of the object being referred to. While a concrete symbol is designed with graphic elements extracted from the apparent or activity characteristics of the object being referred to. Also taking the two symbols of "Emergency" to illustrate. The Chinese symbol of "Emergency" is a concrete one which formed by a nurse's side portrait who is pushing a cart. This design comes from the routine work of emergency rooms: a nurse pushed the emergency patient to the treatment room with a cart. The USA symbol of "Emergency" is an abstract one which formed by a cross figure and the English words "Emergency". The cross is derived from the Red Cross and represents medically relevant meaning. From chi-square test USA symbol of "Emergency" was found to be associated with education level. This also verifies the principle of graphic symbol design principles in ISO 22727, that is, the design of graphic symbols is intuitive and easy to understand, and not affected by language and cultural barriers.

5 Conclusion

Graphic symbols play an increasingly important role in the complex modern architectural environment. The design of graphical symbols should fully consider the prominent features of its information transmission across the language and culture barriers, and use elements that are intuitively related to the reference objects.

The test results showed that concrete symbol is easier to be understood than abstract symbol. According to test results of two different variants of "Emergency", it shows that concrete symbol are more likely to be understood correctly than abstract one. It was also found that Chinese participants' average comprehension level on Chinese healthcare symbols is higher than that of American healthcare symbols, which means through education and learning, the comprehension of graphical symbols can be effectively improved.

The study found that the respondents with higher education level have less difficulty than those with lower education level in comprehending graphical symbols.

Results of this study demonstrate that symbol comprehension can be influenced significantly by the design and respondents' education level.

Acknowledgments. This research was supported by National Key R&D Program of China (2016YFF0201700).

References

1. GB/T 10001 Public information graphic symbol. Standardization Administration of the People's Republic of China (SAC) (2014)
2. GB/T 20501 Public information guidance system – Design elements and requirements. Standardization Administration of the People's Republic of China (SAC) (2014)
3. GB/T 15566 Public information guidance system – Setting principles and requirements. Standardization Administration of the People's Republic of China (SAC) (2012)
4. ISO 7001 Public information graphic symbols. International Organization for Standardization (ISO) (2007)
5. ISO 28564 Public information guidance systems. International Organization for Standardization (ISO) (2016)
6. The SEGD/Hablamos Juntos Healthcare Symbols - Will They Work? SEGD Homepage. https://segd.org/. Accessed 03 Dec 2015
7. Yang, J., Liu, W.: Investigation and analysis on the status of patients' satisfaction with hospital wayfinding system. J. Ability Wisdom **2017**(35), 227 (2017)
8. Hong, S., et al.: Introduction and enlightenment of Taiwan hospital wayfinding systems. J. Mod. Hosp. Manag. **14**(04), 84–86 (2016)
9. Lee, S., et al.: Comprehensibility of universal healthcare symbols for wayfinding in healthcare facilities. Appl. Ergon. **45**(4), 878–885 (2014)
10. ISO 9186-1:2014 Graphical symbols – Test methods – Part 1: Method for testing comprehensibility. International Organization for Standardization (ISO) (2014)
11. ISO 9186-2:2008 Graphical symbols – Test methods – Part 2: Method for testing perceptual quality comprehensibility. International Organization for Standardization (ISO) (2008)
12. ISO 9186-3:2014 Graphical symbols – Test methods – Part 3: Method for testing symbol referent association. International Organization for Standardization (ISO) (2014)
13. ISO/TC 145 Homepage. http://www.iso.org/tc145/sc1
14. ISO 22727:2007 Graphical symbols – Creation and design of public information symbols – Requirements. International Organization for Standardization (ISO) (2007)

Aesthetics and Mindfulness

How Flow and Mindfulness Interact with Each Other in Different Types of Mandala Coloring Activities?

Hao Chen[1]($\boxtimes$), Chao Liu[1]($\boxtimes$), Wen-Ko Chiou[2]($\boxtimes$), and Rungtai Lin[3]($\boxtimes$)

[1] Department of Management, Chang Gung University, Taoyuan City, Taiwan
174673015@qq.com, victory666666@126.com
[2] Department of Industrial Design, Chang Gung University,
Taoyuan City, Taiwan
wkchiu@mail.cgu.edu.tw
[3] Graduate School of Creative Industry Design,
National Taiwan University of Arts, New Taipei City, Taiwan
rtlin@mail.ntua.edu.tw

Abstract. Mandala coloring has been receiving increasing attention in the literature and throughout popular culture. Previous research also indicated that high level of mindfulness may increase flow experience. The literature also suggests that teamwork may moderate the relationship between challenge and flow state, help subjects to overcome challenges and improve their flow state. Therefore based on the previous studies, our study wants to explore: (1) whether mandala coloring can improve mindfulness and flow; (2) what is the relationship between mindfulness and flow during the process of mandala coloring; and (3) whether teamwork can improve the state of flow in mandala coloring activity? Participants were 76 university students, divided into two groups: High-skill (n = 38) and low-skill (n = 38). The two groups performed three mandala coloring experiments in sequence: Structured mandala, Free mandala, and Cooperative mandala. Measurements of state mindfulness and state flow were taken for one pre-assessment of the whole experiment and three pre-assessments of each the three mandala activities. Results indicated that short-term mandala coloring exercises can't improve mindfulness but can significantly improve the flow state. There is a significant positive relationship between mindfulness and some dimensions of flow (e.g., Concentration on task, Unambiguous feedback, Sense of control, Challenge-skill balance, and Autotelic experience). But a negative correlation was found between mindfulness and loss of self-consciousness dimension. Free mandala is challenging for participants in the low-skilled group, but teamwork in cooperative mandala can help them to overcome this challenge. The contribution of this research is to provide a reference for further understanding of the mechanisms that how mandala coloring can help improve subjects' mental state and enhance positive psychology.

Keywords: Mandala coloring · Mindfulness · Flow · Teamwork

© Springer Nature Switzerland AG 2019
P.-L. P. Rau (Ed.): HCII 2019, LNCS 11576, pp. 471–486, 2019.
https://doi.org/10.1007/978-3-030-22577-3_34

1 Introduction

1.1 Mandala Coloring

More recently, mandala coloring has been promoted throughout popular culture as a mindfulness-based antianxiety coloring activity, an increase of mandala use or awareness in popular culture has since emerged (Carsley and Heath 2018). A brief and easy-to-implement mindfulness activity that has emerged in education research and throughout popular media is mindful art making (e.g., Beckwith 2014; Callahan 2016; Carsley et al. 2015). Mindful art making is hypothesized to combine the creative manipulation of materials found in art making (e.g., Abbott et al. 2013) with the benefits of mindfulness meditation (Curry and Kasser 2005). Within the past couple of years, mindfulness-based coloring activities, such as mandala coloring have been incorporated into the school, home, and work environments for test anxiety and stress reduction. These coloring activities are considered to be mindfulness based because individuals have been shown to remain focused and aware of present moment experiences while coloring (Barrett 2015).

1.2 Mindfulness and Flow

Mindfulness as an awareness that emerges through purposefully paying attention in the present moment, non-judgmentally (Kabat-Zinn 1990). Similarly, Bishop et al. (2004) described mindfulness as the self-regulation of attention in an effort to achieve a non-elaborative awareness of the current experience. Both definitions are more aligned to mindfulness practices, which are used to cultivate the ability to be attentive and aware of the present moment in a non-evaluative way.

Flow is an experience that is characterized by complete concentration, heightened sense of control, merging of action and attention, loss of self-consciousness, distortion of time perception, and autotelic experience (Nakamura et al. 2002). Flow seems to be a subjective, psychological state that occurs when an individual becomes so immersed in an occupation that he or she forgets everything except what he or she is doing (Csikszentmihalyi 2002).

Mindfulness and flow had some common features. Both constructs emphasize the importance of focusing on the present moment, not worrying, and performing activities because they were intrinsically rewarding (Wright et al. 2006). Furthermore, both are considered to be indicators of mental health and optimal functioning (e.g., Landhäußer and Keller 2012; Rogatko 2009; Weinstein et al. 2009). Mindfulness may create a basis for the experience of flow (Aherne et al. 2011; Briegel-Jones et al. 2013; Kaufman et al. 2009). Jackson's (1995) evidence suggests that flow requires a present-moment, non-self-conscious concentration on a particular task. Not surprisingly, therefore, a number of authors have recommended that maintaining a present moment focus is an effective strategy for achieving peak performance and flow (Orlick 1990; Jackson and

Csikszentmihalyi 1999). Csikszentmihalyi (1978) explained that flow experiences "are made possible by an unusually intense concentration of attention on a limited stimulus field". Awareness of the present is a core aspect of both mindfulness and flow (Swann et al. 2012).

Research by Cathcart et al. (2014) found that elite athletes with a high level of dispositional mindfulness have a propensity to experience flow. Their research suggests that mindfulness may be a catalyst for flow. Some evidence for the causal role of mindfulness in the mindfulness–flow relationship comes from research with athletes and suggests that mindfulness interventions may increase flow experience (Aherne et al. 2011; Briegel-Jones et al. 2013; Kaufman et al. 2009). Aherne et al. (2011) found that athletes who underwent mindfulness training program experienced greater flow than they did before the program, and experienced greater flow than athletes who did not participate in the training. Kee and Wang (2008) suggests athletes with higher mindfulness scores were more likely to experience the flow state. In addition, elite swimmers have reported being particularly aware and accepting of their bodily sensations during flow experiences reflecting a mindfulness and acceptance state (Bernier et al. 2009). Changes in mindfulness experienced by the intervention participants were positively associated with changes in flow, mindfulness-based interventions tailored to specific athletic pursuits can be effective in facilitating flow experiences (Jackson 2000; Kimiecik and Stein 1992; Scott-Hamilton et al. 2016).

1.3 Flow and Team Work

Jackson and Csikszentmihalyi (1999) stated that the most important characteristic of flow is the balance between the challenge of the occupation and the skills of the individual. According to this theory, to experience flow individuals have to be doing something sufficiently challenging that they make full use of the skills they possess, whereas too much challenge brings frustration, too little challenge brings boredom. In an experimental study, people playing ball games that required more teamwork reported greater joy and more intense flow than those playing the same games that required less teamwork, despite perceiving the game as more challenging (Walker 2010). The study of Tse et al. (2018) explores potential moderating effects of teamwork and flow proneness on the relationship between challenge and flow state. Their findings indicate that although challenge is negatively associated with flow state, this negative association can be mitigated if people work as a team. In organizational psychology, a person's well-being is compromised if job resources cannot meet job demands (Schaufeli and Bakker 2004). One type of resources is social support. Social support is even more important when facing higher challenges because when personal skills do not meet up with the demand on hand, social support can act as an additional resource to maintain engagement and positive experience (Bakker and Demerouti 2007). In a correlational study with music teachers and students, perceived social support, one of the components of job resources, was positively associated with teacher's work enjoyment (Bakker 2005). Their finding serves as preliminary evidence that teamwork may enhance flow and enjoyment when the challenge level is high.

1.4   Research Purpose and Hypothesis

In summary, mandala coloring has been receiving increasing attention in the literature and throughout popular culture, is an example of a brief and simple mindfulness activity (Carsley et al. 2015). Previous research also indicated that high level of mindfulness may increase flow experience. And in the study of Mantzios and Giannou (2018), they suggested future research should explore changes in flow while doing mandala coloring, as the benefits of mandala coloring may be more relevant to flow, rather than open awareness and mindfulness. The literature also suggests that a situational factor, teamwork, and a dispositional factor, flow proneness, may moderate the relationship between challenge and flow state. Therefore based on the previous studies, our study wants to explore: (1) whether mandala coloring can improve mindfulness and flow; (2) what is the relationship between mindfulness and flow during the process of mandala coloring; and (3) whether teamwork can improve the state of flow in mandala coloring activity?

So we divided the subjects into two groups, one group with high painting skills and another group with low painting skills. Different painting skills to match with different challenge levels of activities, structured mandala, free mandala and cooperative mandala.

Structured mandala, which is circular designs composed of symmetrical shapes, facilitate in-depth attention and engagement inherent to mindfulness activities and is believed to create a state of mindfulness (Carsley et al. 2015; Curry and Kasser 2005; Henderson et al. 2007). Filling in the intricate shapes and repeating patterns of the mandala provides individuals with the opportunity to experience a state of focused awareness (Curry and Kasser 2005). The combination of the structure associated with coloring in a mandala and the complexity of the design has been suggested to provide participants with a sense of direction when coloring and in organizing their experience (Carsley and Heath 2018).

Unlike structured mandala, the free mandala has no structure, but only a blank circle. The lack of structure individuals feel during a free mandala activity may be more challenging than structured mandala, and perhaps even anxiety inducing, as they feel the need to create their own structure (Curry and Kasser 2005).

Cooperative mandala is a kind of teamwork which completed by several participants working together. In order to explore whether teamwork can help participants improve their flow when facing the high challenging tasks, the pattern used by the cooperative mandala in this study was modified from the pattern of the free mandala. There are two nested circles, the large outer circle was divided into 4 small parts, each of which colored by an individual, and the middle small circle is colored by four participants together (Fig. 1).

Structured mandala   Free mandala   Cooperative mandala

Fig. 1. Patterns used in three mandala experiments.

Based on all the above theories, we can propose the following hypothesis:

Hypothesis 1, Scores of mindfulness and flow of post-assessment are significant higher than the score of pre-assessment.

Hypothesis 2, There is a positive correlation between mindfulness and flow in the process of mandala coloring.

Hypothesis 3, Cooperative mandala can significantly increase the flow of subjects in the Low-skilled group.

2   Method

2.1   Participants

Participants were 76 university students (72.4% female n = 55 and 27.6% male n = 21) recruited from Chang Gung University located in Taiwan. 55 undergraduate students (67.1%), 17 master students (22.4%), and 8 doctoral students (10.5%). The age of participants ranged from 18 to 49 years old (M = 22.51, SD = 5.56). According to their painting skills, participants were divided into 2 groups: High - skill (Design students or who have spent more than 6 months studying in painting skills training institutions, n = 38), and Low- skill (Students who are not design majors or who have studied in painting skills training institutions for less than 6 months, n = 38). In the High – skill group, there are 32 females (84.2%) and 6 males (15.8%), mean age is 20.61 (SD = 3.15) years old. In the Low – skill group, there are 23 females (60.5%) and 15 males (39.5%), mean age is 24.42(SD = 6.73) years old.

2.2   Measures

State Mindfulness Scale (SMS; Tanay and Bernstein 2013). The State Mindfulness Scale is a state-like measurement tool that includes 21 items, with responses ranging from 1 (not at all) to 5 (very well). The SMS measure consists of two sub-scales that relate to bodily sensations or mental events. Sample items are "I noticed some pleasant and unpleasant physical sensations" and "I noticed emotions come and go." Higher scores reflect greater levels of state-mindfulness. This scale was judged to be more inclusive of present moment awareness and a non-judgmental attitude, compared to the alternative scale that is evaluating mindful attention and awareness of the present moment (see Brown and Ryan 2003 for alternative scale). The study of Mantzios and Giannou (2018) produced an alpha of 0.95/0.94 for pre- and post- measurements of the overall score; and 0.82/0.85 for the bodily sensations and 0.94/0.93 for the mental events subscales.

The Short Dispositional Flow Scale 2 (SDFS-2). This nine item self-report measure (Jackson et al. 2008) is an abbreviated version of the long DFS-2. It is purported to include nine dimensions (one item for one dimensions): challenge-skill balance, action-awareness merging, clear goals, unambiguous feedback, concentration on task, sense of control, loss of self-consciousness, time transformation, and autotelic experience. Items are rated on a 5-point Likert scale, ranging from 1 (never) to 5 (always), to measure the frequency with which the flow characteristics are experienced. A total dispositional flow score is generated by summing the item responses, yielding a possible range in scores from 9 to 45. Higher scores indicate greater levels of dispositional flow. Preliminary research has demonstrated that the short scale provides a good representation of the previously validated longer version, suggesting it is an appropriate and reliable empirical measure of dispositional flow (Jackson et al. 2008). Coefficient alpha estimates of reliability for the DFS-2 ranged from .74 to .81, with acceptable goodness of fit indices, showing the DFS-2 to be a suitable short measure of flow.

2.3 Coloring Material

Both groups were exposed to an A4 size page, and the page with the pattern corresponding to the type of mandala used in the experiment (Fig. 1). All participants were exposed to a box of 12 colored pencils, and a pencil sharpener.

2.4 Procedure

Participants were kept blind to the study, and were informed that they signed-up to volunteer at a study that was investigating "Personality and Art." Pre-screening questions to allow participation evaluated color-blindness, medication use, and former and current diagnoses of affective disorders. In this study, three experiments were conducted with two groups of participants. Three experiments were performed in a chronological order for structured mandala coloring, free mandala coloring and cooperative mandala coloring. One week interval between two adjacent experiments. Before the first experiment started participants received simultaneously a participant information form, a consent form, and the demographics page with the questionnaire (i.e., the SMS and SDFS-2 scales) for the pre-assessment. Next, participants commenced a 30-min mandala coloring. After the 30 min, participants were given a questionnaire again for the post-assessment, and were debriefed and thanked for their participation. In the next two experiments, there was no pre-assessment, but only 30-min mandala coloring and post-assessment. Measurements of state mindfulness and state flow were taken for one pre-assessment of the whole experiment and three pre-assessments of each the three mandala activities. In the third experiment, four participants (2 with high painting skill, and 2 with low painting skill) formed a small team working together to color a cooperative mandala. Participants had the opportunity to record an arbitrary number assigned to their questionnaires and drawing, to allow them to withdraw at a later stage and retain the anonymity of participation. Ethical approval was granted by the Ethical Committee based within the University and was scrutinized to strictly adhere to ethical guidelines set by the Taiwan Psychological Society.

Data were analyzed by utilizing three 2×4 mixed ANOVAs, post hoc paired sample t-tests, independent sample T tests, and linear regressions. The sample size recruited matched or exceeded previous studies. Analyses were conducted by utilizing SPSS version 22 (IBM 2013) and a significance threshold was set at $p < 0.05$.

3   Results

In order to explore the impact of different mandala on the challenge-skill balance, we took out the challenge-skill balance dimension of the SDFS-2 scale, and analyzed it with SMS and SDFS-2 together. We set the pre-assessment as Time 0, post-assessment of structured mandala as Time 1, post-assessment of free mandala as Time 2, and post-assessment of cooperative mandala as Time 3.

Three 2(Group Type: High-skill, low-skill) $\times$ 4(Time: Time 0, Time 1, Time 2, Time 3) ANOVA with repeated measures on the Time was conducted on the Mindfulness (SMS), Overall flow (SDFS-2) and Challenge-skill balance dimension.

For Mindfulness, there was no significant main effect of Time: $F(3,222) = 2.339$, $p = 0.074$, and there was no significant main effect of Group Type: $F(1,74) = 0.469$, $p = 0.495$, and there was also no significant interaction between Time and Group Type, $F(3,222) = 0.649$, $p = 0.585$. Although the effect of time on mindfulness was not significant, the mindfulness scores decreased slightly with time from Time 1 to Time 3 (Table 1).

Table 1. Means and standard deviations for the High-skill group (n = 38) and Low-skill group (n = 38), pre- and post- assessment on the four Times.

Group	Measures	Mean (SD)			
		Time 0	Time 1	Time 2	Time 3
High-skill	SMS	3.72(0.55)	3.82(0.66)	3.65(0.56)	3.64(0.63)
	SDFS-2	3.18(0.61)	3.51(0.71)	3.52(0.51)	3.53(0.64)
	Challenge-skill	2.90(0.92)	3.40(0.89)	3.61(0.76)	3.58(0.79)
Low-skill	SMS	3.85(0.45)	3.80(0.57)	3.76(0.48)	3.70(0.57)
	SDFS-2	3.28(0.50)	3.45(0.50)	3.27(0.44)	3.59(0.53)
	Challenge-skill	3.16(0.95)	3.53(0.86)	3.18(0.73)	3.55(0.72)

SMS, State Mindfulness Scale; SDFS-2, The Short Dispositional Flow Scale 2; Challenge-skill, Challenge-skill balance dimension of SDFS-2.

Time 0, Pre-assessment; Time 1, Post-assessment of structured mandala; Time 2, post-assessment of free mandala; Time 3, Post-assessment of cooperative mandala.

For Flow, there was a significant main effect of Time: $F(3,222) = 11.918$, $p < 0.001$, $\eta_p^2 = 0.139$, with both groups increasing over time in their Flow scores (Table 1). There was no significant main effect of Group Type, $F(1,74) = 0.131$ $p = 0.719$. However, a significant interaction was found between Time and Group Type, $F(3,222) = 3.755$, $p = 0.012$, $\eta_p^2 = 0.048$. Results indicated that mandala coloring produced an increase in flow levels, but both groups produced similar outcomes. Set Time 0 as the baseline, post hoc paired sample t-tests revealed that the only case flow state not significantly increased but slightly decreased in Low-skill group on Time 2, $t(37) = 0.140$, $p = 0.890$, which was not observed in the High-skill group or on other Time conditions. Set Time 2 as the baseline, post hoc paired sample t-tests revealed that there was a significant decrease of flow state compared with Time 1 ($t(37) = -2.423$, $p = 0.020$), and Time 3 ($t(37) = -4.004$, $p < 0.001$). Such significant drop was not found in the High-skill group (Fig. 2).

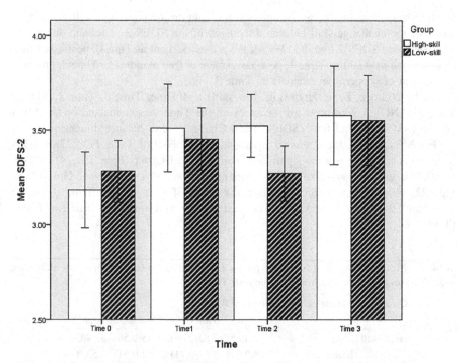

Fig. 2. Means of SDFS-2 for High-skill group and Low-skill group on the four Times.

For Challenge-skill balance dimension, there was a significant main effect of Time: $F(3,222) = 8.216$, $p < 0.001$, $\eta_p^2 = 0.100$. There was no significant main effect of Group Type, $F(1,74) = 0.011$, $p = 0.918$. However, a significant interaction was found between Time and Group Type, $F(3,222) = 3.284$, $p = 0.022$, $\eta_p^2 = 0.042$. Results indicated that mandala coloring produced an increase in score of Challenge-skill balance dimension, but both groups produced similar outcomes (Table 1). Set Time 0 as the baseline, post hoc paired sample t-tests revealed that the only case the score not significantly increased in Low-skill group on Time 2, $t(37) = -0.141$, $p = 0.889$, which was not observed in the High-skill group or on other Time conditions. Set Time 2 as the baseline, post hoc paired sample t-tests revealed that there was a significant decrease of the score compared with Time 3, $t(37) = -2.488$, $p = 0.017$. Such significant drop was not found in the High-skill group (Fig. 3).

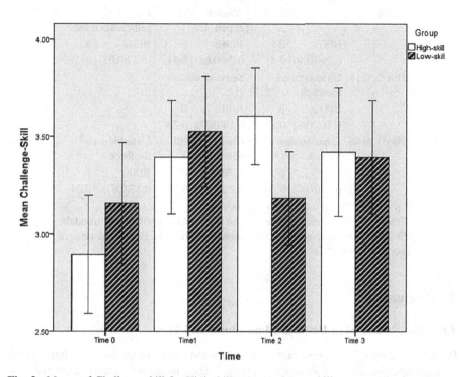

Fig. 3. Means of Challenge-skill for High-skill group and Low-skill group on the four Times.

The results of independent sample T test showed that only on Time 2, there was a significant difference of overall flow state (SDFS-2) between high-skill group and low-skill group, $t(74) = 2.307$, $p = 0.024$. Similar results was found in Challenge-skill balance dimension, there was a significant difference between high-skill group and low-skill group only on Time 2, $t(74) = 2.472$, $p = 0.016$.

We set the mindfulness scores of different time condition as the dependent variables, and the corresponding nine dimensions of flow as the independent variables, then used the stepwise linear regression method to analyze the relationship between mindfulness and flow. The results were shown in Table 2.

Table 2. Stepwise linear regression method to analyze the relationship between mindfulness and cognitive nine dimensions of flow on the four Times.

Time	R^2	Predictors selected by stepwise linear regression					
Time0	0.23	Concentration on task		Unambiguous feedback			
		B(SE)	β	B(SE)	β		
		0.18(0.07)	0.30*	0.17(0.07)	0.27*		
Time1	0.33	Sense of control		Autotelic experience		Loss of self-consciousness	
		B(SE)	β	B(SE)	β	B(SE)	β
		0.29(0.08)	0.43***	0.24(0.08)	0.31**	-0.13(0.05)	-0.26*
Time2	0.16	Unambiguous feedback		Sense of control			
		B(SE)	β	B(SE)	β		
		0.18(0.08)	0.27*	0.14(0.07)	0.23*		
Time3	0.46	Concentration on task		Challenge-skill balance		Unambiguous feedback	
		B(SE)	β	B(SE)	β	B(SE)	β
		0.27(0.07)	0.36***	0.22(0.08)	0.28**	0.17(0.07)	0.24*

* $p < 0.05$; ** $p < 0.01$; *** $p < 0.001$.
Time 0, Pre-assessment; Time 1, Post-assessment of structured mandala; Time 2, post-assessment of free mandala; Time 3, Post-assessment of cooperative mandala

4   Discussion

4.1   The Relationship Between Mindfulness and Flow

Positive psychology is a quest in part to understand optimal experience (Seligman and Csikszentmihalyi 2000). Two forms of optimal experiencing have received the majority of attention within the literature, that is mindfulness and flow (Sheldon et al. 2015). A high level of mindfulness is associated with a greater frequency of the key flow dimensions of challenge–skill balance, clear goals, concentration, unambiguous feedback and sense of control, and loss of self-consciousness (Kee and Wang 2008). This is similar to the results of linear regression in this study, that mindfulness is positively associated with flow dimensions of challenge-skill balance, concentration on task, unambiguous feedback, and sense of control.

But a negative correlation was found between mindfulness and loss of self-consciousness dimension. This finding is similar to the study of Sheldon et al. (2015). Their study found that boosting a person's ability to remain mindful during an activity might actually undermine their ability to get absorbed in that activity. It is important to note, however, that this negative relationship was found only for the absorption facet of flow, that is, the feeling of being carried away by activity, with an altered sense of time and a loss of self-awareness (Sheldon et al. 2015). Mindfulness is typically construed as a mental practice that requires self-discipline and a commitment to trying to maintain reflective awareness of each passing moment. Flow involves intense task concentration, a loss of self-awareness, an altered sense of time, and merging of activity and awareness (Csikszentmihalyi 1990; Nakamura and Csikszentmihalyi 2009). At first glance, mindfulness and flow seem very similar, both involve using the mind in an efficient high-quality way, and both are seen as signals of good mental hygiene and health. Thus, many researchers have assumed that boosting people's ability to be mindful should also boost their ability to experience flow (Aherne et al. 2011; Kaufman et al. 2009; Thienot et al. 2014). But at a second look, the two states seem a little different. Mindfulness involves cultivating an observer of consciousness, trying to maintain reflective awareness of each moment. In contrast, flow involves losing the inner observer within an altered state of consciousness in which the moment blurs into a continuous stream of activity. Flow is an absorbing mental state that arises spontaneously when one is engrossed within optimally challenging activity. Absorption is an important component of flow states, one that is plausibly limited by mindfulness (Sheldon et al. 2015). In terms of William James' (1890) famous metaphor of the "stream of consciousness," mindfulness seems to entail standing on the bank of the stream without falling in; in contrast, flow entails jumping into the stream and tackling a challenging task or problem.

4.2 Why Is Mindfulness not Significant?

The results of data analysis showed that Time has no significant effect on mindfulness, suggests that there was no significant difference found in state mindfulness levels between pre and post of the three mandala interventions. Although mandala coloring has been associated with mindfulness, however, the question of whether they do increase mindfulness has not been addressed (Mantzios and Giannou 2018). Empirical support for the benefits of this activity is limited and the findings are mixed (Carsley et al. 2015; Curry and Kasser 2005; Van der Vennet and Serice 2012). Carsley and Heath (2018) investigated the effectiveness of mandala coloring activity compared with a free draw coloring activity on test anxiety in 152 children. Results revealed an overall significant decrease in test anxiety and an overall significant increase in state mindfulness. In the studies of Mantzios and Giannou (2018), they attempted to identify whether the mindfulness level of 88 university students was increased by doing mandala coloring, and whether there was a need for ongoing guidance while coloring. Results indicated that there were no significant differences between mandala coloring and free-drawing in reducing anxiety. Furthermore, no change was observed in mindfulness and no significant differences between mandala coloring and free-drawing were found in state mindfulness levels. But they found for the participants who liked the ongoing mindfulness guidance while coloring displayed an increase in state mindfulness, while the majority of participants who disliked the ongoing mindfulness guidance while coloring displayed a decrease in state mindfulness. The findings may be explained through the presence of flow, and the immersion onto the task that was disrupted by the meditation teacher who was talking in the background to guide participants to color mindfully (Mantzios and Giannou 2018).

Mandala could be a useful mindfulness tool, especially when considering their popularity. But mindfulness may be enriched through a long time of practice (Carsley and Heath 2018). MBSR (Mindfulness based stress reduction) is an eight weeks mindfulness training program which is generally considered to be effective in improving mindfulness. Eight-week mindfulness training of MBSR in attentional and emotional regulation skills has been found to increase mindfulness (Kabat-Zinn 1982, 2009). Maybe several times of 30-min mandala colorings are not enough to improve mindfulness, it needs time to train to see the effects.

On the other hand, as mentioned above, the increased flow of mandala activity may offset the improvements of mindfulness in some dimensions (e.g., loss of self-awareness). The flow scores increasing over time, while the mindfulness scores decreased slightly with time. After all, flow involves losing self-awareness and immerse into an activity, but mindfulness needs maintaining self-awareness throughout of each moment.

4.3   Cooperative Mandala

The results of the data analysis found that the overall flow score of the high-skilled group increased steadily with time. But the flow score of the low-skilled group dramatically dropped at Time 2, and rose again at Time 3, even higher. Similar trends were also found in Challenge-skill balance dimension. This result indicate that the free mandala is challenging for participants in the low-skilled group, but teamwork in cooperative mandala can help them to overcome this challenge. The study of Tse et al. (2018) examined the moderating effects of teamwork and flow proneness on the relationship between challenge and flow state. Their findings indicate that although challenge is negatively associated with flow state, this negative association can be mitigated if people work as a team. The literature suggests that a situational factor, teamwork, and a dispositional factor, flow proneness, may moderate the relationship between challenge and flow state (Tse et al. 2018). People with a disposition toward flow are described as those who enjoy activities regardless of external rewards (Csikszentmihalyi 2000) and who seek out difficult tasks with the objective of keeping perceived challenges high (Baumann and Scheffer 2011). They are also confident in their ability to master these challenges, in order to keep perceived skills high. These people tend to seek out activities which result in flow states (Asakawa 2004). While highly challenging activities often result in low positive affect (seeing difficulty), those high in dispositional flow tend to be resilient to this state in which overcoming the challenge (mastering difficulty) leads to a high positive affect (Baumann and Scheffer 2011). In contrast, non-autotelic people require external incentives to be motivated (Csikszentmihalyi 2000) and tend to see only difficulty in challenging tasks (Nakamura and Csikszentmihalyi 2002). This was necessary because playing as a team with high interdependence among team members provided better enjoyment and flow experience (Walker 2010). Therefore, encouraging cooperation among teammates, rather than letting teammates play independently, appears to be the underlying factor in making challenge flow-inducing.

4.4   Limitations and Future Research

Both the use of students and the small sample size suggest that (a) caution should be used when interpreting the results, and (b) future research with a larger and more diverse sample is required. In addition, the prolonged and repetitive use of coloring books has not been investigated, and may well indicate different findings. Also, the participants consisted mostly of females. Future research should explore more male participants. Although explorations around gender during this study did not signify any differences and did not deviate the original results reported. Another limitation that should be accounted for in future research is that the gender and age components of High-skilled groups and low-skilled were not strictly matched. Although data analysis showed that gender and age did not have a significant impact on the results of the study. Such similar situation has also been found in other studies. The majority of studies examining the relation between some demographic variables (e.g., gender and age) and mindfulness have not found significant differences (e.g., Shapiro et al. 2007; Shorey et al. 2014; Tan and Martin 2012). Neither age and gender correlated with flow state (Tse et al. 2018).

Many studies have confirmed that mandala can reduce anxiety. Finding indicate that the use of mandala coloring assists in reducing anxiety and in improving mood (Curry and Kasser 2005; Babouchkina and Robbins 2015). Many studies have also pointed out that mindfulness and flow can help to reduce anxiety. Mindfulness interventions have benefits ranging from reductions in anxiety and depression (Cayoun 2011; Grossman et al. 2004; Hofmann et al. 2010; Hölzel et al. 2011; Kabat-Zinn 2003). Some flow experts suggest that flow may be difficult to achieve when one is anxious because anxiety can invoke a negative self-conscious focus that disrupts concentrated attention (Csikszentmihalyi 1990; Jackson and Csikszentmihalyi 1999). Based on the results of this study, it seems to be inferred that the short-term effects of mandala coloring on reducing anxiety may be due to increased flow rather than mindfulness. The long-term practice of mandala coloring to reduce anxiety may be due to the combination of mindfulness and flow. The mechanisms of these actions and causalities need to be further confirmed in future studies.

5   Conclusion

This study found that short-term mandala coloring exercises can't improve mindfulness but can significantly improve the flow state. There is a significant positive relationship between mindfulness and some dimensions of flow (e.g., Concentration on task, Unambiguous feedback, Sense of control, Challenge-skill balance, and Autotelic experience). But a negative correlation was found between mindfulness and loss of self-consciousness dimension. Free mandala is challenging for participants in the low-skilled group, but teamwork in cooperative mandala can help them to overcome this challenge. The contribution of this research is to provide a reference for further understanding of the mechanisms that how mandala coloring can help improve subjects' mental state and enhance positive psychology.

References

Abbott, K.A., Shanahan, M.J., Neufeld, R.W.: Artistic tasks outperform nonartistic tasks for stress reduction. Art Therapy **30**(2), 71–78 (2013)

Aherne, C., Moran, A.P., Lonsdale, C.: The effect of mindfulness training on athletes' flow: an initial investigation. Sport Psychol. **25**(2), 177–189 (2011)

Asakawa, K.: Flow experience and autotelic personality in Japanese college students: how do they experience challenges in daily life? J. Happiness Stud. **5**(2), 123–154 (2004)

Babouchkina, A., Robbins, S.J.: Reducing negative mood through mandala creation: a randomized controlled trial. Art Therapy **32**(1), 34–39 (2015)

Bakker, A.B.: Flow among music teachers and their students: the crossover of peak experiences. J. Vocat. Behav. **66**(1), 26–44 (2005)

Bakker, A.B., Demerouti, E.: The job demands-resources model: state of the art. J. Manag. Psychol. **22**(3), 309–328 (2007)

Barrett, C.A.: Adult Coloring Books: Patterns for Stress Relief. Paper presented at the Phi Kappa Phi Forum (2015)

Baumann, N., Scheffer, D.: Seeking flow in the achievement domain: the achievement flow motive behind flow experience. Motiv. Emot. **35**(3), 267–284 (2011)

Beckwith, P.: Mindfulness and mandalas: alternative therapeutic techniques for AOD adolescents. Capital Univ. Undergraduate Res. J., 1–5 (2014)

Bernier, M., Thienot, E., Codron, R., Fournier, J.F.: Mindfulness and acceptance approaches in sport performance. J. Clin. Sport Psychol. **3**(4), 320–333 (2009)

Bishop, S.R., et al.: Mindfulness: a proposed operational definition. Clin. Psychol. Sci. Pract. **11**(3), 230–241 (2004)

Briegel-Jones, R.M., Knowles, Z., Eubank, M.R., Giannoulatos, K., Elliot, D.: A preliminary investigation into the effect of yoga practice on mindfulness and flow in elite youth swimmers. Sport Psychol. **27**(4), 349–359 (2013)

Callahan, M.J.: Mindfulness Based Art: The Sparks Guide for Educators and Counselors. FriesenPress, Victoria (2016)

Carsley, D., Heath, N.L.: Evaluating the effectiveness of a mindfulness coloring activity for test anxiety in children. J. Educ. Res., 1–9 (2018)

Carsley, D., Heath, N.L., Fajnerova, S.: Effectiveness of a classroom mindfulness coloring activity for test anxiety in children. J. Appl. School Psychol. **31**(3), 239–255 (2015)

Cathcart, S., Mcgregor, M., Groundwater, E.: Mindfulness and flow in elite athletes. J. Clin. Sport Psychol. **8**(2), 119–141 (2014)

Cayoun, B.A.: Mindfulness-Integrated CBT: Principles and Practice. Wiley, Hoboken (2011)

Csikszentmihalyi, M.: Intrinsic rewards and emergent motivation. In: The Hidden Costs of Reward: New Perspectives on the Psychology of Human Motivation, pp. 205–216 (1978)

Csikszentmihalyi, M.: Flow: The Classic Work on How to Achieve Happiness. Random House, New York (2002)

Curry, N.A., Kasser, T.: Can coloring mandalas reduce anxiety? Art Therapy **22**(2), 81–85 (2005)

Grossman, P., Niemann, L., Schmidt, S., Walach, H.: Mindfulness-based stress reduction and health benefits: a meta-analysis. J. Psychosom. Res. **57**(1), 35–43 (2004)

Henderson, P., Rosen, D., Mascaro, N.: Empirical study on the healing nature of mandalas. Psychol. Aesthetics Creativity Arts **1**(3), 148 (2007)

Hofmann, S.G., Sawyer, A.T., Witt, A.A., Oh, D.: The effect of mindfulness-based therapy on anxiety and depression: a meta-analytic review. J. Consult. Clin. Psychol. **78**(2), 169 (2010)

Hölzel, B.K., Lazar, S.W., Gard, T., Schuman-Olivier, Z., Vago, D.R., Ott, U.: How does mindfulness meditation work? Proposing mechanisms of action from a conceptual and neural perspective. Perspect. Psychol. Sci. **6**(6), 537–559 (2011)

Jackson, S.A.: Factors influencing the occurrence of flow state in elite athletes. J. Appl. Sport Psychol. **7**(2), 138–166 (1995)

Jackson, S.A.: Joy, fun, and flow state in sport. In: Emotions in Sport, pp. 135–155 (2000)

Jackson, S.A., Csikszentmihalyi, M.: Flow in Sports. Human Kinetics, Champaign (1999)

Jackson, S.A., Martin, A.J., Eklund, R.C.: Long and short measures of flow: the construct validity of the FSS-2, DFS-2, and new brief counterparts. J. Sport Exerc. Psychol. **30**(5), 561–587 (2008)

Kabat-Zinn, J.: Full Catastrophe Living: The Program of the Stress Reduction Clinic at the University of Massachusetts Medical Center. Delta, New York (1990)

Kabat-Zinn, J.: Mindfulness-based interventions in context: past, present, and future. Clin. Psychol. Sci. Pract. **10**(2), 144–156 (2003)

Kaufman, K.A., Glass, C.R., Arnkoff, D.B.: Evaluation of mindful sport performance enhancement (MSPE): a new approach to promote flow in athletes. J. Clin. Sport Psychol. **3**(4), 334–356 (2009)

Kee, Y.H., Wang, C.J.: Relationships between mindfulness, flow dispositions and mental skills adoption: a cluster analytic approach. Psychol. Sport Exerc. **9**(4), 393–411 (2008)

Kimiecik, J.C., Stein, G.L.: Examining flow experiences in sport contexts: conceptual issues and methodological concerns. J. Appl. Sport Psychol. **4**(2), 144–160 (1992)

Landhäußer, A., Keller, J.: Flow and Its Affective, Cognitive, and Performance-Related Consequences (2012)

Mantzios, M., Giannou, K.: When did coloring books become mindful? Exploring the effectiveness of a novel method of mindfulness-guided instructions for coloring books to increase mindfulness and decrease anxiety. Front. Psychol. **9**, 56 (2018)

Nakamura, J., Csikszentmihalyi, M.: Flow theory and research. In: Handbook of Positive Psychology, pp. 195–206 (2009)

Nakamura, J., Csikszentmihalyi, M., Snyder, C., Lopez, S.J.: Handbook of Positive Psychology. Oxford University Press, New York (2002)

Rogatko, T.P.: The influence of flow on positive affect in college students. J. Happiness Stud. **10** (2), 133 (2009)

Schaufeli, W.B., Bakker, A.B.: Job demands, job resources, and their relationship with burnout and engagement: a multi-sample study. J. Organ. Behav.: Int. J. Ind. Occup. Organ. Psychol. Behav. **25**(3), 293–315 (2004)

Scott-Hamilton, J., Schutte, N.S., Brown, R.F.: Effects of a mindfulness intervention on sports-anxiety, pessimism, and flow in competitive cyclists. Appl. Psychol.: Health Well-Being **8**(1), 85–103 (2016)

Seligman, M.E., Csikszentmihalyi, M.: Positive Psychology: An Introduction, vol. 55. American Psychological Association, Washington, D.C. (2000)

Shapiro, S.L., Brown, K.W., Biegel, G.M.: Teaching self-care to caregivers: effects of mindfulness-based stress reduction on the mental health of therapists in training. Training Educ. Prof. Psychol. **1**(2), 105 (2007)

Sheldon, K.M., Prentice, M., Halusic, M.: The experiential incompatibility of mindfulness and flow absorption. Soc. Psychol. Pers. Sci. **6**(3), 276–283 (2015)

Shorey, R.C., Anderson, S., Lookatch, S., Moore, T.M., Stuart, G.L.: The relation between moment-to-moment mindful attention and anxiety among young adults in substance use treatment. Subst. Abuse Off. Publ. Assoc. Med. Educ. Res. Subst. Abuse **36**(3), 374–379 (2014)

Swann, W.B., Jetten, J., Gómez, A., Whitehouse, H., Bastian, B.: When group membership gets personal: a theory of identity fusion. Psychol. Rev. **119**(3), 441 (2012)

Tanay, G., Bernstein, A.: State mindfulness scale (SMS): development and initial validation. Psychol. Assess. **25**(4), 1286 (2013)

Thienot, E., Jackson, B., Dimmock, J., Grove, J.R., Bernier, M., Fournier, J.F.: Development and preliminary validation of the mindfulness inventory for sport. Psychol. Sport Exerc. **15**(1), 72–80 (2014)

Tse, D.C., Fung, H.H., Nakamura, J., Csikszentmihalyi, M.: Teamwork and flow proneness mitigate the negative effect of excess challenge on flow state. J. Positive Psychol. **13**(3), 284–289 (2018)

Van der Vennet, R., Serice, S.: Can coloring mandalas reduce anxiety? A replication study. Art Therapy **29**(2), 87–92 (2012)

Walker, C.J.: Experiencing flow: is doing it together better than doing it alone? J. Positive Psychol. **5**(1), 3–11 (2010)

Weinstein, N., Brown, K.W., Ryan, R.M.: A multi-method examination of the effects of mindfulness on stress attribution, coping, and emotional well-being. J. Res. Pers. **43**(3), 374–385 (2009)

Wright, J.J., Sadlo, G., Stew, G.: Challenge-skills and mindfulness: an exploration of the conundrum of flow process. OTJR: Occup. Particip. Health **26**(1), 25–32 (2006)

The Aesthetic Pleasure in Design Scale for Spanish Speaking Countries: A Method for the Cross-Cultural Implementation and Adaptation of Psychometric Scales

Luis Miguel Garrido-Possauner[✉] and Jorge Maya

Universidad EAFIT, Medellin, Colombia
{lgarrido,jmayacas}@eafit.edu.co

Abstract. One of the main issues in the field of product aesthetics is the lack of consistency in the instruments and terms being used to assess it. Several scales have been used but with restricted validity and reliability; notwithstanding, the APID (Aesthetic Pleasure In Design) scale developed in English, as part of the UMA (Unified Model of Aesthetics) project, lacks these limitations. Our research, being in a Spanish speaking country, required the scale to be in Spanish to be comprised and applied to domestic respondents. The adaptation of psychometric instruments with conceptual and linguistic challenging constructs, often is difficult, as the items used to assess the construct do not always have a direct translation. Also, it is possible for the adapted version to require different items that were not considered in the original instrument in order to preserve the content's equivalence according to the target culture. A qualitative-quantitative mixed approach is proposed in order to overcome these issues. The resulting instrument has been statistically tested, proving to be both valid and reliable for the measurement of aesthetic pleasure in design. The final scale consists of five items: *bonito, hermoso, agradable, llamativo* and *me gusta*. This paper aims to improve the understanding of how aesthetic pleasure is perceived and therefore expressed by the local respondents gaining insight into how this construct is mentally represented and categorized by the respondents. It also aims to illustrate how psychometric scales based on respondents' vocabulary have a great potential as usability assessment instruments.

Keywords: Cross-cultural research instruments · Cultural differences · Scale adaptation

1 Introduction

1.1 Aesthetics' Assessment

The study of aesthetics has been a topic of growing relevance in the past years. Consequently, there is an increasing interest in trying to improve the current understanding of aesthetics in design and the factors that relate to it. Most studies in the field of product design are focused on the determinants, rather than in the study of aesthetic pleasure itself, because determinants are the variables that can be directly modified by

© Springer Nature Switzerland AG 2019
P.-L. P. Rau (Ed.): HCII 2019, LNCS 11576, pp. 487–505, 2019.
https://doi.org/10.1007/978-3-030-22577-3_35

designers (Blijlevens et al. 2017). It would be nonsense to deny the apparent universality of some aesthetic preferences as the gestalt principles (Hekkert and Leder 2008; Shortess et al. 1997; Fechner 1997), but it could also be harmful to assume them as the only influencing factor. Although many studies have successfully tested the determinants' influence on people's perception of products (Roussos and Dentsoras 2013; Hekkert and Leder 2008), judging a product's aesthetics by evaluating only the determinants has its limitations, as their ability to predict the aesthetic response to a stimulus, is time- (Jacobsen 2010) cultural- (Hekkert and Leder 2008) and product category- (Hekkert 2015) dependent. Not all the determinants have the same influence in every context (Berghman and Hekkert 2017; Hekkert 2015). As Oscar Wild, said "no object is so beautiful that, under certain conditions, it will not look ugly". Most of the empirical studies regarding determinants have been tested on a specific product category, on a single context, and consequently, the methodological differences between studies make it difficult to compare studies across different contexts and product categories (Blijlevens et al. 2017).

Another way to evaluate product aesthetics is to measure the response from the target audience. This aesthetic response is considered to be intangible and therefore latent, as it cannot be directly observed (Blijlevens et al. 2017; Jöreskog and Sörbom 1979). Psychometric instruments have been widely used to assess latent constructs in social sciences, medical care and other fields. However, when it comes to using a psychometric instrument developed in one language, in a translated version, problems might arise as a result of a poor translation process. This paper aims to explain the process behind the adaptation and implementation of an aesthetic pleasure in design scale, originally in English, to a Spanish speaking country.

1.2   Aesthetic Pleasure

Defining the Construct. For many years, researchers have mentioned the existence of a unique underlying factor behind the aesthetic experience (Eysenck 1940; Marty et al. 2003). Despite this, research on how to define and measure the aesthetic pleasure as a construct of interest has received little attention (Blijlevens et al. 2017). For our research, aesthetic pleasure will be understood as the "sensorial **pleasure** and **delight**" (Goldman, 1990) "people derive **from processing** the object for its own sake, as a source of **immediate experiential pleasure in itself**, and not essentially for its utility in producing something else that is either useful or pleasurable" (Dutton 2009, p. 52).

Measuring Aesthetic Pleasure. Many scales have been used to measure aesthetic appreciation (Faerber et al. 2010; Page and Herr 2002; Hung and Chen 2012; Martindale et al. 1990; Hassenzahl and Monk 2010), but with a lack of reliability or validity (Blijlevens et al. 2017). The biggest concerns in this area are summarized in three aspects. One, determinants and/or semantic descriptors are often used inside the scales, which makes it hard to isolate the measurement of the aesthetic response and, therefore, noise is generated in the assessment (Blijlevens et al. 2017; Faerber et al. 2010). Two, the lack of consistency between studies, as the scales used differ from one research project to another, making it difficult to make comparisons between studies

(Blijlevens et al. 2017). This lack of precision in terminology is one of the biggest problems concerning literature on psychological aesthetics, as mentioned by Augustin et al. (Augustin et al. 2012; Faerber et al. 2010). Three, the instruments used in these studies are often used ad hoc or without a mention of their origin or validity (Blijlevens et al. 2017).

In the Latin American context, the problem is even bigger as the number of instruments developed in Spanish is much lower. Many studies use translated items without a former validation. Spanish is an official language in more than 20 countries for more than 400 millions of people (Stewart 2003) and the difference in the lexicon and usage of the language among different countries and cultures makes it difficult to stablish a "standardized language". There is no evidence of a specific instrument for measuring aesthetic pleasure in product design in Spanish. Hernández Belver (1989) carried out a study in which he included the set of items *bonito – feo* (beautiful – ugly), *agradable – desagradable* (pleasing – unpleasing) and *interesante – no-interesante* (interesting – not interesting) to rate artistic related stimuli. Later, Marty et al. (2003) implemented Belver's items after adding the new pair of items *original – común* (original – common), which are actually known determinants (Hekkert and Leder 2008; Berghman and Hekkert 2017), rather than aesthetic responses. Both studies propose interesting items but lack a strong theoretical background. Marty el al. performed a factor analysis inside their study, but its scope was completely exploratory as their objective was to explore search for empirical evidence of an underlying factor behind the aesthetic experience (Marty et al. 2003). Also, the item generation was based on only a few authors' work.

The APID (Aesthetic Pleasure In Design) scale was developed in English as part of the UMA project (Unified Model of Aesthetics). This project aims, as its name suggests, to unify the different theories behind the explanation of aesthetic pleasure (Berghman and Hekkert 2017). This project was developed inside a design-oriented research. Stimuli from different product categories were used to improve the instrument's robustness. The instrument consists of five items (beautiful, attractive, pleasing to see, like to look and nice to look). This scale has been tested proving to be a valid and reliable instrument (Blijlevens et al. 2017). Because of its psychometric properties and its strong theoretical background, it was identified as an ideal instrument to implement in our research. But, in order to be able to use the APID scale in the local context, the instrument had to be in the local language first.

1.3 Translating the APID Scale

Translation of Psychometric Instruments. Translation is the act of rendering knowledge available from one culture to another (Montgomery 2006). Implementing a scale for its use in a different culture is a process that often requires considerable effort by researchers (Brislin 1970; Wang et al. 2006). Contrary to the translation of a text, translating a measurement scale does have rules for correctness (Montgomery 2006). These rules are the same used in the construction of the scale in the source language (see Blijlevens et al. 2017). In other words, it is necessary to follow, in the translation, a method to ensure that the scale in the target language fits all the requirements a scale must fit. Equivalence between the original and the translated version of the instrument must be preserved. In translation studies, equivalence is the notion used to explain what in natural sciences is called precision. The notion of equivalence means that the objective of a translation "is to produce a target language text which is equivalent to the original language text." p. 86 (Sequeiros 2006). According to the Webster dictionary, equivalent means "having the same or similar effect or meaning". In the past decade, there have been increasing numbers of publications on translating and adapting instruments from one culture to another. Eremenco et al. (2005) identified 5 types of equivalence:

1. Content Equivalence: each item's content is relevant in both cultures;
2. Semantic Equivalence: the similarity of meaning of the items in both cultures after translation is emphasized;
3. Technical Equivalence: data collection methods for the 2 versions of the instrument are similar;
4. Criterion Equivalence: scores are interpreted in the same way in their respective cultures;
5. Conceptual Equivalence: the instrument measures the same theoretical construct in each culture.

The so called "free" and "literal" approaches to translation cannot be used in our case because the researchers cannot see if the translated terms really fit (Montgomery 2006). Moreover, "one-to-one correspondence in scientific translation does not exist." (Montgomery 2006, p. 67). Many methods have been proposed in order to protect the equivalence. Here, in Table 1, are some of the most commonly used methods for translating instruments (Brislin 1970).

Table 1. Typically used instrument translation methods

Method	Description	Advantages	Disadvantages
Back-translation	First, a bilingual translator translates an instrument from the original language into the target language; Second, another independent bilingual translator translates the instrument from the target language back into the original language. The two versions of the tool are then compared for concept equivalence. When an error is found in the back-translation, another translator attempts to re-translate it. This procedure continues until the team of bilingual translators agrees that both versions (the	Back translation provides a way to systematically contrast the translated version to the original items.	Some items are more linguistically and conceptually challenging and it might be reflected in a higher difficulty for the experts (Hilton and Skrutkowski 2002) Bilingual translators may be influenced by the source culture when doing the translation (Hilton and Skrutkowski 2002) Translators' lack of expertise in the instrument's knowledge area may affect the equivalence of the translated version

(continued)

Table 1. (*continued*)

Method	Description	Advantages	Disadvantages
	original and its translation) are equivalent (Cha et al. 2007; Brislin 1970; Behling and Law 2000)		Although back-translation is used, the translated version may not be appropriate for its use with the target population, especially for cross-cultural research. (Maneesriwongul and Dixon 2004)
Bilingual technique	Two versions of the same instrument, one in the original and one in the target language, are administered to a group of bilingual participants. Responses to both version are then compared to identify discrepancies (Brislin 1970)	Allows immediate respondent's feedback	Requires a group of bilingual respondents, which is hard to obtain in the local context Bilingual respondents might have a bias regarding their acculturation and may therefore answer differently than local respondents would. (McDermott and Palchanes 1992; Sperber et al. 1994) This method completely relies on the translators' interpretation of the reasons behind the discrepancies
Committee approach	This approach is based on the use of groups as a way to mitigate possible personal mistakes in the translation process. It consists of the implementation of a committee, in which bilingual experts translate the instrument as a team. (Brislin 1970)	The collaborative approach, helps to eliminate time delays between iterations It helps to prevent possible bias from individuals	This method requires a minimum of three bilingual people. Accessibility of bilingual people as translators is a key issue when applying this approach
Pretest procedure	It consists of the implementation of a pilot test, which allows researchers to identify potential issues with the level of understanding of the translated instrument, by testing it with a smaller group (Brislin 1970)	It allows to have a quick look at people's level of understanding of the instrument	Pre-test respondents might not be representative of the target context This method is used to give an insight on possible issues but it is not a translation method by itself

No matter which method is being used, interpretation is always present in translation (Montgomery 2006); the translation of a scale is a question of equivalence though; consequently, interpretation should be ruled out as far as it introduces the translator's subjectivity.

Translating the Scale. The first step in our research was the translation of the reference instrument. As the study's resources and availability of qualified translators were limited, the research team decided to implement a pretest method as a first approach, as it allows researchers to have a diagnosis of possible misunderstandings and mistakes, which is important given that the items have a high loading of cultural content. The original items were translated by two certified translators who used an intra-translation process, meaning that both worked separately and did not see any of the other translator's work until the end of the process, this in order to maximize the variability. Both translators have Spanish as their main language, but one of them is Colombian and the other one Spanish.

Table 2. Technically translated versions of the APID scale

Original item	Translator 1	Translator 2
This is a beautiful product	Este es un excelente/hermoso/ bonito producto	Este es un producto bonito
This is an attractive product	Este es un producto atractivo	Este es un producto atractivo
This product is pleasing to see	Este producto es agradable a la vista	Ver este producto es un placer
This product is nice to see	Da gusto ver este producto	Este producto es visualmente agradable
I like to look at this product	Me gusta ver este producto	Me gusta mirar este producto

As seen in Table 2 both translators reached a similar outcome with small differences. Consequently, the items chosen for the initial translated version were *bonito, atractivo, agradable a la vista, da gusto ver* and *me gusta ver*. The items were then pretested with a small group of people, ten students from the university. This pre-test procedure was not performed systematically and the information gathered was completely qualitative rather than quantitative. Participants were asked to give comments while rating a small number of products with the translated version of the scale. Even though no large discrepancies between the translators' versions had been found, the pretest of the translated version showed that respondents did not understand the instrument and its items properly. It has been noted that data obtained from the general population "are best when the question is clear, and when the respondent knows the answer and is motivated to report it accurately" (Mechanic 1989, p. 150). As mentioned before, items should not only represent theoretical meaning, but they should also be a reflection of how people actually express themselves. For instance, "beautiful" and "attractive" could be defined as two wholly different words according to the dictionary; however, for Colombian people, using them as two different items while assessing a product was difficult. Besides, it is usual in English to define a product as "attractive", but is fairly uncommon in Colombian Spanish to use the words "*atractivo*" or "*atrayente*" with that purpose. This was evidenced before by Deutcher (1973), as he noted that even though a translation is considered equivalent in a back-translation process (e.g. *amigo, ami, tomodachi* for the word "friend"), the original and translated version of the same word may have important differences in their linguistic nuances. Roughly speaking, in a translation task, a semantic network (of the source language term) is activated in the source language; this activated network also includes nodes for the concept and highly salient structures in the target language which exert a "gravitational pull" resulting in an overrepresentation in the translated terms of those salient structures (Halverson 2003). Even if the conceptual and linguistic equivalence is assured, the measurement of the same concept may require different items or indicators across cultures (DeVos 1973). There is also growing evidence that the experiences, expressions, and correlates (e.g. for depressive disorders) are not universal but rather vary depending on the ethno cultural context (Marsella et al. 1973, 1987). The assumption of cultural universality in the construction of research instruments may lead to an inadequate implementation and even an erroneous interpretation of the research findings (González-Calvo et al. 1997).

Hines (1993) proposed a combination of qualitative and quantitative methods as a way to improve the quality of cross-cultural instruments as it helps researchers to create instruments that are more relevant to the target culture. He points out that the use of cognitive techniques may provide information to "better understand how different cultural and ethnic groups construe the world" (Hines 1993), as the information provided by these techniques correspond to the respondents' underlying though processes. Methods such as free listings, frames, rank orders, triad tests and pile sorts are recommended by the author. Other authors also state that the usage of such techniques may protect the instrument's content validity in the target culture by being a source of relevant and appropriate items (González-Calvo et al. 1997). A qualitative-quantitative approach was then adopted by the research team, as this allowed us to overcome the previously found problems: (1) The lack of understanding of the instrument, due to the use of items that were irrelevant in the context; (2) The fact that different items might be needed in the translated version in order to protect the construct's validity.

2 Methodology

Proposed Methodology. For our research, we propose a combination of Free Listing and Card Sorting as the fundamental activities in the item generation phase. The combination of these two methods has been previously proposed and used (González-Calvo et al. 1997; Sinha 2004), proving to be a successful way to explore and understand the respondents' vocabulary and underlying mental models. After the item generation phase, an exploratory factor analysis will be performed in order to test the construct validity of the proposed adapted instrument (Table 3).

Table 3. Overview on the adaptation methodology

Phase	Method	Objective	Inputs	Output
1	Free listing	To identify local respondents' aesthetic relevant vocabulary, to create an initial set of items	Free Listing physical formats	Elicited items ranked by frequency of mention and cognitive saliency indexes
	Card sorting	To visualize the perceived connections between the elicited items in order to understand the relationships between terms and their perceived similarity.	Filtered elicited items	Clusters representing mental connections between items Selection of final items to validate
2	Exploratory factor analysis	To test the instrument validity and reliability.	Proposed items Respondents' evaluations of different products	Exploratory validation of the instrument Final set of items loading the construct of aesthetic pleasure

3   Procedure and Results

The methods for the initial item generation can be deductive or inductive. Deductive methods are based on an extensive literature review and the study of pre-existing scales (Hinkin 1995), while inductive methods are based on qualitative data gathered from the target population (Kapuscinski and Masters 2010). In this case, Free listing and Card Sorting will be used as inductive methods to generate and understand relevant items and their connections.

3.1   Step One: Free Listing

Free listing is an elicitation technique that has been widely used inside the social sciences (Hines 1993). An example of its usage in scale development processes can be evidenced in Kinzie et al. study, as it was used to gather information in the item generation phase for the development of the Vietnamese-language Depression Rating Scale (Kinzie et al. 1982). Free Listing allows researchers to get a better understanding of the knowledge a group of people has about a particular subject and the vocabulary they use to make reference to it. Free Listing is a simple but structured method, which allows researchers to have access to a lot of information about the cultural domain. A cultural domain, as defined by Borgatti (1999), is a set of concepts that seem to belong to the same mental group or category for a specific cultural group. This method consists of asking participants to "list all the adjectives and words of X that they can think of". According to Smith (1999), items with a higher frequency and average position within the lists are the most relevant ones for the target group.

Respondents. A total amount of 332 participants took part in this study, which was conducted in Medellín, Colombia, and its surroundings. Respondents were selected by convenience with pre-defined quotas, as done before by Antmann et al. (2011). Four different companies (a domestic appliances manufacturer, a clothing manufacturer, a textile manufacturer and a bank service provider) collaborated in the study by allowing the research team to conduct the research activities with their employees. Employees from different areas, with different backgrounds, participated within each company. Students from the university also participated in the study. This combined strategy allowed us to reach a high level of diversity, while maintaining pre-defined criteria: One, all participant had Spanish as their main language. Two, none of the respondents had a design or art related job or profession, as the objective was to explore and understand the non-designers' and non-artists' aesthetic vocabulary. Three, the proportion of female and male respondents had to be similar. Of these 332 participants, answers were not considered from people who did not provide all the information (age, gender, main language). The final analysis was performed with a total of 270 participants (mean age 34, SD 14, 140 females).

Procedure. Respondents were asked to write down all the positive terms or expressions they could think of when asked to describe a product's aesthetics. A total amount of 342 items were collected. Lists were then analyzed with the ANTHROPAC software. Colloquialisms were not considered for further analysis in order to protect the scale's generalizability.

Table 4. Twenty elicited words with the highest scores regarding product aesthetics.

Item	Frequency (%)	Salience
Bonito (beautiful)	44.1	356
Lindo (cute/pretty)	20.4	137
Hermoso (gorgeous)	19.3	136
Bueno (good)	15.6	117
Elegante (elegant)	17.8	111
Agradable (nice/pleasant)	11.5	70
Excelente (excellent)	10.7	70
Espectacular (spectacular)	10.4	67
Calidad (quality)	9.6	65
Útil (useful)	10.0	59
Color (color)	9.3	57
Me gusta (I like it)	9.6	52
Práctico (practical)	8.5	52
Cómodo (comfortable)	7.8	50
Me encanta (I love it)	9.3	47
Belleza (beauty)	6.3	44
Rico (tasty)	7.4	42
Divino (divine/adorable)	7.8	41
Súper (super)	7.0	41
Llamativo (eye-catching)	5.9	41

*(Approximate Translations to English)

Most of the elicited items were directly related to aesthetic pleasure. However, as seen in other studies (Antmann et al. 2011), some of the words had more of a descriptive nature than an evaluative one, making reference to specific attributes such as color and size. Also, other words had a semantic nature (comfortable, modern, practical, economic) making reference to products' meanings rather than the perceived aesthetic pleasure. As expected, *bonito* (beautiful) is by far the most relevant term in the domain, as seen before in other studies (Jacobsen et al. 2004; Augustin et al. 2012). However, the assumption of a single explanatory dimension (beautiful-ugly) could harm the construct's content validity, given the huge amount of expressions used to describe it, as evidenced in the item list. Also, as seen in Table 4, the item attractive was not one of the main twenty elicited items, even more, it was one of the least mentioned items. The absence of this term confirms its low relevance when measuring a product's aesthetics in the local context.

A threshold was established and the only items retained were those whose index was higher than the average. The elicited items were then filtered by the research team according to their coherence with the target construct according to the referenced theoretical background. Physical attributes (such as "colors"), semantic concepts (such as "modern") and known determinants (such as "symmetric") were removed from the list. Twelve items were selected as possible candidates for the proposed scale. Finally, six researchers with previous experience in the field of product aesthetics rated the remaining 12 items on the level to which they thought these items were representative of the construct aesthetic pleasure by using a web-based questionnaire. Coherence (the extent to which the term is directly related to the construct of aesthetic pleasure), practicality (the term is easy to understand and use) and relevance (the term's appropriateness for its use within the field of product design) were stablish as the assessing criteria in order to identify the item's representativeness as done before by our reference scale (Blijlevens et al. 2017). All the experts were asked to rate the different items according to these criteria, using a five-point Likert scale. Items with a score higher than three were rounded up while items with a score lower than three were rounded down. Results are presented in Table 4.

Only the items with a score of three points or higher were retained for further analysis (Table 5).

Table 5. 1-least appropriate to measure aesthetic pleasure, 5-most appropriate to measure aesthetic pleasure.

1	2	3	4	5
Bueno	Elegante	Espectacular	Me gusta	Bonito
Excelente	Interesante	Divino	Me encanta	Lindo
Cómodo	Maravilloso		Llamativo	Hermoso
Rico	Delicioso		Estético	Agradable
Genial				Belleza
				Bello

3.2   Step Two: Card Sorting

Card sorting is a clustering method that allows researchers to identify respondents' levels of meaning and mental connections between concepts (Capra 2005; Hines 1993). Similar approaches have used Card Sorting to gain understanding of constructs such as automotive seat comfort (Erol 2018). "According to cognitive anthropologists, uncovering ways in which various cultural groups classify and divide concepts provides valuable insight into the way a particular group defines and organizes reality" (Hines 1993).

Respondents. A total of 24 respondents from Medellin, Colombia participated in this study. 1. All respondents were undergraduate students or workers. 2. None of the respondents has an art or design related job/profession. 3. The proportion of female and male participants had to be similar.

Procedure. Open Card sorting was selected as the best option as it allowed respondents to create their own groups without being biased by a pre-established structure (Spencer and Garrett 2009) Participants were asked to group the different terms according to their similarity. The resulting 12 items from the previous method were used as input. The number of groups was not limited to a maximum or minimum. Data was analyzed using the SynCaps software.

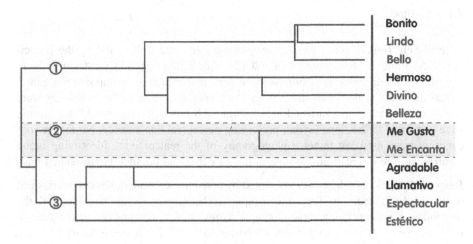

Fig. 1. Cluster analysis after card sorting.

After the cluster analysis three main groups were identified. The research team decided that at least one item from each cluster should be selected in order to have a good content validity. Bonito, me gusta and agradable were then selected as the representative items for each cluster, as they had the highest frequency of mention and its usage was the least age and gender dependent. Hermoso was also selected for further analysis as the research team thought it could provide different information than the item bonito. Many aesthetic theories show the importance of both, the presence of interest and an aesthetic liking inside the aesthetic experience (Graf and Landwehr 2017; Berlyne 1971). Martin also states, from a completely different background, that inside appraisals systems in language there are two different types of reaction when appreciating a stimulus (Martin 2000): impact and quality. Impact is related to the capacity a stimulus has when it comes to captivating the preceptor's attention, while quality describes the positive effect it transmits. For this reason, llamativo (eye-catching) was also selected to be part of the proposed scale, as the research team believed the scale's content validity could be harmed if left out.

As a result, five items are proposed to assess aesthetic pleasure in the local context: *bonito* (beautiful), *hermoso* (gorgeous), *agradable* (nice/pleasing), *llamativo* (eye-catching) and *me gusta* (I like it).

4 Phase Two: Exploratory Factor Analysis

EFA is a commonly used statistical method that allows researchers to evaluate the construct validity of a scale, test, or instrument (Pett et al. 2003; Thompson 2004) by verifying if the proposed items are actually driven by the same underlying latent variables (Field 2009).

4.1 Method

Stimuli Selection. Twenty product images were selected to be rated by the participants. As done by Blijlevens et al. (2017), four different product categories were chosen as stimuli (cameras, motorcycles, chairs, and websites) to improve the generalizability of the scale across different product categories. Five different designs were selected to represent the variety found within each product category. All the stimuli were presented in the same layout, preserving perceptual equivalence. No renders nor concepts were used but rather a photography of the real product. Identifying brand features were removed from the images in order to avoid possible brand related bias.

Respondents. Respondents were recruited by convenience from different contexts and backgrounds in order to keep the sample as heterogeneous as possible. All the respondent's answers that had only extreme scores (1 or 7), neutrals (4), or consecutive responses (e.g., 3, 3, 3…) were deleted before the analysis. Answers in which more than 50% of the scores were assigned to the same value and incomplete answers were also deleted. The final analyses were performed with a total of 142 respondents (85.9% between 19 and 45 years old, 95 females). A minimum amount of 10 respondents per item is recommended while more than 15 is considered ideal (Clark and Watson 1995; DeVellis 2003; Hair Junior et al. 2009).

Procedure. Respondents were asked to view and rate a series of images of products. They were asked to indicate the extent to which they agreed with different statements describing each given stimulus by using a 7-point Likert scale (1 strongly disagree, 7 strongly agree). The aforementioned final items from the generation phase were used for aesthetic pleasure. Items were stated in a way they made a judgment over the stimuli rather than the action (For example, I like the way this product looks, rather than, I like to look at this product). Three items, *novedoso (novel)*, *innovador* (innovative) and *original (original)*, representing the determinant novelty, and one item, *feo* (ugly), representing a commonly used opposite term, were used to assess the discriminant validity of the aesthetic pleasure scale. The questionnaire was created using the web platform Typeforms. This tool is time efficient, as it immediately shows the next question after the participant chooses an answer without having to scroll down. However, this platform does not allow a randomization in the question order so four versions of the questionnaire (with completely different orders) were created to reduce possible bias.

4.2   Results

Correlation Matrix. As the first step of the validation phase a correlation matrix between the nine items was created. Darker colors represent higher correlations between items (closer to 1 or −1). Blue stands for positive correlations while red stands for negatives.

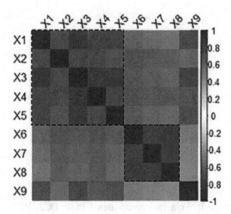

Fig. 2. Correlation matrix – variables measuring aesthetic pleasure and novelty. (Color figure online)

A correlation matrix serves as an indicator to researchers to identify variables that cluster together. "This data reduction is achieved by looking for variables that correlate highly with a group of other variables, but do not correlate with variables outside of that group" (Field et al. 2014). As evidenced in Fig. 1, there are two main data groups that can immediately be recognized. This is a great indicator as the first five variables are the ones supposed to measure aesthetic pleasure and variables X6 to X8 are the ones measuring the determinant "novelty". All correlations within these two groups were above 0,68 and there was not a correlation above 0,9, which means that redundancy was not present. The fact that variables measuring novelty have a medium-high positive correlation with the variables measuring aesthetic pleasure prove the selected items to be a good contrast for discriminant validity. Variable X9, which stands for *feo* (ugly) was also intended to allow a look at the discriminant validity, by standing for an opposite measure. This variable showed a negative correlation to all the variables. As expected, these correlations reach the highest scores when compared to the variables measuring aesthetic pleasure.

PCA and Cluster analysis. A principal component analysis (PCA) was conducted on the 9 items. In order to verify the sampling adequacy for factor analysis, a Kaiser–Meyer–Olkin measure, KMO, was performed. A KMO value of .934 was obtained, which is considered "superb (Field et al. 2014). All KMO values for individual items were >.88, which is highly above the acceptable limit of .5 (Field et al. 2014). Bartlett's test of sphericity = 27102.23, p < .001, indicated that the correlations between items were sufficient for PCA (Bartlett 1950). Eigenvalues for each component in the data were obtained. Three components had eigenvalues over Kaiser's criterion of 1 (Kaiser 1960), explaining, in combination, **87.7%** of the variance. The scree plot showed inflexions that would justify retaining both 2 or 3 components, but as Fig. 3 shows, it was clear that the third component was just an opposite manifestation of the first component as it is located on de same diagonal.

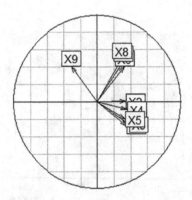

Fig. 3. Principal components PC1, PC2, PC3.

Exploratory Factor Analysis. An exploratory factor analysis with oblique rotation, promax, was performed in order to enhance the differentiation, as the variables loading the different factors were known to have a correlation. Table 2 shows the factor loadings after rotation. The items that cluster on the same factor suggest that factor 1 represents aesthetic pleasure and factor 2 the determinant of aesthetic pleasure, novelty (Table 6).

Table 6. Variable loadings after EFA with oblique rotation

Loadings	Factor 1	Factor 2
Este producto es bonito (this is a beautiful product)	0.96	
Este producto es llamativo (this product is eye-catching)	0.60	
Me gusta como se ve este producto (I like how this product looks)	0.98	
Este producto es hermoso (this is a gorgeous product)	0.74	
Este producto es agradable (this is a nice product)	0.84	
Este producto es feo (this is an ugly product)	−0.79	
Este producto es novedoso (this is a novel product)		0.85
Este producto es original (this is an original product)		0.89
Este producto es innovador (this is a innovative product)		0.99

The five items were retained after the exploratory factor analysis.

Reliability. Cluster analysis revealed that all correlations were above .50 and significant, so all items were retained. Factor in-variance analysis showed no evidence of significant discrepancies between product categories for each factor. Cronbach's alphas were .70 for aesthetic pleasure and .83 for novelty. To assess retest reliability, a subsample (N 40) of the previous sample (N 142) answered the exact same questionnaire after a three-month time period. All correlations between responses from Time 1 and 2 were above .6 and significant for each item. All correlations between the factors at Time 1 and Time 2 were also significant and higher than the recommended level of .7 (Nunnally 1978), aesthetic pleasure (.99) and novelty (.97).

5 Discussion

The exploratory factor analysis showed a good structure among the items constructing the scale. A confirmatory factor analysis is recommended in order to have a more robust validation of the scale. This instrument was created from the local respondents' language, so, although it allowed a much better understanding of the local context and proved to be a valid scale, the scale can only be generalizable inside the local context (Medellín, Colombia). Therefore, a validation of the instrument among different Spanish speakers outside the original context would be a next step. Also, this scale's input was completely visual oriented information, so its performance for other senses should be tested before use.

The results show an adequate fit of the different proposed items. All variables loads were above 0.6 for the factor aesthetic pleasure, and the correlation matrix showed high scores but no redundancy. *Llamativo* (eye-catching) had the lowest correlations inside the group of items, but it had a good theoretical conceptual fit and was still inside the range of desired values, so all of the items measuring aesthetic pleasure were retained. The difference in the correlations and the factor loadings of items measuring "aesthetic pleasure" and the items measuring the determinant "novelty" was clear after PCA and EFA. This is consistent with previous studies (Blijlevens et al. 2017; Marty et al. 2003) and illustrates the importance of differentiating this construct from its determinants when selecting a proper measure. Consequently, five items are proposed to assess aesthetic pleasure in Spanish: *bonito* (beautiful), *hermoso* (gorgeous), *agradable* (nice/pleasing), *llamativo* (eye-catching) and *me gusta* (I like it). Although the final scale consists of five items, researchers could decide if they use a smaller number of items when considered necessary. Content validity should always be considered beforehand.

The adopted method allowed the research team to overcome the adaptation challenges by basing the construction of the instrument both on the respondent's relevant vocabulary and on the underlying aesthetic pleasure theory. The identification of the scale's core items through the elicitation technique allowed the team to gain insight into how aesthetic pleasure is understood and therefore expressed by local respondents. This resulted in a highly relevant initial pool of items, that were then filtered according to previously studied theories, eliminating the initial lack of understanding of the scale's items and their role in product evaluation. The use of the clustering method clarified the connections between items which resulted in a better understanding in the perceived similarities and differences between them. This allowed the research team to have a better picture on the construct's content. The final scale is considered equivalent to the original referenced instrument, as it can be used to measure the same construct under the same methodological considerations. Both instruments were validated inside the realm of product design proving to be reliable and valid instruments.

References

Antmann, G., Ares, G., Varela, P., Salvador, A., Coste, B., Fiszman, S.: Consumers' texture vocabulary: results from a free listing study in three Spanish-speaking countries. Food Qual. Prefer. **22**(1), 165–172 (2011). https://doi.org/10.1016/j.foodqual.2010.09.007

Augustin, M., Wagemans, J., Carbon, C.: All is beautiful? Generality vs. specificity of word usage in visual aesthetics. Acta Psychologica **139**(1), 187–201 (2012)

Bartlett, M.S.: Tests of significance in factor analysis. Br. J. Psychol. **3**(Part II), 77–85 (1950)

Behling, O., Law, K.: Translating Questionnaires and Other Research Instruments (2000). https://doi.org/10.4135/9781412986373

Berghman, M., Hekkert, P.: Towards a unified model of aesthetic pleasure in design. New Ideas Psychol. **47**, 136–144 (2017). Elsevier

Berlyne, D.E.: Aesthetics and Psychobiology. Hemisphere, Washington, DC (1971)

Blijlevens, J., Thurgood, C., Hekkert, P., Chen, L.-L., Leder, H., Whitfield, T.W.A.: The aesthetic pleasure in design scale: the development of a scale to measure aesthetic pleasure for designed artifacts. Psychol. Aesthetics Creativity Arts **11**(1), 86–98 (2017)

Borgatti, S.P.: Elicitation techniques for cultural domain analysis. In: Schensul, J.J., LeCompte, M.D., Nastasi, B.K., Borgatti, S.P. (eds.) Enhanced Ethnographic Methods: Audiovisual Techniques, Focused Group Interviews, and Elicitation Techniques, Ethnographer's toolkit, pp. 115–151, vol. 3. AltaMira, Walnut Creek (1999)

Brislin, R.W.: Back-translation for cross-cultural research. J. Cross Cult. Psychol. **1**, 185–216 (1970)

Capra, M.G.: Factor analysis of card sort data: an alternative to hierarchical cluster analysis. In: Proceedings of the "Human Factors and Ergonomics Society, 49th Annual Meeting, Orlando, Florida, USA (2005)

Cha, E., Kim, K., Erlen, J.: Translation of scales in cross-cultural research: issues and techniques. J. Adv. Nurs. **58**(4), 386–395 (2007). https://doi.org/10.1111/j.1365-2648.2007.04242.x

Clark, L.A., Watson, D.: Constructing validity: basic issues in objective scale development. Psychol. Assess. **7**(3), 309–319 (1995). https://doi.org/10.1037/1040-3590.7.3.309

Deutcher, I.: Asking questions: linguistic comparability. In: Warwick, D., Osherson, S. (eds.) Comparative research methods, pp. 163–186. Prentice Hall, Englewood Cliffs (1973)

DeVellis, R.F.: Scale Development: Theory and Applications, 2nd edn. Sage Publications, Newbury Park (2003)

DeVos, G.: Socialization for Achievement. University of California Press, Berkeley (1973)

Dutton, D.: The Art Instinct. Oxford University Press, New York (2009)

Eremenco, S., Cella, D.S., Arnold, B.: A comprehensive method for the translation and cross-cultural validation of health status questionnaires. Eval. Health Prof. **28**(2), 212–232 (2005)

Erol, T.: Dimensions of holistic automotive seat comfort experience: a card sorting approach. In: Proceedings of "The Human Factors and Ergonomics Society" Annual Meeting, vol. 62, no. 1, pp. 1007–1011 (2018). https://doi.org/10.1177/1541931218621232

Eysenck, H.: The general factor in aesthetic judgements. Br. J. Psychol. Gen. Sect. **31**(1), 94–102 (1940). https://doi.org/10.1111/j.2044-8295.1940.tb00977.x

Faerber, S., Leder, H., Gerger, G., Carbon, C.: Priming semantic concepts affects the dynamics of aesthetic appreciation. Acta Physiol. **135**(2), 191–200 (2010). https://doi.org/10.1016/j.actpsy.2010.06.006

Fechner, G., Höge, H.: Various attempts to establish a basic form of beauty: experimental aesthetics, golden section, and square. Empirical Stud. Arts **15**(2), 115–130 (1997). https://doi.org/10.2190/djyk-98b8-63kr-kudn

Field, A.: Discovering Statistics Using SPSS, 3rd edn. Sage Publications Ltd., London (2009)

Field, A., Miles, J., Field, Z.: Discovering Statistics Using R. Sage, London (2014)

Goldman, Alan H.: Aesthetic qualities and aesthetic value. J. Philos. **87**(1), 23–37 (1990)

González-Calvo, J., González, V., Lorig, K.: Cultural diversity issues in the development of valid and reliable measures of health status. Arthritis Care Res. **10**(6), 448–456 (1997). https://doi.org/10.1002/art.1790100613

Graf, L., Landwehr, J.: Aesthetic pleasure versus aesthetic interest: the two routes to aesthetic liking. Front. Psychol. **8**. https://doi.org/10.3389/fpsyg.2017.00015

Hair Junior, J.F., Black, W.C., Babin, N.J., Anderson, R.E., Tatham, R.L.: Análise multivariada de dados, 6th edn. Bookman, São Paulo (2009)

Halverson, S.L.: The cognitive basis of translation universals. Target **15**(2), 197–241 (2003)

Hassenzahl, M., Monk, A.: The inference of perceived usability from beauty. Hum.-Comput. Interact. **25**, 235–260 (2010). https://doi.org/10.1080/07370024.2010.500139

Hekkert, P.: Aesthetic responses to design: a battle of impulses. In: The Cambridge Handbook of the Psychology of Aesthetics and the Arts, pp. 277–299 (2015). https://doi.org/10.1017/cbo9781139207058.015

Hekkert, P., Leder, H.: Product aesthetics. In: Schifferstein, H.N.J., Hekkert, P. (eds.) Product Experience, pp. 259–285. Elsevier, San Diego (2008)

Hernández Belver, M.: Psicología del arte y criterio estético. Amarú, México (1989)

Hilton, A., Skrutkowski, M.: Translating instruments into other languages: development and testing processed. Cancer Nurs. **25**(1), 1–7 (2002)

Hines, A.M.: Linking qualitative and quantitative methods in cross-cultural survey research: techniques from cognitive science. Am. J. Commun. Psychol. **1993**(21), 72946 (1993)

Hinkin, T.R.: A review of scale development practices in the study of organizations. J. Manag. **21** (5), 967–988 (1995). https://doi.org/10.1177/014920639502100509

Hung, W., Chen, L.: Effects of novelty and its dimensions on aesthetic preference in product design. Int. J. Des. **6**, 81–90 (2012)

Jacobsen, T.: Beauty and the brain: culture, history and individual differences in aesthetic appreciation. J. Anat. **216**(2), 184–191 (2010). https://doi.org/10.1111/j.1469-7580.2009. 01164.x

Jacobsen, T., Buchta, K., Köhler, M., Schröger, E.: The primacy of beauty in judging the aesthetics of objects. Psychol. Rep. **94**(Suppl. 3), 1253–1260 (2004). https://doi.org/10.2466/ pr0.94.3c.1253-1260

Jöreskog, K.G., Sörbom, D.: Advances in Factor Analysis and Structural Equation Models. Abt Books, Cambridge (1979)

Kaiser, H.F.: The application of electronic computers to factor analysis. Educ. Psychol. Meas. **20**, 141–151 (1960)

Kapuscinski, A.N., Masters, K.S.: The current status of measures of spirituality: a critical review of scale development. Psychol. Relig. Spirituality **2**(4), 191–205 (2010). https://doi.org/10. 1037/a0020498

Kinzie, J.D., Manson, S.M., Vinh, D.T., Tolan, N.T., Anh, B., Pho, T.N.: Development and validation of a Vietnamese-language depression rating scale. Am. J. Psychiatry **139**(10), 1276–1281 (1982)

Maneesriwongul, W., Dixon, J.K.: Instrument translation process: a methods review. J. Adv. Nurs. **48**(2), 175–186 (2004). https://doi.org/10.1111/j.1365-2648.2004.03185.x

Marsella, A.J., Hirschfield, R.M., Katz, M. (eds.): Measurement of Depression. Guilford, New York (1987)

Marsella, A.J., Kinzie, D., Gordon, P., et al.: Ethnocultural variations in expression of depression. J. Cross Cult. Psychol. **4**, 435–458 (1973)

Martin, J.: Beyond exchange: APPRAISAL systems in English. In: Hunston, S., Thompson, G. (eds.) Evaluation in Text: Authorial Stance and the Construction of Discourse, pp. 142–175. Oxford University Press, Oxford (2000)

Martindale, C., Moore, K., Borkum, J.: Aesthetic preference: Anomalous findings for Berlyne's psychobiological theory. Am. J. Psychol. **103**, 53–80 (1990). https://doi.org/10.2307/1423259

Marty, G., Conde, C.J.C., Munar, E., Rosselló, J., Roca, M., Escudero, J.T.: Dimensiones factoriales de la experiencia estética [Factorial dimension of aesthetic experience]. Psicothema **15**(3), 478–483 (2003)

McDermott, M.A., Palchanes, K.: A process for translating and testing a quantitative measure for cross-cultural nursing research. J. New York State Nurs. Assoc. **23**, 12–15 (1992)

Mechanic, D.: Medical sociology: some tensions among theory, method, and substance. J. Health Soc. Behav. **30**, 147–160 (1989)

Montgomery, S.L.: Translation of scientific and medical texts. In: Encyclopedia of Language & Linguistics, vol. 13. Elsevier, Amsterdam (2006)

Nunnally, J.C.: Psychometric Theory, 2nd edn. McGraw-Hill, New York (1978)

Page, C., Herr, P.M.: An investigation of the processes by which product design and brand strength interact to determine initial affective and quality judgments. J. Consum. Psychol. **12**, 133–147 (2002). https://doi.org/10.1207/S15327663JCP1202_06

Pett, M.A., Lackey, N.R., Sullivan, J.J.: Making Sense of Factor Analysis: The Use of Factor Analysis for Instrument Development in Health Care Research. Sage Publications Inc., Thousand Oaks (2003)

Roussos, L., Dentsoras, A.: Formulation and use of criteria for the evaluation of aesthetic attributes of products in engineering design. In: International Conference on Engineering Design, ICED 2013, pp. 1–10 (2013)

Shortess, G., Clarke, J., Shannon, K.: The shape of things: but not the golden section. Empirical Stud. Arts **15**(2), 165–176 (1997). https://doi.org/10.2190/3ubv-2lju-t2t9-d7xn

Sinha, R., Boutelle, J.: Rapid information architecture prototyping. In: Proceedings 2004 Conference on Designing Interactive Systems Processes, Practices, Methods, and Techniques - DIS 2004 (2004). https://doi.org/10.1145/1013115.1013177

Smith, J.J.: Using ANTHROPAC 3.5 and a spreadsheet to compute a free list salience index. Cogn. Technol. Work **1**, 179–196 (1999)

Spencer, D., Garrett, J.: Card Sorting, pp. 82–85. Rosenfeld Media, Brooklyn (2009)

Sperber, A.D., DeVellis, R.F., Boehlecke, B.: Cross-cultural translation. J. Cross Cult. Psychol. **25**, 501–524 (1994)

Stewart, M.: The Spanish Language Today. Routledge, London (2003)

Thompson, B.: Exploratory and Confirmatory Factor Analysis: Understanding Concepts and Applications. American Psychological Association, Washington, DC (2004)

Wang, W., Lee, H., Fetzer, S.: Challenges and strategies of instrument translation. West J. Nurs. Res. **28**, 310–321 (2006)

Sequeiros, X.R.: Translation: pragmatics. In: Encyclopedia of Language & Linguistics, vol. 13. Elsevier, Amsterdam (2006)

Selective Preference in Visual Design:
A Case Study of Cover Designs
of Industrial Design Magazine

Rungtai Lin[1(✉)], Ming-Xean Sun[2(✉)], Jianping Huang[1(✉)],
and Jiede Wu[1(✉)]

[1] Graduate School of Creative Industry Design,
National Taiwan University of Arts, New Taipei City, Taiwan
rtlin@mail.ntua.edu.tw, 50516059@qq.com,
125082357@qq.com
[2] Institute of Applied Arts, National Chiao Tung University,
Hsinchu, Taiwan
buddasfox@gmail.com

Abstract. The cover designs of professional magazines can reflect trends in visual design. Based on the cover designs of 27 issues of "Industrial Design" magazine from 1967 to 1974, the purpose of this study is to study how people recognize cover designs which purposely reflect Taiwan's design development and visual design trends. In particular the study explores the empirical selective preference of "Industrial Design" magazine's cover design and how matches between the designer's intension and user's preference support the assumption that visual design trend exists in these cover designs. In this study, the stimulus materials are cover designs as an "encoding" process, and the subjects are viewers as a "decoding" process, both of which draw on the visual significance of the cover design in terms of "Creativity in Layout" and "Balance in Proportion." Results showed that the selective preference of viewers differs with age, gender and education background. This study also purposes an approach of using MDS analysis to understand user perceptions and demonstrate that the results are worthy of further study.

Keywords: Visual design · User perception · Industrial Design Magazine · Taiwan design development

1 Introduction

Social communication (e.g. networking) is a relatively new term that has emerged over the last decade. It may appear to be a new concept that is a regrouping of the previously known concepts of social interaction, communication and language [5, 7, 9, 17, 18, 26, 30]. In this study, visual design was viewed as a form of social communication [1]. What is the point of visual design? Is it graphic design or is it art? What purpose does it serve in our society and culture? After studying how meaning and identity are at the core of every visual design definition, this study argues that the role and function of visual design is social communication [1, 6, 29, 35, 36].

© Springer Nature Switzerland AG 2019
P.-L. P. Rau (Ed.): HCII 2019, LNCS 11576, pp. 506–518, 2019.
https://doi.org/10.1007/978-3-030-22577-3_36

Recently, social communication has received increased attention from the academic and business communities [17]. Both academics and practitioners emphasized that social communication in relationship development relates not only to the human community, but also to aspects such as business, management, arts, and even in different fields of therapy [7, 18, 26, 34]. Since social communication is constantly alert to the spoken and written appearance of novel words, the question presents itself: How did they miss visual design? How is it that the words denoting them and the work they produce are not included in a form of design work? Based on the communication and semiotic theory, this study argues that visual design should be approached semiologically and treated as a semiotic language rather than a form of art [1, 10–12, 27, 28].

The study analyzed how the meaning of visual design is constructed and communicated, and explains how visual design relates to construction of meaning by the designer and reproduction of meaning by the viewer [32–34], taking examples from advertising, magazines, illustration, website design, comics, greetings cards and packaging. Visual design as social communication looks at the ways in which visual design contributes to the formation of social and cultural identities, discussing the ways in which age, gender and education groups are represented in visual design, as well as how images and texts communicate with different cultural groups [1, 35, 36].

This study is carried out to test the hypothesis that subjects prefer a specific visual appearance of "Industrial Design (ID)" magazine cover design. It explores how visual design relates to both culture and human society, and investigates visual design as an integral part of our society and culture, which needs to be studied, acknowledged and understood as art is.

2   Background

2.1   A Research Framework for Visual Design as Communication

After examining a range of communication theoretical approaches, including those of Shannon and Weaver [31], Lasswell [16], Barthes [2], Derrida and Foucault [3], Lin et al. [22] a research framework combining communication theory with semiology and mental models was proposed to explore the issue of visual design (e.g. graphic, painting) as communication. In Lin's research framework, three levels of problems are identified in the study of communication: technical, semantic, and effectiveness. Jakobson's [15] communication model of six constitutive factors with six functions are included in the framework. The six constitutive factors are as follows: addresser, addressee, context, message, contact, and code. Each of these factors determines a different function in each act of communication: emotive, conative, referential, poetic, phatic, and metalingual [8, 15]. In addition, Norman's [24, 25] conceptual model that proposed three levels of design processing—visceral, behavioral, and reflective design - was also taken into account. Thus, to explore the issue of visual design as communication, communication theory should be combined with mental models. Based on previous studies [22], a research framework was proposed to explore the issue of visual design as social communication as shown in Fig. 1.

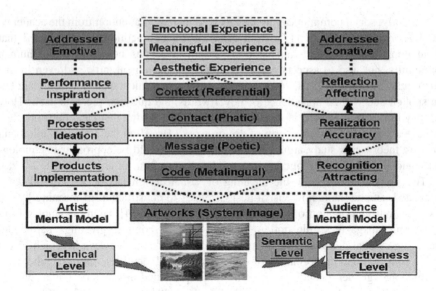

Fig. 1. A framework for social communication research [19]

For social communication, the artist goes through three key stages to express significance through his or her artworks: performance (inspiration), process (ideation), and product (implementation). For the viewer, there are three key steps to understanding the meaning of an artwork: recognition (attracting), realization (accuracy), and reflection (affecting). Recognition requires letting the viewer receive a message through perception in which the viewer can accurately receive a message through the artwork. The degree of realization measures how accurately the transmitted message expresses the desired meaning. Reflection concerns the ways in which the viewer's actions are influenced, thus showing how effectively the message affects conduct in the expected way [4, 19].

2.2   Taiwan Design Development

The evolution of Taiwan design development is a process of adaptive design, specifically a fusion of Dechnology (Design-Technology) and Humart (Humanity-Art). Taiwan design development is a fusion of Dechnology and Humart which could be represented as a smile curve as shown in Fig. 2 [23], from OEM (Original Equipment Manufacturer), ODM (Original Design Manufacture), to OBM (Original Brand Manufacture). The three stages also reflect the tendency of Taiwan craft and product design development, from "use" to "user", from "function" to "feeling", and from "hi-tech" to "hi-touch". Lin's study [23] is intended to explore the relationship between product designs (dechnology) and craft design (humart) which were merged into Taiwan design development. However, we now live in a small world with a large global market. While the market heads toward "globalization", design tends toward "localization" so we must "think globally" for the market, but "act locally" for design.

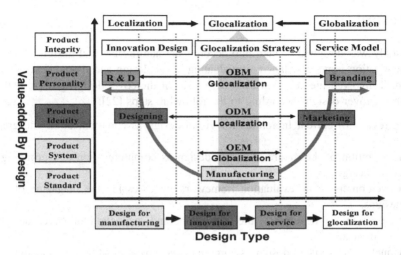

Fig. 2. Briefing diagram of Taiwan design development [23]

2.3   Industrial Design Magazine

Alongside the development of Taiwan design, the ID magazine has been published for over half a century. It is the first design related professional magazine that focused on Taiwan design development and documents completely and comprehensively the development of Taiwan's design and related subjects. ID magazine is the only publication among all the academic publications which focuses on the design field, obviously its influence on the development of Taiwan design has been significant. The first issue of ID magazine was published in December 1967; after publication of issue No. 27 on July 1974, it was suspended until January 1980. Issue No. 136 was published on July 2017 to celebrate the magazine's 50th anniversary as shown in Fig. 3. The front cover designs reflected Taiwan's design development; for example, from social development, technique advancement, and technological influence to international design interaction. Therefore, the cover designs of ID magazine were selected as examples in this study, some of which are shown in Fig. 4.

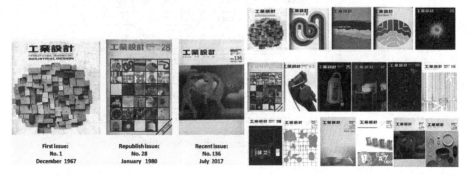

Fig. 3. Three main issues of ID cover designs magazine

Fig. 4. Some cover designs of ID magazine

3 Method

This study was designed to take into account the nature of visual design as a social communication issue, resistance to evaluating cover design and the context of visual design. It involved literature reviews, derivation of the cover design groups, and validation on cover designs according to the following steps [22]:

(a) A review of current literatures for visual design as communication and graphic design.
(b) Exploration of the nature of visual design as communication and grouping the cover design.
(c) Development of an evaluation framework for assessing the magazine of cover designs.
(d) Discussion for developing the framework and evaluation of cover design as communication.
(e) Conclusion of visual design as communication by evaluating cover designs.

Three different sessions were used as shown in Fig. 5. Session 1 conducted a literature review and established a research framework. In Session 2, a pilot study of evaluating "Industrial Design" magazine cover designs was conducted to group the stimulus and test the utility of the framework shown in Fig. 1. Then, a rating approach was used to evaluate cover designs with a questionnaire via website in Session 3. Multivariate data and protocol analysis were applied to study the visual design as social communication and the results of evaluating "Industrial Design" magazine cover designs were explored [4, 19].

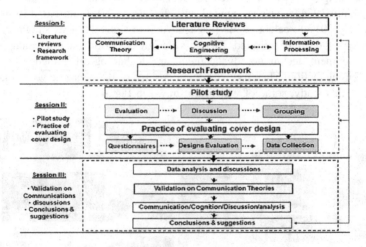

Fig. 5. Research framework for this study

3.1   Pilot Study for Identifying the Stimuli

The pilot study involved using questionnaires and interviews to identify the category of "Industrial Design Magazine" cover designs for evaluation. Cover designs from 27 issues of IDM served as the stimuli and were arranged randomly as shown at the left of Fig. 6. Forty professional designers and experts in visual design served as the subjects and were asked to group 27 issues of cover design into three categories then feedback on the reason why. The data provided by these 40 experts was collected and analyzed identifying three categories namely, graphic design, local feature and product design as shown at the right of Fig. 6. By analyzing the results from each category that reflected the changes in design which and utilized the design elements for the Taiwan design development in 1960s, the three categories of 27 cover designs were used as the stimuli for questionnaire interview.

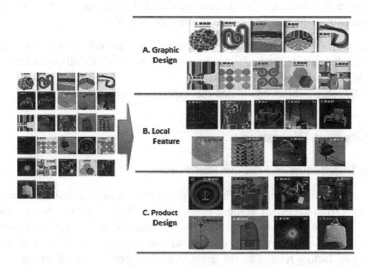

Fig. 6. The three categories of stimuli for 27 cover designs

3.2   Participants

All the study participants were from the web community (e.g. FB, LINE) in Taiwan. There was a total of 490 participants of whom 259/53% were male and (231/47%) female; ages of under 20 (193/39%), 21–45 (139/28%), 46–60 (102/21%) and 61–65+ (56/12%); backgrounds design-related (195/40%), engineering-related (58/12%), business-related (60/12%) and others (177/36%); education backgrounds undergraduate (142/28.98%), graduate (161/32.86%), and other (187/38.16%). The participants were told the purpose of the study and were then asked to select their preference based on their understanding of content of each cover design based on the questions.

3.3   Procedure

This study was conducted on the internet. Social network groups were invited to participate as subjects and those who agreed were instructed to follow the experimental procedure [22]. On the website, the purpose of the experiment was explained to the subjects and the 27 issues of ID cover designs in three categories were presented. The subjects were then asked to identify the total image of the ID cover designs and then rate them with the following five questions:

1. Please identify which best fits the concept "Harmony in Color" for the cover design?
2. Please identify which best fits the concept "Creativity in Layout" for the cover design?
3. Please identify which best fits the concept "Balance in Proportion" for the cover design?
4. Please identify which best fits the concept "Overall in Design" for the cover design?
5. Please identify which cover design do they most prefer?

The 27 issues of ID Magazine cover designs together with the questionnaire were published on the website: https://docs.google.com/forms/d/1YVgOIPbJy9hZttrZauXOF-HA-rzoIsACj1QghsFI3_s/edit?ts=5bcdd7ba

Typically, each subject completed the experiment within 5 min.

4   Results and Discussion

4.1   The Distribution of Selective Preference

Results from experiments indicate that it is possible to draw conclusions regarding the cover designs from data such as those obtained [14, 36]. The distribution of responses to 27 issues of cover design by gender, age, education and background were summarized and analyzed. In order to understand visual design, many studies have proposed the key factors related to the graphic design principles such as color, layout, proportion, balance, rhythm etc. In this study, the participants were asked to select the most fitness of "Harmony in Color", "Creativity in Layout", "Balance in Proportion" and "Overall in Design", then select their most preferred cover design. Taken gender as an example, Fig. 7 summarized the distribution of all participants' responses to the 27 cover designs.

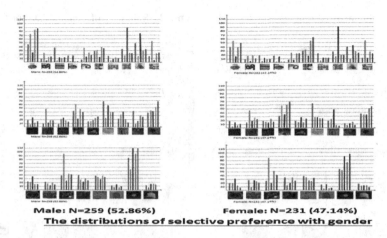

Male: N=259 (52.86%)   **Female: N=231 (47.14%)**
The distributions of selective preference with gender

Fig. 7. The three categories of stimuli for 27 cover designs (Color figure online)

Table 1 summarized the first three and the last three rank issues of cover design for the male subjects, while Table 2 is for the female subjects. In the Table 1, "Q1-5" represents the five questions and 26(32%) in second column indicates that the cover design of issue no. 26 issue was preferred by 32% respondents. The information of Table 2 is the same as Table 1.

A stepwise multiple regression analysis was used to establish the regression model of the most preferred cover design. The results are as follows:

The most preferred (male) $= -0.010 - 0.060 * f1$ (Harmony in Color) $- 0.059 * f2$
(Creativity in Layout) $+ 0.051 * f3$ (Balance in Proportion) $+$
$1.153 * f4$ (Overall in Design)   (1)
$R2 = 0.961$, $p < 0.001$

The most preferred (female) $= -0.033 - 0.159 * f1$ (Harmony in Color) $- 0.068 * f2$
(Creativity in Layout) $+ 0.043 * f3$ (Balance in Proportion) $+$
$1.164 * f4$ (Overall in Design)   (2)
$R2 = 0.930$, $p < 0.001$

The model showed that "Harmony in Color" and "Creativity in Layout" had a negative correlation to the most preferred, while "Balance in Proportion" was slightly linked to the most preferred; so the most preferred of cover design was mainly affected by the overall in design rating. The higher the "overall in design" rating was, the higher the most preferred was.

Table 1. Summary of ranking data for male   **Table 2.** Summary of ranking data for female

Male	Rank no. 1	Rank no. 2	Rank no. 3	......	Rank no. 25	Rank no. 26	Rank no. 27
Q1	26 (32%)	16 (26%)	09 (19%)	....	02 (4%)	13 (3%)	05 (3%)
Q2	22 (37%)	01 (28%)	14 (24%)	....	25 (3%)	03 (2%)	27 (2%)
Q3	26 (42%)	08 (34%)	09 (28%)	....	03 (4%)	07 (3.5%)	02 (1%)
Q4	26 (37%)	01 (32%)	19 (20%)	....	03 (4%)	25 (3.1%)	04 (0.1%)
Q5	26 (42%)	01 (34%)	22 (16%)	....	17 (4.2%)	07 (3.9%)	04 (0.4%)

Female	Rank no. 1	Rank no. 2	Rank no. 3	......	Rank no. 25	Rank no. 26	Rank no. 27
Q1	16 (27%)	26 (24%)	01 (17%)	....	18 (5%)	02 (4%)	05 (3%)
Q2	22 (38%)	14 (25%)	01 (24%)	....	18 (3%)	07 (2%)	04 (0.4%)
Q3	08 (39%)	26 (35%)	09 (19%)	....	07 (5.2%)	18 (4.8%)	02 (3%)
Q4	26 (32%)	14 (26%)	22 (22%)	....	07 (6%)	03 (4%)	04 (0.4%)
Q5	26 (41%)	14 (30%)	01 (21%)	....	18 (4%)	25 (3%)	04 (0.4%)

01 02 03 04 07 08 09

10 12 16 22 25 26

01 02 03 04 05 07 08

09 14 16 18 22 25 26

4.2   Discussions

In this study, the selective preference data were subjected to the MDPREF procedure, and a cognitive space was constructed [13, 20, 21]. The purpose of MDPREF analysis is to transform the selective preference data into a multidimensional configuration. How well the configuration fits the real differences of paired objects depends on the stresses and dimensions. The higher the number of dimensions is, the lower the stress is and the better the configuration fits the preference of the stimulus. The stress values of two-dimensional configurations are .678 and .224 for the male subjects, and .664 and .208 for the female subjects, respectively. The stress values indicate that the two-dimensional space seemed most appropriate for the preference data. The locations of 27 cover designs on the plane defined by the dimensions 1 and 2 are plotted in Fig. 8 for the male subjects, and Fig. 8 for the female subjects [13, 20, 21].

In Figs. 8 and 9 the distance between any two plotted points (cover designs) can be interpreted as an indicator of similarity or dissimilarity. The projections of 27 cover designs aligned to the five questions (attributes) are shown in Figs. 10 (male subjects) and 11 (female subjects) ranked according to the first three and the last three. The features for grouping cover designs together can be used to interpret the meanings of dimensions [20, 21].

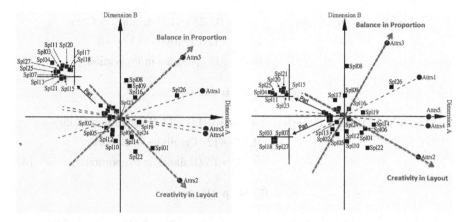

Fig. 8. The cognitive space of male subjects   **Fig. 9.** The cognitive space of female subjects

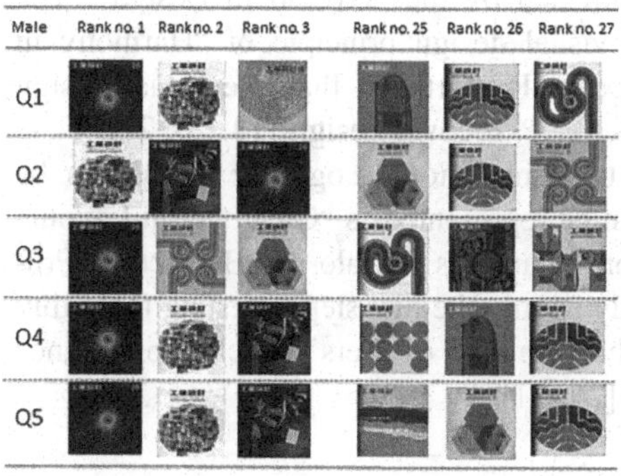

Fig. 10. Projections of ranking data for males 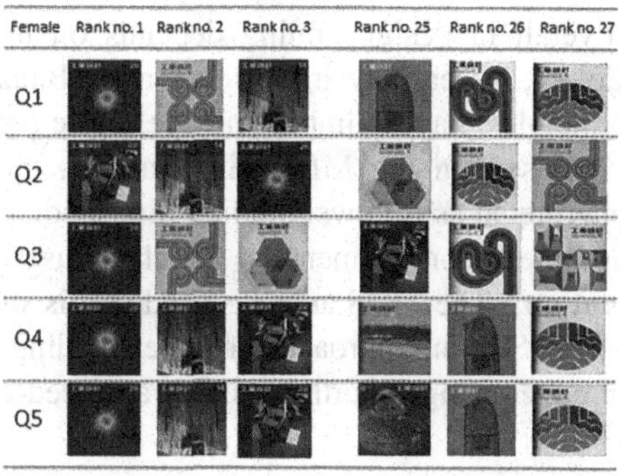   **Fig. 11.** Projections of ranking data for females

The meanings of dimensions also can be interpreted directly according to the relationship of attributes in the cognitive space. The dimensions can be interpreted by attaching the attributes' transformed vectors to the cognitive space more objectively through MDPREF analysis. For example, the correlation between the "Balance in Proportion" and "Creativity in Layout" is .0736 corresponding to an angle of 86° [20, 21]. Thus, the vectors of "Balance in Proportion" and "Creativity in Layout" can be represented as a two-dimension cognitive space as shown in the Figs. 7 and 8 for male and female subjects respectively. However, the correlation between "overall in design" and "the most preferred" is .978 and .957 for the male subjects and female subjects which means that the two attributes are almost the same. Therefore, another stepwise multiple regression analysis was used to establish the regression model's "overall in design" for the selective preference of cover design. The results are as follows:

$$\text{Overall in Design (male)} = -.017 + 0.623 * f1 \text{ (Harmony in Color)}$$
$$- 0.455 * f2 \text{(Creativity in Layout)}$$
$$+ 0.075 * f3 \text{ (Balance in Proportion)} \qquad (3)$$

$$R2 = 0.786, \ p < 0.001$$

$$\text{Overall in Design (female)} = -0.009 + 0.451 * f1 \text{ (Harmony in Color)}$$
$$+ 0.539 * f2 \text{ (Creativity in Layout)}$$
$$+ 0.092 * f3 \text{ (Balance in Proportion)} \qquad (4)$$

$$R2 = 0.734, \ p < 0.001$$

The model shows that the "Harmony in Color" and "Creativity in Layout" were the key attributes for the overall in design while "Balance in Proportion" had a slight effect on "Overall in Design". The previous result showed that the most preferred by the subject's selective preference was mainly affected by the "Overall in Design". The "overall in design" rating depends on the visual design principle of "Harmony in Color", "Creativity in Layout" and "Balance in Proportion", thus the visual design principles play an important role in the preference in cover design [14, 20, 21].

Based on the MDPREF analyses, the two-dimensional cognitive space can be interpreted as follows: the first dimension can be represented as "Creativity in Layout" and the second dimension which focuses on balance is a scale of "Balance in Proportion." The MDS analysis used in this study is only the first step in testing the utility of MDS as an approach for understanding the cognition of users' selective preference in cover design. Further studies are needed [20, 21].

5 Conclusion and Suggestion

Along with the rapid growth and development in information technology and multimedia, the question of whether the traditional visual design principles will change or not is an issue worthy of in-depth study.

Therefore, this case study of comparisons between the cover design intentions and viewer's preferences are purposely a reflection of visual design trend. An approach was proposed that applies some techniques of Multidimensional Scaling to study the cover designs of ID magazine from 1967 to 1974. The methods of this study included pilot study, expert interview, questionnaire and Multidimensional Scaling to analyze the visual features of ID magazine's cover design in order to understand the visual design trend. Results from the experiments indicate that a two-dimensional cognitive space of exploring cover design was configured. Two key factors "Creativity in Layout" and "Balance in Proportion" which affect the cover designs are identified and discussed.

Throughout this study, the totality of graphic language and its specifically graphic variables are emphasized. Although this study may appear to be subjective theoretically, it is suggested that the MDS approach will be validated by more testing and evaluation of cover design and exploring the visual design trend in the further study.

References

1. Barnard, M.: Graphic Design as Communication. Routledge, Abingdon (2013)
2. Barthes, R.: Mythologies (1957). Trans. Annette Lavers, pp. 302–306. Hill and Wang, New York (1972)
3. Boyne, R.: Foucault and Derrida: The Other Side of Reason. Routledge, Abingdon (2013)
4. Chen, S.J., Lin, C.L., Lin, R.: A cognition study of turning poetry into abstract painting. In: The Fifth Asian Conference on Cultural Studies (ACCS 2015), Kobe, Japan (2015)
5. Craig, R.T.: Communication theory as a field. Commun. Theory 9(2), 119–161 (1999)
6. Crilly, N., Moultrie, J., Clarkson, P.J.: Seeing things: consumer response to the visual domain in product design. Des. Stud. 25(6), 547–577 (2004)
7. Dwyer, C., Hiltz, S., Passerini, K.: Trust and privacy concern within social networking sites: a comparison of Facebook and MySpace. In: AMCIS 2007 proceedings, p. 339 (2007)
8. Fiske, J.: Introduction to Communication Studies. Routledge, London (2010)
9. Gameren, K., Vlug, M.: The content and dimensionality of communication styles. Commun. Res. 36, 178–206 (2009)
10. Gibson, J.J.: The Ecological Approach to Visual Perception: Classic Edition. Psychology Press, London (2014)
11. Goldman, A.: Evaluating art. In: The Blackwell Guide to Aesthetics, pp. 93–108 (2004)
12. Goldschmidt, G.: On visual design thinking: the vis kids of architecture. Des. Stud. 15(2), 158–174 (1994)
13. Green, P.E., Carmone Jr., F.J., Smith, S.M.: Multidimensional Scaling: Concepts and Applications. Allyn and Bacon, Boston (1989)
14. Isaacowitz, D.M., Wadlinger, H.A., Goren, D., Wilson, H.R.: Selective preference in visual fixation away from negative images in old age? An eye-tracking study. Psychol. Aging 21(1), 40 (2006)
15. Jakobson, R.: Language in literature. The Belknap Press of Harvard U. P., Cambridge (1987)
16. Lasswell, H.D.: The theory of political propaganda. Am. Polit. Sci. Rev. 21(3), 627–631 (1927)
17. Lenhart, A., Madden, M.: Social Networking Websites and Teens: An Overview, pp. 1–7. Pew/Internet (2007)
18. Livingstone, S.: Taking risky opportunities in youthful content creation: teenagers' use of social networking sites for intimacy, privacy and self-expression. New Media Soc. 10(3), 393–411 (2008)
19. Lin, C.L., Chen, J.L., Chen, S.J., Lin, R.: The cognition of turning poetry into painting. J. US-China Educ. Rev. B 5(8), 471–487 (2015)
20. Lin, R., Lin, C.Y., Wong, J.: An application of multidimensional scaling in product semantics. Int. J. Ind. Ergon. 18(2–3), 193–204 (1996)
21. Lin, R., Lin, P.C., Ko, K.J.: A study of cognitive human factors in mascot design. Int. J. Ind. Ergon. 23(1–2), 107–122 (1999)
22. Lin, R., Qian, F., Wu, J., Fang, W.-T., Jin, Y.: A pilot study of communication matrix for evaluating artworks. In: Rau, P.-L.P. (ed.) CCD 2017. LNCS, vol. 10281, pp. 356–368. Springer, Cham (2017). https://doi.org/10.1007/978-3-319-57931-3_29
23. Lin, R., Kreifeldt, J., Hung, P.-H., Chen, J.-L.: From Dechnology to Humart – a case study of Taiwan design development. In: Rau, P.L.P. (ed.) CCD 2015. LNCS, vol. 9181, pp. 263–273. Springer, Cham (2015). https://doi.org/10.1007/978-3-319-20934-0_25
24. Norman, D.A.: Emotional Design: Why We Love (or Hate) Everyday Things. Basic Books, New York (2005)

25. Norman, D.A.: The Design of Everyday Things: Revised and Expanded Edition. Basic Books, New York (2013)
26. Pempek, T.A., Yermolayeva, Y.A., Calvert, S.L.: College students' social networking experiences on Facebook. J. Appl. Dev. Psychol. **30**(3), 227–238 (2009)
27. Peterson, R.A.: Sociology of the arts exploring fine and popular forms. Contemp. Sociol.: J. Rev. **33**(4), 454–455 (2004)
28. Pratt, H.J.: Categories and comparisons of artworks. Br. J. Aesthetics **52**(1), 45–59 (2012)
29. Rettie, R., Brewer, C.: The verbal and visual components of package design. J. Prod. Brand Manag. **9**(1), 56–70 (2000)
30. Rowland, C.: Using the communication matrix to assess expressive skills in early communicators. Commun. Disord. Q. **32**, 190–201 (2011). 1525740110394651
31. Shannon, C.E., Weaver, W.: The Mathematical Theory of Communication, Urbana (1949)
32. Sullivan, G.: Research acts in art practice. Stud. Art Educ. **48**(1), 19–35 (2006)
33. Trivedi, S.: Artist-audience communication: Tolstoy reclaimed. J. Aesthetic Educ. **38**(2), 38–52 (2004)
34. Trusov, M., Bucklin, R.E., Pauwels, K.: Effects of word-of-mouth versus traditional marketing: findings from an internet social networking site. J. Mark. **73**(5), 90–102 (2009)
35. Twyman, M.: A schema for the study of graphic language (tutorial paper). In: Kolers, P.A., Wrolstad, M.E., Bouma, H. (eds.) Processing of Visible Language, pp. 117–150. Springer, Boston (1979). https://doi.org/10.1007/978-1-4684-0994-9_8
36. Vitz, P.C.: Preference for different amounts of visual complexity. Behav. Sci. **11**(2), 105–114 (1966)

Design for Aesthetic Pleasure

Po-Hsien Lin[1(✉)], Mo-Li Yeh[2], and Hsi-Yen Lin[1]

[1] Graduate School of Creative Industry Design,
National Taiwan University of Arts, Daguan Road, Banqiao District,
New Taipei City 22058, Taiwan
t0131@ntua.edu.tw, p3yann@gmail.com
[2] Department of Cultural Creativity and Digital Media Design,
Lunghwa University of Science and Technology,
No. 300, Sec. 1, Wanshou Road, Guishan District, Taoyuan City 33306, Taiwan
1101moli@gmail.com

Abstract. The theoretical articulation of functionalism has been a dominant influence in modern industrial design. Though practical function of a product is always the industrial designer's main concern, aesthetic effect is still a critical issue for the development of a new product. How a product was perceived as pleasurable? Jordan (1998) in a study titled "Human Factors for Pleasure in Product Use" concluded eight pleasure factors: (1) Security, (2) Confidence, (3) Pride, (4) Excitement, (5) Satisfaction, (6) Entertainment, (7) Freedom, and (8) Nostalgia. Through the quantitative investigation, this study intends to construct an accessible criticism model of cultural creative products based on the perspective of Jordan's theory. The framework provides a foundation for design industries to establish design strategies.

Keywords: Aesthetic pleasure · Product design

1 Introduction

The theoretical articulation of functionalism has been a dominant influence in modern industrial design. Though practical function of a product is always the industrial designer's main concern, aesthetic effect is still a critical issue for the development of a new product.

The Taiwanese government has been aggressively promoting culture creative industries in recent years. The goal of this policy is to develop a new economic model and better the living environment through attracting consumers with cultural products and aesthetic experiences. Many studies pointed out that designing products which emphasize local features to increase their cultural value has become a significant facet of the design process [8].

In addition to mass production products, handicrafts are very important articles for daily life. Crafts industries have become one of the most significant domains in culture creative industries of Taiwan. The exquisite techniques and various materials combine to form a typical aura of craftsmanship, through which to attract the public. According to Culture Statistics Report published by Ministry of Culture, the crafts industries

© Springer Nature Switzerland AG 2019
P.-L. P. Rau (Ed.): HCII 2019, LNCS 11576, pp. 519–530, 2019.
https://doi.org/10.1007/978-3-030-22577-3_37

created a revenue of 77,289,767 thousand NT dollars in 2017 as shown in Fig. 1 [9]. It was ranked number five among all 15 domains of cultural creative industries of Taiwan.

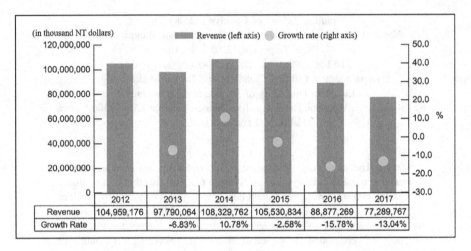

Fig. 1. Annual revenue and growth rate of Taiwan crafts industries 2012–2017

Among all fields of different materials, the products of wooden crafts had an excellent performance in the same year as shown in Table 1 [9].

Table 1. Annual revenue and growth rate of Taiwan wooden crafts industries 2012–2017

Year	2012	2013	2014	2015	2016	2017
Revenue	72,267	77,475	105,770	127,476	110,267	117,908
Growth rate		−7.21%	36.52%	20.52%	−13.50%	6.93%

(in thousand NT dollers)

Wooden crafts have typical attractions. Most of the people were fascinated by the natural texture of woods. One could hardly resist the varied colors, beautiful grains and distinctive scents of wooden products.

2 Research Purpose

The Fig. 2 shows a set of wooden crafts created by Po-Hsien Lin, one of the authors of this paper. The technique applied in these products is called woodturning, which was employed the wood lathe machine, the instrument designed specially for creating objects of symmetry about the axis of rotation.

Fig. 2. Wooden crafts created by Po-Hsien Lin

Fig. 3. The assemblage and the parts of the works (Color figure online)

This set of wooden crafts is an imitation of human figure. Four different woods were used in this set of works. The heads with bright color is Corkwood, the brown wood is Formosan Michelia, the red color is Rosewood, and black wood is Ebony. They could be taken apart and used as a sectional container (Fig. 3).

Though these products are functional, a common response of the first glance at these works is "cute". Many beholders expressed their appreciations because of the pleasure derived from the works. How a product was perceived as pleasurable? What elements of a work could be the main factor that resulted in viewers' preference?

The purpose of this study is to construct an accessible criticism model of cultural creative products. The framework provides a foundation for design industries to establish design strategies. An aesthetic paragon connecting to cultural context is addressed based on the output of the study, through which to promote aesthetic value of Taiwanese modern cultural products, enhances aesthetic literacy of the people.

3 Literature Review

3.1 A Historical Exploration of the Theories of Pleasure

In the book "Design for the Real World," Papanek (1971) brought up the idea of "Function Complex." He announced six parts of the function complex, including method, use, need, telesis, association, and aesthetics [11]. In Norman's (2002) book "Emotional Design", he suggested three critical components of product design: usability, aesthetics, and practicality [10].

Nevertheless, when aesthetics was addressed in the practice of design, it usually referred to beautiful appearance. Two thousand years ago when discussing the topic of "beauty" in his "Major Hippias", Plato emphasized that he intended to explore "what beautiful is" instead of "what is beautiful" [12]. Plato's argument lifted the discussion of beauty up to the level of a philosophical inquiry. Aesthetics becomes a convention discipline of "the branch of philosophy dealing with such notions as the beautiful, the ugly, the sublime, the comic, etc., as applicable to the fine arts...the study of the mind and emotions in relation to the sense of beauty" [1].

During the eighteenth century, some empiricist philosophers such as Edmund Burke and David Hume established their aesthetics theories stressing the connection between sense of beautiful and sensational pleasure [3, 5]. Based on the empiricist aspect of beauty, a product demonstrates its aesthetic feature by evoking users' feelings or emotions of pleasure. Design for pleasure should therefore be a significant approach to create aesthetic value of a product.

3.2 Contemporary Discussions of Pleasure in Product Design

How a product was perceived as pleasurable? Jordan (1998) in a study titled "Human Factors for Pleasure in Product Use" concluded eight pleasure factors: (1) Security, (2) Confidence, (3) Pride, (4) Excitement, (5) Satisfaction, (6) Entertainment, (7) Freedom, and (8) Nostalgia. He also suggested seven displeasure factors: (1) Aggression, (2) Feeling Cheated, (3) Resignation, (4) Frustration, (5) Contempt, (6) Anxiety, (7) Annoyance [7].

Jordan's study evoked many scholars engaged in further exploration of pleasure in design. In Taiwan, Chang and Wu developed a scale for the assessment of consumer pleasure evoked by appearance of products. He extended 17 items for the assessment of consumer pleasure. Chang conceived some pleasure factors based on consumers' practical actions such as "I would like to share this product with others", "I feel I want to have this product", and "I like to play with this product" [2].

In a study on cognition of pleasure images, Hsiao and Chen conducted a factor analysis to reduce 17 items into four factors of emotional effects of pleasure including relaxed & humorous, reliable & familiar, attractive, and behavioral [4].

Based on the perspective of pleasure theories and empirical approaches of cognition inquiry, a questionnaire was developed to obtain information required for this study.

4   Research Methodology

4.1   Research Instrument

This study intends to construct an accessible criticism model of cultural creative products with an emphasis of the pleasure in products design. Based on the perspective of Jordan's theory, a questionnaire of the five-point scale was developed to examine Jordan's eight human factors for pleasure in product use.

Another four questions were designed to explore participants' general impression to the products (Table 2).

Table 2. Five points scale of pleasure attributes and impression assessment of the product

	descriptions	1	2	3	4	5
	Security	☐	☐	☐	☐	☐
	Confidence	☐	☐	☐	☐	☐
	Pride	☐	☐	☐	☐	☐
	Excitement	☐	☐	☐	☐	☐
	Satisfaction	☐	☐	☐	☐	☐
	Entertainment	☐	☐	☐	☐	☐
	Freedom	☐	☐	☐	☐	☐
	Nostalgia	☐	☐	☐	☐	☐
Degree of technique demonstrated in the product		☐	☐	☐	☐	☐
Degree of creativity demonstrated in the product		☐	☐	☐	☐	☐
Degree of pleasure when contemplating the product		☐	☐	☐	☐	☐
Preference of the product		☐	☐	☐	☐	☐

4.2   Research Stimuli

As for the selection process of the research object, the products were chosen from a set of wooden crafts created by Po-Hsien Lin. In order to have an in-depth exploration of participants' reactions to the stimuli, a statistical technique of "Conjoint Analysis" was employed in this study.

Conjoint analysis is a survey-based tool of SPSS used in market research for developing effective product design. It helps to determine what product attributes are important or unimportant to the consumer? What levels of product attributes are the most or least desirable in the consumer's mind [6]?

Based on the prior observation on viewers' reactions to the works, three basic attributes were considered to be the important components for constructing the profile of the works. The first is the color of the material, which is separated into three levels of brown, red, and black. The second is the proportion of the form, which is divided into two levels of tall and stout. The third is the shape of the curve, including two levels of rectangle and round. As shown in Table 3, the information presents a fraction of all possible combinations of the factor levels, which is an orthogonal array designed to capture the main effects for each factor level [6].

Based on the data of Table 4, an "Orthogonal Design" procedure was conducted in SPSS. The program randomly generated a "Card List", which is a reduced set of product profiles that is small enough to include in a survey but large enough to assess the relative importance of each factor.

Table 3. Basic attributes of the works

Attributes	Levels
Color	Brown
	Red
	Black
Proportion	Tall
	Stout
Shape	Rectangle
	Round

Table 4. Card List generated for conjoint analysis

Card list			
Card ID	Shape	Proportion	Color
1	Round	Stout	Brown
2	Round	Tall	Black
3	Rectangle	Stout	Black
4	Rectangle	Tall	Brown
5	Rectangle	Tall	Red
6	Round	Stout	Red
7	Rectangle	Stout	Brown
8	Round	Tall	Brown

After obtaining the card list, eight products were selected from Lin's works as shown in Fig. 4. A survey was added in the questionnaire asking respondents to rank product profiles by order in accordance their preferences for the works.

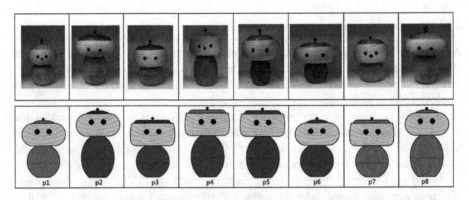

Fig. 4. Eight chosen products in accordance with the card list generated by SPSS

5   Research Results and Data Analysis

5.1   Conjoint Analysis for Relative Importance of Each Attribute of the Products

The importance of attributes of the products was summarized from the results of conjoint analysis as shown in Table 5 and Fig. 5. The outcomes of the statistics exhibited that the conjoint model performed in this study was considerably fit. Pearson's R was .935 (p < .001) and Kendall's tau was .857 (p < .01). All three attributes affected consumers' preference. The most important attribute is color (49.5%), while less important attributes are proportion (26.7%) and shape (23.8%). The relative importance of each attribute was calculated from the utilities given in Table 5 and Fig. 6.

In regard to the overall utility of color, the statistics data suggested that black wood was preferred among the other attribute levels (r = .582). As for the proportion and shape, stout (r = .378) was more preferred than tall and round (r = .087) was more preferred than rectangle.

Table 5. Importance value and utility of the attribute levels

Factor	Level	Utility	Importance value
Color	Brown	−.327	49.482
	Red	−.255	
	Black	.582	
Proportion	Tall	−.378	26.715
	Stout	.378	
Shape	Rectangle	−.087	23.804
	Round	.087	
Pearson's R: .935***		Kendall's tau: .857**	

p < 0.01*p < 0.001

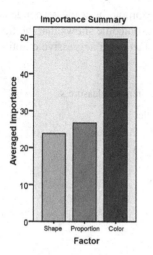

Fig. 5. Average importance of product attributes (Color figure online)

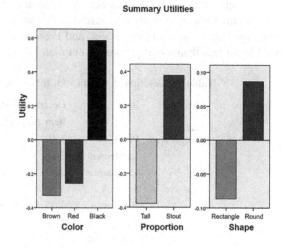

Fig. 6. Preference levels associated with color, proportion, and shape (Color figure online)

5.2   Factor Analysis of Pleasure of the Products

Based on the perspective of Jordan's theory, this study explores viewers' response of pleasure to the selected products. An exploratory factor analysis (EFA) was conducted to search for latent variables within eight items of pleasure. Two factors were extracted with eigenvalues greater than 1.0 and total variance explained 64.579 as shown in Table 6. The first dimension included three items of Pride, Excitement, and Confidence. The second dimension included five items of Security, Freedom, Satisfaction, Entertainment, and Nostalgia. The first group of emotions tend to be strong and aggressive. The second group of emotions tend to be mild and passive.

Table 6. Factor analysis for pleasure attributes

Item	Factor Loading		Communalities	
	f1	f2	f1	f2
Pride	.931	-.009	.867	
Excitement	.905	.149	.842	
Confidence	.761	.383	.726	
Security	-.069	.933		.875
Freedom	.170	.741		.578
Satisfaction	.414	.529		.452
Entertainment	.382	.382		.291
Nostalgia	.066	.202		.045
Eigenvalue	2.796	1.868		
% of Variance	38.712	25.867		
Cumulative %	38.712	64.579		

A basic descriptive statistics set was computed to examine how the respondents react to Jordan's eight items of pleasure in this study. The outcome shows that the first three are Satisfaction, Entertainment, and Freedom. The factors of aggressive emotion tend to be less than those of passive emotion (Table 7).

Table 7. Descriptive statistics for the factor and item of pleasure s

Factor	Item	Descriptive statistics		
		Item mean	SD	Factor mean
Aggressive	Pride	3.40	1.067	3.38
	Excitement	3.41	1.079	
	Confidence	3.33	1.068	
Passive	Security	3.31	1.084	4.00
	Freedom	4.04	.815	
	Satisfaction	4.41	.788	
	Entertainment	4.33	.747	
	Nostalgia	3.92	.886	

5.3   Eight Items of Pleasure to Predict Degree of Products Preferences

To explore how eight items of pleasure affected the respondents' reaction when reviewing the products, this study conducted multiple regression analyses, taking eight items of pleasure as independent variables and the participant's degree of preference to the products as a dependent variable. The multiple regression model with all eight predictors produced $R^2 = .715$, $F = 12.571$, suggesting a statistically significant association between independent variables and the dependent variable ($p < .001$). As can be seen in Table 8, all seven items, except Nostalgia, have significant correlations between the degree of preference. Freedom and Satisfaction had significant positive regression weights, indicating the product with higher scores on these two items was expected to have the strongest degree of preference.

Table 8. Multiple regression analyses for pleasure attributes to predict preference of the product

Independent variable	Predictor variable	B	r	β	t
Preference of the product	Security	−.099	.297**	−.133	−1.183
	Confidence	.085	.485***	.112	.835
	Pride	.136	.470***	.178	1.187
	Excitement	.036	.517***	.048	.319
	Satisfaction	.235	.610***	.229	2.080*
	Entertainment	.000	.418**	.000	−.008
	Freedom	.608	.735***	.613	5.342***
	Nostalgia	.011	.159	.012	.141
	R = .846			R2 = .715	F = 12.571***

*p < 0.05 **p < 0.01 ***p < 0.001

Taking eight items of pleasure as independent variables and the participant's overall degree of pleasure to the products as a dependent variable. The multiple regression model with all eight predictors produced $R^2 = .678$, $F = 10.513$, suggesting a statistically significant association between independent variables and the dependent variable ($p < .001$). As can be seen in Table 9, all seven items, except Nostalgia, have

Table 9. Multiple regression analyses for pleasure attributes to predict degree of pleasure

Independent variable	Predictor variable	B	r	β	t
Degree of pleasure when contemplating the product	Security	−.052	.327*	−.073	−.611
	Confidence	.042	.445**	.058	.406
	Pride	.103	.415**	.142	.888
	Excitement	.085	.489***	.120	.753
	Satisfaction	.203	.599***	.209	1.784
	Entertainment	−.098	.346**	−.096	−.877
	Freedom	.602	.731***	.640	5.240***
	Nostalgia	−.014	.126	−.016	−.175
	R = .823			R2 = .678	F = 10.513***

*p < 0.05 **p < 0.01 ***p < 0.001

significant correlations between the degree of pleasure. Freedom is the only item which had significant positive regression weights.

Taking two factors of pleasure emotions as independent variables and the participant's overall degree of pleasure to the products as a dependent variable, the multiple regression model with two predictors produced $R^2 = .487$, $F = 21.807$, suggesting a statistically significant association between independent variables and the dependent variable ($p < .001$). As can be seen in Table 10, both factors have significant correlations between the degree of pleasure. Additionally, both factors had significant positive regression weights. Passive emotion shows greater effect than Aggressive emotion.

Table 10. Multiple regression analyses for pleasure factors to predict degree of pleasure

Independent variable	Predictor variable	B	r	β	t
Degree of pleasure when contemplating the product	Aggressive emotion	.241	.507***	.300	2.608*
	Passive emotion	.715	.641***	.522	4.539***
	R = .698		R2 = .487	F = 21.807***	

*p < 0.05 ***p < 0.001

Taking three items of technique, creativity, and pleasure as independent variables and the participant's overall degree of preference to the products as a dependent variable. The multiple regression model with all three predictors produced $R^2 = .790$, $F = 56.543$, suggesting a statistically significant association between independent variables and the dependent variable ($p < .001$). As can be seen in Table 11, all three items have significant correlations between the degree of preference and had significant positive regression weights.

Table 11. Multiple regression analyses for product features to predict degree of pleasure

Independent variable	Predictor variable	B	r	β	t
Preference of the product	Skill	.329	.829***	.352	2.872***
	Creativity	.334	.842***	.406	3.235***
	Pleasure	.209	.788***	.199	1.665***
	R = .889		R2 = .790	F = 56.543***	

***p < 0.001

6   Conclusion and Recommendations

6.1   Discussion of Findings

This study used the perspective of Jordan's theory on human factors for pleasure in product use to examine how customers perceived pleasure of products, and the connection between pleasure and appreciation of products. Discussed below are some important findings:

1. Through an evaluation to explore how eight items of attitudinal pleasure affected the respondents' reaction when reviewing the products, the outcome showed that all seven items, except Nostalgia, have significant correlations between their integrated perception of pleasure. Jordan's theory of pleasure in product offered a sufficient support in this study.
2. In this study, Jordan's eight items of pleasure were further reduced to two groups of distinct emotions through an Exploratory Factor Analysis. The first group of emotions tend to be strong and aggressive, including Pride, Excitement, and Confidence. The second group of emotions tend to be mild and passive, including Security, Freedom, Satisfaction, Entertainment, and Nostalgia.
3. Both aggressive and passive emotions have significant correlations between respondents' integrated perception of pleasure when contemplating the products, however passive emotion shows greater effect than that of aggressive emotion.
4. Through an evaluation to explore how eight items of attitudinal pleasure affected the respondents' attitude toward the products, the outcome showed that all seven items, except Nostalgia, have significant correlations between their preference of the products. Among eight pleasure items, Freedom and Satisfaction shows greater effect than that of the other.
5. This study conducted a survey asking respondents to rank product profiles by order in accordance their preferences for eight pieces of selected works. The outcome of a Conjoint Analysis demonstrated that three basic attributes of color, proportion, and shape affected consumers' preference. Among these three attributes, color is the most important item. A further analysis suggested that in this study the participants tend to selected black, stout, and round woodturning works.
6. Through Multiple Regression Analysis, this study employed participants' perception of technique, creativity, and pleasure demonstrated in the products to predict their degree of preference. The outcome showed all three predictors have significant correlations between the degree of preference. Among three elements, the effect of creativity is greater than technique, and pleasure is less important than the other two items.

6.2   Conclusion

This study attempted to employ Jordan's theory of pleasure in product to explore the connection between reviewers' attitudinal pleasure and preference of the products, trying to answer how a product was perceived as pleasurable.

In order to construct an accessible criticism model of cultural creative products with an emphasis on the pleasure in products design, this study use eight pieces of wooden craft as research stimuli. Though Jordan's theory offered a sufficient support in this study, a further finding suggests that passive emotion (security, freedom, satisfaction, entertainment, and nostalgia) could have a stronger effect than aggressive emotion (pride, excitement, and confidence) to evoke human factors for pleasure in products.

The characteristics of the handicraft could evoke different sensations of pleasure compared to those of the industrial product. Nevertheless, the finding is valuable for the development of craft industries. In addition to creativity and technique, pleasure is a very important attribute for a cultural creative product. This study also employed Conjoint Analysis as an instrument to explore consumer's concerns about product attributes. Through a full-profile approach, this study demonstrated a practical model for investigating different preferences met by distinct product offerings.

Whether pleasure is an objective attribute of an object or a subjective sensation of the viewers has been a dilemma in the field of aesthetics. An in-depth discussion of this topic could be very philosophical. However, many modern theories of cognitive psychology and neuroscience are very helpful in the related research. A further study of applying these new scientific domains to investigate the topic about pleasure in product design is strongly suggested.

References

1. The American Heritage Dictionary of the English Language, 5th edn. Houghton Mifflin Harcourt Publishing Company, Boston (2019)
2. Chang, W.C., Wu, T.Y.: the development of a scale for the assessment of consumer pleasure evoked by product appearance. Psychol. Test. **56**(2), 207–233 (2009)
3. Burke, E.: A Philosophical Enquiry into the Origin of Our Ideas of the Sublime and Beautiful. Oxford University Press, New York (2015). (Original work published in 1757)
4. Hsiao, K.A., Chen, P.Y.: Cognition and shape features of pleasure images. J. Des. **15**(2), 1–17 (2010)
5. Hume, D.: A Treatise of Human Nature. Penguin Books, London (1985). (Original work published in 1738)
6. IBM: IBM SPSS Conjoint 22 (2013). http://www.sussex.ac.uk/its/pdfs/SPSS_Conjoint_22.pdf
7. Jordan, P.W.: Human factors for pleasure in product use. Appl. Ergon. **29**(1), 25–33 (1988)
8. Lin, P.-H., Yeh, M.-L.: The construction of cultural impressions for the idea of cultural products. In: Rau, P.-L.P. (ed.) CCD 2018. LNCS, vol. 10912, pp. 212–224. Springer, Cham (2018). https://doi.org/10.1007/978-3-319-92252-2_16
9. Ministry of Culture: Taiwan cultural creative industries annual report 2018. Culture Statistics from Ministry of Culture (2019). https://stat.moc.gov.tw/Research.aspx?type=5
10. Norman, D.A.: Emotional Design: Why We Love (or Hate) Everyday Things. Basic Books, New York (2004)
11. Papanek, V.: Design for the Real World: Human Ecology and Social Change. Chicago Review Press, Chicago (2005)
12. Plato, A., Woodruff, P.: Hippias Major. Hackett Publishing Co., Indianapolis (1982)

Mindfulness Meditation: Investigating Immediate Effects in an Information Multitasking Environment

Na Liu[1], Yubo Zhang[2], Gloria Mark[3], Ziyang Li[2],
and Pei-Luen Patrick Rau[2(✉)]

[1] School of Economics and Management,
Beijing University of Posts and Telecommunications, Beijing, China
liuna18@bupt.edu.cn
[2] Department of Industrial Engineering, Tsinghua University, Beijing, China
yubo-zhang@foxmail.com, lisa_ziyangli@163.com,
rpl@tsinghua.edu.cn
[3] Department of Informatics, University of California, Irvine, Irvine, USA
gmark@uci.edu

Abstract. Interventions to increase focus and decrease stress in the workplace are beginning to receive research attention. At the same time, extensive training in meditation techniques show promising results. This study aimed to investigate the effects of mindfulness meditation on stress, focus, affect, workload, behavior and performance in an information multitasking environment. Participants worked on a proofreading task while being allowed to switch to use Facebook. Stress and focus were measured with heart rate variability and EEG signals respectively. Self-reported affect and workload were measured by questionnaire. Behavior was measured with computer log activity and performance was measured with proofreading accuracy. The results suggest that mindfulness meditation can increase arousal level and decrease stress level after a single session. Positive affect tends to decline without any form of work break. However, a single engagement in meditation has limited impact on regulating people's task switching behavior nor altering the focus level. Design implications for intervention tools are discussed.

Keywords: Mindfulness meditation · Multitasking · Intervention · Interruption

1 Introduction

The proliferation of smart devices in the workplace may serve to encourage multitasking among information workers. People's focus duration on just the computer screen is found to be quite short. The average number of switches per minute between different contents is 0.95 and the average staying length on one content is 65 s [1]. Social media contributes significantly to multitasking in the workplace, e.g. a person switches from a Word document to Facebook. It was found that information workers check Facebook about 21 times a day in the course of working [2]. Among college students, who are potential future information workers, it was found that they check

P.-L. P. Rau (Ed.): HCII 2019, LNCS 11576, pp. 531–542, 2019.
https://doi.org/10.1007/978-3-030-22577-3_38

Facebook 52 times a day, and considering other types of social media, checking rises to 118 times a day [3]. Students who multitask due to checking social media most often report falling behind on schoolwork, and feel more distracted and lack control over online behavior [3].

Social media checking is associated with computer screen or device switching, and this type of multitasking has been found to be associated with stress [4], and negatively impact productivity [2] as well as people's affect [5]. It has also been proved that multitasking is associated with the alteration of brain structures such that individuals performing high multitasking activities have smaller gray matter density in the anterior cingulate cortex [6]. The alteration of brain structures correlates with the decreased cognitive control performance and affect regulation among heavy multitaskers [6]. Thus, it is necessary to propose intervention methods to help information workers maintain productivity and focus duration and to promote workplace well-being. The current study aims to investigate whether mindfulness meditation can bring immediate benefits for people who work in a multitasking environment.

Neuroscience studies have shown that mindfulness meditation can increase control over the distribution of limited brain resources [7] and regulate affect [8]. Mindfulness is a state of consciousness in which attention is focused on present-moment phenomena [9]. Intensive meditation training can improve sustained attention against a decrement in vigilance [10]. In the workplace, mindfulness is associated with positive engagement in work and well-being [11]. Meditation training can also assist in treating for addiction [12]. The mediation practices are beneficial for controlling attention in an environment with distraction. Practicers are able to focus their attention on the primary task with the help of meditation and switch the attention back on the primary task from distracting interruptions.

The effects of mindfulness meditation on people's attention and affect can come into play via continuous practices with a period of training. In the study by Nielsen and Kaszniak [8], the researchers recruited meditators following the Buddhist tradition, who had undergone long-term meditation practices. In another study, participants were given three months' meditation training with five hours to meditate every day [10]. The results of the two studies both showed positive effect of meditation, either on emotional feelings or on task vigilance. In an experiment about multitasking and meditation [13], participants were given meditation training for eight weeks. The researchers found that after the training, participants stayed longer on the primary task and made fewer switches between tasks. These studies suggest that meditation training may be a feasible way to make people more focused in a distracting environment.

However, undergoing a long period of training in mindfulness meditation may not be practical for many people. While research is slowly suggesting that longer training can produce effects, many people may not be able to attend such training. At the same time, the human-computer interaction field is experiencing a surge of studies to investigate how short-term interventions can bring benefits [14]. However, it is unclear what effects a single experience of meditation can bring, in a person's mental states or behavior. Understanding the effects of a single meditation session on mental states and performance is beneficial for proposing useful interventions that can counteract people's stress and increase their focus.

In short, this study simulated an information environment where people multitask extensively and aimed to investigate the immediate effects of mindfulness meditation on people's stress, focus, affect, workload, multitasking behavior and performance. The results will provide implications on designing intervention tools for information multitaskers to increase focus and reduce stress.

2 Method

2.1 Participants

Thirty-six students (17 males and 19 females)from a U.S. west-coast university were recruited in the experiment. A five-point Likert scale was used to measure the overall Facebook usage intensity ("to what extent do you agree or disagree you are a heavy Facebook user?") in the recruitment questionnaire. Only "heavy Facebook users" (rating four or five points in this scale) were finally selected to participate in the experiment.

The average age of the participants was 21.4 (SD = 1.2) years old. All of them were native English speakers, with sufficient capability in English proofreading. The average Facebook age of all participants was 6.4 (SD = 1.6) years. According to their self-reported answers, they used Facebook for 3.7(SD = 2.3) hours daily and checked Facebook for 18.8 (SD = 19.9) times every day on average. Their Facebook intensity score as measured by with a five-point Likert scale was 3.9 (SD = 0.8). Participants were paid 20 dollars as the incentive.

2.2 Experiment Task

In this study, an information environment in the laboratory where multitasking occurs frequently were simulated, which was similar to previous studies [13, 15]. Participants were assigned to proofread Word documents on the U.S. California law codes about public utilities, which was the primary task. One 13-inch Dell Studio XPS laptop computer was provided to complete all the experiment tasks. The length of each document ranged from 1.5 pages to 2 pages, with Times New Roman as the font type and 12 points (pt) as the font size. The line spacing of the document was set 1.5 times. The page layout was A4 (21 cm × 29.7 cm). The top and bottom margins were 2.54 cm and the side margins were 3.18 cm. Each page contained nine spelling errors which were randomly distributed within the page. Participants were instructed to correct the errors directly in the document with the Word processor. Facebook browsing was the secondary task in the experiment. Participants were allowed to take a break whenever they needed it by switching to their own Facebook pages, but no other webpages should be browsed.

2.3 Design and Measurements

A between-subject experiment was designed to conduct this study. The independent variable was the intervention form with three levels: guided focus attention meditation, listening to a piece of arousing dance music remixes, and no intervention. Participants were randomly assigned to three groups corresponding to the three intervention forms. The dependent variables were stress, focus level, affect, workload, task switching behavior and task performance.

The participant's stress level was measured by heart rate variability (HRV) with a digital heart rate monitor including a Polar RS800CX wristwatch receiver and a chest strap sensor. The sensor samples data with a frequency of 1 Hz and the HRV is calculated with the standard deviation of the R-R intervals between consecutive heart beats. The lower the standard deviation, the higher stress level is experienced [16].

The participant's focus level was measured with EEG signals via a MuseTM brain sensing headband with seven electrodes [17]. The headband samples the EEG signal with a frequency of 220 Hz and the data are transmitted to a paired laptop computer. The developer kit of MuseTM supports exporting EEG data after the Fast Fourier Transform, status indicators of the four EEG data electrodes and the timestamp of each data frame. The status indicators of each electrode have three levels: 1 = good, 2 = ok, ≥ 3 bad. Only data frames with indicators of 1 or 2 were retained for further analysis. The EEG signals are categorized into different wave patterns with corresponding frequency intervals. In each data frame, the band powers of alpha (8–13 Hz), beta (13–30 Hz) and theta (4–8 Hz) waves were calculated for each electrode and the average band powers of the three types of brain waves were calculated across the four electrodes. The focus level is calculated according to Eq. (1), where alpha, beta and theta represent the average band powers of different waves [18].

$$Focus = beta/(alpha + theta) \tag{1}$$

Affect was measured via a two-dimensional grid scale which was based on Russell's Circumplex model which includes valence and arousal [19]. The scale has been proved to have adequate reliability, convergent validity and discriminant validity in measuring people's affect [20]. Two orthogonal rating scales (610 px × 610 px) were represented on the laptop screen to measure the subjects' valence and arousal respectively (Fig. 1). The horizontal scale measures valence from unpleasant (0 px) to pleasant (610 px). The vertical scale measures arousal from deactivated (0 px) to activated (610 px). In the experiment, participants were required to click the mouse in the two dimensional map presented in the browser and to click on the position that best represented their affect at that moment. The coordinates in pixels were then normalized to values ranging from 0 to 1 for the data analysis.

Workload was measured with a seven-point Likert scale adapted from the NASA-TLX [21], which contained six dimensions: physical demand, mental demand, time pressure, frustration, performance and effort. The scale about workload was produced and presented with Google Forms.

The data of the computer activity included the window switching frequency (window switching times divided by the time length of computer use) and the average duration of time on the proofreading windows. KidLogger was used to record the participant's computer activity. The log records of KidLogger contain the start time and duration of the active window, the name of the window and a URL if applicable. The timestamp was recorded to the second. Computer activity data was calculated based on

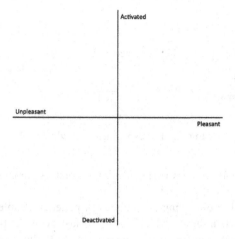

Fig. 1. Affect measurement map based on Russell's Circumplex model.

the log records. In addition, the accuracy rate of the proofreading task was adopted as the performance indicator.

2.4 Procedure

The experiment was conducted in a university laboratory and lasted about 1.5 h. Participants were randomly assigned to three groups which corresponded to the three intervention forms and were numbered group M, group A and group C respectively. In group M, participants were given a 12-minute session of guided focus attention meditation using the breath as the focus point. The meditation session was instructed by a pre-recorded gentle female voice accompanied with a sound of a sea wave. "Sit in a comfortable position and close your eyes. Allow your back to be straight and relax your shoulders. Take a few moments to relax by becoming aware that you are breathing. No need to change your breathing. Your body knows how to breathe." This paragraph of instructions was adapted from those used in the MuseTM headband's accompanied meditation application [17]. Participants were required to follow the instructions from the audio file to meditate until the instructions ended. In group A, participants listened to a piece of arousing club dance music remixes for 12 min, without engaging in any other activities until the music ended. Group C was a control group without any interventions.

The experiment procedure was illustrated in Fig. 2. Upon arrival, participants signed a consent form, read the instructions and filled out a general survey including their demographics, computer and Facebook experience, Facebook usage intensity. The Facebook usage intensity was measured with a five-point Likert scale. Afterwards, they put on the headband and heart rate monitor with the assistance of an experimenter.

Then, participants were informed of the experiment instructions. In order to ensure the ecological validity and avoid bringing too many distortions on the behavior, the instructions omitted the real purpose of the experiment. Participants were informed that the purpose of the experiment was to test the impact of environment settings on

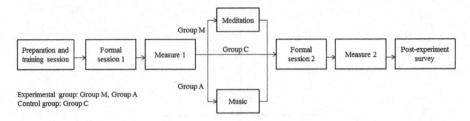

Fig. 2. The experiment procedure.

university students' working performance and workload. A paragraph was provided in the instructions as follows:

"We are interested in observing people's work patterns. People often work on one task and take breaks when they need it. During the task, you can freely take a break at any time by switching to your own Facebook page. NO other new windows or web-pages are allowed to open during the experiment. Please work with your natural pattern."

What followed next was a training session with five sample documents to proof-read. During the training session, the experimenter left the laboratory and the partici-pants were not allowed to use Facebook. Upon the completion of the training task, the participants needed to inform the experimenter with a microphone. Then the experi-menter would come and guide the participants to start the first formal session, in which participants needed to proofread the assigned documents and browse their own Face-book pages when they needed to relax. Participants were asked to pause the proof-reading task after 30 min from the beginning of the formal session (session 1). Then affect and workload were measured in a questionnaire for the first time (measure 1). Participants in group M and group A were required to either did the meditation or listened to the club music. Afterwards, they were required to continue the proofreading task. Participants in group C were required to return to the proofreading task after the measure of affect and workload. After 30 min from the beginning of the second half session (session 2), participants finished the second half session and affect and work-load were measured for the second time (measure 2). At the end of the experiment, participants rated their satisfaction level with the environment. In order to avoid the situation that participants did not browse Facebook during the experiment, they were asked to report one interesting Facebook post they had read at the end of the experi-ment. The recordings of the bio-signals and the computer activity was conducted throughout the formal session.

3   Results

The average age of participants in the three groups was 21.4 ($SD = 1.1$), 21.6 ($SD = 1.0$) and 21.3 ($SD = 1.4$) respectively, showing on significant inter-group difference ($F (2, 31) = 0.32$, $p = 0.729$, $\eta^2 = 0.02$). There was also no significant inter-group difference on the gender ratio ($\chi^2(2) = 0.22$, $p = 0.895$), with 6, 5 and 6 male partic-ipants in the three groups respectively.

According to the self-reported data, there was no significant difference among participants in the three experimental groups on Facebook age (F (2, 31) = 1.02, p = 0.373, η^2 = 0.07), daily usage frequency (F (2, 33) = 2.15, p = 0.132, η^2 = 0.12), daily usage time span (F (2, 33) = 0.70, p = 0.505, η^2 = 0.04), as well as their Facebook usage intensity (F (2, 33) = 0.82, p = 0.450, η^2 = 0.05).

3.1 Stress and Focus

For participants in the two experimental groups (group M and group A), their EEG focus level and HRV were compared between session 1 and the intervention break in order to check the effect of mindfulness meditation and listening to the arousing club music. The HRV data in group A passed the normality test while the other data failed to pass the normality test.

For participants in group M, the EEG focus level and the HRV were 0.65 (SD = 0.42) and 73.74 ms (SD = 36.58 ms) on average in session 1, and were 0.40 (SD = 0.17) and 86.07 ms (SD = 36.15 ms) during the meditation. Wilcoxon signed rank test showed that the EEG focus level decreased and the HRV increased significantly during the meditation (W = 12.0, p = 0.034, r = 0.43; W = 8.0, p = 0.015, r = 0.50).

For participants in group A, the EEG focus level and the HRV were 0.53 (SD = 0.25) and 71.62 ms (SD = 17.18 ms) on average in session 1, and were 0.51 (SD = 0.22) and 85.26 ms (SD = 16.61 ms) while listening to arousing club music. Wilcoxon signed rank test and pairwise T-test showed that the HRV data increased significantly and the focus level remained the same while participants were listening to music (W = 29.0, p = 0.433, r = 0.16; $t(11)$ = 3.42, p = 0.006, d = 0.34).

The above comparison means that both mindfulness meditation and listening to arousing club music took effect on the subject's bio-signals when they were undergoing the intervention. What follows next is the comparison between session 2 and session 1 in the EEG focus level and the HRV level.

In the aspect of the EEG focus level, the data failed to pass the normality test. In session 1, the EEG focus levels of participants in group M, group A have been reported as above and that in group C was 0.49 (SD = 0.23). There was no significant inter-group difference ($H(2)$ = 0.32, p = 0.854, η^2 = 0.01) for the EEG focus level. In session 2, the EEG focus levels of participants in group M, group A and group C were 0.73 (SD = 0.57), 0.54 (SD = 0.29) and 0.48 (SD = 0.22). Wilcoxon signed rank test showed there was no significant differences between session 1 and 2 in terms of the EEG focus level in three groups (group M: W = 30.0, p = 0.480, r = 0.14; group A: W = 36.0, p = 0.814, r = 0.05; group C: W = 36.0, p = 0.814, r = 0.05) (Fig. 3a).

In the aspect of the HRV level, the data failed to pass the normality test. In session 1, the HRV data in group M and group A have been reported as above and that in group C was 72.83 ms (SD = 36.49 ms). There was no significant inter-group difference ($H(2)$ = 0.25, p = 0.881, η^2 = 0.01). In session 2, the HRV of participants in group M, group A and group C were 79.55 ms (SD = 31.98 ms), 89.23 ms (SD = 39.74 ms) and 73.76 ms (SD = 40.73 ms). Wilcoxon signed rank test indicated that the HRV level in session 2 increased marginally significantly in group M (W = 16.0, p = 0.071, r = 0.37), increased significantly in group A (W = 4.0, p = 0.006, r = 0.56) and remained the same in group C (W = 37.0, p = 0.875, r = 0.03) (Fig. 3b).

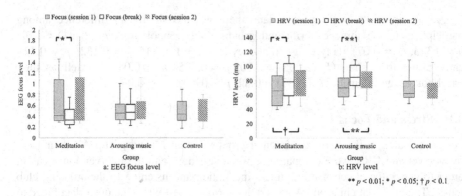

Fig. 3. EEG focus and HRV level (ms) in the three groups.

3.2 Affect and Workload

The data of self-reported valence and workload passed the normality test and the test of variance homogeneity while the data of self-reported arousal failed to pass the normality test.

There was a significant interaction effect of session and group on the valence of participants in the three groups ($F(2, 33) = 5.94$, $p = 0.006$, $\eta^2 = 0.27$), as well as a marginally significant main effect of session ($F(1, 33) = 3.42$, $p = 0.073$, $\eta^2 = 0.09$). In session 1, the valence levels of participants in group M, group A and group C were 0.56 ($SD = 0.20$), 0.61 ($SD = 0.19$) and 0.68 ($SD = 0.10$), showing no significant inter-group difference ($F(2, 33) = 1.46$, $p = 0.246$, $\eta^2 = 0.08$). In session 2, the valence levels of participants in group M, group A and group C were 0.62 ($SD = 0.21$), 0.57 ($SD = 0.19$) and 0.55 ($SD = 0.09$). Simple effect analysis showed that mindfulness meditation and listening to club music had no significant influence on valence ($F(1, 33) = 1.95$, $p = 0.172$, $\eta^2 = 0.06$; $F(1, 33) = 1.27$, $p = 0.269$, $\eta^2 = 0.04$). However, the valence level of participants in group C decreased significantly in session 2 ($F(1, 33) = 12.07$, $p = 0.001$, $\eta^2 = 0.27$). The comparison results of valence are depicted in Fig. 4a.

The arousal levels of participants in group M, group A and group C were 0.57 ($SD = 0.19$), 0.63 ($SD = 0.23$) and 0.63 ($SD = 0.20$) in session 1, showing no significant inter-group difference ($H(2) = 0.65$, $p = 0.723$, $\eta^2 = 0.02$). In session 2, the arousal level of participants in group M increased to 0.67 ($SD = 0.24$), which was a marginally significant effect on increasing the arousal level ($W = 15.0$, $p = 0.060$, $r = 0.38$). The arousal levels of participants in group A and group C were 0.59 ($SD = 0.24$) and 0.57 ($SD = 0.21$) in session 2, showing no significant difference compared with the arousal levels in session 1 ($W = 29.5$, $p = 0.456$, $r = 0.15$; $W = 25.5$, $p = 0.289$, $r = 0.22$). The comparison results of arousal are depicted in Fig. 4b.

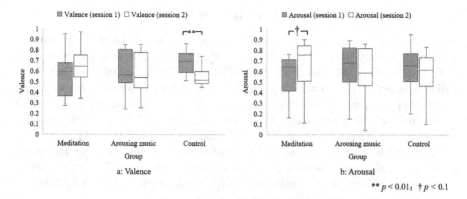

Fig. 4. Self-reported affect in the three groups.

The workload levels of participants in group M, group A and group C were 3.6 ($SD = 0.8$), 3.4 ($SD = 0.9$) and 3.3 ($SD = 1.0$) in session 1, showing no significant inter-group difference ($F(2, 33) = 0.35$, $p = 0.705$, $\eta^2 = 0.02$), and were 3.4 ($SD = 1.1$), 3.7 ($SD = 1.1$) and 3.3 ($SD = 1.1$) in session 2. There was no significant inter-session difference in workload among the three groups ($F(2, 33) = 1.48$, $p = 0.242$, $\eta^2 = 0.08$). With a further analysis on the six dimensions of NASA-TLX, it was found that interventions had different effect on frustration among the three groups ($F(2, 33) = 4.85$, $p = 0.014$, $\eta^2 = 0.23$), as shown in Fig. 5. Mindfulness meditation significantly decreased frustration ($F(1, 33) = 4.68$, $p = 0.038$, $\eta^2 = 0.12$), from 4.1 ($SD = 1.6$) to 3.1 ($SD = 1.9$), while listening to club music significantly increased frustration ($F(1, 33) = 4.68$, $p = 0.038$, $\eta^2 = 0.12$), from 3.2 ($SD = 1.3$) to 4.2 ($SD = 1.3$). For participants in group C, the frustration level was 2.8 ($SD = 1.6$) in session 1 and 3.2 ($SD = 1.5$) in session 2, showing no significant difference ($F(1, 33) = 0.52$, $p = 0.476$, $\eta^2 = 0.02$). Inter-group comparison showed that there was no significant difference in frustration in session 1 among the three groups ($F(2, 33) = 2.24$, $p = 0.123$, $\eta^2 = 0.12$).

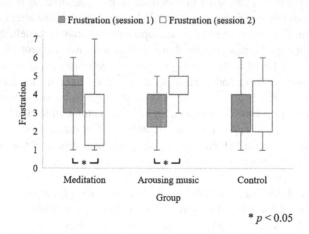

Fig. 5. Self-reported frustration in the three groups.

3.3 Task Switching Behavior and Performance

There was no significant inter-group difference in session 1 in terms of the window switching frequency ($F (2, 33) = 0.08$, $p = 0.919$, $\eta^2 = 0.01$), the average staying time on the proofreading windows ($F (2, 33) = 0.24$, $p = 0.789$, $\eta^2 = 0.02$) and the proofreading accuracy ($F (2, 33) = 1.19$, $p = 0.318$, $\eta^2 = 0.07$). In session 2, task switching behavior of participants did not change significantly among the three groups in terms of the window switching frequency ($F (2, 33) = 0.27$, $p = 0.763$, $\eta^2 = 0.02$) and the average staying time on the proofreading windows ($F (2, 33) = 0.11$ $p = 0.893$, $\eta^2 = 0.01$). Different interventions had no significantly different effect on the proofreading accuracy among the three groups ($F (2, 33) = 0.99$, $p = 0.384$, $\eta^2 = 0.06$).

In summary, there was no significantly different intervention effect on the subject's task-switching behavior as well as the performance in the task.

4 Discussion

The present study investigated whether mindfulness meditation could have immediate effects on a person's mental states or behavior in an information multitasking environment. The results showed some immediate effects of mindfulness meditation and listening to arousing club music on people's stress, affect and frustration. A brief meditation session could decrease a person's stress level and increase the arousal level. Meditation could also significantly decrease a person's frustration level and retain the valence level, but it has no significant effects on a person's focus level, workload, task switching behavior and task performance. Listening to arousing club music could decrease a person's stress level, but the side effect was that the frustration level was increased. Besides, listening to arousing club music had no significant influence on a person's affect, focus level or task switching behavior.

In the experiment, the valence of multitaskers was maintained by meditation, but tended to decline if no break was taken, despite the fact that the valence was still kept positive on average in the control group. This is consistent with previous findings [13], indicating that meditation can resist the decrease of positive affect. It is worth noticing that other forms of breaks might have effects in keeping the positive affect as well, such as exposure to music. This suggests that appropriate break may be beneficial to increase workplace wellbeing. In terms of arousal, meditation increased the arousal level, but no obvious change was found in the other two groups. The results suggest that meditation holds promise in refreshing and energizing people even though they have not experienced long-term training. It was also found that although listening to club music could significantly decrease people's stress level in an information multitasking environment, it had a side effect of strengthening the frustration. The music type adopted in this experiment was club music which was arousing with a fast beat. Future research can investigate the effect of music type on improving people's mental states in a multitasking environment.

We also found that the multitasking computer activity, primary task performance, the EEG focus level and workload were not influenced by mindfulness meditation nor exposure to club music. Considering that previous findings on meditation's role in increasing attention and decreasing task switches were all based on long-term training [10, 13], we infer that the instant effect of a brief intervention may be limited in changing a person's focus level or too frequent task switching behavior. That highlights the necessity of professional training and discipline with meditation. Meditation should not be counted on to be able to correct inappropriate multitasking behavior or increase attention without continuous and disciplined engagement. Another possible reason for the limited effect of meditation is that the multitasking in this experiment involved mainly internal interruptions [22]. Previous study proved that meditation could change task switching frequency given that the interruptions were external [13]. Due to different mechanisms behind the two types of interruptions, the effect of meditation may be different and further exploration is warranted.

Our results have implications for product design aiming to regulate people's attention and behavior. As assistive tools for meditation, products need to provide scientific guidance to guarantee that users meditate in the right way. In addition, assistive products for meditation should increase user stickiness and continuous engagement by introducing some mechanism such as gaming or social media sharing. Otherwise, the influence of such products on mental health and behavior is limited for short-term users. In fact, the headband MuseTM has a corresponding mobile application to allow users to share their meditation progress, forming a mutual competition and motivation among their social relations. These functions are beneficial for motivating users to engage in long-term meditation practices and regulating their mental states. However, it is worth noticing that the function of gaming or social media sharing should not cause users to be addicted, otherwise it may exacerbate task switching or distracted mental states for information workers.

Our study investigated whether a meditation intervention can have immediate effects on people's mental states and behavior, using a simulated work environment. Mindfulness meditation appears to show promise when training is undergone for extended periods. Yet despite the widespread interest in developing short-term interventions for improving workplace wellbeing, our results suggest that single instances of meditation may have only limited effects. We hope that our results can spark others to investigate ways to alleviate workplace stress and increase focus in the modern information work environment.

Acknowledgements. This work was supported by a National Key Resource and Development Plan grant 2016YFB1001200-2.

References

1. Yeykelis, L., Cummings, J.J., Reeves, B.: Multitasking on a single device: arousal and the frequency, anticipation, and prediction of switching between media content on a computer. J. Commun. **64**(1), 167–192 (2014)
2. Mark, G., Iqbal, S., Czerwinski, M., Johns, P.: Focused, aroused, but so distractible: temporal perspectives on multitasking and communications. In: 18th ACM Conference on Computer Supported Cooperative Work & Social Computing, pp. 903–916. ACM, New York (2015)

3. Zywica, J., Danowski, J.: The faces of Facebookers: investigating social enhancement and social compensation hypotheses; predicting Facebook™ and offline popularity from sociability and self-esteem, and mapping the meanings of popularity with semantic networks. J. Comput.-Mediat. Commun. **14**(1), 1–34 (2008)

4. Barley, S.R., Meyerson, D.E., Grodal, S.: E-mail as a source and symbol of stress. Organ. Sci. **22**(4), 887–906 (2011)

5. Mark, G., Wang, Y., Niiya, M.: Stress and multitasking in everyday college life: an empirical study of online activity. In: SIGCHI Conference on Human Factors in Computing Systems, pp. 41–50. ACM, New York (2014)

6. Loh, K.K., Kanai, R.: Higher media multi-tasking activity is associated with smaller gray-matter density in the anterior cingulate cortex. PLoS ONE **9**(9), e106698 (2014)

7. Slagter, H.A., et al.: Mental training affects distribution of limited brain resources. PLoS Biol. **5**(6), 1228–1235 (2007)

8. Nielsen, L., Kaszniak, A.W.: Awareness of subtle emotional feelings: a comparison of long-term meditators and nonmeditators. Emotion **6**(3), 392–405 (2006)

9. Dane, E.: Paying attention to mindfulness and its effects on task performance in the workplace. J. Manag. **37**(4), 997–1018 (2011)

10. MacLean, K.A., et al.: Intensive meditation training improves perceptual discrimination and sustained attention. Psychol. Sci. **21**(6), 829–839 (2010)

11. Malinowski, P., Lim, H.J.: Mindfulness at work: positive affect, hope, and optimism mediate the relationship between dispositional mindfulness, work engagement, and well-being. Mindfulness **6**(6), 1250–1262 (2015)

12. Brewer, J.A., Elwafi, H.M., Davis, J.H.: Craving to quit: psychological models and neurobiological mechanisms of mindfulness training as treatment for addictions. Psychol. Addict. Behav. **27**(2), 366–379 (2013)

13. Levy, D.M., Wobbrock, J.O., Kaszniak, A.W., Ostergren, M.: The effects of mindfulness meditation training on multitasking in a high-stress information environment. In: Graphics Interface, pp. 45–52, Toronto, ON, Canada (2012)

14. Paredes, P., Chan, M.: CalmMeNow: exploratory research and design of stress mitigating mobile interventions. In: SIGCHI Conference on Human Factors in Computing Systems, pp. 1699–1704, Vancouver, BC, Canada (2011)

15. Mark, G., Gonzalez, V.M., Harris, J.: No task left behind? Examining the nature of fragmented work. In: SIGCHI Conference on Human Factors in Computing Systems, pp. 321–330, Portland, Oregon, USA (2005)

16. Hjortskov, N., Rissén, D., Blangsted, A.K., Fallentin, N., Lundberg, U., Søgaard, K.: The effect of mental stress on heart rate variability and blood pressure during computer work. Eur. J. Appl. Physiol. **92**(1/2), 84–89 (2004)

17. Interaxon: Muse: The brain sensing headband (2015). http://www.choosemuse.com/

18. Huang, J., et al.: FOCUS: enhancing children's engagement in reading by using contextual BCI training sessions. In: SIGCHI Conference on Human Factors in Computing Systems, pp. 1905–1908, Toronto, ON, Canada (2014)

19. Russell, J.A.: A circumplex model of affect. J. Pers. Soc. Psychol. **39**(6), 1161–1178 (1980)

20. Russell, J.A., Weiss, A., Mendelsohn, G.A.: Affect grid: a single-item scale of pleasure and arousal. J. Pers. Soc. Psychol. **57**(3), 493–502 (1989)

21. Hart, S.G., Staveland, L.E.: Development of NASA-TLX (Task Load Index): results of empirical and theoretical research. Adv. Psychol. **52**, 139–183 (1988)

22. Miyata, Y., Norman, D.A.: Psychological issues in support of multiple activities. In: Norman, D.A., Draper, S.W. (eds.) User Centered System Design: New Perspectives on Human-Computer Interaction, pp. 265–284. L. Erlbaum Associates Inc., Hillsdale (1986)

Effects of Mandala Coloring on Mindfulness, Spirituality, and Subjective Well-Being

Chao Liu[1](✉), Hao Chen[1](✉), Wen-Ko Chiou[2](✉), and Rungtai Lin[3](✉)

[1] Department of Management, Chang Gung University, Taoyuan City, Taiwan
174673015@qq.com, victory666666@126.com
[2] Department of Industrial Design, Chang Gung University,
Taoyuan City, Taiwan
wkchiu@mail.cgu.edu.tw
[3] Graduate School of Creative Industry Design,
National Taiwan University of Arts, New Taipei City, Taiwan
rtlin@mail.ntua.edu.tw

Abstract. This study investigated the effects of Mandala coloring on subjective well-being, mindfulness, and spirituality, and the relationship between mindfulness, spirituality and subjective well-being. Methods: Recruited 80 students from Chang gung university in Taiwan, measures of the three main variables were administered at pre–test and post-test. Results: Subjective well-being significantly increased (mean score of 3.96 and 4.67 at pre- and post-test, respectively), there is a positive correlation between mindfulness, spirituality and SWB. Spirituality would mediate the relationship between mindfulness and SWB. Conclusion: These results suggest that Mandala coloring can have a positive effect on the subjective well-being. However, further research concerning its effects on mindfulness, spirituality and SWB, as well as other psychological constructs, is warranted to better understand the effects of Mandala coloring.

Keywords: Mandala coloring · Mindfulness · Spirituality · Subjective well-being

1 Introduction

In addition to studying the difficulties and problems people may face in life and how to alleviate them, it is important to know what makes people happiness. What influences a person's opinion of life is good or bad. Mandala coloring, spirituality and mindfulness have been correlated with subjective well-being (Kim et al. 2008; Cappellen et al. 2016; Wilber 2000). Mandala is used as a meditation tool in various religions, but most famously in Tibetan Buddhism, it is a circular design that is believed to facilitate psychotherapy and integration during personal creation. The use of the mandala as a therapeutic tool was first supported by Carl Jung, who believed that the act of painting the mandala had a calming and healing effect on its creator, while promoting spiritual integration and the meaning of personal life (Jung 1973). Mindfulness refers to a

© Springer Nature Switzerland AG 2019
P.-L. P. Rau (Ed.): HCII 2019, LNCS 11576, pp. 543–554, 2019.
https://doi.org/10.1007/978-3-030-22577-3_39

quality of consciousness characterized by the clarity and vividness of present experience (Kabat-Zinn 1994). Spirituality refers to the ability to create meaning based on an
understanding of practical problems (Vaughan 2002). SWB is a long-lasting spiritual
satisfaction, which is used in psychological or emotional States, including positive or
pleasant emotions, from satisfaction to intense Subjective well-being (Diener 2000).

1.1 Mandala

Previous research on mandala art therapy has shown that it has positive psychological
effects on different groups. The application of mandala coloring to the general population has found that it improves the SWB of college students (Pisarik and Larson
2011), improve the self-consciousness of nursing college students (Mahar, Iwasiw and
Evans 2012), improve the negative emotions of healthy adults (Babouchkina and
Robbins 2015), improve the self-ability and self-consciousness of hospice professionals
and palliative therapists, and ultimately reduce job burnout (Potash et al. 2014). In
addition, studies have explored the use of mandala art therapy in groups with physical
or psychological problems, showing that it can reduce the stress of breast cancer
survivors while improving their SWB (Elkisa-Abuhoff, Gaydos, Goldblatt, Chen and
Rose 2009). The mandala, as a meditation tool in various religions but most famously
in Tibetan Buddhism, is a circular design that is thought to facilitate psychotherapy and
the integration by an individual at the time. The use of the mandala as a therapeutic tool
was first championed by Carl Jung, who showed that the mandala's actions painted
calming and healing effects on its creator, while promoting both psychological integration and the meaning of individual life (Jung 1973), which are fundamental to the
work of using them for traumatic information disclosure. Siegel (2000) found that
spontaneous drawings can help determine patients' emotional state and their progress
toward recovery. Spontaneous drawings originates from unconsciousness and plays a
role in the formation of images under the influence of external factors (Furth 2002).The
use of mandala as therapeutic tools for finding self-awareness, expression, conflict
resolution, and healing (Henderson et al. 2007),he regard the mandala as a symbol
means "the material of laden and conflict". Thus, they can provide a sense of order and
integration, as well as the discovery of balance and inner peace despite external conflicts. Curry and Kasser (2005) found that mandala provide a sense of peace, balance
and wholeness in times of pain.

1.2 Mindfulness

Mindfulness therapy was founded by Kabat-Zinn, an honorary professor at the
University of Massachusetts. Mindfulness is a completely open self-awareness that
focuses on the present. Instead of a self-critical attitude, mindfulness embraces every
thought in the heart and mind with curiosity and acceptance, which emphasizes facing
up to the present and awareness (Kabat-Zinn 1994). Mindfulness practitioners clearly
live at the present moment but are not involved in it (Bishop et al. 2004). Mindfulness
meditation increased the meaning and peace of spirituality (Carmody et al. 2008),
facilitated a sense of meaning, peacefulness, and many aspects of spirituality in cancer
patients (Greeson et al. 2011; Garland et al. 2007). The relationship between

mindfulness and quality of life is mediated by increased spirituality (Silva and Pereira 2017; Greeson et al. 2011).

Mindfulness technology is effective in treating a series of mental health difficulties (Baer 2003) and promoting SWB (Brown and Ryan 2003). Therefore, mindfulness is increasingly used as a form of psychological intervention, which originates from the meditation practice of Eastern Buddhism, which uses concepts related to everything (Baer 2003) and is considered related to spiritual intelligence (Kornfield 1993). Mindfulness is effective in promoting SWB (Brown and Ryan 2003). Carmody and Bae (2007) found that regular meditation cultivates mindfulness skills in daily life, thus improving psychological function and increasing SWB. Similarly, Brown and Ryan (2003) reported that mindfulness is negatively related to negative emotions such as anxiety, depression and anger, and positively related to SWB.

1.3   Spirituality

Spirituality is defined as the ability to connect meaning by observing the interconnection between the experience of the living world and the inner world (Rogers 2003; Young 2006) and the ability to create meaning based on an understanding of practical problems (Vaughan 2002). The findings suggest that there is an important relationship between meaning and subjective well-being. Schnell (2010) found that those who were indifferent to life had lower levels of positive emotions and life satisfaction than those who had meaningful lives. Sahin et al. (2012) found in the study of Turkish university students that the two dimensions of life meaning, namely existence meaning and searching meaning, significantly predicted subjective well-being. Dogan et al. (2012) found similar results in a sample of Turkish university students. These findings indicate that the existence of meaning has a positive predictive effect on subjective well-being, while the search for meaning has a negative predictive effect. A study conducted by Cohen and Cairns (2012) in Australia confirmed the negative correlation between high pursuit of life meaning and subjective well-being. Halama and Dedova (2007) found that life meaning significantly predicts life satisfaction of slovak teenagers. A study of Hong Kong adolescents found a significant correlation between life meaning and life satisfaction (Ho et al. 2010). As can be seen from relevant literature, there is a strong relationship between life meaning and subjective well-being.

1.4   Subjective Well-Being (SWB)

SWB in a broad sense is the label of a happy emotional family, such as joy, amusement, satisfaction, gratification, euphoria, and triumph. SWB is broadly defined as a person's cognition and emotional evaluation of his life (Diener, Lucas and Oishi 2002). SWB seems to be a broad structure, including emotional response and cognitive assessment of life satisfaction (Diener et al. 1999). Dina et al. (2002) assumed that each element forming SWB (positive emotion, negative emotion, and life satisfaction) should be measured by researchers individually, rather than attempting to use single or compound measurements, in order to ensure that all aspects of SWB are captured. More and more evidences show the importance of SWB (Sheldon and Lyubomirsky 2004). SWB is a protective factor for the elderly against disability (Ostir, Markides, Black and

Goodwin 2000). On the contrary, low SWB is associated with increased depression (Keyes and Magyar-mow 2003). An increasing number of interventions are aimed at enhancing SWB while reducing symptoms of pain and emotional distress (Diener et al. 2002). The importance of SWB means that we must understand the cognitive and emotional processes and experiences that may sustain and enhance it.

1.5   Research Purpose and Hypothesis

The main purpose of this study is to explore the influence of mandala coloring on mindfulness, spirituality and subjective well-being, and the relationship between mindfulness, spirituality and subjective well-being.

Based on all the above theories, we can propose the following hypothesis:

Hypothesis 1, Mindfulness score of post-assessment is significant higher than the score of pre-assessment.

Hypothesis 2, Spirituality score of post-assessment is significant higher than the score of pre-assessment.

Hypothesis 3, SWB score of post-assessment is significant higher than the score of pre-assessment.

Hypothesis 4, There is a positive correlation between mindfulness, spirituality and SWB.

Hypothesis 5, Spirituality have a mediator effect on the relationship between mindfulness and SWB.

2   Method

2.1   Participants

Participants were 80 university students (72.5% female n = 58 and 27.5% male n = 22) recruited from Chang Gung University located in the northwest of Taiwan. The age of participants ranged from 18 to 49 years (M = 22.53, SD = 5.53).

2.2   Instruments

State Mindfulness Scale (SMS; Tanay and Bernstein 2013). The State Mindfulness Scale is a state-like measurement tool that includes 21 items, with responses ranging from 1 (not at all) to 5 (very well). The SMS measure consists of two sub-scales that relate to bodily sensations or mental events. Sample items are "I noticed some pleasant and unpleasant physical sensations" and "I noticed emotions come and go." Higher scores reflect greater levels of state-mindfulness. This scale was judged to be more inclusive of present moment awareness and a non-judgmental attitude, compared to the alternative scale that is evaluating mindful attention and awareness of the present moment (see Brown and Ryan 2003 for alternative scale). The study of Mantzios and

Giannou (2018) produced an alpha of 0.95/0.94 for pre- and post- measurements of the overall score; and 0.82/0.85 for the bodily sensations and 0.94/0.93 for the mental events subscales.

Spiritual Attitude and Involvement List (SAIL, Meezenbroek et al. 2008). SAIL consists of 26 items arranged in 7 dimensions: meaningfulness, trust, acceptance, caring for others, connectedness with nature, transcendent experiences, spiritual activities. Psychometric properties were tested in five samples differing in age, spiritual and religious background, and physical health. Factorial, convergent and discriminant validity were demonstrated, and each subscale showed adequate internal consistency and test retest reliability (Meezenbroek et al. 2008). SAIL can be employed as a continuous measure ranging from 1 to 6 with higher scores indicating higher levels of spiritual attitude/involvement or it can be employed as a binary variable whereby high spiritual attitude/involvement is indicated by a SAIL score > 4.

The Positive and Negative Affect Scales (PANAS; Watson, Clark and Tellegen 1988) and Satisfaction with Life Scale (SWLS; Diener et al. 1985). As suggested by Diener et al. (1999), measurements of hedonic well-being can be divided into emotional and cognitive components. Following this suggestion, we used the Positive Affect Negative Affect Scale (PANAS; Watson et al. 1988) to assess the emotional component of SWB and the Satisfaction with Life Scale (SWLS; Diener et al. 1985) to assess the cognitive component of SWB. Items on the PANAS range from 1 (not at all) to 5 (all the time) for both positive (10 items; e.g., "interested," "strong") and negative (10 items; e.g., "ashamed," "irritable") affect. The SWLS is a 7-item scale (e.g., In most ways, my life during the past month was close to ideal) with scores on each item ranging from 1 (strongly disagree) to 7 (strongly agree). Following the recommendations of Diener et al. (1999), we calculated each subscale score (PA, NA, and SWLS) and computed a composite subjective well-being (SWBC) score by taking the sum of the positive affect and life satisfaction items and subtracting the negative affect items. The Cronbach's alpha coefficient of the subjective well-being index in Study ranged from 0.79 to 0.86.

2.3 Coloring Material

Participants were exposed to an A4 size page, and the page was a structured mandala, which is circular design composed of symmetrical shapes. All participants were exposed to a box of 12 colored pencils, and a pencil sharpener.

2.4 Procedure and Design

Potential participants responded to an advertisement at a University in the northwest of the Taiwan. Participants were kept blind to the study, and were informed that they signed-up to volunteer at a study that was investigating "Personality and Art." Pre-screening questions to allow participation evaluated color-blindness, medication use, and former and current diagnoses of affective disorders. Participants received simultaneously a participant information form, a consent form, and the demographics page with the questionnaire (i.e., the four scales) for the pre-assessment. Next, participants commenced a 30-min mandala coloring. After the 30 min, participants were given a questionnaire again for the post-assessment, and were debriefed and thanked for their participation. Participants had the opportunity to record an arbitrary number assigned to their questionnaires and drawing, to allow them to withdraw at a later stage and retain the anonymity of participation. Ethical approval was granted by the Ethical Committee based within the University and was scrutinized to strictly adhere to ethical guidelines set by the Taiwan Psychological Society.

Data was performed at the description level with statistics of the mean, standard deviation and Pearson correlation matrix. At the inferential level, paired samples t-test and Sobel test were used. The sample size recruited matched or exceeded previous studies. Analyses were conducted by utilizing SPSS version 22 (IBM 2013) and a significance threshold was set at $p < 0.05$.

3 Results

Paired samples t-test with repeated measures on the Time was conducted on the Mindfulness, spirituality, and SWB scales (Table 1).

Table 1. Means and standard deviations for the measurements, pre- and post-intervention.

Measures	Mean(SD)			t	p
	Pre	Post	Post-Pre		
SMS	3.77(0.53)	3.80(0.62)	0.03(0.45)	0.61	0.55
SAIL	4.28(0.54)	4.33(0.61)	0.05(0.34)	1.33	0.19
PANAS	1.04(1.01)	1.54(0.99)	0.50(0.82)	5.46	<0.001
SWLS	3.88(1.09)	4.20(1.05)	0.32(0.23)	12.53	<0.001
SWB	3.96(1.46)	4.67(1.41)	0.71(0.09)	7.52	<0.001

SMS, State Mindfulness Scale; SAIL, Spiritual Attitude and Involvement List; PANAS, Positive and Negative Affect Scales; SWLS, Satisfaction with Life Scale; SWB, Subjective well-being.

For Mindfulness, Post-Pre was not significant: $t(79) = 0.608$, $p = 0.545$. For spirituality, Post-Pre was also not significant: $t(79) = 1.334$, $p = 0.186$. For SWB, there was a significant difference between post and pre: $t(79) = 7.523$, $p < 0.001$. Results indicated that mandala coloring produced a significant increase in SWB levels.

Use Pearson correlation analysis to reveal the relationship between mindfulness, spirituality, and happiness (Table 2).

Table 2. Pearson correlation matrix for mindfulness, spirituality, subjective well-being, and the subscales of spirituality (Post-assessment of mandala coloring).

	1	2	3	4	5	6	7	8	9	10
1	1									
2	0.58**	1								
3	0.57**	0.63**	1							
4	0.35**	0.11	0.13	1						
5	0.52**	0.48**	0.67**	0.39**	1					
6	0.47**	0.39**	0.55**	0.19	0.45**	1				
7	0.47**	0.40**	0.55**	0.28*	0.52**	0.47**	1			
8	0.36**	0.31**	0.53**	−0.01	0.39**	0.54**	0.54**	1		
9	0.66**	0.64**	0.81**	0.40**	0.78**	0.71**	0.81**	0.72**	1	
10	0.31**	0.58**	0.56**	0.01	0.34**	0.39**	0.29**	0.39**	0.51**	1

1, SMS; 2 to 8 are the subscales of SAIL (2, Meaningfulness; 3, Trust; 4, Acceptance; 5, Caring for others; 6, Connectedness with nature; 7, Transcendent experiences; 8, Spiritual activities); 9, SAIL; 10, SWB
*, $p < 0.05$; **, $p < 0.01$

Mindfulness, spirituality, and almost all subscales of spirituality except acceptance were positively correlated with subjective well-being.

Sobel test was used to test the mediator effect of spirituality on mindfulness and subjective well-being. The results showed that the mediator effect was significant ($Z = 3.61$, $p < 0.001$), indicating that mindfulness through spirituality to affect subjective well-being. The standardized mediator effect $d = 0.35$, that is, each standard deviation increase of mindfulness will increase subjective happiness for 0.35 standard deviation through affecting spirituality.

4 Discussion

We examined the effectiveness of mandala coloring on subjective well-being, mindfulness, and spirituality, and the relationship between subjective well-being, mindfulness, and spirituality. From the results of the data analysis we can indicated that:

1. Mandala art therapy may effectively increase subjective well-being.
2. There is a positive correlation between mindfulness, spirituality and SWB
3. Spirituality have a mediator effect on the relationship between mindfulness and SWB.

While these results correspond with the research findings of (PISARIK 2011; Elkis-Abuhoff et al. 2009) that mandala coloring boosts subjective well-being. Huyser (2002) concluded through experience that individuals will experience peace, satisfaction, love and subjective well-being when mandala coloring. The reason is that the outline of the mandala creates a protective space in which the painter can use his imagination to create. From the quantitative research, the average of pre-test subjective well-being of mandala coloring is 3.96, and the average of post-test subjective well-being is 4.67. The post-painting emotion is obviously better than that before painting, which is consistent with their research.

In addition, our findings confirm the views of Ryan et al. (2008). Based on previous research, individuals' life satisfaction of subjective well-being are met primarily by the support of others, such as a support supervisor in a work environment (Deci et al. 2001), a close partner (Patrick et al. 2007). However, our research suggests that one possible way for individuals to meet subjective well-being is to enhance mindfulness rather than rely on others. Compared with the interpersonal processes discussed above that support the realization of life satisfaction of subjective well-being, mindfulness can support the realization of needs through meditation or other internal processes of mindfulness oriented intervention (Eberth and Sedlmeier 2012; Keng et al. 2011). Therefore, improving the individual's mindfulness ability can improve the degree of subjective well-being.

Spirituality is fertile ground for experiencing positive emotions (Van Cappellen and Rime 2014). Through their participation in spiritual practice, they may experience positive emotions every time. Over time, the amplification effect of positive emotions will accumulate and compound, thus establishing corresponding personal and social resources (Fredrickson 2013). Understanding the mechanisms by which spirituality affects well-being is important because it can inform future interventions seeking to improve well-being. In the context of buddhistic mandala, these findings emphasize that the degree, type (and likely frequency) of positive emotions is not trivial, but can improve an individual's well-being. It is important, however, that while awe, gratitude, love and peace are particularly easily felt in the spiritual realm, they also occur outside the non-religious. For example, these emotions have been discussed in the literature of peak experience (Maslow 1964), flow (Csikszentmihalyi 1991) or chaironic happiness (Wong 2011). This means that the connection between mind and happiness can be explained, at least in part, by a mechanism that is not confined to the mind/environment. However, spirituality may be a protective factor for well-being, as they provide a unique basis for creating these positive emotions of self-transcendence, many of which are characterized by spirituality as powerful motivators. An interesting question is whether non-believers can also reap some of the benefits of spirituality without resorting to religion or spirituality, as long as they can find reliable sources of awe, gratitude, love and peace in their daily lives. Another interesting question is whether positive emotions of self-transcendence are more conducive to happiness than other positive emotions, even for non-spiritual people. All positive emotions expand and build (see "expanding and building theory", Fredrickson 2013), but it's also possible that some of them lead to greater happiness. Given that positive emotions of self-transcendence don't focus on the self or promote pro-social behavior, they may be particularly prone to promoting happiness through feedback loops (Weinstein and Ryan 2010).

Maslow (1943) first proposed the hierarchy of human needs theory. A person needs to meet basic physiological needs, including food, warmth and rest, followed by personal safety. Then there is the psychological sense of belonging and the need for love. People need intimate relationships and friendship, and all human beings want warm and harmonious interpersonal relationships. These, along with the need to be respected, represent accomplishments, reputations, status and opportunities for advancement. In his early theory of hierarchy, there were only five layers, which put the need of human beings to pursue self-realization, that is, to fully exert the full potential of life (including spiritual quotient and creation), at the top. Think that the bottom needs to be met, talent has the mind to pay attention to the pursuit of higher level. Tay and Diener (2011) for 2011 people in The Three Kingdoms, made a cross-cultural study, to investigate the relationship between the demand to satisfy and happy, they found that the bottom first, then the order of the top is not the necessary condition, economically underdeveloped areas of the people, even if is not fully satisfy the physiological needs, also can through the way of relationships, be happy in more satisfied the demand of the upper. Maslow (1969) put forward the demand level model of the complete expression should be six levels, namely the physiological needs, security needs, belonging needs, respect and love the need, the needs of self-realization and transcendence, transcendence need can also be called spirituality or beyond the need of self-realization, his absence beyond sexual motivation on the significance of using the concept of transcendence motivation, on the other hand, has carried on the important supplement to the concept. He defined the "self" in the concept of self-realization as not only the individual existence of the "ego", but also the "expanded self" that has expanded to include all aspects of the world and transcended the distinction between ego and non-ego. Transcendence refers to the highest and most extensive or overall level of human consciousness. Transcendence functions as an end rather than a means and has relations with a person, other people with important relations, ordinary people, nature and the universe. According to Rivera and Mark (2006), Maslow has expanded the hierarchy of needs from five to six. In addition to the needs of physiology, security, belonging, love, respect and self-realization, there is also the need for transcendence. Among them, the needs of self-realization and transcendence are all about the transformation of consciousness. Romeu and Albert (2010) believe that people can achieve self-transcendence to the greatest extent, such as altruism or spiritual improvement.

However, there were no significant differences in terms of mindfulness and spirituality. Although not significant, scores of post-assessment are still higher than the score of pre-assessment. We suggest that the duration of the Mandala coloring was too short for students to develop sufficient mindfulness and spirituality. Nevertheless, while Mandala coloring failed to produce a desirable change in participants' mindfulness and spirituality scores, we did observe that the program helped participants become an abiding state in which mind becomes very still, and is thus able to gain insight in their life experience (Gordon et al. 2017). This was a notable change from noisy state before their mandala coloring.

5   Future Research

With the development of science and technology, human beings will enter the AI era, which will bring unprecedented wealth: according to PWC, artificial intelligence will bring 16 trillion dollars of global GDP growth by 2030, and it will also bring huge challenges of unemployment and employment. In the era of industrial revolution, science and technology to create more job because the manual craftsmen work is broken down into the production of all kinds of work online, but artificial intelligence make water online individual work completely be replaced by robots, which not only take place in the factory, truck drivers, the driver, telephone sales, customer service, onset and radiologists work, in the next 15 years will be gradually replaced by artificial intelligence. And only creative work is guaranteed work, because artificial intelligence can only be optimized but not created. Even worse than losing a job is losing meaning, because the work ethic of the industrial revolution era has convinced humans that work gives them a reason to exist and that work gives them a meaning to live. Humans should reexamine how artificial intelligence affects work and co-exists with humans. Artificial intelligence is taking away a lot of repetitive work, but humans are not people because they are good at repetitive work. How do humans distinguish themselves in the age of artificial intelligence? Only the development of creativity and compassion and other aspects of the soul, those are artificial intelligence can't do. Humans will be pleased when artificial intelligence replaces them in repetitive tasks. Artificial intelligence will be a good tool for creators, so scientists, artists, musicians and writers can become more creative. With their unique minds and hearts, humans will do the work that only humans are good at, winning on the spiritual level of human creativity and compassion. The development of artificial intelligence is a serendipity. Its arrival will liberate human from routine work, and it also reminds human beings why they are human, and human beings need to further study mindfulness, spirituality and happiness.

References

Babouchkina, A., Robbins, S.J.: Reducing negative mood through mandala creation: a randomized controlled trial. Art Ther. **32**(1), 34–39 (2015)

Baer, R.A.: Mindfulness training as a clinical intervention: a conceptual and empirical review. Clin. Psychol. Sci. Pract. **10**(2), 125–143 (2003)

Bishop, S.R., et al.: Mindfulness: a proposed operational definition. Clin. Psychol. Sci. Pract. **11** (3), 230–241 (2010)

Broom, B.C.: Medicine and story: a novel clinical panorama arising from a unitary mind/body approach to physical illness. Adv. Mind-Body Med. **16**(3), 161 (2000)

Brown, K.W., Ryan, R.M.: The benefits of being present: mindfulness and its role in psychological well-being. J. Pers. Soc. Psychol. **84**(4), 822 (2003)

Cappellen, P.V., Toth-Gauthier, M., Saroglou, V., Fredrickson, B.L.: Religion and well-being: the mediating role of positive emotions. J. Happiness Stud. **17**(2), 485–505 (2016)

Carmody, J., Reed, G., Kristeller, J., Merriam, P.: Mindfulness, spirituality, and health-related symptoms. J. Psychosom. Res. **64**(4), 393–403 (2008)

Cohen, K., Cairns, D.: Is searching for meaning in life associated with reduced subjective well-being? Confirmation and possible moderators. J. Happiness Stud. **13**(2), 313–331 (2012)

Da, S.J., Pereira, A.M.: Perceived spirituality, mindfulness and quality of life in psychiatric patients. J. Relig. Health **56**(1), 130–140 (2017)

Diener, E.: Subjective well-being. The science of happiness and a proposal for a national index. Am. Psychol. **55**(1), 34 (2000)

Diener, E., Emmons, R.A., Larsen, R.J., Griffin, S.: The satisfaction with life scale. J. Pers. Assess. **49**(1), 71–75 (1985)

Diener, E., Lucas, R.E., Oishi, S.: Subjective well-being: the science of happiness and life satisfaction. In: Snyder, C.R., Lopez, S.J. (eds.) Handbook of Positive Psychology, pp. 63–73. Oxford University Press, Oxford (2002)

Diener, E., Suh, E.M., Lucas, R.E., Smith, H.L.: Subjective well-being: three decades of progress. Psychol. Bull. **125**(2), 276 (1999)

Doğan, T., Sapmaz, F., Tel, F.D., Sapmaz, S., Temizel, S.: Meaning in Life and subjective well-being among Turkish University students. Proc. – Soc. Behav. Sci. **55**(55), 612–617 (2012)

Elkis-Abuhoff, D., Gaydos, M., Goldblatt, R., Chen, M., Rose, S.: Mandala drawings as an assessment tool for women with breast cancer. Arts Psychother. **36**(4), 231–238 (2009)

Furth, G.M.: The Secret World of Drawings: A Jungian Approach to Healing Through Art (Studies in Jungian Psychology By Jungian Analysts). University of Toronto Press, Toronto (2002)

Garland, S.N., Carlson, L.E., Cook, S., Lansdell, L., Speca, M.: A non-randomized comparison of mindfulness-based stress reduction and healing arts programs for facilitating post-traumatic growth and spirituality in cancer outpatients. Support. Care Cancer **15**(8), 949–961 (2007)

Greeson, J.M., et al.: Changes in spirituality partly explain health-related quality of life outcomes after Mindfulness-Based Stress Reduction. J. Behav. Med. **34**(6), 508–518 (2011)

Halama, P., Dedova, M.: Meaning in life and hope as predictors of positive mental health: do they explain residual variance not predicted by personality traits? Studia Psychologica **49**(3), 191 (2007)

Henderson, P., Rosen, D., Mascaro, N.: Empirical study on the healing nature of mandalas. Psychol. Aesthetics Creativity Arts **1**(3), 148–154 (2007)

Ho, M.Y., Cheung, F.M., Cheung, S.F.: The role of meaning in life and optimism in promoting well-being. Pers. Individ. Differ. **48**(5), 658–663 (2010)

Huyser, A., Boeke, W.: Mandala Workbook for Inner Self-development. Binkey Kok Publications (2002)

Jung, C.: Mandala Symbolism (3rd Printing) (RFC Hull, Trans.). Bollingen Series. Princeton University Press, Princeton (1973)

Kabat-Zinn, J.: Wherever You Go, There You Are: Mindfulness Meditation in Everyday Life. Hachette Books (2009)

Kasser, T.: Can coloring mandalas reduce anxiety? Art Ther. **22**(2), 81–85 (2005)

Keyes, C.L., Magyar-Moe, J.L.: The measurement and utility of adult subjective well-being (2003)

Kim, H., Kim, S., Choe, K., Kim, J.S.: Effects of mandala art therapy on subjective well-being, resilience, and hope in psychiatric inpatients. Arch. Psychiatr. Nurs. **32**(2), 167–173 (2018)

Koltko-Rivera, M.E.: Rediscovering the later version of Maslow's hierarchy of needs: self-transcendence and opportunities for theory, research, and unification. Rev. Gen. Psychol. **10** (4), 302–317 (2006)

Kornfield, J.: A Path With Heart: A Guide Through the Perils and Promises of Spiritual Life New York. Bantam Books (1993)

Labelle, L.E., Lawlorsavage, L., Campbell, T.S., Faris, P., Carlson, L.E.: Does self-report mindfulness mediate the effect of Mindfulness-Based Stress Reduction (MBSR) on spirituality and posttraumatic growth in cancer patients? J. Positive Psychol. **10**(2), 153–166 (2015)

Lopez, S.J., Snyder, C.: Positive Psychol. Assess. APA, Washington (2003)

Mahar, D.J., Iwasiw, C.L., Evans, M.K.: The mandala: first-year undergraduate nursing students' learning experiences. Int. J. Nurs. Educ. Scholarsh. **9**(1), 22–23 (2012)

Meezenbroek, E.D.J., et al.: measuring spirituality as a universal human experience: development of the spiritual attitude and involvement list (SAIL). J. Psychosoc. Oncol. **30**(2), 141–167 (2012)

Ostir, G.V., Markides, K.S., Black, S.A., Goodwin, J.S.: Emotional well-being predicts subsequent functional independence and survival. J. Am. Geriatr. Soc. **48**(5), 473–478 (2000)

Pisarik, C.T., Larson, K.R.: Facilitating college students' authenticity and psychological well-being through the use of mandalas: an empirical study. J. Humanistic Couns. **50**(1), 84–98 (2011)

Potash, J.S., et al.: Mandalas as indicators of burnout among end-of-life care workers. J. Appl. Arts Health **4**(3), 363–377 (2014)

Şahin, M., Aydın, B., Sarı, S., Kaya, S., Pala, H.: Öznel iyi oluşu açıklamada umut ve yaşamda anlamın rolü. Kastamonu Eğitim Dergisi **20**(3), 827–836 (2012)

Schnell, T.: Existential indifference: Another quality of meaning in life. J. Humanistic Psychol. **50**(3), 351–373 (2010)

Sheldon, K.M., Lyubomirsky, S.: Achieving sustainable new happiness: prospects, practices, and prescriptions. Positive Psychol. Pract. 127–145 (2004)

Silva, J.P.D., Pereira, A.M.S.: Perceived spirituality, mindfulness and quality of life in psychiatric patients. J. Relig. Health **56**(1), 130–140 (2017)

Tanay, G., Bernstein, A.: State mindfulness scale (SMS): development and initial validation. Psychol. Assess. **25**(4), 1286–1299 (2013)

Tay, L., Diener, E.: Needs and subjective well-being around the world. J. Pers. Soc. Psychol. **101**(2), 354–365 (2011)

Vaughan, F.: What is spiritual intelligence? J. Humanistic Psychol. **42**(2), 16–33 (2002)

Watson, D., Clark, L.A., Tellegen, A.: Development and validation of brief measures of positive and negative affect: the PANAS scales. J. Pers. Soc. Psychol. **54**(6), 1063 (1988)

Wilber, K.: Integral Psychology: Consciousness, Spirit, Psychology, Therapy. Shambhala Publications (2000)

Zernicke, K.A., et al.: The eCALM trial: eTherapy for cancer applying mindfulness. exploratory analyses of the associations between online mindfulness-based cancer recovery participation and changes in mood, stress symptoms, mindfulness, posttraumatic growth, and spirituality. Mindfulness **7**(5), 1–11 (2016)

Assessment of the Sense of Pleasure in Public Artwork in Living Environment

Taking the Streets Near the Taipei University in Sanxia District as an Example

Hsienfu Lo[✉], I-Ting Wang[✉], and Gao Yang[✉]

Graduate School of Creative Industry Design, College of Design, National Taiwan University of Arts, New Taipei City, Taiwan
hsienfulo@gmail.com, etinw@ms43.hinet.net,
Lukegao1991@gmail.com

Abstract. We can often see a lot of art works set in our living environment, and the "Act on Setting of Public Art" has also been promulgated by government for more than 20 years. However, our people still have a smattering of knowledge about the integration of public art into living environment. Setting of public art is a kind of artistic activities that combine the public and the public living space. It can also allow people to walk out of the room and interact with the natural and human environment, increase human's understanding of the urban environment, let art enter people's life and practice the art of living. This research has studied the public art works on Xueqin Road near the New Taipei City Senior High School Affiliated to Taipei University in Sanxia District in Taiwan, which are originally expected to enhance the public's appreciation of aesthetics, and also explored and tried to understand how the residents living here feel about the giant 12 artworks. It is hoped that the results of this research can be used as a reference for public art setting. This research has explored (1) whether there is a difference in the pleasure of the viewers' perceptions of public art, and (2) whether the aesthetic experience have an impact on pleasant response of the public to public art. And it has invited students, teachers and parents from schools adjacent to the public art setting to answer the questionnaire as subjects, so as to understand the relationship between art and pleasure, enhance students' theoretical knowledge of artistic appreciation and to realize the social function of effective art teaching in the cultural and creative industry development.

Keywords: Public art · Artistic symbols · Pleasure · Aesthetic experience

1 Introduction

Public art is an artistic activity that combines the concept of artistic creation with the public living space of the people. At first, public art was to transform and bring forth new ideas to traditional art, break the way of viewing art creations and combine art with outdoor natural and humanistic environments. On January 26, 1998, the Cultural Development Committee of the Executive Yuan promulgated the "Act on Setting of

© Springer Nature Switzerland AG 2019
P.-L. P. Rau (Ed.): HCII 2019, LNCS 11576, pp. 555–569, 2019.
https://doi.org/10.1007/978-3-030-22577-3_40

Public Art". However, the general public is still strange to and/or unfamiliar with the integration of public art into the environment. In school, there are few courses set for landscape or public art appreciation. However, the style or form of public art in life is numerous, and when it is set in different environments, the people have a polarized reaction to the landscape. This research is hoped to deepen the knowledge and appreciation of public art in art education and improve the understanding of middle school students about aesthetics.

1.1   Research Motives

The open space type and attributes of the setting of public art works are diverse and varied. So for public art works set in different environments in the light of local conditions, people have polarized responses. By viewing the evolution of public art setting in public fields, from "environmental art" in the initial period to the later "artistic environment" and the current "integrated shaping", its setting emphasizes that public art needs to be integrated with people, matters and things in the environment, and that works must be closely related to the locations. The public art originated from the city-states of the Western Empire. At that time, in order to demonstrate their dominant power, the rulers override and controlled the livelihood of ordinary citizens by public art works characterized by political representation and religious representation. There are dozens of public art works on the streets near the school, which are originally expected to enhance the public's appreciation of aesthetics. This research has been expected to explore and try to understand how the residents living here (parents, teachers and students) feel about pleasure brought by the giant 12 artworks.

1.2   Research Objective

Based on the above research motives, this research has studied citizens (students/teachers/parents) with different backgrounds, exploring what kind of environment and what kind of public art will bring the public with pleasant feelings and by analysis of visual variables and by use of visual communication theories discussing the impact of public art on the emotional experience of the people. It is hoped that the results of this research can be used as a reference for public art setting.

This research has explored (1) whether there is a difference in the pleasure of the viewers' perceptions of 12 public art works, and (2) whether the aesthetic experience have an impact on pleasant response of the public to public art.

1.3   Research Background

The author is a teacher from New Taipei Municipal Senior High School Affiliated to Taipei University in Taiwan. The school is located in the center of Taipei University special zone in Sanxia District in New Taipei City. Nowadays, the town has a high maturity, not only the overall street profile has been formed, but also the merchants and the immigration population have been in place. Compared with other North Tai-wan re-planed zones, this zone is progressing very rapidly. Since 2003, the land sales of Taipei University special zone have gradually reached its peak. The Taipei University special zone employs a low-density development and has planned a total of 17 major streets by design concept of setback, plus the green landscape planted, forming the trend of "Going Green" which is pursued by the modern people and focuses on the integration of rest and outdoor landscapes. By adopting a model similar to that of overseas forest cities, the town's green coverage rate has been greatly improved, and residents can enjoy greenery at close range. There are nearly 300 pieces of art works in just 1.3 km. In this research, course description has been done for the students to know the locations and basic creative concepts of the top 12 large works, and studies of designed research indices are based on the accumulated life experience, thus trying to understand the sense of pleasure in visual and psychological that public art brings to middle school students.

Art Environment and Cultural Resources

Sanxia Zushiye Temple

The Sanxia Zushiye Temple is located in the center of Sanxia District and is the interfaith center of immigrants from Anxi County. It was sketched in the thirty-fourth year of Emperor Qianlong (AD 1769). In the thirty-sixth year since foundation of the Republic of China, the Zushiye Temple was in a state of total disrepair. Therefore, Professor Li Meishu was appointed as art design and engineering guidance for the reconstruction. He combined the styles of different genres of artisans and contemporary artists, making the temple earn the reputation of "Folk Arts Center" and "Oriental Arts Center".

New Taipei City Yingge Ceramics Museum

The New Taipei City Yingge Ceramics Museum was officially opened on November 26, 2000. It is the first ceramic-themed professional museum in Taiwan. It is dedicated to the investigation, collection, preservation and maintenance of Taiwanese ceramic culture and engaged in research, collection, display, education and promotion. It also actively promotes international exchanges and cooperation.

Li Meishu Memorial Gallery

The museum was established in 1990 and was originally called "Physician Liu Qinggang and Professor Li Meishu Brothers Memorial Gallery"; in April 1995, it was moved to the current site and officially named "Li Meishu Memorial Gallery". The purpose of the memorial gallery is to commemorate the predecessor painter Professor Li Meishu. Professor Li Meishu (1902–1983), who devoted himself to artistic creation and art movement during his lifetime, insisted on embracing the beauty of Taiwan's native land by the realistic route he learned at Tokyo Art School for a lifetime.

Present Status of Education

Aesthetic education is an education that refines individual aesthetic literacy. Through participating in art courses in school, students must start from the mastery of basic aesthetics in life and can recognize the true, the good and the beautiful from the form and connotation of people, matters and things in daily life, thus cultivate the ability to perceive, imagine, interpret, speculate, practice and communicate, and the development of related habits. These abilities and habits cannot be obtained by one-shot but must be cultivated for a long time. Through a good artistic environment, students can deeply experience the relationship between art and life and enhance their aesthetic literacy.

2   Literature Review

The Provisions of the United States on Public Art define the functions and values of public art as (1) sense of belonging and identity, (2) participation in communication and understanding, and (3) improvement of environmental quality. France defines them by itself as (1) expressing local cultural characteristics, (2) improving environmental quality, (3) improving the city's appearance and landscape, and (4) developing educational opportunities [6]. The function of public art is to (1) beautify buildings and the environment, (2) let art workers develop their expertise to contribute to society, (3) benefit the people, (4) create public monuments, (5) construct historical and cultural objects, (6) enhance the national aesthetic literacy, and (7) influence social and cultural development [7]. Public art is an artistic activity that combines the concept of artistic creation with the public living space of the people. The purpose of this research is to explore the role of public art in the environment. The literatures discussed in this research include three major parts, that is, "Public Art", "Sense of Pleasure" and "Art Communication Theories".

2.1   Discussion on Relationship Between Public Art and Environment

Public art is set up to improve the quality of public space environment, playing a role in the environment in beautifying the environment and enhancing the aesthetic temperament of the public. The public art originated from the city-states of the Western Empire. At that time, in order to demonstrate their dominant power, the rulers override and controlled the livelihood of ordinary citizens by public art works characterized by political representation and religious representation. Appropriate public art can help the open space to achieve the interaction between environment, public art and human. The quality of interaction is related to the way that public art is presented, and public art with good interaction can make people feel happy when they gathers here to take activities and achieve the purpose of communication [13].

Taiwan is lacking neither in art nor in extensive "public" art works. However, the concept of public art is rarely debated. Professor Chen Qinan pointed out that "of course, many architects and landscape designers will insist that public art should include the building itself and the environmental landscapes [12]; some other think that public art should include the dynamic performing arts presented in the square space; however, there will be more people who after watching Taiwan's streetscapes and living spaces may advocate that it will be the best choice to leave nothing but more open vision for the most rare visual enjoyment." [5].

2.2   Discussion on Sense of Pleasure

The Mandarin Chinese Dictionary revised by the Ministry of Education defines pleasure as meaning of happiness and joy [2]. Most of the research shows that pleasure means that the experience is mostly positive, pleasant, delightful and interesting, and for pleasure Jordan also pointed out that products of pleasant images should be usable, aesthetical, achievable and credible, and Jordan suggested that based on the pleasure design of products, the discussion about future design should not only stay in physiological or cognitive research on general product functions but also emphasize human-oriented studies which promote the design of a more comprehensive relationship between people and products. Podilchak [11] argues that "sense of pleasure is often confused with the depiction of tourist fun, but studies find that sense of pleasure is primarily defined as personal and intrinsic experience and unique personal perception." [10] argues that the concept of sense of pleasure should be limited to the feelings of happiness, joy, delightfulness, etc. in the experience of seeing, listening, taste, smell or feeling when one performs an activity or engages in something while researches on psychology and neuroscience most often use happy words to describe the general pleasant response. Most communication researchers use the word of 'sense of pleasure' to describe and explain this positive response to media contents [8].

2.3 Discussion on Art Communication Theories

Art communication refers to the delivery of art works, concepts, ideas, etc. created by artists to the appreciators of art through various channels, in which the main body of art communication is art works. The decoding process for the viewer is (1) a sensory impression whether the reader/listener sees and produces shape perception or not; (2) a thinking mode whether the reader/listener understands and does meaning cognition or not; and (3) a psychological activity whether the reader/listener is moved and achieves inner feelings or not [9]. The outdoor public art has gone out of the exhibition space inside the museum and gradually turned to the open public space. With the mission of breaking the space authority of the museum, it brings the works to the surrounding environment of the citizens' life, eliminating the sense of alienation between art and the viewer and increasing exposure opportunities. The venue of creation is the field of exhibition, letting art live in our environment, and we can even touch the material everywhere and experience it by ourselves. In the implementation of public art, France identifies it by whether it can (1) express local cultural characteristics, (2) improve environmental quality, (3) improve the city's appearance and landscape, and (4) develop educational opportunities [6]. Through the art communication mode, people can see, understand and then get moved, combining the art with life. Art communication is a process and is also a complex organic system. From birth, display to reception, art involves creation, appreciation, evaluation, circulation and guidance. The appreciation of art communication is the most prominent part with the most research potential [4].

3 Research Architecture

Through the art communication mode, people can see, understand and then get moved. From sensory stimulation (formal beauty), exploring the unknown (symbolic beauty), social interaction (ideal beauty) and self-growth (conceptual beauty), the feelings reader/listener gets when he/she see these public art works can be explored [1]. The research is divided into three stages; the first stage includes literature discussion and theoretical construction, as described above; the second stage is to make a questionnaire test on samples, and after the preliminary test and expert consultation, the test is formally carried out; the third stage is to sort out the results of questionnaire test, conduct relevant statistical analysis, discuss related results and obtain possible results and recommendations. The research architecture is shown in the figure (Table 1).

3.1   Research Architecture

3.2   Research Methods

Table 1. Research architecture diagram

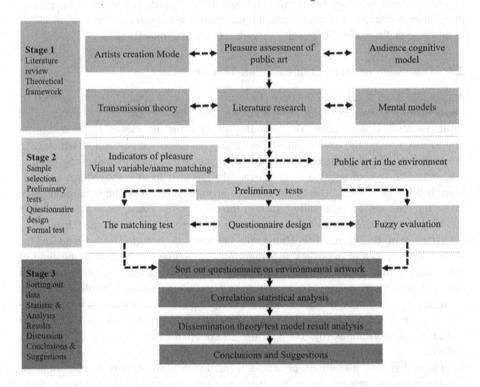

This research has been conducted by use of research architecture indicated in the figure, combined with questionnaires and results analysis. A total of 151 valid questionnaires are obtained, including 59 males and 92 females, to explore high school students' understanding of the sense of pleasure through art works in life and understand the relationship between the meaning of art communication mode in technical level, semantic level and effect level and the reader/listener's sense of pleasure. The samples are the following 12 public works, and the subjects are invited to fill questionnaires by subjectively evaluating the strength of the factor preference (1–5 points) according to the following factors; the questionnaire is divided into three parts: sensory stimulation (formal beauty), exploration of unknown (symbolic beauty), social interaction (ideal beauty) and self-growth (conceptual beauty). Each piece of works is designed from 4 dimensions and with 12 questions.

3.3   Sample Selection

The streets of a city are the best representation of a town's styles. The builders of Taipei University zone have taken the concept of "10 billion towns and art streets" as the blueprint. They have planned landscapes of 30,000 square meters costing more than 10 billion yuan. By the joint strength of government and private enterprises, they build the country's first University City full of artistic atmosphere in Taipei University special zone in Sanxia district as well as an art street on Qinxue Road that is comparable to the Champs Elysees in Paris. The research has studied 12 large-scale public art works on Qinxue Road, which are listed in the following figure (Table 2) and described in the diagram (Table 3).

Table 2. List of public art works on Qinxue road (12 in total)

No.1	No.2	No.3

No.4	No.5	No.6

No.7	No.8	No.9

No.10	No.11	No.12

Table 3. Description of public art works (12 in total)

No.	Name	Works	Description
01	Open Wings		This work has different beauty from different angles. It means that one should open his/her wings and fly against the wind to seek for the special things he/she wants.
02	Poseidon		"Poseidon" takes the theme of the Renaissance sculpture, which makes people feel like they are in an artistic Western country.
03	Parent-child Tree		The Parent-child Tree is the work of Harada Yoshihiro, producer of Japan's Love Expo. These three pine trees represent father, mother and child, symbolizing a happy family and meaning that the new life will continue.
04	Rising Sound of Rhyme		Using the symbol of the string, the rotating shape shows the sound lingering and uploading, which seems to make the people who see it follow the rhyme.
05	Flying Birds Over Bamboo Forest		"Flying Birds Over Bamboo Forest" is created by Chridstine Macy, planner of the Canadian World Music Festival. It requires harmony between nature and all things. The huge bamboo shape makes people feel like they are in the bamboo forest and they can appreciate the cool breeze.
06	Space Coordinates		The high vertical direction of the "Space Coordinates" makes the work magnificent, and it catches people's eyes through bright colors. There is a wind detector at the top to tell you where the wind comes from.
07	Mother and Son		The work "Mother and Son" expresses by a semi figure that the mother holds the child in her arms and takes care of it. Mother turns her faces to the child, watching and guarding the child for a lifetime.
08	Plum Pavilion		The Plum Pavilion is on Meijie street. It is designed by Sergio A. Pelleroni, winner of the National Design Awards of the United States who believes that this work represents a passage that leads to a certain memory of people.

(Continued)

Table 3. *(Continued)*

09	Circle of Life		Ceramic art work "Circle of Life" presents the wonderful structure of the marine food chain with the concept of natural ecological conservation. Large and small fishes such as dolphins, whales and flying fish are set in undulating layers of waves, symbolizing the infinite circulation of marine ecology.
10	Window of the Universe		The "Window of the Universe" expects a different kind of stimulation in the boring life and unchanging scene. Its key ring opens a mysterious sub-dimensional window and lets people enter a vision of different feelings.
11	Tranquil Sea		The use of white marble material creates a view in which people are leisurely and peaceful watching the sea in the city jungle. This blue sea washes away the hustle and bustle of heavy traffic, allowing people to read the peace of mind.
12	New Vision		In life, different people have different positions for a same thing; people will have different degrees of feeling from different angles in the same environment. For a lot of things, the key is whether you can feel the life with your heart and then turn it into creative inspiration.

3.4   Guidance on Aesthetic Course

There are many ways in which human beings can understand and recognize the world they live in, such as by philosophical way, political way, economic way, scientific way, etc., and changes can be made when human understand and recognize the world through artistic appreciation activities. Philosophy attracts people to deeply ponder the underlying and abstract implication of the world, which is profound and speculative; politics informs people and their groups of their status and interests, which is witty and practical; economy expands people's desire for wealth, which is ordinary and realistic; and science systematically analyzes and exposes everything visible in the world and some invisible objects, making people understand their true features. Art, on the other hand, selectively aggregates and synthesizes the unique characteristics of the above-mentioned several ways, and presents a huge picture of survival in a comprehensive, emotional and visual way, which is magnificent and amazing.

In a nutshell, the significance of art appreciation to people is that it can greatly enrich people's spiritual life, and over time, it will form a spiritual spring that nourishes life. By appreciating the works of art, people further their own vision of life and deepen their understanding of life and social reality. At the same time, people will have a variety of complex emotional reactions in art appreciation activities when facing the changes in the characters and their destiny in the works. In this emotional ups and downs, the appreciators gain a rich sense of beauty. The research guides students to observe and recognize environmental art (material, size, location, color, shape and creative ideas), and then select their favorite artworks by visual evaluation.

3.5 Questionnaire Design

The content of the questionnaire in this research is based on the communication theories discussed earlier. After watching each piece of work, the subjects will answer the questionnaire in an intuitive way (a questionnaire with 16 questions is designed for each piece of work) and select the favorite one. Analysis has been done on sense of pleasure in dimensions of formal beauty, symbolic beauty, ideal beauty and conceptual beauty.

Questionnaire

The format of the questionnaire is as follows (Table 4):

Table 4. Questionnaire format (example)

Art Work	Questionnaire Content
 **NO.01 Open Wings** This work has different beauty from different angles. It means that one should open his/her wings and fly against the wind to seek for the special things he/she wants.	I. Please subjectively evaluate the strength of the factor preference according to the following factors: (weak 1☐2☐3☐4☐5☐ strong) **Sensory Stimulation (Formal Beauty)** 1. Degree that this piece of art works makes me feel new and interesting. Weak 1☐ 2☐ 3☐ 4☐ 5☐ Strong 2. Degree that this piece of art works makes me feel humanity. Weak 1☐ 2☐ 3☐ 4☐ 5☐ Strong 3. Degree that this piece of art works makes me feel artistic. Weak 1☐ 2☐ 3☐ 4☐ 5☐ Strong 4. Degree that this piece of art works makes me feel I want to collect it. Weak 1☐ 2☐ 3☐ 4☐ 5☐ Strong V. The Number of your favorite art works: ( )

Questionnaire Content

In the face of rapid changes in society and the ever-changing trends and challenges, the talents needed in the future must have a modern citizenship and civility with both local care and global vision. The artistic and aesthetic literacy of citizenship must be cultivated and implemented through a sound artistic and aesthetic education system, administrative support system, empowerment of teachers, development of curriculum and teaching materials, integration of social resources and shaping of social goodness and beauty. The subjects participate in this research by giving subjective evaluation of the strength of factor preference according to the following factors. The contents of the questionnaire are as follows:

I. Sensory Stimulation (Formal Beauty)
1. This piece of art works makes me feel bright and strong colors.
2. This piece of art works makes me feel smooth streamlined appearance.
3. This piece of art works makes me feel the position of the work is suitable.
4. This piece of art works makes me feel the material used is proper.
II. Exploring the Unknown (Symbolic Beauty)
5. Degree that this piece of art works makes me feel distinct themes.
6. Degree that this piece of art works makes me feel a sense of space.
7. Degree that this piece of art works makes me feel abstraction
8. Degree that this piece of art works makes me feel realism.
III. Social Interaction (Ideal Beauty)
9. Degree that this piece of art works makes me feel emotional integration.
10. Degree that this piece of art works makes me feel social care.
11. Degree that this piece of art works makes me feel story-telling.
12. Degree that this piece of art works makes me feel I want to touch it.
IV. Self-growth (Conceptual Beauty)
13. Degree that this piece of art works makes me feel new and interesting.
14. Degree that this piece of art works makes me feel humanity.
15. Degree that this piece of art works makes me feel artistic.
16. Degree that this piece of art works makes me feel I want to collect it.

3.6 Test Results

This research uses the holistic question as assessment criteria and carries out analysis on the fourth part: "Symbolic Beauty"; it conducts a preliminary assessment of pleasure sense on the basis of " degree of novelty and interestingness", "degree of humanity", " degree of artistic sense" and "degree of possible collection", and does analysis from three dimensions: the mean and standard deviation of overall evaluation results, the statistics of highest pleasure sense by male and female separately and the favorite art work.

Statistics of Mean and Standard Deviation of Overall Evaluation Results

Reliability analysis has been done on answers given by all subjects to the 48 questions. And the analysis results show that the internal consistency coefficient of cronbach's alpha is 0.95; it is an acceptable reliability. The mean and standard deviation of overall evaluation is listed (see Table 5), for example: for question "Degree that this piece of art works makes me feel new and interesting" (Q1), the average of the work No. 01 is 3.25 points, and the standard deviation is 1.11 points listed in the brackets below.

Table 5. Statistics of mean and standard deviation of overall evaluation results by all subjects

Questions	Work No. 01	Work No. 02	Work No. 03	Work No. 04	Work No. 05	Work No. 06	Work No. 07	Work No. 08	Work No. 09	Work No. 10	Work No. 11	Work No. 12
Q1	3.25	3.19	2.99	3.04	3.12	3.32	2.73	3.11	**3.40**	3.30	3.33	3.19
	(1.11)	(1.13)	(1.09)	**(1.17)**	(1.13)	(1.11)	(0.98)	(1.17)	(1.11)	(1.07)	(1.11)	**(1.17)**
Q2	2.12	2.17	2.68	2.06	2.34	2.09	**3.86**	2.37	2.49	2.03	2.48	2.00
	(0.92)	(0.97)	**(1.19)**	(0.96)	(1.02)	(0.88)	(1.06)	(1.20)	(1.08)	(0.96)	(1.11)	(0.93)
Q3	3.94	**4.05**	3.07	3.74	3.36	3.27	3.47	3.33	3.59	3.61	3.55	3.36
	(0.92)	(0.93)	(1.00)	(0.97)	(1.06)	(1.14)	(0.91)	(1.05)	(1.07)	(1.06)	(0.97)	**(1.15)**
Q4	2.47	**3.45**	2.15	2.55	2.52	2.62	2.63	2.63	2.90	2.72	2.92	2.53
	(1.21)	(1.27)	(1.07)	(1.19)	(1.27)	**(1.28)**	(1.16)	(1.26)	(1.24)	(1.22)	(1.26)	(1.23)

From Table 5, we can see for question "degree that this piece of art works makes me feel new and interesting" (Q1), the highest average is work No. 09 (with 3.4 points), and the maximum standard deviation is work No. 04 and No. 12 (with 1.17 points); for question "degree that this piece of art works makes me feel humanity" (Q2), the highest average is work No. 07 (with 3.86 points), and the maximum standard deviation is work No. 07 (with 1.19 points); for question "degree that this piece of art works makes me feel artistic" (Q3), the highest average is work No. 02 (with 4.05 points), and the maximum standard deviation is work No. 12 (with 1.15 points); and for question "degree that this piece of art works makes me feel I want to collect it" (Q4), the highest average is also work No. 02 (with 3.45 points), and the maximum standard deviation is work No. 06 (with 1.28 points).

T Verification Summary of Independent Samples by Male and Female in Overall Pleasure Assessment

As shown in Table 6, the results show there is a significant difference in work No. 06 "Space Coordinates" ($t = -2.186$, $p < .05$), work NO. 07 "Mother and Child" and work NO. 10 "Window of the Universe" ($t = -2.842$, $p < .05$).

Table 6. T verification summary of independent samples by male and female in overall pleasure assessment

Level	Gender	Number of Subjects	M	SD	df	T	Difference Comparison
No.6 -Q2	F	92	1.957	.8108	108.192	-2.189*	F>M
	M	59	2.288	.9658			
No.7 -Q4	F	92	2.478	1.0637	149	-2.009*	F>M
	M	59	2.864	1.2792			
No.10 -Q4	F	92	2.489	1.0843	104.183	-2.842**	F>M
	M	59	3.085	1.3556			

F (Fe-male) ; M (Male)   *p<.05 **p<.01 ***p<.001

Favorite Works

As shown in Table 7, work No. 02 "Poseidon" is the one most liked by subjects, with a total of 43 votes (including 24 females and 19 males) in this research. Therefore, the researcher gives the follow conjectures for the reason: (1) Poseidon is a Greek and Roman mythology, which is a classic story and is relatively well-known, (2) there are many films in the name of Poseidon, which also affects the degree of likeness, (3) this is a virtual age of information media, and there are many online games on the background of mythological stories, which have a considerably high effect on the middle school students, and (4) the artist completes the work by anthropomorphic and realistic methods, which makes the subjects can easily accept the ideas that the artist wants to convey.

Table 7. Statistics of favorite works

NUMBER	01	02	03	04	05	06	07	08	09	10	11	12
VOTES	06	43	04	08	10	11	07	14	21	04	19	05

4 Conclusions and Recommendations

With social progress, the promotion of people's spiritual life after the improvement of material life level will definitely contribute to the development of one's body and mind. It is especially important to appreciate art, know art, understand art and thus improve artistic value. The epochal situations including people's ideology, social value judgment, cultural uniqueness and transformation of aesthetic concepts have indirectly contributed to the promotion of Taiwan's public art and shaped the appearance of Taiwan's public art today. It may be a good way to guide the education of art appreciation. The research comes up with the following conclusions:

1. There are quite a lot of artworks in life. Through educational viewpoints, middle school students can better understand the importance of improving campus art environment and life quality. It is hoped that everyone can see, understand, and then move and act to shape an aesthetic environment that all people participate in.
2. In the evaluation of the overall joy of public art by males and females, there is a significant difference in work No. 6 in the degree of humanity expression, female > male. There is also a significant difference in both work No. 7 "Mother and Child" and work No. 10 "Window of the Universe" in the degree of desire for collection. There is no significant difference in other dimensions, which can provide follow-up research directions.
3. In this research, work No. 02 "Poseidon" is the one most liked by subjects, with a total of 43 votes (sharing a proportion of 28.4%), which has a lot to do with life experience. Besides aesthetic view points and Greek and Roman mythology, it also has a lot to do with current online games and cartoon culture popular among and loved by students, affecting the popularity of public art.
4. For communication between people in daily life, although the language is direct and powerful, it is often too explicit; the text is relatively gentle and indirect, but the words fail to express the idea, the effect will be greatly reduced. For expressing the intentions by creation of public art, using its image as a material to interpret the symbolic meaning behind it, even though social culture has given a certain meaning, people's interpretation has more flexible cognitive space, which will constitute a subtle interaction and relationship with the viewer so as to produce another communication language.
5. This research combines questionnaire feedback, statistical analysis, subjective conjectures and comparative analysis. Although it is not exhaustive as it only analyzes from aspect of overall perception. Its preliminary research results can provide reference for artists and teachers. In the future, regression studies can be made to conduct further analysis from dimensions of formal beauty, symbolic beauty and ideal beauty.

References

1. Chen, X., Yan, H., Li, X., Lin, Z.: Case study of curatorial design–a case study of the poetic picture–the beauty of immortal clouds painting exhibition. J. Des. **21**(4), 1–24 (2016)
2. Chen, H.: Public art and school education. Public Art Newsl. **31**, 1 (2002)
3. Committee on cultural development of the executive yuan: Reference manual for public art setting operations. Civil society, Taipei (1998)
4. Shao, P.: Phase of Contemporary Cultural Arts. Artist Press, Taiwan (1992). Astringent

5. Guo, M.C.: The study of public art Settings in schools: a case study of the public art Settings in Taipei city's fuxing elementary school. Master's thesis, institute of visual arts, Taipei normal university, Taipei (2003)
6. Huang, J.: American public art. Artist, Taipei (1992)
7. Wang, P., Li, J.: Education, art and public implication. Public Art Newsl. **40**, 13–14 (2007)
8. Kandinsky: Spirituality of Art. Artist Press, Taipei City (1998). Trans. by M. Wu
9. Lin, R.: Outsider art, national aesthetics-enrichment of retirement with art. Hum. Soc. Sci. Newsl. **18**(3), 13–26 (2017)
10. Lu, C.: Reading the guide to the public art festival. National Taichung Library, Taiwan (2012)
11. Trancik, R.: Finding Lost Space – Theories of Urban Design. Pastoral city cultural, Taipei (1991)
12. Wu, S.: The relationships among Public art and Urban space (2006)
13. Yan, C.: Urban walking Study, vol. 59, pp. 64–65. Eslite Published, Taipei (2005)
14. Yom, J.J.: Public art in Chicago's Millennium Park as a model for the new Civic Park in Los Angeles. Doctoral dissertation, University of Southern California 2007. Dissertation Abstracts International, vol. 45, no. 5 (2007)

Research and Extraction on Intelligent Generation Rules of Posters in Graphic Design

Hao Tan[1], Biwen Xu[2(✉)], and Aiqi Liu[3]

[1] State Key Laboratory of Advanced Design and Manufacturing
for Vehicle Body, Hunan University, Changsha, China
htan@hnu.edu.cn
[2] School of Design, Hunan University, Changsha, China
877588112@qq.com
[3] Hunan University, Changsha, China
3316647479@qq.com

Abstract. With the advent of the intelligent era, artificial intelligence has gradually played an important role in the generation of design. That's why it is particularly essential that how to use artificial intelligence to make a design output. This study aims to explore the rules of machine-generated graphic design. Take the intelligently generated film poster as an example, designers use professional knowledge to train the machine for multiple rounds and evaluate the machine-generated results. Then explore and improve the machine intelligently generated film poster for multiple rounds to let the machine generate movie posters which fit the public's aesthetic. In the end, through the evolution of designers, we determined the measurement dimension of aesthetic. We also summarized several important rules for machine-generated movie posters and design, as well as provided reference for machine-generated graphic design and human-machine cooperation design in the future.

Keywords: Machine learning · Graphic design · Universal aesthetics

1 Introduction

The roots of artificial intelligence in the 50-ies and 60-ies AI lab of the MIT [1]. In general, it is not a very new technology. In recent years, artificial intelligence technology has been widely used. Similarly, the demand for design in various industries is expanding, for example, it has already been designed using artificial intelligence technology especially in the field of applied graphic design, such as packaging, books, advertising posters, and website banners, etc. [2]. Thus, the designers are freed from the original production chain and become a role of summary whilst the machine is doing a design.

In order to make artificial intelligence better for design, this paper takes the intelligently generated poster design as an example to explore the rules of machine intelligent generation of graphic design. The artistic and aesthetic goals in the poster design are quantified as measurable rules, and through the evaluation of the

P.-L. P. Rau (Ed.): HCII 2019, LNCS 11576, pp. 570–582, 2019.
https://doi.org/10.1007/978-3-030-22577-3_41

intelligently generated posters by the designers, the evaluation criteria finally summarized into five dimensions.

Through the exploration of the rules, the efficiency of designing with artificial intelligence can be improved. And evaluating the final design output can also facilitate the design cooperation between designers and machines at this stage. What's more, shift from research design to research machine support, use rules to train more intelligent machines efficiently and quantify the steps of working with machines can lower the threshold for using machine learning. Thus through design, everyone can use artificial.

2 Inquiry

2.1 Participants

In this study, we have 5 designers, 100 participants in the aesthetic assessment and 6 developers familiar with artificial intelligence algorithms. The age ranges from 20 to 48 years old.

2.2 Inquiry Arrangements

Currently most of the systems that acquire images with aesthetic value need human judgement. These can be grouped into The search for a general, or universal, sense of aesthetics, and learning from examples of human judgments [3]. The whole study is divided into three rounds of inquiry. In the first round of inquiry, we asked the five designers to conduct a desk research of the existing poster design to analyze the design rules of the poster combining with the previous literature, Intent to find a general aesthetic. Then we imported the rules into the machine to further help the machine learn from human judgment, and evaluated the final machine-generated posters. The second round consists of two parts: rule adjustment and aesthetic assessment. In the third round, we improved the rules and established the evaluation criteria of aesthetic assessment based on the previous results of public aesthetic assessment to help improve and perfect the rules. In the meantime, the training machine continues to improve itself (Fig. 1). Because exploration and refinement are critical and complementary tasks in design [4].

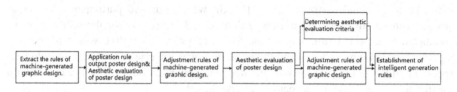

Fig. 1. Experiment process

2.3   Inquiry

The First Round of Inquiry. The poster design rule extraction phase. We searched more than 100 literatures, downloaded and sorted out more than 2,000 movie poster designs. Then we extracted and refined the layout rules, the hierarchy of movie posters and color classification and matching [5].

Layout Rule Extraction. We used the grid system to summarize and explore the layout of the movie posters in the following six dimensions, and finally generate the rules of eight types of layout. 1. The spatial position of the layout image. 2. The size of the space of the layout image. 3. The combination relationship and separation form between the various parts of the layout image, the main image and the accompanying image. 4. The combination relationship and separation form between the layout image and space. 5. The visual impact and power generated by the layout image. 6. The form of beauty law and aesthetics produced. The final result is a style specification rule for six types of layouts (Fig. 2).

Poster Layer Classification and Rule Extraction. Then we classified the layer of poster design further, which is mainly divided into background elements, theme objects, text elements, and decoration elements. What's more, the background elements were divided into colored background (including a single color, a gradient color, a repeating texture, a color block combination, a multi-color pattern, etc.) and scene background (the subject-related background and the general-purpose background) (Fig. 3).

Color and Style Rules Extraction. There exist universally for humans eleven basic perceptual color categories [6]. Based on the hue, color, brightness and purity of the poster color, we did color division and matching for the final generated movie poster. At the same time, taking the use of the poster into account, summary of the overall color matching (Fig. 4).

Aesthetic Assessment. To build learning models one can focus on the judgments of a single person or attempt to get aggregated judgments for a number of people [3].

We firstly invited 30 participants to evaluate the satisfaction for 600 posters produced by the machine. Secondly, we asked the participants, including14 males and 16 females, aged from 20 to 48 years old to rate the poster on the Likert-Scale [7], the score of which is ranging from 1 (very bad) to 5 (very good). Related scholars and others suggest that people's emotional reactions should be used as a source of evaluating the artistic and aesthetic works [8]. So we encouraged participants to use an adverb with an adjective description to think aloud the reason for the score. And we conducted a statistical summary of the high-frequency descriptive words in the oral reports. The participants who used the evaluation was interviewed in order to judge the specific attitude of the user towards the machine-generated poster. Finally, five criteria for the public aesthetic assessment were concluded.

Summary. We summarized and sorted the ten keywords that appeared the most frequently in the oral description of the participants. Key word1 was the keyword that appeared the most frequently, and key word was the tenth keyword that appeared the most frequently. participants' comments on the poster with a score of 1 are mostly "the

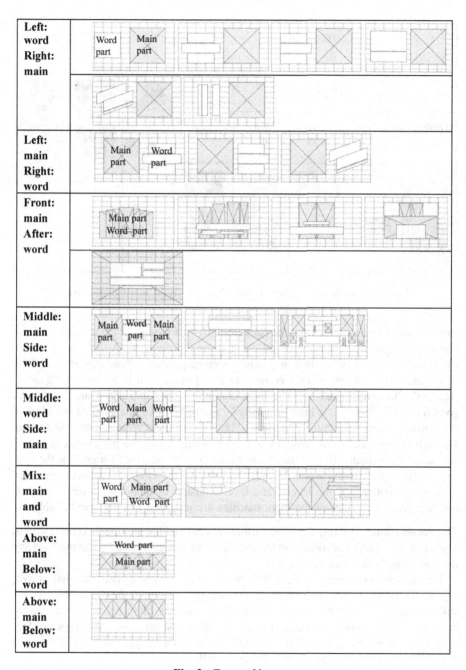

Fig. 2. Types of layouts

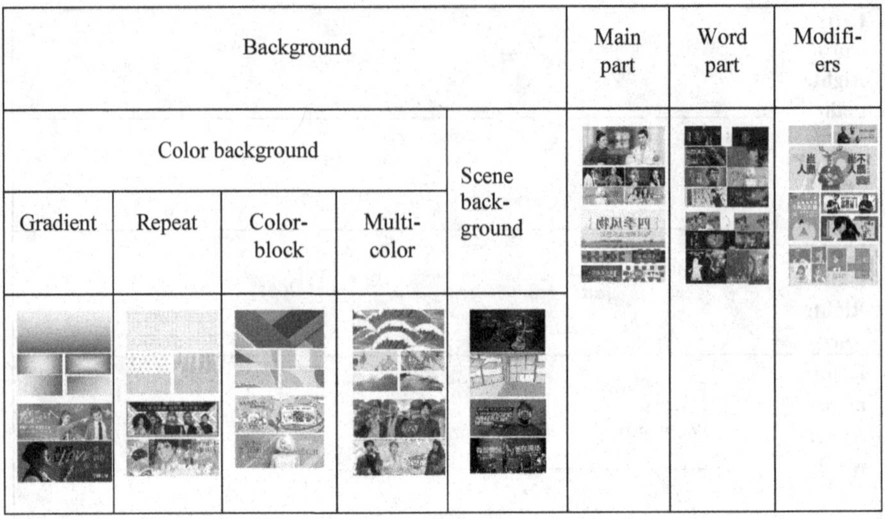

Background					Main part	Word part	Modifi- ers
Color background				Scene back- ground			
Gradient	Repeat	Color- block	Multi- color				

Fig. 3. Classification and extraction of poster layer (Color figure online)

content cannot be separated from the background", "it's too big", "it's a little close", "it doesn't look good", "it's not focused", and so on. In the score 2, the most common words are "too flowered", "unclear words", "strange position", "too scattered", "a little ugly", etc.; Most of the score 3 comments are "just ok", "a little messy", "gaudy", "strange", "just mediocre" etc. The most common words in grade 4 are "a little bit good-looking", "better", "a little bit gaudy", "not bad", "like this" and so on. Most of the words in score 5 are "nice", "perfect", "bravo", "so great", "reasonable" and so on. Through the interview and summary after participant rating, the posters generated by the machine are finally divided into the following five grades: the fifth grade is the best, and the first grade is the worst. In order to improve the effect of machine generated posters, we finally took the level 5 and level 4 posters as qualified posters. Based on this, the generation rules of the input machine are modified and improved (Table 1).

The Second Round of Inquiry. We further summarized the previously complex rules. The rules are adjusted according to the recognition rules generated by the machine and the participant's oral description (Fig. 5).

For the "cannot be separated", "a little messy", "too scattered" and other issues were adjusted. Instead of stratifying the characters and background of the poster, we used the stills of the film to generate the poster. We classified films according to content intention, and explored the matching rules of serif, non-serif and other types of font styles [9]. Then we corresponded different fonts in different types of films to maintain the unified style of the final poster (Table 2) [10].

At the same time, in order to make better use of the following rules in other graphic design, we have sorted the content elements in poster design according to their importance. The most important are the first level, then the second level, and so on. In the design of the movie poster, the first level content is the background of the stills. The second level content is the main character and the third level content is the name of the film. The fourth

Color	Match		Mood board
Red		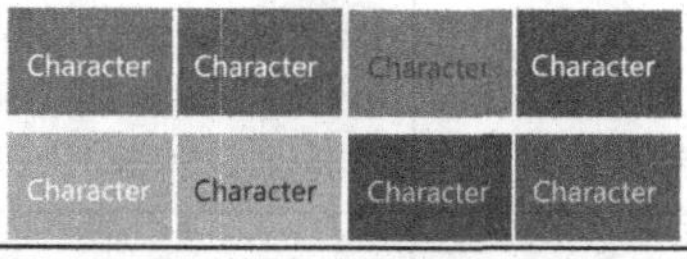	Dangerous bloody powerful majestic ...
Brown		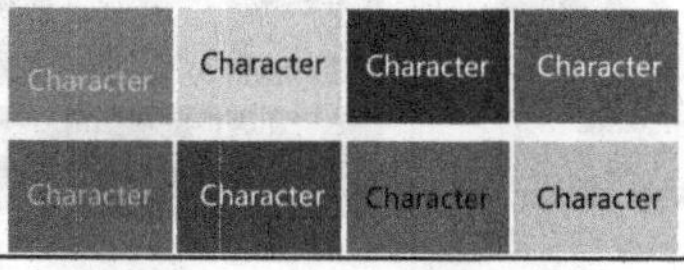	Vicissitude nostalgic martial arts ...
Orange		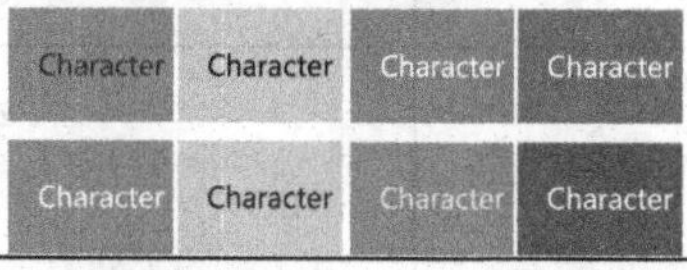	Endurance warm ignorant dull ...
Yellow		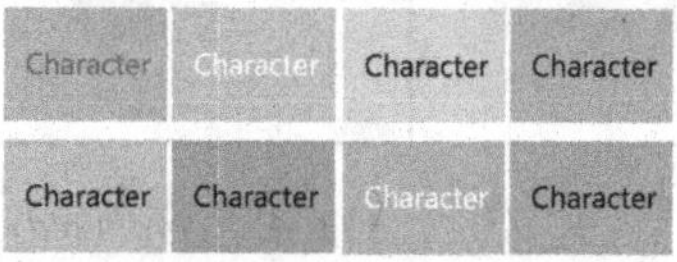	Happy logical innovative spiritual hopeful ...
Green		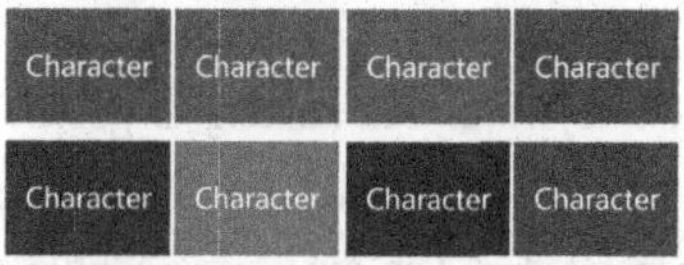	Natural vital youthful monetary quiet ...
Light blue		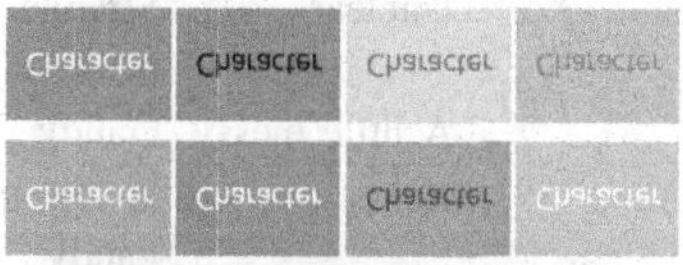	Peaceful cold depressed sad lonely ...
Dark blue		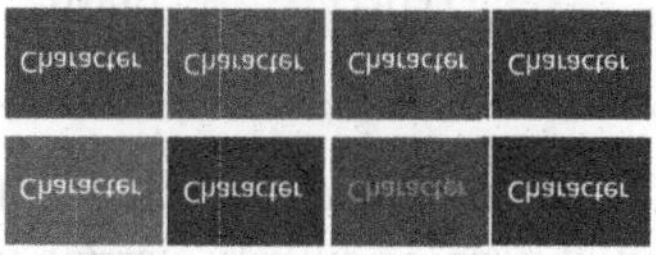	Calm intelligent loyal safe masculine brave ...
Purple		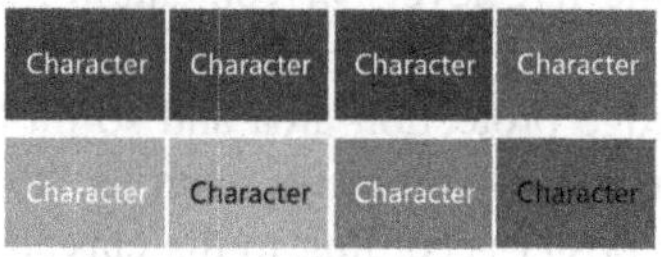	Aristocratic luxurious ambitious mysterious moody ...

Fig. 4. Color classification and matching and corresponding intention (Color figure online)

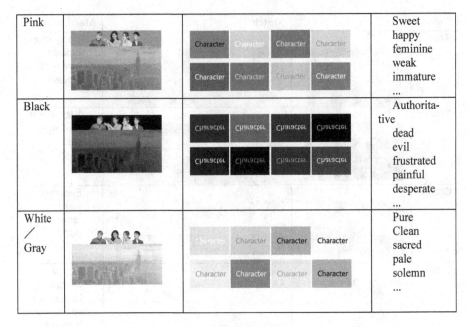

Fig. 4. (*continued*)

Table 1. Evaluation keywords and ranking of posters of different levels by participants

	Key word 1	Key word 2	Key word 3	Key word 4	Key word 5
Score 1	Cannot be separated	Too big	A little close	Not good	Not focused
Score 2	Too flowered	Unclear	Strange position	Too scattered	A little ugly
Score 3	Just ok	A little messy	Gaudy	Strange	Just mediocre
Score 4	A little bit Good-looking	Better	A little bit gaudy	Not bad	Like this
Score 5	Nice	Perfect	Bravo	So great	Reasonable

level content is the introduction of the film and the fifth level content is other elements, such as the information of winning awards, starring information and so on.

Comments aimed at participants include "unclear"," blocked face " and "too scattered". For each of the five levels of content, we explored areas where the level of content could not be placed in the entire poster, for instance, the background subject protection area, the edge protection area and so on (Fig. 6).

In response to participant comments such as "too gaudy" and "too flowered", we added a mask for the poster according to the classification of the film content to unify the tone of the whole picture (Fig. 7).

Fig. 5. Machine identification of characters in the background of the poster

Table 2. Matching rules between different types of fonts and different types of movies

Style	Fonts
Science fiction, action	Serif, Decorative font
horror, suspense	Decorative font, Calligraphy font
Youth, love	Serif, Handwritten font, Decorative font
Comedy, cartoon	Sans-serif, Decorative font
Kung Fu	Serif, Handwritten font
War, Sci-Fi	Sans-serif, Calligraphy font

Serif	Chinese	SimSun	FangSong	NSimSun
		KaiTi	STFangsong	STZhongsong
	English	Bookman old style.	Baskerville	Times New Roman
		Caslon	Courier	
Sans-serif	Chinese	SimHei	Lantinghei SC	STHeiti
		Microsoft Yahei	Microsoft JhengHei	PingFang SC
	English	Helvetica	Formata	Din
		Frutiger	Verdana	
Others	special design	Decorative font (word and shape combination)		
		Handwritten font (free writing)		
	Calligraphy font	Calligraphy font		
		Brush font		

About aesthetic assessment, we input the modified rules into the machine again, and generated 600 different movie posters. Once again we invited the previous 30 participants to score the movie posters generated by the machine and to give oral reports on

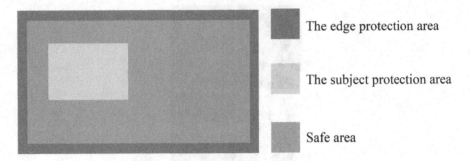

The edge protection area

The subject protection area

Safe area

Fig. 6. Area exploration of second level content

Back-ground style	Science fiction、 action	horror、 suspense	Youth 、 love	Comedy 、 cartoon	Kung Fu
Filter style	 ...	 ...	 ...	 ...	 ...

Fig. 7. Filter effect matching content style

Table 3. Participant score results for 600 posters

Scores	Numbers
Score 1	41
Score 2	39
Score 3	120
Score 4	202
Score 5	198

the five-point Likert-Scale. In this poster generation result, we got 402 posters that were rated as score 4–5 by participants (Table 3). But some participants still mentioned problems such as "too much separation of text messages".

The Third Round of Inquiry. In response to the questions raised by the participants, we tried to combine the text information. Combine the three levels of content and the four levels of content into the same level of content, and give several combination templates for machine reference and learning (Fig. 8).

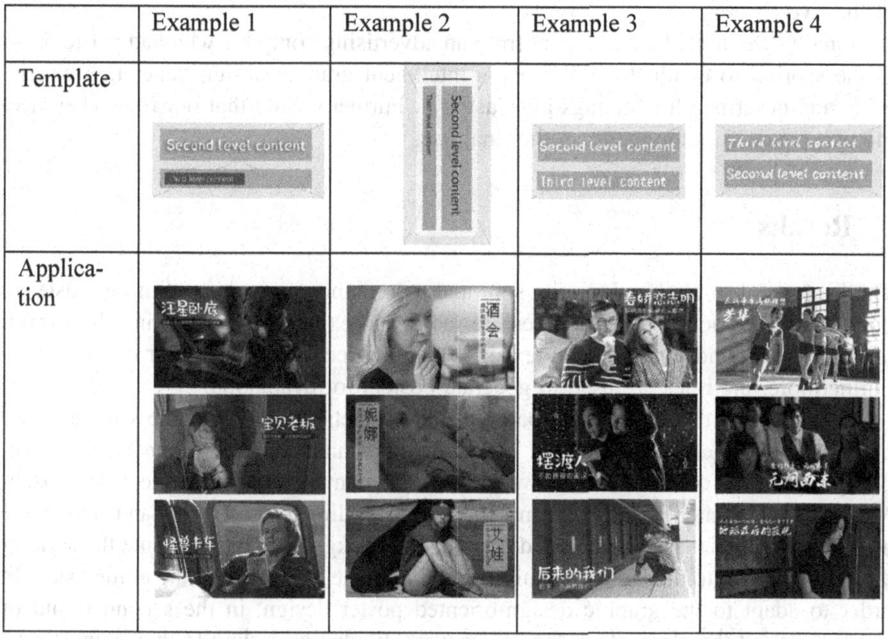

	Example 1	Example 2	Example 3	Example 4
Template				
Application				

Fig. 8. Third and fourth level content combination templates and applications (Color figure online)

Although creating a new design is more artistic, creating a series of designs with public aesthetic significance must conform to some measurable rules [11]. So we established the standard of public aesthetic assessment according to the classification and corresponding description of the previous two participants' aesthetic assessment of posters. First of all, we determined the evaluation criteria of the five levels, and then chose the fifth and fourth levels, which were ranked highly, as the eligibility criteria for the machine generated posters.

Through analysis, we summarize the criteria for public aesthetic assessment. It can be concluded that only posters that meet the following requirements can be classified into the fifth level: the characters in the background are not blocked. The text and other elements are clear. The overall picture is harmonious in tone with a gathering and dispersing relationship and prominent theme. The fourth level is slightly worse compared with the fifth level. It should meet: the characters in the background is not obscured. The text and other elements are clear. The overall picture is tonal harmony, accumulation and dispersion relations or outstanding theme. The third level should meet the characters in the background is not obscured, clear text and other elements. The overall picture is tonal harmony or have a relationship between accumulation and dispersion or outstanding theme. The poster of the second level is the one in which the characters in the background are not blocked. The text and other elements are clear. The overall picture is harmonious in tone. And there is a gathering and dispersing relationship. The theme is prominent. The first level is a poster that meets only a little of the five criteria.

Finally, we invited a participant from an advertising company who had participated in the scoring to conduct a full-process intelligent graphic design generation experience, and described the feelings after using it. Further ensure that our rules also meet the participant's requirements in the final use.

3   Results

The first round of exploration is to split and recombine every element in the poster to build a suitable poster design. Rules are made and explored by exploring the overall layout, background, main object, text information, decoration and color of the poster. Furthermore, the rules are used to generate posters for evaluation.

According to the feedback of participants' aesthetic assessment, the second round of inquiry changed the extraction of background and character elements into still background and combined them with other elements to generate the final poster. Meanwhile, it matched the font and the corresponding poster scene and added the auxiliary effect of mask. That is to determine the background, to determine the style of the text, and then to the layout planning, and finally the color tone of the unified step. In order to adapt to the graphic design-oriented poster design, in the second round of exploration, all the elements in the poster were divided according to their importance. The use of rules is simplified by dividing the most important level of content into the least important level of content.

Finally, through the perfection of the third round of exploration, we conclude that the final rule extraction should be the determination of the first-level content, such as the determination of the background; Second content such as text style collocation; Third levels of content such as text color style collocation. Fourth level is matching of other elements such as actors and crew; The fifth level is the determination of the overall tone of the mask. Finally, the aesthetic assessment criteria can be used to evaluate the aesthetics of the poster using the rules, so as to ensure the quality of the final output.

4   Conclusion

Due to the increasing demand for design in various industries, the original design method and cost can no longer meet the existing design requirements. This paper proposed a rule based on artificial intelligence generating design to reduce the burden on designers. At the same time, intelligent rule extracting reduces the threshold for users to use graphic design and artificial intelligence technology which contributes to meet the design needs of all walks of life and the popularity of artificial intelligence. When using this rule, the user can not only control the elements in the graphic design, but also select and control the final output design style in the early stage. In addition, the designer can also use the graphic design generated based on the rule as a basis of his own design, and make further modifications and adjustments if he need. From a broad perspective, the exploration process and formulation of the rule can be applied to other areas where artificial intelligence and designers collaborate.

5 Future Work

The experimental study in this paper is limited to applied film poster and graphic design, so there are still several problems to be solved. First of all, when selecting posters for summary, most of the posters we chose are online applied posters, that is, they focus more on the expression and presentation of content and lack diversified artistic effects. Secondly, there are only a limited number of fonts we can match, so there should be more fonts that can be applied to the poster, which may also have an impact on the final rule we summarized. There is also much more work to be done to help us explore the details of machine learning to generate graphic design rules.

- analyze and summarize more artistic posters and designs to add diversity and artistry to the final graphic design.
- design and compare more different machine generation approaches to refine current rules from more different perspectives.

Acknowledgments. We would like to express our gratitude to Wenliang LI, Aiqi Liu, Shenglan Peng and her team who helped us during the experiment with his professional skill.

References

1. Bratteteig, T., Verne, G.: Does AI make PD obsolete?: exploring challenges from artificial intelligence to participatory design. In: Proceedings of the 15th Participatory Design Conference (2018)
2. Odonovan, P., Agarwala, A., Hertzmann, A.: Learning layouts for single-page graphic designs. IEEE Trans. Visual Comput. Graphics **20**(8), 1200–1213 (2014)
3. Ciesielski, V., Barile, P., Trist, K.: Finding image features associated with high aesthetic value by machine learning. In: Machado, P., McDermott, J., Carballal, A. (eds.) EvoMUSART 2013. LNCS, vol. 7834, pp. 47–58. Springer, Heidelberg (2013). https://doi.org/10.1007/978-3-642-36955-1_5
4. O'Donovan, P., Agarwala, A., Hertzmann, A.: DesignScape: design with interactive layout suggestions (2016)
5. Jahanian, A., Liu, J., Lin, Q., et al.: Recommendation system for automatic design of magazine covers. In: International Conference on Intelligent User Interfaces. ACM (2013)
6. Berlin, B., Kay, P.: Basic Color Terms: Their Universality and Evolution (2013)
7. Breffle, W.S., Morey, E.R., Thacher, J.A.: A joint latent-class model: combining likert-scale preference statements with choice data to harvest preference heterogeneity. Environ. Resource Econ. **50**(1), 83–110 (2011)

8. Belke, B., Leder, H., Augustin, M.D.: Mastering style–effects of explicit style-related information, art knowledge and affective state on appreciation of abstract paintings. Psychol. Test Assess. Model. **48**(2), 115–134 (2006)
9. Jung, M.C., Shin, Y.C., Srihari, S.N.: Multifont classification using typographical attributes. In: International Conference on Document Analysis & Recognition. IEEE (1999)
10. Dürst, M.J.: Prolog for structured character description and font design. J. Log. Program. **26**(2), 133–146 (1996)
11. Zhang, Y., Hu, K., Ren, P., et al.: Layout style modeling for automating banner design. In: Proceedings of the on Thematic Workshops of ACM Multimedia 2017 ACM, New York, pp. 451–459 (2017)

Exploring Semantic Space for Kawaii Design

Chien-Wen Tung, Nan Qie, and Pei-Luen Patrick Rau[✉]

Department of Industrial Engineering,
Institute of Human Factors and Ergonomics, Tsinghua University, Beijing, China
rpl@mail.tsinghua.edu.cn

Abstract. Kawaii has drawn the attention of people both in and out of Japan. In order to investigate Kawaii semantics and find typical Kawaii design features, we conducted a survey of Kawaii semantics and an experiment to verify the findings of the survey. The survey finds Kawaii semantics from visual, acoustic, tactile, movement and emotional aspects. Explorative factor analysis is conducted to find typical factors and to establish a six-dimensional model of Kawaii semantics. The experiment is based on the survey and intends to examine the effects of Kawaii factors on Kawaii design of furniture, household appliances and robots. The results indicate that roundness is effective to make all three products Kawaii. Interaction effects between factors are significant, indicating that Kawaii is integrated but not simply aggregated by Kawaii features. Kawaii design guidelines are put forward from the results to improve design efficiency and improve user experience in Kawaii design in the future. This research for the first time fuses Kawaii features from multiple aspects and provides a structural foundation for further study of Kawaii design.

Keywords: Kawaii design · Semantic questionnaire · Factor analysis

1 Introduction

Through the circulation of the global economy, Kawaii, has drawn the attention of people both in and out of Japan. By outputting many ACG industry, Kawaii has fevered the whole world and become a sub-culture in the world. There were many popular Kawaii image such as Doraemon, the character in the comic of Fujiko • F • Fujio, Hello kitty which designed by Shimizu Yuko, as well as Sailormoon which swept the Europe in 1944, and the Pokemon just made a hit in 2016 (Allison 2003; Perez 2016). These widely known characters and their affiliated products flooded in our life and also brought great commercial value. According to the list of best-selling entertainment products unveiled by Forbes, Hello Kitty made $800 million in 2011 and tightly seized the world's fifth (Goudreau 2012). The effects of Kawaii are not only in the animation, comics, and games but also in the entertainment industry, public facilities, transportation, industrial products, consumer goods and even food.

The description of Kawaii debuted during Heian era in 8th -12th AC. An archaic word, utsukushi, was denoted the meaning of Kawaii and the meaning changed to beautiful in modern time. At the end of Heian era, the word, kawayui, arose as predecessor of Kawaii which meant ashamed or blushing due to a twinge of conscience or pity and pitiable during medieval era in 12th–16th AC. Till 1945 in Taisho era, Kawaii

© Springer Nature Switzerland AG 2019
P.-L. P. Rau (Ed.): HCII 2019, LNCS 11576, pp. 583–591, 2019.
https://doi.org/10.1007/978-3-030-22577-3_42

was printed in Japanese dictionaries as kawayuishi and later changed to kawayui (Cheok and Fernando 2012; Nittono 2016). As the sweeping trend of Kawaii, the word Kawaii has been added in to the Collins English Dictionary in October 2014.

Recently, a new concept called Kawaii+ arose, where the plus mark means that Kawaii can evoke human being positive emotions, and has a lot of positive meanings based on experiments in previous studies. Kawaii refers to a special positive emotion whose features are related to smiling and approaching behavior (Nittono and Tanaka 2010). Kawaii can reduce people's fear and make uninteresting information more acceptable such as a bitter pill with a layer of sugar (Cheok and Fernando 2012). Results of previous experiments showed that viewing Kawaii images can help improve performance on tasks that need carefulness, narrow the breadth of attentional focus, and reduce the global precedence effect. When viewing Kawaii images, people's motor behaviors were more physically tender, and it furthermore increased perceptual care-fulness (Nittono et al. 2012; Sherman et al. 2009). People had great interest and predilection for Kawaii objects. They were sensitive about, drawn to and excited by something Kawaii, which can bring them positive feeling of comfort. There was gender difference in Kawaii perception. Japanese females were more positive and sensitive to Kawaii objects than males, and female used the word Kawaii more often. (Tokosumi and Teng 2011; Nittono 2016).

Previous researchers have found stimulus factors of Kawaii from tactile, visual, motional and auditory aspects. The tactile textures which make people feel Kawaii such as yarn, cotton, and sheep fabric are bushy, flurry, soft, smooth, and elastic. As for visual stimuli, the visual textures which are tangible, flurry, and soft are commonly considered Kawaii (Ohkura and Komatsu 2013). As for colors, experiments showed that warm colors were generally chosen as more Kawaii than cold colors. The yellow and purple hues were chosen as Kawaii most frequently. The combinations of hue and brightness or saturation were important for evaluating Kawaii degrees of colors (Ohkura et al. 2014; Ohkura et al. 2008). The color in pink or basically like pink were chosen as Kawaii colors, while dark brown and dark green were chosen as non-Kawaii colors in previous experiments. Objects with small size were generally chosen as more Kawaii than larger objects. The curved shapes were chosen as more Kawaii than shapes with straight lines in two-dimensional space. While in the three-dimensional space, round objects were chosen as most Kawaii in general. The effect of shape on Kawaii perception is also dependent on color (Ohkura et al. 2011; Ohkura et al. 2014). In a study of Roomba, motions that were rotational, slow, and sudden changes in accel-eration by collisions were evaluated Kawaii (Sugano et al. 2013). In a word, a Kawaii object is in bright, primary, pure, and warm colors (i.e. red, orange, and yellow), soft and with nature longer pile tactile texture, has animal like movements and small steps in motions, higher pitch in sounds, small size, baby like or bigger head in proportion, and roundness in shapes. These characters are all connected to the natural world. Newborn babies with these characters evoke Kawaii feelings and the feelings such as young, innocent, vigorous, pure, harmless and friendly (Cheok 2010). Kawaii features found in literature were summarized in Table 1.

The features mentioned above contribute to Kawaii from various aspects. Does a simple combination of these features lead to a perfect Kawaii design? If not, how do these features interact with each other in Kawaii design? Up to our knowledge there has

Table 1. Variables contributing to Kawaii in previous literature

Factor	References
Color	Cheok (2010), Komatsu and Ohkura (2011), Ohkura et al. (2014, 2008)
Size	Cheok (2010), Ohkura et al. (2011, 2014)
Shape	Cheok (2010), Ohkura et al. (2008)
Body proportion	Cheok (2010)
Visual texture	Ohkura and Komatsu (2013)
Tactile texture	Cheok (2010), Ohkura and Komatsu (2013)
Tone	Cheok (2010)
Pitch	Cheok (2010)
Onomatopoeias	Hashiguchi and Ogawa (2011), Ohkura and Komatsu (2013)
Object motion	Cheok (2010), Sugano et al. (2013)

been little research so far focusing on the integration of Kawaii features. In this study, we aim to explore Kawaii semantic space from an integration view. First, we conducted semantic questionnaires to find factors of Kawaii features. Then we conducted a full factorial experiment to explore the interactions between the factors.

2   Study I: Exploring the Semantic Space

2.1   Methodology

A semantic differential scale was used to construct the questionnaire of this survey. The semantic differential scale was proposed by Osgood and was used to measure the semantics or meaning of words, particularly adjectives and their referent concepts (Osgood 1952). The questionnaire contained two parts. The first part was constructed by 36 pairs of adjectives with opposite meanings. The adjectives were chosen according to the findings in pervious literatures. A five-point scale was used to construct the questionnaire (1-agree to the first adjective; 5-agree to the second adjective). The adjectives were 14 pairs in visual subpart containing color, size, shape, proportion, and textures; five pairs in acoustic subpart containing pitch, tone and volume; five pairs in tactile texture subpart; six pairs in motion subpart; and six pairs in motion subpart. The second part was to collect demographic information of the subjects and their willingness in purchasing something with Kawaii design. The demographic information included subjects' gender, age, and their nationality.

An online questionnaire was used and each participant can have the opportunity to win a lottery draw as a reward. There were 125 questionnaires collected and 118 of them were valid. There were 51 male subjects, and 61 female subjects. Their ages range from 19 to 28 years old (M = 23.6, SD = 2.1). All subjects were Chinese. There were 90 subjects (76.3%) willing to buy something with Kawaii design.

2.2   Survey Results

For the survey results, if the average rating on one pair of subjects is smaller than 3.0, it means that the first adjective was considered more Kawaii than the second one; and vice versa. Following are the results of the survey.

Visual. The visual aspect included color, size, shape, proportion, and visual texture. The mean ratings of both male and female subjects indicated that warm, pure, saturated, bright color, small size, curved line, orderliness, round shape, disproportion, babylike, soft and furry looked, tangible and natural features contribute to visually Kawaii. Gender difference existed. Although both genders rated on the same side on all the objectives, male subjects (M = 2.29, SD = 1.19) agreed more on pure color than female participants (M = 2.81, SD = 1.35, F = 4.61, p = .034) as Kawaii, while female participants agreed more on babylike (Female M = 2.10, SD = 0.90; Male M = 1.64, SD = 0.67; F = 10.00, p = .002) and furry look (Female M = 1.39, SD = 0.60; Male M = 1.71, SD = 0.80; F = 5.61, p = .020) than male participants as Kawaii.

Acoustic. The acoustic aspect included pitch, volume and tone. The mean ratings of both male and female subjects indicated that high pitch, smooth, whispered, lightly and soft features contribute to acoustically Kawaii. Gender difference on acoustic aspect was not found.

Tactile. For tactile aspect, the mean ratings of both male and female subjects indicated that bushy, soft, smooth, elastic and fluffy features contribute to tactilely Kawaii. Female subjects (M = 1.46, SD = 0.64) agreed more on fluffy than male subjects (M = 1.73, SD = 0.75, F = 4.23, p = .042) as a Kawaii feature.

Movement. In movement aspect, the mean ratings of both male and female subjects indicated that rotational, obedient, liquid movement, obtuse and tardy features contribute to movement Kawaii. Female subjects agreed that brave is more Kawaii (M = 3.40, SD = 1.12) while male subjects agreed that shrinking is more Kawaii (M = 2.63, SD = 1.15), which was significantly different (F = 13.65, p < .001)

Emotional. For emotional profile, the mean ratings of both male and female subjects indicated that innocent, harmless, cheerful, sympathy, young and vitality features contribute to emotionally Kawaii. Female subjects (M = 1.09, SD = 0.29) agreed more on cheerful than male subjects (M = 1.25, SD = 0.56, F = 4.34, p = .039) as Kawaii.

2.3   Factor Analysis

Exploratory factor analysis was applied to find the dimensional semantic space of Kawaii. The KMO measure of samplings adequacy was 0.78 > 0.70. The principle component analysis was conducted as extracting method and the factor whose Eigenvalue was more than 1.0 were extracted. Varimax rotation with Kaisar normalizing was operated as a rotation with the items, and the lower limit of the factor loading was 0.50 (Hair et al. 1995). The extracted factors were named by the common meanings of the comprising item. Six factors were extracted and 67.78% of overall variance were explained. The results were summarized in Table 2.

The Cronbach's alpha of the six factors were 0.78 (baby schema), 0.75 (acoustics), 0.64 (sense of obedience), 0.61 (movement), 0.55 (sense of harmony), 0.37 (color), respectively. Four of them were larger than 0.60 (Hair et al. 2010). The fact that the last two alphas failed to reach 0.60 may due to the limited number (only 2) of items within those two factors.

Table 2. Factor analysis of Kawaii features

Items	Factors					
	Factor I Baby schema	Factor II Acoustics	Factor III Sense of obedience	Factor IV Movement	Factor V Sense of harmony	Factor VI Color
Curved/straight-lined	0.75					
Furry/bald	0.74					
Babylike/non-babylike	0.72					
Soft/hard	0.71					
Round/angled	0.64					
Soft/strong		0.79				
Light/heavy		0.79				
Whispered/loud		0.77				
Obedient/rebellious			0.85			
Smooth/ragged			0.76			
Sensitive/obtuse				0.82		
Shrinking/brave				0.81		
Pure/mixed color					0.81	
Orderliness/messy					0.76	
Bright/dim						0.79
Saturated/unsaturated						0.77
Variance explained	0.17	0.13	0.10	0.10	0.09	0.08

3 Study II: Exploring Design Element Portfolio

3.1 Methodology

Based on the result of semantic questionnaire, we selected one typical element in each factor as experiment factors and applied them on three types of product design. In the experiment, 3D models of furniture (chair), household appliances (microwave oven), and robots were created by 3D blender 2.78 and showed to the participants. To control the number of factors, the item obedient was merged into sense of harmony and smooth was merged into acoustics. Thus, the five factors of Study II were baby schema (roundness), acoustics (soft sound), movement (obtuse movement), sense of harmony (pure color), and color (brightness). A 2 k-full-factorial experiment design was used. Table 3 showed the high and low levels defined for each factorial design object. The low and high levels for the factors were selected according to some preliminary experiments. There were 2 * 3 treatments in chair, 2 * 4 treatments in microwave oven, and 2 * 5 treatments in robot. For each type, a non-colored and unchanged prototype was used as the compared object. Participants watched a total of 56 trails and scored on whether the treatment is more Kawaii than compared object.

An 11-point Likert scale was conducted to measure whether the design is more Kawaii than compared object (1-relatively not Kawaii; 6-neutral; 11-relatively Kawaii). Figure 1 was part of designs used in the experiment. In the experiment, chair prototype

Table 3. Experiment design of Study II

Object	Levels	Baby schema	Sense of harmony	Brightness	Acoustics	Movement
Chair	High	Roundness	YR	#f29135	–	–
	Low	Non-roundness	YR and White	#b26b27	–	–
Microwave Oven	High	Roundness	BG	#4cfcc4	With	–
	Low	Non-roundness	BG and White	#084D15	Without	–
Robot	High	Roundness and 1.8 times head	YR	#f29135, #d9cf10	With	With
	Low	Non-roundness	YR Y and White	#b26b27, # b2aa0d	Without	Without

refers to the general office chair design, microwave oven refers to the Media microwave oven prototype design, and the robot is a reference to the Japanese animation character Gundam as a prototype design.

In this stage, 30 Chinese students from Tsinghua university (15 males and 15 females) who aged 20–29 (M = 23.9, SD = 2.2) were invited to participate in the experiment. Each participant was given 80 RMB as a reward.

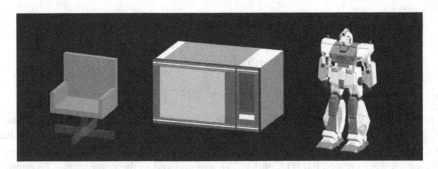

Fig. 1. Examples of prototypes used in Study II

3.2 Results of the Experiment

Repeated measured ANOVA was used to determine the main and interaction effects of factors and Mauchly's test was used to test the sphericity assumption. In cases in which the sphericity assumption was violated, the degrees of freedom were corrected using Greenhouse-Geisser estimates of sphericity. Effect size was measured with a generalized eta-squared ($\eta2$) which proposed by Olejnik and Algina (2003). Paired t-tests with Bonferroni adjustment were used for post hoc analysis. The main results are as following.

Furniture (Chair). The means of ratings on all designs were higher than neutral point 6.0, except for design 1 (not rounded, not pure color, not bright) and design 3 (not rounded, pure color, not bright). The results of ANOVA indicated that the effect of roundness and brightness were significant on Kawaii ratings. Rounded design (M = 8.08, SD = 2.61) was rated significantly more Kawaii than non-rounded design (M = 6.78, SD = 2.89, p < .001, η2 = 0.12). Design with highly bright color (M = 8.39, SD = 1.88) was rated significantly more Kawaii than design without bright color (M = 6.47, SD = 2.62, p < .001, η2 = 0.25).

Household Appliances (Microwave Oven). The means of all designs were higher than neutral point 6.0. The results of ANOVA indicated that the effect of roundness, the interaction effects of roundness * pure-color, roundness * brightness, pure-color * brightness, and roundness * sound were significant. Rounded design (M = 8.08, SD = 1.93) was rated significantly more Kawaii than non-rounded design (M = 6.70, SD = 2.22, p < .001, η2 = 0.15). The effect sizes of interaction effects of roundness * pure-color, roundness * sound were too small (less than 0.10) so they were not discussed further. Post-hoc tests showed that the effect of brightness was only significant when the design was not rounded or when the design was not pure color. When the design was not rounded, design with highly bright color (M = 7.05, SD = 2.33) was rated significantly more Kawaii than design without bright color (M = 6.34, SD = 1.86, p = .002, d = 0.34). When the design was not pure colored, design with highly bright color (M = 7.98, SD = 1.97) was rated significantly more Kawaii than design without bright color (M = 7.13, SD = 2.47, p < .001, d = 0.38).

Robot. The means of all designs were higher than neutral point 6.0. The results of ANOVA indicated that the effect of roundness, movement, brightness, sound, the interaction effects of pure-color and brightness, roundness * pure-color * sound, movement * brightness * sound, roundness * movement * pure-color * brightness * sound were significant. Only the effect of roundness had an acceptable effect size (larger than 0.10). Rounded design (M = 8.31, SD = 1.45) was rated significantly more Kawaii than non-rounded design (M = 7.36, SD = 1.37, p < .001, η2 = 0.17).

4 General Discussion

To our knowledge, this research for the first time fuses multiple Kawaii features from visual, acoustic, tactile, movement and emotional aspects. Previous research on Kawaii perception are mainly conducted with Japanese participants, while the involved participants in this research are all Chinese, providing insights of Kawaii perception beyond Japanese culture. The first study examines Kawaii perception between Chinese male and female, as well as establishes a six-dimension Kawaii model. The second study in further investigates Kawaii design features of different product types with experimental approach.

The survey confirms that for Chinese participants, warm, pure, saturated and bright color, small size, curved line, orderliness, round shape, disproportion, babylike, soft, furry, tangible, natural looked; high-pitch, smooth, whispered, lightly and soft sound or voice; bushy, soft, smooth, elastic and fluffy touched; rotational, obedient, liquid, obtuse and tardy movement; innocent, harmless, cheerful, sympathy, young and vitality emotions contribute to a Kawaii design. Chinese understand Kawaii nearly the same way as Japanese do (Cheok 2010; Ohkura and Komatsu 2013; Ohkura et al. 2014, 2008). Gender difference exists in some aspects. In general, female Chinese agree more on furry (both visually and tactilely), baby schema and cheerful as Kawaii and male

Chinese agree more on pure color as Kawaii, although the tendency for both genders are the same on these features. The divergence is in movement, where female think brave as Kawaii while male think shrinking as Kawaii. The survey establishes a full-scale semantic space for Kawaii, can provide detailed guidelines for Kawaii design, and help extends Kawaii definition from microcosmic perspective.

The six-dimensional Kawaii model is an integration of previous studies on Kawaii features and points out the six most important facets of Kawaii design. According to the model, a Kawaii design should consider baby schema, acoustic aspects, sense of obedience, movement, sense of harmony and color.

The experiment involves three types of products: furniture (chair), household appliances (microwave oven), and robots. Results of the experiment indicates that for all three products, roundness in shape is a key element to make a design Kawaii. Bright color is effective to make a furniture Kawaii. The results of effects on household appliance Kawaii is noteworthy. The analysis shows that only when roundness and pure-color level is low, the brightness in color is effective to make a household appliance Kawaii, while when the design is already rounded and pure-colored the effect of brightness fails to be significant. This finding is valuable to point out that Kawaii features do not simply accumulate to make a design Kawaii, but their influences interact with each other. Kawaii is not a result of aggregated Kawaii features, but an integrated concept. Change in one feature of a design can influence the Kawaii in other features. Kawaii is a Kansei concept (Ohkura et al. 2008). Designers should take full consideration of the relationship among every design element to provide a product with Kawaii value.

The research has some limitations. First, the participants are all Chinese. Although these years Chinese young people are highly influenced by Japanese culture and every participant in this research claims that they know Kawaii, there is still doubt that whether the model and the experiment results can be generalized and represent the "Kawaii" as its original meaning. Second, due to the difficulties to make real products with different designs, 3D models are used in the experiment. Previous research indicates that Kawaii perception in real and virtual presentation may differ (Ohkura et al. 2009). Third, the sample size of the survey is only 118 and this is not sufficient to confirm the factor analysis. Further investigation with sample from Japanese or other cultures, and experiments with real objects are needed in generalization of the findings of this research.

5   Conclusion

This research provides a dimensional semantic model of Kawaii design features. The experiment further tests the semantic model with controlled designs of typical artificial product types. The results of this study provides an integrated picture of what a Kawaii design should be like, and provide valuable guidelines for designers who want to take advantage of the power of Kawaii into their product design.

References

Allison, A.: Portable monsters and commodity cuteness: Pokemon as Japan's new global power. Postcolonial Stud. 6(3), 381–395 (2003)

Cheok, A.D.: Kawaii/cute interactive media. In: Cheok, D. (ed.) Art and Technology of Entertainment Computing and Communication, pp. 223–254. Springer, London (2010). https://doi.org/10.1007/978-1-84996-137-0_9

Cheok, A.D., Fernando, O.N.N.: Kawaii/cute interactive media. Univ. Access Inf. Soc. **11**(3), 295–309 (2012)

Goudreau, J.: Disney Princess Tops List Of The 20 Best-Selling Entertainment Product's. Forbes (2012). Accessed Https://Www.Forbes.Com/Sites/Jennagoudreau/2012/09/17/ Disneyprincess-Tops-List-of-the-20-Best-Selling-Entertainment-Products

Hair, J.F., Black, W.C., Babin, B.J., Anderson, R.E.: Multivariate Data Analysis: A Global Perspective. Pearson Education, Upper Saddle River (2010)

Hair, J.F., Anderson, R.E., Tatham, R.L., Black, W.C.: Multiple discriminant analysis. Multivariate Data Analysis, pp. 178–256 (1995)

Hashiguchi, K., Ogawa, K.: Proposal of the Kawaii search system based on the first sight of impression. In: Salvendy, G., Smith, M.J. (eds.) Human Interface 2011. LNCS, vol. 6772, pp. 21–30. Springer, Heidelberg (2011). https://doi.org/10.1007/978-3-642-21669-5_3

Komatsu, T., Ohkura, M.: Study on evaluation of Kawaii colors using visual analog scale. In: Smith, Michael J., Salvendy, G. (eds.) Human Interface 2011. LNCS, vol. 6771, pp. 103–108. Springer, Heidelberg (2011). https://doi.org/10.1007/978-3-642-21793-7_12

Nittono, H.: The two-layer model of 'kawaii': a behavioural science framework for understanding kawaii and cuteness. East Asian J. Popular Cult. **2**(1), 79–95 (2016)

Nittono, H., Fukushima, M., Yano, A., Moriya, H.: The power of Kawaii: viewing cute images promotes a careful behavior and narrows attentional focus. PloS one **7**(9), e46362 (2012)

Nittono, H., Tanaka, K.: Psychophysiological responses to Kawaii (cute) visual images. Int. J. Psychophysiol. **3**(77), 268–269 (2010)

Ohkura, M., Goto, S., Aoto, T.: Systematic study for "Kawaii" products (fifth report): relation between Kawaii feelings and biological signals. In: ICCAS-SICE 2009, pp. 4343–4346. IEEE (2009). Accessed http://ieeexplore.ieee.org/abstract/document/5332844/

Ohkura, M., Goto, S., Higo, A., Aoto, T.: Relationship between Kawaii feeling and biological signals. Trans. Japan Soc. Kansei Eng. **10**(2), 109–114 (2011). https://doi.org/10.5057/jjske. 10.109

Ohkura, M., Komatsu, T.: Basic study on Kawaii feeling of material perception. In: Kurosu, M. (ed.) HCI 2013. LNCS, vol. 8004, pp. 585–592. Springer, Heidelberg (2013). https://doi.org/ 10.1007/978-3-642-39232-0_63

Ohkura, M., Komatsu, T., Aoto, T.: Kawaii rules: increasing affective value of industrial products. In: Watada, J., Shiizuka, H., Lee, K.-P., Otani, T., Lim, C.-P. (eds.) Industrial Applications of Affective Engineering, pp. 97–110. Springer, Cham (2014). https://doi.org/ 10.1007/978-3-319-04798-0_8

Ohkura, M., Konuma, A., Murai, S., Aoto, T.: Systematic study for "Kawaii" products (the second report)-comparison of "Kawaii" colors and shapes. In: SICE Annual Conference, pp. 481–484. IEEE (2008). http://ieeexplore.ieee.org/abstract/document/4654703/

Olejnik, S., Algina, J.: Generalized eta and omega squared statistics: measures of effect size for some common research designs. Psychol. Methods **8**(4), 434 (2003)

Osgood, C.E.: The nature and measurement of meaning. Psychol. Bull. **49**(3), 197–237 (1952). https://doi.org/10.1037/h0055737

Perez, S.: Pokémon Go passed 100 million installs over the weekend. Tech Crunch, 1 August 2016

Sherman, G.D., Haidt, J., Coan, J.A.: Viewing cute images increases behavioral carefulness. Emotion **9**(2), 282–286 (2009)

Sugano, S., Miyaji, Y., Tomiyama, K.: Study of Kawaii-ness in motion – physical properties of Kawaii motion of Roomba. In: Kurosu, M. (ed.) HCI 2013. LNCS, vol. 8004, pp. 620–629. Springer, Heidelberg (2013). https://doi.org/10.1007/978-3-642-39232-0_67

Tokosumi, A., Teng, F.: Ontological approach to aesthetic feelings: a multilingual case of *Cutism*. In: Smith, M.J., Salvendy, G. (eds.) Human Interface 2011. LNCS, vol. 6771, pp. 161–164. Springer, Heidelberg (2011)

Research on the Influence of Interactivity on the Aesthetic Cognition of Art

Gao Yang$^{(\boxtimes)}$, I-Ting Wang, Hsienfu Lo, and Rungtai Lin

Graduate School of Creative Industry Design,
National Taiwan University of Arts, Banqiao, Taiwan
Lukegao1991@gmail.com, etinw@ms43.hinet.net,
hsienfulo@gmail.com, rtlin@mail.ntua.edu.tw

Abstract. The art participation of the public has been declining year by year, and art has become more and more difficult to understand. However, the complex pressure of modern life has made people's spiritual needs getting urgent. How to let art re-enter into the daily life of the public is a problem that art workers need to face. Interactive art seems to be a good medium to attract the public to participate in art activities, but the impact of interactivity on the audience's aesthetic cognition remains to be explored. This study takes the art work "Iron Bird" as the object, uses Norman's emotional design theory, and uses questionnaires to understand the audience's perception situation of "iron bird" from the three levels of "instinct", "behavior" and "reflection", also to explore the impact of interaction on the aesthetic perception of art. The research shows that: 1. The influence of interaction on cognition is mainly reflected in the instinct level and behavior level. 2. Compared with pleasure, the influence of interaction on cognition is less and weaker. 3. Interactivity has no significant effect on the preference. 4. Interaction can significantly improve viewer's sense of pleasure. 5. Interaction can enhance the viewer's rational cognition and make them judge in a more objective way. The sense of pleasure can influence the viewer's perceptual cognition and subjective recognition.

Keywords: Interactivity · Cognition

1 Introduction

The change of lifestyle and the change of population composition have caused the decline of artistic participation of the public year by year, especially in visual art [1]. At the same time, the art works created by artists are becoming more and more difficult to understand, and the distance between art and life has become increasingly farther away. The complex life pressure faced by modern people makes them gradually regain the sensory experience and spiritual needs. How to make art re-enter into daily life is a problem that art workers need to face. Howard Gardner emphasizes in his research on seven intelligence in the brain: interactivity can stimulate the understanding of different learning individuals and greatly enhances their memory [2]. It can be seen that interaction can positively influence audience perception, interactive art work seems to be a good medium to guide the public into the art activities, but how the influence of

© Springer Nature Switzerland AG 2019
P.-L. P. Rau (Ed.): HCII 2019, LNCS 11576, pp. 592–601, 2019.
https://doi.org/10.1007/978-3-030-22577-3_43

interaction on the audience's aesthetic cognition remains to be explored. This study takes the art apparatus "Iron Bird" as the research object, based on the emotional design theory proposed by Norman, through questionnaires, in order to understand the influence of interactivity on aesthetic cognition, in order to provide theory reference for related art creators.

2   Literature Review

2.1   Cognition of Art

Art creation is a process of continuous exchange. When evaluating works, we must understand the communication between artists and audiences, not only in the social context but also in the interactive experience between artists and audiences [3, 4]. Audience is the key to understanding art, because the meaning that art creates depends on how it is used by its consumers, rather than by creators [5]. When appreciating works of art, the audiences feels the medium, form and content of art in a mingled state of perceptual emotion and rational cognition, and perceives the image and characteristics of the works of art, which in turn produces inner feelings and resonance [6].

2.2   The Different Levels of the Brain

Roger Fly in Discussion on Aesthetic Sense said that most of human life consists of instinctive reactions to perceptible things and the accompanying emotions. Humans can evoke and relive this experience again in consciousness. In this way, we get different levels of value standards and different types of feelings [7]. Norman, Andrew Ortony and William Revelle, suggest that these human attributes result from three different levels of the brain: the visceral level, the behavioral level and the reflective level. The three levels can be mapped to product characteristics like this:

Visceral design .⟩ Appearance
Behavioral design ⟩ The pleasure and effectiveness of use
Reflective design. ⟩ Self-image, personal satisfaction, mwmories

At the visceral level, physical features—look, feel, and sound—dominate. There are four components of good behavioral design: function, understandability, usability, and physical feel. Reflective design is all about message, about culture, and about the meaning of a product or its use [8].

2.3   Installation Art Work "Iron Bird"

The Iron Bird (Fig. 1) is a piece of installation art work in steel as the main material and kraft paper on the wings. The creation was inspired by the toy "flying bird moble" (Fig. 2). In order to adapt to the processing technology of metal bars and to make the wings can be folded and unfolded, the author designed a new modeling form. It is characterized by a linear shape, a simple mechanical structure, some movable parts and a sense of life.

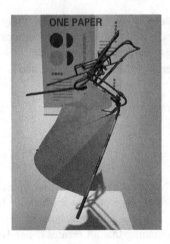

Fig. 1. Iron bird   **Fig. 2.** Flying bird moble

3 Research Method

This study adopted a questionnaire survey method, selected the guests and audiences participated in the OPOP Forum 2018 as subjects, through the questionnaire to find out the audience's cognition of the art work "Iron Bird". The OPOP Forum is an academic event integrated exhibition of Works and publication of Papers, organized by the Graduate School of Creative Industry Design of the National Taiwan University of Arts. It is an one-week academic activity. A total of 120 valid questionnaires were collected during the event. There were 45 males and 75 females; 4 people under 19 years old, 101 people aged 20–39 and 15 people aged 40–59. Professional background: 14 people in sculptures, 3 in mechanics, 10 in artists, 30 in design and 63 in others. Academic background: 86 students, 29 institute researchers and 4 others. Interaction with "Iron Bird": 68 people (56.7%) did not operate it while 52 (43.3%) operated. Based on the questionnaire information, the study is divided into three stages: the first stage tests the reliability and validity of the assessment questionnaire; the second stage detects the influence of interaction on the cognition of the work and the third stage corrects the results obtained in the second stage. The study process is shown in Fig. 3.

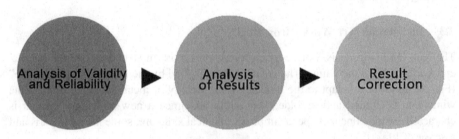

Fig. 3. The study process

4 Questionnaire Design

The assessment questionnaire is divided into three parts: basic information work evaluation and general rating. The basic information includes: gender, age, professional background, education level and interaction. The evaluation of the work takes the form of a 5-point scale. According to the emotional research conducted by Norman and his colleagues, the evaluation project is divided into: Visceral level, Behavioral level and Reflection level [4]. To be specific, the Visceral level takes color, material, form, texture and sound as the evaluation item; The Behavioral level is evaluated by technic, operability, structure and narration; The Reflection level is based on emotion, resonance, style, nostalgia, culture and pleasure. And the level of preference was added as a general rating (Fig. 4).

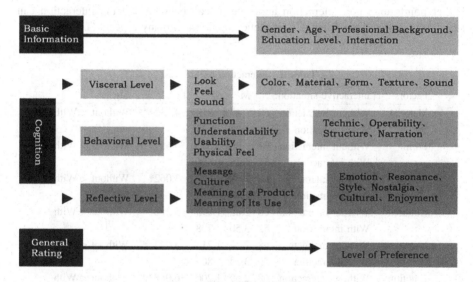

Fig. 4. Questionnaire design

5 Analysis and Discussion of Results

5.1 Analysis of Validity and Reliability

The reliability analysis of the questionnaire is to explore the internal consistency of each facet of the present scale and the reduction of the Cronbach-α coefficient of the dichotomous degree after deleting the single-question, and is set as the reference standard of the selected topic and the reliability of the questionnaire. The questionnaire analysis found that the Cronbach-α coefficient was .945. The total correlations of the single article correction is between .498–.848, the "α coefficient after deletion" is between .937–.944, therefore the internal consistency between the selected questions is quite high, and the question selection is reasonable. Though the validity analysis we found that the KMO coefficient is .942, which means a higher value. The Sig value is .000, which is significant. The characteristic value is 8.352, which can explain 59.657% of the variation of the preset use. The factor loading of every test article is between .553–.873, and commonality is between .457–.762, overall this questionnaire has good construction validity.

5.2 General Evaluation of the Works

Taking the interaction between the subject and the work as the self-variation, the 15 factors and the general evaluation of the work as dependent variables, the independent sample t-test is used to analyze the influence of interaction on the cognition of the work. The results are summarized in Table 1. Among them, the audience has significant differences in material, form, technic, culture, narration, emotion, resonance, style, nostalgia, pleasure and preference. The audience interacted with the work rated notable higher points than non interaction audience. It can be seen that the interaction can significantly affect the audience's aesthetic cognition in many aspects (Table 1).

Table 1. Interaction differences

Factors	Interactive situation	N	M	SD	T	Sig
Material	Without interaction	68	3.47	.819	-4.132^{***}	Without < With
	With interaction	52	4.04	.685		
Form	Without interaction	68	3.66	.840	-4.607^{***}	Without < With
	With interaction	52	4.25	.556		
Technic	Without interaction	68	3.63	.790	-3.062^{*}	Without < With
	With interaction	52	4.06	.725		
Culture	Without interaction	68	2.62	1.093	-5.296^{***}	Without < With
	With interaction	52	3.50	.728		
Narration	Without interaction	68	2.44	1.214	-5.943^{***}	Without < With
	With interaction	52	3.54	.803		
Emotion	Without interaction	68	2.59	1.200	-6.088^{***}	Without < With
	With interaction	52	3.69	.781		
Resonance	Without interaction	68	2.31	1.225	-6.380^{***}	Without < With
	With interaction	52	3.48	.779		
Style	Without interaction	68	2.93	1.319	-4.654^{***}	Without < With
	With interaction	52	3.87	.886		
Nostalgia	Without interaction	68	3.10	1.295	-4.309^{***}	Without < With
	With interaction	52	3.96	.885		
Pleasure	Without interaction	68	2.69	1.123	-7.177^{***}	Without < With
	With interaction	52	3.90	.721		
Preference	Without interaction	68	3.49	.782	$-4,303^{***}$	Without < With
	With interaction	52	4.02	.577		

$^{*}p < .05$ $^{***}p < .001$

5.3 T-Test Result Correction

However, according to Table 1, the interaction caused a significant difference in pleasure. Compared with the non interaction audience, the average of interacted audience's enjoyment value increased by 1.21 (45%). Psychologist Alice Isen pointed out that happiness can expand ideas and promote creative thinking [9]. It shows that the sense of pleasure affects the perception of the audience. Therefore, the factors with significant differences in Table 1 may not be directly caused by interaction, but because the interaction aroused the audience's pleasure and thus affected the audience's perception of the work. In order to accurately detect the impact of interaction on cognition, it is necessary to get rid of the disturbance of the result of pleasure (Fig. 5).

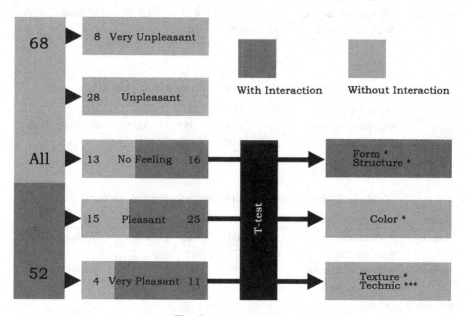

Fig. 5. Result correction

1. Grouping questionnaires of the same level of enjoyment the following results are obtained:

   - A total of 29 questionnaires selected "have no feeling", of which there were 13 with interactions and 16 non interactions.
   - A total of 40 questionnaires selected "feeling pleasant", of which there were 15 with interactions with and 25 non interactions.
   - A total of 15 questionnaires selected "feeling very pleasant", of which there were 11 with interactions and 4 non interactions.
   - The audience who chose "feeling unpleasant" and "feeling very unpleasant" did not interact with the work so the results of which could not be compared with the other questionnaires. Therefore, they were not included in the consideration.

2. Taking the interaction between the subject and the work as the self-variation, the 15 factors and the general evaluation of the work as dependent variables, the independent sample t-test is used to analyze the influence of interaction on the cognition of the work. The results were arranged in order as follows: (Table 2: Audience without obvious pleasure, Table 3: Audience feeling pleasant, Table 4: Audience feeling very pleasant).

Table 2. InterAction differences (Audience without obvious pleasure)

Factors	Interactive situation	N	M	SD	T	Sig
Form	Without interaction	13	3.69	.751	−1.570*	Without < With
	With interaction	16	4.06	.443		
Structure	Without interaction	13	3.77	.439	−1.517*	Without < With
	With interaction	16	4.00	.365		

$*p < .05$

Table 3. Interaction differences (Audience feeling pleasant)

Factors	Interactive situation	N	M	SD	T	Sig
Color	Without interaction	15	4.00	.353	.935*	Without > With
	Without interaction	25	3.80	.816		

$*p < .05$

Table 4. Interaction differences (Audience feeling very pleasant)

Factors	Interactive situation	N	M	SD	T	Sig
Texture	Without interaction	4	4.00	.000	1.000*	Without > With
	With interaction	11	3.73	.905		
Technic	Without interaction	4	5.00	.000	2.887***	Without > With
	With interaction	11	4.55	.522		

$*p < .05 \ ***p < .001$

The results show:

- Audience without obvious pleasure has significant differences in the recognition of the two evaluation factors of form and structure. The audience with interaction has significantly higher recognition than those who did not interact.
- The audience that felt pleasant has significant differences in the recognition of color. The audience without interaction has a significantly higher recognition than the interacted audience.
- The audience who felt very pleasant has significant differences in the recognition of the two aspects of "texture" and "technic". The audience without interaction has significantly more recognition than the audience with interaction.

3. The comparison of above results with Table 1 gives the following differences:

- The total number of factors showing significant differences in Table 1 is 10 (excluding pleasure), and the total number of factors showing significant differences in Tables 2, 3 and 4 is 5. It can be seen that when the difference caused by pleasure is excluded, the scope of influence of interaction on cognition is narrowed.
- Interactivity has no significant effect on the "preference".
- Table 2 (Group of audience without obvious pleasure) has an intensity of "form" factor (−1.570*, non interaction < with interaction) significantly lower than Table 1 (−4.607***, non interaction < with interaction); The "structure" factor (−1.517*, with interaction > non interaction) that shows significant differences in Table 2 did not appear in Table 1. It can be seen that compared with pleasure, the influence of interaction on cognition is weaker. When both pleasure and interaction exist, the influence of interaction is difficult to be shown.
- Table 3 (Group of audience feeling pleasant) has a significant difference in the "color" factor (.935*, non interaction > with interaction), which is not shown in Table 1, it means no significant difference.
- Table 4 (Group of audience feeling very pleasant) showed a significant difference in the "texture" factor (1.000*, non interaction > with interaction), which did not appear in Table 1. The "technic" factor (2.887***, non interaction > with interaction) shows a significantly higher intensity than that in Table 1 (−3.062*, non interaction < with interaction), and the ratio relationship is reversed. Tables 3 and 4 present the situation in which the viewers are pleasant, compared with Table 1, there are two differences.

The first type is the difference in the "technic" factor. As shown in Table 2, the impact of pleasure on cognition is much greater than that of interactivity, so the "technic" factor (2.887***, non interaction > with interaction) that was originally expressed as a strongly significant difference in Table 4, is changed to (−3.062*, non interaction < with interaction) in Table 1 when the pleasure effect was added, meanwhile, the ratio relationship is reversed and a significant difference is presented.

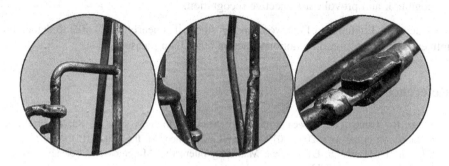

Fig. 6. Iron bird details (Color figure online)

The second type: interaction under the premise of pleasure reduces the audience's sense of identity to the work. This phenomenon did not appear in Table 1 or Table 2. Factors that reduced identity are: color, texture and technic. From the appearance of the "Iron Bird" in Fig. 6, we can see the uneven color of the steel surface due to high temperature, the traces left by the welding not carefully polished and the convex or concave on surface due to the inferior welding technique. These details are consistent with the identity reducing factors in Tables 3 and 4. The "Iron Bird" is not outstanding in terms of color, texture and technic. The high recognition in Table 1 is derived from the pleasant emotions that caused the viewer's perceptual cognition, which made them subjectively tolerate the deficiencies of the art work, thus increasing the recognition of it (the viewers without obvious pleasure in Table 2 did not make similar judgments can prove this from the side), while the interaction enhances the viewers' rational cognition and makes them see a more objective reality through emotions.

6 Conclusion and Suggestion

Given the influence of interactivity on cognition, interaction has become a hot trend in art. More and more interactive art works are exhibited in art galleries and are sought after by artists and spectators. However, interactivity is not as powerful as what we think or what we see. Simple interaction is even hard to touch the viewer's heart. The expression that the artistic creators hope to engage the public in participating in artistic activities through interaction is difficult to achieve. The detailed conclusions are as follows:

1. The influence of interactivity on cognition is reflected in the level of instinct and behavior.
2. Compared with pleasure, interactivity has less impact on cognition and weaker intensity.
3. Interactivity has no significant effect on the preference.
4. Interaction can significantly improve the viewer's sense of pleasure.
5. Interaction can enhance the viewer's rational cognition and make him see things in a more objective way; The sense of pleasure can affect the viewer's perceptual cognition and provoke a subjective recognition.

Due to the limitations of the work, in this study, it is nearly impossible to detect the influence of interaction on emotional factors other than pleasure.

References

1. Silber, B., Triplett, T.: A decade of arts engagement: findings from the Survey of Public Participation in the Arts, 2002-2012. National endowment for the arts (2015)
2. Caulton, T.: Hands-On Exhibitions: Managing Interactive Museums and Science Centres. Routledge, London (1998)
3. Goldman, A.: Evaluating art. In: The Blackwell Guide to Aesthetics, pp. 93–108. Wiley-Blackwell, Oxford (2004)

4. Trivedi, S.: Artist-audience communication. Tolstoy Reclaimed **38**, 38–52 (2004)
5. Alexander, V.D.: Sociology of the Arts Exploring Fine and Popular Forms, 1st edn. Blackwell Publishing Ltd., Oxford, pp. 193–210 (2003)
6. Zhou, P.Y.: Aisina jiaoyu piping lilun zhi yanjiu (Unpublished master's thesis). National TaiwanNormal University, Taipei City (1995)
7. Roger, F.: Vision and Design. Chatto & Windus, London (1920)
8. Norman, D.A.: Emotional design: why we love (or hate) everyday things. Basic Civitas Books, pp. 21–83 (2004)
9. Isen, A.M.: Positive affect and decision making. In: Lewis, M., Haviland, J.M. (eds.) Handbook of emotions, pp. 261–277. Guilford, New York (1993)

Author Index

Printed in the United States
By Bookmasters